AWS Certified Security

Study Guide

Specialty (SCS-C0

AWS Certified Security

Study Guide

Specialty (SCS-C01) Exam

Dario Goldfarb, Alexandre M. S. P. Moraes,
Thiago Morais, Mauricio Muñoz, Marcello Zillo Neto,
Gustavo A. A. Santana, Fernando Sapata

About the Authors

Dario Goldfarb is a security solutions architect at Amazon Web Services in Latin America with more than 15 years of experience in cybersecurity, helping organizations from different industries to improve their cyber-resiliency. Dario enjoys sharing security knowledge through speaking at public events, presenting webinars, teaching classes for universities, and writing blogs and articles for the press. He has a significant number of certifications, including CISSP, the Open Group Master IT Architect, and the AWS Security Specialty certification, and holds a degree in systems engineering from UTN (Argentina) and a diploma on cybersecurity management from UCEMA (Argentina).

Alexandre M. S. P. Moraes, CCIE No. 6063, worked as a systems engineer and consulting systems engineer for Cisco Brazil from 1998 to 2014, in projects involving not only security and VPN technologies but also routing protocol and campus design, IP multicast routing, and MPLS networks design. He is the author of *Cisco Firewalls* (Cisco Press, 2011) and has delivered many technical sessions related to security in market events such as Cisco Networkers and Cisco Live (Brazil, United States, United Kingdom). In 2014, Alexandre started a new journey as a director for Teltec Solutions, a Brazilian systems integrator that is highly specialized in the fields of network design, security architectures, and cloud computing. Alexandre holds the CISSP, the CCSP, and three CCIE certifications (routing/switching, security, and service provider). He graduated in electronic engineering from the Instituto Tecnológico de Aeronáutica (ITA–Brazil) and holds a master's degree in mathematics (group theory) from Universidade de Brasília (UnB–Brazil).

Thiago Morais is the leader of solutions architecture teams at Amazon Web Services in Brazil. With more than 20 years of experience in the IT industry, he has worked at startups, advertising agencies, and information security companies, developing and implementing solutions for various industries. In recent years, Thiago has been focused on cloud computing and has specialized in serverless architectures, leading a team that works with large startups and software vendors to help them build solutions in the cloud. He currently holds five AWS certifications and is a regular speaker at local and global technology conferences. Thiago holds a degree in computer science from Universidade Ibirapuera (UNIB–Brazil) and an MBA degree from Insper (Brazil).

Mauricio Muñoz is senior manager of a specialist solutions architects team at Amazon Web Services in Latin America. Mauricio started more than 20 years ago working in information security and has been CISSP certified since 2005. Throughout his career, Mauricio has extended his field of expertise by working on projects for enterprise customers in areas such as networking, application integration, analytics, and cloud computing. Passionate about learning and sharing knowledge, Mauricio was an authorized instructor for CISSP and CEH certification training, as well as for other related technical certifications (including more recently AWS training on the delivery of architecting). He is a frequent speaker for both cloud computing and industry events in Latin America. Currently, Mauricio holds seven

AWS certifications. Mauricio has developed his professional career in different countries around Latin America, holding the title of electronics engineer from Pontificia Universidad Javeriana (PUJ–Colombia) and executive MBA from Insper (Brazil).

Marcello Zillo Neto is a chief security advisor and former chief information security officer (CISO) in Latin America. He has over 20 years of experience in information security, network security, cybersecurity, risk management, and incident response, helping banks, service providers, retail customers, and many other verticals to create their security journey to the cloud. Marcello is a frequent speaker at cloud computing and security events and holds a degree in computer engineering from Universidade São Francisco (USF), an executive MBA from Insper (Brazil), and executive training in digital business strategy and machine learning at MIT. He is also a professor, teaching information security, cloud security, incident response, and security strategy, among other cybersecurity disciplines in universities in Brazil such as Fundação Instituto de Administração (FIA). He also has the following certifications: Certified Information Systems Security Professional (CISSP), AWS Certified Solutions Architect, AWS Certified Security Specialist, and Lead Auditor–ISO 27001.

Gustavo A. A. Santana is the leader of the specialist and telecommunications solutions architecture teams at Amazon Web Services in Latin America. With more than 20 years of experience in the IT industry, Gustavo has worked on multiple enterprise and service provider data center projects that required extensive integration across multiple technology areas such as networking, application optimization, storage, servers, end-to-end virtualization, automation, and cloud computing. A true believer in education as a technology catalyst, he has also dedicated himself to the technical development of IT professionals from multiple customers, partners, and vendors. A frequent speaker at cloud computing and data center industry events, Gustavo holds a degree in computer engineering from Instituto Tecnológico de Aeronáutica (ITA–Brazil), an MBA in strategic IT management from Fundação Getúlio Vargas (FGV–Brazil), six AWS certifications, VMware Certified Implementation Expert in Network Virtualization (VCIX-NV), and three Cisco Certified Internetwork Expert (routing/switching, storage networking, and data center) certifications. He is also the author of three books: *Data Center Virtualization Fundamentals* (Cisco Press, 2013), *CCNA Cloud CLD-FND 210-451 Official Cert Guide* (Cisco Press, 2016), and *VMware NSX Network Virtualization Fundamentals* (VMware Press, 2018).

Fernando Sapata is a principal business development manager for serverless at Amazon Web Services in Latin America. Fernando started developing software in Clipper Summer 87 at 13 years old, and today he has more than 19 years of experience in the IT industry. Fernando has worked with multiple segments such as Internet service providers, telecommunications, consulting services, storage, and now, cloud computing. With solid experience in software development and solutions architecture, Fernando worked as a principal solutions architect at AWS for four years, helping customers in their cloud journey. He is an active member of serverless advocacy, frequently speaking in cloud computing and community events worldwide. He is a teacher, writer, podcaster, and a believer that knowledge and technology can transform lives.

About the Technical Editors

Daniel Garcia is a principal security SA in Amazon Web Services, currently holds six AWS certifications, and has more than 20 years of experience in networking, network security, and cybersecurity. During his career, he has helped companies in multiple verticals such as telecom, banking, insurance, retail, oil and gas, government, and education, among others, to successfully craft and implement their networking and cybersecurity strategies, always striving to design efficient architectures to protect, detect, and respond. Daniel holds an electrical engineering degree from Universidade de São Paulo (USP–Brazil), and a master's degree in business administration from Fundação Getúlio Vargas (FGV–Brazil).

Todd Montgomery is a senior data center networking engineer for a large international consulting company, where he is involved in network design, security, and implementation of emerging data center and cloud-based technologies. He holds six AWS certifications, including the Big Data specialty certification. Todd holds a degree in electronics engineering, as well as multiple certifications from Cisco Systems, Juniper Networks, and CompTIA. Todd also leads the AWS certification meetup group in Austin, Texas.

Contents at a Glance

Contents

Table of Exercises

Introduction

As the pioneer and world leader of cloud computing, Amazon Web Services (AWS) has positioned security as its highest priority. Throughout its history, the cloud provider has constantly added security-specific services to its offerings as well as security features to its ever-growing portfolio. Consequently, the AWS Certified Security–Specialty certification offers a great way for IT professionals to achieve industry recognition as cloud security experts and learn how to secure AWS environments both in concept and practice.

According to the AWS Certified Security Specialty Exam Guide, the corresponding certification attests your ability to demonstrate the following:

- An understanding of specialized data classifications and AWS data protection mechanisms
- An understanding of data encryption methods and AWS mechanisms to implement them
- An understanding of secure Internet protocols and AWS mechanisms to implement them
- A working knowledge of AWS security services and features of services to provide a secure production environment
- The ability to make trade-off decisions with regard to cost, security, and deployment complexity given a set of application requirements
- An understanding of security operations and risks

Through multiple choice and multiple response questions, you will be tested on your ability to design, operate, and troubleshoot secure AWS architectures composed of compute, storage, networking, and monitoring services. It is expected that you know how to deal with different business objectives (such as cost optimization, agility, and regulations) to determine the best solution for a described scenario.

The AWS Certified Security–Specialty exam is intended for individuals who perform a security role with at least two years of hands-on experience securing AWS workloads.

What Does This Book Cover?

To help you prepare for the AWS Certified Security Specialty (SCS-C01) certification exam, this book explores the following topics:

Chapter 1: Security Fundamentals This chapter introduces you to basic security definitions and foundational networking concepts. It also explores major types of attacks, along with the AAA architecture, security frameworks, practical models, and other solutions. In addition, it discusses the TCP/IP protocol stack.

Chapter 2: Cloud Security Principles and Frameworks This chapter discusses critical AWS Cloud security concepts such as its shared responsibility model, AWS hypervisors,

AWS security certifications, the AWS Well-Architected Framework, and the AWS Marketplace. It also addresses both security *of* the cloud and security *in* the cloud. These concepts are foundational for working with AWS.

Chapter 3: Identity and Access Management This chapter discusses AWS Identity and Access Management (IAM), which sets the foundation for all interactions among the resources in your AWS account. It also covers the different access methods to the AWS IAM services, including AWS Console, AWS command-line tools, AWS software development kits, and the IAM HTTPS application programming interface. Furthermore, the chapter addresses how to protect AWS Cloud environments using multifactor authentication and other best practices.

Chapter 4: Detective Controls This chapter discusses how to gather information about the status of your resources and the events they produce. It also covers the four stages of the detective controls flow framework: resources state, events collection, events analysis, and action. It also discusses Amazon EventBridge and several AWS Cloud services supporting multiple detective activities.

Chapter 5: Infrastructure Protection This chapter explores AWS networking concepts such as Amazon VPC, subnets, route tables, and other features that are related to network address translation (NAT gateways and NAT instances) and traffic filtering (security groups and network access control lists). It also addresses AWS Elastic Load Balancing and how security services such as AWS Web Application Firewall can provide secure access to your cloud-based applications. Finally, it discusses the AWS Shield and AWS's unique approach to mitigate distributed denial-of-service attacks.

Chapter 6: Data Protection This chapter discusses protecting data using a variety of security services and best practices, including AWS Key Management Service (KMS), the cloud hardware security module (CloudHSM), and AWS Certificate Manager. It also covers creating a customer master key (CMK) in AWS KMS, protecting Amazon S3 buckets, and how Amazon Macie can deploy machine learning to identify personal identifiable information (PII).

Chapter 7: Incident Response This chapter introduces the incident response maturity model's four phases—developing, implementing, monitoring and testing, and updating—and provides best practices for each phase. It also discusses how to react to a range of specific security incidents such as abuse notifications, insider threats, malware, leaked credentials, and attacks.

Chapter 8: Security Automation This chapter provides an overview of event-driven security and a range of techniques for identifying, responding to, and resolving issues, using tools and techniques such as AWS Lambda, AWS Config, AWS Security Hub, and AWS Systems Manager. It also discusses WAF security automation and isolating bad actors' access to applications.

Chapter 9: Security Troubleshooting in AWS This chapter discusses using AWS CloudTrail, Amazon CloudWatch logs, Amazon CloudWatch events, and Amazon EventBridge to help troubleshoot the operation of AWS Cloud environments. It also presents access control, encryption, networking, and connectivity scenarios that result from common misconfigurations and integration mishandling.

Chapter 10: Creating Your Security Journey in AWS This chapter discusses security in AWS and mapping security controls. It also exemplifies a security journey through three phases: infrastructure protection, security insights and workload protection, and security automation.

Appendix A: Answers to Review Questions This appendix provides the answers to the review questions that appear at the end of each chapter throughout the book.

Appendix B: AWS Security Services Portfolio This appendix provides an overview of the 18 AWS cloud services dedicated to security, identity, and compliance.

Appendix C: DevSecOps in AWS This appendix introduces DevSecOps, the AWS family of services that implement DevOps practices, and how security controls can be implemented in an automated pipeline.

How to Contact the Publisher

If you believe you've found a mistake in this book, please bring it to our attention. At John Wiley & Sons, we understand how important it is to provide our customers with accurate content, but even with our best efforts an error may occur.

In order to submit your possible errata, please email it to our Customer Service Team at `wileysupport@wiley.com` with the subject line "Possible Book Errata Submission."

Interactive Online Learning Environment and Test Bank

Studying the material in the *AWS Certified Security Study Guide: Specialty (SCS-C01) Exam* is an important part of preparing for the AWS Certified Security Specialty (SCS-C01) certification exam, but we provide additional tools to help you prepare. The online test bank will help you understand the types of questions that will appear on the certification exam. The online test bank runs on multiple devices.

Sample Tests The sample tests in the test bank include all the questions at the end of each chapter as well as the questions from the assessment test. In addition, there are two practice exams with 50 questions each. You can use these tests to evaluate your understanding and identify areas that may require additional study.

Flashcards The flashcards in the test bank will push the limits of what you should know for the certification exam. There are 100 questions that are provided in digital format. Each flashcard has one question and one correct answer.

Glossary The online glossary is a searchable list of key terms introduced in this exam guide that you should know for the AWS Certified Security Specialty (SCS-C01) certification exam.

Go to www.wiley.com/go/sybextestprep to register and gain access to this interactive online learning environment and test bank with study tools.

To start using these tools to study for the AWS Certified Security Specialty (SCS-C01) exam, go to www.wiley.com/go/sybextestprep, register your book to receive your unique PIN, then once you have the PIN, return to www.wiley.com/go/sybextestprep, find your book and click register or login and follow the link to register a new account or add this book to an existing account.

AWS Certified Security Study Guide–Specialty (SCS-C01) Exam Objectives

This table shows the extent, by percentage, of each domain represented on the actual examination.

Domain	% of Examination
Domain 1: Incident Response	12%
Domain 2: Logging and Monitoring	20%
Domain 3: Infrastructure Security	26%
Domain 4: Identity and Access Management	20%
Domain 5: Data Protection	22%
Total	100%

Exam objectives are subject to change at any time without prior notice and at AWS's sole discretion. Please visit the AWS Certified Security–Specialty website (aws.amazon.com/certification/certified-security-specialty) for the most current listing of exam objectives.

Objective Map

Objective	Chapter
Domain 1: Incident Response	
1.1 Given an AWS abuse notice, evaluate the suspected compromised instance or exposed access keys	7

Objective	Chapter
1.2 Verify that the Incident Response plan includes relevant AWS services	1, 2, 7, 10
1.3 Evaluate the configuration of automated alerting, and execute possible remediation of security-related incidents and emerging issues	8, 10
Domain 2: Logging and Monitoring	
2.1 Design and implement security monitoring and alerting	1, 4, 10
2.2 Troubleshoot security monitoring and alerting	9
2.3 Design and implement a logging solution	4, 10
2.4 Troubleshoot logging solutions	9
Domain 3: Infrastructure Security	
3.1 Design edge security on AWS	1, 5, 8, 10
3.2 Design and implement a secure network infrastructure	1, 5, 10
3.3 Troubleshoot a secure network infrastructure	5, 9
3.4 Design and implement host-based security	2, 4, 10
Domain 4: Identity and Access Management	
4.1 Design and implement a scalable authorization and authentication system to access AWS resources	1, 3, 10
4.2 Troubleshoot an authorization and authentication system to access AWS resources	3, 9
Domain 5: Data Protection	
5.1 Design and implement key management and use	6, 10
5.2 Troubleshoot key management	6, 9
5.3 Design and implement a data encryption solution for data at rest and data in transit	1, 6, 10

Assessment Test

1. Which one of the following components should not influence an organization's security policy?
   - **A.** Business objectives
   - **B.** Regulatory requirements
   - **C.** Risk
   - **D.** Cost–benefit analysis
   - **E.** Current firewall limitations

2. Consider the following statements about the AAA architecture:
   - I. Authentication deals with the question "Who is the user?"
   - II. Authorization addresses the question "What is the user allowed to do?"
   - III. Accountability answers the question "What did the user do?"

   Which of the following is correct?
   - **A.** Only I is correct.
   - **B.** Only II is correct.
   - **C.** I, II, and III are correct.
   - **D.** I and II are correct.
   - **E.** II and III are correct.

3. What is the difference between denial-of-service (DoS) and distributed denial-of-service (DDoS) attacks?
   - **A.** DDoS attacks have many targets, whereas DoS attacks have only one each.
   - **B.** DDoS attacks target multiple networks, whereas DoS attacks target a single network.
   - **C.** DDoS attacks have many sources, whereas DoS attacks have only one each.
   - **D.** DDoS attacks target multiple layers of the OSI model and DoS attacks only one.
   - **E.** DDoS attacks are synonymous with DoS attacks.

4. Which of the following options is incorrect?
   - **A.** A firewall is a security system aimed at isolating specific areas of the network and delimiting domains of trust.
   - **B.** Generally speaking, the web application firewall (WAF) is a specialized security element that acts as a full-reverse proxy, protecting applications that are accessed through HTTP.
   - **C.** Whereas intrusion prevention system (IPS) devices handle only copies of the packets and are mainly concerned with monitoring and alerting tasks, intrusion detection system (IDS) solutions are deployed inline in the traffic flow and have the inherent design goal of avoiding actual damage to systems.

D. Security information and event management (SIEM) solutions are designed to collect security-related logs as well as flow information generated by systems (at the host or the application level), networking devices, and dedicated defense elements such as firewalls, IPSs, IDSs, and antivirus software.

5. In the standard shared responsibility model, AWS is responsible for which of the following options?

   A. Regions, availability zones, and data encryption

   B. Hardware, firewall configuration, and hypervisor software

   C. Hypervisor software, regions, and availability zones

   D. Network traffic protection and identity and access management

6. Which AWS service allows you to generate compliance reports that enable you to evaluate the AWS security controls and posture?

   A. AWS Trusted Advisor

   B. AWS Well-Architected Tool

   C. AWS Artifact

   D. Amazon Inspector

7. Which of the following contains a definition that is not a pillar from the AWS Well-Architected Framework?

   A. Security and operational excellence

   B. Reliability and performance efficiency

   C. Cost optimization and availability

   D. Security and performance efficiency

8. Which of the following services provides a set of APIs that control access to your resources on the AWS Cloud?

   A. AWS AAA

   B. AWS IAM

   C. AWS Authenticator

   D. AWS AD

9. Regarding AWS IAM principals, which option is not correct?

   A. A principal is an IAM entity that has permission to interact with resources in the AWS Cloud.

   B. They can only be permanent.

   C. They can represent a human user, a resource, or an application.

   D. They have three types: root users, IAM users, and roles.

10. Which of the following is not a recommendation for protecting your root user credentials?

   A. Use a strong password to help protect account-level access to the management console.

   B. Enable MFA on your AWS root user account.

C. Do not create an access key for programmatic access to your root user account unless such a procedure is mandatory.

D. If you must maintain an access key to your root user account, you should never rotate it using the AWS Console.

11. In AWS Config, which option is not correct?

A. The main goal of AWS Config is to record configuration and the changes of the resources.

B. AWS Config Rules can decide if a change is good or bad and if it needs to execute an action.

C. AWS Config cannot integrate with external resources like on-premises servers and applications.

D. AWS Config can provide configuration history files, configuration snapshots, and configuration streams.

12. AWS CloudTrail is the service in charge of keeping records of API calls to the AWS Cloud. Which option is not a type of AWS CloudTrail event?

A. Management

B. Insights

C. Data

D. Control

13. In Amazon VPCs, which of the following is not correct?

A. VPC is the acronym of Virtual Private Cloud.

B. VPCs do not extend beyond an AWS region.

C. You can deploy only private IP addresses from RFC 1918 within VPCs.

D. You can configure your VPC to not share hardware with other AWS accounts.

14. In NAT gateways, which option is not correct?

A. NAT gateways are always positioned in public subnets.

B. Route table configuration is usually required to direct traffic to these devices.

C. NAT gateways are highly available by default.

D. Amazon CloudWatch automatically monitors traffic flowing through NAT gateways.

15. In security groups, which option is not correct?

A. Security groups only have allow (permit) rules.

B. The default security group allows all inbound communications from resources that are associated to the same security group.

C. You cannot have more than one security group associated to an instance's ENI.

D. The default security group allows all outbound communications to any destination.

16. In network ACLs, which option is not correct?
    A. They can be considered an additional layer of traffic filtering to security groups.
    B. Network ACLs have allow and deny rules.
    C. The default network ACL has only one inbound rule, denying all traffic from all protocols, all port ranges, from any source.
    D. A subnet can be associated with only one network ACL at a time.
17. In AWS KMS, which option is not correct?
    A. KMS can integrate with Amazon S3 and Amazon EBS.
    B. KMS can be used to generate SSH access keys for Amazon EC2 instances.
    C. KMS is considered multitenant, not a dedicated hardware security module.
    D. KMS can be used to provide data-at-rest encryption for RDS, Aurora, DynamoDB, and Redshift databases.
18. Which option is not correct in regard to AWS KMS customer master keys?
    A. A CMK is a 256-bit AES for symmetric keys.
    B. A CMK has a key ID, an alias, and an ARN (Amazon Resource Name).
    C. A CMK has two policies roles: key administrators and key users.
    D. A CMK can also use IAM users, IAM groups, and IAM roles.
19. Which of the following actions is not recommended when an Amazon EC2 instance is compromised by malware?
    A. Take a snapshot of the EBS volume at the time of the incident.
    B. Change its security group accordingly and reattach any IAM role attached to the instance.
    C. Tag the instance as compromised together with an AWS IAM policy that explicitly restricts all operations related to the instance, the incident response, and forensics teams.
    D. When the incident forensics team wants to analyze the instance, they should deploy it into a totally isolated environment—ideally a private subnet.
20. Which of the following actions is recommended when temporary credentials from an Amazon EC2 instance are inadvertently made public?
    A. You should assume that the access key was compromised and revoke it immediately.
    B. You should try to locate where the key was exposed and inform AWS.
    C. You should not reevaluate the IAM roles attached to the instance.
    D. You should avoid rotating your key.
21. Which of the following options may not be considered a security automation trigger?
    A. Unsafe configurations from AWS Config or Amazon Inspector
    B. AWS Security Hub findings
    C. Systems Manager Automation documents
    D. Event from Amazon CloudWatch Events

22. Which of the following options may not be considered a security automation response task?
    - **A.** An AWS Lambda function can use AWS APIs to change security groups or network ACLs.
    - **B.** A Systems Manager Automation document execution run.
    - **C.** Systems Manager Run Command can be used to execute commands to multiple hosts.
    - **D.** Apply a thorough forensic analysis in an isolated instance.

23. Which of the following may not be considered a troubleshooting tool for security in AWS Cloud environments?
    - **A.** AWS CloudTrail
    - **B.** Amazon CloudWatch Logs
    - **C.** AWS Key Management Service
    - **D.** Amazon EventBridge

24. Right after you correctly deploy VPC peering between two VPCs (A and B), inter-VPC traffic is still not happening. What is the most probable cause?
    - **A.** The peering must be configured as transitive.
    - **B.** The route tables are not configured.
    - **C.** You need a shared VPC.
    - **D.** You need to configure a routing protocol.

25. A good mental exercise for your future cloud security design can start with the analysis of how AWS native security services and features (as well as third-party security solutions) can replace your traditional security controls. Which of the options is not a valid mapping between traditional security controls and potential AWS security controls?
    - **A.** Network segregation (such as firewall rules and router access control lists) and security groups and network ACLs, Web Application Firewall (WAF)
    - **B.** Data encryption at rest and Amazon S3 server-side encryption, Amazon EBS encryption, Amazon RDS encryption, and other AWS KMS-enabled encryption features
    - **C.** Monitor intrusion and implementing security controls at the operating system level versus Amazon GuardDuty
    - **D.** Role-based access control (RBAC) versus AWS IAM, Active Directory integration through IAM groups, temporary security credentials, AWS Organizations

Answers to Assessment Test

1. E. Specific control implementations and limitations should not drive a security policy. In fact, the security policy should influence such decisions, and not vice versa.
2. D. Accountability is not part of the AAA architecture; accounting is.
3. C. When a DoS attack is performed in a coordinated fashion, with a simultaneous use of multiple source hosts, the term distributed denial-of-service (DDoS) is used to describe it.
4. C. It's the other way around.
5. C. AWS is responsible for its regions, availability zones, and hypervisor software. In the standard shared responsibility model, AWS is not responsible for user-configured features such as data encryption, firewall configuration, network traffic protection, and identity and access management.
6. C. AWS Artifact is the free service that allows you to create compliance-related reports.
7. C. Availability is not a pillar from the AWS Well-Architected Framework.
8. B. AWS Identity and Access Management (IAM) gives you the ability to define authentication and authorization methods for using the resources in your account.
9. B. IAM principals can be permanent or temporary.
10. D. If you must maintain an access key to your root user account, you should regularly rotate it using the AWS Console.
11. C. AWS Config can also integrate with external resources like on-premises servers and applications, third-party monitoring applications, or version control systems.
12. D. CloudTrail events can be classified as management, insights, and data.
13. C. You can also assign public IP addresses in VPCs.
14. C. You need to design your VPC architecture to include NAT gateway redundancy.
15. C. You can add up to five security groups per network interface.
16. C. The default network ACL also has a Rule 100, which allows all traffic from all protocols, all port ranges, from any source.
17. B. Key pairs (public and private keys) are generated directly from the EC2 service.
18. D. IAM groups cannot be used as principals in KMS policies.
19. B. To isolate a compromised instance, you need to change its security group accordingly and detach (not reattach) any IAM role attached to the instance. You also remove it from Auto Scaling groups so that the service creates a new instance from the template and service interruption is reduced.

20. A. As a best practice, if any access key is leaked to a shared repository (like GitHub)—even if only for a couple of seconds—you should assume that the access key was compromised and revoke it immediately.

21. C. Systems Manager Automation documents are actually a security automation response task.

22. D. A forensic analysis is a detailed investigation for detecting and documenting an incident. It usually requires human action and analysis.

23. C. AWS KMS is a managed service that facilitates the creation and control of the encryption keys used to encrypt your data, but it doesn't help you to troubleshoot in other services.

24. B. VPC peering requires route table configuration to direct traffic between a pair of VPCs.

25. C. Monitor intrusion and security controls at the operating system level can be mapped to third-party solutions, including endpoint detection and response (EDR), antivirus (AV), host intrusion prevention system (HIPS), anomaly detection, user and entity behavior analytics (UEBA), and patching.

Security Fundamentals

THE AWS CERTIFIED SECURITY SPECIALTY EXAM OBJECTIVES THAT LEVERAGE CONCEPTS EXPLAINED IN THIS CHAPTER INCLUDE THE FOLLOWING:

✓ **Domain 1: Incident Response**

- 1.2. Verify that the Incident Response plan includes relevant AWS services

✓ **Domain 2: Logging and Monitoring**

- 2.1. Design and implement security monitoring and alerting

✓ **Domain 3: Infrastructure Security**

- 3.1. Design edge security on AWS
- 3.2. Design and implement a secure network infrastructure

✓ **Domain 4: Identity and Access Management**

- 4.1. Design and implement a scalable authorization and authentication system to access AWS resources

✓ **Domain 5: Data Protection**

- 5.3. Design and implement a data encryption solution for data at rest and data in transit

Introduction

An understanding of the concepts explained in this chapter will be critical in your journey to pass the AWS Certified Security Specialty exam. We will introduce the following topics:

- Basic security definitions
- Foundational networking concepts
- Main classes of attacks
- Important security solutions and services
- Well-known security frameworks and models

In this chapter, you will learn about basic security concepts and some foundational terminology that comes from the information technology (IT) infrastructure knowledge domain. Even if your sole objective is to conquer the AWS Certified Security Specialty certification, this chapter is relevant for any professional, particularly for the officially accredited ones, to demonstrate a good level of general education on the security subject matter (be it related to cloud-based or to traditional on-premises environments).

If you are already an experienced information security expert, you can still use this chapter for concept review purposes.

Understanding Security

The world of data communications has evolved considerably over the years, irrevocably impacting learning methods, business models, human interaction possibilities, and even the dynamics of most day-to-day activity. The networks of today are powerful, enabling individuals and companies to quickly transport data, voice, and video in an integrated fashion, thus providing access from multiple types of devices to all kinds of applications, which may reside anywhere in the globe.

On one hand, virtually limitless use cases are brought to existence by the omnipresent *network of networks*. On the other hand, this almighty global entity, which came to be known as *the Internet*, turned out to be a platform that embeds dangerous characteristics such as user anonymity, the ability to simultaneously control multiple remote computing devices, and the possibility to automate execution of tasks. Unfortunately, from a technical perspective, this all-encompassing network may be used for both good and evil.

Being aware of the adverse results that may be derived from widespread connectivity, it is natural to look for ways to ensure that only the legitimate or noble usages of the networked systems are allowed. Effective resources that compensate for the absence of natural boundaries in the Internet must be implemented. There should be structured means of defining what the acceptable activities are, from either a productivity or a protection standpoint. Conditional access to networked resources should be put in place, instead of simply providing unrestricted access and naively relying on inherent humankind's goodwill. Dealing with this variety of challenges is what the security practice lends itself to.

But where to start your security learning journey? Well, the first step in solving a problem is recognizing that there is one. The second most effective step is ensuring that you understand what needs to be solved or, in other words, *what is the problem?* And if you are presented with questions for which there may be multiple answers (or multiple choices, as in your certification exam), a good starting point is to eliminate all those options that do not apply. In an attempt to summarize what the practice of security could signify, it is probably easier to begin by defining *what it is not*:

- **Security is neither a product nor a service.** First of all, there is no single product that can act as a "magic black box" that will automatically solve every problem. Moreover, the available capabilities of a given product will be helpful only when they are properly enabled for actual use.
- **Security is not a technology.** Technologies, including those that provide visibility and the ability to block traffic as well as respond to attack situations, may be grouped to form an important *defensive system*. However, the threat matrix is an ever-changing object, meaning that several techniques and tools that have been largely employed on well-known attack scenarios may prove ineffective when facing the newest challenges.
- **Security is not static.** It is not something that you do once and quickly forget. Processes must exist for dealing with planning, implementation, testing, and updating tasks. And all of these items must involve people and discipline.
- **Security is not a check box.** You should know what you are protecting against and, once you determine that, look for resources that can demonstrate true *security effectiveness*.
- **Security is not made only by nominal security elements.** In spite of the existence of dedicated security hardware and software products, security is not limited to them. For example, there are countless contributions that can be given to the overall security process by well-configured network infrastructure devices such as routers.
- **Security is not a beautiful graphical user interface (GUI).** You should always understand what is going on behind the scenes—what is in the brain of the system and not relying blindly, for instance, on reports that state "you are protected."

Now that you've learned what security is not about, it is time to start getting acquainted with what it can be. One general principle that has proved valuable in many fields is to move from global concepts to specifics, and not in the opposite direction. In that sense, if the assigned duty is to protect the relevant digital assets of a particular organization, it is highly advisable that you understand its vision, mission, objectives, and also the possible competitors. All of these items will be considered in a high-level document known as the *organizational security policy*, which establishes the foundation for all initiatives and tasks pertaining to security.

Among the typical pieces of information that are used to guide policy creation, some deserve special mention:

Business Objectives The main references for policy definition, these are related to the classic "*Why we are here?*" and "*What are we trying to achieve?*" questions that are answered in mission statements or company strategies for a period.

Regulatory Requirements These are specific to the industry sector to which the organization belongs and must be always considered. These requirements are normally able to give a clue to what type of data is valuable in that particular industry.

Risk The acceptable level of risk, from the point of view of senior leadership, should be included in the policy. There can be various categories of risks, such as direct financial loss, improper disclosure of intellectual property, strategic information theft, or damages to the public image of the organization.

Cost/Benefit Analysis This analysis should always be evaluated for the mitigation of the identified risks. The cost/benefit ratio of implementing a certain control must always be taken into consideration, and this calculation involves not only investment in products but also the cost of specialized personnel to make it possible.

A security policy is related to an organization's business strategy and, as such, is normally written using broader terms. To have practical applicability, the general rules and principles it states need to be carefully described in a set of companion documents, which are tactical in nature. The most common of these elements are as follows:

Standards These specify *mandatory* rules, regulations, or activities.

Guidelines These encompass sets of recommendations, reference actions, and operational guides to be considered under circumstances in which standards are not applicable.

Baselines These documents are meant to define the minimum level of security that is required for a given system type.

Procedures These include step-by-step instructions for performing specific tasks. They define how policies, standards, and guidelines are implemented within the operating environment.

Figure 1.1 depicts the relationship of the security policy with its companion documents and main sources of information. It also displays some important attributes that must be present in the policy.

You should be aware of several important principles, especially if you are in charge of defending important digital assets. First, you should be aware that *attacks happen*. It does not matter whether or not you detect them. It is not even important whether those attacks have already been successful (even if they haven't, they might be someday—it's just a matter of time). In dealing with security, it is critical to have an attack-and-defense culture in place so that you are always reflecting on potential exposures and how to mitigate the associated risk.

FIGURE 1.1 Positioning the security policy

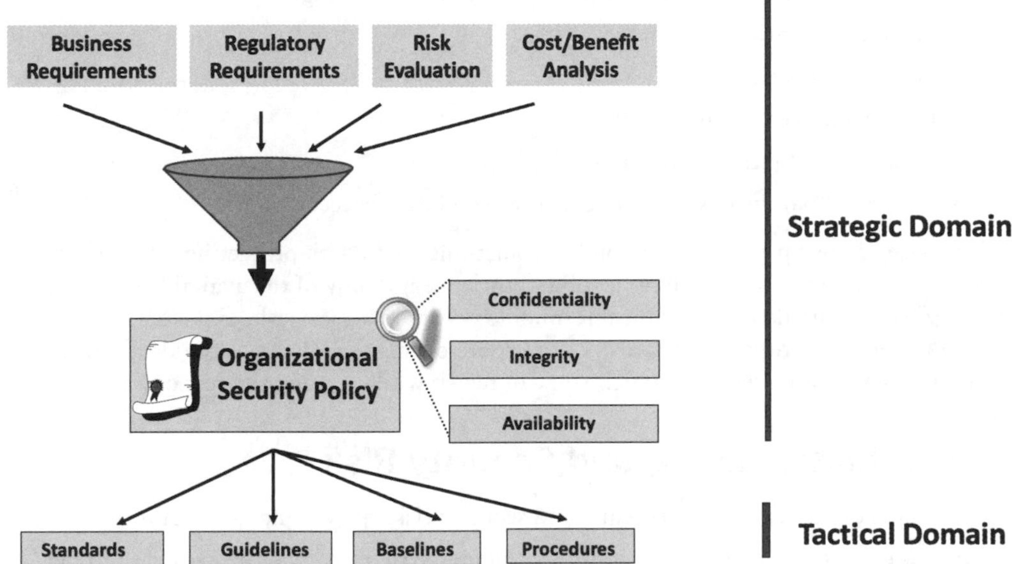

You should also notice that every networked element is a potential attack target. This is the case with servers (web, application, database servers, and so on), client devices of any kind, and even infrastructure devices, such as routers, switches, and wireless access points.

Hope is not a strategy. You should make sure your security strategy directly states the access policies and clarifies what types of traffic are permitted and under what conditions. There should be precisely documented network topologies that provide easy understanding of allowed connections, from sources to destinations. You should deploy elements acting as established *policy enforcement points*, instead of assuming that users and devices will behave properly.

Much like onions, security is built in layers. By considering the hypothesis that a certain defense may be circumvented, you should build additional protection layers along the path that leads to your valuable hosts.

At this point of the discussion, some questions may arise, such as: How can you link the macro statements from the overarching security policy to those down-to- earth requirements of configuring a certain access control rule? Or, for instance: What does a particular traffic flow permission have to do with a given business objective of an organization?

To respond to such inquiries, begin by identifying the critical business systems of your organization. What communication protocols are involved in connecting to those systems? What are the inherent risks of having these protocols running in your network? Are there reported vulnerabilities that could be exploited? What are the suitable security measures for risk mitigation?

Basic Security Concepts

Imagine that you have been assigned a mission and that you are truly committed to accomplish it. Before you begin executing the specific tasks that compose the major objective of your journey, you must understand, at a minimum, the following:

- What rules are involved?
- What are the restrictions?
- What is available in your toolkit?
- What kind of help can you count on?
- What are the parameters that indicate that you have succeeded?

Likewise, if your particular mission has something to do with protecting a given computing environment, you must have a solid knowledge not only of the available security building blocks but also of the typical terminology that relates to risk, exposure, threats, and the absence of proper safeguards. The purpose of this section is to provide a reference, within the realm of IT security, which you can revisit while reading the rest of this book.

Vulnerability, Threat, and Security Risk

The concepts of vulnerabilities, threats, and security risks are distinct and yet interrelated:

- A *vulnerability* is a weakness within a computer system that can be exploited to perform unauthorized actions.
- A *threat* is defined by any entity (such as a person or a tool) that can exploit a vulnerability intentionally or by accident. Such an entity is also known as a *threat actor* or *threat agent*.

The concept of *security risk* relates to the probability of a certain vulnerability being exploited by a threat actor. A risk also depends on the value of the digital asset under analysis. For instance, if the same software bug (an example of vulnerability) is present on both a lab virtual machine and a production application server, a higher security risk should be associated with the latter.

Security Countermeasures and Enforcement

Within a computing environment, the mechanisms aimed at risk mitigation are called *security countermeasures* (or *security controls*). They can come in multiple formats, including the following:

- Software patching (to eliminate a previously detected vulnerability).
- Implementation of security capabilities that are specifically designed as defensive resources (thus avoiding vulnerability exploitation). Some examples of such capabilities

will be explored in the "Important Security Solutions and Services" section later in this chapter.

- Verification of user identity before granting access to critical data.

The mere process of defining access policies and their component rules is not sufficient for effective security. You must have a means to ensure that those rules are implemented and obeyed—or, in other words, there must be *enforcement*.

Confidentiality, Integrity, and Availability

The following are foundational attributes that you should consider not only for policy definition but also for evaluation of security effectiveness:

Confidentiality This principle is concerned with preventing unauthorized disclosure of sensitive information and ensuring that a suitable level of privacy is ensured at all stages of data processing. Encryption is a typical example of a technology designed with confidentiality in mind.

Integrity This principle deals with the prevention of unauthorized modification of data and with ensuring information accuracy. Hash message authentication codes, such as HMAC-MD5 and HMAC-SHA (largely employed by the Internet Protocol Security [IPsec] framework), are mathematical functions conceived to provide integrity for the data transmitted in Internet Protocol (IP) packets.

Availability This principle focuses on ensuring reliability and an acceptable level of performance for legitimate users of computing resources. Provisions must be made against eventual failures in the operating environment, which includes the existence of well-designed recovery plans at both the physical and logical levels.

In many publications, the confidentiality, integrity, and availability security principles are also referred as the *CIA triad*.

Accountability and Nonrepudiation

Accountability is an attribute related to a certain individual or organization being held responsible for its actions. The idea is to ensure that all operations performed by systems or processes can be identified and precisely associated with their author.

Nonrepudiation is the property of ensuring that someone cannot deny that they have performed an action in an effort to avoid being held accountable. In the IT security world, repudiation examples are someone denying that a certain system transaction has been carried out or a user denying the authenticity of its own signature.

Authentication, Authorization, and Accounting

Authentication, authorization, and accounting are three security functions that are usually combined to deliver access control services. This interaction inspired the creation of the *AAA architecture*, in which the meaning of each "A" is more easily grasped when associated with the question it was designed to answer:

Authentication Deals with the question "*Who is the user?*" The process to find this answer basically involves extracting user-related information (such as a username and its corresponding password) from an access request to a system and comparing it to a database of previously defined valid users. Certain environments may treat non-registered users as *guests* or *generic users*, thus granting a basic level of access.

Authorization Addresses the question "*What is the user allowed to do?*" This user should have been authenticated before authorization occurs in order to differentiate the access privileges, or *authorization attributes*. The authorization failures that appear on an AAA service report can help characterize improper access attempts.

Accounting Answers the question "*What did the user do?*" Through this process, an accounting client—for instance, a networking device—collects user activity information and sends it to an accounting server (or service in the case of the AWS Cloud). This function serves not only to provide statistics about legitimate use but also to spot unexpected user behavior (in terms of traffic volume or abnormal access hours, for instance).

Visibility and Context

It is certainly much easier to protect your computing systems from the threats that are visible. Fortunately, in today's computing environments, *visibility* is not restricted to what you are able to directly see. Tools and techniques have been specifically developed to provide information about many parameters of packet flows, including the hidden ones.

Another important concept for the current security practice is *context*. Providing context relates to the ability to gather additional pieces of information around the main one so that ambiguity removal is possible before making policy decisions. Here are some examples:

- The same user may be granted different levels of access to corporate resources, depending on the device being used. On a domain-registered personal computer, the user will be provided with full access, whereas on a personal device the same user will have only basic access to applications.
- Access to certain strategic systems may be deemed normal only for a specific time of day or day of the week. Any deviation from what is considered standard may indicate a misuse and should trigger further investigation.
- A certain traffic pattern may be deemed an attack according to the source IP address that it comes from.

Foundational Networking Concepts

Chances are that you may be the security architect in charge of protecting companies that view the AWS Cloud as an interesting disaster recovery option for its critical workloads. You may also be responsible for providing security for companies that are adapting applications so that they can be migrated to the AWS Cloud. Or you may be the security consultant for a cloud-native organization. In any of these scenarios, it is important to keep in mind that, although hosted in a *special network place*, your cloud-based systems will still be reachable through the Internet using standard data communication protocols. Consequently, it is not possible to perform *cloud security* well without a good knowledge of *network security*, which, in turn, is not achievable unless you are familiar with the basics of networking.

This section will visit two network communication models: the *Open Systems Interconnection* (OSI) model as well as what came to be the most prevalent and successful standard for network-based communications, the *TCP/IP protocol stack*. This approach will prove insightful and allow you to quickly locate the layer(s) over which an attack is taking place, thus making it easier to figure out what types of protection mechanisms may prove the most suited.

The OSI Reference Model

The OSI model was developed by the International Organization for Standardization (ISO, from the Greek word *iso*, which means *equal*) in 1984. This example of a divide-and-conquer approach for explaining network-based communications was aimed at reducing the overall perception of complexity and, undoubtedly, has contributed to generations of professionals and students working in this field. OSI divides the communication system into seven abstract layers, each of which is in charge of a well-defined job, while working in a collaborative way, in order to achieve data transmission between two given systems.

Some of the OSI benefits are listed here:

- It allows the standardization of interfaces among devices, making interoperability possible between diverse systems, even those created by distinct vendors.
- It enables modularity, from engineering and development standpoints, making it possible to design features that belong to a particular layer, without worrying, at least momentarily, about what happens on another.
- It makes it possible to build specialized devices that may act on a specific layer or, eventually, on just some of them.
- It allows more direct isolation of problems, which is useful not only for troubleshooting efforts but also for security planning.

Now that you know the motivation behind the creation of this famous conceptual model, whose hierarchy is illustrated in Figure 1.2, we'll briefly describe the main functions associated with each of the seven layers:

FIGURE 1.2 The OSI model

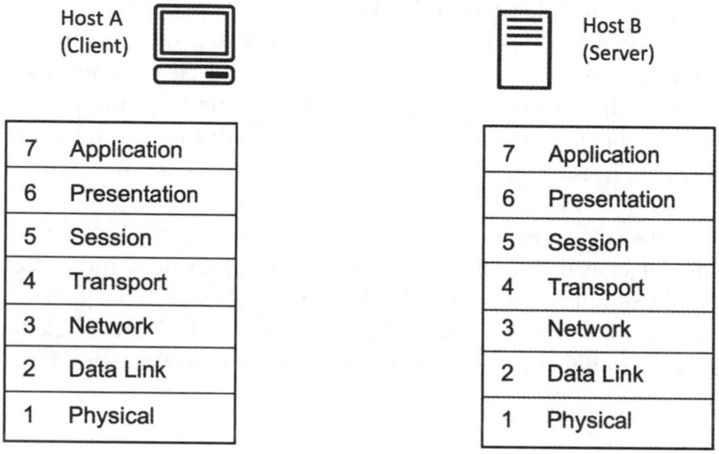

Host A (Client)

Host B (Server)

Host A	Host B
7 Application	7 Application
6 Presentation	6 Presentation
5 Session	5 Session
4 Transport	4 Transport
3 Network	3 Network
2 Data Link	2 Data Link
1 Physical	1 Physical

Physical Layer (Layer 1) The lowest layer is responsible for the physical connection between the devices and is concerned with transmitting raw bits over a communication channel. The main design issues include dealing with mechanical, electrical, optical, and timing interfaces as well as with ensuring that when one side sends a 1 bit, it is accurately received by the other side as a 1 bit, and not as a 0 bit.

Data Link Layer (Layer 2) This layer is in charge of node-to-node delivery of the message in the form of larger and sequential units of data called *frames*. For proper identification of end hosts, it defines a physical addressing scheme, which has only local significance, such as the 48-bit MAC address used by the Ethernet network interface cards (NICs). Some of the issues this layer deals with are error-free delivery, flow control (thus avoiding a fast transmitter from overwhelming a slow receiver), and controlled access to shared media (such as those that allow broadcast transmission).

Network Layer (Layer 3) The main task of this layer concerns *routing* a unit of data (the so-called Layer 3 *packet*) from one given source to a destination that resides on a different network, potentially connected by means of a different Data Link layer technology. This layer introduces the concept of the *logical address*, of which the IP address is the most important example. This addressing paradigm, which treats an individual host as part of a larger logical entity (known as a Layer 3 *subnet*), is what makes global delivery of packets accurate, scalable, and flexible, independently of the Layer 2 media (and the correspondent Layer 2 address of the destination node).

Transport Layer (Layer 4) This layer is aimed at providing reliable message delivery, from the source to the destination host, irrespective of the types, and number, of physical or logical (Layer 3) networks traversed along the path. The Transport layer is also able to confirm (or acknowledge) the successful data transmission and to trigger retransmission if errors are detected. Layer 4 introduces the concepts of source and destination ports, thus allowing multiple service processes to run (and be identified) within the same computing node. The most common transport protocols are Transmission Control Protocol (TCP) and User Datagram Protocol (UDP), both of them belonging to the TCP/IP stack, which will be discussed later in the "The TCP/IP Protocol Stack" section.

Session Layer (Layer 5) A session consists of the coordinated exchange of requests and responses between application processes running on endpoint machines. The main functions associated with this layer are session handling (establishment, maintenance, and termination), controlling the dialogue between the two communicating parties (half-duplex and full-duplex transmission), and inserting synchronization control points into the data flow (which makes it possible for a large transfer to be restarted from the point where it was interrupted, rather than retransmitting everything).

Presentation Layer (Layer 6) This layer is sometimes referred to the as the *translation layer*, because it deals with the syntax and semantics of the data being transmitted. This is what makes it possible for devices that employ different data representations to communicate. The data structures being exchanged can be defined in an abstract way, along with a standard encoding to be used over the transmission media.

Application Layer (Layer 7) This is the top layer of the OSI reference model and the closest to the end user. Many examples of application protocols are very well known for the typical end user; the most common are the Hypertext Transfer Protocol (HTTP), the File Transfer Protocol (FTP), and the auxiliary Domain Name System (DNS), which acts as the mapping agent between site names and IP addresses before the actual application connection takes place.

The TCP/IP Protocol Stack

Sponsored by the U.S. Department of Defense, the academic network known as the ARPANET (Advanced Research Projects Agency Network) is considered the ancestor of today's Internet. It already employed packet switching (instead of circuit switching) and was the first network to implement the TCP/IP protocol suite.

Even though it is always instructive during the learning process to contrast a certain protocol stack with the OSI model, you should not forget that other suites of protocols were already in use before OSI was established. This was the case of the TCP/IP stack, which survived the test of time and, despite any eventual criticism, became the de facto standard for internetworking. Due to the practical importance of protocols such as IP, TCP, and UDP, we'll provide a dedicated analysis that, although brief, may be useful to you later. Figure 1.3 compares TCP/IP and the OSI layers.

FIGURE 1.3 Comparison between the OSI model and the TCP/IP stack

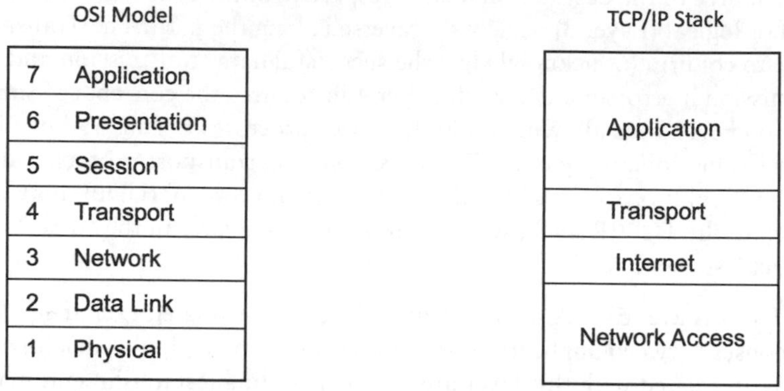

OSI Model

7 Application
6 Presentation
5 Session
4 Transport
3 Network
2 Data Link
1 Physical

TCP/IP Stack

Application
Transport
Internet
Network Access

The *Internet Protocol* (IP) is almost a synonym of the OSI network layer; packet routing is its most relevant task. IP routing deals with the choice of a path over which the IP packets (or datagrams), destined to a particular host, will be sent. Even though some techniques employ additional attributes (the *source IP address*, for example), the classic definition of routing considers the *destination IP address* as the only criterion for path selection. The IP routing function can be divided into four basic activities:

1. **Gathering routing information:** This can be achieved by manual definition of static routes or by using dynamic routing protocols, such as *Open Shortest Path First* (OSPF), *Routing Information Protocol* (RIP), or *Border Gateway Protocol* (BGP).
2. **Building the routing table:** Before installing a path in this table, a router sequentially performs two comparisons: (1) If more than one *equal-length* network prefix is available to a destination, the router will prefer the one with the lowest *administrative distance* (a measure of the trustworthiness among static routes, dynamic routes originated from routing protocols, or a mixture of both), and (2) for two equal-length prefixes that have the same value for the administrative distance parameter, a router will choose the one with the *lowest cost* under the perspective of the particular routing protocol.
3. **Searching for the longest prefix match:** When a packet arrives at the incoming interface, its destination IP address is extracted and compared with the available entries in the routing table. The comparison that results in the longest *bitwise* match for the network mask is selected. The last possibility of finding such a match is to use a *default route*, if one is configured.
4. **Forwarding the packet on the outgoing interface:** When a match happens in step 3, it will point to an entry in the routing table that has a corresponding *outgoing interface*. This last step involves building the appropriate Layer 2 header for this interface.

The TCP/IP model defines two end-to-end transport layer protocols: TCP and UDP. The choice will depend on the requirements of the application protocol being used. TCP is connection-oriented, is reliable, and includes flow control, while UDP is a much simpler option that provides *best effort* delivery of individual packets. UDP is connectionless and unreliable, but nevertheless well suited for real-time traffic (such as voice and video) and other applications that use a client-server communication model with simple request-reply queries.

The types of field included in the header of a communication protocol can tell a lot about its operational capabilities and flexibility. The way a packet with such a header is processed by end hosts or routers along the path can also reveal insightful information about potential protocol vulnerabilities that, if exploited, may lead to security issues. You should therefore have a good understanding of the IP, TCP, and UDP headers. We also recommend that you pay attention to header elements whenever a new protocol is introduced.

Figure 1.4 shows the IPv4 header and Figure 1.5 shows the UDP and TCP headers, with a special reference to the TCP flags field.

FIGURE 1.4 The IPv4 header

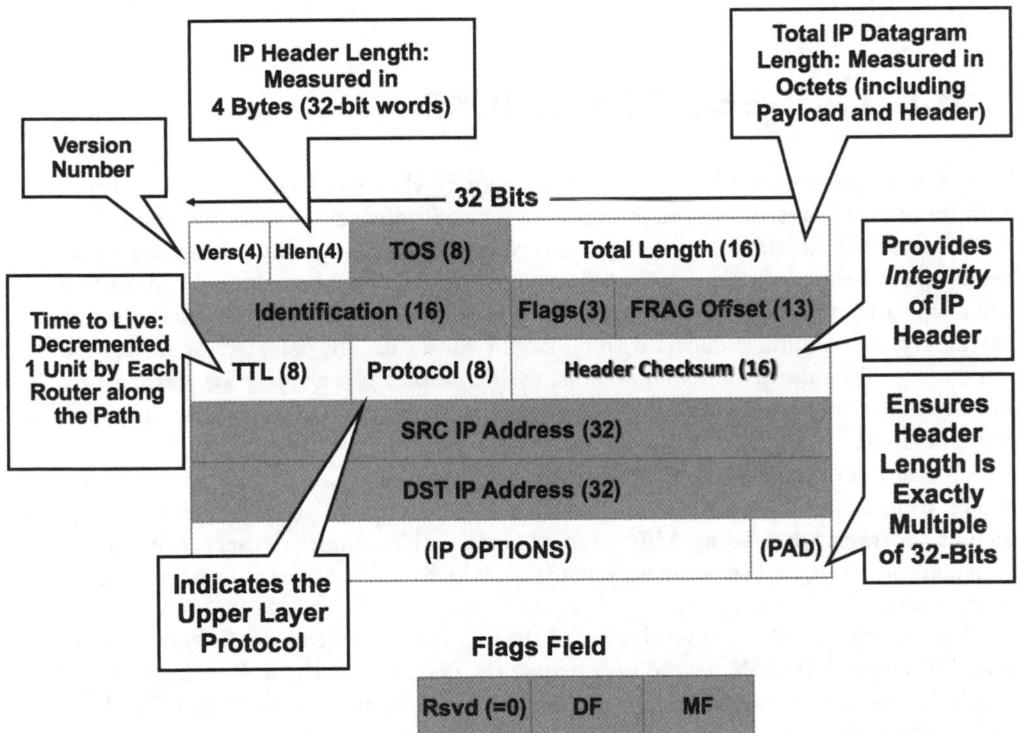

FIGURE 1.5 UDP and TCP headers

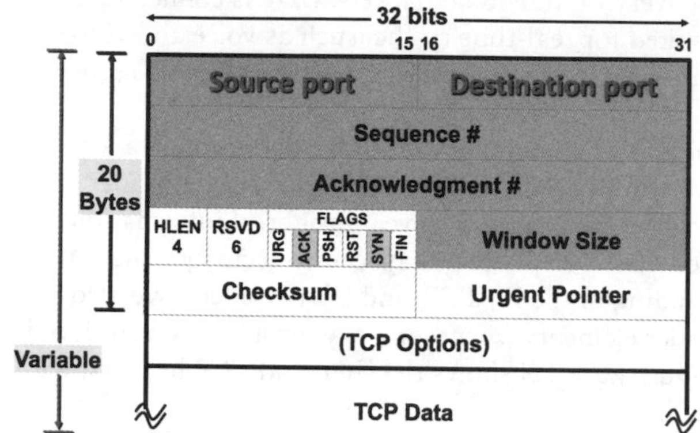

TCP Flags Field

Flag	Meaning
URG	Urgent Pointer field is valid
ACK	Acknowledgment field is valid
PSH	This segment requests a push
RST	Reset the connection
SYN	Synchronize sequence numbers
FIN	End of byte stream for sender

UDP Header

0 15 16 32

Source Port (16)	Destination Port (16)
Length (16)	UDP Checksum (16)
Data (if any)	

Main Classes of Attacks

Even though cyberattacks have always been around, when you compare current threats with those of the Internet's humble beginnings, the difference is essentially related to the intent of the individuals (or groups) carrying out the exploitation attempts. If in the beginning notoriety was the main motivation, the possibility of quick personal profit is what typically attracts more on today's threat landscape. Stealing intellectual property, having access to digital products without paying for it, illegally transferring money from someone else's bank account, and even using the Internet as a weapon for warfare between nations (or specific political groups within a country) are just a few examples of what could be done.

Another relevant challenge faced by the security professionals of today is that new exploit tools are made available daily, whereas the technical knowledge required to operate them is constantly decreasing. Most of them come with examples of use, scripts for attack automation, and sometimes even a GUI, which can make the cyberattack an even simpler task.

This section provides an overall view of the main classes of threats. Before starting the actual discussion, though, a word of warning: the descriptions that follow by no means should be deemed complete, mainly because this is a dynamic subject matter. Furthermore, it is common to find some types of attacks falling within more than one class.

Reconnaissance

Reconnaissance is normally defined as an attack preparation phase rather than an attack class on its own. The underlying goal is to obtain as much information as possible about potential targets without actually interacting with their main application. Internet Control Message Protocol (ICMP) ping sweeps, port scanning (both on UDP and TCP), the observation of a host's behavior under particular conditions (such as exposure to fragmented IP packets), and even *social engineering* are mechanisms that belong to the class of reconnaissance attacks.

Frequently considered harmless (and, as such, overlooked), this practice may be an indicator that attacks are about to happen.

Password Attacks

It is very natural for inside users to have more access rights to the systems of an interconnected organization. Being aware of this characteristic, many attackers leverage techniques that allow them to be authenticated as regular privileged users in such environments. Two possible ways of accomplishing such a goal are

- Creating a new privileged account
- Compromising an existing account and elevating its privileges

Brute-force attacks are those in which all possible combinations of letters are sequentially tried by a program. A *dictionary* attack assumes that users tend to select a common word (typically small) to build their passwords. If the attacker gets access to an encrypted file that contains all the passwords, it will be possible to apply the same encryption to a dictionary of frequently used passwords and compare the results.

Eavesdropping Attacks

Network eavesdropping, also called *sniffing*, is an attack targeted at the *confidentiality* attribute of data. One typical goal here is to obtain valid username and password combinations. In passive eavesdropping, the attacker listens to the message exchange that takes place over the network. This is achievable in many ways: by installing a wiretap; by connecting to shared media, such as an Ethernet hub; or by configuring switch port mirroring (using the attacker's machine as the destination). In active eavesdropping, the attacker tries to produce the mirroring effect but does not need to configure it. Some examples are the exploitation of weaknesses in auxiliary local area network (LAN) protocols such as Dynamic Host Configuration Protocol (DHCP) or Address Resolution Protocol (ARP).

IP Spoofing Attacks

IP spoofing is the act of copying or falsifying a trusted source IP address. It is frequently used as an accessory resource for performing innumerable types of attacks. Typical motivations behind IP spoofing are

- Impersonating a trusted user (or host) and taking advantage of the privileges associated with this trust relationship
- Diverting attention away from the actual attack originator in an attempt to remain undetected
- Casting suspicion on a legitimate host

Man-in-the-Middle Attacks

Man-in-the-middle (MitM) is a broad class of attacks that involve a hacker maliciously inserting a third system into a two-part network conversation or transaction. To achieve this, the attacker establishes independent connections with the victim machines and relays the exchanged messages, thus tricking both victim machines into believing they are directly communicating.

Denial-of-Service Attacks

Since the early days of computer networking, attackers have employed many different techniques to take advantage of system vulnerabilities. Whereas many of the attack categories are focused on compromising the confidentiality or integrity attributes, there are also attempts to affect the availability of services. This last form of doing harm to networked organizations is the practice of *denial of service* (DoS), which induces exhaustion of processing resources (on either connectivity devices or computing hosts), thus keeping legitimate users from accessing the intended applications. DoS attacks can occur in many layers of the OSI reference model, as illustrated in the following examples:

Layer 4 DoS The *TCP SYN flood* is a classic attack that exploits the *three-way handshake* that TCP uses for connection setup. Normally, a TCP three-way handshake consists of a client sending a SYN message to the server, which acknowledges it by sending a SYN-ACK back to the client, causing the client to establish the connection via an ACK message. In this DoS attack, the client never sends the ACK message, creating a substantial number of half-open connections on the server that may exhaust its computing resources.

Layer 3 DoS Earlier examples of Layer 3 DoS attacks were the *Ping of Death* (where a large ICMP Echo message is maliciously sent to a host to cause buffer overflow when it attempts to reassemble the malformed packet), the *Smurf* attack (where an attacker broadcasts an ICMP Echo message using a target host IP as its source and causing all other hosts to flood this host with ICMP Echo Reply messages), and the *teardrop* attack (where an attacker sends fragmented IP packets to a target host, which may crash when trying to reassemble them).

Layer 2 DoS The Spanning Tree Protocol (STP) was created to remove looped connections in an Ethernet LAN. Switches deploying the same STP version exchange communication during a time interval to decide which links must be blocked to avoid such loops. An attacker may send false messages to initiate STP recalculations that can lead to a LAN environment becoming unavailable.

When a DoS attack is performed in a coordinated fashion, with simultaneous use of multiple source hosts, the term *distributed denial-of-service* (DDoS) is used to describe it.

Malware Attacks

Broadly speaking, *malware* is a software program designed to perform unauthorized actions on computer systems, sometimes reaching the limit of causing irreversible damage to them. Malware enters the network through vulnerabilities and can perform multiple types of malicious actions, including blocking access to network elements; installing additional hostile software on the initial target; propagating to neighboring hosts; creating communication channels with remote control machines in order to perpetuate illegal access; and, eventually, rendering systems unusable. Reflecting their main purpose or the way they act, malware is known under various names:

Virus A specific type of malware that depends on some kind of human action to start its job. A virus replicates itself by inserting its code into other programs and files, or even into a computer's boot sector. Viruses may be distributed through peripheral devices (such as flash drives), email attachments, or infected websites.

Worm This malware type does not require a program to trigger its execution, self-replication, and propagation. Once installed in a victim system, it can create multiple copies of itself and spread through the network, infecting any devices that do not have suitable protection in place.

Trojan Horse This is a destructive program that deceives the user by posing as a genuine application. It is very common for Trojans to create backdoors, thus providing attackers with continuous access to the infected system and allowing, for instance, the theft of information.

Adware This malware class is focused on presenting unwanted advertising to users and is typically bundled with free software or browser toolbars.

Launcher This accessory malware is used to download other malicious software. It is normally used for the initial compromise of a target.

Keylogger This malware is designed to stealthily record everything that is typed on a computer keyboard and transmit the data to a remote agent.

Ransomware This type of malware encrypts all user files on the target machine. After the initial compromise, the victim receives a message offering to restore access in return for the payment of a ransom.

Phishing Attacks

Phishing is the practice of sending fraudulent emails that appear to have come from trusted sources with the objective of obtaining personal information or inducing the victim to perform some action, such as clicking on a hyperlink that will install malware.

Spear phishing is a more advanced technique in which the attackers include information that looks personal and is meaningful for the victims. With this investment in time and special preparation, the received message is more likely to be considered genuine.

Risk Management

Now that you have an understanding of common attack categories and how they operate, it is time to start working on the defense-related activities. Such practices involve, but are not limited to, the following:

- Understanding what each of the security technologies in your protection toolbox can bring to the game
- Knowing your key security personnel and determining the level of security education in your organization
- Designing the security processes to be implemented
- Spreading the security culture inside your team and organization

Important Security Solutions and Services

This section provides a quick review of the main security solutions and services available in the market. You can use this section as a reference that you can return to while you read the remaining chapters of this study guide.

Firewalls

In the context of networking, a *firewall* is a security system aimed at isolating specific areas of the network and delimiting domains of trust. The firewall acts as a sort of *conditional gateway*, specifying the traffic types allowed to go from one domain to another by means of access control policies. It is important to keep in mind that a firewall is capable of controlling only the traffic that *passes through* it. Therefore, you must have a clear knowledge of the location of clients (*connection initiators*) and servers in the network before defining your policy.

Firewalls are the classic example of a specialized (and dedicated) security device and are pivotal elements in any defense system. Their evolution, through decades of service, has a lot to do with the OSI layers in which they act. Here's a brief review of the various generations of firewalls:

Packet Filters Packet filters focus their access control efforts on static parameters related to the network and transport layers. They are *stateless* in essence, acting only over individual packets instead of connections.

Circuit-Level Proxies (or Generic Proxies) These proxies establish *sessions*, as defined in Layer 5 of the OSI model, to the intended destinations on behalf of requesting source hosts. The classic implementation of this category is the SOCKS5 software.

Application-Level Proxies (or Dedicated Proxies) These proxies understand and interpret the commands within the application protocol they are providing services for. Given their application awareness, they are able to provide functionality such as caching, detailed logging, and user authentication. The trade-offs are the need to develop specific client software for each protected application and their CPU-intensive nature.

Stateful Firewalls These firewalls incorporate the concept of connections and *state* to the original packet filters. Their access control rules act on *groups of packets* that belong to the same connection (or *flow*), rather than on individual packets. This class of firewalls has been widely deployed, not only because their capabilities are much more advanced than those of packet filters but also because they provide much higher performance than dedicated proxies.

Next-Generation Firewalls (NGFWs) NGFWs have been developed using stateful inspection as a departure point. They include the critical capability of identifying applications, regardless of the TCP or UDP service port they use for transport. This is quite relevant because, with the advent of Web 2.0, many applications try to disguise themselves inside HTTP flows (which are always allowed through stateful firewalls), thus avoiding the use of their originally assigned service ports. This modern class of firewalls also includes easy ways of creating user-based rules and integration with auxiliary tools that dynamically analyze the content inside the IP packets, thus helping overall malware detection and prevention efforts. They are also capable of categorizing and filtering uniform resource locators (URLs) and decrypting Secure Sockets Layer (SSL) channels to inspect the content in the communication data payload. Many NGFWs also deploy intrusion-mitigation techniques, which will be explained in the "Intrusion Detection and Intrusion Prevention" section later in this chapter.

Web Proxies

A *web proxy* (also known as a web gateway) is an important example of an application-level firewall, typically used to control the access of internal corporate users to outside web servers (*outbound* access control). Among many other features, this class of device is capable of blocking malware, enforcing acceptable-use policies, categorizing and filtering URLs, and controlling content based on the reputation of the sites hosting it. The main objective of web proxies is to keep external content requested by internal clients from harming the organization. Nevertheless, given the evolution of NGFWs, this well-known security element is falling into obsolescence.

Web Application Firewalls

The web application firewall (WAF) is a specialized security element that acts as a full-reverse proxy, protecting applications that are accessed through the HTTP protocol. Whereas web proxies protect the client side, WAF devices protect the server side of the connection from application layer attacks. A typical WAF analyzes each HTTP command, thus ensuring that only those actions specified in the security policy can be performed. A reference for WAF action is compensating for the top vulnerabilities identified by OWASP (*Open Web Application Security Project*). Among the most common vulnerabilities are code injection and cross-site scripting. Figure 1.6 contrasts the insertion of web proxies and WAF devices in the network topology.

FIGURE 1.6 Contrasting WAF and a web proxy

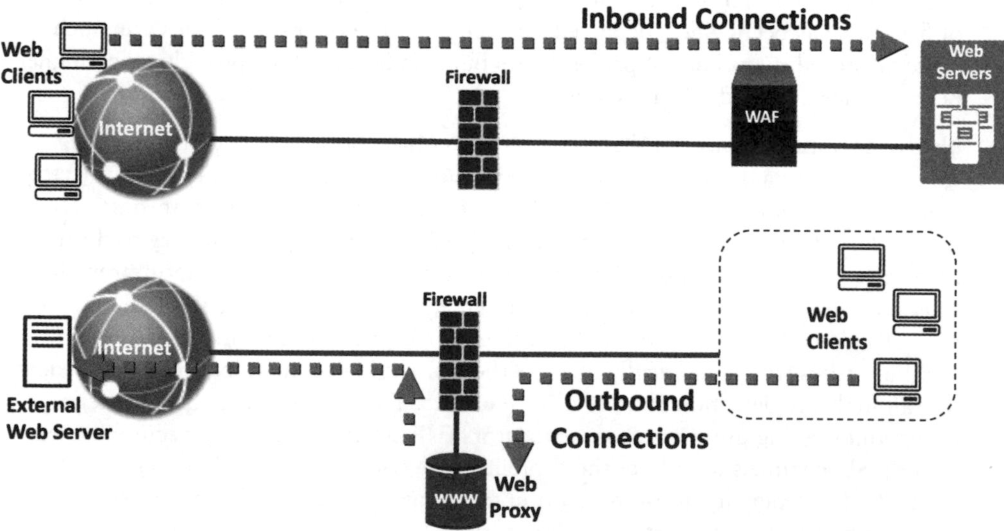

You should not confuse the *Application Visibility and Control* (AVC) capabilities of NGFWs, which are focused on controlling outbound user access, with the services provided by WAFs. Instead of replacing one with another, they can actually work in tandem.

Intrusion Detection and Intrusion Prevention

Intrusion-detection and intrusion-prevention technologies provide in-depth inspection capabilities so that the occurrence of malicious traffic can be discovered inside network packets, at either their header or data portion. While *intrusion-detection system* (IDS) devices handle only copies of the packets and are mainly concerned with monitoring and alerting tasks, *intrusion-prevention system* (IPS) solutions are deployed inline in the traffic flow and have the inherent design goal of avoiding actual damage to systems.

IDSs and IPSs can look for well-known attack patterns within packet streams and take an action according to the configured policy. Some typical actions are packet drop, connection block, denying further access to the address that sourced the attack, and sending an alert when an attack indication (*signature*) is spotted.

IPSs act as a normal companion to stateful firewalls, mainly for data center protection (inbound traffic). They provide detailed analysis for the connections permitted by firewalls, thus complementing their work. An IPS concentrates most of its analysis at the Network, Transport and Application layers, possibly maintaining state (*stateful pattern matching*) and executing traffic anomaly detection.

There are many possible formats for practical IPS deployment:

- As a dedicated appliance
- As a dedicated hardware (or software) module inside a stateful firewall
- As a resource that is enabled on a per-firewall rule basis on NGFWs

Figure 1.7 displays a typical coordination of protection devices that are well suited for controlling *inbound* access.

FIGURE 1.7 Sample inbound topology

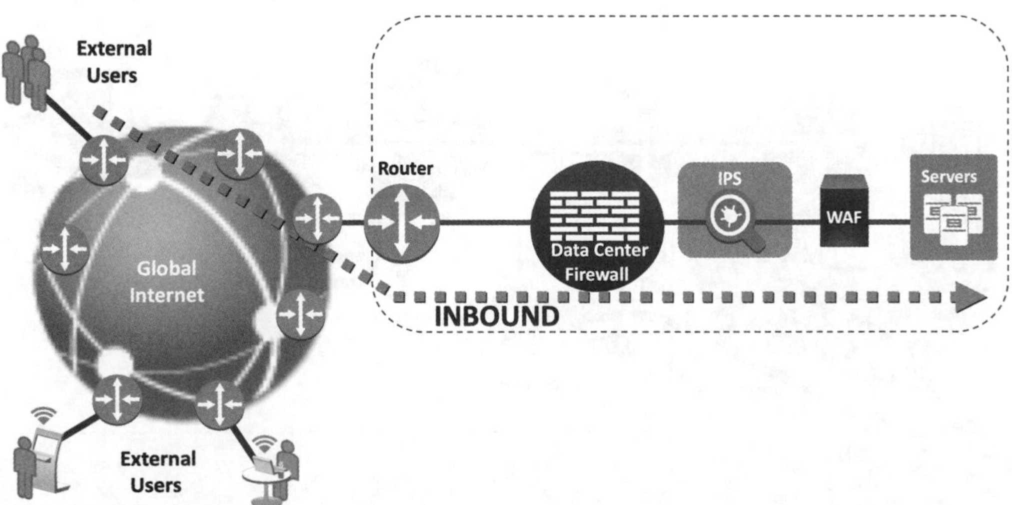

Virtual Private Networks

The term *virtual private network* (VPN) is used to refer to technologies that reproduce the characteristics of a private corporate network, even when traffic is being transported over a shared network infrastructure. VPNs were created to provide a secure extension of corporate networks, without requiring a dedicated infrastructure based on expensive WAN circuits.

But security has a broad meaning and may represent very different resources when considered from the standpoint of a particular VPN technology. To further your understanding, we'll summarize the main categories.

The IPsec framework provides answers for questions such as confidentiality, integrity, and authentication of VPN participants and management of cryptographic keys. All of these tasks are accomplished by using standardized protocols and algorithms, a fact that contributed to render IPsec ubiquitous. IPsec supports both client-to-site (or *remote access VPN*) and site-to-site (also known as *LAN-to-LAN*) deployment models. IPsec operates at the Network layer (Layer 3) and, as such, is able to protect native IP protocols (ICMP, for instance) or any application carried over TCP or UDP.

SSL VPN is another remote access VPN technology that does not require a dedicated client. When it was created, SSL VPN was even considered a synonym of *clientless access* (because web browsers are considered a sort of universal client that is available on any networked machine). And this possibility of providing secure remote access, even for those stations that were not managed by corporate IT, sounded appealing for administrators. Not long after the inception of SSL, customers started to request a *client-based* SSL-VPN option that could eventually replace IPsec as the standard remote-access VPN solution. One benefit is the fact that SSL is used everywhere (mainly for HTTP protection) and, as a result, is permitted through firewalls and routers along the path. A classic topology for VPN termination (either IPsec or SSL-based) is shown in Figure 1.8.

FIGURE 1.8 Classic topology for VPN termination

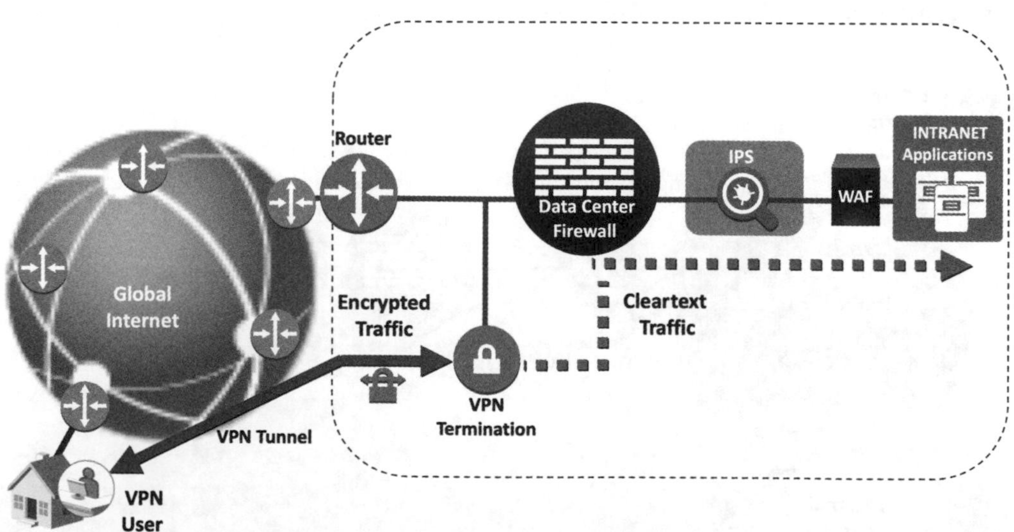

A third common use of the term VPN relates to the *Multiprotocol Label Switching* (MPLS) space, where the service known as *MPLS VPN* was designed to achieve logical network segmentation and optimized routing (in an *any-to-any* or *full-mesh* topology). Although segmentation means providing native traffic isolation among tenants that are transported through the MPLS backbone, there is no provision for the security mechanisms that IPsec deals with (integrity, confidentiality, and authentication). IPsec can be used to add security services for the virtual circuits that characterize MPLS VPN. Although MPLS VPN is primarily used by telecommunications providers to isolate tenant traffic in a shared backbone, we included it here to show you how flexible the term *VPN* is.

Protecting DNS and Using Insights from DNS

The Domain Name System (DNS) is a hierarchical and decentralized directory that maps the assigned hostnames of resources connected to the Internet or other IP networks to their corresponding IP addresses. The motivation is to simplify access to applications by using (ideally) easy-to-remember names, thus avoiding the need for the end user to know the machine-readable IP addresses. This name-to-IP association process, which precedes the actual application request, lies at the heart of the Internet's operation. This official distributed database is constructed in a collaborative way, and the exchange of information pertaining to this process relies on the DNS protocol.

Given the foundational role played by DNS in the Internet architecture, research on two mutually complementary fields has increased:

- Understanding how the protocol operates and its inherent vulnerabilities so that not only message exchange (client-to-server and server-to-server) can be secured but also access can be provided to a directory whose data integrity can be ensured
- Leveraging the information on such a large and dynamic database to keep users from connecting to well-known malicious domains in an attempt to minimize the likelihood that a legitimate user brings harmful content inside the organization

Tools for Vulnerability Analysis and Management

As defined in the earlier section "Basic Security Concepts," a vulnerability is a weakness that can be exploited. It may be seen as a sort of *door that should not be open*. In the context of IT, the *vulnerability assessment* process involves identifying and classifying vulnerabilities in the digital entities that compose the computing environment under analysis (such as end-user machines, operating systems, applications, and key networking elements). After this information-gathering phase, the findings should be presented in a structured fashion so that the corrective actions can be prioritized according to the risk level. Although the grouping of topics may vary among vendors, the typical tasks included in the process may be summarized as follows:

Inventory Compiling *It is very difficult to protect a resource you are not aware of.* Building a hardware and software inventory of the environment is a basic step toward the goal of minimizing the attack surface. The assets that are mission-critical must be identified and grouped according to their business value.

Identification of Vulnerabilities Running scanning tools throughout the inventory will help you create a list of current vulnerabilities (mainly software bugs and misconfigurations) and where they reside.

Definition of Priorities Not all vulnerabilities have the same criticality level and, as such, must not be deemed equally urgent. Considering the business relevance of each potential target will guide the IT staff on prioritizing efforts. If your tool of choice is able to automate the categorization of vulnerabilities and assign some sort of *risk rating*, instead of just presenting a long list of affected entities, it will be much more useful.

Remediation By using the risk-oriented list of the previous step, you can build a road map of actions to be taken so that you reduce the exposure level. If the chosen tool automatically identifies the corrections that must be made, it will be even more useful.

Effectiveness Measurement Knowing that you took the right path, and having some perception of progress, positively affects the morale of the team. "*How much did we reduce the exposure level?*" and "*How does our company compare with our competitors in the same market segment?*" are two simple evaluations that should follow remediation. Again, this can be done manually or, ideally, by selecting a tool that automates it.

Security is not just about technology. It is a continuous process. It involves people. Irrespective of the particular tool you eventually choose and the way it structures and presents the vulnerability data, going through the typical steps we've just described must be a part of your security team's routine. Furthermore, there should be a suitable periodicity.

Correlation of Security Information and Events

Security information and event management (SIEM) solutions are designed to collect security-related logs as well as flow information generated by systems (at the host or application level), networking devices, and dedicated defense elements such as firewalls, IPSs, IDSs, and antivirus software. They work by aggregating, normalizing, and categorizing the received information and then applying intelligence algorithms that allow them to correlate events that refer to particular sessions. Here are some reasons you might employ SIEM solutions:

- To lower the volume of data that must be dealt with by removing ambiguous session information and avoiding the generation of events for legitimate resource use
- To provide real-time insights on security alerts, clearly separating what is meaningful in an attempt to minimize the occurrence of false positives
- To prioritize response actions so that the most critical issues are treated first (according to associated risk level)

Modern SIEM solutions include *artificial intelligence* (AI) and *user behavior analytics* (UBA) so that they can quickly spot deviations from the normal network activity profile for a particular user, which may indicate intentional misuse or, eventually, derive from system compromise. In a sense, SIEM solutions tend to complement the vulnerability management practice. Whereas the latter deals with the somehow *static* measures of closing the doors that do not need to remain open, the former is more dynamic in nature, providing real-time visibility of what is flowing through the doors.

One critical thing you can do to make your SIEM project successful is to devote time for event filtering so that you can limit the amount of data that will be collected. This approach not only improves performance but also impacts on cost, because most products (and services) are charged based on storage amount or *events per second* (EPS). Another factor in your SIEM selection is to understand *how ready it is* for the correlation tasks pertaining to the systems within your environment. To determine that, ask the following questions:

- Are there native integration agents so that my systems start sending logs to the SIEM?
- Do I need to send every log to the system and then select the security events? Is it possible for the systems of interest to send only security-related information?
- How *plug-and-play* is the solution? What is the average customization time for putting it to work?
- How does the system scale?
- Does the SIEM integrate with incident response tools?

SIEM is a classic example of a solution that has a tremendous potential for alleviating the operational burden of security monitoring. But, to really benefit from it, you will need to invest in training, thus making sure that the team gets acquainted with the capabilities of the tool. It is also advisable to ensure that a detailed documentation of the environment is available and what types of logs and flow data are generated by each of the monitored sources. *This process is not only about acquiring a product or service.*

TLS/SSL Offload and Visibility

The *Secure Sockets Layer* (SSL) protocol was developed to provide services such as data integrity, confidentiality, and peer authentication for application protocols that are carried over TCP. The motivation behind the construction of such a generic layer of security was to avoid the need for embedding security for every application. SSL was updated up to version 3.0, which was deprecated in 2015 and replaced by the standards-based *Transport Layer Security* (TLS) protocol.

Some studies show that TLS/SSL usage is growing continuously. What should be deemed an evolution of the overall security practice brings the collateral effect of lack of visibility, thus allowing malicious traffic to hide inside the encrypted channels. To cope with this new challenge, many security solutions, such as NGFWs, WAFs, and IPSs, started supporting decryption of the TLS streams before going through the analysis activities they were designed for.

By deploying TLS-offload operations, these solutions can provide the following benefits:

- Web servers can be offloaded from any encryption duties (or leverage less-intensive encryption algorithms), which allow them to serve more concurrent clients with a better response time.

- The security solutions can now process and analyze Layers 5–7 information that was originally encrypted (and therefore, reaching application services without any protection).
- The security solutions can centralize public certificates and allow the use of private certificates (which are less expensive and easier to maintain) in the web servers.

TLS Orchestration

Because TLS decryption can be relatively CPU-intensive, it can negatively impact the performance of specialized on-premises appliances that deploy TLS offload (such as NGFWs, WAFs, and IPSs) and introduce latency in their filtering operations. To deal with such a scenario, a solution known as *TLS orchestration* was devised. The idea is to provide a centralized TLS decryption service whose operations include the following:

1. TLS traffic arriving on a centralized device called *TLS orchestrator*, where such traffic is decrypted.
2. The cleartext traffic is dynamically steered to the inspection elements, according to their individual capabilities.
3. After going through the chain of inspection services, the legitimate traffic is sent back to the TLS orchestrator.
4. Traffic is re-encrypted by the orchestrator and delivered to the original destination.

Handling Security Incidents

In the context of information security, an *incident* is defined as a violation (or a threat of violation) of security policies, acceptable-use policies, or standard security practices. Among the actions that may follow from the occurrence of an incident are a negative impact on its reputation, a loss of intellectual property, or unauthorized access to data.

To deal with these sorts of events, you should establish an *incident handling program*. For instance, you should define the meaning of "incident" within your organization. Another important step is to assign an incident response team, with clearly defined responsibilities, among which creating an incident response plan deserves special mention.

As in other domains, incident response may also leverage some tools in order to make the daily tasks of security administrators a bit easier. For example, a new class of products, grouped under the term *security orchestration, automation, and response* (SOAR), has been developed. SIEM solutions are a natural source of information to SOAR systems, which focus on coordinating and automating response actions among multiple protection elements using the concept of playbooks. The ability to create response templates for those incidents that happen often may free a significant amount of time for administrators, thus allowing them to focus on what is different or new.

Structured Malware Protection

As discussed before, there are various categories of computer programs that can be grouped under the name *malware*. There is no absolute strategy for providing protection against malware attacks. Therefore, the next section will introduce an approach for *structured malware protection* as a practical usage example of a security model.

Well-Known Security Frameworks and Models

The concept of security risk is based on the likelihood of a certain vulnerability being exploited, and its respective impact potential, which depends on the value of the digital asset under analysis.

The underlying goal of reducing risk inspired the creation of *security frameworks*, which are published materials that typically include standards, guidelines, sample policies, recommended security safeguards and tools, risk management approaches, relevant technologies, and recognized best practices for protection of certain computing environments.

At a tactical level, the contents inside the framework will translate into *security controls*, which must map to the specific threats a company may be exposed to. A basic design principle that will help in selecting the appropriate controls is to add more layers of defense according to the criticality of the asset being protected.

Many frameworks were developed with a particular goal in mind, such as providing guidance for a given industry segment (according, for instance, to the type of data that is more relevant for that sector, the most valuable systems, and the associated communication protocols). On the other hand, there are examples of frameworks that are meant for more general use. Among the various examples that are in use, some deserve special mention:

Payment Card Industry Data Security Standard (PCI DSS) Created with the goal of increasing the level of protection for issuers of credit cards by requiring that merchants meet minimum levels of security when they process, store, and transmit card holder data.

Health Insurance Portability and Accountability Act (HIPAA) A set of security standards for protecting certain health information that is transferred or held in electronic form.

National Institute for Standards and Technology Cybersecurity Framework (NIST CSF) A publication that results from a collaborative work among industry, academia, and the U.S. government. The framework recognizes that the cybersecurity activities inside an organization should be guided by its business drivers. It also establishes that the overall risk management process should include the risks pertaining to the cybersecurity domain. The CSF assembles standards, guidelines, and practices that have proved effective and may be used by entities belonging to any market segment.

General Data Protection Regulation (GDPR) A set of rules created by the European Union (EU) that requires businesses to protect the personal data and privacy of EU citizens. GDPR not only applies to transactions that occur within the EU members but also governs the transfer of personal data outside the EU. This regulation states that foreign entities willing to conduct business with EU companies also need to demonstrate their compliance with GDPR. This fact motivated the creation of GDPR-like standards outside Europe.

Instead of focusing on security standards that apply to the type of organization you are in charge of protecting, you should become familiar with those principles that can be employed in a broader sense.

Sample Practical Models for Guiding Security Design and Operations

Security controls are implemented to reduce the level of risk to which an organization is exposed. Generically speaking, they are divided into three main categories:

Physical Controls Designed to protect facility, personnel, and material resources. Some examples are locks, fencing, monitoring cameras, and security agents. This type of control is inherently present in the data centers belonging to the large cloud service providers such as AWS.

Logical Controls Many examples of this category of controls are provided in the section "Important Security Solutions and Services" earlier in this chapter.

Administrative Controls Some examples of this class are risk management process, security documentation, and training (not only specific to operations but also to promote overall security awareness within the organization).

The Security Wheel

Figure 1.9 portrays the *security wheel*, a closed-loop model for security operations that is centered on the foundational concept of security policy, discussed earlier in the "Understanding Security" section. This model recognizes that the security practice has a continuous and cyclical nature and is structured in five basic stages:

1. **Develop a Security Policy:** Start with a high-level policy that clearly establishes and documents the strategic goals that relate to the business drivers or mission of the organization. The policy should refer to the appropriate standards, guidelines, procedures, and baselines that will guide the actual implementation.
2. **Implement Security Measures:** Having defined the assets that need to be protected and the appropriate protection level (according to business relevance), you next deploy the

security controls that will contribute to risk mitigation. Many layers of defense, such as those described in the "Important Security Solutions and Services" section, may be coordinated to provide better security.

FIGURE 1.9 The security wheel

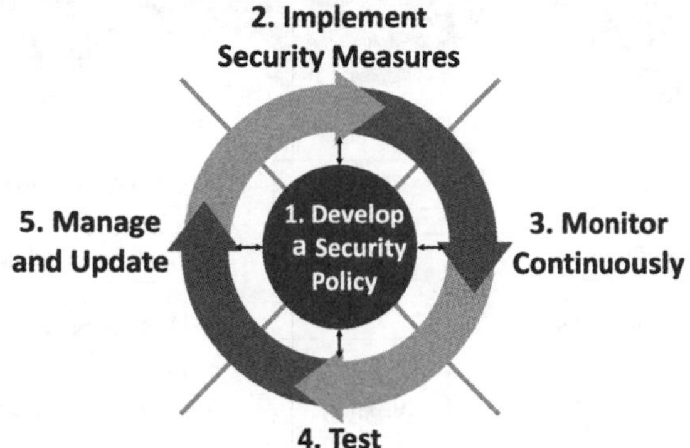

3. **Monitor Continuously:** At this stage, resources such as logging, intrusion detection, and SIEM are employed to spot violations of the access policies.
4. **Test:** Even though you may have invested a lot in protection and monitoring capabilities, *you should not take them for granted.* Systems evolve rapidly and new ways to exploit their weaknesses will be readily available. Vulnerability analysis and management apply well to this stage.
5. **Manage and Update:** Taking as a departure point the feedback that comes from stages 3 and 4, improvements can be applied to stage 2 in the form of new or updated controls. Depending on the specific findings, you may need to review the security policy (for instance, in case it was too permissive or too simple in its original definitions and that reference led to exposure and high risk to the organization's assets).

The Attack Continuum Model

Security is a moving target. No matter the investment of time, effort, and financial resources to protect the organization, new challenges will be faced every day. And attack attempts keep happening all around. Despite the security structure you might have in place, falling victim to a cyberattack is just a matter of time. Of course, the more solid the construction of your layered defense system, the lower the probability of the attack effects being spread throughout the company.

Building on the axiom that *attacks happen*, the attack continuum model associates the security controls with the phase to which they relate most: *before*, *during*, or *after* the attack. Figure 1.10 represents the attack continuum model and suggests some security solutions that may fit each of the model phases:

FIGURE 1.10 The attack continuum model

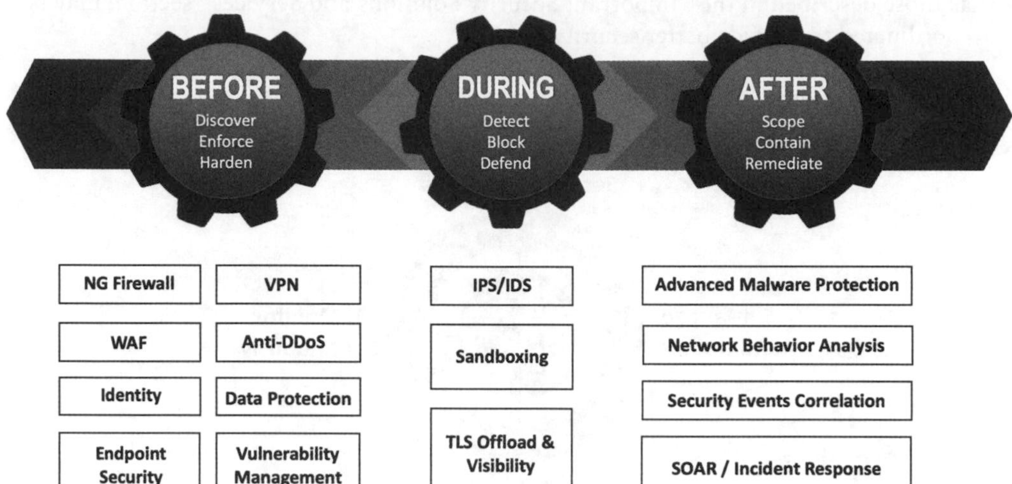

- **Before:** The tools and methods used here refer mainly to attack *prevention* tasks. The motivation is to have the controls that allow you to minimize the attack surface.
- **During:** *Detection* and monitoring tools, which provide visibility and awareness of what is going on during live packet flow, are the key types of resources for this stage.
- **After:** It is increasingly common that modern attack tools are programmed to have an initial *dormant phase*, with the underlying goal of remaining undetected for a certain period. A good defense implementation needs retrospective security capabilities so that these intentionally delayed threats can be detected (and stopped) before any damage. The protection mechanisms for this phase should identify the point of entry, understand its reach, contain the propagation, and remediate any eventual damage or disruption.

Of course, once a threat is found in the *after the attack* stage, the implicit feedback loop of this model must be used so that the prevention resources of the *before the attack* stage are updated to avoid reinfection.

Applying the Attack Continuum Model for Structured Malware Protection

As a practical illustration, a range of protection mechanisms that can be effective in fighting against malware are positioned within the attack continuum model, as shown in Figure 1.11.

- **Before the Attack:** Avoiding the connection of internal users to well-known malicious domains, and to IP addresses that have been used to host domains with bad reputations, proves to be an effective antimalware measure. To achieve that, tools that provide insights about the current DNS infrastructure and help with identifying domain generation algorithms are very useful. NGFWs and modern IPSs that can block traffic after evaluating the content being transported can also contribute to this effort. For instance, they can block files that are deemed harmful, based on hash information that comes from cyberintelligence sources, thus avoiding their entry into the organization. TLS orchestration systems can play the important auxiliary role of providing visibility for all the inspection devices.

FIGURE 1.11 The attack continuum model applied to malware protection

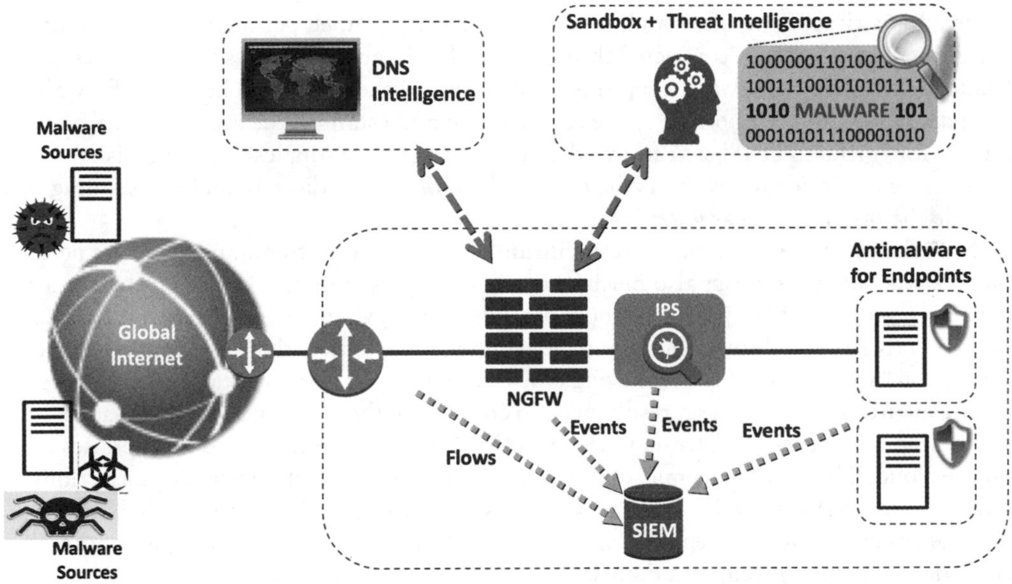

- **During the Attack:** While the allowed packets are flowing through the network, monitoring tools should be in place. For instance, IPSs should be searching for attack patterns, and files that come through email or web vectors (and whose reputation are not known) can be dynamically evaluated by interaction with *sandbox* solutions, which execute untrusted applications in a separate environment without risking production systems.
- **After the Attack:** Even after all the efforts carried out in the previous phases, some attacks may still be successful. Instead of getting depressed about such an occurrence, consider this an invitation to invest even more in an organized work method. A good start here relates to answering questions such as: Was the attack a result of misconfiguration of one of my protection elements? Was it a result of an unpatched vulnerability? Was the attack totally unknown? In the two first cases, it is a matter of hard and structured work to apply the appropriate corrections. In the last case, a good option is to have antimalware software running on the endpoints, which should be considered

the last line of defense. By looking for abnormal behavior, this kind of element can block malicious activities taking place on end hosts, without need of specific previous knowledge. An access attempt to an external *command and control* source, from a dormant threat on the inside, can also be an indicator of a new threat; DNS insight tools are useful for that purpose. SIEM solutions can also be handy to identify that certain actions, when combined, represent an attack.

The Zero-Trust Model

Once upon a time, in an ideal land, there existed clearly defined perimeters for corporate networks. Branch offices connected through leased lines or IPsec VPNs to the company headquarters, and there was a central point of access to the Internet. The classic firewalls were able to delimit the borders of the organization and establish the access control conditions for traffic to flow between two domains of trust. The simplest logical division was to consider the inside networks as the *trusted domain* and all those IP addresses falling outside the organization as *untrusted.*

Nonetheless, times have changed significantly and computer communication has not only become ubiquitous but also much more complex. The options of access technologies have been multiplied, and each user now possibly owns several devices. Branch offices connect directly to the Internet, thus greatly expanding the frontiers that need supervision and protection. Most companies are moving at least a portion of their workloads to cloud computing environments and, as a result, need to coordinate the security efforts so that they have compatible levels of defense, independently of the data being located on-premises or on the cloud. The extranet connections that, on one hand, simplify business transactions among partners, on the other hand may create shared vulnerabilities, especially if one of the companies is less experienced about security. These are only a few examples of the common challenges faced, on a daily basis, by network administrators.

To adapt to this context, a relatively recent framework, *zero trust,* has established itself as a reference for security design. The model is based on the *principle of least privilege*, which states that organizations should grant the minimal amount of permissions that are strictly necessary for each user or application to work. Therefore, they should not implicitly trust any entity, at any time, no matter if it resides outside or inside the organization domains.

The great philosophy change brought about by zero trust is concerned with avoiding a blind trust of inside hosts and networks. The typical assumption that internal systems are reliable is flawed, because if a single inside host is compromised, lateral movement and associated threat spread will become easy tasks. From a network traffic standpoint, this new security paradigm advocates heavy use of network segmentation, encryption technologies, and identity-based access controls, both at the user and the device levels.

The zero-trust approach is an interesting architecture for cloud environments, which are usually *multitenant* by design and, as such, do not allow you to implicitly trust a shared network. Some relevant controls guided by this model are as follows:

- Using advanced authentication and authorization resources, before granting access, is key for avoiding undesired use of your computing resources or, even worse, unauthorized access to data under your control.
- Promoting granular segmentation of the network, up to the point where you are able to define access control rules down to a single instance level (when necessary), is another key measure associated with the new "shared land" reality. This fine-grained rule-building practice is frequently called *microsegmentation*.
- The use of encryption technologies everywhere is key to bring the confidentiality and integrity attributes to the scene, thus helping you to ensure that data privacy has not been compromised and that data remains unaltered.

Summary

In this chapter, we reviewed general concepts and terminology that are indispensable, both for demonstrating a good level of general education on the security subject matter and for a better understanding of the upcoming chapters.

After exploring basic networking and security definitions, we introduced the main classes of attacks as well as the typical elements that can be used to protect against them. Taking into consideration the critical axiom that *security is not a product*, we reviewed some well-known security frameworks. These particular security models have been selected among the countless options available, not only for being very practical in nature but also because they are complementary to each other.

We discussed the *security wheel*, designed to remind you of the importance of building a security policy and having processes in place to deal with daily security challenges. We next examined the *attack continuum model*, which shows you how to position the available security controls according to their capability of adding value to dealing with a particular attack stage. Finally, we introduced the *zero-trust* paradigm, which is based on the principle of least privilege, thus providing the recommended mindset for creating controls on the shared computing environments that are so characteristic of cloud computing.

Exam Essentials

Understand basic security definitions. A *vulnerability* is a weakness within a computer system that can be exploited to perform unauthorized actions. A *threat* is a potential danger that may derive from the exploitation of a vulnerability. *Security risk* relates to the probability of a certain vulnerability being exploited and the corresponding impact, which will depend on the value of the digital asset under analysis. *Accountability* is an attribute related to a certain individual or organization being held responsible for its actions. *Nonrepudiation* is ensuring that someone cannot deny an action that has already been performed to avoid attempts of not being accountable.

Understand confidentiality, integrity, and availability. *Confidentiality* is concerned with preventing unauthorized disclosure of sensitive information and with ensuring a suitable level of privacy at all stages of data processing. *Integrity* deals with the prevention of unauthorized modification of data and with ensuring information accuracy. *Availability* focuses on ensuring reliability and an acceptable level of performance for legitimate users of computing resources. Together, these security principles form the *CIA triad*.

Know the components of the AAA architecture. In the AAA architecture, *authentication* deals with the question "Who is the user?"; *authorization* has to do with defining "What is the user allowed to do?"; and *accounting* relates to the question "What did the user do?"

Understand the OSI model. The *OSI model* was developed by the International Organization for Standardization (ISO) and divides data communication into seven layers: Physical, Data Link, Network, Transport, Session, Presentation, and Application.

Understand the TCP/IP stack. The *TCP/IP stack* is a suite of network protocols that was developed to support ARPANET and is largely used on the Internet today. Because it precedes the OSI model, it does not match the OSI's division of seven layers. The main TCP/IP stack protocols are the Internet Protocol (IP), Transmission Control Protocol (TCP), and User Datagram Protocol (UDP).

Understand reconnaissance and eavesdropping attacks. *Reconnaissance* attacks aim to obtain as much information as possible about potential targets, without actually interacting with their main application. Such attacks use resources such as ICMP ping sweeps, port scanning, and even social engineering for their objective. *Eavesdropping* attacks analyze network traffic with the objective of obtaining valid username and password combinations or other relevant user information.

Understand common classes of attacks. *Password* attacks attempt to obtain access rights to the systems of a networked organization through brute force (testing all combinations) or dictionary techniques (using common words). *IP spoofing* is the act of copying or falsifying a trusted source IP address. *Man-in-the-middle* attacks involve a hacker inserting itself into a two-part network conversation or transaction as a way of accessing all information. *Denial-of-service* attacks are focused on compromising the availability of services. Finally, *phishing* is the practice of sending fraudulent emails that appear to have come from trusted sources, with the objective of obtaining personal information or inducing the receivers to perform some action, such as clicking on a hyperlink that will install malware.

Be able to define malware. *Malware* is a software program designed to perform unauthorized actions on computer systems, sometimes reaching the limit of causing irreversible damage to them. According to the way malware acts, it may be classified as virus, worm, Trojan horse, adware, launcher, keylogger, or ransomware.

Understand firewalls and their related technologies. A *firewall* is a security system aimed at isolating specific areas of the network and delimiting domains of trust. Throughout their development history, firewalls were classified as packet filters, circuit-level proxies, application-level proxies, stateful firewalls, and next-generation firewalls. A *web proxy* is an example of an application-level firewall that is used to control the access of internal corporate users to outside web servers. A *web application firewall* (WAF) is a specialized security element that protects applications that are accessed through HTTP.

Know the difference between IDS and IPS technologies. Intrusion-detection and intrusion-prevention technologies were conceived to provide in-depth inspection capabilities so that the occurrence of malicious traffic can be determined inside network packets at either their header or data portions. While *intrusion-detection system (IDS)* devices handle only copies of the packets, being mainly concerned with monitoring and alerting tasks, *intrusion-prevention system (IPS)* solutions are deployed inline in the traffic flow and have the inherent design goal of avoiding actual damage to systems.

Be able to define VPNs. *Virtual private networks (VPNs)* refer to technologies that reproduce the characteristics of a private corporate network, even when traffic is being transported over a shared network infrastructure.

Be familiar with SIEM solutions. *Security information and event management (SIEM)* solutions collect security-related logs, as well as flow information, generated by end systems (at the host or the application level), networking devices, and dedicated defense elements, such as firewalls, IPSs, IDSs, and antivirus.

Know the main security frameworks. The *Payment Card Industry Data Security Standard (PCI DSS)* was created with the goal of increasing the level of protection for issuers of credit cards by requiring that merchants meet minimum levels of security when they process, store, and transmit card holder data. The *Health Insurance Portability and Accountability Act (HIPAA)* is a set of security standards for protecting certain health information that is transferred or held in electronic form. The *National Institute for Standards and Technology Cybersecurity Framework (NIST CSF)* is a framework that assembles security standards, guidelines, and practices that have proved effective and may be used by entities belonging to any market segment. The *General Data Protection Regulation (GDPR)* is a set of rules created by the European Union (EU), requiring businesses to protect the personal data and privacy of EU citizens.

Know the main security models. The *security wheel* is a closed-loop practical model that has a continuous and cyclical nature and is structured in five basic stages: develop a security policy, implement security measures, monitor and respond, test, and manage and improve. The *attack continuum model* is based on the axiom that attacks happen and associates the security controls with each phase they relate to the most: before, during, or after the attack. Finally, the *zero-trust* security model is based on the *principle of least privilege*, which states that organizations should grant the minimal amount of permissions that are strictly necessary for each user or application to work. Therefore, they should not implicitly trust any entity, at any time, no matter if it resides outside or inside the organization domains.

Review Questions

1. Read the following statements and choose the correct option:
   - a. A vulnerability is a weakness within a computer system that can be exploited to perform unauthorized actions.
   - b. A security risk is defined as any entity (such as a person or a tool) that can exploit a vulnerability intentionally or by accident.
   - c. A threat relates to the probability of a certain vulnerability being exploited by a threat actor, which will depend on the value of the digital asset under analysis.

   A. Options a, b, and c are correct.
   B. Only option a is correct.
   C. Only option b is correct.
   D. Only option c is correct.

2. Read the following statements and choose the correct option:
   - a. Confidentiality can be addressed through data encryption.
   - b. Integrity can be addressed via hashing algorithms.
   - c. Availability can be addressed with recovery plans.

   A. Options a, b, and c are correct.
   B. Only option a is correct.
   C. Only option b is correct.
   D. Only option c is correct.

3. What better defines "the property of ensuring that someone cannot deny an action that has already been performed so that you can avoid attempts of not being accountable"?

   A. Accountability
   B. Nonrepudiation
   C. Responsibility
   D. Verification
   E. Authentication

4. Which option correctly defines the AAA architecture?

   A. Accountability, authorization, availability
   B. Authentication, authorization, anonymity
   C. Authentication, authorization, accountability
   D. Authentication, authorization, accounting
   E. Authorization, anonymity, accountability

5. Which option represents the seven OSI model layers in the correct order?
   - **A.** Physical, Data Link, Network, Transport, Session, Presentation, and Application
   - **B.** Physical, Data Link, Network, Transport, Session, Application, and Presentation
   - **C.** Physical, Data Link, Routing, Transport, Session, Presentation, and Application
   - **D.** Bit, Frame, Packet, Connection, Session, Coding, and User Interface
   - **E.** Physical, Media Access Control, Network, Transport, Session, Presentation, and Application

6. Which of the following options is not correct?
   - **A.** UDP is part of the TCP/IP stack.
   - **B.** IP can be related to the Network layer of the OSI model.
   - **C.** ICMP, OSPF, and BGP are dynamic routing protocols.
   - **D.** TCP is a connection-oriented and reliable transport protocol.
   - **E.** UDP is a connectionless and unreliable transport protocol.

7. Which well-known class of cyberattacks is focused on affecting the availability of an application, connectivity device, or computing hosts?
   - **A.** Man-in-the-middle
   - **B.** Phishing
   - **C.** Malware
   - **D.** Reconnaissance
   - **E.** Denial of service

8. Which of the following options is not correct?
   - **A.** A firewall is a security system aimed at isolating specific areas of the network and delimiting domains of trust.
   - **B.** A typical WAF analyzes each HTTP command, thus ensuring that only those actions specified on the security policy can be performed.
   - **C.** All VPNs were created to provide a secure extension of corporate networks, without the need of using a dedicated infrastructure but ensuring data confidentiality.
   - **D.** IPsec deals with integrity, confidentiality, and authentication.
   - **E.** SIEM stands for security information and event management.

9. Which security framework was created with the goal of increasing the level of protection for issuers of credit cards?
   - **A.** HIPAA
   - **B.** GDPR
   - **C.** PCI DSS
   - **D.** NIST CSF
   - **E.** CS STAR

10. Which concept guides the zero-trust security model?
    A. Develop, implement, monitor continuously, test, and improve
    B. Before, during, and after an attack
    C. Principle of least privilege
    D. In transit and at rest
    E. Automation

Cloud Security Principles and Frameworks

THE AWS CERTIFIED SECURITY SPECIALTY EXAM OBJECTIVES THAT LEVERAGE CONCEPTS EXPLAINED IN THIS CHAPTER INCLUDE THE FOLLOWING:

✓ **Domain 1: Incident Response**

- 1.2. Verify that the Incident Response plan includes relevant AWS services

✓ **Domain 3: Infrastructure Security**

- 3.4. Design and implement host-based security

Introduction

In this chapter, you will learn critical cloud security concepts that will help you create the foundation to go deeper into all the topics covered in the next chapters.

These concepts will be critical in your journey to pass the AWS Certified Security Specialty exam. We will introduce the following topics:

- Cloud security principles
- The Shared Responsibility Model
- AWS compliance programs
- AWS Well-Architected Framework
- AWS Marketplace

Cloud Security Principles Overview

As a general rule, the concepts and controls studied in Chapter 1, "Security Fundamentals," apply to both on-premises and cloud-based environments. Nonetheless, before moving your workloads to the cloud, you must determine what tasks will remain under your control and what tasks will be taken care of by the *cloud service provider* (CSP) of your choice. The sum of these efforts is usually referred to as the *Shared Responsibility Model.*

One noticeable challenge regarding cloud security is the inherent perception of loss of control. This initial suspicion may be a result of the lack of visibility into the provider's environment or incompatibility of security tools and rules used in the cloud, as compared to those resources your company is familiar with. Although it may sound obvious, you should not move to a provider that you do not trust. And moving from doubt to trust does not mean simply verifying that the CSP has a famous security certification or accreditation displayed on its website. It is *essential* to understanding the security practices and controls available on the provider's infrastructure and, even more important, how to enable and enforce those controls.

Generally speaking, physical controls are more readily available and consistent in the cloud. That happens because, in order to sound attractive and reliable to their potential customers, CSPs must invest in highly available data centers and enforce restrictive rules for physical access to facilities. Doing so might prove to be impracticable for most companies, which will, most frequently, have third parties in charge of those activities. Moreover, some IT security teams from more traditional organizations may frown at the need to take care of these physical aspects or even consider them as secondary concerns for someone who is in charge of *infrastructure specifics*.

As the pioneer and clear leader of the cloud service provider market, Amazon Web Services (AWS) has focused its development efforts on embedding security controls in each of its cloud services (such as Amazon EC2, Amazon S3, and Amazon VPC). In addition, AWS created innovative security services such as AWS Identity and Access Management (IAM), AWS Security Hub, Amazon GuardDuty, AWS Shield, AWS Web Application Firewall (WAF), AWS Key Management Service (KMS), Amazon Macie, AWS Artifact, Amazon Detective, and AWS Secrets Manager, among others. Moreover, AWS offers hundreds of industry-leading products from third-party security-focused partners to leverage existing controls and skills that are already in place in your organization.

Therefore, before you decide to move your first workload to the AWS Cloud, it is crucial that you familiarize yourself with the AWS security and compliance services, tools, best practices, and responsibilities, as well as have a good understanding of your own duties during your organization's cloud adoption journey. With this background, you will be able to maintain and steadily improve your security posture using the AWS Cloud, creating a better security plan and implementing your security controls based on industry best practices, frameworks, and regulations with which your organization must be compliant.

The Shared Responsibility Model

AWS provides a global IT secure infrastructure, with compute, storage, networking, database, and higher-level services, like artificial intelligence (AI), machine learning (ML), analytics, and Internet of Things (IoT). To access the company's more than 175 available services (at the time of this writing), you can use the AWS Console, shown in Figure 2.1.

If you have ever watched an AWS presentation, you have probably observed that security is stated as AWS's "job zero," because of the company's mission to release cloud services with embedded security controls and divulge best practices on how to use them. Embedding security controls in the cloud services and establishing best practices for them will ensure that your cloud environments are compliant with security evaluations and certifications based on the AWS Information Security Management System (ISMS). This includes a set of AWS information security policies, and processes, as well as industry-specific security and compliance frameworks.

FIGURE 2.1 Services available from the AWS Console

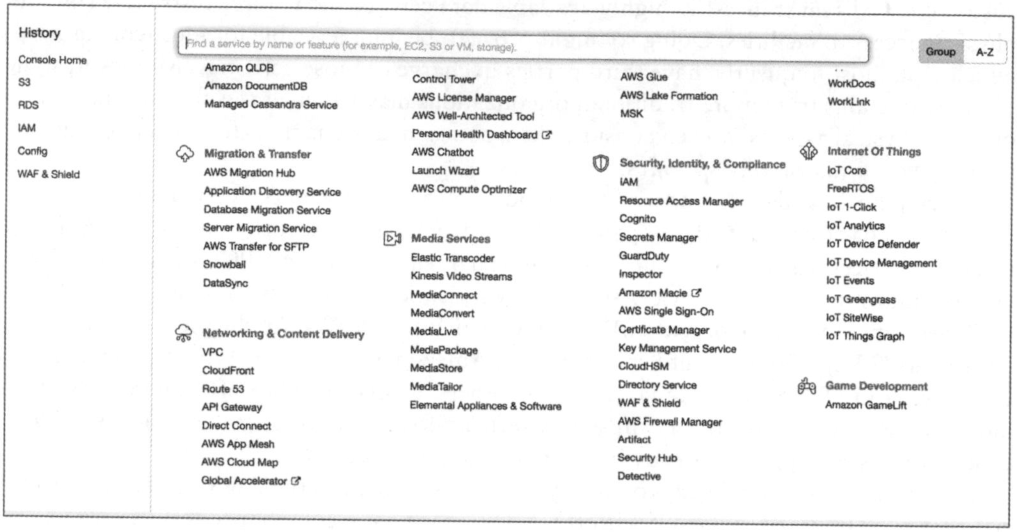

The Shared Responsibility Model defines the boundaries and responsibilities belonging to AWS and those belonging to the customer regarding security and compliance. Generally speaking, AWS is in charge of security and compliance *of the cloud*, and customers are in charge of security and compliance *in the cloud*. But what exactly does that mean in real-life scenarios?

Because it is responsible for the security of the cloud, AWS controls (and is accountable for) the security and compliance aspects of its infrastructure, which includes hardware and software, as you can see in Figure 2.2.

AWS is in charge of physical security and compliance of all data center facilities, in all regions, availability zones, and edge locations. AWS is also responsible for hardware security in all of its facilities around the globe, as well as for compute, storage, database, and networking security. For instance, AWS executes patch management in all routers, switches, and network equipment that are part of the AWS network infrastructure. In the same way, customers own the security management in all storage and computing resources that they have requested and that were provisioned by the AWS Cloud.

As you can see in Figure 2.2, AWS is responsible for implementing the security of the software layer that runs on top of the hardware components. One example of this layer is a *hypervisor*, which is the underlying platform that virtualizes CPU, storage, and networking infrastructure. Through such software, AWS leverages a rich set of management capabilities and also controls how these hardware systems will serve each AWS customer.

Consequently, when you create your Amazon EC2 instance, AWS is in charge of implementing the security patches, hardening guidelines, and best practices in the hypervisor

FIGURE 2.2 Standard Shared Responsibility Model

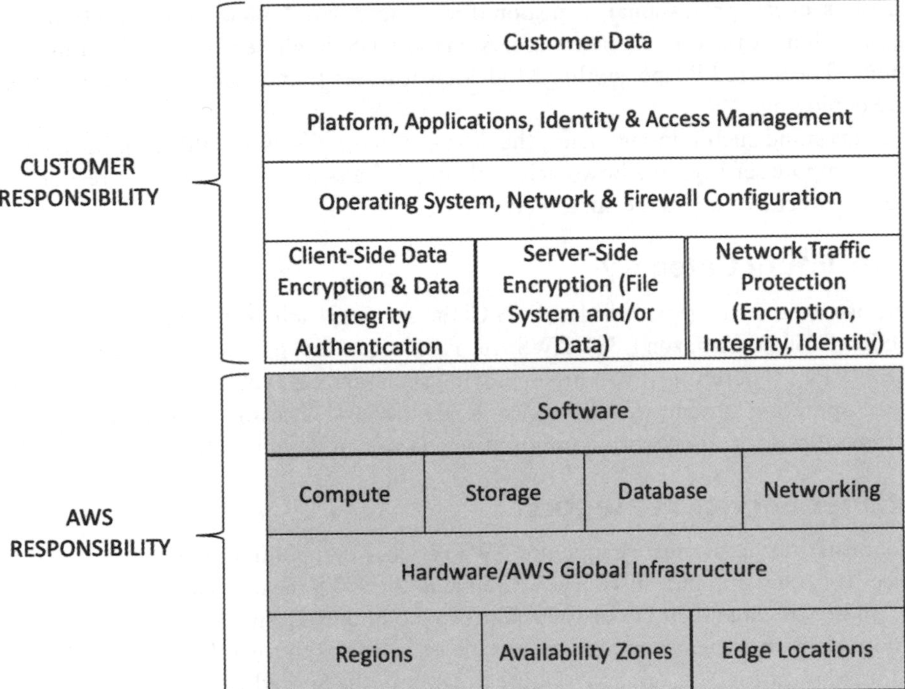

layer. You are in charge of updating the instance's operating system (OS) patches, implementing system configuration best practices, and creating security policies that align with your organization's security policy.

AWS uses two different hypervisors: Nitro and Xen. The launch of C5 instances introduced a new hypervisor for Amazon EC2, the Nitro Hypervisor, that is built on core Linux Kernel-based Virtual Machine (KVM) but that does not include general-purpose OS components. Eventually, all new instance types will use the Nitro Hypervisor, but in the short term, some new instance types will continue to use Xen depending on the requirements of the platform. Note that AWS uses a customized and hardened version of the Xen hypervisor.

In Figure 2.2, you can see that you (as an AWS customer) are always in charge of data encryption, OS security (in the case of Amazon EC2 instances), network firewall rules and configurations, IAM throughout your AWS Cloud environment (including your Amazon VPCs and AWS accounts), and your own application security that is running in the AWS Cloud.

Different Powers, Different Responsibilities

As a cloud security professional, you should remember that AWS offers a variety of cloud services, such as Amazon EC2 instances, Amazon RDS databases, and AWS Lambda functions. The Shared Responsibility Model has features that depend on the type of service you are deploying.

To understand such idiosyncrasies, the next sections will discuss three main categories of AWS compute services and how each of them produces a slightly different responsibility division between AWS and the customer.

Infrastructure Category

The infrastructure category includes AWS Cloud services such as Amazon EC2, Amazon Elastic Block Store (Amazon EBS), AWS Auto Scaling, and Amazon Virtual Private Cloud (Amazon VPC). Therefore, if you are deploying such services, you are in charge of the deployed operating system, security controls, identity and access management, data encryption, firewall rules, and network configuration, as shown in Figure 2.2.

Container Services Category

The container services category includes AWS services that commonly run on Amazon EC2 instances (or other compute instances available in the AWS Cloud) where you, as a customer, do not manage their OS or their platform components. In such services, AWS manages more elements when compared to services that belong to the infrastructure category, providing application "containers." Figure 2.3 shows the Shared Responsibility Model for container services.

This AWS definition is distinct from the concept of "container platforms" such as Docker and Linux Containers (LXC).

As you can see in Figure 2.3, customers are in charge of data protection and encryption, network traffic protection, firewall access rules definitions, and IAM administration of their AWS accounts and environments. And in such scenarios, AWS takes care of the container platform and management (including patching), and OS security controls, as well as all other lower-layer-based controls.

The AWS shared responsibility for container services applies to AWS services such as Amazon RDS and Amazon Elastic MapReduce (EMR) because AWS manages the underlying infrastructure, the OS, and their application platform. Because they are *managed* services, their AWS-controlled application platform also offers more sophisticated features such as data backup and recovery tools. Nonetheless, it is up to you to define and configure your disaster recovery and business continuity policy.

FIGURE 2.3 Shared Responsibility Model for container services

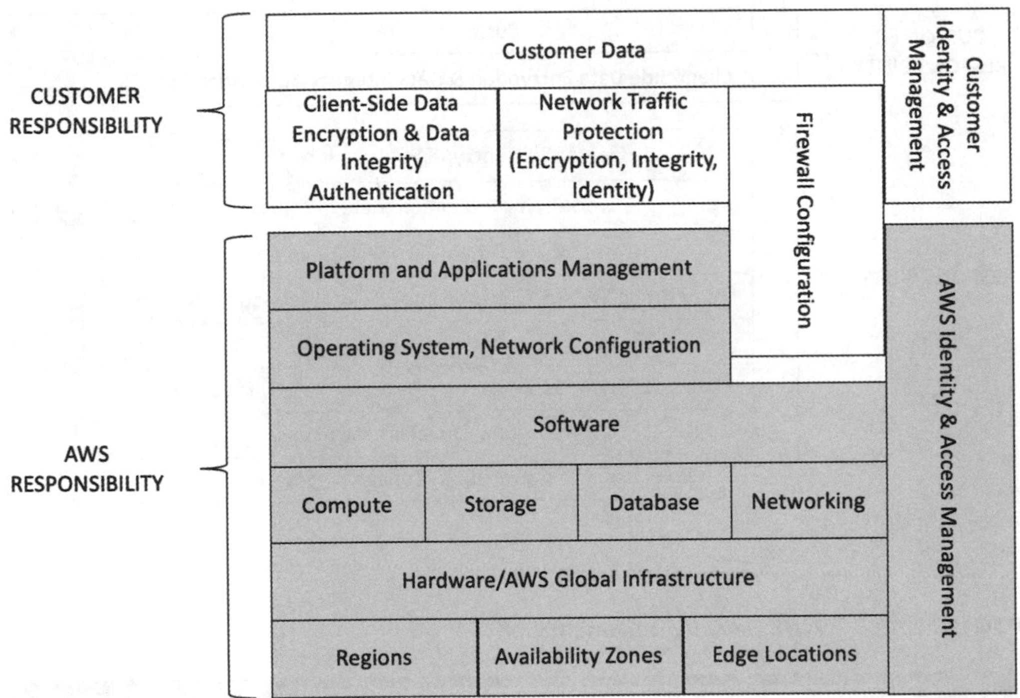

Abstracted Services Category

The abstracted services category encompasses higher-level services such as Amazon S3, Amazon DynamoDB, Amazon Simple Queue Service (SQS), and Amazon Simple Email Service (Amazon SES). As a customer, in these cases you are interacting with only AWS endpoints and APIs whereas AWS manages all of their components, applications, and the operating system. As a customer, you are using a multitenant platform that is configured to securely isolate your data.

In Figure 2.4, you can see that, as a customer, you are still in charge of data protection using encryption as well as IAM policies and rules definitions in services that belong to the abstracted services category.

AWS provides a set of documents with security best practices for each one of its cloud services. These documents are intended to help you implement your controls in your cloud environments on the AWS Cloud platform (Figure 2.5). You will find this web page at docs.aws.amazon.com/security.

FIGURE 2.4 Shared Responsibility Model for abstracted services

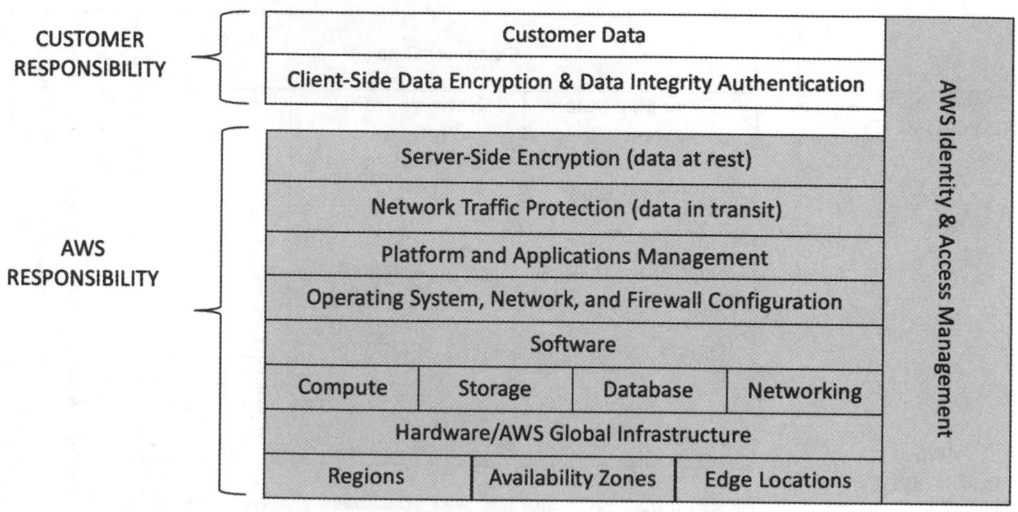

FIGURE 2.5 AWS Security Documentation

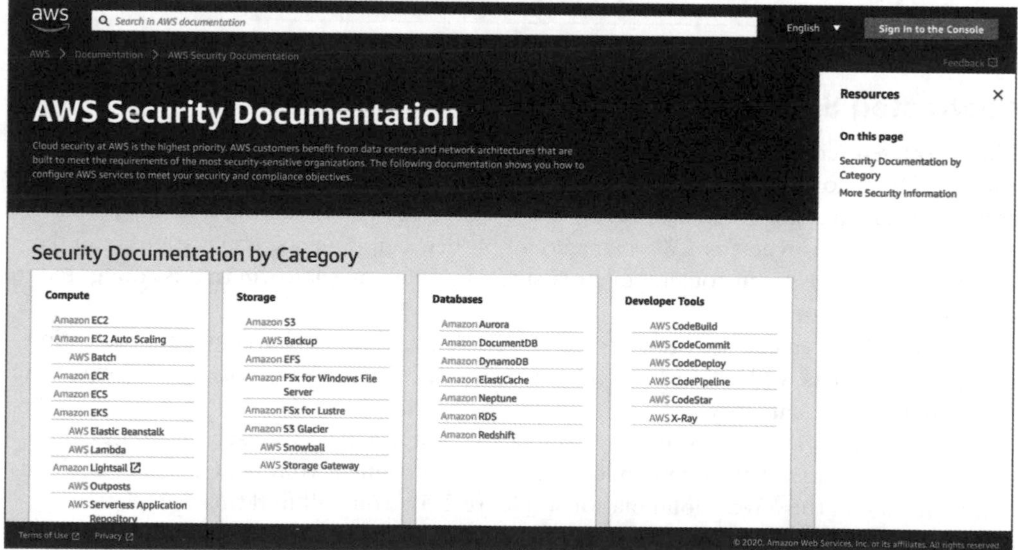

AWS Compliance Programs

When you are running your workloads in the AWS Cloud, you inherit all the security controls and compliance best practices that AWS has developed for its most security-demanding customers. Also, due to its global presence, AWS must comply with various regulations and best practices for security, compliance, and data protection around the world.

All certifications and compliance programs that AWS supports can be found in the AWS Compliance Programs site (`aws.amazon.com/compliance/programs`), as you can see in Figure 2.6.

FIGURE 2.6 AWS Compliance Programs site

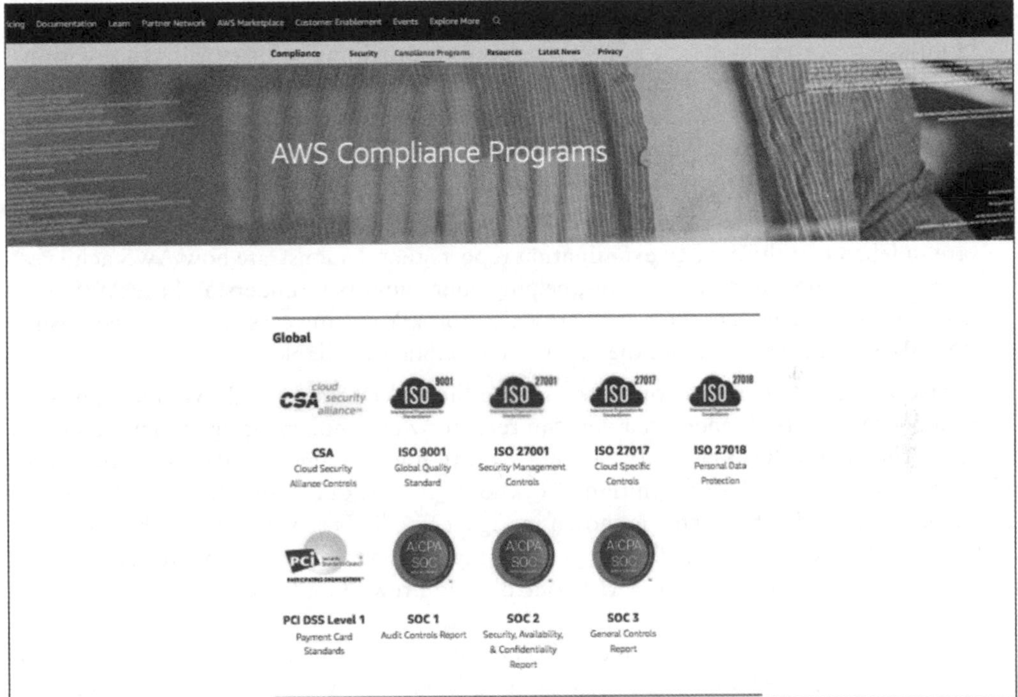

The process of defining the cloud service provider that will be used to run your workloads should include an evaluation of the provider's security controls, best practices, and certifications that are relevant to your industry and organization. Some of the security best practices and standards you must consider are as follows:

- **ISO 27001:** A standard from the International Organization for Standardization, ISO 27001 is part of the ISO 27000 information security standards family. It is used to define and implement an information security management system (ISMS), which helps companies to manage information assets that include sensitive data. This standard also leverages ISO 27002 as the basis for security controls best practices.

- **ISO 27017:** Another standard that is part of the ISO 27000 family, ISO 27017 is focused on the information security practices for cloud computing. It defines the best practices and security controls that a cloud service provider must implement, supplementing the guidance explained in ISO 27002.
- **ISO 27018:** This standard establishes commonly accepted control objectives, controls, and guidelines to protect *personally identifiable information* (PII) for public cloud computing environments.
- **PCI DSS:** As briefly mentioned in Chapter 1, the Payment Card Industry Data Security Standard is an information security standard for organizations that handle and store credit card information.
- **CSA STAR:** The Cloud Security Alliance (CSA) is a not-for-profit organization with a mission to promote the use of best practices for providing security assurance within cloud computing environments. The CSA Security, Trust, Assurance, and Risk (STAR) level 3 standard helps cloud service providers, customers, auditors, and consultants to verify that available cloud security controls meet the adequate level of assurance required to protect data.
- **SOC 1, SOC 2, and SOC 3:** The System and Organization Controls (SOC) reports are independent third-party examination reports that demonstrate how AWS achieves compliance and controls objectives, helping your auditors to understand the AWS security control models. There are four critical reports. You can access three of them using the AWS Artifact portal, and the other one is publicly available.

In case you decide to focus your attention on the PCI DSS standard, AWS has published a very interesting report that you can refer to when implementing security controls based on the Shared Responsibility Model. You can find the report at d1.awsstatic.com/whitepapers/compliance/AWS_Anitian_Workbook_PCI_Cloud_Compliance.pdf, and a glimpse of its table of contents is shown in Figure 2.7. This report can also help you understand the technical controls that you must implement as a part of your responsibility. Such technical controls are IAM controls and firewall and network access rules, among many others.

In Figure 2.8 (and at aws.amazon.com/compliance/csa), you can see that AWS is in compliance with the CSA STAR while also providing the CSA STAR Consensus Assessment, which explains how AWS is implementing the controls the standard requires (Figure 2.9). The latter can be found here: d1.awsstatic.com/whitepapers/compliance/CSA_Consensus_Assessments_Initiative_Questionnaire.pdf.

The AWS SOC 1 Type 2 Report evaluates the effectiveness of AWS controls that might affect internal controls over financial reporting (ICFR), and the auditing process is aligned to the SSAE 18 and ISAE 3402 standards. The AWS SOC 2 Privacy Type I Report assesses the AWS controls that meet the American Institute of Certified Public Accountants (AICPA)

FIGURE 2.7 AWS PCI DSS Anitian Report

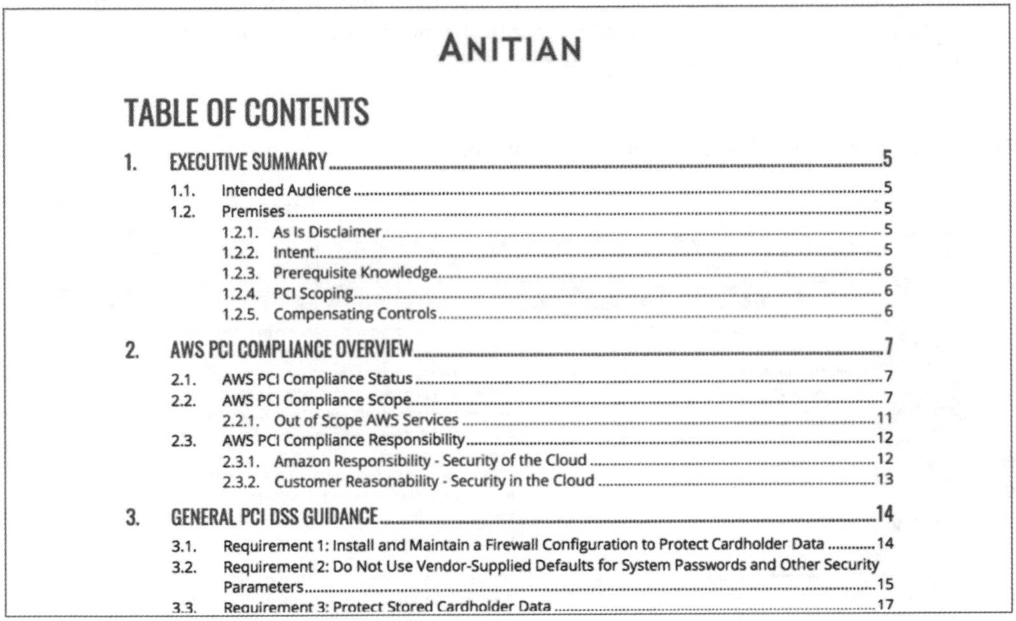

ANITIAN

TABLE OF CONTENTS

1. EXECUTIVE SUMMARY 5
   - 1.1. Intended Audience 5
   - 1.2. Premises 5
     - 1.2.1. As Is Disclaimer 5
     - 1.2.2. Intent 5
     - 1.2.3. Prerequisite Knowledge 6
     - 1.2.4. PCI Scoping 6
     - 1.2.5. Compensating Controls 6
2. AWS PCI COMPLIANCE OVERVIEW 7
   - 2.1. AWS PCI Compliance Status 7
   - 2.2. AWS PCI Compliance Scope 7
     - 2.2.1. Out of Scope AWS Services 11
   - 2.3. AWS PCI Compliance Responsibility 12
     - 2.3.1. Amazon Responsibility - Security of the Cloud 12
     - 2.3.2. Customer Reasonability - Security in the Cloud 13
3. GENERAL PCI DSS GUIDANCE 14
   - 3.1. Requirement 1: Install and Maintain a Firewall Configuration to Protect Cardholder Data 14
   - 3.2. Requirement 2: Do Not Use Vendor-Supplied Defaults for System Passwords and Other Security Parameters 15
   - 3.3. Requirement 3: Protect Stored Cardholder Data 17

criteria for privacy. The AWS SOC 2 Security, Availability, & Confidentiality Report assesses the AWS controls that meet the American Institute of Certified Public Accountants (AICPA) criteria for security, availability, and confidentiality. Finally, the AWS SOC 3 Security, Availability, & Confidentiality Report summarizes the AWS SOC 2 report.

FIGURE 2.8 AWS CSA Compliance site

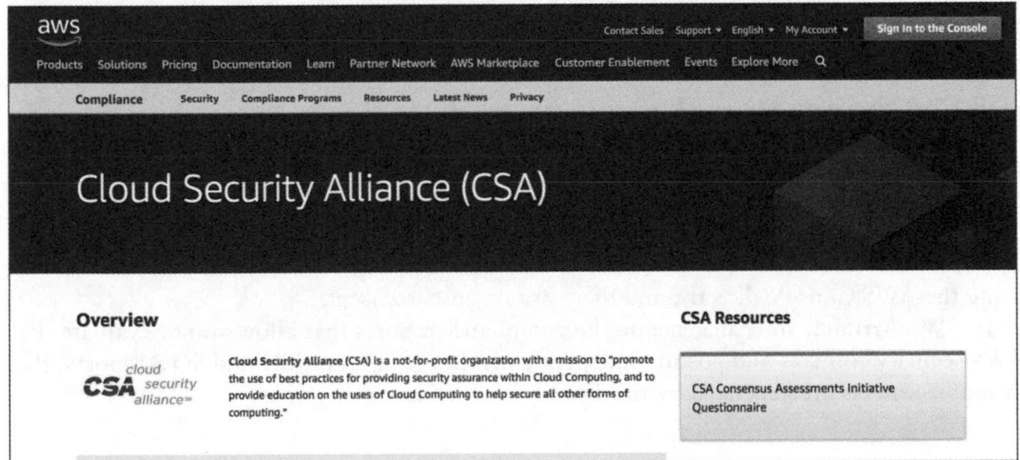

Using the ISO 27000 certifications, SOC Reports, and other necessary regulations and accreditation models, you can evaluate how the security controls are implemented in the AWS data centers and services, and thus determine whether the level of compliance will achieve the protection you desire for your business.

FIGURE 2.9 CSA Consensus Assessment site

Amazon Web Services — *CSA Consensus Assessments Initiative Questionnaire (CAIQ)*

Question ID	Consensus Assessment Questions	Answer			Notes	Control Responsibility
		Yes	No	N/A		
AIS-01.2	Do you use an automated source code analysis tool to detect security defects in code prior to production?	X			Automated code analysis tools are run as a part of the AWS Software Development Lifecycle, and all deployed software undergoes recurring penetration testing performed by carefully selected industry experts. Our security risk assessment reviews begin during the design phase and the engagement lasts through launch to ongoing operations. Refer to the AWS Overview of Security Processes for further details. That whitepaper is located here. https://d1.awsstatic.com/whitepapers/Security/AWS_Security_Whitepaper.pdf	AWS
AIS-01.3	Do you use manual source-code analysis to detect security defects in code prior to production?		X		Manual source-code analysis is not employed. Automated code analysis tools are run as a part of the AWS Software Development Lifecycle.	N/A

Even if PCI DSS is not a requirement for your business, the security controls discussed in the standard can and should be used as a basis for you to define the controls needed for your environment, especially when you are dealing with sensitive data.

AWS Artifact Portal

Once you define the controls, certifications, and regulations necessary to meet your business protection requirements, you will need to perform periodic assessments and audits of those controls in AWS. Using a model based on total transparency and self-service principles, AWS created a service portal called AWS Artifact. You can access the Artifact portal using the AWS Console directly, and there are no costs to use it.

In AWS Artifact, you can generate the compliance reports that allow you to evaluate the AWS security controls and posture independently. In the cases of ISO and SOC reports, the available reports are generated by third-party independent companies.

In Figure 2.10, you can see how the AWS Artifact portal appears in the AWS console. Exercise 2.1 shows how to use the AWS Artifact portal to generate a PCI DSS report.

FIGURE 2.10 AWS Artifact portal

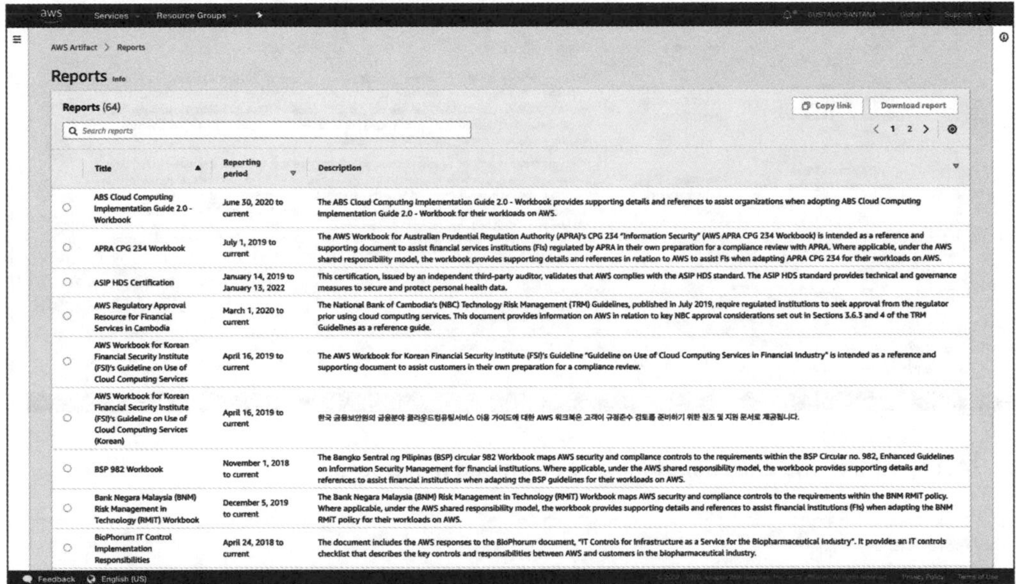

EXERCISE 2.1

Generating the PCI DSS Report in the AWS Artifact Portal

In this exercise, you will use the AWS Artifact portal available on the AWS Console to generate a PCI DSS report and also evaluate what your (and AWS's) responsibilities for each requirement are. For assistance in completing this exercise, please refer to the AWS Artifact documentation at `docs.aws.amazon.com/artifact`.

1. Open the AWS Console.
2. Search for the Artifact service.
3. Open the Artifact service.
4. Search for the report PCI DSS Attestation of Compliance (AOC) and Responsibility Summary – Current and click Get This Artifact.

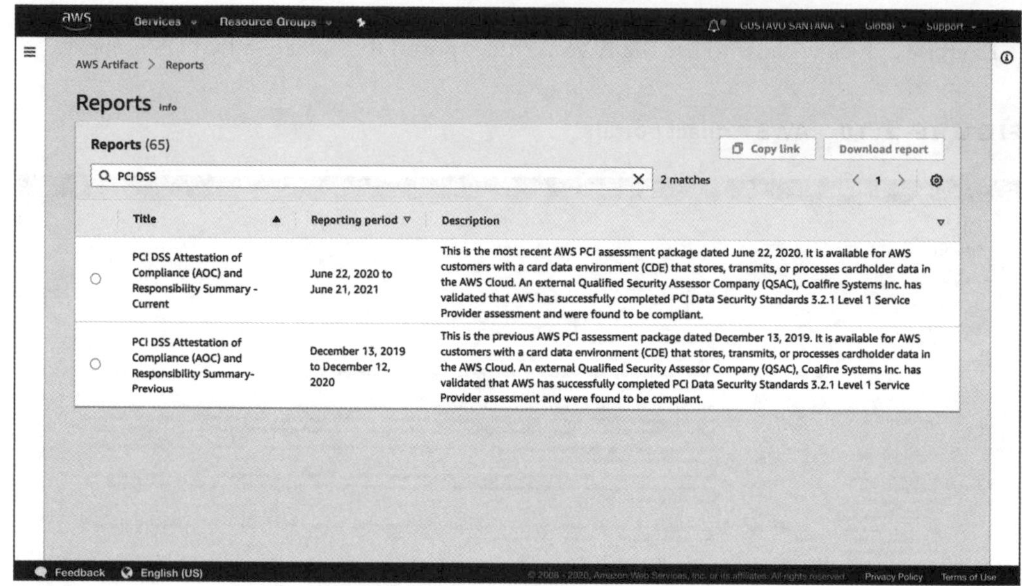

5. Accept the terms and conditions and download the report.

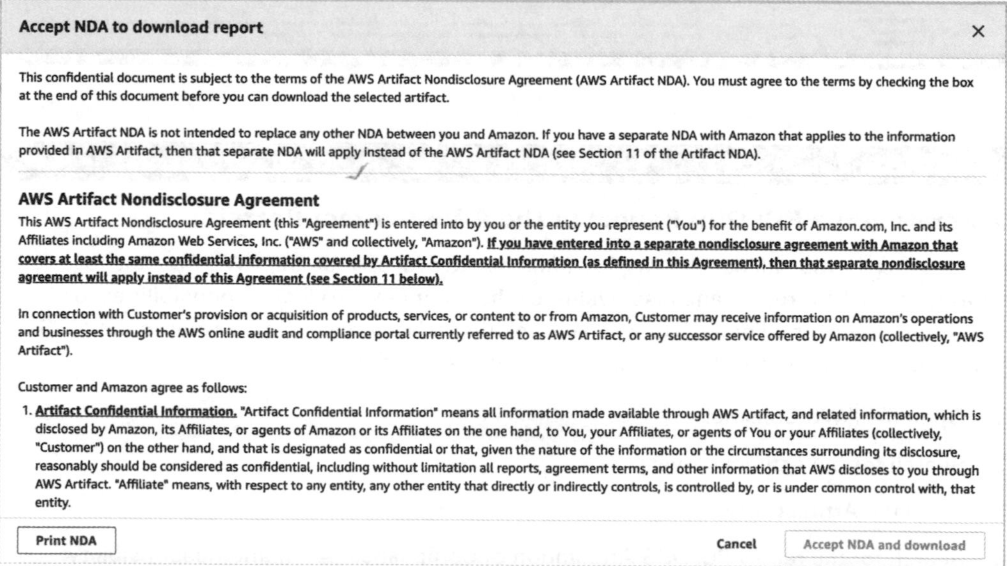

6. Open the generated PDF using Adobe Acrobat Reader. (Be sure to use Adobe Acrobat or Adobe Reader to reliably view the files within the download.)

7. In the PDF, follow the instructions to open the artifact.

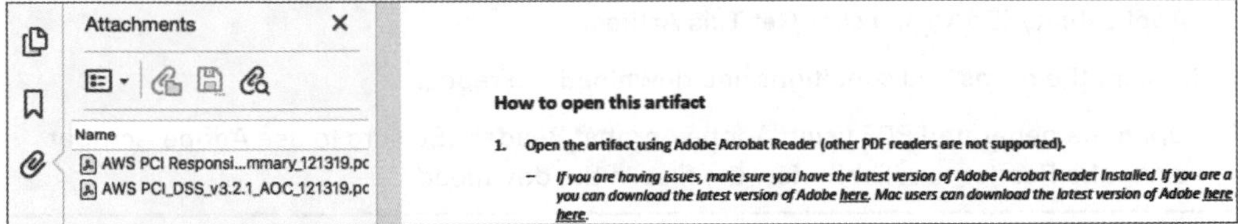

8. You can explore the PCI Responsibility Summary PDF report as well as the Microsoft Excel file with all the necessary security controls, explaining in detail all requirements and the AWS and customer responsibilities.

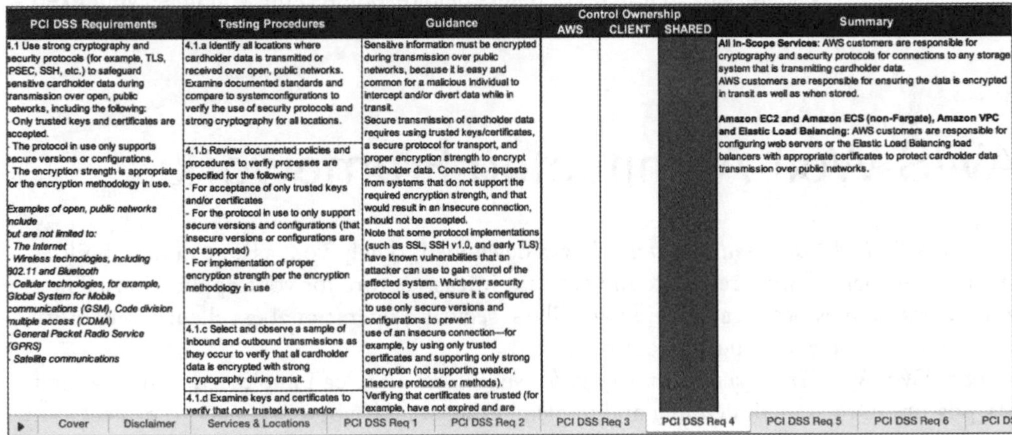

PCI DSS Requirements	Testing Procedures	Guidance	Control Ownership AWS	CLIENT	SHARED	Summary
4.1 Use strong cryptography and security protocols (for example, TLS, IPSEC, SSH, etc.) to safeguard sensitive cardholder data during transmission over open, public networks, including the following: - Only trusted keys and certificates are accepted. - The protocol in use only supports secure versions or configurations. - The encryption strength is appropriate for the encryption methodology in use. *Examples of open, public networks include but are not limited to:* *- The Internet* *- Wireless technologies, including 802.11 and Bluetooth* *- Cellular technologies, for example, Global System for Mobile communications (GSM), Code division multiple access (CDMA)* *- General Packet Radio Service (GPRS)* *- Satellite communications*	4.1.a Identify all locations where cardholder data is transmitted or received over open, public networks. Examine documented standards and compare to systemconfigurations to verify the use of security protocols and strong cryptography for all locations. 4.1.b Review documented policies and procedures to verify processes are specified for the following: - For acceptance of only trusted keys and/or certificates - For the protocol in use to only support secure versions and configurations (that insecure versions or configurations are not supported) - For implementation of proper encryption strength per the encryption methodology in use 4.1.c Select and observe a sample of inbound and outbound transmissions as they occur to verify that all cardholder data is encrypted with strong cryptography during transit. 4.1.d Examine keys and certificates to verify that only trusted keys and/or	Sensitive information must be encrypted during transmission over public networks, because it is easy and common for a malicious individual to intercept and/or divert data while in transit. Secure transmission of cardholder data requires using trusted keys/certificates, a secure protocol for transport, and proper encryption strength to encrypt cardholder data. Connection requests from systems that do not support the required encryption strength, and that would result in an insecure connection, should not be accepted. Note that some protocol implementations (such as SSL, SSH v1.0, and early TLS) have known vulnerabilities that an attacker can use to gain control of the affected system. Whichever security protocol is used, ensure it is configured to use only secure versions and configurations to prevent use of an insecure connection—for example, by using only trusted certificates and supporting only strong encryption (not supporting weaker, insecure protocols or methods). Verifying that certificates are trusted (for example, have not expired and are				**All In-Scope Services:** AWS customers are responsible for cryptography and security protocols for connections to any storage system that is transmitting cardholder data. AWS customers are responsible for ensuring the data is encrypted in transit as well as when stored. **Amazon EC2 and Amazon ECS (non-Fargate), Amazon VPC and Elastic Load Balancing:** AWS customers are responsible for configuring web servers or the Elastic Load Balancing load balancers with appropriate certificates to protect cardholder data transmission over public networks.

Cover | Disclaimer | Services & Locations | PCI DSS Req 1 | PCI DSS Req 2 | PCI DSS Req 3 | PCI DSS Req 4 | PCI DSS Req 5 | PCI DSS Req 6 | PCI D

Exercise 2.2 shows how to use the AWS Artifact portal to check the ISO 27001 and ISO 27017 reports.

EXERCISE 2.2

Checking the ISO 27001 and ISO 27017 Reports

In this exercise, you will check the ISO 27001 and ISO 27017 reports using the AWS Artifact portal in your AWS Console. For assistance in completing this exercise, please refer to the AWS Artifact documentation at `docs.aws.amazon.com/artifact`.

1. Open the AWS Console.
2. Search for the Artifact service.
3. Open the Artifact service.

4. Search for the reports ISO 27001:2013 Certification, ISO 27001:2013 Statement of Applicability (SoA), SO 27017:2015 Certification, and ISO 27017:2015 Statement of Applicability (SoA), and click Get This Artifact.
5. Accept the terms and conditions and download the report.
6. Open the generated PDF using Adobe Acrobat Reader. (Be sure to use Adobe Acrobat or Adobe Reader to reliably view the files in the download.)

In some cases, there are costs to execute the labs, so please check the price and costs before you perform any exercise from this certification guide. Also, be sure to turn off or delete paid resources after you finish your exercises.

AWS Well-Architected Framework

The *AWS Well-Architected Framework* was developed to help you, as a customer, build secure, high-performing, resilient, and efficient infrastructure for your applications. The framework defines best practices in five pillars: security, operational excellence, reliability, performance efficiency, and cost optimization.

The *AWS Well-Architected security pillar* shows how you can implement a strong security posture in the cloud, defining and implementing security best practices to protect systems and information, while also generating business value for your organization.

The security pillar has seven security design principles:

- **Implement a Strong Identity Foundation:** Use the least privilege principle (which is based on the zero-trust security model explained in Chapter 1) by creating *segregation of duties* (SoD), using the proper IAM roles and permissions, defining the appropriate authorization for each resource that will interact with the AWS Cloud, and limiting and centralizing privileged accesses and eliminating long-term credentials when possible.
- **Enable Traceability:** Enable audit logs by centralizing log collection, ingestion, protection, and enrichment, and by creating alerts that should be monitored by one or several teams that will respond to each kind of alert, based on required runbooks and playbooks.
- **Apply Security at All Layers:** Defense-in-depth is a must; you cannot use just one layer of protection but must implement network security, OS security, load balancer security, application security, and so on. You must implement security best practices in all AWS Cloud services and components that will be a part of your application.

- **Automate Security Best Practices:** Automation is a key function in cloud security. The best way to deploy an agile and secure environment is to leverage automation, implement security as code, and transform your paper security policies into real and coded security controls. As you create infrastructure as code and insert embedded security controls to achieve automated security, you can scale your cloud environments while maintaining the same level of protection.
- **Protect Data in Transit and at Rest:** You must understand your data in order to protect sensitive information in both data exchange and storage, using encryption, tokenization, and masking resources to achieve it. You should also create and enforce access control policies to limit access to sensitive data wherever it is.
- **Keep People Away from Data:** You must create mechanisms and tools to reduce or eliminate manual and human access to production data, thus reducing operation risks related to human mistakes when handling sensitive data.
- **Prepare for Security Events:** You must define an incident response management practice, running incident simulations, creating tools, using automation, and running playbooks to improve the security incident capabilities.

The security design principles from the AWS Well-Architected Framework's security pillar also define five best practice areas for security in the cloud that will be covered in the following chapters of this study guide:

- Chapter 3: "Identity and Access Management"
- Chapter 4: "Detective Controls"
- Chapter 5: "Infrastructure Protection"
- Chapter 6: "Data Protection"
- Chapter 7: "Incident Response"

Using the AWS Well-Architected Tool

Since November 2018, you can execute automated assessments in your AWS environments using the AWS Well-Architected Tool.

Figure 2.11 shows the tool, which has no associated cost and is available for every AWS user.

Although the AWS Certified Security Specialty certification does not explicitly require a deep knowledge of the AWS Well-Architected Framework, it is essential to read and study the framework to deepen your expertise in the best practices not only in security but in the other pillars as well.

FIGURE 2.11 AWS Well-Architected Tool

Exercise 2.3 shows you how to use the Well-Architected Tool to simulate an evaluation.

EXERCISE 2.3

Using the Well-Architected Tool

In this exercise, you will simulate a Well-Architected evaluation using the AWS Well-Architected Tool inside the console. For assistance in completing this exercise, please refer to the AWS Well-Architected Tool documentation at `docs.aws.amazon.com/wellarchitected`.

1. Open the AWS Console.
2. Search for the Well-Architected Tool in the console.
3. Open the Well-Architected Tool Service.

4. Click Define Workload (the orange button).

5. Create a Security Evaluation Assessment by completing all the fields.

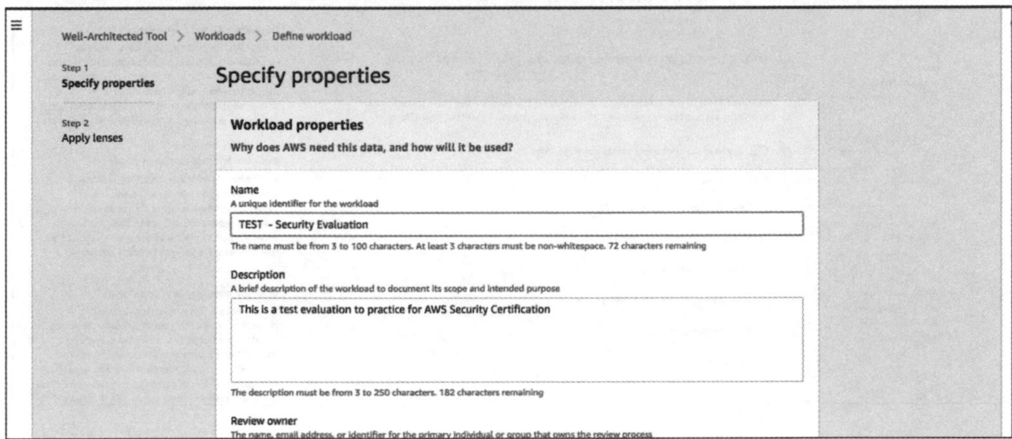

6. When you have finished completing the form, you can start executing the assessment by clicking Start Reviewing.

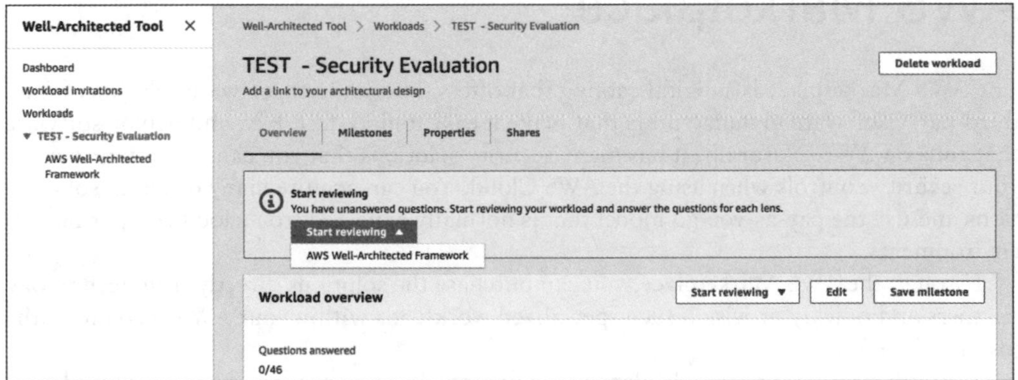

7. For each Well-Architected pillar, you will need to answer specific questions. Videos are available to help you understand the context and how to evaluate and implement the recommended best practices. Comprehending the Well-Architected Framework security pillar will help you go deeper and understand the security concepts and tools that will help you not only pass the AWS Certified Security Specialty exam but also implement better security environments in the future.

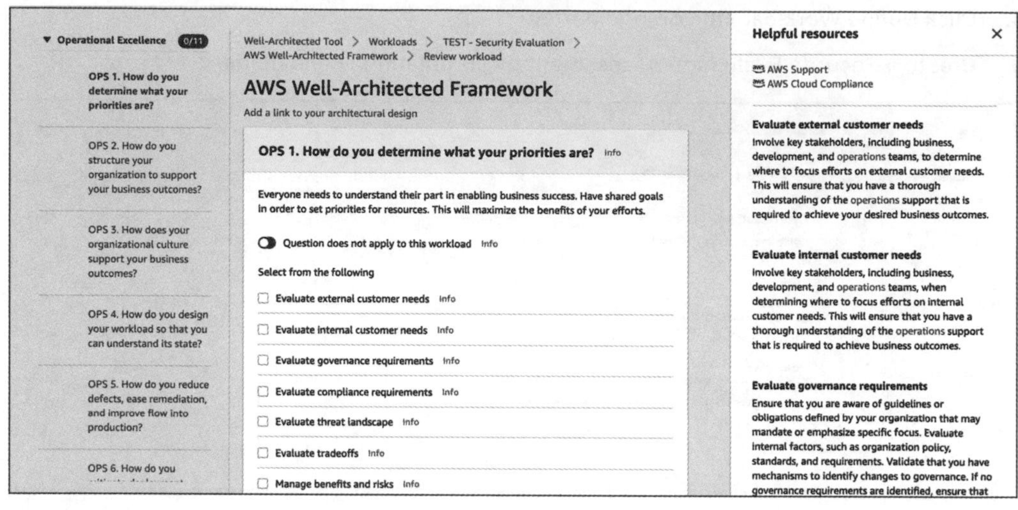

AWS Marketplace

The AWS Marketplace is a digital catalog that offers thousands of software solutions from third-party software manufacturers that make it easy to find, test, buy, and deploy software that runs on AWS. Naturally, it has many security solutions that you can use to improve your security controls when using the AWS Cloud. You can acquire many different solutions and use the pay-as-you-go model that is normally expected from cloud computing environments.

Through the AWS Marketplace, you can purchase the solutions directly from technology partners and quickly provision such specialized workloads within your AWS account, with just a few clicks.

As an illustration, Figure 2.12 depicts the first results of a search using the keyword "Security" in AWS Marketplace.

The solutions available from the marketplace are broken into various categories and are available from several strategic partners, enabling you to replicate and migrate security solutions from your on-premises environment to the AWS Cloud with little effort. Furthermore, many solutions allow you to use your previously available licenses on a process that is also known as the Bring Your Own License (BYOL) model.

To keep up to date with the latest releases, be sure to regularly visit the AWS Marketplace.

FIGURE 2.12 AWS Marketplace Security Solutions

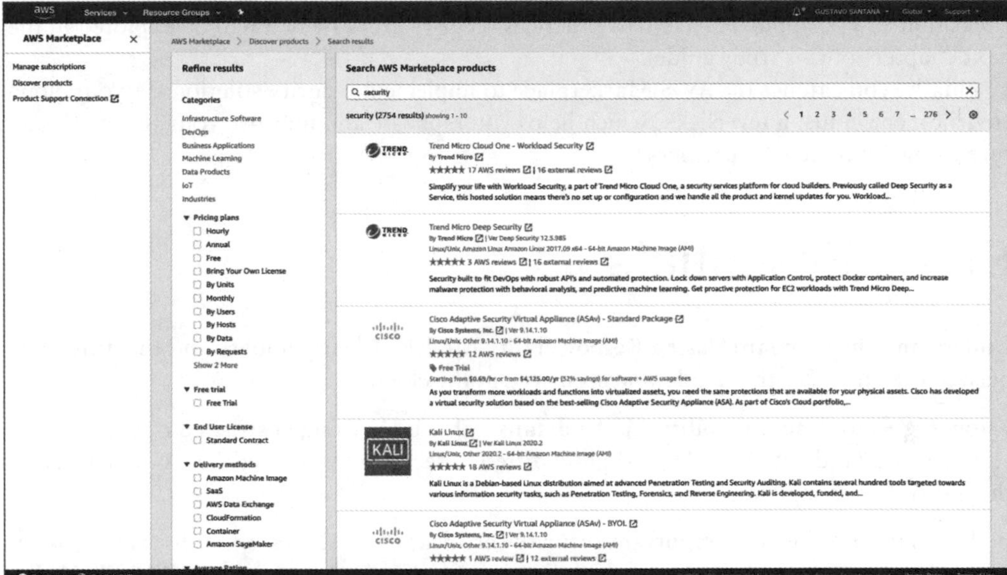

Summary

In this chapter, you learned how important it is to understand the Shared Responsibility Model and its guidance when adopting different types of services in the AWS Cloud.

Based on the model, AWS remains responsible for the security *of* the cloud, while you (the customer) are always responsible for security *in* the cloud. This means you are responsible for securing your workloads running in your AWS environments while leveraging the security services and features AWS offers, including data protection and encryption, application security, network security configuration, and access control to your AWS environment.

Depending on the type of service you are using, you may have more or fewer security responsibilities. For example, if you are using managed services such as AWS Lambda, Amazon RDS databases, and Amazon S3, you have to deal with fewer security controls than you would if you were only using Amazon EC2 instances. Still, you will always be responsible for controlling access to your data and for protecting your applications.

AWS adopts security best practices to comply with various rules and regulations from different countries around the globe, and all certifications and reports are available on the AWS Artifact portal inside the AWS Console. Amazon offers this portal as a free service to allow you to access information about AWS compliance and security practices using AWS and third-party reports.

You can also use the AWS Well-Architected Tool in the AWS Console to evaluate the security and compliance of your workloads. Both resources are based on seven design principles that can be applied to five best practices security areas (which will be explored in the next chapters of this study guide).

Finally, you can use the AWS Marketplace to implement security solutions in your cloud environment in just a few clicks, which helps you replicate and improve your security posture using AWS security partners.

Exam Essentials

Understand the Standard Shared Responsibility Model. Clearly understand the difference between security "of the cloud" and security "in the cloud."

Know the Shared Responsibility Model details. If you are using abstracted or container services, you (and AWS) will have slightly different security responsibilities. Understand these differences in detail.

Be familiar with the most important security certifications. It is essential for you to understand the objectives and context of the following certifications and reports: ISO 27001, ISO 27002, PCI DSS, SOC (1,2,3), and CSA STAR.

Know how to use the Well-Architected Framework. Understand that the AWS Well-Architected Framework has five pillars, one of which is security. In the security pillar, there are seven security design principles:

1. Implement a strong identity foundation.
2. Enable traceability.
3. Apply security at all layers.
4. Automate security best practices.
5. Protect data in transit and at rest.
6. Keep people away from data.
7. Prepare for security events.

Also defined as part of the Well-Architected security pillar are five security best practices areas:

- Identity and access management
- Detective controls
- Infrastructure protection
- Data protection
- Incident response

Be familiar with the AWS Marketplace. You can find many security solutions in the AWS Marketplace that you can use to improve your security posture. You can use strategic AWS security partners. You can use your own licenses in a *Bring Your Own License* model. The pay-as-you-go model is another option available to you.

Review Questions

1. In an Amazon EC2 instance deployment, who is in charge of the data center facilities security, based on the Shared Responsibility Model?

   A. AWS

   B. The customer

   C. The responsibility is shared

   D. Depends on the region

2. In a database implementation of Amazon RDS running MySQL, who is in charge of the operating system security patching, based on the Shared Responsibility Model?

   A. The customer

   B. The responsibility is shared

   C. AWS

   D. Depends on the region

3. From where can you download ISO 27001, ISO 27017, ISO 27018, and other certification files in PDF format?

   A. AWS Security Portal

   B. AWS Artifact

   C. AWS GuardDuty

   D. AWS public website

4. What is the SOC-1 Type 2 report?

   A. It evaluates the effectiveness of AWS controls that might affect internal controls over financial reporting (ICFR).

   B. It is a summary of the AWS SOC 2 report.

   C. It evaluates the AWS controls that meet the American Institute of Certified Public Accountants (AICPA) criteria for security, availability, and confidentiality.

   D. None of the above

5. What is the SOC 2 Security, Availability, & Confidentiality report?
   A. It evaluates the effectiveness of AWS controls that might affect internal controls over financial reporting (ICFR).
   B. It is a summary of the AWS SOC 2 report.
   C. It evaluates the AWS controls that meet the American Institute of Certified Public Accountants (AICPA) criteria for security, availability, and confidentiality.
   D. None of the above
6. Which option best defines the AWS Well-Architected Framework?
   A. It is a framework developed by AWS that describes best practices to help customers implement security best practices in their environments.
   B. It is a paid service developed by AWS that defines best practices to help customers implement best practices in their environments, improving security, operational excellence, reliability, performance efficiency, and cost optimization.
   C. It is a no-cost framework developed by AWS that defines best practices, helping the customer to implement their environments, improving security, operational excellence, reliability, performance efficiency, and cost optimization.
   D. It is a tool in the AWS console that helps customers automatically implement architecture best practices.
7. What are the design principles defined in the AWS Well-Architected security pillar?
   A. Identity and access management, detective controls, infrastructure protection
   B. Data protection, identity and access management
   C. Implement a strong identity foundation, enable traceability, apply security at all layers, automate security best practices, keep people away from data, and prepare for security events
   D. Implement a strong identity foundation, enable traceability, apply security at all layers, automate security best practices, protect data in transit and at rest, keep people away from data, and prepare for security events
   E. Identity and access management, detective controls, infrastructure protection, data protection
8. Who is in charge of the AWS hypervisor security when you, as a customer, are deploying Amazon EC2 instances in the AWS Cloud?
   A. AWS is always in charge of the hypervisor security.
   B. The customer is in charge of the hypervisor security.
   C. It depends on the type of instance.
   D. There is a Shared Responsibility Model, so the customer and AWS have the responsibility of the hypervisor security.

9. What are the best practices areas for security in the cloud covered by the Well-Architected security pillar? (Choose all that apply.)
   - **A.** Identity and access management
   - **B.** Infrastructure protection
   - **C.** Security awareness
   - **D.** Incident response
   - **E.** Security automation
   - **F.** Detective controls
   - **G.** Authentication and authorization
   - **H.** Data protection

10. You are looking for an endpoint protection solution, and you want to use the same solution that you are using on-premises today to improve your workload protection running on your Amazon EC2 instances. Where can you find endpoint protection solutions to protect your servers running in the AWS Cloud?
    - **A.** AWS Console
    - **B.** AWS website
    - **C.** AWS Security Services
    - **D.** AWS Marketplace

Identity and Access Management

THE AWS CERTIFIED SECURITY - SPECIALTY EXAM OBJECTIVES THAT LEVERAGE CONCEPTS EXPLAINED IN THIS CHAPTER INCLUDE THE FOLLOWING:

✓ **Domain 4: Identity and Access Management**

- 4.1. Design and implement a scalable authorization and authentication system to access AWS resources
- 4.2. Troubleshoot an authorization and authentication system to access AWS resources

Introduction

In this chapter, you will learn what AWS Identity and Access Management (IAM) is and how it sets the foundation for all interactions among the resources in your AWS account. We'll also cover the various access methods to the AWS IAM services:

- AWS Console
- AWS command-line tools
- AWS software development kits
- IAM HTTPS application programming interface (API)

You will also learn how to protect and secure your AWS Cloud environments using features such as multifactor authentication (MFA) and other best practices.

IAM Overview

AWS Identity and Access Management (IAM) provides a set of APIs that control access to your resources on the AWS Cloud. AWS IAM gives you the ability to define authentication and authorization methods for using the resources in your account.

When you create your account, you receive a single identity that gives you full access to the resources in the account. The login information is in the form of an email address. This identity is called the *root account* or *root user*, and due to its high set of permissions, AWS recommends restricting the access to these credentials to a few people and using it only on rare cases. For additional security, AWS recommends that you enable MFA on your root account and don't create root access keys to make programmatic requests to AWS. You cannot reduce the permissions associated with your AWS root account, unless service controls policies (SCPs) are used in accounts different from the admin account in an AWS Organization.

AWS IAM empowers you to define strict access rules for individuals and other systems for manipulating resources in a specific account. For example, you can specify that a user can call a specific API from a specific IP address only during a certain period of the day. AWS

IAM makes access to AWS resources possible for applications that are running on-premises or in the AWS Cloud. Such granularity allows systems administrators to comply with security and regulations that are relevant for their organizations.

We will also cover the various *principals* that can interact with AWS and how they are authenticated. We will then discuss how to write policies that define permitted access to services, actions, and resources, and how to associate these policies with authenticated principals. Finally, we will explore additional AWS IAM features that can help you secure your infrastructure, including MFA, rotating keys, federation, resolving of multiple permissions, and AWS IAM roles.

AWS IAM is designed to protect the resources in your AWS account and it should not be used as an identity provider (IdP) for your applications. If you are planning to migrate your on-premises application to the AWS Cloud and it already has its own IdP, you should continue to use it. For example, if your application uses Microsoft Active Directory (AD) as its IdP, you can extend it into AWS by using the AWS Directory Service, an Active Directory–compatible directory service that is capable of integrating with your on-premises AD. On the other hand, if you plan to implement a new web application or mobile app, you may consider *Amazon Cognito* for identity management for your application.

How AWS IAM Works

The AWS IAM service provides the necessary infrastructure for you to implement authentication and authorization in your AWS account. To better understand the AWS IAM architecture, let's explore the main elements that comprise it.

Principals

A *principal* is an AWS IAM entity that has permission to interact with resources in the AWS Cloud. Whether it is permanent or temporary, this principal can represent a human user, a resource, or an application. There are three types of principals: *root users*, *IAM users*, and *roles* (or temporary security tokens).

Root Users

When you create your first account on AWS, the account is known as the root user identity, since it allows you to sign in to AWS. You can log into the AWS Console using the email address and password that you provided when you created your account. This set of information is also known as your *root user credentials*.

The root user credentials give you unrestricted access to all the AWS resources in your account. This access covers (but is not limited to) viewing billing information, changing your root account password, and performing the complete termination of your account and deletion of its resources.

For daily operations in your AWS account, it is not necessary to use the *root user*. Moreover, AWS highly recommends that you not share the root user credentials with anyone, simply because doing so gives them unrestricted access to your account. There is no way to restrict the access given to the root user in the master account. However, if the account is a member of an AWS Organization, it's possible to use SCPs to restrict root user account permissions.

Once you have set up your AWS account, the most important thing that you should do is protect your root user credentials by following these recommendations:

- Use a strong password to help protect account-level access to the management console.
- Enable MFA on your AWS root user account.
- Remember that you should not create an access key for programmatic access to your root user account unless such a procedure is mandatory. You can create another IAM user with the required permissions to perform the necessary actions on your account. It is possible to give administrative permissions to an IAM user.
- In case you must maintain an access key to your root user account, you should regularly rotate it using the AWS Console. You need to log in using your account's email address and password to rotate (or even delete) your access keys credentials for your root account.
- Remember, never share your root user password or access keys with anyone. Anyone with access to the root user account can terminate and destroy all resources in your AWS account.

Resetting Root Users

You must be signed in as the root user to change the root user password or anything else related to the user. To execute such a procedure, take the steps shown in Exercise 3.1.

EXERCISE 3.1

Change the Root Account Password

In this exercise, you will reset the root account password.

1. Use your email address and password to log into the AWS Console as the root user.
2. Click on the name of your account in the upper-right corner.
3. Choose My Security Credentials.
4. In the Password pane, click the link Click Here.

5. Once you click, you will be redirected to the Login page to confirm your root credentials. From the options presented, choose Root User and enter the email registered for your root account.
6. Click Next, and on the following screen, enter your root password and click the Sign In button.
7. If you have MFA enabled on your root account, enter the MFA code at the prompt.
8. After you confirm your root credentials, you'll see the Update Account Settings page. Click the Edit button next to the Password field.
9. Use a strong password for your account, with a minimum of 8 and a maximum of 128 characters. It should contain a combination of the following character types: uppercase, lowercase, numbers, and special characters. Don't use simple passwords, such as *january, password, p4ssw0rd,* or your *date of birth,* that could be easily cracked through dictionary attacks.

You'll change user account names, passwords, and email settings on the Update Account Settings page, which is shown in Figure 3.1.

FIGURE 3.1 Update Account Settings page

In case you need to reset the root account credentials, remember to delete the previous two-factor authentication information, as well as any access and secret keys that might exist for the root account. It's important to remember to reenable MFA on the account and avoid creating root access keys.

In Exercise 3.2, you can take your root account security management further by setting up MFA.

EXERCISE 3.2

Enable Multifactor Authentication for the Root Account

In this exercise, you will enable MFA for the root account.

1. Log into your AWS account using your root account credentials.
2. Click the name of your account and then select My Security Credentials.
3. On the Your Security Credentials screen, expand the Multi-factor Authentication (MFA) section, and then click Activate MFA.
4. On the Manage MFA Device screen, select the Virtual MFA Device option and then click Continue.
5. Ensure that you have an authenticator app on your mobile phone or computer.
6. On the next screen, click Show QR Code and scan it using your authenticator app.
7. Enter the two consecutive codes in the MFA Code 1 and MFA Code 2 fields.
8. Click Assign MFA. Now, every time you log in with your root credentials, you must provide an MFA Code as part of the login process.

IAM Users

IAM users are people or applications in your organization. They persist within the AWS accounts where they were created, but may have cross-account permissions if configured to do so. Each IAM user has its own username and password that give them access to the AWS Console. Additionally, it's also possible to create an access key to provide users with programmatic access to AWS resources.

IAM users is a concept that gives administrators the granularity required to control how users should interact with AWS resources. You should notice that an IAM user is not necessarily a person. It can be an application (such as *SalesApp*) that runs on AWS or on your corporate network and needs to interact with resources in your account. If your application is running on AWS, you should use IAM roles to provide temporary credentials for the application to access AWS resources. However, if your application is running on your corporate network, you can create an IAM user and generate access keys, so *SalesApp* can have the required credentials to access your resources.

In order to avoid using your root user account, you should create an IAM user for yourself and then assign administrator permissions for your account so that you can add more users when needed. Figure 3.2 shows such a scenario. In the figure, you can see the user details page as well as the list of policy permissions attached to the user.

FIGURE 3.2 IAM users and account permissions

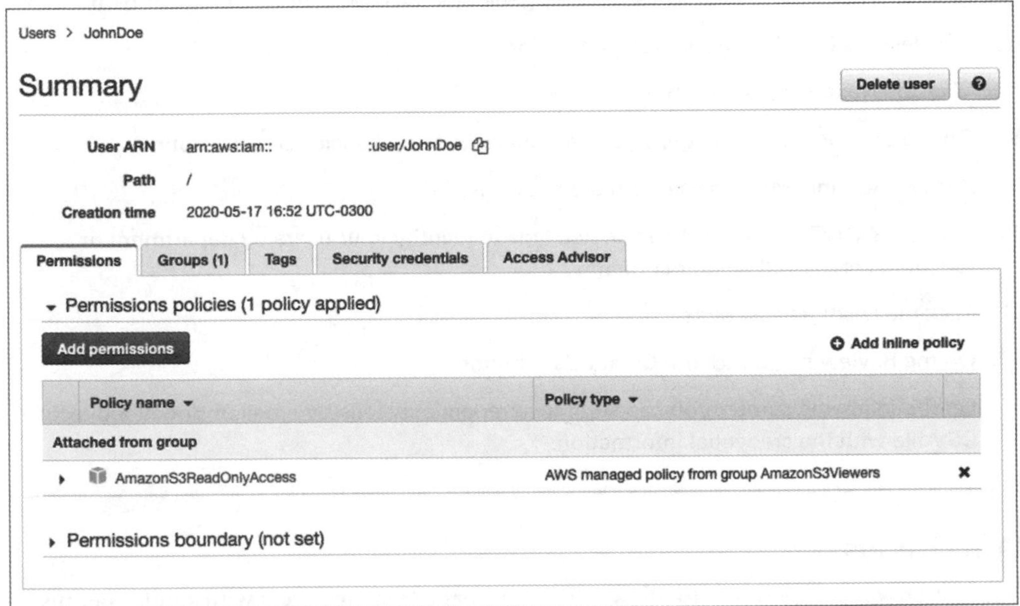

Always remember to enforce the zero trust model's principle of least privilege when creating your users—that is, users should have only the minimum required permissions to perform the tasks they need. You should define fine-grained policies associated with your IAM users. Policies will be covered later in this chapter in the "Access Management with Policies and Permissions" section.

You can create IAM users and set whatever permissions are necessary. Exercise 3.3 shows you how to create an IAM user with administrator access.

EXERCISE 3.3

Create an IAM User with Administrator Access Permissions

In this exercise, you will learn how to create a new IAM user with administrator permissions.

1. Open the IAM Console and select Users from the left-side menu.

EXERCISE 3.3 *(continued)*

2. Click Add User.
3. In the User Name field, type **MyAdminUser**.
4. For Access Type, assign AWS Management Console access.
5. Choose whether you want to use an autogenerated password or provide your own.
6. Deselect the Require Password Reset option.
7. Click the Next: Permissions button.
8. On the Set Permissions page, select the Attach Existing Policies Directly option.
9. Choose AdministratorAccess from the policy list.
10. Click the Next: Tags button. You can use tags to identify your users by department or functional areas within your company.
11. Click the Next: Review button.
12. On the Review page, click the Create User button.
13. On the following screen, you can send the credential details by email or download a CSV file with the credential information.

IAM Groups

An *IAM group* is a good way to allow administrators to manage users with similar permissions requirements. Administrators can create groups that are related to job functions or teams such as administrators, developers, QA, FinOps, operations, and so on. They can then assign fine-grained permissions to these groups.

When you add IAM users to a group, they inherit the group's permissions. With such a simple practice, it becomes easier to manage bulk changes in your environment and move IAM users around as they change or gain new responsibilities in the company.

One important thing for you to note: An IAM group is not an *identity* because it cannot be referred to as a *principal* when you're setting up permission policies. It is just a logical organization that allows you to attach policies to multiple users all at once.

Try to avoid assigning permissions directly to IAM users since these permissions are hard to track when your organization scales and users move to different organizational positions.

Figure 3.3 describes the relation between users and groups with their related permissions.

FIGURE 3.3 Groups and IAM users

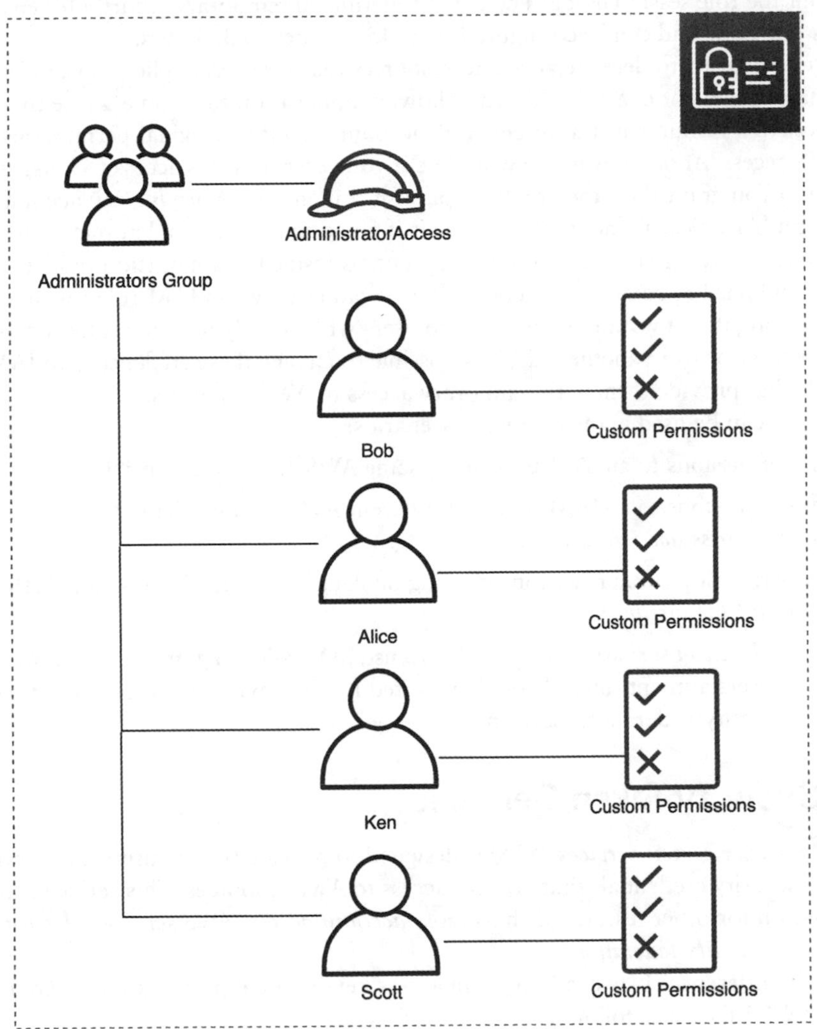

IAM Roles

Similar to IAM users, *IAM roles* can have a permission policy that determines what the IAM role can and cannot do in AWS. IAM roles are not exclusively associated with an IAM user or group; they can also be assumed by other entities, such as applications or services.

Additionally, IAM roles do not have long-term credentials or access keys directly assigned to them during creation. When a role is assumed, it is granted temporary credentials by a service called *AWS Security Token Service (STS)*. Such temporary credentials are valid throughout the role session usage. The default lifetime of temporary security tokens issued by STS is one hour and can be configured from 15 minutes to 36 hours.

Roles can be used to delegate access to resources that services, applications, or users do not normally have. For example, you can allow an application to assume a role that provides access to a resource in a different AWS account even if its original permissions did not allow such access. Another example would be if your user only has access to a *development account* and you grant them the ability to publish content in the *production* account by assuming an IAM role. Yet another example is if you grant an external application access to AWS resources, but instead of using fixed credentials inside the application (which are easy to extract and hard to rotate once deployed), you can leverage an IAM role for this purpose.

Furthermore, if you want to give access to users who already have identities on your corporate directory or from another IdP, it is possible to change these credentials to IAM role credentials that provide them with temporary access to AWS resources.

IAM roles can be used in the following scenarios:

- Grant permissions to an IAM user in the same AWS account as the role.
- Grant permissions to an IAM user in a different AWS account than the role, which is also called *cross-account access*.
- Grant permissions to applications running on Amazon EC2, which is called *AWS service role for an EC2 instance*.
- In user *federation* scenarios, it's possible to use IAM roles to grant permissions to external users authenticated through a trusted IdP. You will learn more about federation in the "Identity Federation" section.

AWS Security Token Services

The *AWS Security Token Services (STS)* is designed to provide trusted users and services with temporary security credentials that control access to AWS resources. This service provides the foundation for other features such as *cross-account access, AWS service roles for an EC2 instance,* and *identity federation*.

The main differences between long-term access keys and temporary security credentials issued by AWS STS are as follows:

- When you issue a temporary security credential, you can specify the expiration interval of that credential, which can range from a few minutes to several hours. Once expired, these credentials are no longer recognized by AWS, and any API requests made with them are denied.
- Temporary credentials are dynamic and generated every time a user requests them. A user can renew the temporary credentials before their expiration if they have permission to do so.

Roles for Cross-Account Access

Roles for cross-account access grant users of one AWS account access to resources in a different account. Such a procedure enables a different set of scenarios such as API or CLI calls or AWS Console access.

One common use case can be two AWS accounts, such as *Dev* and *Prod*, where users from the Dev account must access the Prod account. The regular permissions to a developer in the Dev account do not allow them to directly access the resources in the Prod account. However, it's possible to define a trust policy that allows a developer in the Dev account to assume a role in the Prod account. Once the trust policy is attached to the Prod role, a Dev account with the permission to assume the production role (with a `sts:AssumeRole` directive) can access the Prod account with the permissions defined by the role assumed.

In Example 3.1, the trust relationship policy definition attached to the role ProdAccess in the Prod account allows an IAM user or role in the Dev account to perform the `AssumeRole` action. Note that the policy is specifying the Dev AWS account identifier in its definition.

Example 3.1: ProdAccess role trust relationship policy definition in the Prod account

```
{
"Version": "2012-10-17",
"Statement": {
  "Effect": "Allow",
  "Principal": { "AWS": "arn:aws:iam::dev-aws-account-id:root" },
  "Action": "sts:AssumeRole",

}
```

In Example 3.2, it is the policy definition attached to the user or role in the Dev account that allows them to perform the `AssumeRole` action on the ProdAccess role in the Prod account.

Example 3.2: Assume role permission policy

```
{
  "Version": "2012-10-17",
  "Statement": [{
    "Effect": "Allow",
```

```
    "Action": ["sts:AssumeRole"],
    "Resource": "arn:aws:iam::prod-account-id:role/ProdAccess"
  }]
}
```

In Example 3.3, the policy definition attached to the `ProdAccess` role provides Amazon S3 bucket operations in the `production-bucket`.

Example 3.3: `ProdAccess` permission policy

```
{
    {
      "Effect": "Allow",
      "Action": [
        "s3:ListBucket",
        "s3:GetBucketLocation"
       ],
      "Resource": "arn:aws:s3:::production-bucket"
    },
    {
      "Effect": "Allow",
      "Action": [
        "s3:GetObject",
        "s3:PutObject",
        "s3:DeleteObject"
      ],
      "Resource": "arn:aws:s3:::production-bucket/*"
    }
  ]
}
```

AWS Service Role for an EC2 Instance

AWS service role for an EC2 is an IAM role that can be attached to multiple Amazon EC2 instances, which allows your applications to securely make API requests from your instances without the need to manage the security credentials that applications use.

To further understand what this feature actually does, imagine a scenario where an application running on an Amazon EC2 instance needs to post a message to Amazon Simple Queue Service (SQS). In this scenario, you do not need to set up an IAM user with the required policies to post a message to Amazon SQS and then share the user's access keys with the developer to manage directly inside the application configuration file. Instead, you can create a *role for an EC2 instance* and attach a policy to the role (with the required permission to access Amazon SQS), allowing the application to assume the role and perform the actions with temporary credentials.

When running your applications on Amazon EC2 instances, always use AWS service roles for an EC2 instance to give your applications access to AWS resources.

Access Management with Policies and Permissions

Access to AWS resources is managed through *policy documents*, which are attached to IAM identities or AWS resources. A policy is a JavaScript Object Notation (JSON) file that defines all the permissions that an identity or a resource has. When an identity or a resource makes an API request to other services, the AWS Cloud evaluates its permissions and allows the request to go through or denies it, based on a policy definition.

Here are the key points you should learn to understand how the AWS Cloud evaluates policies during API requests:

- All requests are denied by default because they follow the *principle of least privilege.*
- If your policy has an explicit allow directive, it will override the default.
- Permissions boundaries, service control policies, and session policies can override the permissions defined in policy documents.
- If you place an explicit deny on your policy, it will override any allow directive present in the document.

JSON Policy Documents

The AWS Certified Security – Specialty exam requires you to understand the JSON syntax and the policy document structure. When designing simple policies, you can use the *visual editor* available in the AWS Console, which covers most of the everyday scenarios. Nonetheless, in situations where you need to write more complex policies, you should leverage the JSON editor that is also available in the AWS Console.

The JSON policy document consists of the following elements:

- **Version:** This is the version of the policy language. The latest version is 2012-10-17.
- **Statement:** This contains the remaining elements of the policy.

- **Sid (Optional):** This is an identifier used to differentiate statements. As a best practice, for complex or more customized policies, use this field as a small description of that statement.
- **Effect:** Use this element to specify whether the policy *allows* or *denies* something.
- **Principal:** Use this element only when defining resource-based policies, where you define which principal is affected by that specific statement. In identity-based policies, the principal is implicit.
- **Action:** This is the list of methods that the policy allows or denies.
- **Resource:** This is required only when you're defining identity-based policies and you need to specify the resources that the policy statement applies.
- **Condition (Optional):** This element allows you to implement custom logic to test values of specific keys in the context of the request. For example, you can use it to test whether the user making the request has MFA enabled (`aws:MultiFactorAuthPresent`).

Example 3.4 shows a JSON policy that allows full read access to Amazon S3.

Example 3.4: S3 read-only JSON policy

```
{
    "Version": "2012-10-17",
    "Statement": [
        {
            "Effect": "Allow",
            "Action": [
                "s3:Get*",
                "s3:List*"
            ],
            "Resource": "*"
        }
    ]
}
```

As you can see in Example 3.4, the JSON policy allows full access to all `Get` and `List` operations on Amazon S3. Additionally, this policy is not restricted to a specific resource because it is using the * directive on the `Resource` element.

If you are not comfortable editing JSON documents to create your policies, you can use the visual editor from the AWS Console. You can see a summary of the permissions, which helps you troubleshoot and fix common errors encountered when creating IAM policies.

AWS provides a set of policy types that are available to use in different scenarios. For the remainder of this section, we are going to cover the most common ones.

Identity-Based Policies

Identity-based policies are JSON permissions policies that you can attach to an identity such as IAM users, IAM groups, or IAM roles. These policies define the actions that the principal can perform, and for which resources and in which conditions it might do so. AWS categorizes these policies into three different types:

AWS-Managed Policies These are policies provided and managed by AWS. They are essentially curated policies that allow you to quickly start setting up permissions to IAM entities and cover the most common use cases. For example, you can find policies by job function such as Administrator, Billing, and Database Administrator. These policies may change based on AWS's discretion, such as when a change to the actual policy might impact customers if applied to an existing policy.

Customer-Managed Policies These are policies that you create and manage in your AWS account. Once you have better understanding of your users and applications, you can start defining fine-grained permissions policies that are reusable within your AWS account.

Inline Policies This type of policy is directly embedded in the entity. For example, when you create an IAM user and attach an inline policy to it, that policy will live within that entity and cannot be shared. If you delete the entity, the policy is also deleted. This type of policy gives the administrators a 1-to-1 relationship between the IAM entity (user, group, or role) with its permission policy.

Managed policies provide you with features that make the day-to-day administration activities easier. These policies are as follows:

- Reusability
- Central change management
- Versioning and rollback
- Delegate permission management

Resource-Based Policies

A *resource-based policy* allows you to directly attach permissions to AWS resources, such as an Amazon SQS queue or an Amazon S3 bucket. It also allows you to specify who has access to that resource even if it does not have an explicit identity-based policy that says so. Figure 3.4 shows an example of a resource-based policy for Amazon S3.

FIGURE 3.4 Resource-based policy example

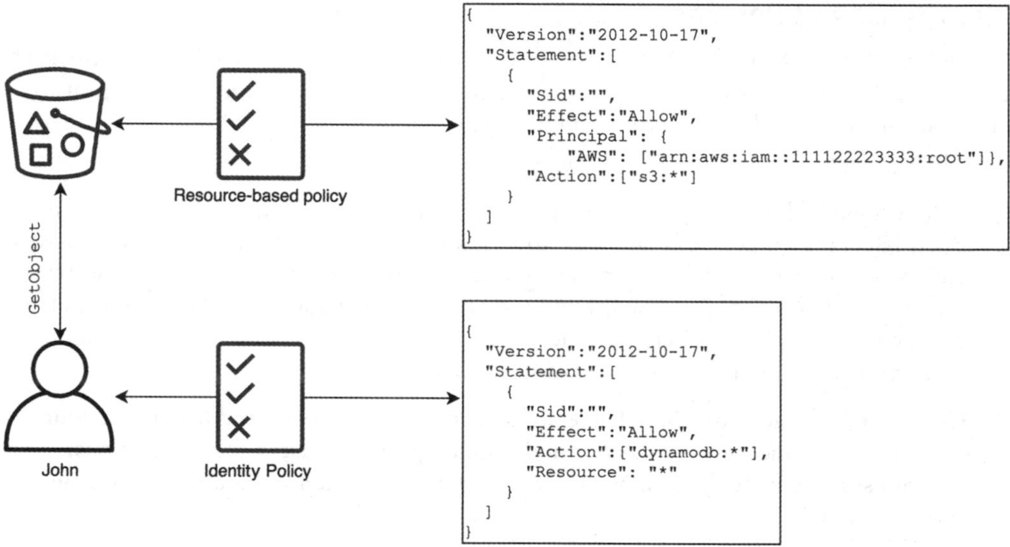

In Figure 3.4, user John does not have explicit permissions to perform the `GetObject` operation on the Amazon S3 bucket. However, the policy attached to the Amazon S3 bucket allows full access to the user John within the AWS account, which allows the request to complete successfully.

Cross-account resource access is used in scenarios where you need to access resources in different accounts. For example, say SalesApp needs to send a message (`SendMessage`) to an Amazon SQS queue in the Message Broker AWS account. You should explicitly allow the role attached to SalesApp to make requests to the Amazon SQS queue on the Message Broker account. Additionally, you must add a resource-based policy to the Amazon SQS queue that allows SalesApp to perform the actions required, in this case `SendMessage`.

Defining Permissions Boundaries

Permissions boundaries allow you to define the maximum permissions a user or application can be granted by IAM identity-based policies. You can use a customer-managed or an AWS-managed policy to set the permissions boundaries for an IAM user or role.

The boundaries assigned to the user or role do not give them permissions, but rather define the limits of the permissions attached to them, as shown in Examples 3.5 and 3.6.

Example 3.5: Administrator user policy

```
{
    "Version": "2012-10-17",
    "Statement": [
        {
            "Effect": "Allow",
            "Action":"*",
            "Resource": "*"
        }
    ]
}
```

Example 3.6: Permissions boundary to restrict access to Amazon S3 operations

```
{
    "Version": "2012-10-17",
    "Statement": [
        {
            "SID": "AllowAmazonS3AccessOnly",
            "Effect": "Allow",
            "Action":["s3:*"],
            "Resource": "*"

         } }
        }
    ]
}
```

In Example 3.5, a permission policy allows administrative permission to a user or role. However, the permissions boundary assigned to the user John restricts access only to Amazon S3 operations for any given bucket. Although the user John has a permission policy that gives administrator access, if he tries to access any other resources or services besides Amazon S3, it fails due to the permissions boundary assigned to him.

Figure 3.5 shows how the effective permissions work when you are using permissions boundaries. You can see that IAM determines the effective permissions for one specific IAM user or role; they must be allowed on both its policies and permissions boundaries.

FIGURE 3.5 Effective permissions example

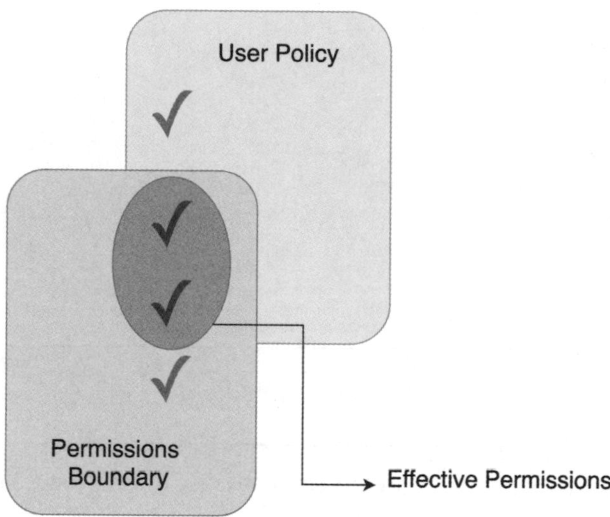

Access Management in Amazon S3

On top of the AWS IAM permission policies that you can attach to users and roles to manage AWS resources, Amazon S3 offers a specific set of resource-based policies that allows even finer-grained control over your Amazon S3 environment. Such resource-based policies are divided into two types:

Access Control Lists (ACLs) An ACL is a list of grants and users who have permission for them. It is possible to define cross-account read or write permissions using ACLs. Unlike IAM policies, ACLs use an Amazon S3–specific XML schema. AWS generally recommends that you leverage IAM policies rather than ACLs. However, if you need to define object-specific permissions, you must use ACLs. Example 3.7 shows an Amazon S3 ACL.

Example 3.7: Amazon S3 ACL definition

```
<?xml version="1.0" encoding="UTF-8"?>
<AccessControlPolicy xmlns="http://s3.amazonaws.com/doc/2006-03-01/">
  <Owner>
    <ID>*** Owner-Canonical-User-ID ***</ID>
    <DisplayName>owner-display-name</DisplayName>
  </Owner>
  <AccessControlList>
    <Grant>
      <Grantee xmlns:xsi="http://www.w3.org/2001/XMLSchema-instance"
               xsi:type="Canonical User">
        <ID>*** Owner-Canonical-User-ID ***</ID>
        <DisplayName>display-name</DisplayName>
      </Grantee>
      <Permission>FULL_CONTROL</Permission>
    </Grant>
  </AccessControlList>
</AccessControlPolicy>
```

Bucket Policy Provides you with a simple way to define cross-account access to your S3 buckets without setting up IAM roles. It also gives you centralized management of your bucket permissions. Just like IAM, these policies are defined using a JSON file. You should be diligent with bucket policies to avoid making your files publicly accessible by accident. These policies can be managed per user-level, which means that you can create a bucket policy that sets specific permissions per user within a bucket. Example 3.8 shows one bucket policy that allows full read permissions to anonymous users. Bucket policies are applied at the bucket level and do not extend to object-level granularity.

Example 3.8: Amazon S3 bucket policy

```
{
    "Version":"2012-10-17",
    "Statement": [
```

```
        {
            "Effect":"Allow",
            "Principal": "*",
            "Action":["s3:GetObject"],
            "Resource":["arn:aws:s3:::my-bucket/*"]
        }
    ]
}
```

Be very cautious when granting anonymous access to your Amazon S3 bucket. If you do, anyone on the Internet can access the contents of your bucket. Never grant anonymous access to your buckets unless required to do so—for example, when you're doing static website hosting.

In Example 3.8, when specifying resources on your bucket policy statement, pay attention to the specified resource ARN of your bucket. It should contain the /* notation at the end; otherwise, you'll get an error stating that the action does not apply to any resources.

There are many ways you can manage access management from the AWS Management Console and the IAM Console. You can create IAM groups and set their level of access to Amazon S3, as shown in Exercise 3.4.

EXERCISE 3.4

Create an IAM Group with Amazon S3 Read-Only Access Role

In this exercise, you will create an IAM group and attach a role allowing read-only access to Amazon S3.

1. Log into the AWS Management Console using the MyAdminUser credentials.
2. Go to the IAM console and select Groups from the left-side menu.
3. Click Create New Group.
4. For the group name, enter **AmazonS3Viewers**; then click Next Step.
5. On the Attach Policy screen, search for the `AmazonS3ReadOnlyAccess` policy, and then click the Next Step button.
6. On the review screen, click Create Group.

You can also create Amazon S3 buckets, as shown in Exercise 3.5.

EXERCISE 3.5

Create an Amazon S3 Bucket

In this exercise, you will create an Amazon S3 bucket and block all public access to it.

1. Using the MyAdminUser, log into the AWS Management Console and go to the Amazon S3 console.
2. Click Create Bucket.
3. Choose a name for your bucket. Remember that Amazon S3 buckets must be unique.
4. Choose the region where you want to create the bucket.
5. Leave the option Block All Public Access selected.
6. Click Create Bucket.

Exercise 3.6 shows you how to add users to your S3 groups as well.

EXERCISE 3.6

Add a User to the AmazonS3Viewers Group

In this exercise, you will create a user and add it to the AmazonS3Viewers group.

1. Open the IAM Console.
2. Select Users from the left-side menu.
3. Click Add User.
4. For the username, enter **JohnDoe**.
5. For Access Type, select AWS Management Console access.
6. Define a custom password and deselect the Require Password Reset option.
7. Click Next: Permissions.
8. Click Add User To Group, and from the group list, select AmazonS3Viewers.
9. Click Next: Tags.
10. On the Tags screen, add any tags that you want to identify this user. Then click Next: Review.
11. On the review screen, click Create User.

Policy Conflicts

When Amazon S3 needs to authorize a request to a bucket or object, it evaluates all access policies, such as user policies and resource-based policies (bucket policy, bucket ACL, and object ACL) associated with the respective target of the request.

You should always remember that when dealing with policy conflicts on Amazon S3, the AWS Cloud follows the *principle of least privilege* where everything is denied by default, unless instructed otherwise by an *allow*. You should also observe that any explicit *deny* overrides any other *allow* policy statement.

In your preparation for the exam, remember the following steps when evaluating the policy conflicts:

1. Every bucket and object is private by default (principle of least privilege).
2. Access policies, user policies, and resource-based policies (bucket policy, bucket and object ACLs) are all evaluated.
3. If an explicit deny is found, evaluation stops and the request is denied.
4. If an explicit allow is found, evaluation stops and the request is allowed.
5. In any other case, the request is denied.

Secure Data Transport in Amazon S3

Amazon S3 supports HTTP and HTTPS requests by default. However, if you want to guarantee that all data is encrypted in transit, you must create a specific bucket policy that denies any requests that meet the condition `"aws:SecureTransport":"false"`. Example 3.9 shows such a condition in action in an Amazon S3 bucket policy.

Example 3.9: Enforce HTTPS (TLS) bucket policy

```
{
    "Version": "2012-10-17",
    "Statement": [
        {
            "Sid": "AllowRequests",
            "Effect": "Allow",
            "Principal": "*",
            "Action": "s3:*",
            "Resource": "arn:aws:s3:::your-s3-bucket/*"
        },
```

```
        {
            "Sid": "ForceSSLRequests",
            "Effect": "Deny",
            "Principal": "*",
            "Action": "s3:*",
            "Resource": "arn:aws:s3:::your-s3-bucket/*",
            "Condition": {
                "Bool": {
                    "aws:SecureTransport": "false"
                }
            }
        }
    ]
}
```

In Example 3.9, the policy starts by allowing all requests to the bucket. In the following statement, we use a condition to deny all the requests that match the `"aws:SecureTransport":"false"` condition.

Another thing you can do is force SSL encryption for an Amazon S3 bucket, as Exercise 3.7 shows.

EXERCISE 3.7

Force SSL Encryption for an Amazon S3 Bucket

In this exercise, you will learn how users can access your bucket files using SSL encryption through bucket policies.

1. Log into the AWS Management Console using the MyAdminUser credentials.
2. Open the Amazon S3 console and select the bucket that you created in Exercise 3.5.
3. Select the Permissions tab.
4. Click Block Public Access.
5. Click Edit, deselect the Block All Public Access, and then click Save.
6. Click Bucket Policy.
7. In the Bucket Policy Editor, add the following bucket policy:

```
{
    "Version": "2012-10-17",
    "Statement": [
```

EXERCISE 3.7 *(continued)*

```
            {
                "Sid": "AllowRequests",
                "Effect": "Allow",
                "Principal": "*",
                "Action": "s3:*",
                "Resource": "arn:aws:s3:::your-s3-bucket/*"
            },
            {
                "Sid": "ForceSSLRequests",
                "Effect": "Deny",
                "Principal": "*",
                "Action": "s3:*",
                "Resource": "arn:aws:s3:::your-s3-bucket/*",
                "Condition": {
                    "Bool": {
                        "aws:SecureTransport": "false"
                    }
                }
            }
        ]
    }
```

8. Replace `your-s3-bucket` with the name of your bucket.
9. Click Save. The console will present you with a warning saying that your bucket has public access now.
10. Create a file named **hello.txt**, enter the text **AWS Security Specialty Exam**, and then click Save.
11. Upload the `hello.txt` file to your bucket.
12. Click the file `hello.txt` in the bucket.
13. In the Overview panel, search for the Object URL field and copy and paste this address into your web browser. The message "AWS Security Specialty Exam" should appear.
14. Change the protocol from HTTPS to HTTP in the Object URL. It should present an Access Denied message, confirming that the policy is working.

Cross-Region Replication in Amazon S3

Cross-region replication (CRR) replicates objects from one region to another in an asynchronous fashion. Such replication can happen between buckets owned by the same AWS account or by different accounts. Consequently, CRR allows cloud environment administrators to meet compliance requirements that demand aggregating logs into a single bucket in a different AWS account and region miles away from the original stored data.

Additionally, you can use CRR to change object ownership at the destination bucket, restricting access to the replicated objects. This guarantees that once the object is replicated, it cannot be changed. Moreover, you can change the class of objects at your destination to achieve more cost-effective storage designs.

Replication only happens in a one-to-one relation, or simply, from one source to one destination. Once the object is replicated, it is not possible to replicate it again. Furthermore, when you enable CRR, you do not need to write custom policies to enforce SSL encryption during the replication, because this is done by default.

The following items detail *what is replicated* when CRR is enabled:

- New objects created after the replication is activated. Old objects will not be replicated unless they are changed after the replication was activated.
- Unencrypted objects.
- Encrypted objects by SSE-S3-managed keys or customer-managed keys (CMKs) stored in Amazon KMS (SSE-KMS). The latter should be explicitly enabled to work.
- Object metadata, ACL updates, any existing tags, and lock retention information.
- If you perform a `delete` operation to mark the object as deleted, this marker will be replicated.

On the other hand, the following items represent *what is not replicated* by the CRR:

- Objects created before the CRR was enabled.
- Any objects created with SSE-C, or customer-provided encryption keys.
- Objects deleted through a `delete` operation with a version ID specified. This prevents malicious deletion of your data.

For cross-region replication to work, you should pay attention to key requirements such as the following:

- *Versioning* should be enabled in both buckets (source and destination).
- Make sure that the *replication role* specified gives all the necessary permissions to replicate and access the objects on the source bucket.
- If the destination bucket is owned by a different AWS account, the *account owner of the destination* must grant the required permission to store the replicated objects. It is also possible to change object ownership during replication to the destination bucket.

- If the owner of the source bucket does not have permissions on the stored objects, the read and read_acp permissions should be granted; otherwise, replication of these objects will fail.
- Bucket owner must have permissions to access objects (ACLs) to perform the replication.

Amazon S3 Pre-signed URLs

As mentioned in the "Policy Conflicts" section earlier, all objects in your Amazon S3 bucket are private by default, unless you set up policies to make them accessible. However, there are situations in which you need to share objects with other users, services, or even the whole Internet through a finer-grained approach.

For such scenarios, you can leverage *pre-signed URLs*, which allow users and applications to access private objects for a limited period of time. It is important that you observe that anyone who has access to a pre-signed URL will have access to the object.

To create pre-signed URLs, you must provide security credentials, the bucket name, and the object key that you want to share. Keep in mind that the credentials being used to generate the pre-signed URL must have the right permissions to access the Amazon S3 object. The permissions defined by the pre-signed URL are scoped at the object level and do not allow any other operations at the bucket level.

You can use the AWS API, the AWS CLI, or one of the AWS SDKs available to generate a pre-signed URL. Example 3.10 uses the AWS CLI to generate a pre-signed URL from an Amazon EC2 instance with an IAM role attached that has the `AmazonS3FullAccess` policy attached to it.

Example 3.10: Generating a pre-signed URL using AWS CLI

```
> aws s3 presign s3://security-bucket-example-0009/hello.txt

# Command Output

> https://security-bucket-example-009/hello.txt?AWSAccessKeyId=AKIAEXAMPLEACCESS
KEY
&Signature=EXHCcBe%EXAMPLEKnz3r8O0AgEXAMPLE&Expires=1555531131
```

Example 3.10 uses the `presign` command, assuming that we have a file `hello.txt` in the `security-bucket-example-0009` bucket. The command output is the pre-signed URL that can be shared with other users and applications.

The `presign` command has a parameter called `--expires-in` that allows you to change the expiration time of a pre-signed URL. Although it has a default value of 3600 seconds, you can increase it to up to seven days.

Identity Federation

Identity federation provides you with the ability to perform access management of your AWS account at one single place. In simpler terms, it allows you to exchange valid credentials from external IdPs, such as Microsoft Active Directory, through open standards, such as Security Assertion Markup Language 2.0 (SAML), for temporary AWS credentials provided by the Amazon Security Token Service (STS).

To grasp the main aspects of deploying identity federation in the AWS Cloud, study these key terms:

Identity A user in your corporate or web identity store such as Microsoft Active Directory or Facebook.

Identity Store Central location where identities are stored. It represents services such as Microsoft Active Directory, Amazon, Apple, Facebook, and Google.

Identity Broker A client application that performs the authentication of the users against the IdPs, then obtains AWS temporary security credentials, and finally provides the users with access to the AWS resources.

Figure 3.6 explains the identity federation process with Microsoft Active Directory to allow login into the AWS Console.

FIGURE 3.6 Identity federation workflow

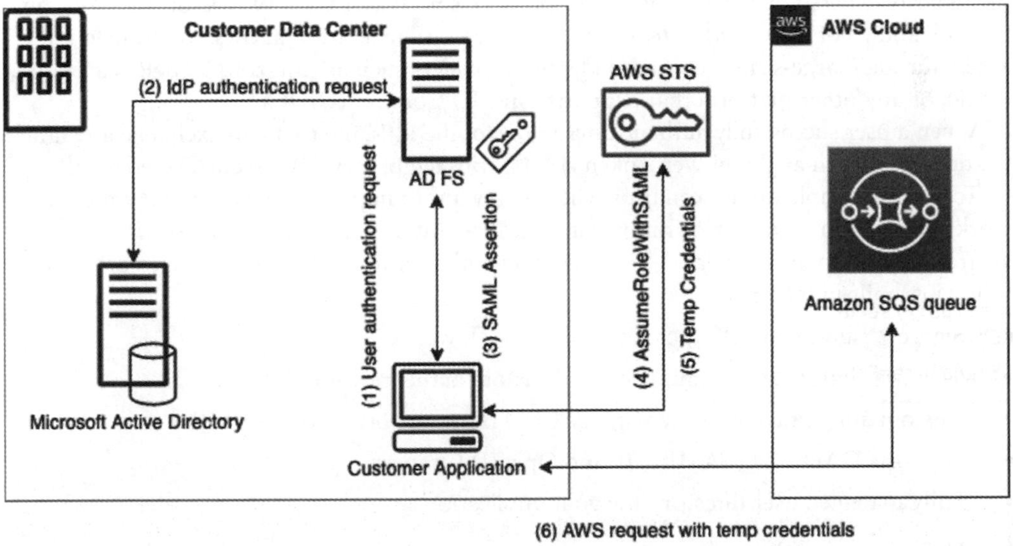

The identity federation process shown in Figure 3.6 follows these steps:

1. The user logs into an identity broker using their corporate credentials.
2. The IdP authenticates the user against the LDAP-based identity store.
3. The IdP generates a SAML assertion with all the required user information and submits the assertion to the identity broker.
4. The identity broker calls the `AssumeRoleWithSAML` STS API, passing the SAML assertion and the role ARN to assume.
5. The API response, if successful, includes AWS temporary security credentials with its associated permissions.
6. With the temporary credentials, the client application can perform operations on AWS resources.

In order to help your organization scale, you can take advantage of the *AWS Single Sign-On (SSO)* service, which allows you to manage single sign-on access to multiple AWS accounts in a central place. The service also integrates with *AWS Organizations,* which will be covered in the section "Multi-Account Management with AWS Organizations," later in this chapter.

Amazon Cognito

In scenarios where your mobile or web applications need access to AWS resources, you can take advantage of *web identity federation*. Web identity federation allows you to federate access through large-scale web-based identity providers such as Amazon, Google, Facebook, Apple, or any other platform that supports OpenID Connect (OIDC).

When a user successfully authenticates in one of the IdPs, the user can exchange an authentication code, such as JSON Web Token (JWT), with temporary AWS security credentials.

To reduce complexity in scenarios where you want to implement custom authentication workflows within your web or mobile applications, AWS created *Amazon Cognito,* which abstracts all heavy lifting related to application authentication. Amazon Cognito offers the following built-in features:

- Sign-up, sign-in, and "forgot my password" flows
- Web user interface customization and custom authentication domain
- Custom authentication flow with CAPTCHA or any other form of MFA
- Supports OAuth 2.0, SAML 2.0, and OpenID Connect
- Fully managed user directory for your application.
- Guest user support
- Access control using role-based access control (RBAC)
- User data synchronization between devices

Amazon Cognito User Pools

A *user pool* is a secure directory within Amazon Cognito that allows you to manage the users of your web or mobile applications in one single place.

Users in a user pool can sign in with their registered credentials or by using a social identity from web providers such as Amazon, Google, Facebook, or Apple. Additionally, they can use SAML 2.0 or OpenID Connect with enabled identity providers.

Upon successful authentication, Amazon Cognito returns a set of JWTs that the application developer can use to secure and authorize access to application APIs or use to obtain AWS temporary credentials. Figure 3.7 describes the sign-in flow using the Amazon Cognito user pool.

FIGURE 3.7 User pool authentication flow

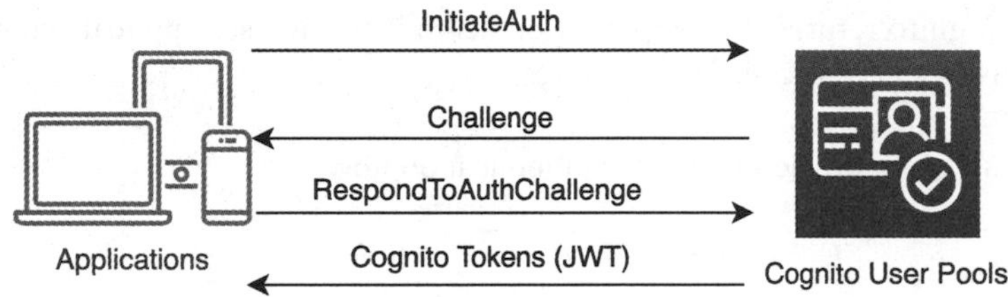

In Figure 3.7, a user from the Amazon Cognito user pool performs a successful authentication and receives JWTs in exchange that they can use in the application.

Amazon Cognito Identity Pools

Amazon Cognito *identity pools* allow you to create unique identifiers for guest users who access your application and authenticate these users with identity providers. You can then exchange these identities with temporary, limited-privilege AWS credentials to access other AWS services.

Identity pools specify two types of identities: authenticated and unauthenticated, with both of them always associated with an IAM role. *Authenticated identities* represent the users who are verified by a web identity provider (Amazon Cognito user pools, Facebook, Amazon, Google, or Apple) or a custom backend authentication process. *Unauthenticated identities* represent guest users.

Figure 3.8 depicts the authentication flow for Amazon Cognito identity pools using an external provider. It illustrates the following steps:

1. The user application logs in by using one of the supported web identity providers (Login Provider).
2. Upon successful authentication, the Login Provider returns a session key for the user.

3. With the session key for the user, the application issues a call to the Amazon Cognito `GetId` API to retrieve a unique identifier for the user.
4. Amazon Cognito validates the provided session key against the Login Provider.
5. If the session key provided is valid, the `GetId` API returns a unique identifier for the user.
6. The user application then sends a request to the Amazon Cognito `GetCredentialsForIdentity` API, passing the unique identifier returned by the `GetId` API, the session key from the Login Provider, and the role ARN (Amazon Resource Name).
7. Amazon Cognito validates the provided session key against the Login Provider and the unique identifier.
8. Upon successful validation, Amazon Cognito issues a call to the AWS STS service to retrieve temporary credentials for the user based on the role permissions specified in step 6.
9. Amazon Cognito returns the temporary credentials to the user application, which in turn can use them to access AWS resources.

FIGURE 3.8 Cognito identity pools authentication flow

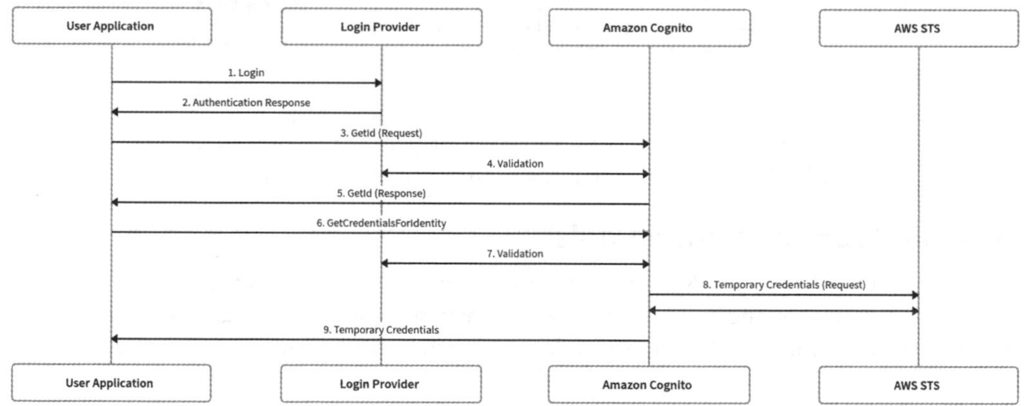

Multi-Account Management with AWS Organizations

You can use the *AWS Organizations* cloud service to manage all your AWS accounts in one single place. This service provides you with a centralized view of billing, access control, and the ability to share cross-account resources. Furthermore, you can automate account provisioning by using the AWS Organizations APIs and quickly add AWS accounts to their respective groups.

Using AWS Organizations, you can group your AWS accounts into organizational units (OU) and attach SCPs to limit the permissions within that account.

OUs allow you to group accounts and other organizational units in a hierarchical structure. Such a composition gives you the ability to mimic your own organizational structure and break down the OUs into teams, while using SCPs to limit the service usage per team.

Figure 3.9 illustrates a sample account hierarchy using AWS Organizations.

FIGURE 3.9 AWS Organizations account hierarchy

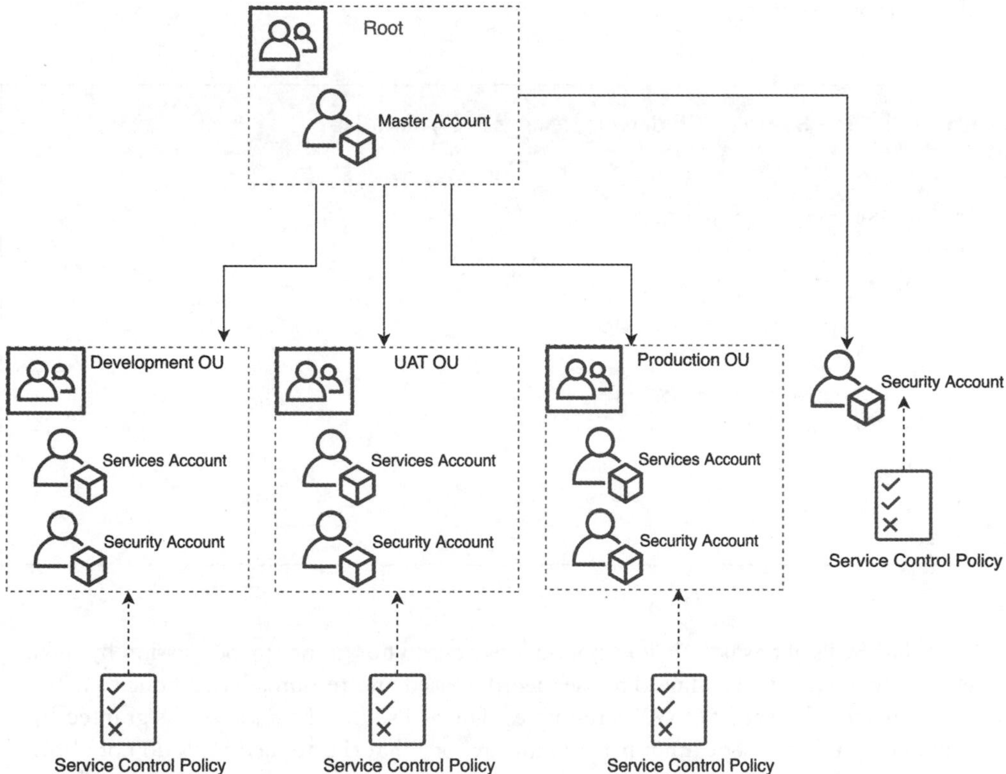

In Figure 3.9, there are three OUs (Development, UAT, and Production). Attached to each OU is an SCP that limits the access to AWS services. You can also note that there is a separate account, "Security Account," that is not under any OU but has a corresponding SCP attached to it.

Service Control Policies

You can use SCPs to centrally manage the availability of service actions across multiple AWS accounts within your AWS Organizations deployment. SCPs are similar to IAM policies and have the same syntax.

In truth, an SCP is more akin to an *IAM permissions boundary*, which restricts the actions that users, groups, and roles within that account can actually perform (including the root account).

Example 3.11 shows a sample SCP that denies access to any Amazon DynamoDB (AWS's NoSQL database service) actions.

Example 3.11: Sample SCP denying access to DynamoDB

```
{
    "Version": "2012-10-17",
    "Statement": [
        {
            "Sid": "DenyDynamoDBAccess",
            "Effect": "Deny",
            "Action": "dynamodb:*",
            "Resource": "*"
        }
    ]
}
```

Note that SCPs act as permissions boundaries and do not grant any permission by themselves. Consequently, you still need to use identity-based and resource-based policies within your account to allow access to AWS resources. The SCPs filter the permissions granted by these policies, and the user cannot perform any actions that the applied SCPs do not allow.

Also remember to validate which services and actions are allowed in the SCP attached to the account when you are dealing with debugging permission issues. The SCP boundaries always take precedence over the permissions defined through identity and resource-based policies. Last, it's important to note that in member accounts of an AWS Organization, the root user is also affected by SCP boundaries.

Service control policies are not available if you only enabled consolidated billing in your organization.

AWS Single Sign-On

AWS Single Sign-On (AWS SSO) is a single sign-on managed service that provides a centralized place for your users to access AWS accounts and other cloud applications. AWS SSO can manage access for all AWS accounts under your AWS Organizations.

AWS SSO supports identity federation using SAML 2.0, allowing integration with AWS Managed Microsoft AD and third-party applications such as Azure Active Directory, Office 365, Concur, and Salesforce.

AWS SSO can also integrate with your on-premises Microsoft Active Directory (AD). In such a scenario, you must create a two-way trust relationship between your AWS Managed Microsoft AD deployment and the on-premises AD.

Another available option is using the *AD connector*, which is a feature from the AWS Directory Service. In essence, the AD connector is a directory gateway that routes requests to your on-premises AD. Additionally, AWS SSO provides support for the System for Cross-Domain Identity Management (SCIM) v2.0 standard. Using SCIM, your AWS SSO identities are kept in sync with your IdP, providing automatic provisioning, updates, and deprovisioning of users between your IdP and AWS SSO.

Microsoft AD Federation with AWS

AWS enables you to implement identity federation to sign in to AWS Console using Microsoft Active Directory (AD) credentials. With identity federation, you can use an existing corporate AD to perform all user administration and thus skip manually creating user credentials in AWS. Such federation reduces the administration overhead and enables users to use single sign-on in the AWS Console.

When implementing AD federation, you should be aware of some key terms that it uses:

Microsoft Active Directory Federation Services (AD FS) A Microsoft solution that provides single sign-on access and acts as the identity broker between AWS and the Microsoft Active Directory. It resides inside your on-premises infrastructure.

Two-Way Trust For the SAML 2.0 federation to work, you need to set up a trust between your AWS account and AD FS. This setup manually exchanges SAML metadata between the two parties; the metadata contains the issuer name, creation date, expiration date, and keys that AWS can use to validate the authentication information (assertions) issued by AD FS.

Although the AWS Certified Security – Specialty exam does not require you to configure a Microsoft AD federation with AWS, you should have a clear understanding of how the process works. Figure 3.10 is a visual representation of the authentication workflow using identity federation with AD and your AWS account.

FIGURE 3.10 Authentication workflow using federation between AWS account and Microsoft AD

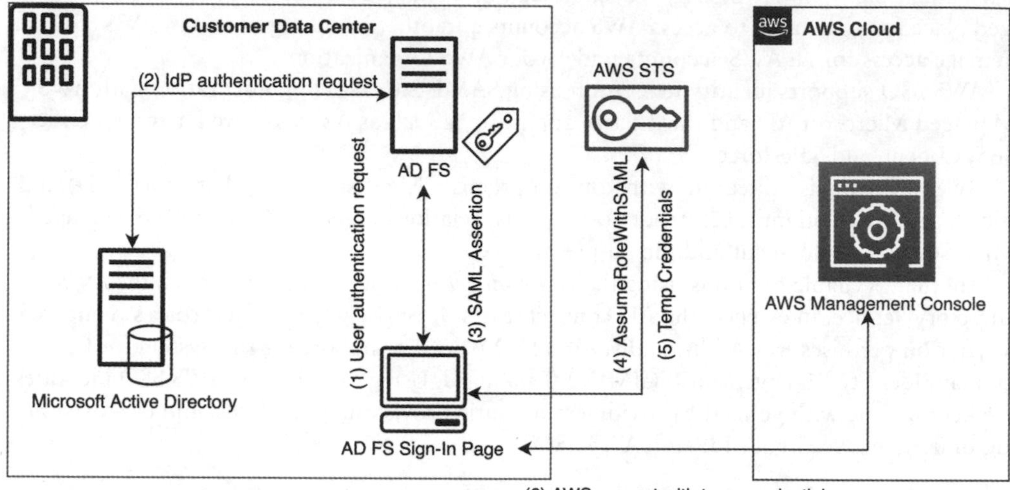

In Figure 3.10, you can observe the user authentication process in an identity federation with Microsoft AD following these steps:

1. A user from your corporate network logs into AD FS, providing their Active Directory credentials.
2. Active Directory validates the user credentials.
3. Upon a successful login, AD FS returns a SAML 2.0 assertion containing all the necessary user information.
4. The user is redirected to the AWS sign-in page, which extracts the SAML 2.0 assertion.
5. The AWS sign-in page then exchanges the SAML assertion with AWS temporary credentials using the `AssumeRoleWithSAML` API.
6. With the credentials obtained in the previous step, the user is then redirected to the AWS Management Console authenticated with their AD credentials.

Protecting Credentials with AWS Secrets Manager

AWS Secrets Manager is a managed service that allows developers, IT, and security administrators to rotate, manage, and retrieve database credentials (RDS and non-RDS), API keys, and other secrets throughout their lifecycle.

It is a critical step to follow in order to guarantee the integrity of your whole system in case your application code is compromised. Using AWS Secrets Manager, you can remove hard-coded credentials, passwords, and any other type of sensitive information in your code, with an API call to the AWS Secrets Manager to retrieve and store secrets programmatically. AWS Secrets Manager provides integration with AWS CloudFormation through resource types that enable you to create secrets as part of an AWS CloudFormation template.

AWS Secrets Manager uses Amazon Key Management Service (KMS) to encrypt your secrets at rest. Every secret stored has a corresponding AWS KMS customer master key (CMK) associated with it. Consequently, users can use the default AWS Secrets Manager CMK for the account or provide one of their own.

Secrets Permission Management

You can manage the permissions associated with the secrets stored in Secrets Manager by using identity-based and resource-based policies. You should always assess your environment to evaluate which type of policies to use. Keep in mind that you should choose the type that reduces your administration work and evolves as your organization scales.

If you use *identity-based policies*, you can grant access to many secrets for that identity, which is useful when you are setting up an IAM role for an application that requires access to more than one secret.

On the other hand, using *resource-based policies* enables you to grant access to multiple principals to a secret. Additionally, you can define cross-account permissions for your secrets, especially in scenarios where you have a centralized security account containing all secrets your applications require.

Automatic Secrets Rotation

AWS Secrets Manager also enables you to rotate your credentials automatically for select AWS services and databases. The rotation process takes advantage of AWS Lambda functions to orchestrate the secret rotation process.

The following database services support automatic secrets rotation:

- Amazon Aurora on Amazon RDS
- MySQL on Amazon RDS
- PostgreSQL on Amazon RDS
- Oracle on Amazon RDS
- MariaDB on Amazon RDS
- Microsoft SQL Server on Amazon RDS
- Amazon DocumentDB
- Amazon Redshift

Moreover, you can implement your custom AWS Lambda rotation function for third-party services and other unsupported databases.

When you turn on automatic rotation for your Amazon RDS database, AWS Secrets Manager will immediately rotate the secret once you save the configuration. Keep in mind that before enabling rotation, you need to update all of your application code to retrieve credentials from AWS Secrets Manager. Otherwise, your application will break.

Choosing between AWS Secrets Manager and AWS Systems Manager Parameter Store

In the scenarios in which you need to store database credentials for AWS or third-party databases, manage credential rotation, and provide cross-account access, you should choose AWS Secrets Manager because it has these functionalities already built in. In fact, at the time of this writing, AWS charges AWS Secrets Manager as follows:

- US$ 0.40 per secret per month
- US$ 0.05 per 10,000 API calls

On the other hand, AWS Systems Manager Parameter Store offers a central place to store environment configuration for your applications, user-defined parameters, and any other type of encrypted or plain-text information with no additional charge. Additionally, you can use AWS Systems Manager Parameter Store to reference secrets in AWS Secrets Manager.

Summary

An essential part of the success of your cloud journey is how you leverage the ability to experiment with new ideas and create solutions to quickly respond to business demands. At the same time, as the administrator of a new cloud environment, you want to maintain or improve your organization's existing security.

AWS Identity and Access Management (IAM) lets you build a scalable and easy-to-manage solution. With JSON-based policies, you can define fine-grained permissions for the resources in your AWS accounts. Furthermore, using IAM roles, you can control access between resources that are located in different AWS accounts.

When designing your multi-account strategy, you can take advantage of AWS Single Sign-On (SSO) to provide a single place for your users to access all of your company's AWS accounts. With AWS Organizations, you have a central location for managing all your AWS accounts, implementing automatic account provisioning, and defining permissions boundaries for the users with service control policies (SCPs).

If you are building mobile or web applications that need to scale to hundreds of millions of users, you can use Amazon Cognito to integrate users with identity providers such as Google, Facebook, and Amazon. And in case you need to continue to use your corporate identity provider (IdP) for such applications, you can use SAML 2.0 federation methods available on AWS. Additionally, you can take advantage of AWS Secrets Manager to rotate, manage, and retrieve database credentials and other service secrets.

Finally, Amazon S3 provides security features that allow you to use resource-based and identity-based policies to define who can access the data in your buckets and how it is accessed. You can also use these policies in conjunction with access control lists (ACLs) to create fine-grained per-object permissions. You can also replicate data across regions and accounts using cross-region replication (CRR) to meet compliance requirements that might dictate that you store data in different AWS regions.

Exam Essentials

Understand the criticality of the root account user. The root account user provides complete unrestricted access to all the services and resources in your account. It is crucial that you use a strong password policy, enable multi-factor authentication (MFA) for your root account user, and keep the usage of this account to a minimum. Unless you *must* have a root user access key, it is best not to create one. If an administrator leaves the company, make sure that you create a new password, re-create the MFA, and delete any access key ID and secret access key. Additionally, review IAM users to guarantee that they are valid; otherwise remove them.

Understand how IAM works. AWS Identity and Access Management (IAM) provides the constructs and necessary infrastructure for you to manage authentication and authorization for your AWS account and all the resources in it. Principals can represent a person or an application that uses an IAM user or an IAM role to send requests to the AWS Cloud. When you create a user or role, by default, it does not have permission to perform any actions on your account. You define permissions by using IAM policies, which are JSON documents that specify the resources and actions that the specified principal can perform. AWS has three types of IAM policies:

AWS-Managed Policies A curated list of policies created and managed by AWS with a wide range of policies for all AWS services.

Customer-Managed Policies Policies created and managed by you in your account. Fine-grained policies designed for your use case.

Inline Policies Policies created and managed by you that are directly attached to a user, group, or role. As your organization scales, it is harder to manage inline policies. If you delete the entity that the policy is attached to, the policy is deleted as well.

Understand Amazon S3 bucket policies. Bucket policy is a type of resource-based policy directly attached to your Amazon S3 bucket and is limited to 20 KB in size. When using bucket policies, you have a central location to manage how principals access your bucket. Moreover, you use bucket policies to define cross-account access to your bucket. These policies can be fine-grained to the user level. For example, user John can only make `PUT` requests whereas Mike can perform `READ` and `PUT` actions. Finally, it is essential for you to remember that when troubleshooting permission issues, an explicit `DENY` overrides any `ALLOW` policies.

Know about Amazon S3 access control lists (ACLs). Amazon S3 ACLs are a legacy mechanism to manage permissions for your Amazon S3 bucket and objects. Different from JSON policies, ACLs use XML syntax to define permissions. You can use Amazon S3 ACLs to define permissions to individual objects, whereas Amazon S3 bucket policies only apply to the bucket level. For the exam, remember that Amazon S3 ACLs can only grant permissions to other AWS accounts—you cannot use them to define permissions to users in your account. Finally, you cannot explicitly define `DENY` permissions using Amazon S3 ACLs.

Understand how Amazon S3 authorizes requests. AWS follows the principle of least privilege, which denotes that any permission evaluation defaults to a `DENY` unless an explicit `ALLOW` exists. When authorizing a request, Amazon S3 evaluates whether the principal performing the request action has all the permissions to perform that action. It gathers all access policies, user policies, and resource-based policies to validate if the request can complete successfully. If any of the policies evaluated have an explicit `DENY` for the specified action in the request, the evaluation process stops, and the requisition is not allowed.

Know about Amazon S3 cross-region replication (CRR). Cross-region replication allows you to copy objects across Amazon S3 buckets between regions and AWS accounts. The replication process retains object metadata, deletion markers (the deletes for versions are not retained), and storage classes. You can specify different storage classes for your objects during replication (for example, putting objects directly in S3 Glacier). All the replication has SSL/TLS enabled by default. You don't have to use the `aws:SecureTransport` policy to enforce encryption in transit. CRR enables you to fulfill compliance requirements that you store your data across regions or implement WORM (write-once-read-many) for your application access logs.

Be familiar with Amazon pre-signed URLs. All objects in your bucket are private by default. In case you need to share objects with others without changing your bucket or object permissions, you can take advantage of pre-signed URLs. You can create these pre-signed URLs by using the AWS CLI or one of the available SDKs. The user generating these URLs must have the required permissions to access the object represented by the pre-signed URL. Otherwise, the request is going to fail. Pre-signed URLs can be valid from one hour up to seven days. You can customize the expiration configuration by using the `--expires-in` modifier, specifying the expiration time in seconds.

Understand identity federation using Microsoft Active Directory. AWS allows you to implement identity federation using identity providers (IdPs) that support Security Assertion Markup Language (SAML) 2.0 standards, providing access for your corporate users to the AWS Console or the AWS CLI. To enable identity federation with Microsoft Active Directory, you are required to create a SAML provider in AWS to establish a two-way trust with Microsoft Active Directory Federation Services (Microsoft AD FS). In addition, you need to create IAM roles that map to Microsoft Active Directory groups. This way, when a user logs in, the AWS Security Token Services (AWS STS) creates temporary security credentials based on the permissions defined in the assigned role. Finally, with the provided temporary credentials, the federated user can access resources and services in your AWS account.

Review Questions

1. When you first create your AWS account, what are the steps you take to protect your root account and provide secure, limited access to your AWS resources? (Choose three.)
   A. Create access keys and secret keys for the root account.
   B. Create an IAM user with the `AdministratorAccess` role to perform day-to-day management of your AWS resources.
   C. Create a strong password for the root account.
   D. Enable multifactor authentication for the root account.
2. When you're creating resource-based policies, can you use IAM groups as principals?
   A. Yes.
   B. No.
   C. This relationship does not make sense.
   D. More information is needed.
3. When writing a resource-based policy, which are the minimum required elements for it to be valid?
   A. Version, Statement, Effect, Resource, and Action
   B. Version, Statement, Effect, Principal, SID, and Action
   C. Version, Statement, Effect, Principal, and Action
   D. Version, Statement, Effect, Resource, and Condition
4. What IAM feature can you use to control the maximum permission an identity-based policy can grant to an IAM entity?
   A. Service control policy (SCP)
   B. Session policies
   C. Permissions boundary
   D. All the options above
5. How do you enforce SSL when you have enabled cross-region replication for your Amazon S3 bucket?
   A. In the configuration wizard, you must select Use SSL when you enable cross-region replication.
   B. Create a bucket policy that denies requests with a condition where `aws:SecureTransport` is `false`.
   C. SSL is enabled by default when using cross-region replication.
   D. Enable `SecureTransport` in the Amazon S3 console.

6. You created an S3 bucket and assigned it a resource-based policy that allows users from other AWS accounts to upload objects to this bucket. What is the only way to manage the permissions for the uploaded objects?
   A. Create a bucket policy specifying the path where the objects were uploaded.
   B. Create an IAM role that gives full access permissions to users and groups that have this role attached.
   C. The owner of the objects must use ACLs to manage the permissions.
   D. None of the above.

7. Which of the following is *not* true of the temporary security credentials issued by AWS Security Token Services (STS)?
   A. Temporary credentials are dynamic and generated every time a user requests them.
   B. Once expired, these credentials are no longer recognized by AWS, and any API requests made with them are denied.
   C. A user can never under any conditions renew the temporary credentials.
   D. When you issue a temporary security credential, you can specify the expiration interval of that credential that can range from a few minutes to several hours.

8. You created a new AWS Organization for your account using Consolidated Billing. Later you learn about service control policies (SCPs). Now you want to use them in your organization. What do you need to do to take advantage of SCPs?
   A. You can start using SCPs without any change in the configuration of your AWS Organization.
   B. You should use the master account to start creating SCPs.
   C. You must log in with the root account credentials to use SCPs.
   D. You should open the AWS Organizations Management Console and on the Settings tab choose Begin Process To Enable All Features.

9. Developers in your company are building a new platform where users will be able to log in using their social identity providers and upload photos to an Amazon S3 bucket. Which actions should you take to enable the users to authenticate to the web application and upload photos to Amazon S3? (Choose two.)
   A. Configure the SAML identity provider in Amazon Cognito to map attributes to the Amazon Cognito user pool attributes.
   B. Configure Amazon Cognito for identity federation using the required social identity providers.
   C. Create an Amazon Cognito group and assign an IAM role with permissions to upload files to the Amazon S3 bucket.
   D. Create an Amazon S3 bucket policy with public access to upload files.
   E. Create an IAM identity provider, with Provider Type set to OpenID Connect.

10. One of your administrators created an Amazon S3 pre-signed URL and shared it with an external customer to upload system logs. However, the user receives Access Denied when they try to upload the logs. What are the possible reasons that the user cannot upload the logs? (Choose two.)

    A. Users uploading the files are not providing the correct access and secret keys.

    B. The administrator who generated the pre-signed URL does not have access to the S3 bucket where the logs need to be uploaded.

    C. There is a bucket policy not allowing users to access the bucket using pre-signed URLs.

    D. The pre-signed URL has expired.

Detective Controls

THE AWS CERTIFIED SECURITY SPECIALTY EXAM OBJECTIVES THAT LEVERAGE CONCEPTS EXPLAINED IN THIS CHAPTER INCLUDE THE FOLLOWING:

✓ **Domain 2: Logging and Monitoring**

- 2.1. Design and implement security monitoring and alerting
- 2.3. Design and implement a logging solution

✓ **Domain 3: Infrastructure Security**

- 3.4. Design and implement host-based security

Introduction

An important part of the security cycle is being able to understand what is actually happening in an environment. Think about this: if a tree falls in the middle of the forest and nobody hears it, does it make a sound?

Well, as a security professional, it is important for you to notice when trees go down, even if there seems to be no sound or other consequences. Such observation can be an indicator of something not working as expected or a warning of a future, undesired consequence. That is why security experts put effort into having sensors in the right place to learn what is happening. At some point, even if you cannot see inside a system, you should at least infer what is happening within it through its generated events. This practice is known as *observability.*

Think of *resources* in your AWS account as observable objects. These resources and the information they manage (extract, process, store, transmit, analyze, generate, or archive) are the ultimate goal of your protection. These resources follow a lifecycle and are also executing actions as part of their job inside a system. In consequence, these resources are dynamic and continually experiencing changes.

In this chapter, you will learn how to gather information about the status of your resources and, most importantly, the *events* they produce. These events represent how the resources are changing and how they are interacting with external elements and also among themselves.

Detecting actions and presenting them in the form of *observable records* is not the end of the detection process. In the AWS Cloud, you have great capabilities, such as big data analytical capabilities and automation, that add value to the detection process. Big data analytical capabilities provide tools to extract *findings* out of the huge amount of raw detected information and deliver as processed events in the form of observable records. Automation allows you to evolve from being a mere viewer to a security enforcer. Although remediating controls are not part of the scope of this chapter, you will learn about some of them since they are closely related to detective controls. Blend these capabilities with the enlarged visibility the AWS Cloud provides and you will understand one of the main reasons multiple professionals acknowledge that they are more secure in the cloud.

To explain the various detective controls, this chapter will follow the *framework* presented in the form of a flow in Figure 4.1.

FIGURE 4.1 Detective controls flow framework

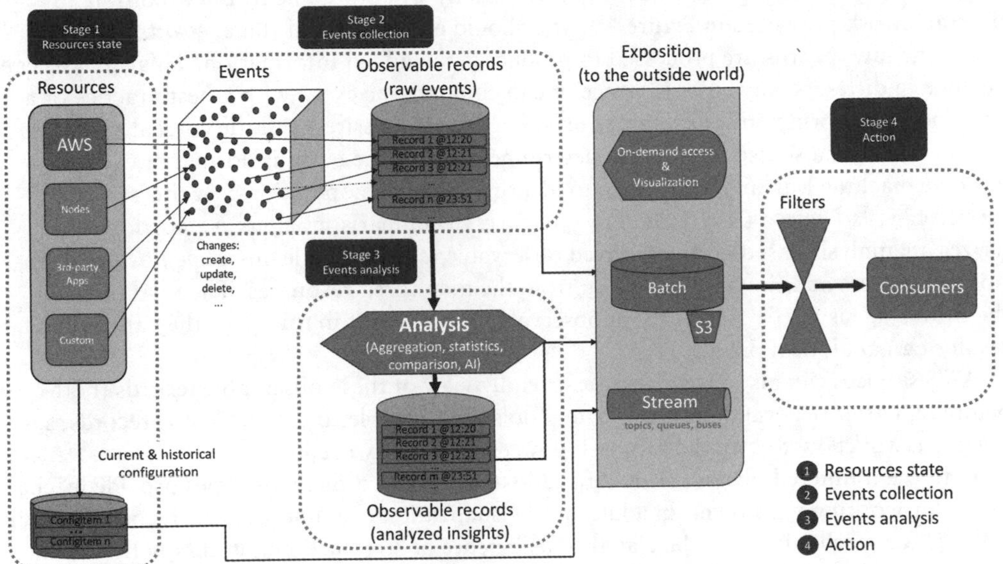

As you can see in Figure 4.1, the framework is split into four main stages: resources state, events collection, events analysis, and action.

The flow starts with a collection of resources and the act of keeping track of its configuration and status over time. These resources are the "objects" that are under observation. They can be AWS resources (such as Amazon EC2 instances or REST APIs published on Amazon API Gateway), external resources (such as software-as-a-service [SaaS] or custom applications), or AWS Cloud services themselves (for example, a service reporting the API calls it receives).

In essence, these services do not focus on detecting changes but on establishing a series of static pictures. Just like in a movie, if you have enough snapshots over a period of time, you can observe movement by watching the sequence of these pictures. This resource collection is the first stage, the *resources state*.

Because these resources commonly serve business processes, they change over time due to the intrinsic automation nature of cloud computing environments or the request processing intended to generate outcomes. All of it represents movement, or simply, modifications in the environment.

An *event* is the representation of such a change or an action on the environment. Just like a tree falling in the middle of a forest, an event can happen at any time and you need the right tools to record it as an *observable record*. The second stage, *events collection*, deals with registering the events occurring in the environment. The creation of these records can be passive or active. A record is *passively* created when external sources are responsible for sending event notifications to the detective control. By contrast, a record is *actively* created if the detective service intentionally looks for information. And, yes, there are AWS Cloud services that use both methods.

Because detective services can provide a large amount of information, it may be challenging to any security professional to know exactly what to do next. But according to the framework presented in Figure 4.1, you should enter the third stage, *events analysis*, where the raw records are processed to produce value-added information. This analysis can be done in different ways. For instance, it can compare the event with a best practice or a baseline and inform you if differences exist between the desired and the current situation.

A service can also use statistics to determine whether the event is normal or even leverage machine learning techniques to identify suspicious operations. At this stage, the service can also have a passive or active posture. In comparison, a *passive posture* characterizes an analysis based on the received observable records, while an *active posture* intentionally gathers additional information from the monitored resources. The final result of the third stage is also a repository of observable records, but in this case, they are a direct result of an analytical process.

AWS services can also provide a user-friendly view of these observable records (both before and after the event analysis stage). Tools are available to manage those records, supporting a workflow to give the proper follow-up to security events.

Both the unfiltered observable records and analyzed records repositories provide mechanisms for working with them, in addition to visualization or requesting the records via API calls. These mechanisms can be classified as batches or streams in light of how they grant access to the information. Processing as a *batch* means producing a historical view of the records that you can work on. Services can also provide access to observable records as a *stream*, which allows you to act as soon as the event is reported.

In the fourth stage, the *action* stage, you will connect the detection controls with reactive actions, through the magic of automation in the cloud. Chapter 8, "Security Automation," will focus on automatic reactions, but this chapter will introduce you to how some detective services can generate a response to observable events. In the action stage, Amazon EventBridge is arguably one of the most powerful tools in the AWS Cloud. The role of EventBridge is to connect the source of events with consumers who can respond to those events.

In this chapter, you will be introduced to several AWS Cloud services supporting multiple detective activities. Although most of them carry out tasks for different stages in the detective controls flow framework, you will analyze each one in light of its primary goal within the framework. So, keep your eyes and mind open and enjoy the ride.

Stage 1: Resources State

The first stage in the detective framework focuses on knowing the state of the monitored resources. AWS provides tools that assess the current situation of resources at different levels and keep historical track of their state. Of course, having that kind of information enables AWS services to dabble into other stages via trigger actions and calls to other services.

AWS Config

AWS resources inside your account have their own configuration at each point in time. AWS Config is the service that allows you to keep track of the configuration of these AWS resources.

In Chapter 2, "Cloud Security Principles and Frameworks," you learned about the shared responsibility model. In detection, the observability of events is heavily based on that model. Hence, you cannot react to what you do not see—and what you see depends on what you have permission to access. AWS Config allows you to gather information about monitored resources, and such information belongs to the part assigned to AWS in the shared responsibility model. For example, according to the AWS Shared Responsibility Model, AWS Config can obtain information like Instance ID, IAM role, IP addresses, and security groups from Amazon EC2 instances, but it does not have access to the processes that are running inside the instance.

AWS Config allows you to monitor several types of resources inside your account, including compute, serverless, databases, storage, and security, among many others. It starts monitoring by turning on a *configuration recorder.* This component's mission is to keep track of *configuration items* (document containing the configuration information of a resource) for the monitored resources, updating them each time a resource is created, updated, or deleted. The service provides one configuration recorder per account per region. Within this configuration, you can define the resources you want to monitor as a choice between all supported resources or a defined subset of them. This collection of resources is called the *recording group.* Once you have the configuration recorder created, you can stop and start it via API calls or through the AWS Console. After the configuration recorder is successfully started, it is in "recording on" mode and tracks changes of the monitored resources by recording a new configuration item when a change in the configuration is detected, either in the monitored resource itself or in the configuration of any of its related monitored resources (*relationships,* which you will learn about in this section). The CLI command `describe-configuration-recorder-status` returns the status of the configuration recorder.

The configuration recorder captures information by calling the APIs of the monitored resources. It takes a few minutes to record the changes after they occurred.

In essence, the configuration recorder saves each monitored resource's configuration and updates the information according to the detected changes. The information gathered from the monitored resources is stored in a construct called the *configuration item.* You can think of a configuration item as a JSON object that contains the configuration of a resource from the AWS point of view. In fact, this JSON file contains the following information: metadata, attributes (including tags, resourceID, resource type, creation time, ARN, and availability zone), *relationships,* and *current configuration.* The *current configuration* section corresponds to the information that is retrieved by calling the describe or list APIs of the resource.

Relationships are descriptions of connections among different resources. For example, an Amazon EC2 instance has a relationship with a network interface. From the network interface's standpoint, the relationship has the name "is attached to" (the instance); from the instance's point of view, the relationship has the name "contains" (the network interface). Such information is described as part of the JSON object. The available relationships are described in detail in the AWS Config documentation, if you are looking for more information.

You can define the retention period for the configuration items, from 30 days to 2,557 days (7 years, the default configuration).

AWS Config provides you with a repository of configurations for each monitored resource. You can look for a specific resource (or group of resources) and ask for their current configuration item. You can do it through the AWS Config management console, under the Resources menu, or you can use the `BatchGetResourceConfig` API.

You can also use a SQL-like syntax to query information from the current configuration state of a monitored resource. This feature, called *advanced query*, allows you to look for resource information directly inside the configuration items, without directly calling APIs to the resource. The queries can be executed directly within the management console or by calling the `SelectResourceConfig` API.

Moreover, AWS Config can provide a holistic picture of the current configuration: a *configuration snapshot*. In practice, a configuration snapshot is a JSON file that contains the current configuration for all the monitored resources. This file is delivered into an Amazon S3 bucket you own. You can manually create such a snapshot by calling the `DeliverConfigSnapshot` API at any time or by scheduling a periodic delivery to occur every 1, 3 , 6, 12, or 24 hours.

At this point, you have seen AWS Config recording static configurations; however, these resources are not static in nature. As they change their configuration over time, AWS Config (with its configuration recorder on) keeps track of those changes. Not only that, but AWS Config also correlates the changes in a resource with the events that produced it (for example, the API call that produced a change in the resource's configuration). AWS Config takes a "photo" of the new configuration each time a detected change happens and stores that new configuration in conjunction with information about what caused the change. This sequence of "pictures" for a specific resource is known as a *configuration timeline*.

Consequently, AWS Config keeps the observable records of events along with configuration items. The service acts in a passive way when resources inform AWS Config that a change occurred, but it also acts in an active way because at that point, AWS Config calls the APIs to get information about the new status of the resource.

You can see the complete list of configuration items (current and past) for a specific resource, which provides the evolution of its configuration and changes over time. In the AWS Config console, click the Configuration Timeline button for the resource details (as shown in Figure 4.2). You can also call the `GetResourceConfigHistory` API to obtain the same information.

FIGURE 4.2 AWS Config Management console – Configuration Timeline

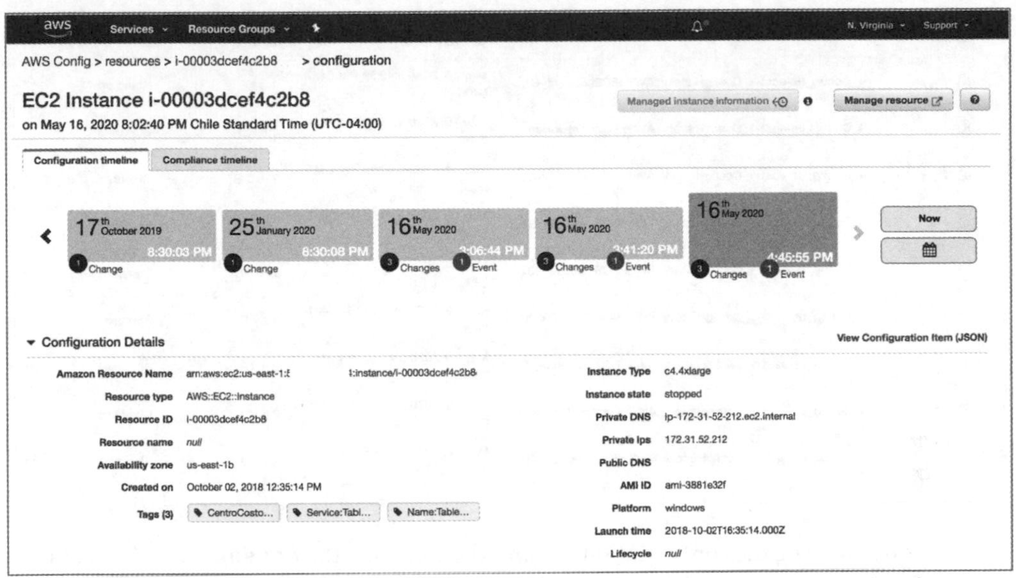

As you can see, AWS Config records very useful information. To expose such information to the external world, the service leverages the concept of a *delivery channel*. The delivery channel defines an S3 bucket and an SNS topic that AWS Config uses to deliver information (such as the *configuration snapshots*) and notifications. This component is mandatory when using AWS Config. You can have one delivery channel per region, per account. You can create a delivery channel by calling the `PutDeliveryChannel` API or by configuring the settings page in the AWS Config management console.

Depending on how the information is organized and delivered through the delivery channel, you can have different views. Besides configuration snapshots and configuration timelines, AWS Config also provides a *configuration history:* a collection of recorded configuration items that changed over a time period. AWS Config automatically delivers *configuration history files* every six hours to the S3 bucket configured in the delivery channel. Such a collection contains all configuration items of the monitored resources that changed since the last history delivery (if there were several changes during that period, all the configuration items would be part of the configuration history files). Each configuration history file corresponds to a different resource type.

To better illustrate this, you can see an example of AWS Config history files delivered to an S3 bucket in Figure 4.3.

The information collected by AWS Config can also be provided in a stream, which means being notified as soon as a change is detected. This method is called a *configuration stream* and it uses the topic defined in the delivery channel. The same topic is used to deliver several notifications (like the creation of a historical record or a snapshot), so AWS Config uses the key `messageType` inside the message body to signal which information the

FIGURE 4.3 Config history files delivered to an S3 bucket

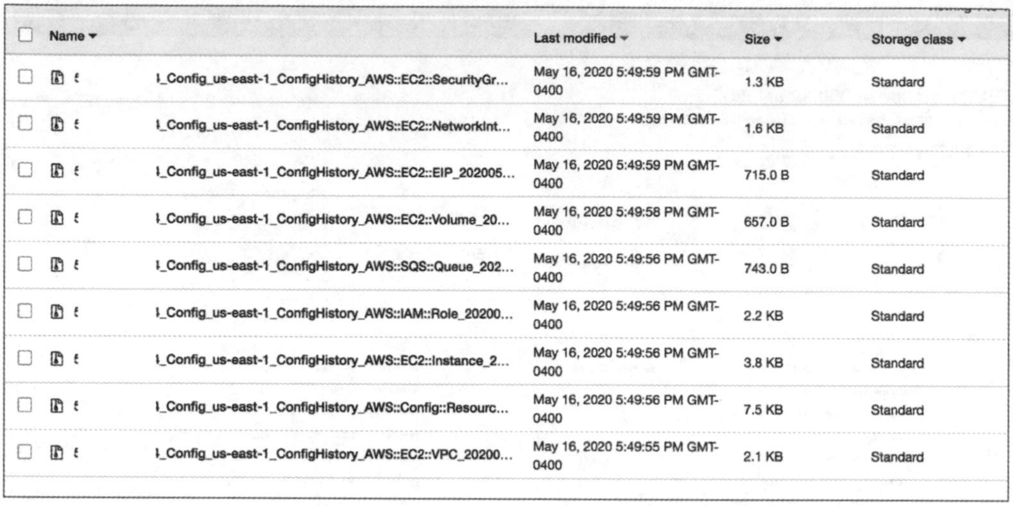

Name		Last modified	Size	Storage class
	_Config_us-east-1_ConfigHistory_AWS::EC2::SecurityGr...	May 16, 2020 5:49:59 PM GMT-0400	1.3 KB	Standard
	_Config_us-east-1_ConfigHistory_AWS::EC2::NetworkInt...	May 16, 2020 5:49:59 PM GMT-0400	1.6 KB	Standard
	_Config_us-east-1_ConfigHistory_AWS::EC2::EIP_202005...	May 16, 2020 5:49:59 PM GMT-0400	715.0 B	Standard
	_Config_us-east-1_ConfigHistory_AWS::EC2::Volume_20...	May 16, 2020 5:49:58 PM GMT-0400	657.0 B	Standard
	_Config_us-east-1_ConfigHistory_AWS::SQS::Queue_202...	May 16, 2020 5:49:56 PM GMT-0400	743.0 B	Standard
	_Config_us-east-1_ConfigHistory_AWS::IAM::Role_20200...	May 16, 2020 5:49:56 PM GMT-0400	2.2 KB	Standard
	_Config_us-east-1_ConfigHistory_AWS::EC2::Instance_2...	May 16, 2020 5:49:56 PM GMT-0400	3.8 KB	Standard
	_Config_us-east-1_ConfigHistory_AWS::Config::Resourc...	May 16, 2020 5:49:56 PM GMT-0400	7.5 KB	Standard
	_Config_us-east-1_ConfigHistory_AWS::EC2::VPC_20200...	May 16, 2020 5:49:55 PM GMT-0400	2.1 KB	Standard

message contains. For the configuration stream, the value for the `messageType` key is `ConfigurationItemChangeNotification`.

In Table 4.1, you will find a comparison of the different views AWS Config provides.

TABLE 4.1 Comparison of different "views" for configuration items

Configuration view	Contains	Frequency	Delivery channel
Configuration History Files	Files with all configuration items (grouped by resource type) of resources that changed since last delivery	6 hours (fixed)	Amazon S3 bucket (`ConfigHistory` prefix)
Configuration Snapshot	One file with all the current configuration items	Manual or configurable to 1, 3, 6, 12, 24 hours	Amazon S3 bucket (`ConfigSnapshot` prefix)
Configuration Stream	Configuration items as messages in a topic, delivered as soon as they were detected by Config	Continuous (within minutes)	Amazon SNS topic; `messageType`: `ConfigurationItemChangeNotification`

With what you have learned, you can already insert the AWS Config capabilities in the detective framework proposed in this chapter's introduction. In Figure 4.4 you can see the AWS Config concepts we have presented so far and how they are related to the framework.

FIGURE 4.4 AWS Config and the detective framework

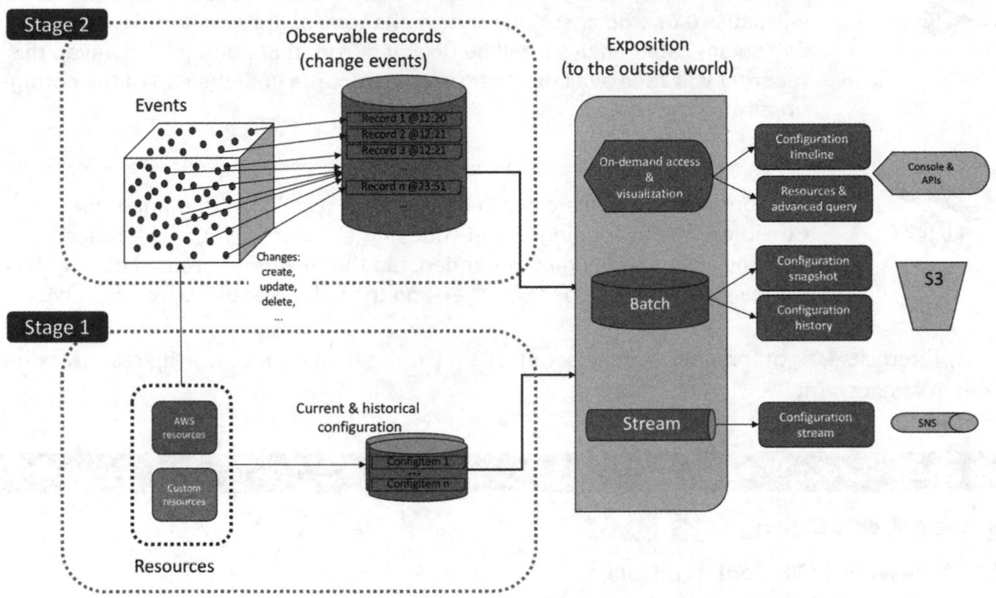

The main goal of AWS Config is to record configuration and changes of the resources and not analyze them. In other words, AWS Config does not judge if a change is good or bad or if it needs to execute an action. Such a role will be accomplished by a component called *AWS Config Rules*, which will be discussed in the "Stage 3: Event Analysis" section.

When considering multiple regions, AWS Config provides the concept of *aggregator* as a component that allows you to access information about resources and compliance outside the current region and account. You can choose one account and region to host the aggregator and all other regions inside the account, and other accounts (and regions in those accounts) will be sources that can share their information with it. An aggregator can read configuration and compliance data recorded by AWS Config, but it cannot modify a resource's configuration. AWS Config integrates with the concept of AWS Organizations, so you can easily make all the accounts inside one organization report to an aggregator.

AWS Config can also integrate with external resources like on-premises servers and applications, third-party monitoring applications, or version control systems. You can publish configuration items for these resources to AWS Config, so you can manage the resource inventory. You can also have the resources registered with AWS CloudFormation; in this case, if you apply changes to the resources using AWS CloudFormation templates, they will be recorded by AWS Config.

The AWS Config recorder component can be disabled at any time, which will cause it to stop checking for new changes of the monitored resources, and so any other analysis will be disabled from that point on. However, the recorder will keep available the previous records until the end of the configured retention period.

For completing the exercises in this chapter, use the AWS Management Console. Start by logging in and choosing a region of your preference. Optionally, but highly recommended, tag the resources created during these exercises with a key `Cost Center` and the value `security-chapter4`.

In Exercise 4.1 you practice how to set up AWS Config to start monitoring resources in your AWS account.

EXERCISE 4.1

Set Up AWS Config

1. Access the AWS Config console.
2. If this is the first time you've configured AWS Config in the chosen region, use the Get Started wizard. Otherwise, open the Settings menu.
3. Under the "Resource types to record" section, choose All Resources (Including Global Resources) to be monitored by AWS Config.
4. Under the "Amazon S3 bucket" section, create a new bucket to receive files delivered by AWS Config. Use **`security-chapter4`** as the prefix for the bucket.
5. Under the "Amazon SNS topic" section, establish the configuration changes to be streamed to a new SNS topic. Name the topic **config-security-chapter4**.
6. Choose to use an existing AWS Config service-linked role for the service. If you are using the Get Started wizard, click Next to finish the first part of the configuration. Otherwise, click Save and skip to Step 9.
7. Skip the AWS Config Rules page (at this point, don't configure any AWS Config rules).
8. Review the final page. Submit the configuration.
9. Subscribe an email account to the Amazon SNS topic you created in Step 5.
10. Execute changes in your account: create a new EC2 instance, apply a security group, and modify the security group configuration.
11. Wait 15 minutes.
12. In the AWS Config console, open the Resources menu and look for the monitored resources.

13. Choose the monitored resource. Check the configuration item information and the configuration timeline.
14. (Optional) Using AWS CLI, execute the **deliver-config-snapshot** command to have a snapshot delivered. Check the S3 bucket for snapshot files. (Use the **describe-delivery-channels** command to gather information about Config delivery channels.)
15. (Optional) Wait for 6 hours and check the S3 bucket for history files.

AWS Systems Manager

AWS Systems Manager is a comprehensive service that assembles an admirable collection of capabilities. The service's features share the objective of helping the administration of large fleets of instances (which can be Amazon EC2 instances, on-premises servers, or even instances running in other cloud providers), especially for operational activities. In the past, this service had different names such as AWS EC2 Simple Systems Manager, or simply SSM (an acronym you will find in this book as well as in the AWS official documentation).

Because of its myriad features, when approaching the AWS Systems Manager service, it is easier to analyze through the lens of its capabilities instead of the whole service. AWS Systems Manager's capabilities are grouped under these four categories:

Operations Management Refers to the capability of understanding the current state of your environment and how its components are performing. It covers features such as Explorer, OpsCenter, CloudWatch Dashboard, and Personal Health Dashboard (PHD).

Application Management Helps with the administration of applications that are distributed along several components and AWS accounts.

Actions & Change Allows you to specify a sequence of actions to be executed on your managed instances and how to control its execution.

Instances & Nodes Capabilities under this category are oriented to manage instances and nodes at scale.

Some SSM capabilities allow you to interact with monitored resources (instances) at deeper levels (like gathering information directly from the operating system or applications, executing commands inside the operating system, or establishing a terminal administration channel into the instances). This deeper interaction is possible due to a software component called the *SSM agent*. The agent acts as the representative of the service inside the instance.

One of the SSM's capabilities, called *inventory*, leverages the SSM agents in the instances to extract metadata information (such as installed software and applications), enabling the state tracking of these resources. Once the information is collected, SSM can export it to an S3 bucket you own (by configuring a component called *resource data sync*). In SSM Inventory, you can define how frequently you want the inventory data to be collected; resource data sync will keep the information in your Amazon S3 bucket updated according with that frequency.

To access such information, you can query the Inventory capability in SSM (via console or API calls) or the information in S3 (through Amazon Athena, AWS Glue, or Amazon QuickSight). You can also use an embedded functionality in the SSM console called *detailed view*, which provides a way to query inventory information in your S3 bucket (exported by a resource data sync) without leaving the SSM console. This functionality in fact uses Amazon Athena, Amazon QuickSight, and AWS Glue under the hood.

Next, the *resource groups* capability (under the Application Management category) provides you with a better view of AWS resources in your account by grouping them. These groups are created based on common attributes shared by resources such as tags or the originating CloudFormation stack. Therefore, if you use a tagging strategy to identify resources that share attributes, you can leverage SSM resource groups to show information about those grouped resources at the same time in the same console. This information contains data provided by other services like AWS Config, AWS CloudTrail, and Amazon CloudWatch, as well as other SSM capabilities.

The Operations Management category is entirely applicable to stage 1 of the detective framework. The capabilities grouped under this category (Explorer, OpsCenter, CloudWatch dashboards, and PHD), share in common the fact that they do not create or analyze new information. Their focus is to provide a central point of view for several operational metrics, like CloudWatch dashboards, a list of created operational tickets (*opsitems*), and the status of PHD checks. As such, this capability is a visualization tool that aggregates different information into a single pane of view.

Stage 2: Events Collection

Events are at the core of the detection task. These events represent the activities that are happening, affecting the resources and producing changes. In a dynamic environment, these changes are constantly occurring. A detective system will capture those changes and convert them into observable records.

At the second stage of the framework presented in the chapter's introduction, the focus is not on deciding if the event is good or bad but on capturing as many *interesting* events as possible and representing them as records in a repository. Therefore, the collection of events into observable records is at the core of a detective control in this stage.

AWS CloudTrail

As per the access model defined by the AWS Cloud, interactions with services happen through authenticated and authorized API calls. AWS CloudTrail is the service in charge of keeping records of these calls. The service also records non-API events related to service actions and to sign-in attempts to the AWS Console, AWS Discussion Forums, and AWS Support Center.

Actions taken by an IAM principal (such as a user, a role, or an AWS service) are recorded as events in AWS CloudTrail. The basic unit of activity recording in AWS

CloudTrail is called an *event*, which is represented by the record that contains the logged activity. There are three different types of events:

- **Management:** Operations performed on AWS resources, or control plane operations, and non-API events like sign-in operations.
- **Insights:** "Meta-events," generated by CloudTrail when it detects unusual management API activity.
- **Data:** Logs of API operations performed within a resource, also known as data plane operations (for example, `PutObject` or `GetObject` operations on an Amazon S3 object or an `Invoke` operation on an AWS Lambda function).

The fields of a recorded event (as shown in Example 4.1) describe the activity and also include metadata. They provide information about *what* was done (for example, `eventName`, `requestParameters`, `responseElements`, `requestID`, `eventType`, `resources`), *who has* done it (information about the principal and how it was authenticated; for example: `userIdentity`, which itself includes other attributes like `type`, `principalID`, `arn`, or `accountID`), *when* (`eventTime`), and *where* (for example: `eventSource`, `awsRegion`, `sourceIPAddress`, `userAgent`, `recipientAccountId`). In addition, there is context information about the event itself like `eventVersion`, `eventType`, `apiVersion`, `managementEvent`, and `readOnly` attributes.

Example 4.1 AWS CloudTrail event


```
{
  "Records": [
    {
      "eventVersion": "1.05",
      "userIdentity": {
        "type": "AssumedRole",
        "principalId": "AEIOUUEDLRTHJNMAUHIJK:ecs-service-scheduler",
        "arn": "arn:aws:sts::123456789012:assumed-role/AWSServiceRoleForECS/ecs-
service-scheduler",
        "accountId": "123456789012",
        "accessKeyId": "AAMERICARTVPIMD4MYNOR",
        "sessionContext": {
          "sessionIssuer": {
            "type": "Role",
            "principalId": "AEIOUUEDLRTHJNMAUHIJK",
            "arn": "arn:aws:iam::123456789012:role/aws-service-role/ecs.amazonaws.
com/AWSServiceRoleForECS",
            "accountId": "123456789012",
            "userName": "AWSServiceRoleForECS"
```

```
        },
        "webIdFederationData": {},
        "attributes": {
          "mfaAuthenticated": "false",
          "creationDate": "2020-04-21T23:48:58Z"
        }
      },
      "invokedBy": "ecs.amazonaws.com"
    },
    "eventTime": "2020-04-21T23:58:57Z",
    "eventSource": "servicediscovery.amazonaws.com",
    "eventName": "GetInstancesHealthStatus",
    "awsRegion": "us-east-1",
    "sourceIPAddress": "ecs.amazonaws.com",
    "userAgent": "ecs.amazonaws.com",
    "requestParameters": {
      "serviceId": "srv-abcdef3nnytkte1f"
    },
    "responseElements": null,
    "requestID": "8044381c-70ae-430b-af05-7a9d0290a525",
    "eventID": "656e695e-0532-48a5-9ed5-8ab94a3f4e76",
    "eventType": "AwsApiCall",
    "recipientAccountId": "123456789012"
  }
 ]
}
```


AWS CloudTrail is enabled at the creation of an AWS account. Management events recorded within the past 90 days are available in the Event History menu of AWS CloudTrail. This feature (available through the AWS Management Console or via the `LookupEvents` API) allows you to view, search, and download management events related to the account during that timeline.

AWS CloudTrail event history only shows management events, and not all management events are supported to appear in event history.

In addition to AWS CloudTrail's focus on events recording, the service also provides the extended functionality of giving awareness on the events, looking for an abnormally high volume of API calls or unusual activity (detected through mathematical models and by continually monitoring write management events). This functionality is called *Insights* and is available through the AWS Management Console and also through the same `LookupEvents` API.

In the Insights console, you will be able to access a list of Insights events recorded for the last 90 days, see details of the unusual activity, and view a timeseries graph.

Effectively managing an account requires you to keep a record of the events for longer than 90 days. It also requires you to provide a persistent layer to analyze, visualize, and respond to changes or just to have the records as evidence for an audit. A *trail* allows you to store AWS CloudTrail events in an Amazon S3 bucket that you own, in the form of *log files*. This way, you can control the lifecycle policy and the retention and protection policies of the persisted data. Each log file is compressed (in `gzip` format) and contains one or more JSON-formatted records where each record represents an event. AWS CloudTrail delivers log files several times an hour (about every 5 minutes). Typically the log files for management and data events appear in your S3 bucket within 15 minutes after the activity was executed in the account. Insight events typically appear within 30 minutes after detecting the unusual activity.

AWS CloudTrail stores management and data events in different log files than insight events. Insight log files follow the same pattern as trail log files but instead of using the `CloudTrail` prefix, they use `CloudTrail-Insight`. Unlike the recording of management events into the event history console that happens by default, the recording of insight events in the Insights console of AWS CloudTrail has to be intentionally enabled in the trail.

Table 4.2 summarizes the various event types AWS CloudTrail deals with. The table shows where you can visualize the events through the AWS CloudTrail Management console or which AWS CloudTrail API call you should use to access them.

TABLE 4.2 AWS CloudTrail: Event types

Event type	Enabled	Type of activity	AWS CloudTrail console (90 days)	API (90 days)
Management	By default	API activity (control plane), service events, sign-in events	Event History	`LookupEvents`
Insight	Requires configuration (in the Trail)	"Meta-events": unusual activity associated with write APIs	Insights	`LookupEvents` (using the `EventCategory` parameter)
Data	Requires configuration (in the Trail)	API activity (data plane)	Not available	Not available

Note that once the records are stored in Amazon S3, you can use services like Amazon Athena and Amazon QuickSight to visualize and analyze them. Amazon Athena requires the creation of a table to define the structure of the data and its location within S3. Simply enough, AWS CloudTrail provides a way to create that table directly from its console by clicking the Create Athena Table button on the Event History page.

Using the AWS CloudTrail's console for creating the trail's table is not mandatory; you can also manually create the table in Athena.

Following our detection framework, the observable records can also be exposed to the world in a stream of events. AWS CloudTrail integrates with Amazon CloudWatch Logs, Amazon SNS, and Amazon EventBridge to deliver these streams. The first two integrations (Amazon CloudWatch Logs and Amazon SNS) are configured inside the trail, but it is in Amazon EventBridge configuration where you can set up the third integration.

You will learn more about Amazon CloudWatch Logs later in the "Amazon CloudWatch Logs" section and about Amazon EventBridge in the "Stage 4: Action" section. At this point it is important to note that this integration allows you to capture events in Amazon EventBridge for every service supported by AWS CloudTrail.

Configuring an *Amazon SNS* topic for a trail allows you to receive notifications whenever a log file is delivered to the trail's S3 bucket. If you subscribe to an Amazon SNS notification, you can choose a topic residing in your own account or in another account. In any case, the topic must have an access policy that allows AWS CloudTrail to deliver messages to it.

To protect records in AWS CloudTrail, the service provides encryption and integrity validation mechanisms. AWS CloudTrail allows you to implement encryption at rest for the records by choosing an encryption method and key at the trail level. By default, log files are encrypted using the Amazon S3 server-side encryption. You can choose to use your own AWS Key Management Service (KMS) key. In this case the key needs to be created in the same region as the bucket that contains the AWS CloudTrail log files. Key policy must allow the service to encrypt with it and also allow chosen principals in the AWS account to use it for decryption.

You will learn about AWS Key Management Service (KMS) in Chapter 6, "Data Protection."

AWS CloudTrail also embeds a trail *integrity validation* mechanism. This mechanism uses asymmetric cryptographic techniques (digital signatures) applied to the files delivered in S3 buckets. Using these techniques, AWS CloudTrail protects the records and allows you to determine if a delivered log file was modified, deleted, or unchanged. Integrity validation works like this:

1. AWS CloudTrail calculates a 256-bit hash (using SHA-256) for every delivered log file.
2. Each hour, CloudTrail builds a consolidated file that contains a list (in JSON format) of each log file delivered in the previous hour and its corresponding SHA-256 calculated hash. This file is called a *digest file*.

3. AWS CloudTrail calculates both the SHA-256 hash and the digital signature (using RSA with SHA-256) of the digest file, using a private key (part of a public-private key pair) managed by the service. This key pair is periodically rotated, and it is different for each AWS region.
4. AWS CloudTrail delivers the current hour's digest file as an object (to your S3 bucket), including its calculated digital signature, in the metadata (under the `x-amz-meta-signature` key, which is shown in Figure 4.5).

FIGURE 4.5 AWS CloudTrail digest file object metadata

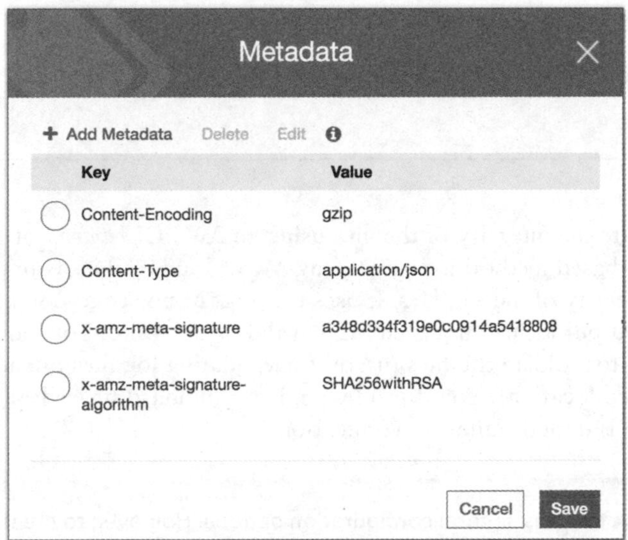

Each digest file includes information about the previous digest file hash and signature, which establishes a sequential chain of digest files. Example 4.2 shows the header of a CloudTrail digest file.

Example 4.2 AWS CloudTrail digest file header

```
{
 "awsAccountId": "123456789012",
  "digestStartTime": "2020-04-21T23:19:16Z",
  "digestEndTime": "2020-04-22T00:19:16Z",
  "digestS3Bucket": "cloudtrail",
  "digestS3Object": "<path to current S3 object>.json.gz",
```

```
  "digestPublicKeyFingerprint": "1234567890b5dc9467b26b16602a50ce",
  "digestSignatureAlgorithm": "SHA256withRSA",
  "newestEventTime": "2020-04-22T00:18:58Z",
  "oldestEventTime": "2020-04-21T23:08:48Z",
  "previousDigestS3Bucket": "cloudtrail",
  "previousDigestS3Object": "<path to previous S3 object>.json.gz",
  "previousDigestHashValue": "<hash value>",
  "previousDigestHashAlgorithm": "SHA-256",
  "previousDigestSignature": "<digest signature>",
  "logFiles": [
   ...
  ]
}
```

You can validate the integrity of the files using an AWS *CLI-based* or a *custom* method. The CLI-based method is provided by AWS CloudTrail as a simple way of validating the integrity of the log files. It uses the `validate-logs` command and produces a text output identifying each file as valid or not valid. You can also use a *custom* method to validate the files (useful for validating log files outside their originally delivered location). You do so by applying standard procedures for public key infrastructure (PKI) digital signature verifications.

A trail has several configuration options. However, to create a new trail you have to provide its name and the Amazon S3 bucket name to store log files. By default, a trail records all *management* events and no *insight* or *data* events. The trail is always encrypted, but other default options differ depending on whether you use the console or the API.

AWS CloudTrail is a regional scoped service: events reported at the event history level are related to your account and region. However, you can consolidate events from different regions in a single trail by creating a multiregion trail. When creating a new trail, you define its scope by choosing the regions the trail covers (options are Current Region or All Regions). When a trail is configured to apply to All Regions (recommended configuration), it will create a multiregion trail. That trail will have the current region as its home region, and it will automatically configure trails for every AWS region enabled in that account. Events at the event history level will be recorded in each region. However, AWS CloudTrail will deliver the log files from all the enabled regions to the centralized Amazon S3 bucket defined in the multiregion trail. Within the Amazon S3 bucket structure, the log files will be delivered under a prefix that identifies the region they come from. If configured, the Amazon SNS topic will receive a notification for each one of those written log files.

If a trail applies for all regions, when a new AWS region is added and enabled in the account, AWS CloudTrail will automatically create the trail for that region.

On the other hand, if a trail is not chosen to apply to all regions, it will exist only in the current region. The trail will receive event logs only from the region where it was created.

In addition to the regional scope, a trail can also have an *organizations* scope. You can create a trail in an organization's master account that will log events from all the accounts under it. This scope is independent of the regional scope. All of the organization's member accounts will be able to see the trail but they won't have privileges to modify it. By default, they won't have privileges to access the trail's S3 bucket either.

Another possible centralization mechanism is to have trails produced by different accounts storing log files in a centralized Amazon S3 bucket (in this case, if you don't use the organizational scope, you will need to configure the right access privileges for different accounts to put objects in the bucket).

Although you cannot disable event history, you can disable the log collection at the trail level. When you disable a trail, you are not going to record events during the period in which the trail is disabled (or deliver trails into the Amazon S3, Amazon SNS, or Amazon CloudWatch logs). You can also disable the collection of only insights or data events at the trail level.

Now that you know about AWS CloudTrail, in Exercise 4.2 you can practice how to create a trail in your AWS account.

EXERCISE 4.2

Set Up a Trail in CloudTrail

1. Access the AWS CloudTrail console.
2. Create a new trail with the name **security-chapter4**.
3. Apply the trail to all regions, and record all management and insight events.
4. Monitor S3 activity related with all S3 buckets in your account.
5. Create a new bucket to store the trail, using a unique name and the prefix **security-chapter4**.
6. Encrypt your log files using a new KMS key called **security-chapter4**.
7. Choose the SNS topic security-chapter4 to send notifications.
8. Generate API activity in your account (access other services, create or modify AWS resources).

9. Wait 15 minutes and check the files in your CloudTrail S3 bucket.
10. Validate that you received SNS notifications related to the delivered files into S3.
11. (Optional) Wait 30 minutes and check for events in Insights (inside your S3 bucket).
12. Wait 1 hour and then validate the integrity of the digest and log files. Use the **validate-logs** CLI command.
13. (Optional) Follow the procedure at this site to manually validate the integrity of the log files: `docs.aws.amazon.com/awscloudtrail/latest/userguide/cloudtrail-log-file-custom-validation.html`.

Amazon CloudWatch Logs

Applications, services, resources, and almost every technological component produce observable records of activity in the form of log records. An important part of monitoring resources is the capability to deal with those logs. Amazon CloudWatch Logs allow you to manage the logs produced by systems throughout their lifecycle, in a scalable, highly available, and managed service.

In the AWS Console, Amazon CloudWatch Logs appear under the CloudWatch visualization console, but they use a different set of APIs.

The basic unit of Amazon CloudWatch Logs is *log events*. These events are generated by external sources and sent to the service using the `PutLogEvents` API. Any external source can ingest log events through an API call. AWS services publish logs to CloudWatch Logs. In addition, AWS provides a way to extract logs from applications running in compute instances and ingest them into Amazon CloudWatch Logs through the unified *Amazon CloudWatch agent*. The agent is supported across different operating systems and allows you to gather both logs (in-guest and custom metrics).

Each log event is a record representing an event reported to the service and contains two main parts: *timestamp* (date and time when the event occurred) and *raw message* (specific data this record is reporting). Every log event is stored in the service, but to make it easier to manage them, incoming records are organized in a structure called a *log stream* (usually, log events inside a log stream come from the same source). Within this structure you can find records in time-sequential order.

To increase manageability of the information stored in log streams, they are hierarchically organized inside another structure: the *log group*. Configuration parameters are usually defined at the log group level, so all log streams inside it share the same set of configuration parameters. You can see a graphical representation of this structure in Figure 4.6.

FIGURE 4.6 Representation of CloudWatch log events hierarchical grouping

As an example, an AWS CloudTrail trail can deliver events to a log group. This log group (created in the same AWS region as the home region of the AWS CloudTrail trail) receives the events the trail is configured to monitor (management, insights, or data events). You can see this integration by completing Exercise 4.3.

EXERCISE 4.3

AWS CloudTrail Integration with Amazon CloudWatch Logs

1. Access the AWS CloudTrail console and edit the trail you created in Exercise 4.2.
2. Configure the trail to send the events to a new Amazon CloudWatch log group called `CloudTrail/security-chapter4`.
3. Generate activity in your AWS account.
4. Access the Amazon CloudWatch console, look for the log group you created, and check that you received events.

You can configure encryption for the data stored in a log group by linking an AWS KMS Customer Master Key (CMK). In a nutshell, a CMK is a cryptographic key stored inside AWS KMS that implements envelope encryption; when integrated with other AWS services, the CMK deals with the process of securely encrypting those services' data. Amazon CloudWatch Logs will decrypt the data when accessing it. If you associate a new CMK to the log group, the events from that moment on will be encrypted based on the new key. If you disassociate a CMK from the log group, the new events after that moment will be kept unencrypted.

Retention is another aspect you can configure at the log group level. You control how long CloudWatch Logs keep the log events. By default, there is no retention limit (configured as Never, meaning that the log events will never be deleted). You can configure the retention period in days, using specific values that range from 1 to 3,653 days.

Once the log events are part of a log stream, you can retrieve those log events through the management console or API calls. Also, you usually like to analyze the ingested information. It is at this point that *Amazon CloudWatch Logs Insights* comes in handy.

Amazon CloudWatch Logs Insights provides a query syntax to apply to one or more (up to 20) log groups. As with any query language, everything starts with how data is structured. Logs Insights automatically discovers the data fields of AWS services logs and any JSON-based logs (including AWS CloudTrail logs); when it cannot detect the specific type of a log, the purpose-built query language provides the `parse` command to define ephemeral fields and to use them in the specific query. Logs Insights is also aware of the system fields that are automatically generated when a log event arrives to CloudWatch Logs: `@message` (raw log event), `@timestamp` (when the event occurred), `@ingestionTime` (when the event was ingested), `@logStream` (the name of the log stream), and `@log` (the unique ID of the log group).

You may also be interested in summarizing information from the data. With that goal in mind, Amazon CloudWatch Logs provides a mechanism: the *metric filter* (defined at the log group level). A metric filter extracts information from an event log and converts it into a number to be plotted in a timeseries representation (in Amazon CloudWatch).

To establish a metric filter, first you define a *filter*. This filter defines how Amazon CloudWatch Logs selects the interesting log events. It is expressed in the form of a filter pattern that looks for attributes in a JSON object. In Example 4.3, the filter pattern looks for a specific event version and user identity type.

Example 4.3 Filter pattern in Amazon CloudWatch Logs

```
{($.eventVersion="1.05")&&($.userIdentity.type="IAMUser")}
```

After selecting the interesting events, the next definition is to create the *metric*. The objective of a metric is to establish what number will be reported to Amazon CloudWatch (to store and plot). The metric is aggregated and reported on a per-minute basis. By default, the number reported is the count of log events matched by the filter (a count of "1" per each matched event); however, you can choose to report any number in a numeric field of the event, or even a fixed floating-point number per matched event.

To finish the definition of a metric filter, you will define both the name of the metric and its namespace. (A metric namespace is a label that allows you to group metrics. Think of it as a folder in a hierarchical structure that contains different metrics: even if there are two metrics that share the same name, they will be considered different metrics if they belong to different namespaces.) You will also establish a default value: the number to be reported for each log event that does not match the filter.

Specifically, by creating metric filters on top of log groups receiving events from AWS CloudTrail, you can monitor and alert according to the number of occurrences of any event reported in a trail.

At the log group level, you can set up how to send log events data outside Amazon CloudWatch Logs. You can *export* the log events to an Amazon S3 bucket you own and manage. Choose the data to export by defining the start and end times, an optional prefix of the log stream (inside the log group), the destination S3 bucket, and an optional bucket prefix. Information in a log group can take up to 12 hours to be available for exporting.

This method will provide you with the batch historic view. Once in Amazon S3, you can use services like Amazon Athena and Amazon QuickSight to create additional analysis and visualization of the data.

For exposing the records in a streamlike fashion, Amazon CloudWatch Logs provide another mechanism: *subscriptions*. In a subscription, Amazon CloudWatch Logs produce a near real-time stream of events and deliver them to a consumer. The consumer can be Amazon Kinesis Data Streams, Amazon Kinesis Data Firehose, or an AWS Lambda function (which allows further customization). The Amazon CloudWatch Logs management console provides a wizard that lets you configure an AWS Lambda function that inserts the feed into an Amazon Elasticsearch Service cluster. When defining a subscription, you will also have the option to define a filter in the same way as described in the previous section. The filter allows you to choose which events are sent to the consumer.

Eventually, you will want to configure subscriptions to feed log events to another account's Amazon CloudWatch Logs structure. This special cross-account subscription is called the *destination*. On the receiving account, you will need to create a CloudWatch Logs destination object (using the `PutDestination` API) that will act as the receiving end of a conduit between the accounts. Figure 4.7 shows the different concepts.

FIGURE 4.7 Schematic representation of log data for cross-account consumption

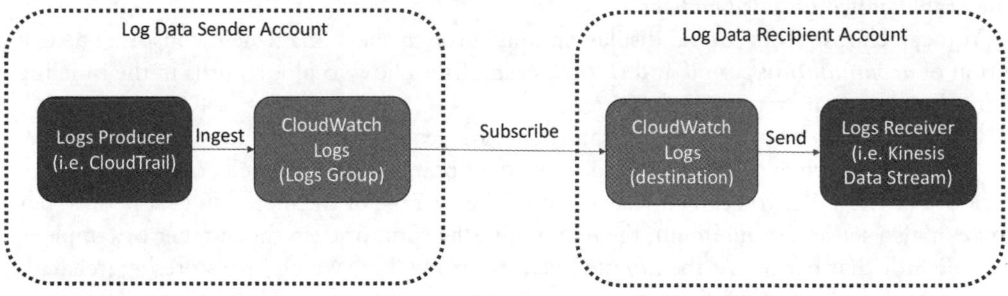

The Amazon CloudWatch Logs destination itself is protected by a resource-level access policy.

At ingestion time, the source defines the *log stream* (and so, the account and region) where a log event belongs. Usually, services send their logs to a log stream inside its own account and region. Using the destinations concept, you can centralize events in a single AWS account. Another common way of centralizing logs is having them exported into an S3 bucket.

Amazon CloudWatch

Amazon CloudWatch provides several functionalities under the same umbrella. It is time for you to learn about Amazon CloudWatch functionalities that deal with detection, in addition to Amazon CloudWatch Logs. As a start, you can understand Amazon CloudWatch as a *metric repository* service. Basically, its function is to record information in a time sequence by storing a number (metric) for each period of time. Amazon CloudWatch receives data either from AWS services or custom data sources (custom metric). You can entrust the Amazon CloudWatch agent to collect internal information from a system (such as memory utilization) or obtain metrics from your own applications.

You can also collect information about specific applications through the Amazon CloudWatch Application Insights functionality. In this case, the information is collected via an AWS SSM agent. Application Insights is powered by Amazon SageMaker and it is compatible with .NET and SQL Server applications.

At the time of ingesting data into Amazon CloudWatch, the sources define a *namespace*, a metric *name*, and (optionally) metric *dimensions* to group the information. For each metric, you will define one of two possible resolutions: Standard or High. Standard resolution stores data with one-minute granularity whereas High resolution metrics have a one-second granularity. By default, AWS Services publish metrics in Standard resolution. At this moment, High resolution metrics are only available for custom metrics.

Then, Amazon CloudWatch retains the metrics for up to 15 months, aggregating data of higher resolution as that data becomes older. Once the metrics are in a repository (a repository of observable records like the one we defined in the detection framework) organized by namespace, dimensions, and metric names, Amazon CloudWatch can plot them in a timeline graph (called *graphed metrics*).

You can choose from several display options through the management console. The definition of *accumulation period* and *statistics* establishes how to plot records in the timeline. This plot is known as a *graphed metric*.

For the *accumulation period* you can choose ranges from one second to 30 days. The *statistic* is the math expression applied to the data points in the selected accumulation period. For example, you can choose to report the average of the metric in that period, but you can also select the minimum, the maximum, the sum, or even the number of samples recorded for that period. At the minute level, Amazon CloudWatch also stores aggregated information of the minimum, maximum, sum, and number of samples. You can also create personalized dashboards that include selected graphed metrics to easily access them at a central location.

You can consume Amazon CloudWatch metrics in a streamlike way by configuring *alarms*. Alarms are defined thresholds for a specific metric. Once a metric crosses the threshold for a custom-defined number of times, the alarm is triggered. You can configure actions to execute and notifications to send (via an Amazon SNS topic or a specific email addresses) when an alarm is triggered.

A static threshold may not be suitable because the behavior of the metric depends on seasonality. In such cases, Amazon CloudWatch offers the option for an alarm to use a dynamic band as a threshold. Amazon CloudWatch's *anomaly detection* functionality determines that dynamic band. Based on machine learning models and statistics, anomaly detection establishes the dynamic range where the metric should normally fall over a period of time.

Now, it is time to consolidate the various concepts in practice. In Exercise 4.4, you will use the Amazon CloudWatch Logs log group created in Exercise 4.3 to create a metric and establish an alarm in Amazon CloudWatch when an S3 bucket is created or deleted.

EXERCISE 4.4

Create an Amazon CloudWatch Alarm

1. In the Amazon CloudWatch Logs console, access the log group you created in Exercise 4.3.
2. Create a metric filter with the following expression:

```
{($.eventSource = s3.amazonaws.com)
&& (($.eventName = CreateBucket) || ($.eventName = DeleteBucket)) }
```

3. Name the filter and the namespace **`security-chapter4`**.
4. Name the metric **`bucket-create-delete`**.
5. Use a metric value of **`1`** and a default value of **`0`**.
6. Once the filter and metric are created, in the Amazon CloudWatch Logs console select the filter you created and click the Create Alarm button.
7. Configure the alarm to alert whenever the metric achieves a value greater than or equal to 1; send notification to the Amazon SNS topic **`security-chapter4`**. Name the alarm **`security-chapter4`**.
8. Wait a few minutes and check in the CloudWatch metrics console that the namespace/metric pair `security-chapter4/bucket-create-delete` was created.
9. Go to the S3 management console and create a new test S3 bucket.
10. Check that the metric reports a number 1 and that the alarm triggered.
11. (Optional) Create an alarm to detect when a root user logs in.
12. (Optional) Follow the examples here: `docs.aws.amazon.com/awscloudtrail/latest/userguide/cloudwatch-alarms-for-cloudtrail.html`.
13. (Optional) Follow these examples to automatically configure best practices in monitoring alarms: `docs.aws.amazon.com/awscloudtrail/latest/userguide/use-cloudformation-template-to-create-cloudwatch-alarms.html`.

In Amazon CloudWatch, you can define a centralized account as a monitoring account and share metrics and dashboards from other accounts with it. It is not necessary for these other accounts to be part of the same organization. On the AWS Management Console of the centralized account, you will have the option to view data for different regions and accounts.

AWS Health

AWS Health provides you with information about issues, notifications, or scheduled changes in the underlying infrastructure (under the AWS portion of the shared responsibility model) that could affect your AWS account.

Such information is uncovered in a dashboard called *Personal Health Dashboard* (PHD) in the AWS Management Console. There, you will find the most recent issues and notifications and the upcoming scheduled changes. AWS Health provides an *event log* console, with a list of the events reported within the past 90 days.

If you subscribed to business or enterprise support plans, you can call the APIs of this service. Doing so allows you to work with information about specific events and aggregations (such as the description of event types and summary counts) in an automated way.

By default, the events reported in the AWS Health service cover all AWS regions within the current AWS account. You can create filters to check only the ones of interest to you. From the master account of an AWS Organization, provided it is covered by a business or enterprise support plan, you can use the *organizational view* API to have a consolidated information about events on all your AWS organization's accounts and to aggregate health events in real time.

Although you cannot disable the AWS Health service for your account, you can enable and disable the *organizational view*.

Stage 3: Events Analysis

According to the detective framework presented in the chapter's introduction, after collecting the events you should focus on analyzing them—or, in other words, use the observable records as raw material and execute an analytical process to produce a list of "processed" events (or findings). These processed events are also records that give you value-added information.

In the following sections, you will learn about AWS Config Rules (continuing your exploration of the AWS Config service), Amazon Inspector, Amazon GuardDuty, AWS Security Hub, AWS Systems Manager, SSM (specifically State Manager, Patch Manager, and Compliance capabilities), and AWS Trusted Advisor.

AWS Config Rules

AWS Config tracks configuration items of your monitored resources (and how they change over time), providing you with a configuration timeline for each of these resources.

AWS Config is notified when a change happens. This notification allows the service to establish if the change leaves the monitored resource in a compliant or noncompliant state by comparing it with a template that defines what the desired configuration is.

An AWS Config rule is the entity that defines such a template, which resources it will evaluate, when the evaluation will occur, and what remediation action to take (if any).

There are three types of AWS Config rules:

- **Custom rules:** Custom rules trigger a custom AWS Lambda function you create and maintain. AWS Config passes the information about the monitored resource to the function at triggering time. You develop the function in a way that returns a status of compliant or noncompliant.
- **Managed rules:** You can choose from a variety of predefined rules instead of creating one yourself.
- **Service-linked rules:** Only AWS services can create and deploy service-linked rules; you cannot edit them. They are considered good practices defined as standards by AWS service development teams.

When is a rule triggered? An AWS Config rule can be configured to trigger in three ways (not mutually exclusive): on a *periodic* basis (you can choose to execute every 1, 3, 6, 12, or 24 hours), when a *configuration change* is detected (creating a sort of continuous audit on your monitored resources), or *on-demand* (either by an API call or via the Management Console). You can restrict the resources the rule will act upon (defining resource types and resource identifiers in the rule configuration).

If the result of an evaluation is a noncompliant status, the rule can apply a remediation action, which you will learn more about in the "Stage 4: Action" section.

Rule parameters (key-value pairs) further extend the flexibility of the execution of AWS Config Rules since they can receive external inputs as part of the rule configuration. For *custom* rules, you define the configuration, parameters, and the AWS Lambda function AWS Config will actually summon. In contrast, *managed* rules predefine (and do not allow you to modify) the configuration related with the trigger type and the parameter's key attributes.

AWS Config keeps a record of the rules' execution. For each rule, the service maintains a list of the monitored resources and their reported status (either compliant or noncompliant). In consequence, you can have a rule-centric view (with a summary of resources and its status on a per-rule basis). You also have access to a resource-centric view, which shows information about the resource and all rules applied to it (with its corresponding status).

In the same way that AWS Config displays a configuration timeline showing the changes on a resource over time, the service also offers a *compliance timeline*. A compliance timeline is a graphical timeseries view to show the compliance status of a resource over time, as shown in Figure 4.8. This visualization allows you to easily understand when a resource modified its compliance state and what changes produced the shift.

FIGURE 4.8 AWS Config Management Console—compliance timeline

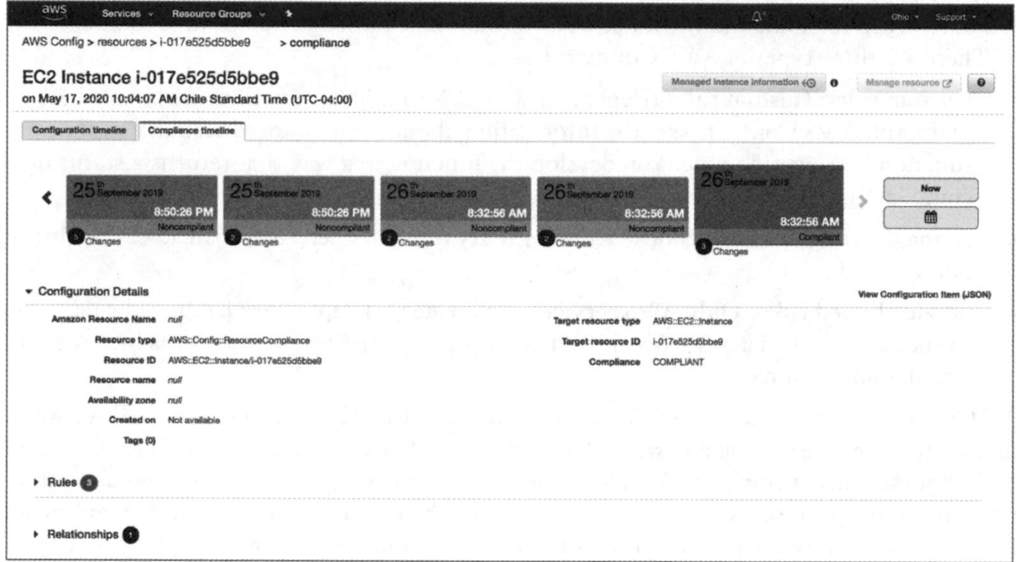

Within the notifications the AWS Config delivery channel sends to the defined Amazon SNS topic, you'll see notifications of when a rule is applied to a resource and when the compliance status of a resource changes.

An AWS Config aggregator also offers a consolidated view of rules in the same way it consolidates information about different resources across accounts, as explained in the "Stage 1: Resources State" section.

In Exercise 4.5, you will practice with AWS Config rules by configuring a rule to check a specific tag in your resources.

EXERCISE 4.5

AWS Config Rules

1. Open the AWS Config console.
2. Choose to add a new rule and use the `required-tags` template.
3. Name the rule **`security-chapter4`**.

4. Set the rule to trigger when detecting a change in the EC2 instance created in Exercise 4.1.
5. Configure the rule to look for a tag with the key **`security-chapter4`**.
6. Wait until the new rule is evaluated.
7. In the AWS Config console, look for the EC2 instance created in the previous exercise and check its compliance status.
8. In the EC2 console, modify the EC2 instance by creating a tag **`security-chapter4`**, and put any non-empty value in the tag.
9. Reevaluate the **`security-chapter4`** AWS Config rule. Check the EC2 instance compliance status regarding this rule.
10. Open the compliance timeline for the EC2 resource. See that the timeline shows the progress of the configuration and how it complied with the rule.

Amazon Inspector

Amazon Inspector focuses on evaluating the security status of an Amazon EC2 instance. It provides insights into security issues or vulnerabilities. The service gathers this information at the network level (*network assessment*) or directly from the instance operating system and applications, through an installed Amazon Inspector agent (*host assessments*). Amazon Inspector uses *automated reasoning technology* (you can find more information at `aws.amazon.com/security/provable-security`) to analyze network access policies and alert about possible breaches.

Rules packages inside Amazon Inspector are collections of rules. A *rule* is a predefined security check to evaluate against an EC2 instance. Each rule has an assigned severity level (high, medium, low, or informational). Grouping rules into rules packages greatly facilitates the configuration of Amazon Inspector.

An *assessment target* is a list of Amazon EC2 instances. This list can consist of all Amazon EC2 instances in the account and region, or it can be a subset defined by all of those Amazon EC2 instances that share a specific key-value tag.

Finally, an *assessment template* defines which rule packages run on which assessment target. Most of the Amazon Inspector configuration happens at the assessment template level (this relationship is depicted in Figure 4.9).

You can run an assessment template as many times as you want, usually on a periodical basis. The results obtained every time you run an assessment template are reported in an *assessment run*. The rules that detect possible security issues will generate findings inside the assessment run.

Each Amazon Inspector finding is actually stored as a JSON file. You can see the list of findings directly in the Amazon Inspector console or by calling the `ListFindings` API. Each finding keeps details such as its severity, the date of the discovery, description, and recommendations on how to deal with it.

FIGURE 4.9 Amazon Inspector: rules packages, assessment target, and assessment template relationship

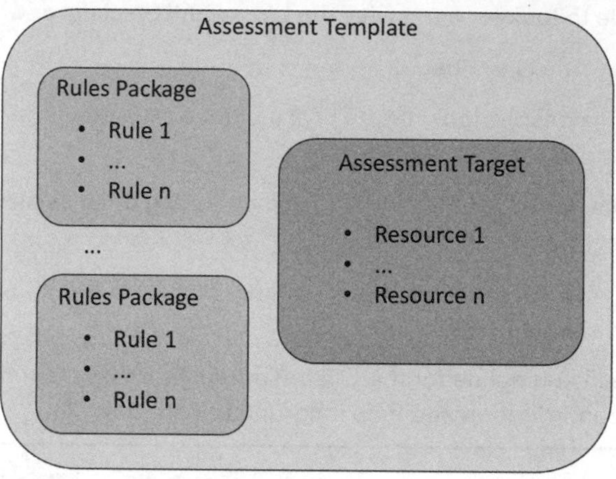

Amazon Inspector also gives you the capability to attach customized attributes (in the form of key-value pairs) to a finding. This capability is helpful to manage the findings as part of a lifecycle process. For example, you can define a filter expression that returns only findings that match specific attributes.

For each assessment run, you can generate a documented report (in either PDF or HTML format) with findings information. Amazon Inspector collects instances' telemetry data in JSON-formatted files and stores them in an Inspector-owned S3 bucket. You cannot access these files (after a 30-day retention period they are automatically deleted).

For exposure of findings in a stream structure, you can define an Amazon SNS topic in the assessment template. The topic will receive notifications when a finding is reported and when an assessment run starts, finishes, or changes its state.

Amazon GuardDuty

Amazon GuardDuty analyzes selected logs to produce observable records of suspicious activities, which are known as *findings*. The logs the service uses come from AmazonVPC Flow Logs, AWS CloudTrail, and DNS queries (specifically, the queries solved by AWS VPC DNS resolvers in the account). Nonetheless, Amazon GuardDuty does not require you to enable VPC Flow Logs, create a trail in AWS CloudTrail, or even configure an Amazon Route 53 zone. Instead, Amazon GuardDuty automatically gathers information from these services, without affecting the performance of your applications.

Amazon GuardDuty's analysis is based on threat intelligence information (such as IP addresses and domain-based lists) as well as machine learning models. You can create your own lists of *trusted IPs* and of malicious IPs (*threat lists*). These lists can consist of publicly routable host or network IPs. Activity from IP addresses on a trusted IP list will not generate any findings. On the other hand, Amazon GuardDuty generates findings from every activity involving IP addresses on threat lists.

The basic entity in Amazon GuardDuty is called a *detector*. In a nutshell, a detector consumes information and generates findings within a specific AWS account and region. An Amazon GuardDuty finding contains several attributes such as ID, time of the finding, severity, finding type, affected resources, and action details. The naming convention adopted for *finding types* is important, since it contains valuable information for security teams. The example in Figure 4.10 illustrates the naming convention.

FIGURE 4.10 Sample finding details in Amazon GuardDuty

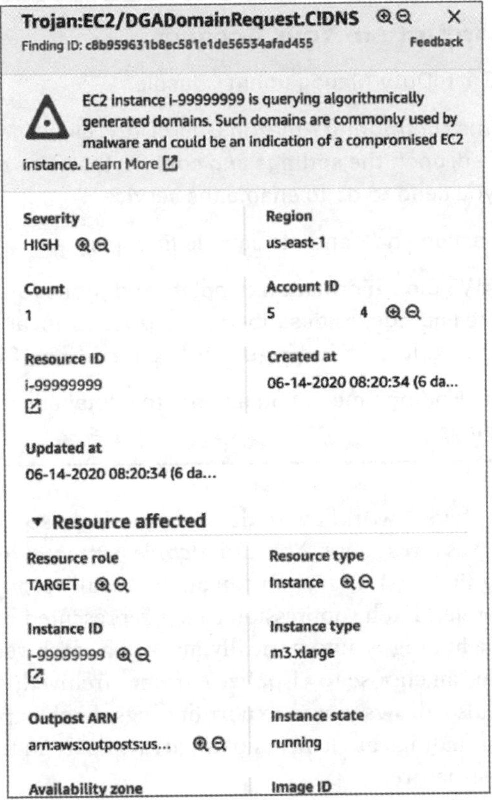

As you can see in the name of this finding, the threat purpose (objective of the attack; in our example it signals a Trojan) appears first; then the string `EC2` represents the resource type affected by the suspicious activity; third, the threat family name (`DGADomainRequest`; it informs that the instance is querying algorithmically generated DNS domains) and variant (not always present; in this case is the known variant "C"). Finally, the artifact indicates the type of resource owned by the attacker (a DNS server in this example).

Events corresponding to the same finding type and affecting the same resource are considered *recurrent occurrences*. Each finding will keep a count of its number of recurrent occurrences.

Once a *detector* is enabled, Amazon GuardDuty starts reporting findings. You can access the list of findings at any time through the management console or via the `GetFindings` API. You can also see findings-related statistics by calling the `GetFindingsStatistics` API.

In Exercise 4.6, you will enable GuardDuty in your account and will check information provided as part of the findings.

EXERCISE 4.6

Enable Amazon GuardDuty in Your Account

1. Open the Amazon GuardDuty Management Console.
2. If this is your first time configuring Amazon GuardDuty, click Enable GuardDuty. If it's already configured, open the settings and confirm that Amazon GuardDuty is enabled. That's all you need to do to enable the service.
3. Go to the Settings section and generate sample findings.
4. (Optional) Use the AWS CloudFormation template and procedure to generate an environment and produce findings, as described here: `docs.aws.amazon.com/guardduty/latest/ug/guardduty_findings.html#guardduty_findings-scripts`.
5. Navigate through the Findings menu and explore the detailed information reported for the different findings.

Amazon GuardDuty offers a workflow to deal with findings so that you can document the manual actions taken as a response. You can *archive* or *unarchive* findings (so you can only focus on interesting findings). Also, you can automatically send findings to an archive by creating *suppression rules*. Each suppression rule is represented by a filter. When a finding matches the filter, the finding is automatically marked as archived. When visualizing GuardDuty findings, you can choose to visualize current, archived, or all findings.

Amazon GuardDuty also allows you to export findings. Each exported file is a JSON-formatted file containing findings as elements of an array. Each finding is represented by all its attributes in a JSON structure.

You can also configure the automatic export of findings to an S3 bucket you own. Amazon GuardDuty will export *active* findings (findings matching suppressed rules will not be exported) within five minutes of its first occurrence. If an active finding receives recurrent events, you can configure how frequently those events are reported (every 15 minutes, every hour, or every six hours). Exported files of findings are encrypted with an AWS KMS key you choose.

Amazon GuardDuty adheres to the concept of a *master* account. The master account receives findings from other (*member*) accounts and has the capability to manage (enable, disable, or suspend) the detectors, manage the findings workflow (archive and create suppression rules), and configure threat lists for those member accounts. You can select the member accounts on a per-account basis (by invitation) or include all the accounts in your AWS Organization.

Amazon GuardDuty allows you to *disable* or *suspend* the detector in an account, on a per-region basis. Suspending a detector stops the detection of new findings but keeps information about previously detected findings. Disabling a detector stops the detection and deletes all related findings.

AWS Security Hub

AWS Security Hub is a service that consolidates security information about your AWS resources and presents it in a single pane. AWS Security Hub receives information from other AWS security services (such as Amazon GuardDuty, Amazon Inspector, Amazon Macie, AWS Firewall Manager, and IAM Access Analyzer) as well as integrated third-party security products or from your own custom security applications.

AWS Security Hub is also able to gather data about the current control implementation and status of your AWS account (via API calls and other services such as AWS Config) to complement its information and to deliver a series of findings and compliance verdicts. In that sense, AWS Security Hub acts as a concentrator of security information, correlator, and processor of data to provide filtered information about the security status of your environment.

Input and output data in AWS Security Hub conforms to a standardized format called AWS Security Finding Format (ASFF).

AWS Security Hub relies on the concept of *security standards* when gathering information from the accounts. Each security standard is composed of a list of security controls and the definition of how those should be configured (best practices). Then, the service compares the current environment status with the expected controls the security standard establishes. As a result of the comparison (or check), AWS Security Hub produces a verdict of compliance for each of the controls. The service has two methods to execute those checks and keep the information up to date: change-triggered and scheduled. Change-triggered checks are run when a change in the monitored resource is detected. This method requires the resource to be supported by AWS Config. When there is no AWS Config support to monitor changes for a check, AWS Security Hub executes a periodic check no later than 12 hours after the last execution.

One of the main benefits of Security Hub is to provide a centralized view of the security findings. Such findings are presented in the Security Hub console (or through the `GetFindings` API). In Figure 4.11 you can see a centralized view of findings in AWS Security Hub, showing an aggregation by different sources of events.

AWS Security Hub also provides a process called a *workflow* to manage the findings. A workflow describes a series of stages in which a finding can be positioned at any point in time. Each finding contains an attribute called `WorkflowStatus`, which has one of the following values: New, Notified, Suppressed, or Resolved. You can modify the workflow status of a finding, giving you the flexibility to implement your own process to deal with the security findings.

FIGURE 4.11 Centralized view in AWS Security Hub grouped by product name

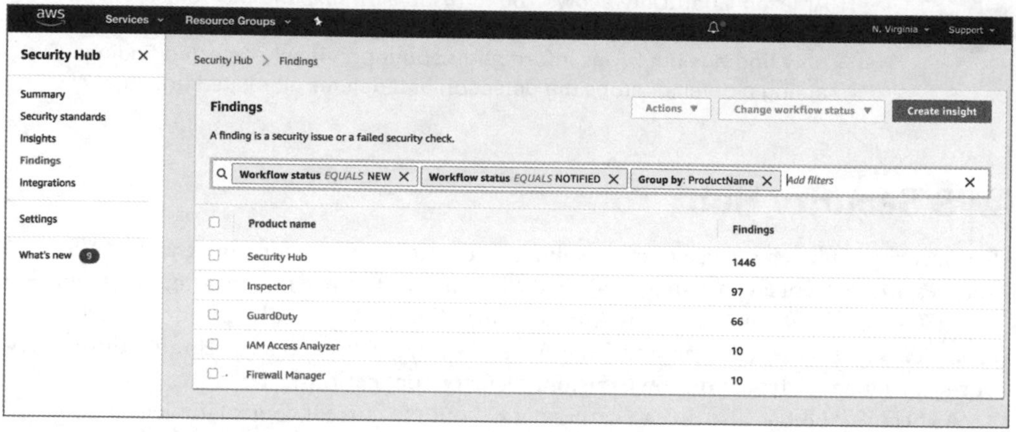

Findings also contain an attribute named `RecordState`. This attribute can take the value Active or Archived. By default, findings with an archived value in the `RecordState` attribute are filtered out from the lists shown in the Management Console (nonetheless, you can modify the visualization filter).

Along with findings, AWS Security Hub presents an additional view to consume the information via *insights*. Insights are filters and groupings that allow you to see affected resources in groups to facilitate the human analysis. AWS Security Hub provides a predefined list of insights, but you can also create your own. For example, in Figure 4.12 you see an example of an insight showing the AWS resources with the greatest number

FIGURE 4.12 AWS Security Hub—insights example

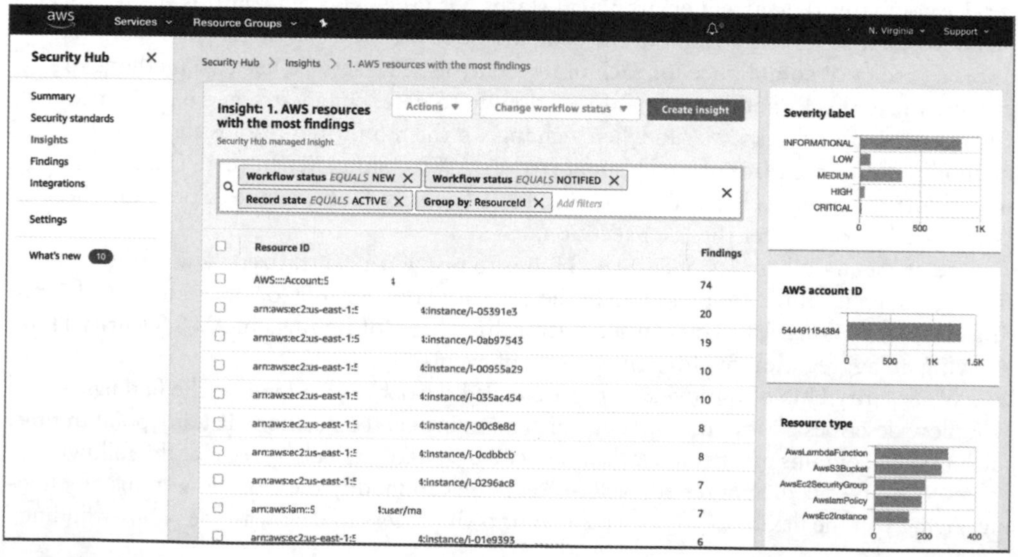

of findings. Each insight is defined by a query on the findings view that uses a `group by` clause, so the result of an insight is a grouped view of findings.

Exercise 4.7 explores the AWS Security Hub concepts, including enabling the service and reviewing findings and insights.

EXERCISE 4.7

Enable AWS Security Hub in Your Account

1. Open the AWS Security Hub Management Console.
2. If this is your first time configuring AWS Security Hub, click Enable Security Hub (confirm that at least the CIS and AWS Foundational security standards are selected). If it's already configured, click Settings, select the General tab, and confirm that AWS Security Hub is enabled. That's all you need to do to enable the service.
3. Navigate to the Security Standards menu and check your account compliance.
4. Go to Findings and confirm that the sample findings from Amazon GuardDuty were also reported in AWS Security Hub. Explore the details provided for these findings.
5. Navigate through the Insights page. In the "AWS resources with the most findings" insight, look for the instance with ID `i-99999999` (generated by the sample findings in Amazon GuardDuty).

Security Hub itself does not provide a way to consume the data generated by it (other than through visualization). Instead, it relies on Amazon EventBridge to integrate with external services.

You will learn about Amazon EventBridge and its integration with AWS Security Hub in the "Stage 4: Action" section.

AWS Security Hub has a regional scope, so you need to enable it on every region where you want to use its capabilities. The service adheres to the master-member concept. A Security Hub master account invites other accounts. An account accepting a request from a master account becomes a member account. The master can view findings from the member accounts and can also execute actions on those findings.

Services that send information to AWS Security Hub can also conform to a master-member concept (like Amazon GuardDuty and Amazon Macie). However, even if the account is configured as master for that sender service, you still need to configure the master-member relationships for all the required source accounts in AWS Security Hub.

AWS Security Hub supports both ingress and egress integrations. Ingress integrations allow external systems (AWS services, third-party applications, or custom applications) to send events to AWS Security Hub and generate findings. On the other side, egress integrations allow AWS Security Hub to send findings to third parties so that you can track your observable records in external systems, such as your own SIEMs.

Disabling AWS Security Hub in a region will stop the generation of new findings but keep existing findings for the retention period of 90 days. AWS Security Hub will also stop the verification of security standards and will remove the master-member relationships.

AWS Systems Manager: State Manager, Patch Manager, and Compliance

These three capabilities of AWS Systems Manager—State Manager, Patch Manager, and Compliance—are categorized under the group *instances & nodes* of the service.

State Manager and *Patch Manager* capabilities work by specifying the desired state of a managed resource (by documenting a set of desired parameters) and constantly act to keep the fleet adhering to that state. *Compliance* capability shows you the current adherence status both for State Manager and Patch Manager.

State Manager relies on the concept of *associations*. An association is a construct that defines the desired state of an instance. State Manager establishes the instance's desired state and the actions to bring the instance to that desired state. This information is included inside an SSM *document*. An association also defines which instances are covered by this desired state and a schedule to periodically execute the checks. For example, you can use a predefined AWS SSM document to check if an antivirus is installed and updated. If it is not installed, the document defines the actions for installing it. If it is already installed, the document defines the actions for updating it. If the two conditions are fulfilled, the system is marked as compliant.

SSM documents are JSON- or YAML-formatted files that describe the actions to be executed and their workflow; they receive parameters at execution time. SSM documents can be of different types. The ones more relevant for our discussion are *command* and *automation*. Command documents are used with the State Manager capability. Automation documents are executed by the Automation capability of SSM. You can create an association that uses an Automation document in State Manager, but it will be triggered by the Automation capability.

State Manager can also use a document of type *policy*. It uses that document to gather inventory information.

Although State Manager intends to keep track of the periodic execution and the status of the associations over time, the Patch Manager capability is oriented to keep instances and nodes in the desired state regarding OS and application patches. Patch Manager relies on the concept of *patching configuration*. A patching configuration contains information about the desired state for patching (a patch baseline with rules and definitions on which patches an instance should have), its target list of instances, the schedule for patching, and whether a specific maintenance window applies. Optionally, Patch Manager can be used only to assess if the patches are up-to-date.

You can also use State Manager with specific AWS SSM documents to execute patch management activities.

To execute the patching actions, Patch Manager will rely on `RunCommand` (for a single execution) or `MaintenanceWindows` (when periodically scheduled) capabilities.

The SSM *Compliance* capability offers an overview of the status of the monitored instances according to the *patch* and *status* compliance definitions (given by the Patch Manager and State Manager capabilities). So, with Patch Manager and State Manager, you define your desired state and constantly compare it with the current state of your monitored resources; with Compliance you have easy access to that information to quickly understand your current situation. You can consume this information either directly through the Compliance Management Console or through API calls.

To consume observable records from AWS SSM Compliance in a batchlike mode, you use the SSM Resource Data Sync feature (part of the Inventory capability of AWS SSM). When setting up a resource data sync, you define an Amazon S3 bucket (from one of your accounts) where the Inventory capability will deliver inventory information (in the form of JSON files). These JSON files contain information about your managed instances. The resource data sync will update the information when new compliance data is gathered.

Compliance capability is focused on the current status of your instances. To access historical information about resource compliance, you can use AWS Config. Specifically, you can configure AWS Config to monitor the SSM-provided resources SSM Patch Compliance and SSM Association Compliance.

AWS Trusted Advisor

Any discussion about gathering security insights on your AWS account would be incomplete without mentioning AWS Trusted Advisor. Available to every AWS account, this service provides a list of checks that compare your current account status against a set of good practices grouped under four categories: security, cost optimization, reliability, and performance. You can control access to specific checks through IAM access control policies. AWS Trusted Advisor also has the capability to monitor how close you are to reaching service limits. Moreover, if your account has a Business or Enterprise support plan, your AWS Trusted Advisor service will cover additional checks such as checking unrestricted access rules in security groups or whether AWS IAM is enforcing a password policy.

AWS Trusted Advisor keeps a list of observations about how you can improve your environment. These observable records are available within the AWS Console (Business and Enterprise support users can also access them via API calls). From the AWS console, you can also download a file containing all the observable records and configure your account contacts to receive a weekly email with a status report.

Finally, AWS Trusted Advisor checks your account resources throughout all regions. It is enabled or disabled at the account level.

Stage 4: Action

Technically speaking, *remediation* can be defined as acting on (or reacting to) an observation as a way of improving a security posture, which is not explicitly part of the detective controls. Consequently, in the following sections, you will focus on learning about services and features that are related to AWS detective controls and that offer a smooth association with remediation actions.

AWS Systems Manager: Automation

The AWS SSM automation capability makes use of the SSM *automation* documents. These documents describe a series of tasks to execute and a target list of resources. The AWS SSM automation capability runs these tasks on several resources at the same time. You can choose to trigger a predefined automation as a response to a detected observable record (for example, through AWS Config Rules remediation).

AWS Config Rules: Remediation

Once an AWS Config Rule executes a check, if a resource is reported as being in a noncompliant state, the service can link that execution to a remediation action. This configuration applies at the rule level; in the AWS Config Rule configuration, you point to an SSM Automation action already defined in your account and enter the parameters required to execute the automation, and execution retries. You can specify to automatically execute the remediation action (in this case, you also define the amount of retries) or keep it for on-demand triggering. As shown in Figure 4.13, the list of remediation actions for the AWS Config Rule matches the automation documents in SSM.

To make it easy for you to apply best practices in an account, AWS Config provides a structure that groups a set of rules under a unique name. This structure is called a *Conformance pack*. This grouping of rules under a unique deployment helps you manage each collection as an individual entity.

A conformance pack is described by a YAML template that contains the list of rules and its remediation actions. AWS provides a list of predefined sample templates, but you can also create your own templates.

FIGURE 4.13 SSM automation documents as remediation actions in AWS Config Rules

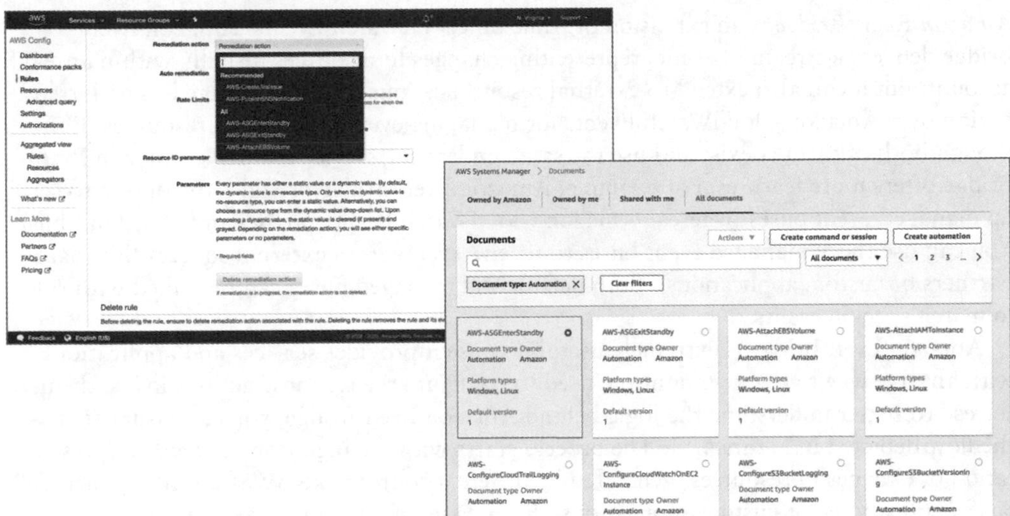

In Exercise 4.8, you will configure an AWS Config Rule to take an action when a resource is reported as being in a noncompliant status.

EXERCISE 4.8

AWS Config Rules Remediation

1. Open the AWS Config console.
2. Edit the rule `security-chapter4` (configured in Exercise 4.5).
3. Under the section Choose remediation Action, configure the rule to take an action of `AWS-PublishSNSNotification`.
4. In the ResourceID Parameter option, choose Message. This means that the `message` parameter sent to the AWS SSM Automation document will contain the `ResourceID` as the message to be sent to the topic.
5. Under the Parameters subsection, in the `TopicArn` parameter, configure as a value the ARN of the Amazon SNS topic `config-security-chapter4` already created in Exercise 4.1. Save the rule (you can keep the rest of configuration by default).
6. Reevaluate the rule, making sure it raises a noncompliant status (if needed, modify the tags of the evaluated resource).
7. Under the Choose Resources In Scope section, select one noncompliant resource. Then, click Remediate.
8. Verify that the topic received the alert.

Amazon EventBridge

Amazon EventBridge is an extension of Amazon CloudWatch Events. Amazon EventBridge delivers a stream of events representing changes to resources (usually within an AWS account, but it can also extend to external resources). Amazon EventBridge is a preferred option over Amazon CloudWatch Events for managing events from AWS resources. Even though both of them coexist and use the same underlying service and API, Amazon EventBridge offers more features. For example, Amazon EventBridge provides the option to set up managed event buses (whereas Amazon CloudWatch Events provide only a default bus). You can use those managed event buses to receive events from external sources (like SaaS partners or custom applications). Both default and managed buses can be linked with rules to match specific events.

Amazon EventBridge is extremely useful because it provides services and applications with an easy way to react without the need to configure the response actions inside themselves. To better understand the logic behind Amazon EventBridge, you can visualize it as the flow depicted in Figure 4.14. The process starts with the ingestion of *events* (representation of changes in resources, generated by different sources like AWS resources, partners' SaaS applications, or custom applications). Events are ingested into an *event bus* (and you can have several types of buses: *default* bus, *partner bus*, and *custom bus*). Finally, you can trigger *actions* as a response to selected events (you select the events defining a rule with a matching filter).

FIGURE 4.14 A generic Amazon EventBridge flow

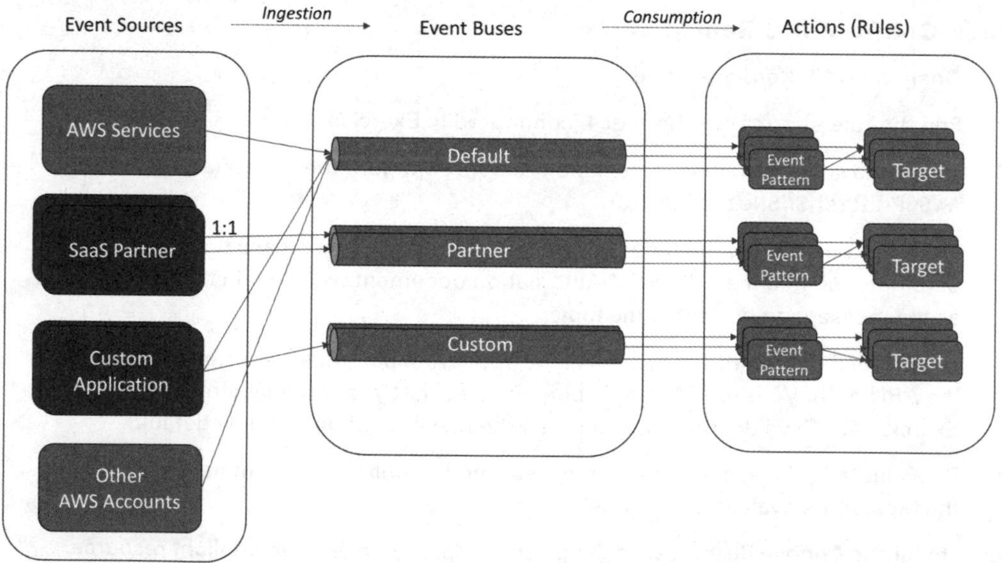

Consequently, you can think of Amazon EventBridge as a service that provides abstracted event buses and adds capabilities to connect sources of events with action executors. In addition, it can also trigger actions at predefined times (scheduled events) on a periodical basis.

As previously mentioned, Amazon EventBridge provides you with three types of buses: default, partners, and custom.

This capability of supporting several buses is one of the differences that distinguishes Amazon EventBridge from Amazon CloudWatch Events (which provides only a default bus). Another difference is the capability of Amazon EventBridge to receive events from AWS partners.

The default event bus automatically receives events from AWS resources. This is a unique bus per region and per account. You don't create it and you cannot delete it because it is part of the Amazon EventBridge infrastructure.

For example, AWS CloudTrail events are captured on the default event bus. Hence, even for services that do not directly deliver events to Amazon EventBridge, you can capture their API activity with it. Amazon EventBridge receives those events according to the configuration of the trails (including the definition of management, insights, and data events).

In Exercise 4.9, you will create a rule attached to Amazon EventBridge's default bus to capture and notify of AWS CloudTrail events related to an Amazon S3 bucket.

EXERCISE 4.9

AWS CloudTrail Integration with Amazon EventBridge

1. Open the Amazon EventBridge Management Console.
2. Create a new rule, applied over the default bus.
3. Configure the rule so that it captures every occurrence of an S3 bucket being created or deleted. The event pattern at the end should be something like this:

```
{
  "source": [
    "aws.s3"
  ],
  "detail-type": [
    "AWS API Call via CloudTrail"
  ],
  "detail": {
    "eventSource": [
      "s3.amazonaws.com"
    ],
    "eventName": [
```

```
            "DeleteBucket",
            "CreateBucket"
        ]
      }
    }
```

4. Send the captured events to the Amazon SNS topic `security-chapter4`.
5. Delete the test S3 bucket you created in Exercise 4.4 (or execute any create or delete bucket action). Confirm that the notification of the action has arrived on the `security-chapter4` topic.

Other AWS services like Amazon GuardDuty and AWS Security Hub rely on Amazon EventBridge to provide access to their findings in a streamlike structure.

Amazon GuardDuty delivers new events to Amazon EventBridge within five minutes of the finding. It updates recurrent events according to the frequency configured for the export of findings to Amazon S3.

AWS Security Hub integrates with Amazon EventBridge at two levels. The first level follows the same pattern discussed before: Amazon EventBridge captures in the default bus the findings reported by AWS Security Hub. The second level is to configure custom actions. A custom action only means that you configured in AWS Security Hub a unique ID related to a custom action name. Then, when dealing with findings or insights in the Management Console, you select findings or insights, click the Action button, and choose a custom action to execute. AWS Security Hub will report an event to Amazon EventBridge, sending the findings or insights information in conjunction with an attribute to distinguish this event as a custom action and another attribute including the custom action's unique ID. This way, Amazon EventBridge allows you to differentiate the events and define patterns to apply different actions.

In AWS Security Hub, you can apply a custom action for up to 20 findings and up to 100 resource identifiers (from insights) at the same time.

For a selected group of third-party solutions, you can configure a partner event source that allows Amazon EventBridge to receive events from SaaS applications. This configuration starts by providing information about your AWS account to the external party. Once you complete the setup, following the instructions provided by the partner, a partner event source will be attached to your Amazon EventBridge implementation. Then you can link that source to a partner event bus. Each partner event source is attached to one, and only one, partner event bus. Conversely, a partner event bus can only receive events from one partner event source.

Finally, Amazon EventBridge gives you the flexibility to create your own buses, called custom event buses. You ingest custom events into Amazon EventBridge, through the `PutEvents` API. These custom events can be sent both to the default event bus or to a custom event bus. In Example 4.4 you can see a sample custom event and then its representation on Amazon EventBridge.

Example 4.4 Amazon EventBridge custom event


```
{
  "Entries": [
    {
      "Detail": {
        "custom-app-id": "id-2131580",
        "role": "accounting"
      },
      "DetailType": "Custom App Sample Event",
      "EventBusName": "my-event-bus",
      "Resources": [
        "chile:santiago:west-1:sensor/12345"
      ],
      "Source": "custom.app.001",
      "Time": 1589627829
    }
  ]
}
```


Ingested events are represented by JSON objects that follow different schemas. Amazon EventBridge keeps a repository for these schemas: the Amazon *EventBridge Schema Registry*. This repository is already populated with event schemas for existing AWS services events. You can update the Schema Registry by uploading your own schemas or by starting the process of discovering schemas on an event bus. For every registered schema, you can download code bindings, embed them in your applications, and send custom events directly from them. Resource-based policies protect access to the EventBridge Schema Registry.

Amazon EventBridge provides the event buses to store records for the events, but it does not provide direct access to such events as observable records. Instead, you create rules that access the stream of events in the bus. Each rule is attached to only one event bus.

In addition to specifying the event bus the rule is linked to, a rule offers two additional definitions: an *event pattern* (an expression to match the events of interest) and a *target* (a service that will be invoked). The event pattern closely follows the structure of the JSON object representing events. It determines the attributes and its values for the events you are interested in. Example 4.5 illustrates an event pattern that matches the previously discussed custom event.

Example 4.5 Event pattern for the sample custom event


```
{
  "account": [
    "123456789012"
  ],
  "source": [
    "mycustom.app.001"
  ],
  "detail-type": [
    "My Custom App Sample Event"
  ],
  "detail": {
    "mycustom-app-id": [
      "id-2131580"
    ]
  }
}
```

When matching an event delivered by AWS CloudTrail, you specify a pattern matching the type "AWS API Call via CloudTrail," as shown in Example 4.6 (in this case, the source service of the events is AWS IAM).

Example 4.6 Amazon EventBridge pattern's configuration to detect AWS IAM events delivered by CloudTrail


```
{
  "source": [
    "aws.iam"
  ],
  "detail-type": [
    "AWS API Call via CloudTrail"
  ],
  "detail": {
    "eventSource": [
      "iam.amazonaws.com"
    ]
  }
}
```

The flexibility of the event patterns allows you to use exact matching, provide a list of values to match, look for null or empty strings, or use expressions for content-based filtering.

Besides event patterns, the other part of a rule is the *target*: the AWS Service that will receive the event. There are several possible targets, including AWS Lambda functions or even an Amazon EventBridge event bus in another account. In any case, the target must be in the same AWS region as the rule. When configuring via the AWS Management Console, the rule requires the definition of at least one target. When configuring via API calls, you use the `put-rule` action to define the rule and the `put-targets` action to specify targets for a rule.

For the same rule, you can configure several targets. And for each target you can define an *event transformation* that describes the JSON object that will be delivered to the target. That JSON object can be exactly the same matched event from the event bus (no transformation) or can be a transformed object based on the event.

You can use this flexibility to accomplish several goals. For example, you can send events to an AWS Lambda function to store in Amazon S3 for future access or send events to a queue and consume them from a stream.

By default, Amazon EventBridge creates a default event bus for every region in an AWS account. That bus will receive internal events from each region. Both default and custom event buses can be configured to allow receiving events from other AWS accounts (and it is easy to add all accounts from an AWS Organization). To accomplish that, you will configure a rule attached to the sender event bus that will send events to a receiver event bus in the destination account. In any case, sender and receiving accounts must be in the same region. So, you need to configure this interaccount relationship for each region you want to share events with.

In short, one of the greatest flexibilities of Amazon EventBridge is that it allows you to ingest events to the event bus from virtually any application, as long as you follow the event structure. To make things easier, Amazon EventBridge supports a list of third-party SaaS applications that are certified to work with it, and the integration is fully documented. This is the way you can integrate with different external services such as monitoring services, ticketing systems, and security services, among others.

There is no specific capability to disable Amazon EventBridge. The default event bus will be available for every region and account. However, you can decide when to create, modify, and delete partner and custom event buses. You can also decide when to turn on and off the Schema Registry discovery on a specific bus.

Summary

Detection services are a fundamental part of AWS Cloud security principles. Because of the high levels of visibility that you reach when implementing your workloads in the cloud, the detection services are able to accomplish its goals in a comprehensive manner. In general, the job of the detection services starts by monitoring resources and keeping an up-to-date picture of their status. AWS services in the detection category allows you to monitor resources not only at the AWS part of the shared responsibility model (such as API calls reported by AWS CloudTrail) but also by gathering information related with the user part of the model (for example, by installing an AWS SSM Agent inside monitored instances). Taking advantage of the automation provided by the cloud, these services are able to capture (as observable records) the events and changes affecting the resources and, using the cloud analytics capabilities, can process those records and produce insights related to security events. But that's not all! Because of the integration capabilities of the cloud, the services can automatically respond to different situations in a way to remediate those findings. These are some of the reasons why most AWS customers say their workloads are more secure in the AWS cloud than in any other environment.

Exam Essentials

Understand how AWS Config establishes a continuous compliance control. AWS Config expands its capabilities through the whole detective spectrum. Configuration items are the JSON-object representation of the monitored resources. They are stored in an AWS Config repository and can be accessed using combined methods like API calls, queries, or processing the files exported into S3 buckets. Configuration stream delivers a constant update of changes occurring to monitored resources, giving the opportunity to be notified or act upon a change in the environment. AWS Config extends its functionality with AWS Config Rules, which apply a sort of comparison with a desired state of configuration, establishing a continuous monitoring control on every monitored resource. In addition to reporting deviations from the desired state in the form of noncompliance status, you can use AWS Config Rules to link a noncompliant report with a remediation action that reacts to an undesired change. Depending on your configuration of the rule, the remediation action can be executed automatically when AWS Config detects that the resource is in a noncompliance state, or you can manually execute the configured action via the AWS Management Console or API call.

Understand how AWS CloudTrail monitors usage. AWS CloudTrail captures information about API calls occurring inside the AWS environment. For quick access to events reported in the last 90 days, AWS CloudTrail offers the event history feature. For longer retention and analysis of the information, a trail provides the mechanism of delivering the information into a S3 bucket. A trail constantly receives event information (usually reporting within 15 minutes of its occurrence). Integration with Amazon EventBridge allows you to create responses for specific API calls. AWS CloudTrail provides the mechanisms for you to protect the trails by applying the least privileged access control and using integrity validation methods.

Distinguish the differences and relationships between Amazon CloudWatch, Amazon CloudWatch Logs, and Amazon EventBridge (formerly Amazon CloudWatch Events). All these capabilities belong to the Amazon CloudWatch family, but each one is responsible for a different functionality. Amazon CloudWatch is a metric repository with the main objective of keeping track of important telemetry produced by monitored resources over time, representing them in timeseries graphs and alerting when they are outside predefined boundaries. Amazon CloudWatch Logs is a managed, centralized repository that receives and stores logs generated by different sources. Amazon CloudWatch Logs offers management capabilities to query the stored log information and to convert logs into metrics to be monitored by Amazon CloudWatch. Amazon EventBridge (an extension of the former Amazon CloudWatch Events) allows sources of events to connect with consumers that act upon the received event. Events are ingested into Amazon EventBridge buses, and from them, using rules to apply a filtering, they are captured and delivered to targets (consumers).

Understand how Amazon GuardDuty protects the environment. Through information from Amazon VPC Flow logs, AWS CloudTrail and DNS requests, and by applying threat intelligence and machine learning models, Amazon GuardDuty detects suspicious activity related to the monitored accounts and reports them in the form of findings. Each finding contains information about the suspicious activity, affected resources, and how to resolve it. Amazon GuardDuty allows you to manage findings directly in the console or via API. It also allows you to export them to an Amazon S3 bucket you own. Amazon GuardDuty automatically sends events to Amazon EventBridge.

Know how AWS Security Hub allows the centralization of security events. AWS Security Hub acts as a central repository for findings produced by several AWS services like Amazon GuardDuty, Amazon Inspector, Amazon Macie, IAM Access Analyzer, or AWS Firewall Manager. It can also integrate findings generated by third-party applications. It keeps a centralized visualization of compliance levels when comparing the environment against security standards. AWS Security Hub can also integrate with selected third-party partner products to complement its functionality. AWS Security Hub can act as a SIEM solution or integrate with external SIEM partners to manage the lifecycle of security events. AWS Security Hub integrates with Amazon EventBridge to provide a way to react in near real time against detected security events.

Be familiar with Amazon Inspector capabilities. Amazon Inspector analyzes the current state of Amazon EC2 instances and reports detected vulnerabilities. Amazon Inspector allows you to choose the assessment to run by offering rules packages of type network or host. Although network rules don't require an agent, executing a host rule is mandatory to run an Amazon Inspector agent inside the target Amazon EC2 instances. You can mix rule packages of different types in a single assessment.

Understand how to use the Personal Health Dashboard. AWS Health notifies about performance or availability issues and planned maintenance activities that affect the underlying infrastructure supporting the workloads in the AWS account. The information is provided through a console called Personal Health Dashboard (PHD), and depending on the support plan that covers the account, it can also be accessed via API calls.

Recognize how AWS Trusted Advisor increases an account's security posture. AWS Trusted Advisor provides actionable items to increase the security posture of the account. By periodically checking and acting based on AWS Trusted Advisor results, an account administrator can increase the security posture of the environment.

Recognize AWS Systems Manager capabilities that contribute to detection of incidents. AWS Systems Manager provides a comprehensive collection of capabilities to better operate instances and applications at scale. Some of these capabilities integrate within detection processes. Inventory, dashboards, and resource groups help organize and provide information about the current status of monitored resources. Compliance, Patch Manager, and State Manager compare the status of the resources with the desired up-to-date situation. Automation allows you to fix a detected deviation from a desired state.

Review Questions

1. Read the following statements and choose the correct option:

   I. By default, a trail delivers management events.

   II. By default, a trail delivers insight events.

   III. By default, a trail delivers data events.

   A. I, II, and III are correct.

   B. Only I is correct.

   C. Only II is correct.

   D. Only III is correct.

2. What is the representation of a point-in-time view of the attributes of a monitored resource in AWS Config called?

   A. Configuration snapshot

   B. Configuration item

   C. Configuration stream

   D. Configuration record

3. Read the following statements about AWS Config Rules and choose the correct option:

   I. A rule can be a custom rule.

   II. A rule can be a managed rule.

   III. A rule can be a service-linked rule.

   A. I, II, and III are correct.

   B. I and II are correct.

   C. Only I is correct.

   D. Only II is correct.

4. Which option do you use to validate the integrity of the log files delivered by AWS CloudTrail?

   A. The Amazon S3 `validate-files` action

   B. The AWS Config `cloud-trail-log-file-validation` managed rule

   C. The AWS CloudTrail `validate-logs` action

   D. There is no way to validate those log files' integrity.

5. How could you centralize AWS CloudTrail log files from different accounts?

   I. Configure the trail as an organization trail.

   II. Configure the trail from different accounts to deliver to the same S3 bucket.

   III. Configure the Consolidate Trails feature in AWS Organizations.

A. I, II, and III are correct.

B. I and II are correct.

C. Only I is correct.

D. Only II is correct.

6. Which of the following is *not* an option to directly subscribe an Amazon CloudWatch Logs log group?

A. Amazon Kinesis Data Streams

B. Amazon Kinesis Data Firehose

C. AWS Lambda

D. Amazon Elasticsearch Service

7. How could you receive "high resolution" metrics in Amazon CloudWatch?

I. Publish a custom metric of type "high resolution."

II. Selected AWS services produce "high resolution" metrics by default.

III. Use the `modify-resolution` request to modify the attribute resolution of a standard metric to `high resolution`.

A. I, II, and III are correct.

B. I and II are correct.

C. Only I is correct.

D. Only II is correct.

8. Which of the following is *not* part of the definition of an Amazon EventBridge rule?

A. Bus

B. Event pattern

C. Remediation action

D. Target

9. How could you automate responses to a finding reported in Amazon GuardDuty?

I. Creating a rule in Amazon EventBridge for findings directly received from Amazon GuardDuty

II. Configuring an event in the S3 bucket, directly receiving the findings from GuardDuty

III. Subscribing to the Amazon SNS topic, directly receiving the findings from Amazon GuardDuty

A. I, II, and III are correct.

B. I and II are correct.

C. Only I is correct.

D. Only II is correct.

10. What is a collection of related findings, grouped by a common attribute and saved as a filter in AWS Security Hub, called?
    A. Findings group
    B. Insights
    C. Security standard
    D. Integrations

Infrastructure Protection

THE AWS CERTIFIED SECURITY SPECIALTY EXAM OBJECTIVES THAT LEVERAGE CONCEPTS EXPLAINED IN THIS CHAPTER INCLUDE THE FOLLOWING:

✓ **Domain 3: Infrastructure Security**

- 3.1. Design edge security on AWS
- 3.2. Design and implement a secure network infrastructure
- 3.3. Troubleshoot a secure network infrastructure

Introduction

Amazon Web Services relies on old and new infrastructure concepts to support applications on the AWS Cloud. And as new networking constructs are introduced (and old ones slightly changed), security policies must also adapt to them accordingly.

In this chapter, you will be introduced to AWS networking concepts such as Amazon VPC, subnets, and route tables, as well as other features that are related to network address translation (NAT gateways and instances) and traffic filtering (security groups and network access control lists). You will also learn how AWS Elastic Load Balancing works and how security services such as AWS Web Application Firewall can provide secure access to your web-based applications deployed in the cloud.

Finally, you will explore AWS's unique approach to mitigate distributed denial-of-service attacks while being introduced to AWS Shield.

AWS Networking Constructs

Computer networking can be understood as an engineering discipline whose objective is to study and analyze data communication among computing resources. Unfortunately, this field of study had sometimes fallen into the well of misunderstood areas due to a lack of comprehension of its most fundamental concepts. Therefore, in order to provide full clarity on how infrastructure security works in the AWS Cloud, this section will focus on the definition of its foundational networking concepts.

AWS has a series of constructs—or objects—that can compose a cloud networking topology. The first one you should know is *Amazon Virtual Private Cloud (Amazon VPC)*, which is an abstraction that represents a virtual network within the AWS Cloud. Within a VPC, you can deploy cloud resources in a logically isolated part of the AWS Cloud, securely apart from other user accounts.

Of course, very few computing resources are created to be totally secluded from other systems. Therefore, within a VPC you will need to employ other network constructs to allow (and, most importantly, control) the communication between cloud resources.

One of the advantages of cloud computing is its agility, which enables you to quickly spin up resources to deploy full applications in minutes. Such a characteristic facilitates experimentation and learning since you can always deprovision these resources without risk or a high amount of investment. Therefore, if you are a novice to AWS Cloud networking concepts, try to repeat the configurations shown in this whole chapter. Even if you are already acquainted with these objects, you can follow the steps, but watch for notes or tips (like this one) to learn the details that fully characterize them.

In the AWS Console, the VPC configuration is currently available in the Networking and Content Delivery part of the list of AWS Cloud Services. After selecting it, you will be automatically taken to your Amazon VPC dashboard, which is shown in Figure 5.1.

FIGURE 5.1 Amazon VPC dashboard

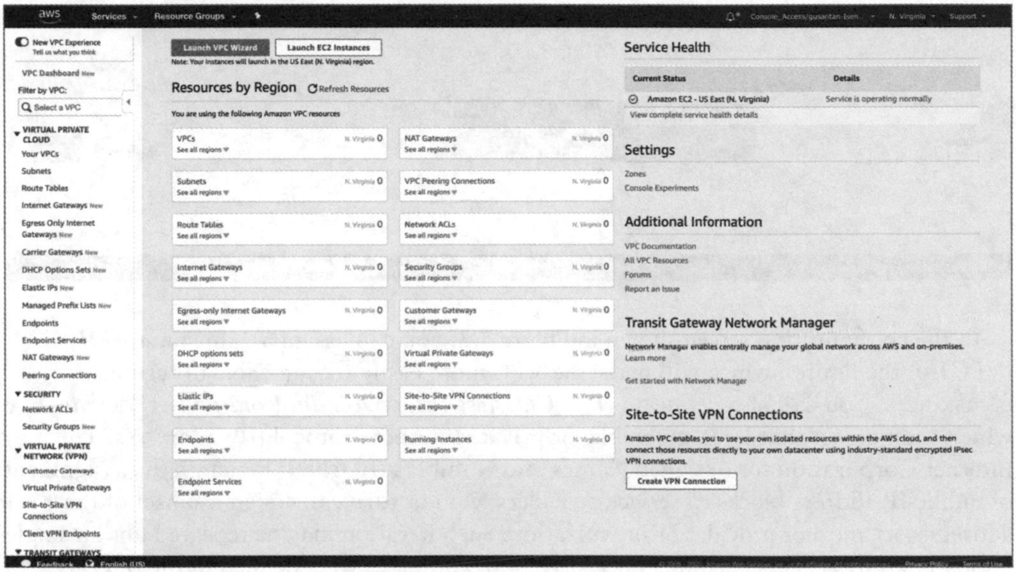

As Figure 5.1 shows, the VPC dashboard presents a considerable variety of VPC-related objects. To fully understand their function, you will not click the Launch VPC Wizard button (which is probably tempting you at the top of the screen). Instead, you will create your network objects one by one.

It is important that you notice that the VPC dashboard in Figure 5.1 is associated with an AWS region (US East, N. Virginia) and therefore shows all VPCs (and their corresponding objects) that are configured within a single region. So, here is an important detail: *VPCs do not extend beyond a region.*

Click Your VPCs in the menu at left to open a screen that shows a list of VPCs you have already created and an inviting button named Create VPC. Figure 5.2 shows the VPC settings you have access to.

FIGURE 5.2 VPC settings

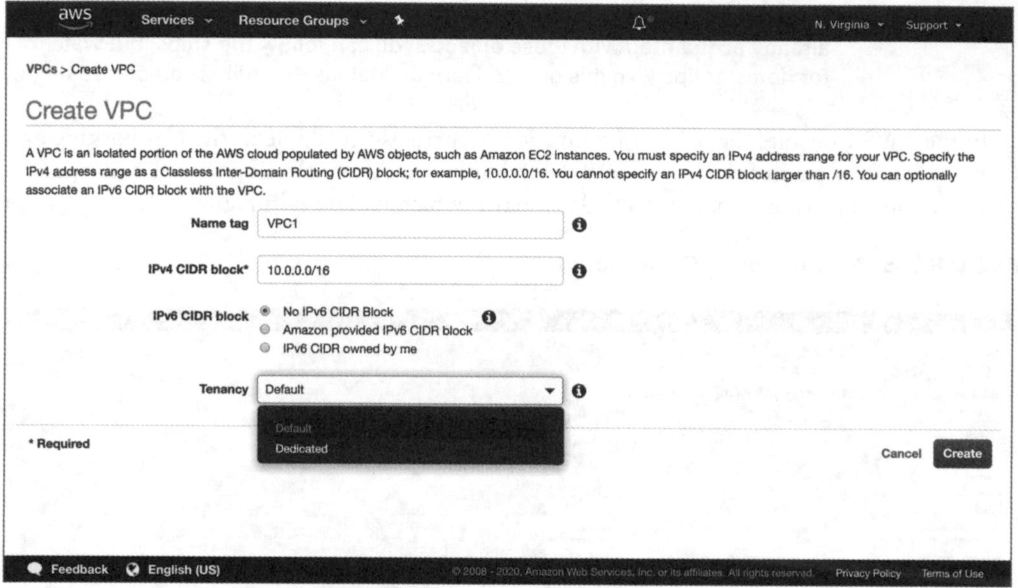

In the configuration screen shown in Figure 5.2, you can assign a name tag to a VPC (VPC1 in the figure), which will make the VPC more easily recognizable in future circumstances. You can also define an *IPv4 Classless Inter-Domain Routing (CIDR) block*, which is an object that leverages public or private Internet Protocol (IP) addresses. The Internet Corporation for Assigned Names and Numbers (ICANN) manages the assignment of public IP address blocks to service providers, who in turn can assign a subset of these addresses to another provider or organization. Such iteration may be repeated until a single public IP address is assigned to a host. Private IP addresses were defined in the Internet Engineering Task Force (IETF) Request for Comments (RFC) 1918 published in February 1996. In summary, these three special IP address blocks (which encompass addresses that are not valid in the Internet) are

- 10.0.0.0 to 10.255.255.255 (10/8 prefix)
- 172.16.0.0 to 172.31.255.255 (172.16/12 prefix)
- 192.168.0.0 to 192.168.255.255 (192.168/16 prefix)

In Figure 5.2, you can see that all IP addresses of VPC1 will belong to CIDR block 10.0.0.0/16. Also notice that you can define the sixth version of the Internet Protocol (IPv6) to be used in VPC1. However, because this chapter focuses on the AWS Cloud's most fundamental networking concepts, this option is not enabled in the examples throughout the chapter.

You can have up to five IPv4 CIDR blocks per VPC (one primary and four secondary CIDR blocks). This quota can be increased up to a maximum of 50, if you request it. Please check the AWS official documentation for complete and current information.

The last VPC configuration setting shown in Figure 5.2 refers to the concept of *tenancy*, which defines how VPC1 will share hardware with other accounts within the AWS Cloud. The options are

- **Default:** Amazon EC2 instances you deploy in this VPC will share hardware with other AWS accounts.
- **Dedicated:** Amazon EC2 instances deployed in a dedicated VPC will run on hardware dedicated to a single tenant (which can be understood as an AWS account).

The choice between either option depends on various factors such as compliance regulations or existing software license specifics. For this example, you should assign VPC1 to the default option. You can conclude the VPC configuration by clicking Create.

There is a quota of five VPCs you can create per region. You can expand it to 100 VPCs, if you request it. Please check the AWS official documentation for complete and current information.

Many seasoned networking engineers have surely heard the sentence "Nothing good comes out of a networking discussion that doesn't have a topology." Consequently, Figure 5.3 summarizes what you have created so far.

FIGURE 5.3 VPC1 network topology

The next concept you will explore is the one called *subnet*. In the AWS Cloud context, this construct represents a range of IP addresses in your VPC. More importantly, deploying resources in a single subnet will make them inherit traffic policies that are applied to the subnet.

Figure 5.4 shows what happens when you access the VPC dashboard again, click Subnets in the menu at left, and then click Create Subnet.

FIGURE 5.4 Subnet creation

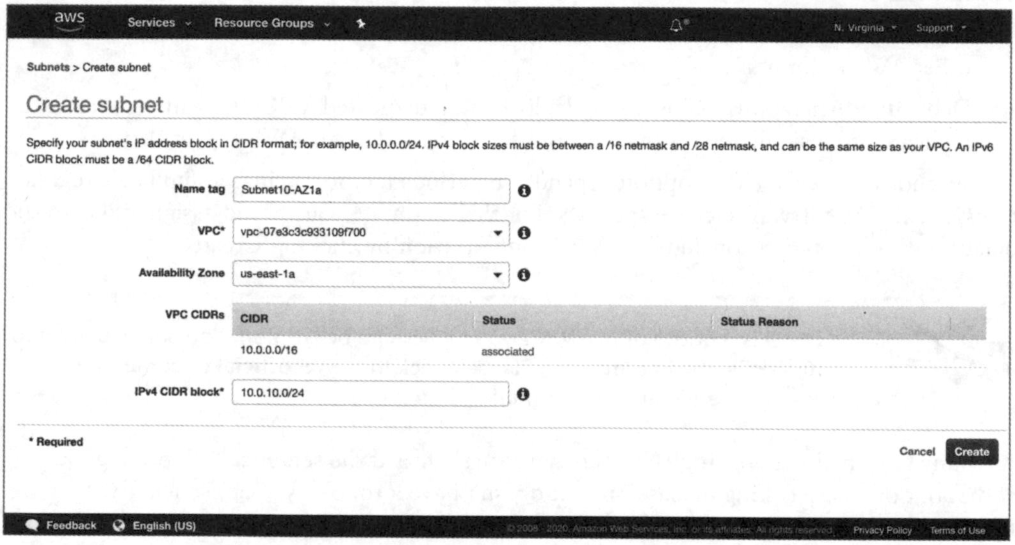

Figure 5.4 shows the creation of a subnet called Subnet10-AZ1a. (The reason for this name will become clear over the next couple of paragraphs.) The subnet belongs to VPC1 (which is referred to by its VPC unique name identifier, vpc-07e3c3c933109f700) and the availability zone (AZ) in which you are deploying this subnet. A subnet is by definition located within a single AZ. This fact will certainly influence your network designs and how you plan high availability for your applications.

Figure 5.4 shows that you can define the subnet's IPv4 CIDR block, which is 10.0.10.0/24. This network topology will use the CIDR block's third byte to differentiate subnets that belong to the defined VPC CIDR range. Hence, the naming convention chosen for Subnet10-AZ1a hopefully will facilitate your reading and quickly highlight which network and associated AZ each subnet is using.

You can have up to 200 subnets per VPC. Please check the AWS official documentation for complete and current information.

Figure 5.5 shows some of Subnet10-AZ1a's parameters immediately after it is created.

FIGURE 5.5 Subnet10-AZ1a parameters

In Figure 5.5, you will notice that Subnet10-AZ1a has a Subnet ID (subnet-06d8d39eba569d28b) that uniquely differentiates it from all other created subnets in the AWS Cloud. Furthermore, the figure shows familiar parameters such as to which VPC (VPC1) the subnet belongs and its configured IPv4 CIDR (10.0.10.0/24). Interestingly, it also depicts the number of available IP addresses in this subnet.

Attentive readers will probably ask why a subnet with a 255.255.255.0 (/24) subnet mask is not showing all 254 addresses that are normally available in such configurations (256 minus 2, where the first is the subnet's network address and the last represents the subnet's broadcast address). The missing three addresses are predefined identifiers that AWS reserves in each subnet:

- **Second address:** Reserved for the VPC router (10.0.10.1 in Subnet10-AZ1a)
- **Third address:** Reserved for the DNS server (10.0.10.2 in Subnet10-AZ1a)
- **Fourth address:** Reserved for future use (10.0.1.3 in Subnet10-AZ1a)

The AWS Cloud automation ensures that these IP addresses defined for the VPC router and DNS server will be automatically inserted in the Amazon EC2 instances as they are deployed on Subnet10-AZ1a.

Unlike traditional networks, AWS does not support IP broadcast communication within a subnet.

Continuing our exploration of Figure 5.5, notice that Subnet10-AZ1a has two parameters that represent its availability zone. The first is simply called Availability Zone, which represents the choice you have made during the subnet creation. In this case, the zone names (such as us-east-1a, us-east-1b, and so on) were randomized per each account so that not everyone would choose the same zones (yes, humans are that predictable). However, some users want to share resources centrally in a single account to leverage the high bandwidth and low latency from putting consumer and provider accounts in the same actual availability zones. For these scenarios, AWS created Availability Zone ID, which is a static reference that provides a cross-account identification of an AZ.

Finally, you will notice a Route Table parameter that points to a route table ID of rtb-0f5b21e026c4c8753 listed with the subnet. In fact, this object represents the main route table associated with VPC1, which is shown in Figure 5.6 (click Route Tables in the menu at left to see it).

FIGURE 5.6 VPC1 default route table

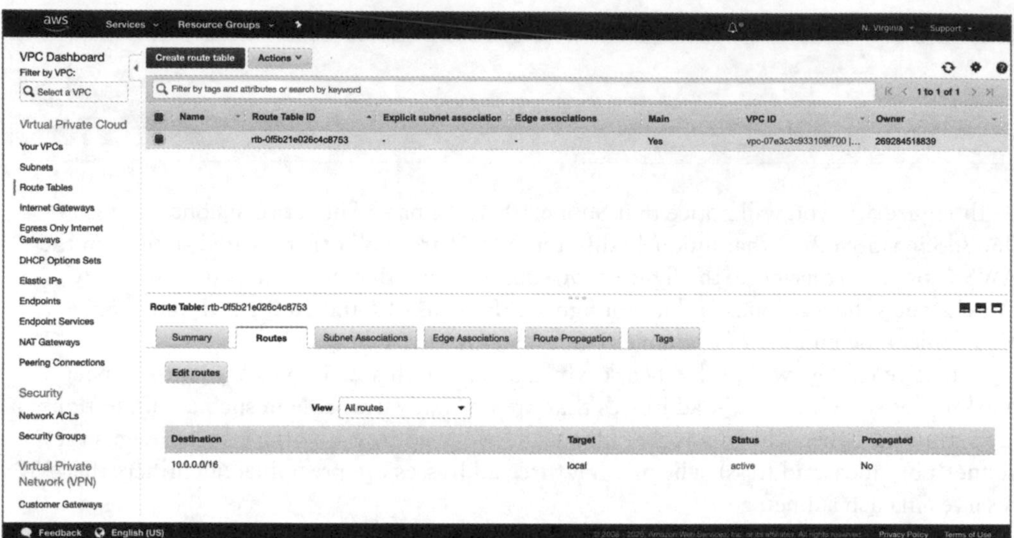

In Figure 5.6, the route table has a single route (10.0.0.0/16) declared to be a *local target*, which means that the VPC router can reach it within the VPC and that this route should not be propagated (or distributed) to external routers.

Moreover, you can notice a subnet association of a route table to a specific subnet, which may surprise some network and security engineers who are more used to traditional on-premises network designs. However, through this noteworthy association, you can implement interesting routing schemes to deviate traffic from its default behavior in specific subnets. You will see some of these scenarios in the "Network Address Translation" and "VPC Endpoints" sections later in this chapter.

Now, create yet another subnet called **Subnet20-AZ1b**, whose name will suggest its address and availability zone. At this stage, both subnets are captive to VPC1 and are not at all accessible to the Internet. To deploy such external connectivity, you will need to create yet another network construct called an *Internet gateway*.

In summary, an Internet gateway is a scalable, redundant, and highly available VPC component that allows communication between instances in your VPC and the Internet. There are two types of Internet gateways in the AWS Cloud:

- **Internet Gateways:** Provide a target in your VPC route tables for Internet-routable traffic (default route). They also perform network address translation (NAT) for instances that have been assigned public IPv4 addresses, and they support IPv6 traffic.
- **Egress Only Internet Gateways:** Are only used to enable outbound IPv6 traffic from the VPC.

In the network topology you are currently building in this chapter, you will insert an Internet gateway to make instances within your VPC accessible to the Internet. Therefore, you can click Internet Gateways in the menu at left in your VPC management console, and then click Create Internet Gateway. Figure 5.7 shows the only parameter required in this step.

FIGURE 5.7 Internet gateway IGW1 creation

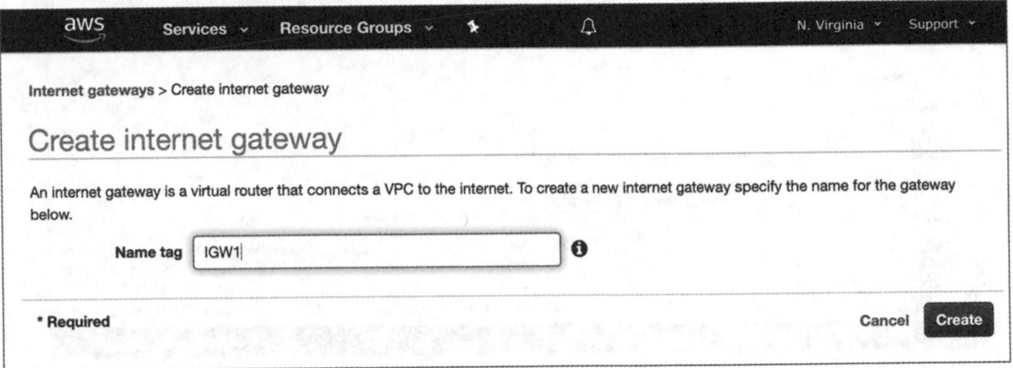

After you click Create, the state of IGW1 is red and is considered to be "detached." Such behavior occurs because you have to explicitly *attach* (or associate) an Internet gateway to a VPC so that it can route traffic from and to the Internet.

There is a biunivocal relationship between these network constructs; therefore, you can have only one Internet gateway attached per VPC and each Internet gateway can only be attached to a single VPC. Moreover, you can have up to five Internet gateways per region by default. Please check the AWS official documentation for complete and current information.

To attach IGW1-VPC1, select IGW1 on the Internet Gateways screen, click the Actions drop-down menu, and select Attach To VPC. After you select VPC1, you will reach the status shown in Figure 5.8.

Figure 5.9 represents the network topology you have built at this point.

In Figure 5.9, notice that IGW1 is serving both subnets in the VPC via the VPC router. To dive a little deeper into the inner workings of the VPC, let's take a peek at the current status of the main route table by clicking Route Tables in the menu at left, as Figure 5.10 shows.

As you can see in Figure 5.10, this route table does not have a route to the Internet yet. Therefore, to leverage the recently created IGW1, you will add a default route (0.0.0.0/0) pointing to the Internet gateway. That way, the VPC router will direct any traffic that is not local (10.0.0.0/16) in VPC1 to the Internet gateway.

FIGURE 5.8 IGW1 is attached to VPC1.

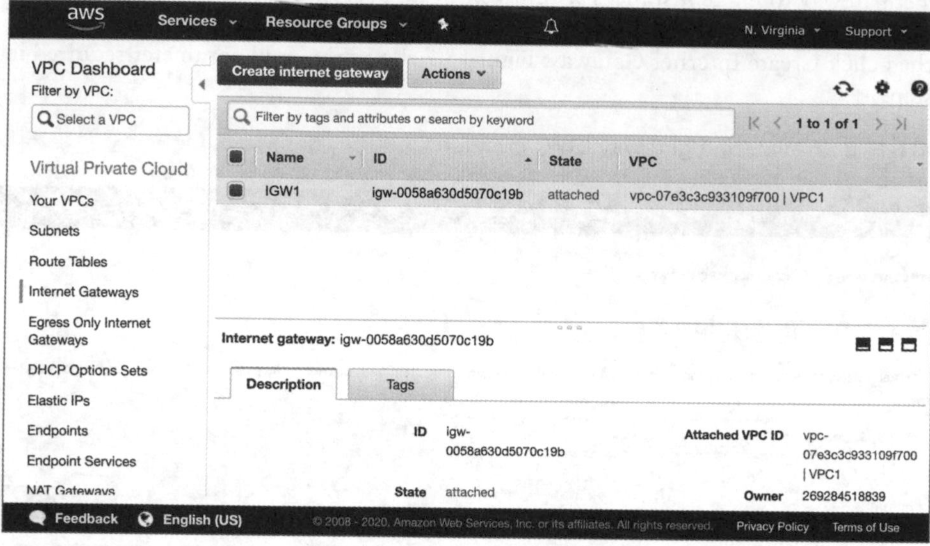

FIGURE 5.9 Updated topology

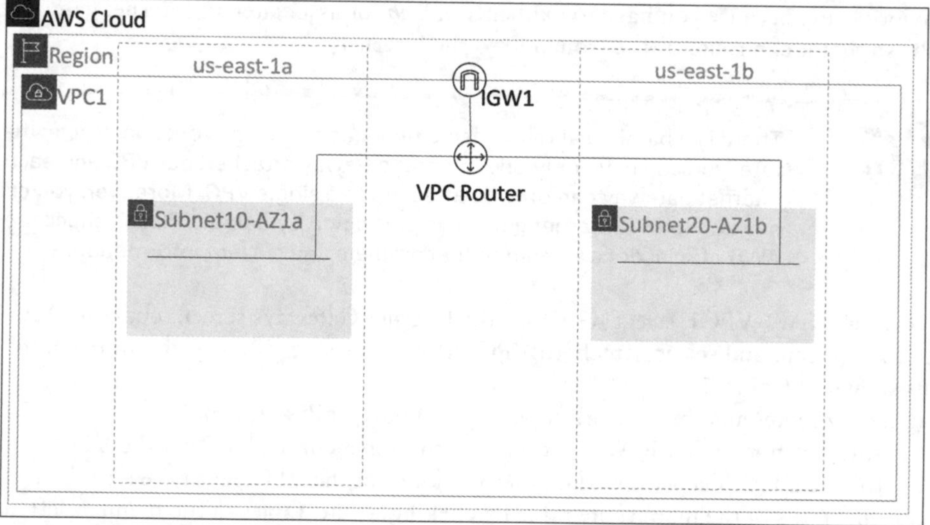

To make it happen, select the main route table, click Edit Routes, and add the *default route* (0.0.0.0/0 as Destination and IGW1 as Target) as shown in Figure 5.11.

Click Save Routes, and you now have ensured that traffic from both subnets in VPC1 will reach IGW1. However, since instances that are deployed on the created subnets will receive addresses within the range of 10.0.0.1 to 10.0.255.254, they cannot be reached on the Internet (these are private addresses, remember?). Therefore, to offer a valid IP address as a target for Internet-sourced traffic, IGW1 will also have to perform network address translation.

FIGURE 5.10 Main route table after IGW1 creation

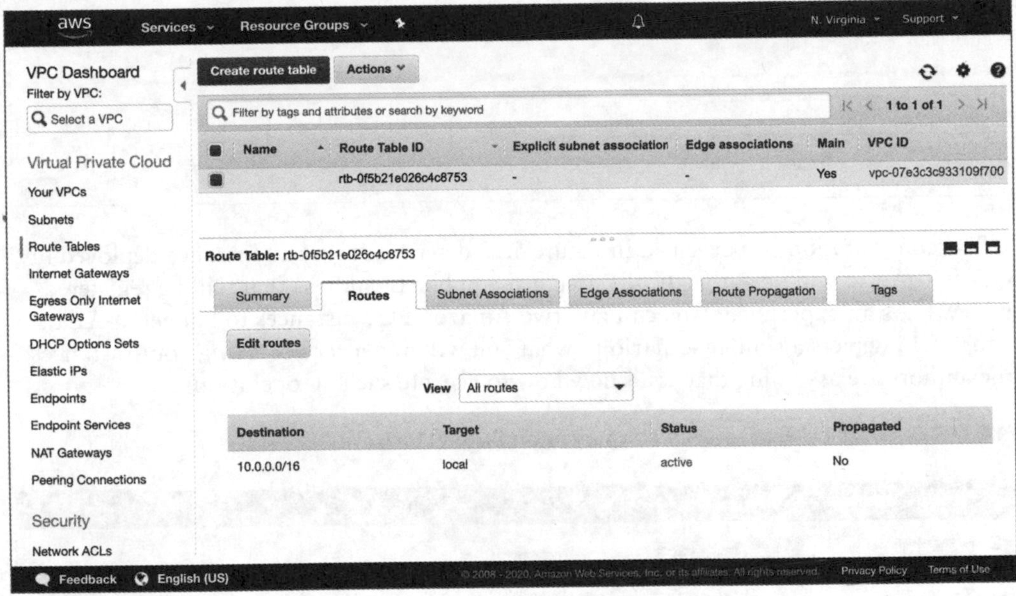

FIGURE 5.11 Adding the default route to the main route table

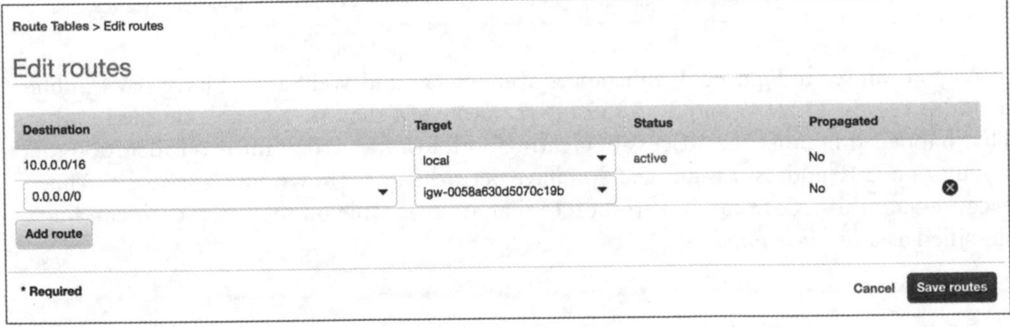

Through NAT, an Internet gateway can receive traffic directed to a public IP address and change it to a private IP address that is assigned to a resource located within a VPC. Such an endeavor can be achieved in different ways in the AWS Cloud, but for the sake of simplicity, you will rely on a simple approach where a public IP address is automatically assigned to instances deployed in a subnet.

Figure 5.12 shows what happens when, on the Subnets screen, you select Subnet10-AZ1a, and from the Actions drop-down menu, you select the Modify Auto-Assign IP Settings option.

FIGURE 5.12 Modifying IP Auto-Assignment on Subnet10-AZ1a

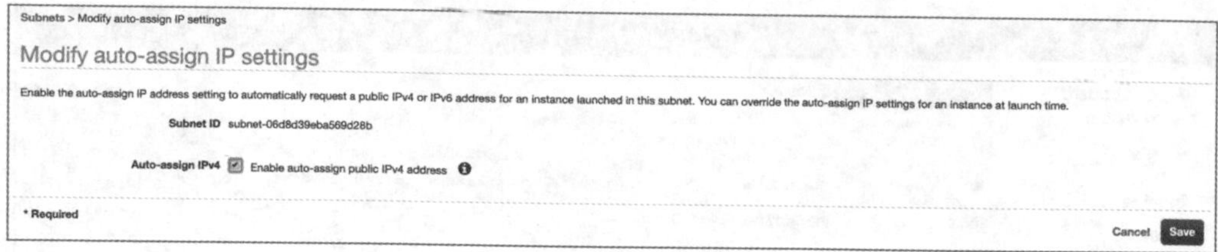

The configuration you executed in Figure 5.12 determines that an instance deployed in Subnet10-AZ1a will be automatically assigned a public IP address that will be registered in IGW1. As an experiment, you can add two Amazon EC2 instances to Subnet10-AZ1. Figure 5.13 depicts a similar scenario to what you will find after deploying your instances (the authors are assuming that you know how to execute such an operation).

FIGURE 5.13 Two instances deployed on Subnet10-AZ1a

aws Services Resource Groups N. Virginia Support

New EC2 Experience
Tell us what you think

EC2 Dashboard New
Events New
Tags
Reports

Launch Instance Connect Actions

Filter by tags and attributes or search by keyword 1 to 2 of 2

Name	Instance ID	Instance Type	Availability Zone	IPv4 Public IP	Private IP Address
WebServer1	i-06e21d7fb55c4f674	t2.micro	us-east-1a	54.162.9.49	10.0.10.153
WebServer2	i-09120ed373672331a	t2.micro	us-east-1a	3.87.159.146	10.0.10.131

As you can see in Figure 5.13, instances WebServer1 and WebServer2 have IPV4 public IP addresses (54.162.9.49 and 3.87.159.146, respectively) that are routable on the Internet. That happened because the process of creating both instances took into consideration the default public IP address assignment you have performed, as shown in Figure 5.12. And because Subnet10-AZ1a can host resources that are reachable on the Internet, it can be classified as a *public subnet*.

The IP addresses assigned to both instances are called *elastic IP addresses*. These Internet-reachable IPv4 addresses are designed for dynamic cloud computing. You can also consider these addresses as a pool of public addresses AWS owns. They can be associated and disassociated to resources deployed within the AWS Cloud to serve different objectives, such as temporary Internet access or application high availability.

A fair question you may have at this moment would be, "What happens when an instance is actually deployed on Subnet20-AZ1b, which does not have auto-assignment of public addresses?" If you create an Amazon EC2 instance named **DBServer1** on Subnet20-AZ1b, it will not have a public IP address and therefore will not be directly accessible from the Internet via IGW1. Subnets such as Subnet20-AZ1b are commonly known as *private subnets*, and they are generally used when you are running a web application that relies on backend servers that are not accessible on the Internet but that can communicate with resources located in the same VPC.

Nonetheless, some resources installed in private subnets (such as application or database servers) may need limited outgoing access to the Internet for various reasons such as software updates. The next section will show how such a need may be addressed in an Amazon VPC.

But first, you will explore working with VPCs in a more hands-on way. In Exercise 5.1, you will create a VPC and four subnets, and in Exercise 5.2, you will create an Internet gateway for your VPC.

EXERCISE 5.1

Create a VPC and Subnets

In this exercise, you will create a VPC with four subnets.

1. Log in to your AWS account and choose a region of your preference.
2. Create a VPC called **SecureVPC** with a CIDR block of **192.168.0.0/16**.
3. Create a subnet called **PublicSubnet-A** in an availability zone that ends with the letter *a* with the following CIDR block: **192.168.1.0/24**. Use the Auto-Assign Public IP Address configuration in this subnet.
4. Create a subnet called **PublicSubnet-B** in an availability zone that ends with the letter *b* with the following CIDR block: **192.168.2.0/24**. Use the Auto-Assign Public IP Address configuration in this subnet.
5. Create a subnet called **PrivateSubnet-A** in an availability zone that ends with the letter *a* with the following CIDR block: **192.168.3.0/24**.
6. Create a subnet called **PrivateSubnet-B** in an availability zone that ends with the letter *b* with the following CIDR block: **192.168.4.0/24**.

EXERCISE 5.2

Create an Internet Gateway

After finishing Exercise 5.1, you will create and attach an Internet gateway to your VPC.

1. Create an Internet gateway called **Internet-Gateway**.
2. Attach it to SecureVPC.

3. Create a route table called **PublicRouteTable**, associate it with Internet-Gateway, and assign it to PublicSubnet-A and PublicSubnet-B.

4. Create two free-tier Amazon EC2 instances (**Web-A** and **Web-B**) located at PublicSubnet-A and PublicSubnet-B, respectively. Allow SSH and web services in these servers and access them via the Internet. Use the following script to enable the web service on instance Web-A (and change it accordingly to Web-B):

```
#!/bin/bash
  sudo -s
  yum update -y
  yum install httpd -y
  echo "Web-A">/var/www/html/index.html
  service httpd start
  chkconfig httpd on
```

Network Address Translation

You can provide egress-only access to the Internet to a resource located at a private subnet through a *NAT gateway* deployed on a public subnet. Select NAT Gateways in the menu at left in the VPC management console, and click Create NAT Gateway to open the screen shown in Figure 5.14.

FIGURE 5.14 The Create NAT Gateway screen

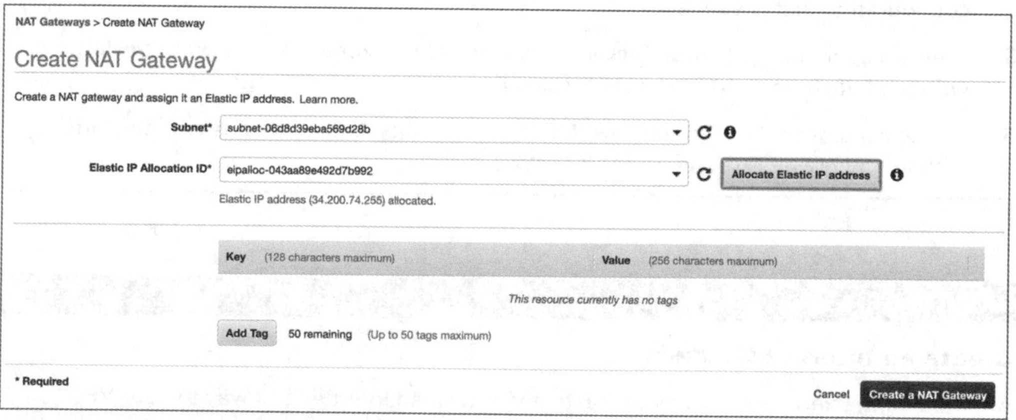

Figure 5.14 shows the required parameters of a NAT gateway. Besides being located at a public subnet such as Subnet10-AZ1a (because the NAT gateway itself needs to access the Internet), a NAT gateway also requires the allocation of an elastic IP address. By clicking Allocate Elastic IP Address, you will be able to assign one IP address to your NAT gateway.

After your NAT gateway is finally instantiated, the AWS Console makes sure that you do not forget to edit your route tables, as shown in Figure 5.15.

FIGURE 5.15 NAT gateway creation

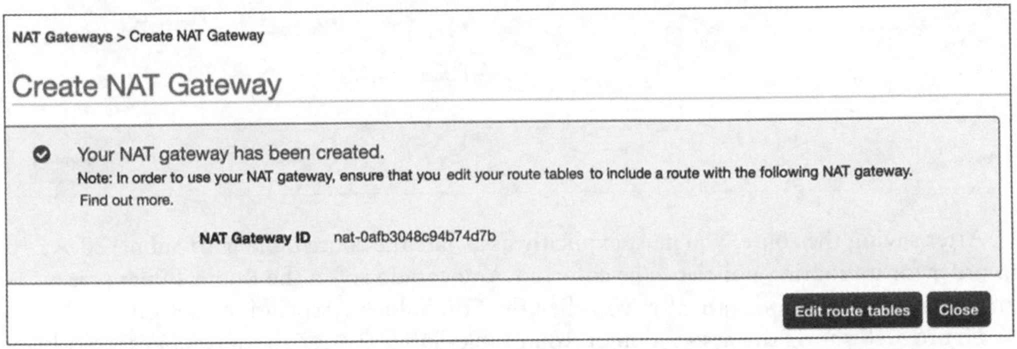

NAT Gateways > Create NAT Gateway

Create NAT Gateway

Your NAT gateway has been created.
Note: In order to use your NAT gateway, ensure that you edit your route tables to include a route with the following NAT gateway.
Find out more.

NAT Gateway ID nat-0afb3048c94b74d7b

Edit route tables Close

The not-so-subtle suggestion on the Create NAT Gateway screen (you can only imagine how many support cases AWS must have received from this issue) comes from the fact that the main route table currently points out to IGW1 whenever an address out of the range 10.0.0.0/16 reaches the VPC router. Therefore, to steer the traffic from Subnet20-AZ1b to NAT-GW1, you will need to create a separate route table and associate it with such a subnet.

Figure 5.16 shows the necessary parameters to create the new route table.

FIGURE 5.16 Route table creation

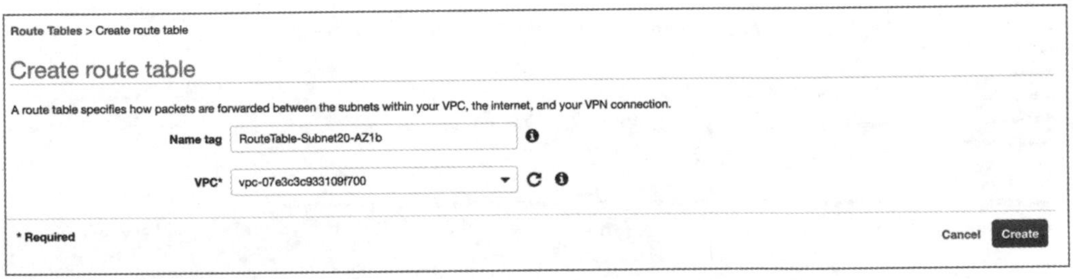

Route Tables > Create route table

Create route table

A route table specifies how packets are forwarded between the subnets within your VPC, the internet, and your VPN connection.

Name tag RouteTable-Subnet20-AZ1b

VPC* vpc-07e3c3c933109f700

* Required Cancel Create

Because RouteTable-Subnet20-AZ1b comes with only one local route (10.0.0.0/16), you should also edit it and include a default route (0.0.0.0/0) pointing out to NAT-GW1 as a target for Internet-bound traffic. If you are on the Route Tables screen of the VPC management console, you can do this by selecting RouteTable-Subnet20-AZ1b, selecting the Routes tab, and clicking Edit Routes.

Figure 5.17 shows the addition of a default route (0.0.0.0/0). But at this time, the default route is pointing to NAT-GW1 (nat-0afb3048c94b74d7b in the figure) right after you click the Add Route button.

FIGURE 5.17 Adding a default route to RouteTable-Subnet20-AZ1b

Route Tables > Edit routes

Edit routes

Destination	Target	Status	Propagated
10.0.0.0/16	local	active	No
0.0.0.0/0	nat-0afb3048c94b74d7b		No

Add route

* Required

Cancel Save routes

After saving the route, you must explicitly associate the route table with Subnet20-AZ1b in order for its routing policies to be enforced. You can do so on the Route Tables screen and Subnet Associations tab, after you click the Edit Subnet Associations button.

Figure 5.18 shows the association of RouteTable-Subnet20-AZ1b to its namesake subnet.

FIGURE 5.18 Subnet association

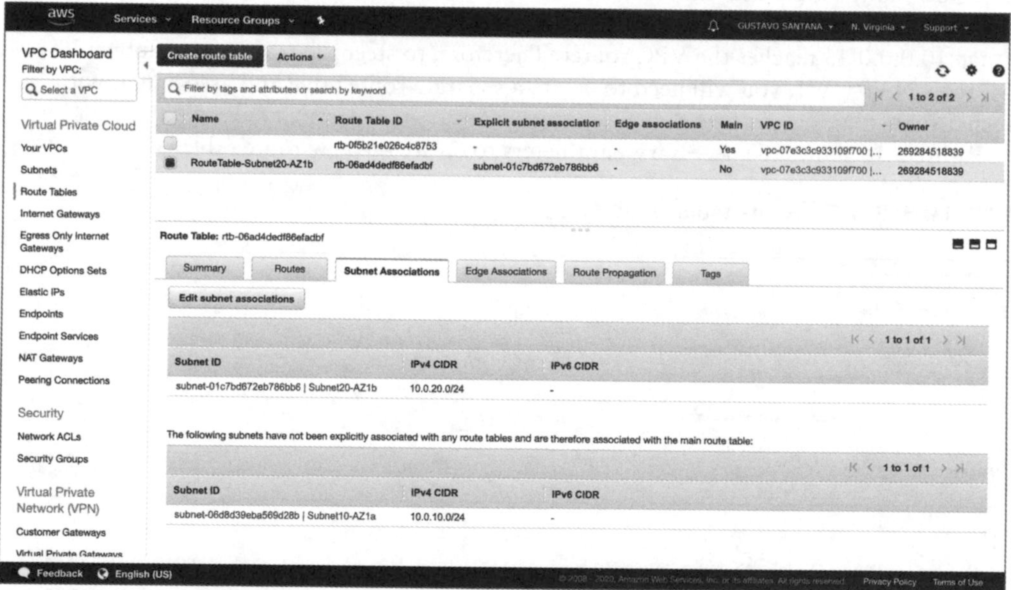

Each subnet can have only one route table associated to it. However, within a VPC each route table can be associated to multiple subnets. (As you have seen, the main route table is associated to all subnets by default.) You can have up to 200 route tables per VPC and 50 routes per route table. However, you may increase this number to a maximum of 1,000 with a compromise in terms of network performance.

Say you've deployed an Amazon EC2 instance called DBServer1 in Subnet20-AZ1b (as suggested in the "AWS Networking Constructs" section earlier). Figure 5.19 shows your current VPC network topology status.

FIGURE 5.19 Topology with NAT gateway

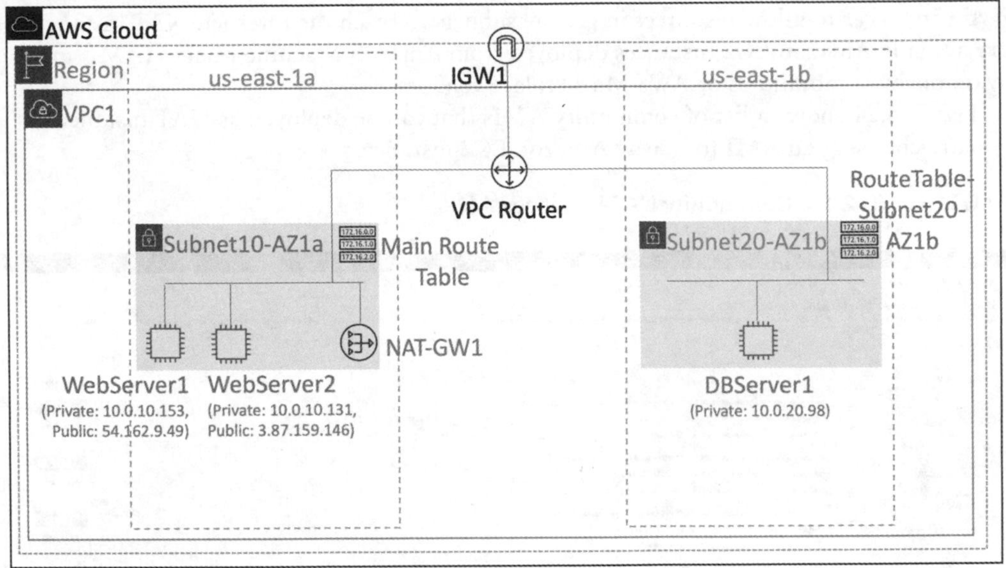

In Figure 5.19, DBServer1 does not have a public address because it is located on a private subnet (Subnet20-AZ1b). Therefore, traffic from DBServer1 has to first reach NAT-GW1 and from there be sent to the Internet using the NAT gateway's public IP address through IGW1 for the whole communication with a host in the Internet.

Figure 5.20 shows how Amazon CloudWatch automatically monitors traffic from DBServer1 flowing through NAT-GW1. You can access these statistics on the Monitoring tab of the NAT Gateways screen.

FIGURE 5.20 NAT-GW1 CloudWatch statistics

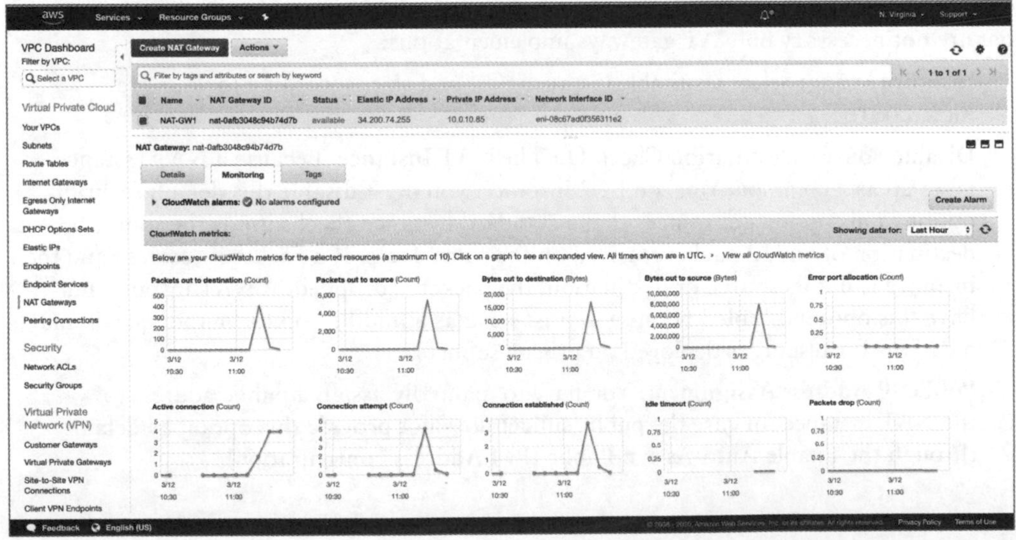

Unfortunately, life was not as easy before NAT gateways were presented on a screen in your VPC management console. Back then, you would have probably had to leverage *NAT instances* to allow resources in private subnets to reach the Internet. NAT instances are actually Amazon EC2 instances deployed from Amazon Machine Images (AMI) made available by communities or AWS Marketplace vendors.

Figure 5.21 shows a list of community AMIs that can be deployed as NAT instances as you are choosing an AMI for a new Amazon EC2 instance.

FIGURE 5.21 Community NAT instances AMIs

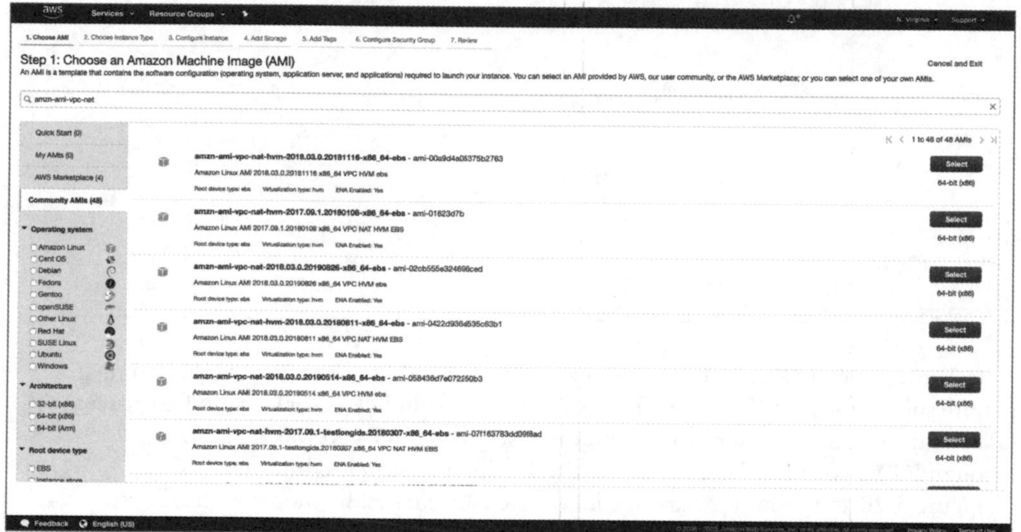

As you can see in Figure 5.21, all images that contain the string `amzn-ami-vpc-nat` in their names can be used as NAT instances. However, their straightforward deployment in a public subnet is not enough for these machines to be ready for their NAT duties. In fact, when you are deploying a NAT instance, you also have to execute the following actions that are not necessary on NAT gateways implementations:

- **Instance Sizing:** Select a suitable instance type and size, according to your predicted traffic.
- **Disable Source/Destination Check On The NAT Instance:** Because a NAT instance is set up as a common Amazon EC2 instance, you must disable this default security option. This option guarantees that a standard instance checks if it is the source or destination of any IP packet received on their interfaces. If a packet is received and the instance is not its source or destination, the packet is dropped. A NAT instance must have this option disabled because it *must* serve as a middle hop for outbound communications for resources deployed on private subnets.
- **Public IP Address Assignment:** You have to manually assign a public address to the NAT instance (in case the public subnet does not provide this option by default through the Enable Auto-Assign Public IPv4 Address configuration).

- **Security Group Assignment:** You have to associate this security construct to your NAT instance (and change it accordingly in the resources located in private subnets) to allow outbound traffic to the Internet. You will learn about security groups in the next section.

As a memory aid, Table 5.1 lists additional differences between NAT gateways and NAT instances from a design standpoint.

TABLE 5.1 Comparison between NAT gateways and NAT instances

Characteristic	NAT instance	NAT gateway
High availability	You have to resort to Auto Scaling groups, multiple subnets in different availability zones, and scripting to manage NAT instance failover.	You must implement a NAT gateway in each availability zone and create a zone-independent architecture with more than one private subnet.
Performance	It depends on the NAT instance type and size.	It can scale up to 45 Gbps.
Maintenance	You have to manage software updates and system patches.	AWS manages it for you.
Type and size	The choice is yours based on your predicted workload.	It is a single consistent offering.
Traffic monitoring	CloudWatch standard instance metrics.	Predefined CloudWatch metrics for NAT gateways.

For the reasons presented in Table 5.1, NAT gateways are considered more appropriate and secure for enterprise-class designs. However, not everything is a drawback when dealing with NAT instances. In fact, you must know about two exclusive characteristics these devices can implement that NAT gateways cannot:

- **Bastion Server:** NAT instances can be used as a primary access point from the Internet and act as a proxy to your Amazon EC2 instances located in your VPC. Consequently, you can log into a NAT instance (via SSH, for example) to access servers on private or protected public networks.
- **Port Forwarding:** NAT instances can be configured to steer inbound Internet traffic to resources on private subnets depending on the destination port the inbound connection is using. For example, a connection to the NAT instance public IP address using port 8000 can be configured to reach a database server listening on port 9000.

In Exercise 5.3, you will create two NAT gateways.

EXERCISE 5.3

Create NAT Gateways

Building on Exercise 5.2, you will create two NAT gateways.

1. Create two NAT gateways called **NAT-GW-A** and **NAT-GW-B** located at PublicSubnet-A and PublicSubnet-B, respectively. Do not forget to allocate elastic IP addresses for them.
2. Create two route tables: **PrivateRouteTable-A** (whose default route has NAT-GW-A as target) and **PrivateRouteTable-B** (whose default route has NAT-GW-B as target). Associate these route tables to PrivateSubnet-A and PrivateSubnet-B, respectively.
3. Create two free-tier Amazon EC2 instances (**DB-A** and **DB-B**) located at PrivateSubnet-A and PrivateSubnet-B, respectively. Prove that they are reaching the Internet via their corresponding NAT gateways.

Security Groups

You can think of a *security group* as a virtual firewall that controls inbound and outbound traffic on an elastic network interface (ENI) that belongs to an Amazon EC2 instance or another resource deployed on a VPC. An ENI is basically a virtual adapter card. Therefore, you can define rules in terms of IP addresses, transport protocols (TCP or UDP), and ports that will define which type of communication your instance can receive or transmit.

During the creation of the instances in the AWS Networking Constructs screen, you had to select (or even create) security groups. To provide communication with the exterior world (in the case of WebServer1 and WebServer2), this chapter uses a group called SG1, as shown in the Security Groups screen in the VPC management console in Figure 5.22.

As you can see in Figure 5.22, SG1 has three inbound rules that allow SSH, HTTP, and HTTPS to instances that are associated to it. Consequently, these rules allow TCP connections that use destination ports 22, 80, and 443, respectively. So, when you are adding inbound rules to a security group, you are actually allowing specific connections to reach instances associated to it. Moreover, in each security group, there is a hidden final rule that denies every other connection that is not defined in previous rules.

If you have a traditional security background, you are probably trying to draw analogies between this cloud networking concept and other security on-premises solutions. However, if you are comparing security groups to agent-based software firewalls, you must be aware that security groups are part of the AWS cloud infrastructure (more specifically, AWS hypervisors) and are not dependent on an operating system installed on an instance.

FIGURE 5.22 Security group SG1

aws Services Resource Groups N. Virginia Support

VPC Dashboard
Filter by VPC:
Select a VPC

Virtual Private Cloud
Your VPCs
Subnets
Route Tables
Internet Gateways
Egress Only Internet Gateways
DHCP Options Sets
Elastic IPs
Endpoints
Endpoint Services
NAT Gateways
Peering Connections

Security
Network ACLs
Security Groups

Virtual Private

Create security group Actions

Filter by tags and attributes or search by keyword 1 to 3 of 3

Name	Group ID	Group Name	VPC ID	Type	Description
	sg-0db0f8bc9453f1dca	SG1	vpc-07e3c3c933109f700	EC2-VPC	Allows SSH, HTTP, and HTTPS
	sg-0f7d3fb9a3500691e	default	vpc-07e3c3c933109f700	EC2-VPC	default VPC security group
	sg-d024a7b9	default	-	EC2-Classic	default group

Security Group: sg-0db0f8bc9453f1dca

Description Inbound Rules Outbound Rules Tags

Edit rules

Type	Protocol	Port Range	Source	Description
HTTP	TCP	80	0.0.0.0/0	Allows HTTP to the instance
SSH	TCP	22	0.0.0.0/0	Allows SSH for administrative pur...
HTTPS	TCP	443	0.0.0.0/0	Allows HTTPS to the instance

Feedback English (US) © 2008 - 2020, Amazon Web Services, Inc. or its affiliates. All rights reserved. Privacy Policy Terms of Use

Security groups are *stateful*, which means that return traffic from an allowed inbound connection is automatically permitted to leave the instance and you do not have to define a corresponding outbound rule to allow it. To illustrate this behavior, Figure 5.23 represents an HTTP connection as it reaches the WebServer1 instance.

FIGURE 5.23 Security groups and an inbound connection

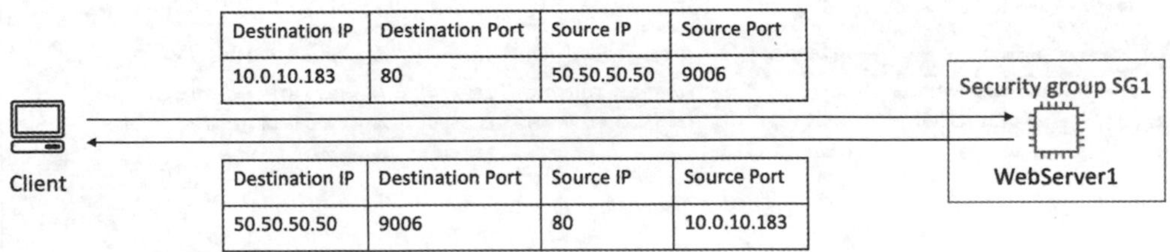

In the figure, SG1 allows the connection due to its destination TCP port (80). The return traffic, whose destination TCP port is 9006, is automatically allowed due to the stateful nature of the security group.

In this chapter's examples, SG1's outbound rules are left unchanged. They allow every single connection from the instances associated with this group, as Figure 5.24 shows.

Of course, because security groups are stateful, the return traffic for the outbound connections is automatically permitted. However, you can change the outbound configuration to limit outbound connections depending on your level of trust on the deployed instance.

FIGURE 5.24 SG1 outbound rules

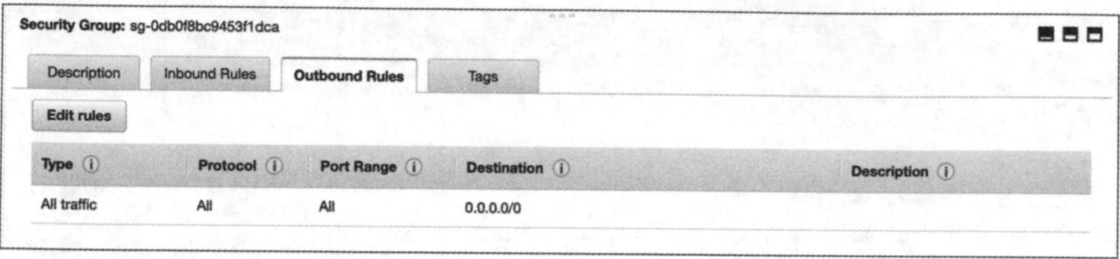

Through security groups, you can deploy the principle of *least privilege*, allowing only expected inbound and outbound connections and nothing else, and thus avoiding attacks and exploits that may generate unexpected traffic.

When you create an instance via the AWS Software Development Kit (SDK) or command-line interface (CLI) and you do not specify a security group, it will be automatically associated to a *default security group* (the AWS Console will ask you to choose the default security group or create one). This special group is shown in Figure 5.25.

FIGURE 5.25 VPC1 default security group

Create security group | Actions

Filter by tags and attributes or search by keyword — 1 to 3 of 3

Name	Group ID	Group Name	VPC ID	Type	Description
	sg-0db0f8bc9453f1dca	SG1	vpc-07e3c3c933109f700	EC2-VPC	Allows SSH, HTTP, and HTTPS
	sg-0f7d3fb9a3500691e	default	vpc-07e3c3c933109f700	EC2-VPC	default VPC security group
	sg-d024a7b9	default	-	EC2-Classic	default group

Security Group: sg-0f7d3fb9a3500691e

Description | Inbound Rules | Outbound Rules | Tags

Edit rules

Type	Protocol	Port Range	Source	Description
All traffic	All	All	sg-0f7d3fb9a3500691e	

As shown in the figure, the default security group (sg-0f7d3fb9a3500691e) has only one inbound rule allowing all connections but with an interesting kind of source: only from other instances that are associated with the *same security group*. Therefore, this rule allows free communication between instances *within* the same security group.

The outbound rule in the default security group is exactly the same as SG1 (all traffic allowed to any destination).

In Figure 5.25, you can also see that yet another default group exists: the *default EC2-Classic* (sg-d024a7b9). This term refers to the original release of Amazon EC2 service that was available before December 4, 2013. Before this date, you could deploy your instances in a single, flat network that you shared with other customers in the AWS Cloud. As a consequence, if you created instances before this date, you can still leverage such a security group for them.

Figure 5.26 exhibits the inbound rules that are defined in the EC2-Classic default security group.

FIGURE 5.26 EC2-Classic default security group

Create security group | Actions

Filter by tags and attributes or search by keyword | 1 to 3 of 3

Name	Group ID	Group Name	VPC ID	Type	Description
	sg-0db0f8bc9453f1dca	SG1	vpc-07e3c3c933109f700	EC2-VPC	Allows SSH, HTTP, and HTTPS
	sg-0f7d3fb9a3500691e	default	vpc-07e3c3c933109f700	EC2-VPC	default VPC security group
	sg-d024a7b9	default	-	EC2-Classic	default group

Security Group: sg-d024a7b9

Description | Inbound Rules | Tags

Edit rules

Type	Protocol	Port Range	Source	Description
All TCP	TCP	0 - 65535	sg-d024a7b9 (default)	
All UDP	UDP	0 - 65535	sg-d024a7b9 (default)	
All ICMP - IPv4	All	N/A	sg-d024a7b9 (default)	

As you can see in Figure 5.26, the EC2-Classic default security group has inbound rules distinct from the VPC security default group: it allows all destination TCP ports (from 0 to 65535), all UDP ports (from 0 to 65535), or all ICMP IPv4 packets to all other instances that share the same security group. Furthermore, the EC2-Classic default security group does not have any outbound rules (because it does not support them).

Of course, you can edit these security groups by creating new rules that will allow traffic to flow through them. Table 5.2 gives you a full picture of what parameters you can use to build a rule in a security group.

TABLE 5.2 Security group rules parameters

Parameter	Description
Type	Describes the protocol that will be allowed. You can choose well-known protocols, such as SSH, RDP, HTTP, or HTTPS. You can also choose to insert a custom TCP or UDP port, or even port ranges.
Protocol	Characterizes the type of transport protocol (TCP or UDP) or ICMP.
Port Range	You can manually enter a port number or a port number range.
Source (for inbound rules) or Destination (for outbound rules)	You can specify an IP address range in CIDR format (for example, 192.168.0.0/16 or 10.1.1.1/32, which represents a single IP address) or your own IP address. You can also specify the name or ID of another security group in the same region, as well as prefix lists. Only for EC2-Classic implementations, you can also specify a security group in another AWS account, using as its prefix the other account ID and a forward slash (example: 111122223333/OtherSecurityGroup).
Description	A string to provide insights for a security group rule.

You can deploy up to 2,500 VPC security groups per region. You can also have 60 inbound and 60 outbound rules per security group (making a total of 120 rules). A rule that references a security group or prefix list ID counts as one rule. Please check the AWS official documentation for complete and current information.

When you are deploying Amazon EC2 instances to subnets in your VPC, you can associate them to previously created security groups or one that you create. You can add up to five security groups per network interface. When you add two or more security groups to the same instance, the rules from each security group are effectively *aggregated* to create a unique set of rules as if they belonged to a single security group. The resulting ruleset will be equal or more permissive when compared to each of the original security groups. As an example, imagine that you create a security group **SG2** with the following inbound rules:

- Allow SSH from a single IP address 1.2.3.4
- Allow MySQL (TCP port 3306) from any source (0.0.0.0/0)

If SG1 and SG2 are associated to the same instance, the resulting set of rules instance would be as follows:

- Allow SSH (TCP port 22) from any source (0.0.0.0/0) due to SG1 permitting SSH from all sources
- Allow HTTP (TCP port 80) from any source (0.0.0.0/0), which is allowed by SG1
- Allow HTTPS (TCP port 443) from any source (0.0.0.0/0), which is also allowed by SG1
- Allow MySQL (TCP port 3306) from any source (0.0.0.0/0), which in turn is permitted by SG2

As you can see, security groups are a very powerful tool to control traffic to and from instances. But as you will learn in the next section, they are not the only resource you can use to provide traffic filtering within your VPC.

Because security group rules only *allow* traffic, the order in which they are inserted is not relevant.

As you may have noticed in Table 5.2, security group inbound rules specify source addresses whereas outbound rules specify destination addresses. Therefore, when you select Source/Destination Check, the destination for inbound rules and the source for outbound rules are tied to the ENI.

In Exercise 5.4, you will create two security groups and associate their instances.

EXERCISE 5.4

Create Security Groups

Building on Exercise 5.3, you will create two security groups and associate their instances.

1. Build a security group named **WebSG** that allows HTTP from any host on the Internet and only allows SSH from your own personal computer's public IP address.
2. Associate WebSG to instances Web-A and Web-B.
3. Build a security group called **DBSG** that permits inbound ICMP Echo requests and replies (also known as "pings").
4. Associate DBSG to instances DB-A and DB-B.
5. Test all communications defined in this exercise.

Network Access Control Lists

Network access control lists (NACLs) are network traffic control objects that act as firewalls when traffic enters or leaves a subnet in your VPC. You can add this extra layer of traffic filtering to avoid unexpected traffic between subnets *regardless of what you have actually deployed on them.*

In fact, the VPC you have created in the "AWS Networking Constructs" section had an associated NACL, as you can see on the Network ACLs screen in the VPC management console (Figures 5.27 and 5.28).

FIGURE 5.27 Default NACL inbound rules

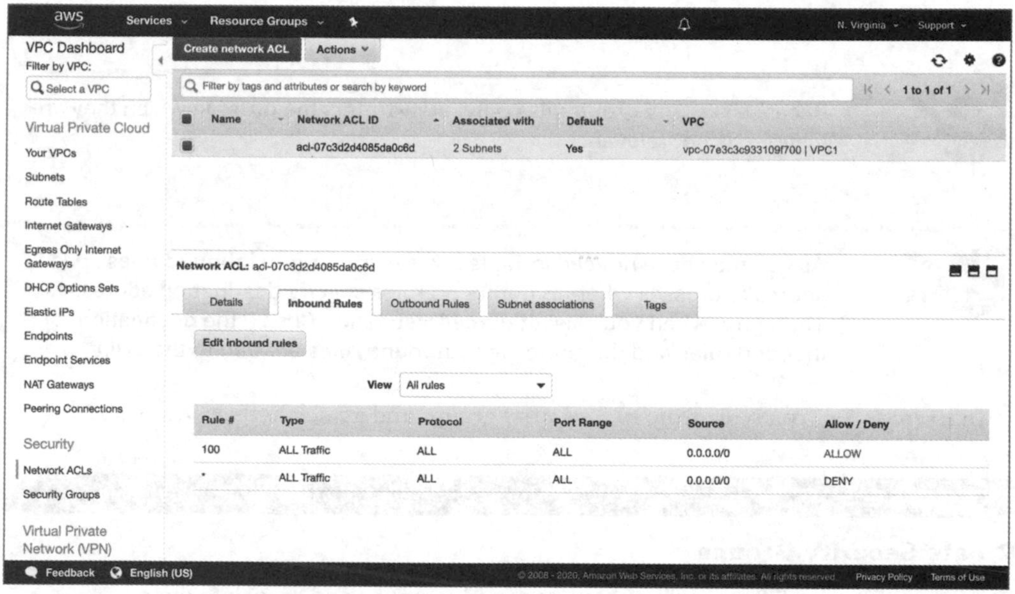

These figures show the inbound and outbound rules from VPC1 default network ACL (acl-07c3d2d4085da0c6d). Because you are already used to how security group rules are built, it will be easier for you to start noticing some of the differences between these security group rules and NACL rules. In both inbound and outbound rules of the default NACL, there are two rules:

- **Rule 100:** Allowing all traffic from all protocols, all port ranges, from any source
- **Rule *:** Denying all traffic from all protocols, all port ranges, from any source

The rule number (such as 100) defines how traffic will be filtered. In NACLs, each traversing packet is compared to each rule and, if there is a match, the action (allow or deny) is performed against that packet and the rule evaluation stops. In the case of the default NACL shown in Figures 5.27 and 5.28, all traffic is allowed in Rule 100, which makes Rule * (which is always the last rule) essentially useless.

FIGURE 5.28 Default NACL outbound rules

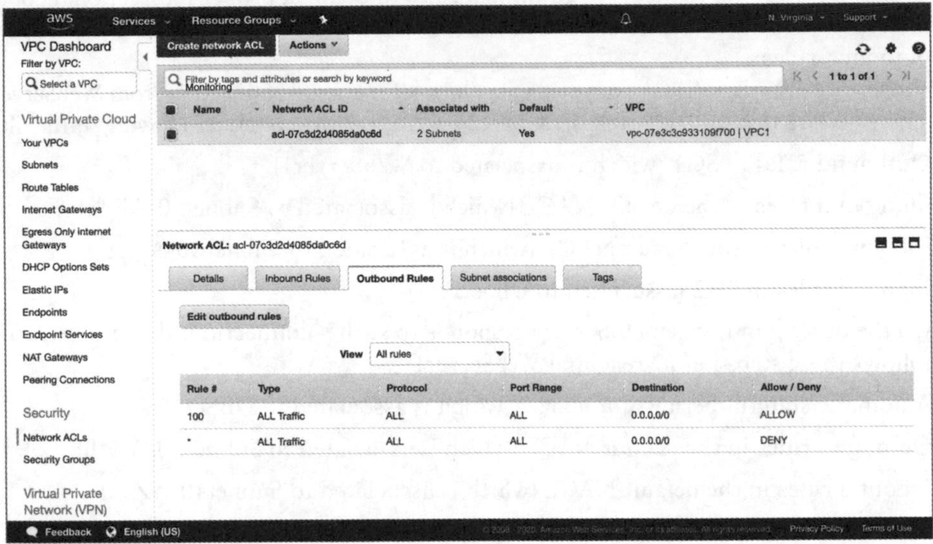

Also notice that you can change the rules of the default NACL at any time.

As its name implies, the default NACL is associated with all subnets. So, considering VPC1, Subnet10-AZ1a, and Subnet20-AZ1b, Figure 5.29 explains how the default NACL is positioned in the VPC1 network topology.

As you can see in Figure 5.29, NACLs are positioned at the border of VPC subnets. Such a mental model will be important when you are troubleshooting connectivity issues.

FIGURE 5.29 Network topology showing the default NACL

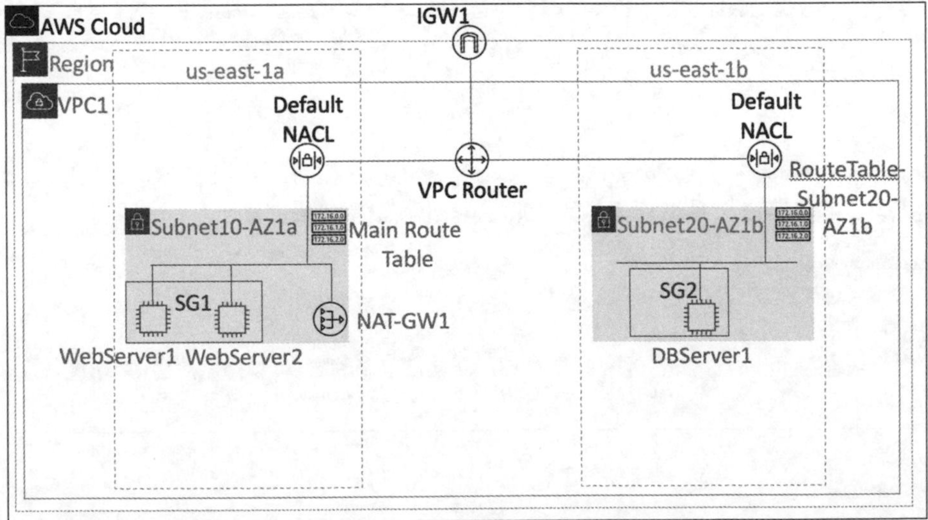

Contrary to security groups, NACLs are *stateless*, which means that return traffic must be explicitly allowed (or denied) via additional rules to define a proper bidirectional communication filter. Therefore, when building NACLs, you must be mindful of both inbound and outbound rules.

Using Figure 5.29 as a visual aid, you can see how a functional connection from WebServer1 in Subnet10-AZ1a toward DBServer1 in Subnet20-AZ2 goes through the following traffic filters:

1. Outbound rules in SG1 (which is associated to WebServer1)
2. Outbound rules in the default NACL (which is associated to Subnet10-AZ1a)
3. Inbound rules in the default NACL (which is associated to Subnet20-AZ1b)
4. Inbound rules in SG2 (associated to DBServer1)

   On the other hand, when DBServer1 responds to such a connection, the return traffic follows these steps before reaching WebServer1:

5. Automatic stateful permission in SG2 (which is associated to DBServer1)
6. Outbound rules in the default NACL (which is associated to Subnet20-AZ1b)
7. Inbound rules in the default NACL (which is associated to Subnet10-AZ1a)
8. Automatic stateful permission in SG1 (which is associated to WebServer1)

You will create an NACL that will be associated to Subnet20-AZ1b allowing specific MySQL communication from Subnet10-AZ1a, ICMP traffic for connectivity testing purposes, and also software updates from a specific IP address (1.2.3.4) on the Internet via HTTPS.

Figure 5.30 shows a new NACL called NACL1 immediately after its creation on the NACL screen (under the Create Network ACL button).

FIGURE 5.30 Recently created NACL1

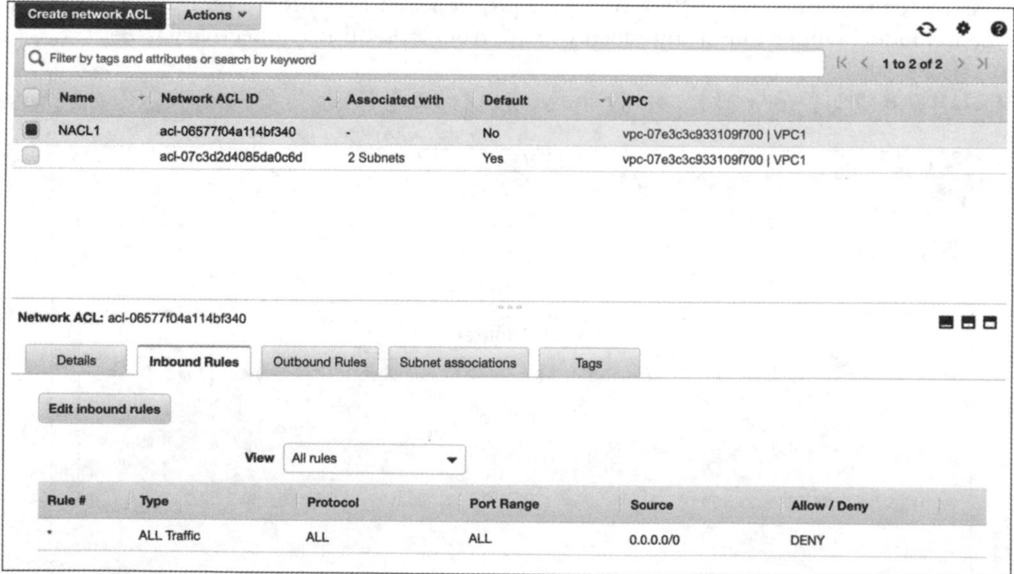

As you can see in Figure 5.30, the only inbound rule in NACL1 is the (explicit) final rule that essentially denies everything. Because NACL1's only outbound rule is the same, if you associate this NACL as it is to Subnet20-AZ1b, it will block any traffic from and to this subnet (which can be an extremely secure approach but not practical for real-world applications).

Consequently, to implement the aforementioned MySQL, ICMP, and software update traffic filtering, Figures 5.31 and 5.32 show the inbound and outbound rules you should add to NACL1.

FIGURE 5.31 NACL1 inbound rules

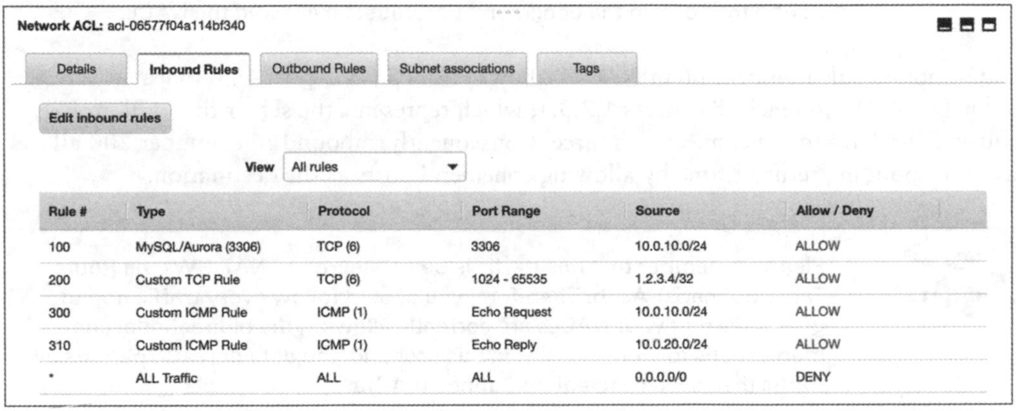

Network ACL: acl-06577f04a114bf340

Details | **Inbound Rules** | Outbound Rules | Subnet associations | Tags

Edit inbound rules

View All rules

Rule #	Type	Protocol	Port Range	Source	Allow / Deny
100	MySQL/Aurora (3306)	TCP (6)	3306	10.0.10.0/24	ALLOW
200	Custom TCP Rule	TCP (6)	1024 - 65535	1.2.3.4/32	ALLOW
300	Custom ICMP Rule	ICMP (1)	Echo Request	10.0.10.0/24	ALLOW
310	Custom ICMP Rule	ICMP (1)	Echo Reply	10.0.20.0/24	ALLOW
*	ALL Traffic	ALL	ALL	0.0.0.0/0	DENY

FIGURE 5.32 NACL1 outbound rules

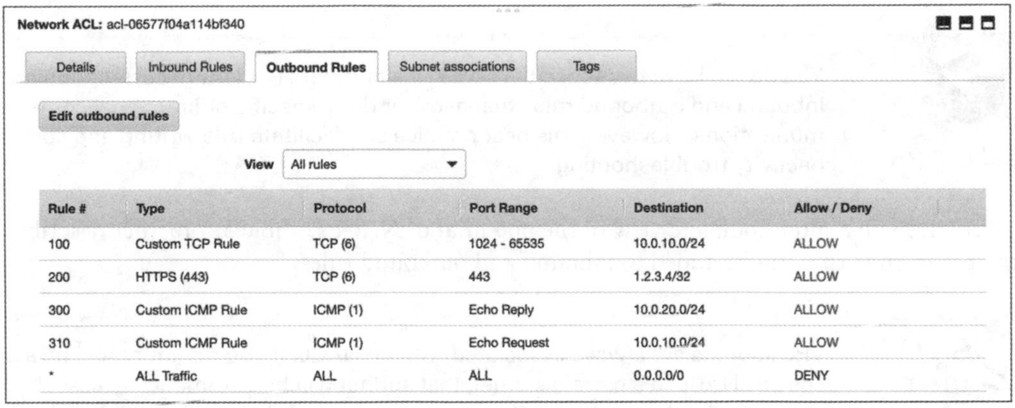

Network ACL: acl-06577f04a114bf340

Details | Inbound Rules | **Outbound Rules** | Subnet associations | Tags

Edit outbound rules

View All rules

Rule #	Type	Protocol	Port Range	Destination	Allow / Deny
100	Custom TCP Rule	TCP (6)	1024 - 65535	10.0.10.0/24	ALLOW
200	HTTPS (443)	TCP (6)	443	1.2.3.4/32	ALLOW
300	Custom ICMP Rule	ICMP (1)	Echo Reply	10.0.20.0/24	ALLOW
310	Custom ICMP Rule	ICMP (1)	Echo Request	10.0.10.0/24	ALLOW
*	ALL Traffic	ALL	ALL	0.0.0.0/0	DENY

It is important that you examine both figures to understand how the NACL's statelessness influences how the rules are built. Because NACL1 will be associated to Subnet20-AZ1b (via the Subnet Associations tab), try to focus on how the NACL allows MySQL/Aurora traffic between Subnet10-AZ1a and Subnet20-AZ1b: Inbound rule number 100 allows all TCP port 3306 traffic (which characterizes the aforementioned database traffic) from IP addresses on the prefix 10.0.10.0/24 (CIDR block from Subnet10-AZ1a). At the same time, outbound rule number 100 permits the return traffic, which is characterized by the use of *ephemeral ports* as destination TCP ports destined for subnet 10.0.10.0/24.

Ephemeral ports are random source port numbers that are generated in TCP connections or UDP communications. When a client establishes these communications with a server, an ephemeral port is chosen from the 1,024–65,535 range to be the client's source port. The designated ephemeral port then becomes the destination port for return traffic from the service, so outbound traffic from the ephemeral port must be allowed the NACLs.

Outbound rule number 200 in NACL1 allows HTTPS (TCP port 443) to leave Subnet20-AZ1b to reach IP address 1.2.3.4, which represents the server that will provide software updates to the connection source. Consequently, inbound rule number 200 allows its corresponding return traffic by allowing ephemeral ports as the destination.

Please remember that this traffic is being steered to NAT-GW1 via Route Table-Subnet20-AZ1b. Therefore, you should follow every traffic hop to guarantee that your NACLs are correctly allowing the bidirectional communications to work. Luckily, in this scenario, the default NACL permits all traffic that leaves and enters Subnet10-AZ1a.

Finally, rules number 300 and 310 were provisioned to allow ICMP Echo (Request and Reply) traffic from Subnet10-AZ1a to Subnet20-AZ1b, and vice versa.

You do not have to choose the same rule numbers to identify corresponding inbound and outbound rules that allow or deny specific bidirectional communications. However, this best practice can facilitate rule writing and connectivity troubleshooting.

To give you a more complete view of the potential of NACLs, Table 5.3 further describes the parameters that can be added to inbound and outbound rules.

VPC subnets are always associated with an NACL. If you do not associate a specific NACL to a certain subnet, that subnet will be automatically associated with the default NACL. You can associate an NACL with multiple subnets. However, a subnet can be associated with only one NACL at a time.

TABLE 5.3 Network ACL rules parameters

Parameter	Description
Rule #	Because rules are evaluated starting with the lowest numbered rule, when a rule matches traffic, it is immediately applied independently of any higher-numbered rule that may contradict it. You should create rules in increments (such as 10 or 100) to allow the later insertion of new rules where necessary. It can be in the 1–32,766 range.
Type	Type can be: Custom TCP rule, Custom UDP rule, Custom ICMP rule, Custom Protocol Rule, ALL TCP, ALL UDP, ALL ICMP – IPv4, ALL ICMP – IPv6, ALL Traffic, or specific protocols such as SSH, telnet, nameserver, DNS (TCP or UDP), HTTP, HTTP, POP3, IMAP, LDAP, SMB, SMTPS, IMAPS, POP3S, MS SQLS, Oracle, MySQL/Aurora, NFS, RDP, PostgreSQL, Redshift, WinRM-HTTP, WinRM-HTTPS, HTTP*, or HTTPS*.
Protocol	Characterizes the IP protocol number for the packets you are referring in the rule. It is automatically defined when you choose the rule type, except for Custom Protocol Rule, which allows the selection of different protocols such as ICMP, IGMP, or GGP, among others.
Port Range	Used on custom rules and protocols, in which you can enter a port number or a port range, such as 443 or 1024-65535.
Source (Inbound rules only) or Destination (Outbound rules only)	Determines the IP address or range that is allowed or denied by the rule via CIDR notation (10.0.10.183/32 for hosts or 10.0.10.0/24 for address ranges).
Allow/Deny	Where you define the rule action according to its characterized traffic.

In Exercise 5.5, you will create an NACL.

EXERCISE 5.5

Create an NACL

Building on Exercise 5.4, you will create an NACL.

1. Create an NACL named **PrivateNACL** that allows Oracle connections (TCP destination port 1521 with ephemeral ports as TCP source) and blocks ICMP Echo communication from PublicSubnet-A and PublicSubnet-B.
2. Associate PrivateNACL to PrivateSubnet-A and PrivateSubnet-B.
3. Test whether the ICMP communications between subnets are working.

Elastic Load Balancing

Server load balancers (SLBs) are network devices that have been present in data centers since the 1990s. These devices were created to provide the following services to applications:

Scalability Whenever an application server saturates one of its hardware resources (e.g., CPU, memory, storage, or connectivity), connected application users may suffer performance impacts such as a higher response time or service unavailability. In these scenarios, SLBs allow a group of application servers to share user requests in order to avoid this situation.

High Availability Even if an application server is not properly functioning, the SLB can direct user traffic to other servers without the users noticing any change.

Content Switching In certain occasions, users that access the same application should be treated differently. For example, a user accessing an application through a mobile device should have a different experience from one doing the same on a desktop. An SLB can analyze data above the Transport layer (such as browser type or complete URL) to determine the best server for each user.

AWS offers three types of server load balancing services under the name *Elastic Load Balancing*. These network services are used to distribute client traffic across multiple targets (such as Amazon EC2 instances or application containers) in distinct availability zones in order to increase application availability and scale.

Elastic Load Balancing implementations follow the same basic architecture, which is represented in Figure 5.33.

In this figure, the following configuration elements are identified:

Target Parameter that represents instances or IP addresses, as well as the transport protocol and port (HTTP, HTTPS, TCP, TLS, UDP) from AWS resources that will receive the connections Elastic Load Balancing is dispatching.

Health Checks Synthetic requests that verify whether an application is available on a server. These requests can leverage communication on HTTP, HTTPS, TCP, TLS, UDP, or even a combination of TCP and UDP.

Target Group A group of instances, IP addresses, or AWS Lambda functions that deploy the same application, use the same health check, and are balanced via a load-balancing algorithm such as *round robin* (each target receives a new connection per time) or *least outstanding requests* (the target with fewer associated connections receives the next connection). You can register a target with multiple target groups.

Listener Entity that checks for connection requests from clients, using the protocol and port that you configure. This configuration element is also informally called virtual IP (VIP).

FIGURE 5.33 Elastic Load Balancing architecture

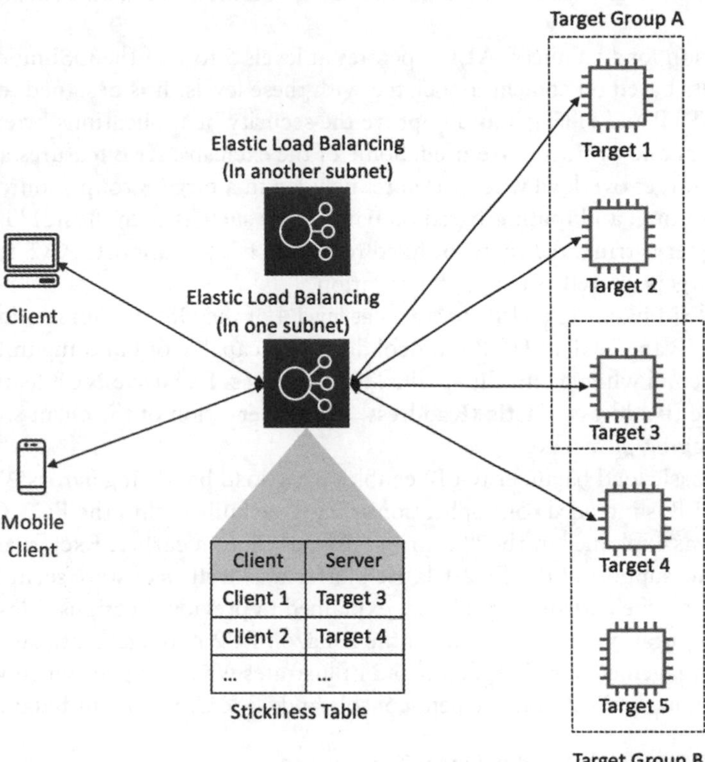

Stickiness An optional feature that enables Elastic Load Balancing to bind a user's session to a specific target. This ensures that all requests from the user during the session are subsequently sent to the same target. The stickiness can have a duration between one second and seven days.

AWS Elastic Load Balancing receives a user connection on one of its listeners and verifies whether the user is already registered in the stickiness table. If the user is not in the table, the elastic load balancer analyzes the target group associated to the listener and determines through health check results which targets have the application healthily working at that specific moment. Using the listener-configured load-balancing algorithm, the elastic load balancer selects the target that will receive the client request. Then, it records a client characteristic (such as IP source) and the selected target in the stickiness table and *splices* both connections (client to elastic load balancer and elastic load balancer to target) until the client receives its intended response from the load-balanced application. If the user is already registered in the stickiness table, the elastic load balancer repeats the splicing process with the preregistered target (meaning that it waives the target selection).

AWS Elastic Load Balancing supports three types of load balancers: *Application Load Balancer, Network Load Balancer,* and *Classic Load Balancer.* All of them support the following features: health checks, Amazon CloudWatch metrics, logging, availability zone failover, cross-zone load balancing, stickiness, SSL offloading, and backend server encryption.

An application load balancer (ALB) operates at levels 5 to 7 of the OSI model, routing traffic to targets based on content associated with these levels. It is designed to load-balance web traffic (HTTP and HTTPS) and improve the security of applications by ensuring that the latest ciphers and protocols are used. Some of the exclusive ALB features are slow start (to avoid target overload when they are included in a target group); source IP address CIDR-based routing; and routing based on parameters such as path, host, HTTP header and method, query string, redirects, or fixed response. It also supports AWS Lambda functions as targets as well as user authentication.

A network load balancer (NLB) operates at level 4 of the OSI model, routing connections based on IP and TCP or UDP protocol data. It is capable of handling millions of requests per second while maintaining ultra-low latencies. Exclusive NLB features include the use of static IP address, elastic IP address, and preservation of the client source IP address (for logging purposes).

Finally, a classic load balancer (CLB) enables basic load balancing across Amazon EC2 instances. A CLB is intended for applications that were built within the EC2-Classic network, which was explained in the "Security Groups" section earlier. Exclusive CLB features include the support of the EC2-Classic platform as well as custom security policies.

Contrary to all the networking services explained in previous sections, Elastic Load Balancing configurations are available on the Amazon EC2 management console and not on the VPC management console. Figure 5.34 illustrates what happens when you select Load Balancing in the EC2 management console and click Create Load Balancer.

FIGURE 5.34 Select Load Balancer Type screen

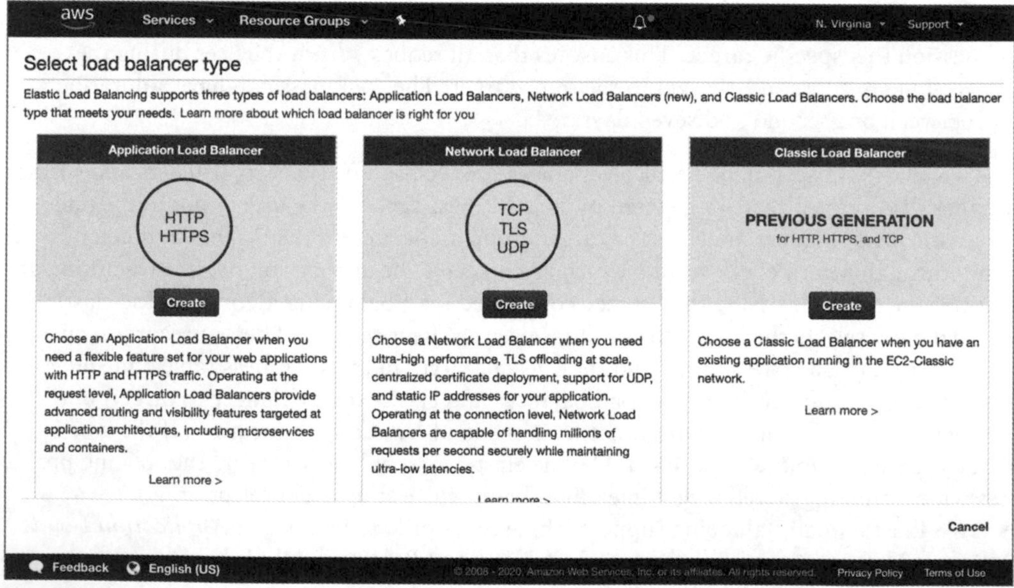

As an experiment, you will configure an ALB to further understand how Elastic Load Balancing works in a VPC. When configuring Elastic Load Balancing, you must start with the definition of at least one target group. Figure 5.35 shows the basic configuration of a simple target group called TG1.

FIGURE 5.35 TG1 basic configuration

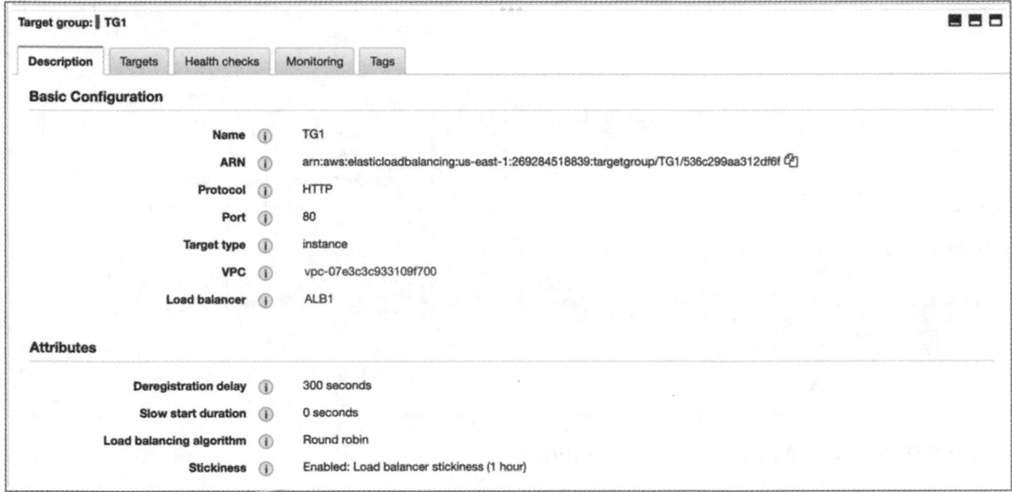

Figure 5.35 shows the group's name (TG1), protocol (HTTP), and TCP port (80) as well as a couple of attributes such as Deregistration Delay (the amount of time the ALB continues to send traffic to a target after it has been removed from this group), Slow Start Duration (whose value is 0 seconds, which means disabled), Load Balancing Algorithm (Round Robin), and Stickiness (which is enabled).

Figure 5.36 shows the registered targets that belong to TG1.

As you can see in Figure 5.36, there are three targets: WebServer1, WebServer2, and WebServer3, where the first two are located in AZ us-east-1a and the last one is instantiated in us-east-1b.

Now, you can finally configure an ALB. The configuration is shown in Figure 5.37.

Figure 5.37 shows the following ALB1 settings: AWS Resource Number (ARN), DNS Name (`ALB1-1534697530.us-east-1.elb.amazonaws.com`), State (Active), Type (Application), Schema (Internet-Facing, rather than internal), IP Address Type (ipv4), and VPC. More importantly, it shows that the ALB is installed in two different availability zones. In case one of them goes through a catastrophic failure, the ALB1 DNS name will direct user connections to the corresponding ALB1 listener IP address in the remaining AZ (without exposing such failure to users).

FIGURE 5.36 TG1 registered targets

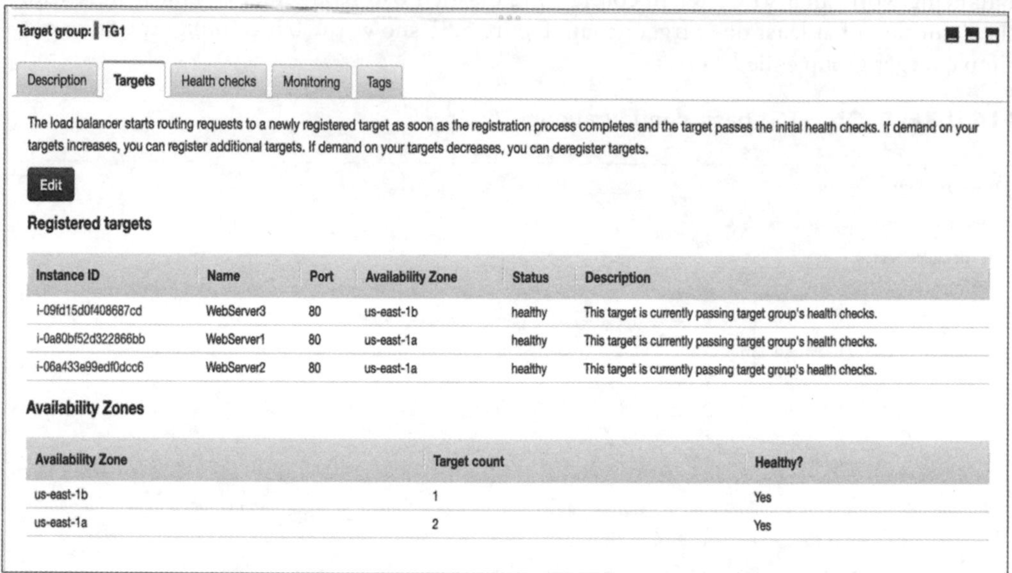

FIGURE 5.37 ALB1 Description settings

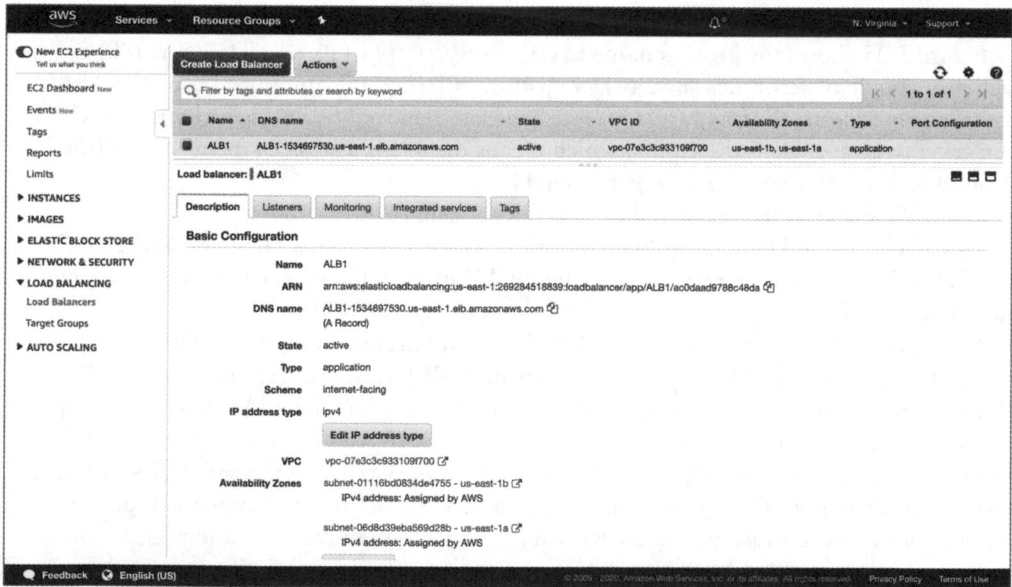

As you start to send HTTP traffic to the ALB1 DNS name, the application load balancer Monitor tab will show Amazon CloudWatch metrics such as Target Response Time, Requests, Rule Evaluations, HTTP 5XXs, HTTP 4XXs, ELB 5XXs, ELB 4XXs, and HTTP 500s. The same tab on the Target Groups screen will show you the following Amazon CloudWatch metrics: Unhealthy Hosts, Healthy Hosts, Target Response Time,

Requests, HTTP 5XX, HTTP 4XXs, Backend Connection Errors, and Target TLS Negotiation Errors. See Figure 5.38 for an example.

FIGURE 5.38 ALB1 Requests Amazon CloudWatch Metric

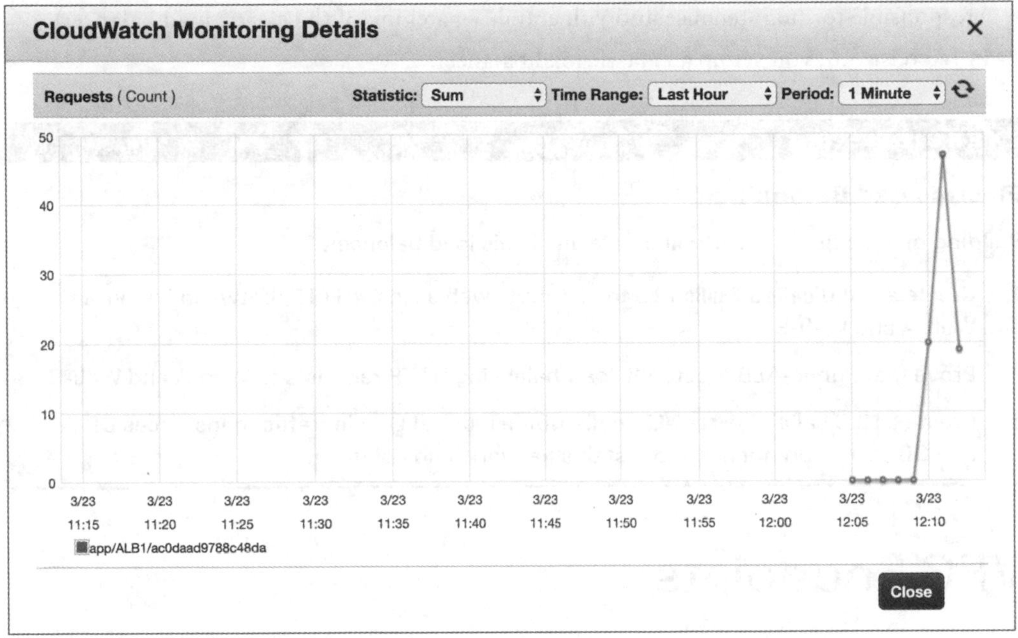

Finally, Figure 5.39 showcases how ALB1 is inserted in the topology that you have built during this chapter.

FIGURE 5.39 Network topology with ALB1

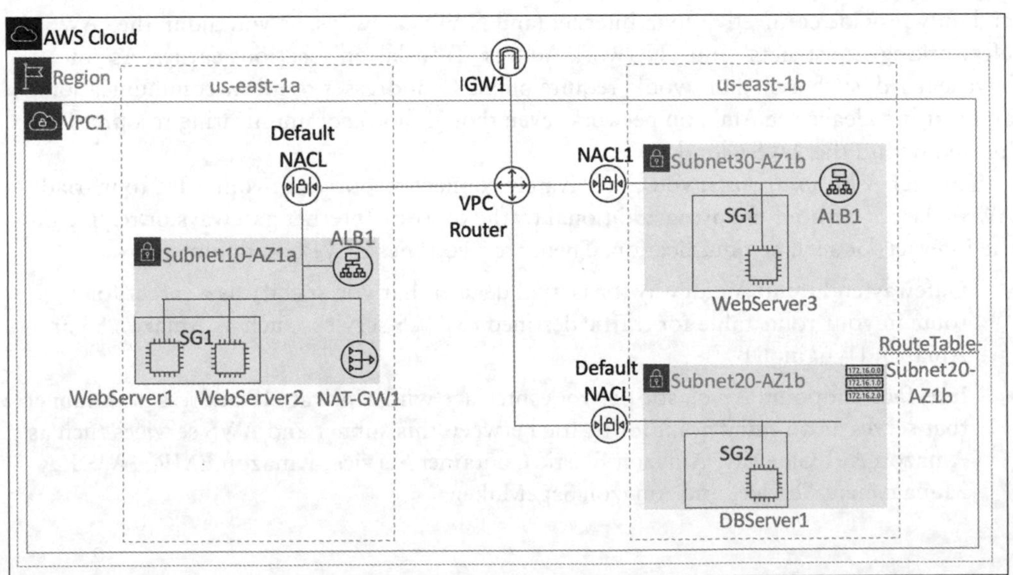

From a security perspective, ALB1 can provide the following benefits to the environment illustrated in Figure 5.39:

- Encryption offload to the web servers
- Operating system and web server isolation from nonconformant traffic (with AWS responsible for maintenance and vulnerability patching of the elastic load balancer)

In Exercise 5.6, you set up an elastic load balancer.

EXERCISE 5.6

Elastic Load Balancing

Building on Exercise 5.5, you will create an elastic load balancer.

1. Create an ALB called **Public-ALB** to distribute web access (HTTP) between instances Web-A and Web-B.
2. Prove that Public-ALB is actually load-balancing HTTP requests to Web-A and Web-B.
3. Create a NLB called **Private-NLB** to distribute internal Oracle traffic to instances DB-A and DB-B. You do not need to test this network load balancer.

VPC Endpoints

One of the main advantages of developing applications on the AWS Cloud is the inherent proximity to other computing, storage, and networking resources deployed in it. Nonetheless, there are different ways you can design internal connectivity for your different services deployed on AWS.

One approach you could adopt is to treat *anything* external to your VPC as the Internet and only provide connectivity via Internet (and NAT) gateways, as you did in the "AWS Networking Constructs" and "Network Address Translation" sections earlier. As you have learned, such a method would require public IP addresses to allow communication and traffic to leave the Amazon network, even though both communicating resources are located within the AWS Cloud.

Through *VPC endpoints*, you can privately connect resources in your VPC to myriad AWS services without imposing additional traffic on your Internet gateways or relying on the Internet for such communication. There are two types of VPC endpoints:

- **Gateway endpoint:** A gateway (or virtual device) that you specify as a target for a route in your route table for traffic destined to AWS services such as Amazon S3 and Amazon DynamoDB
- **Interface endpoint:** An elastic network interface with a private IP address on a subnet that serves as an entry point for traffic between this subnet and AWS services such as Amazon API Gateway, Amazon Elastic Container Service, Amazon EMR, AWS Key Management Service, and Amazon SageMaker

You will put such concepts in action to enable a direct connectivity to an Amazon S3 bucket from an Amazon EC2 instance in the topology you built. In such a scenario, Figure 5.40 illustrates the creation of a gateway endpoint.

FIGURE 5.40 VPC gateway endpoint creation

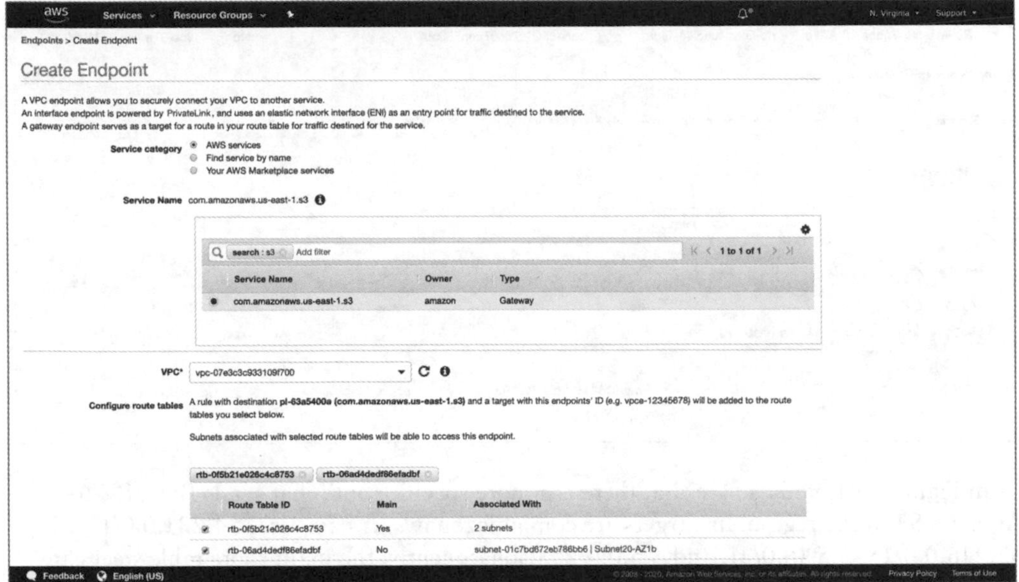

In Figure 5.40, you will notice that the following parameters are required for the gateway endpoint deployment:

- **Service Category:** This allows you to look for different methods to search for services to be connected to your VPCs. Its options include AWS Services, Find Service By Name, and Your AWS Marketplace Services.
- **Service Name:** The console helps you with the reverse DNS name of the service you will connect to using this VPC gateway. Figure 5.40 shows the Amazon S3 service in the N. Virginia region (com.amazonaws.us-east-1.s3).
- **VPC:** This drop-down list allows you to select the VPC where the VPC endpoint will be created (vpc-07e3c3c933109f700 represents VPC1 in our scenario, which will be different in your implementation).

The Create Endpoint screen allows you to define which route tables will be adjusted to detour traffic to this service. Figure 5.41 shows how VPC1's main route table was adapted to send Amazon S3 traffic through the VPC gateway you just created.

FIGURE 5.41 Updated main route table in VPC1

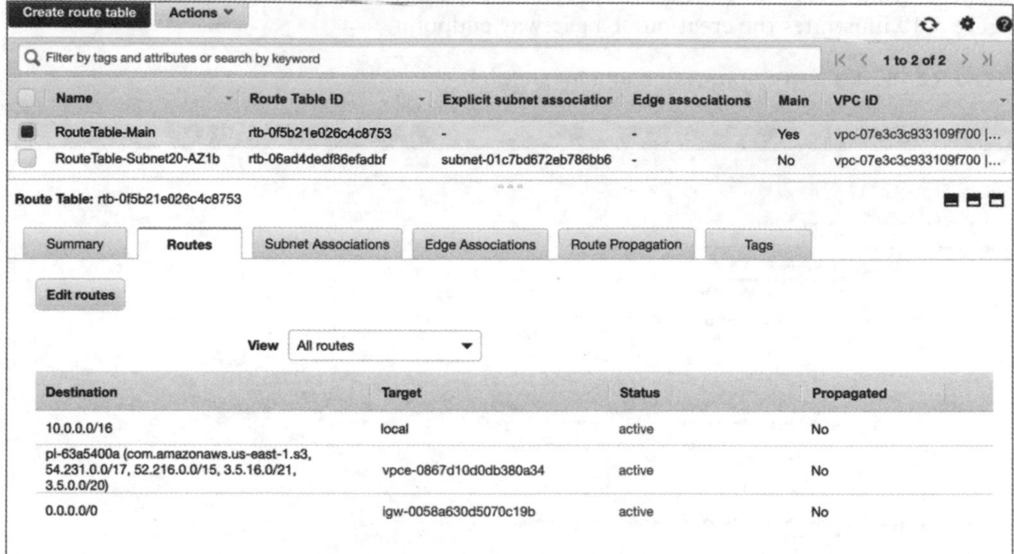

In Figure 5.41, you can see that there is a more specific route that sends IP traffic to Amazon S3 in the region. Its targets are com.amazonaws.us-east-1.s3, 54.231.0.0/17, 52.216.0.0/15, 3.5.16.0/21, and 3.5.0.0/20. Consequently, the main route table steers any IP packets with a destination among these networks toward this VPC endpoint (whose identifier is vpce-0867d10d0db380a34, in this scenario).

You can also create a VPC interface endpoint using a configuration similar to the one shown in Figure 5.42.

In Figure 5.42, you can see that similar parameters from the gateway endpoint are required for the interface endpoint creation: Service Category, Service Name, and VPC. The configuration includes the following:

- **Subnets:** Indicates where the elastic network interfaces will be provisioned
- **Enable DNS Name:** Enables the use of a private DNS name for this endpoint
- **Security Group:** Associates a security group with the endpoint's elastic network interfaces

FIGURE 5.42 VPC interface endpoint creation

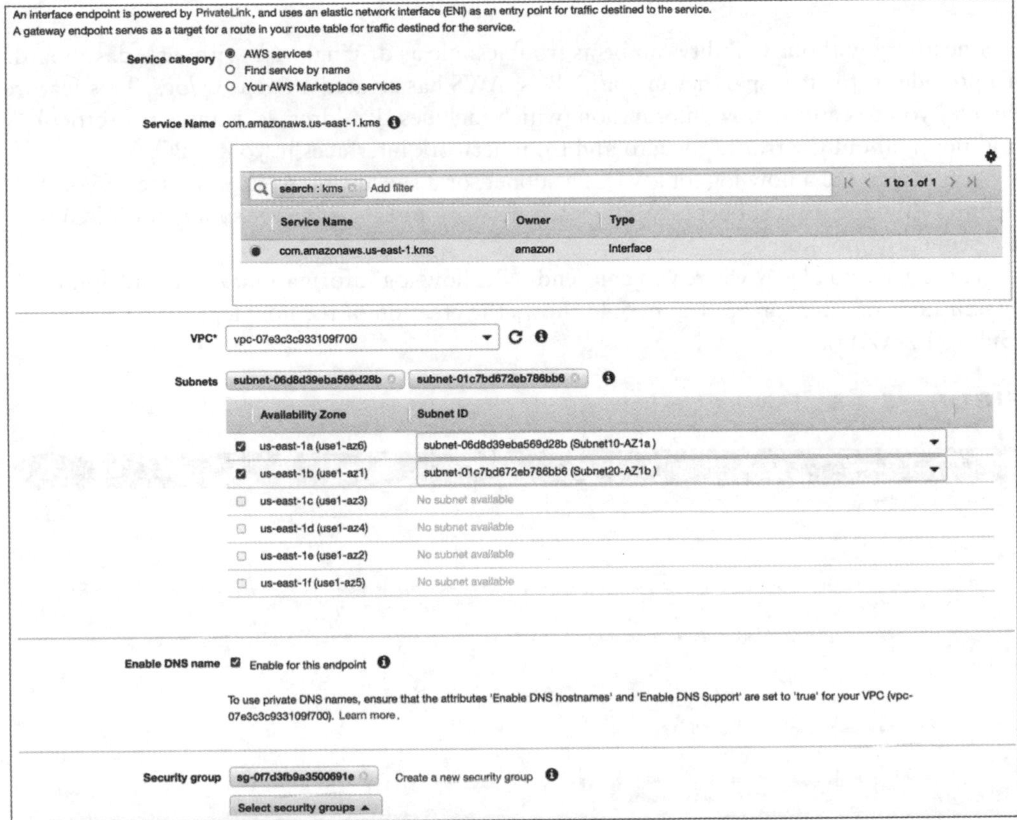

In Exercise 5.7, you will work with VPC endpoints.

EXERCISE 5.7

Work with VPC Endpoints

Building on Exercise 5.6, you will work with VPC endpoints.

1. Create a VPC gateway endpoint called **GW-EP** to connect PrivateSubnet-A and Private-Subnet-B to Amazon S3 in the region you have chosen.
2. Verify that Private-RouteTable-A and Private-RouteTable-B were changed to provide communication between the subnets and the VPC gateway endpoint.

VPC Flow Logs

Connectivity without visibility can be as troublesome as driving a car without a dashboard. To provide traffic transparency in your VPCs, AWS has created *VPC flow logs*. This feature enables you to capture flow information (which includes IP addresses, transport protocol, and ports) about the traffic going to and from network interfaces in your VPC.

You can create a flow log for a VPC, a subnet, or a specific network interface. If you define a flow log for a subnet (or VPC), each network interface in that subnet (or VPC) is consequently monitored.

There are two places where you can send VPC flow log information: Amazon CloudWatch Logs or Amazon S3. Figure 5.43 shows the creation of the flow logs for a subnet (Subnet10-AZ1a).

FIGURE 5.43 Flow log creation

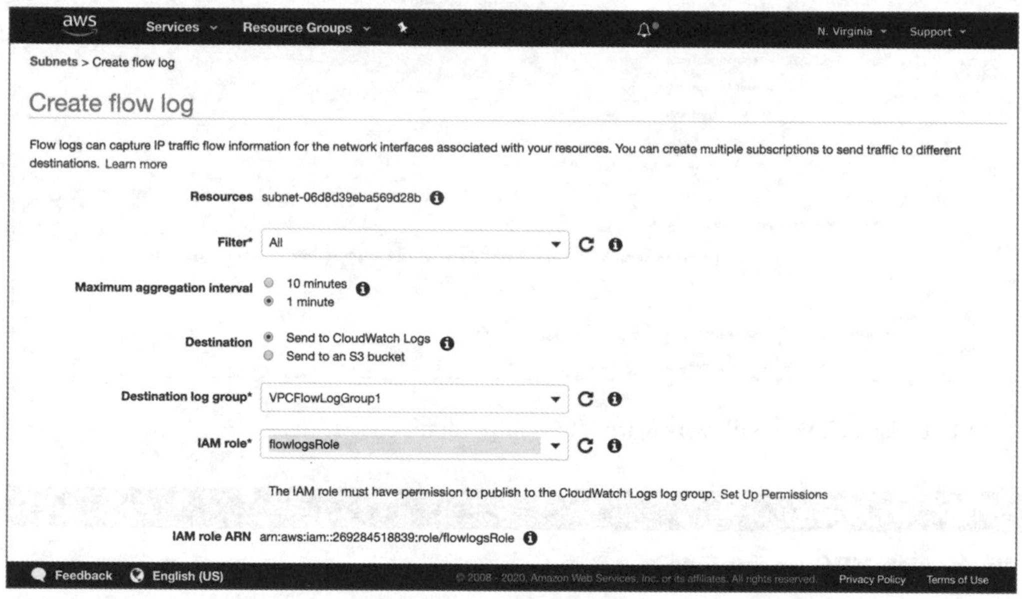

To access the screen shown in Figure 5.43 from the VPC management console, click Subnets in the menu at left and click the Create Flow Log button. You cannot enable flow logs for VPCs that are peered with your VPC (and their subnets) unless the peer VPC belongs to your AWS account.

Figure 5.43 shows the parameters required for AWS to log the IP traffic in this subnet:

- **Filter:** Choose All to log accepted and rejected traffic by the network interface, Rejected to record only blocked traffic, or Accepted to record only forwarded traffic.

- **Maximum Aggregation Interval:** This specifies the time interval during which a flow of packets is captured and aggregated into a flow log record.
- **Destination:** Options are Send To CloudWatch Logs and Send To An S3 Bucket.
- **Destination Log Group:** This specifies the name of the Amazon CloudWatch Logs log group to which the flow log is published. A new log stream is created for each monitored network interface (the figure shows VPCFlowLogGroup1 as the chosen name for the log group).
- **IAM Role:** This specifies the AWS Identity and Access Management role that has permission to publish to the Amazon CloudWatch Logs log group (flowlogsRole, in this scenario). You can create this role at this point by clicking the Set Up Permissions link.

You cannot change the configuration of a flow log after you have created it.

Figure 5.44 shows some flow logs generated via the previously specified configuration as they are visible on Amazon CloudWatch.

FIGURE 5.44 VPC flow log example

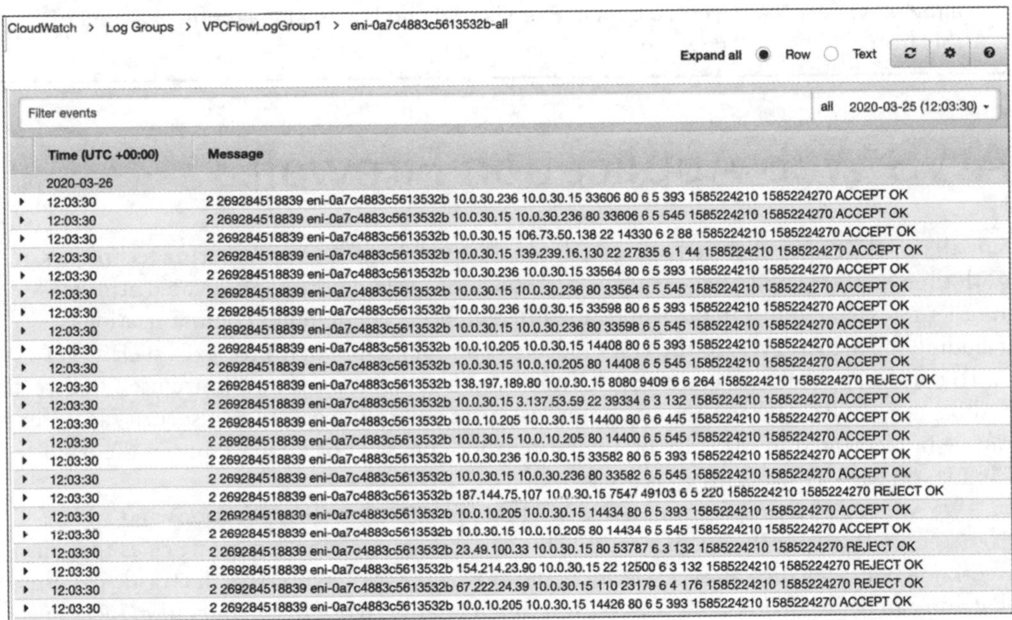

Time (UTC +00:00)	Message
2020-03-26	
12:03:30	2 269284518839 eni-0a7c4883c5613532b 10.0.30.236 10.0.30.15 33606 80 6 5 393 1585224210 1585224270 ACCEPT OK
12:03:30	2 269284518839 eni-0a7c4883c5613532b 10.0.30.15 10.0.30.236 80 33606 6 5 545 1585224210 1585224270 ACCEPT OK
12:03:30	2 269284518839 eni-0a7c4883c5613532b 10.0.30.15 106.73.50.138 22 14330 6 2 88 1585224210 1585224270 ACCEPT OK
12:03:30	2 269284518839 eni-0a7c4883c5613532b 10.0.30.15 139.239.16.130 22 27835 6 1 44 1585224210 1585224270 ACCEPT OK
12:03:30	2 269284518839 eni-0a7c4883c5613532b 10.0.30.236 10.0.30.15 33564 80 6 5 393 1585224210 1585224270 ACCEPT OK
12:03:30	2 269284518839 eni-0a7c4883c5613532b 10.0.30.15 10.0.30.236 80 33564 6 5 545 1585224210 1585224270 ACCEPT OK
12:03:30	2 269284518839 eni-0a7c4883c5613532b 10.0.30.236 10.0.30.15 33598 80 6 5 393 1585224210 1585224270 ACCEPT OK
12:03:30	2 269284518839 eni-0a7c4883c5613532b 10.0.30.15 10.0.30.236 80 33598 6 5 545 1585224210 1585224270 ACCEPT OK
12:03:30	2 269284518839 eni-0a7c4883c5613532b 10.0.10.205 10.0.30.15 14408 80 6 5 393 1585224210 1585224270 ACCEPT OK
12:03:30	2 269284518839 eni-0a7c4883c5613532b 10.0.30.15 10.0.10.205 80 14408 6 5 545 1585224210 1585224270 ACCEPT OK
12:03:30	2 269284518839 eni-0a7c4883c5613532b 138.197.189.80 10.0.30.15 8080 9409 6 6 264 1585224210 1585224270 REJECT OK
12:03:30	2 269284518839 eni-0a7c4883c5613532b 10.0.30.15 3.137.53.59 22 39334 6 3 132 1585224210 1585224270 ACCEPT OK
12:03:30	2 269284518839 eni-0a7c4883c5613532b 10.0.10.205 10.0.30.15 14400 80 6 6 445 1585224210 1585224270 ACCEPT OK
12:03:30	2 269284518839 eni-0a7c4883c5613532b 10.0.30.15 10.0.10.205 80 14400 6 5 545 1585224210 1585224270 ACCEPT OK
12:03:30	2 269284518839 eni-0a7c4883c5613532b 10.0.30.236 10.0.30.15 33582 80 6 5 393 1585224210 1585224270 ACCEPT OK
12:03:30	2 269284518839 eni-0a7c4883c5613532b 10.0.30.15 10.0.30.236 80 33582 6 5 545 1585224210 1585224270 ACCEPT OK
12:03:30	2 269284518839 eni-0a7c4883c5613532b 187.144.75.107 10.0.30.15 7547 49103 6 5 220 1585224210 1585224270 REJECT OK
12:03:30	2 269284518839 eni-0a7c4883c5613532b 10.0.10.205 10.0.30.15 14434 80 6 5 393 1585224210 1585224270 ACCEPT OK
12:03:30	2 269284518839 eni-0a7c4883c5613532b 10.0.30.15 10.0.10.205 80 14434 6 5 545 1585224210 1585224270 ACCEPT OK
12:03:30	2 269284518839 eni-0a7c4883c5613532b 23.49.100.33 10.0.30.15 80 53787 6 3 132 1585224210 1585224270 REJECT OK
12:03:30	2 269284518839 eni-0a7c4883c5613532b 154.214.23.90 10.0.30.15 22 12500 6 3 132 1585224210 1585224270 REJECT OK
12:03:30	2 269284518839 eni-0a7c4883c5613532b 67.222.24.39 10.0.30.15 110 23179 6 4 176 1585224210 1585224270 REJECT OK
12:03:30	2 269284518839 eni-0a7c4883c5613532b 10.0.10.205 10.0.30.15 14426 80 6 5 393 1585224210 1585224270 ACCEPT OK

VPC flow logs can monitor all IP traffic except Amazon DNS server traffic (although all other DNS server traffic can be monitored), Amazon Windows license activation traffic, instance metadata (169.254.169.254) traffic, DHCP traffic, and IP communication directed to the default VPC router's reserved IP address.

You can also create flow logs for network interfaces that belong to other AWS services, such as Elastic Load Balancing, Amazon RDS, Amazon ElastiCache, Amazon Redshift, Amazon WorkSpaces, NAT gateways, and transit gateways.

In Exercise 5.8, you will check how the VPC flow logs present traffic information in your system.

EXERCISE 5.8

Checking VPC Flow Logs

Building on Exercise 5.7, you will view the VPC flow logs.

1. Enable VPC flow logs in Secure-VPC.
2. Observe the flows in Amazon CloudWatch. Test the Echo Reply (ping) communication allowed via the NACL you've built in Exercise 5.5 and locate at least one example of this traffic in the VPC flow logs.

AWS Web Application Firewall

Not all attacks can be detected using traditional Layers 3 and 4 traffic filtering techniques. With time on their hands, hackers have continued to develop more sophisticated attacks in order to exploit vulnerabilities in many different facets of computer communications, including the higher layers of the OSI model to compromise popular protocols such as HTTP.

To defend applications against such attacks, web application firewalls are used to detect and block HTTP malicious activity. In on-premises environments, such a security feature can be implemented in software or appliances (both physical or virtual), but in the AWS Cloud, you can easily deploy it as a service.

AWS Web Application Firewall (AWS WAF) protects your web applications and APIs from known IPv4 and IPv6 web attacks. Through this service, you can create rules that block well-known attacks such as SQL injection and cross-site scripting, or specific traffic patterns that you can define. Within AWS WAF, you can filter any part of the web request, including IP addresses, HTTP headers, HTTP body, and requested uniform resource identifiers (URIs).

The most fundamental object in an AWS WAF implementation is the creation of a *Web Access Control List* (Web ACL). These objects are available on the WAF & Shield management console in the AWS Console.

Figure 5.45 shows the first step in the creation of a Web ACL creatively named WebACL1.

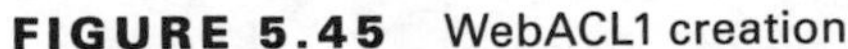

FIGURE 5.45 WebACL1 creation

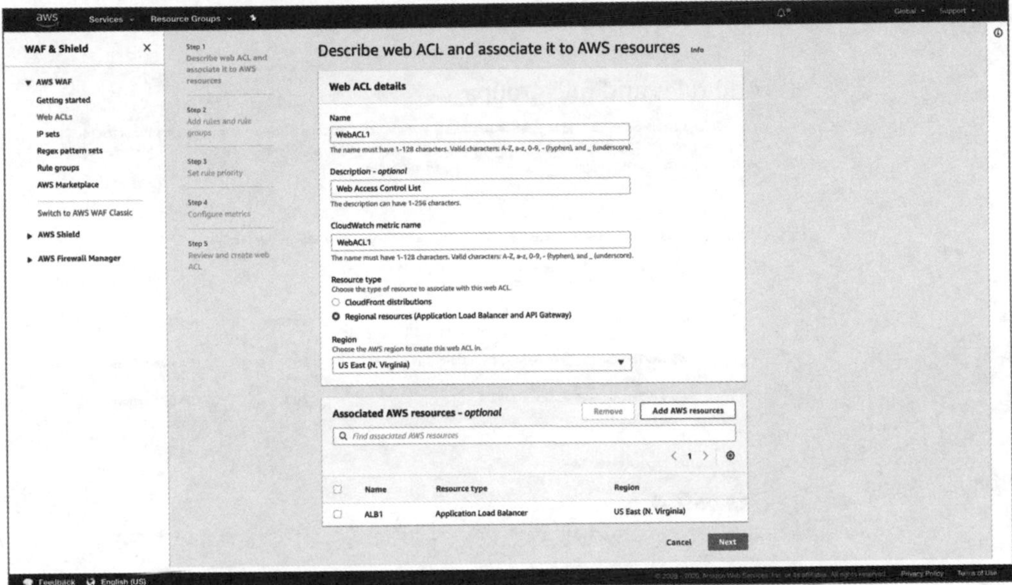

In Figure 5.45, you can already notice some important aspects of the WebACL1 creation. First, its scope is regional and it applies to region us-east-1. WebACL1 is regional because it is associated with application load balancer ALB1, which is firmly established in the Eastern US (N. Virginia) region. If WebACL1 was applied to an Amazon CloudFront distribution, it would have a *global* scope due to the nature of this service.

AWS WAF can also be associated to Amazon API Gateways and also, ingeniously, to Amazon CloudFront distributions that are serving websites that can be hosted outside of the AWS Cloud.

You can do more with WebACL1's configuration. You can add your own rules or *managed rule groups*. This refers to a preconfigured set of rules defined by AWS or AWS Marketplace sellers. These managed rule groups support protection against vulnerabilities defined on the OWASP Top 10 Security Risks, threats specific to content management systems (CMSs), or emerging Common Vulnerabilities and Exposures (CVE).

Figure 5.46 illustrates a configuration step that allows the addition of two managed rule groups.

The managed rule groups shown in Figure 5.46 are as follows:

- **Amazon IP Reputation List (AWS-AWSManagedRulesAmazonIpReputationList):** Contains rules that are based on Amazon threat intelligence to block sources associated with bots or other threats.

FIGURE 5.46 Adding rules to WebACL1

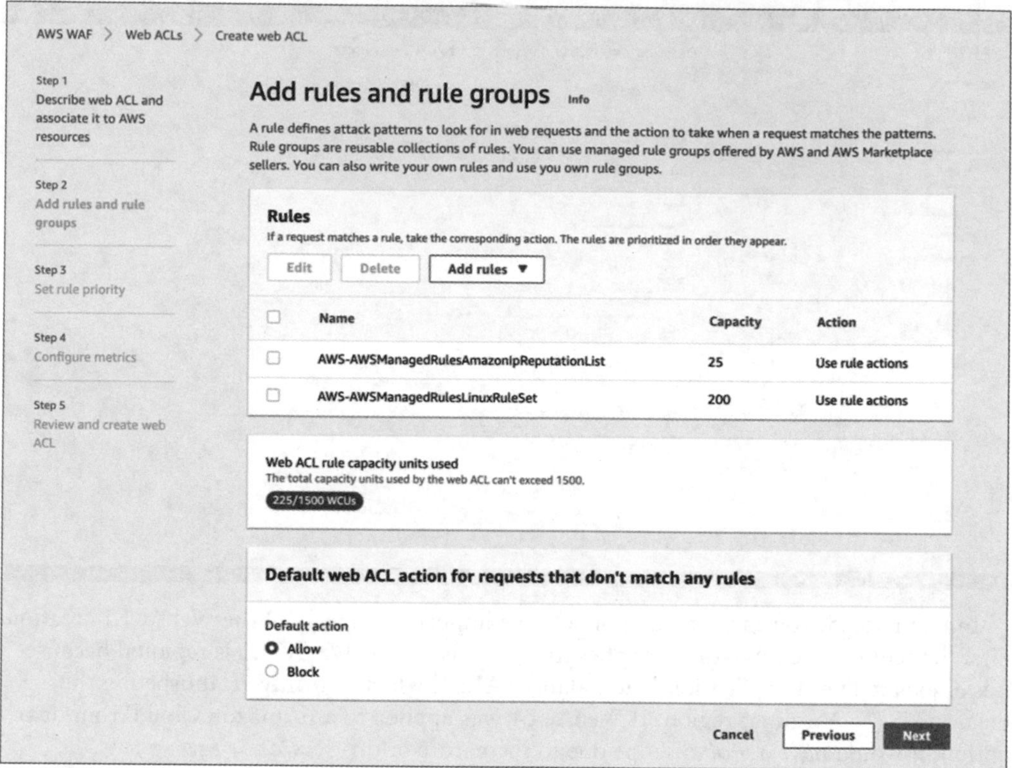

- **Linux Operating System (AWS-AWSManagedRulesLinuxRuleSet):** Specifies rules that block request patterns associated with exploitation of vulnerabilities specific to Linux. It can help prevent attacks that expose file contents or execute code for which the attacker should not have had access.

In Figure 5.46, you can also see that each of these groups has a defined *capacity unit* (25 and 200, respectively). Be aware that each web ACL has a limit of 1,500 capacity units.

You can also deploy 100 Web ACLs per region. There are also other quotas that you should be aware of, such as rule groups (100 per region), IP sets (100 per region), and requests per second per web ACL deployed on an ALB (25,000 per region). Please check the AWS official documentation for complete and current information.

Figure 5.46 shows Allow as the *default action* WebACL1 should take if a web request does not match any of the managed rule groups previously discussed.

In order to make this web ACL even more interesting, you can also create your own rules and rule groups. Figure 5.47 illustrates the creation of a custom rule called BlockAdminPages.

FIGURE 5.47 BlockAdminPages custom rule creation

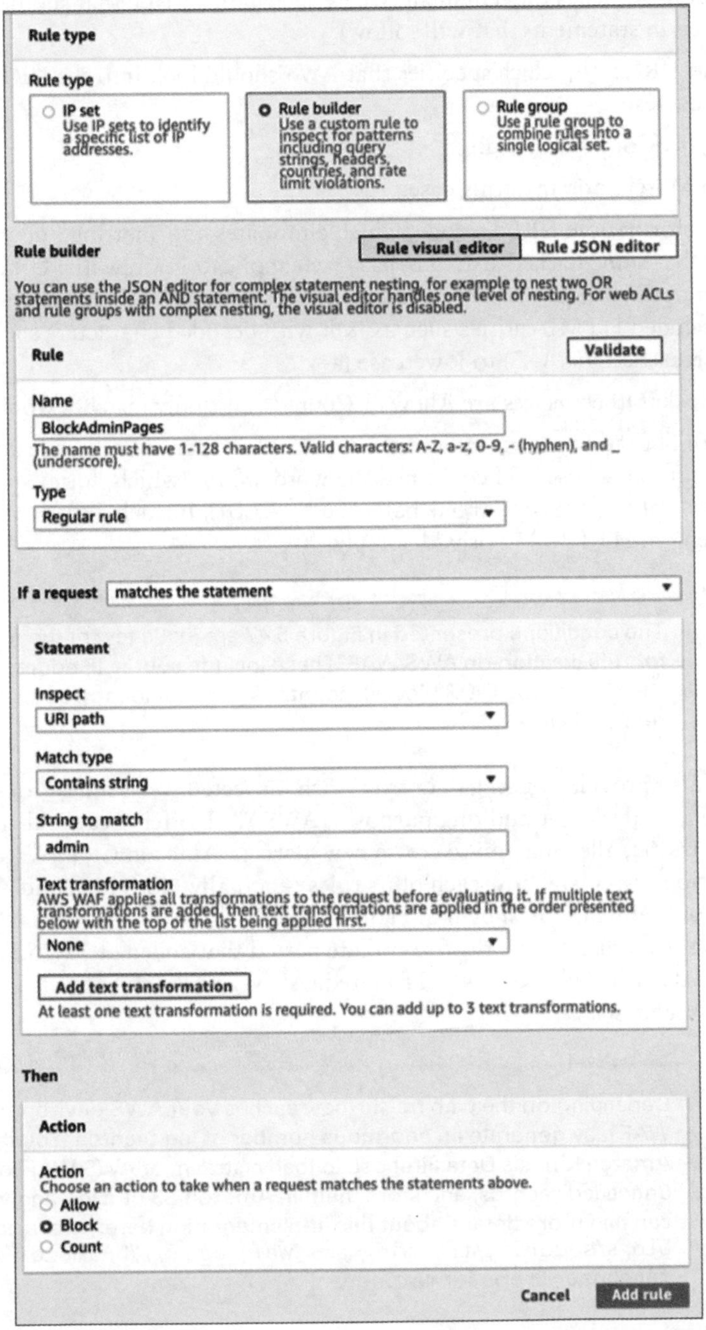

Rule type

Rule type

IP set
Use IP sets to identify a specific list of IP addresses.

Rule builder
Use a custom rule to inspect for patterns including query strings, headers, countries, and rate limit violations.

Rule group
Use a rule group to combine rules into a single logical set.

Rule builder

Rule visual editor | Rule JSON editor

You can use the JSON editor for complex statement nesting, for example to nest two OR statements inside an AND statement. The visual editor handles one level of nesting. For web ACLs and rule groups with complex nesting, the visual editor is disabled.

Rule

Validate

Name

BlockAdminPages

The name must have 1-128 characters. Valid characters: A-Z, a-z, 0-9, - (hyphen), and _ (underscore).

Type

Regular rule

If a request: matches the statement

Statement

Inspect

URI path

Match type

Contains string

String to match

admin

Text transformation

AWS WAF applies all transformations to the request before evaluating it. If multiple text transformations are added, then text transformations are applied in the order presented below with the top of the list being applied first.

None

Add text transformation

At least one text transformation is required. You can add up to 3 text transformations.

Then

Action

Action

Choose an action to take when a request matches the statements above.

Allow

Block

Count

Cancel | Add rule

In Figure 5.47, you can see the following parameters for the creation of this rule:

- **Name:** `BlockAdminPages` string.
- **Type:** Regular Rule, which will resort to string recognition.
- **If A Request:** Matches the statement (where the characteristic that should be matched is described in statements that will follow).
- **Statement:** URI path, which specifies that AWS should look into the URIs of HTTP accesses.
- **Match Type:** Contains String.
- **String To Match:** `admin` in this case.
- **Text Transformation:** URL Decode, which eliminates a formatting known as URL encoding that some hackers use to bypass web application firewalls. Other text transformation options can be added in case you want AWS WAF to compress whitespace, replace encoded HTML entities such as (&)lt with decoded characters such as <, or convert uppercase letters (A–Z) to lowercase (a–z).
- **Action:** Block. Other choices are Allow or Count (where only matches would be counted).

With the configuration shown in Figure 5.47, the BlockAdminPages rule actually obstructs all requests whose URI contained the word *admin* (which, for example, could refer to administrative pages on targets balanced by ALB1). In such a scenario, blocked web accesses are sent an HTTP 403 Forbidden reply.

The conditions presented in Figure 5.47 are just a few of the many available for rule creation on AWS WAF. These include source IP addresses (in /8, /16, /24, and /32 CIDR blocks), countries, request length, and specific HTTP request headers.

AWS WAF also provides logging data from each inspected web request for use in security automation, analytics, or auditing purposes. AWS WAF offers near real-time visibility into your web traffic, allowing you to create new alerts in Amazon CloudWatch. In the case of WebACL1, you can follow how each of its rules is actually "hit" in CloudWatch or in the Overview tab of WebACL1, as shown in Figure 5.48.

Figure 5.48 shows that during the five-minute period that ended at 12:25 P.M. on March 30, 2020, WebACL1 had blocked 148 HTTP requests via its BlockAdminPages custom rule and allowed 33 requests.

Depending on the web traffic that reaches your AWS environment, AWS WAF may generate an enormous number of log records. You can use Amazon Kinesis Data Firehose to load a stream of AWS WAF logging, filter unneeded records, and store them in Amazon S3 or a log analysis tool. You can find more details about this implementation here: `aws.amazon.com/blogs/security/trimming-aws-waf-logs-with-amazon-kinesis-firehose-transformations`.

FIGURE 5.48 WebACL1 Overview graph

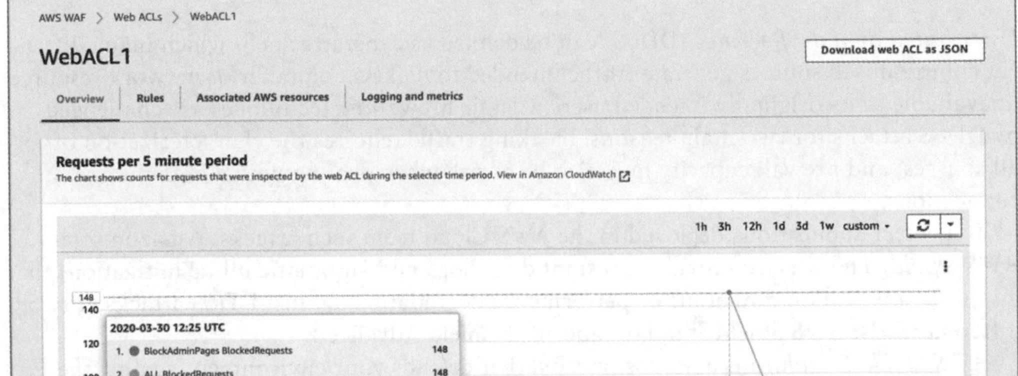

AWS WAF also includes a full-featured API that you can use to automate the creation, deployment, and maintenance of security rules.

In Exercise 5.9, you will create and test a firewall.

EXERCISE 5.9

Create and Test an AWS Web Application Firewall

Building on Exercise 5.8, you will work with an AWS WAF.

1. Create an AWS WAF Web ACL called **Web-ACL** with one managed group rule of your choice and a blocking default action and associate it to Public-ALB, which you created in Exercise 5.6.
2. Test the access to Public-ALB several times in your browser.
3. Create a custom rule allowing HTTP web access to Public-ALB.
4. Again, test the access to Public-ALB several times in your browser.
5. Check both test results via a graphical diagram.

AWS Shield

Distributed denial-of-service (DDoS) can be defined as cyberattacks in which many different compromised sources generate traffic intended to make a computer or network resource unavailable to its originally intended users. Classic firewalling techniques are challenged by DDoS attacks for two main reasons: blocking traffic requires the characterization of all sources, and firewall capacity may also be at risk when dealing with a high number of connections.

To protect applications deployed in the AWS Cloud from such attacks, Amazon offers *AWS Shield*. This service provides constant detections and automatic inline mitigations that minimize application downtime or performance degradation against DDoS attacks at two different levels: AWS Shield Standard and AWS Shield Advanced.

AWS Shield Standard is a no-cost version that defends your environment against the most common Network (Layer 3) and Transport (Layer 4) known infrastructure attacks when you use Amazon CloudFront and Amazon Route 53. It relies on detection techniques such as network flow monitoring, a combination of traffic signatures, and anomaly algorithms. Additionally, it mitigates attacks through inline mechanisms, which include deterministic packet filtering, priority-based traffic shaping, and rules in AWS Web Application Firewall. And more importantly, AWS Shield Standard is activated by default in all AWS accounts.

AWS Shield Advanced enables additional detection and mitigation against larger and more sophisticated DDoS attacks on Amazon EC2, Elastic Load Balancing, Amazon CloudFront, AWS Global Accelerator, and Amazon Route 53. AWS Shield Advanced provides the following distinct features:

- **Near real-time visibility and reporting:** With Layers 3 and 4 attack notifications and attack forensic reports as well as Layer 3, 4, and 7 attack historical reports.
- **Integration with AWS WAF:** You can respond to incidents as they occur via customizable rules that you can deploy instantly in AWS WAF (which is also included in AWS Shield Advanced at no extra cost) to quickly mitigate attacks.
- **24/7 access to the AWS DDoS Response Team (DRT):** For manual mitigation of edge cases affecting your availability such as custom rules intended to mitigate application layer DDoS attacks in your environments.
- **Cost protection:** Against DDoS-related cost spikes in AWS Shield Advanced protected resources, with reimbursement related to Amazon EC2, Elastic Load Balancing, Amazon Route 53, Amazon CloudFront, and AWS Global Accelerator.

AWS Shield Advanced provides enhanced detection through network flow inspection, resource specific monitoring, resource and region-specific granular detection of DDoS attacks, Application layer DDoS attacks like HTTP floods or DNS query floods by baselining traffic, and identification of anomalies. It offers advanced attack mitigation via routing techniques, DRT manual mitigations, and attack notifications via Amazon CloudWatch, as well as postattack analysis.

AWS Shield Advanced is not activated by default. As of this writing, AWS charges $3,000 per month (with a 12-month commitment) for AWS Shield Advanced plus additional data transfer fees.

Summary

As infrastructure evolves from manual configurations in on-premises data centers to automated functions in cloud computing, infrastructure security is developing accordingly. In the AWS Cloud, objects such as Amazon VPC, subnets, route tables, Internet gateways, and NAT gateways help millions of users deploy their network topologies with simplicity and agility. Furthermore, traffic filter techniques such as security groups and NACLs allow fine-grained traffic control within these topologies in order to protect resources from unexpected connections.

Infrastructure protection in the AWS Cloud is further reinforced by the following services:

- **AWS Elastic Load Balancing:** Provides scalability, high availability, and content switching to your applications deployed in Amazon EC2 instances, containers, or AWS Lambda functions
- **VPC Endpoints:** Provide direct connectivity between your VPCs and AWS Cloud services you have deployed in the same region
- **VPC Flow Logs:** Enable historical traffic visibility in your VPCs, subnets, or network interfaces
- **AWS Web Application Firewall:** Protects your applications against well-known web attacks through the identification of data in the higher layers of the OSI model
- **AWS Shield:** Defends your applications against DDoS attacks with two levels of protection (AWS Shield Standard and AWS Shield Advanced)

Exam Essentials

Know the AWS main network constructs. The Amazon *VPC* (Virtual Private Cloud) represents a virtual network within the AWS Cloud. VPCs were created to isolate cloud resources from other systems, networks, or accounts. Within these abstractions, one or more CIDR blocks are distributed among subnets, which characterize a range of IP addresses in a VPC. Each subnet has assigned traffic policies such as a route table, which defines how IP traffic will be handled by the VPC router. A subnet belongs to a single availability zone, and their design must take application high availability into account. An Internet gateway provides a target in route tables for Internet-routable traffic.

Understand the various methods of network address translation (NAT). Although Internet gateways can provide NAT services to resources located in public subnets, other methods of IP address translation are used for instances and other cloud resources located in private subnets. NAT gateways are enterprise-class specialized virtual devices that AWS manages to enable NAT services in such scenarios. NAT instances are Amazon EC2 instances developed by communities and AWS Marketplace vendors to also provide NAT services. When compared to NAT gateways, NAT instances require additional care from an infrastructure and operations standpoint.

Understand the differences between security groups and NACLs. There are two main ways of implementing traffic filtering within an Amazon VPC. Security groups are a set of inbound and outbound stateful rules that control traffic on elastic network interfaces (ENIs) that belong to Amazon EC2 instances or other cloud resources (such as VPC interface endpoints) in terms of IP addresses as well as transport protocols and ports. NACLs are traffic filters that control traffic that traverses from one subnet to another through inbound and outbound stateless rules.

Understand how Elastic Load Balancing works. AWS provides Elastic Load Balancing as a network service to ensure application scalability, high availability, and forwarding decisions based on higher-layer information from user requests. AWS Cloud currently offers Elastic Load Balancing in three different formats: application load balancer (ALB), network load balancer (NLB), and classic load balancer (CLB).

Know about VPC endpoints. VPC endpoints enable direct connectivity, within the Amazon network, between resources in your VPC and other AWS Cloud services. They are available in two different types: interface endpoint and gateway endpoint. An interface endpoint is an elastic network interface that extends a private IP address from a subnet to services such as Amazon API Gateway and AWS Key Management Service (KMS). A gateway endpoint is a virtual device that offers a route target to AWS services such as Amazon S3 and Amazon DynamoDB.

Understand VPC flow logs. VPC flow logs provide traffic capture on network interfaces from specific AWS services (such as Amazon EC2, Elastic Load Balancing, Amazon RDS, Amazon ElastiCache, Amazon Redshift, Amazon WorkSpaces, NAT gateways, and transit gateways), subnets, or VPCs. You can send and review VPC flow logs in two different places: Amazon CloudWatch Logs or Amazon S3.

Be familiar with the AWS Web Application Firewall. AWS WAF protects web applications and APIs from known higher-layer attacks that exploit systems via HTTP and HTTPs malicious activity. The service leverages web ACLs (with managed and custom rules) that are applied to application load balancers, Amazon API gateways, or Amazon CloudFront distributions.

Understand AWS Shield and its offerings. AWS Shield protects applications deployed in the AWS Cloud from DDoS attacks with two different levels of services: AWS Shield Standard and AWS Shield Advanced.

Review Questions

1. Read the following statements and choose the correct option:

   I. A VPC can extend beyond AWS regions.

   II. A VPC can extend beyond AWS availability zones.

   III. A subnet can extend beyond AWS availability zones.

   A. I, II, and III are correct.

   B. Only I is correct.

   C. Only II is correct.

   D. Only III is correct.

2. Considering that you gave the CIDR block 172.16.100.128/25 to a subnet, which option is correct?

   A. The IP address of the VPC router is 172.16.100.128.

   B. The IP address of the DNS server is 172.16.100.130.

   C. The IP address 172.16.100.131 is the first one available for use in the subnet.

   D. You cannot assign this CIDR block to a subnet.

3. Read the following statements and choose the correct option:

   I. Internet gateways and egress-only Internet gateways allow Internet-outbound traffic.

   II. Both Internet gateways and egress-only Internet gateways support IPv4 and IPv6 traffic.

   III. Internet gateways and egress-only Internet gateways support network address translation.

   A. Only I is correct.

   B. I and III are correct.

   C. I and II are correct.

   D. I, II, and II are correct.

4. Which statement about NAT gateways and NAT instances is not correct?

   A. You have to size and manage NAT instances.

   B. You can use NAT instances for port redirection.

   C. You do not have to disable the source/destination check on NAT gateways.

   D. You must assign a security group to a NAT gateway.

   E. You can use NAT instances as Bastion hosts.

5. Read the following statements about security group rules and choose the correct option:

   I. You can allow HTTP from 10.0.40.0/24.

   II. You can block HTTP from your own public IP address.

   III. You can allow HTTP from any source.

   A. I, II, and III are correct.

   B. I and III are correct.

   C. II and II are correct.

   D. Only III is correct.

6. Which statement about security groups and NACLs is not correct?

   A. You can configure inbound and outbound rules on both.

   B. You have to explicitly configure outbound rules to allow return traffic from permitted connections to instances associated to a security group.

   C. You can use a CIDR block as the source in NACLs.

   D. You can use other security groups as the source in security groups.

7. Read the following statements about AWS Elastic Load Balancing and choose the correct option:

   I. ALBs, NLBs, and CLBs support health checks, CloudWatch metrics, and AZ failover.

   II. NLBs can support AWS Lambda functions as targets.

   III. CLBs can only be used with EC2-classic implementations.

   A. Only I is correct.

   B. I and II are correct.

   C. II and III are correct.

   D. I, II, and III are correct.

8. What can the VPC Flow Logs monitor?

   A. Amazon DNS traffic

   B. DHCP traffic

   C. Traffic from a Windows instance

   D. Traffic destined to the VPC router's reserved IP address

9. AWS WAF web ACL rules cannot detect which of the following conditions?

   A. SQL injection attacks

   B. Cross-site scripting attacks

   C. Length of requests

   D. HTTP response headers

   E. Country that requests originate from

10. Which statement about AWS Shield is correct?
    A. AWS Shield Standard offers support of the AWS DDoS response team (DRT).
    B. AWS Shield Advanced is charged per month.
    C. AWS Shield Standard is disabled by default.
    D. AWS Shield Advanced is enabled by default.

Data Protection

THE AWS CERTIFIED SECURITY SPECIALTY EXAM OBJECTIVES THAT LEVERAGE CONCEPTS EXPLAINED IN THIS CHAPTER INCLUDE THE FOLLOWING:

✓ **Domain 5: Data Protection**

- 5.1. Design and implement key management and use
- 5.2. Troubleshoot key management
- 5.3. Design and implement a data encryption solution for data at rest and data in transit

Introduction

In this chapter, you will learn how to leverage the AWS-native security services and best practices available in the AWS Cloud to protect your data. We'll address the following:

- Working with the AWS Key Management Service (KMS)
- Creating a customer master key (CMK) in AWS KMS
- Understanding the cloud hardware security module (CloudHSM)
- Using AWS Certificate Manager
- Protecting Amazon S3 buckets
- Understanding how Amazon Macie deploys machine learning to identify personal identifiable information

Using a variety of AWS cloud security controls, services, and practices, a security team aims to create the mechanisms and implement the necessary controls to protect sensitive data stored in the AWS Cloud, thus meeting regulatory, security, and data privacy needs. With such measures, this team can adequately protect the most valuable asset of companies in the digital age: data and information.

With the emergence of data privacy and protection regulations around the world such as the European Union's General Data Protection Regulation (GDPR), which came into force in May 2018, data protection and privacy are becoming even more strategic topics for all kinds of business and governmental organizations.

Different regulations all over the world are being used to enforce severe financial penalties to address information leaks and even negligence in implementing security controls, best practices, and reporting security incidents. In such scenarios, the use of data protection mechanisms—especially cryptographic mechanisms—is fundamental in increasing the resilience of information technology systems. *Cryptography* is defined as the ability to transform standard text information into ciphertext using cryptographic algorithms and keys, as in the symmetric encryption operation shown in Figure 6.1.

FIGURE 6.1 Cleartext and ciphertext

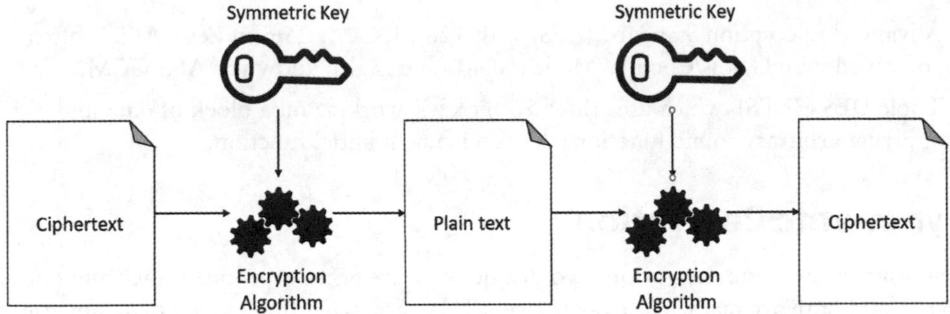

In Figure 6.1, on the left is plain text (unprotected data) that is passing through an encryption algorithm using a symmetric key, generating a ciphertext (protected data) in the middle of Figure 6.1. The same algorithm and symmetric key are applied again (on the right) to open the ciphertext, generating the same plain text (unprotected data) again.

When deploying encryption, you have two types of cryptographic algorithms you can implement, symmetric and asymmetric, which we will explore next.

Symmetric Encryption

Keys are strings of data that are used to encrypt and decrypt data. In symmetric encryption algorithms, the same key is used in both operations, as shown in Figure 6.1. The size of such keys also determines how hard it is for an attacker to try all possible key combinations when attempting to decrypt a protected message. Table 6.1 presents some examples of symmetric cryptographic encryption algorithms.

TABLE 6.1 Symmetric cryptographic encryption algorithms

Name	Key size
Advanced Encryption Standard (AES)	128, 192, and 256 bits
Twofish	128, 192, and 256 bits
Serpent	128, 192, and 256 bits
Blowfish	32 to 448 bits
Carlisle Adams and Stafford Tavares (CAST5)	40 to 128 bits
Data Encryption Standard (DES)	64 bits
Triple Data Encryption Standard (3DES)	128 and 192 bits, effectively 56, 112, and 168
IDEA	128 bits

The AWS cryptographic tools and services support two widely used symmetric algorithms:

- Advanced Encryption Standard (AES) with 128-, 192-, or 256-bit keys. AES is often combined with Galois/Counter Mode (GCM) and is also known as AES-GCM.
- Triple DES (3DES), which uses three 56-bit keys, working on a block of data and applying arbitrary round functions derived from an initial function.

Asymmetric Encryption

When using asymmetric encryption, two distinct keys are necessary—one public and one private—and both are mathematically derived. There are two different uses of symmetric encryption to guarantee confidentiality and authenticity/nonrepudiation. Let's use an example of a scenario where we have two users, defined here as Alice and Bob. In this scenario, Alice wants to send information to Bob, protecting the data using asymmetric encryption mechanisms to guarantee that only Bob will be able to access the protected data.

To achieve the desired confidentiality protection, Alice will encrypt the data using Bob's public key, as shown in Figure 6.2, and Bob will decrypt the data information using his private key.

FIGURE 6.2 Asymmetric encryption

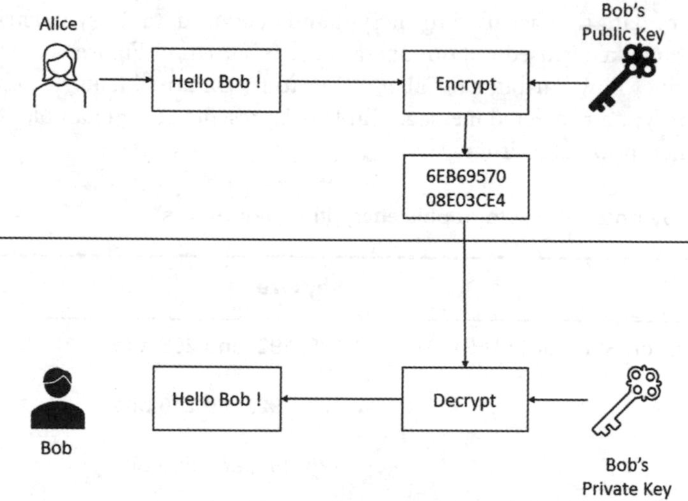

In this scenario, only the owner of the respective private key can decrypt the information encrypted by the public key. Consequently, the private key must be adequately protected against any improper access, which could include unexpected visibility of encrypted information.

In the same scenario, if Bob then wants to send data back to Alice, using encryption to protect the data confidentiality, Bob must encrypt the data using Alice's public key, and Alice will decrypt the data using her private key.

AWS services typically support Rivest–Shamir–Adleman (RSA) for asymmetric cryptographic key algorithms. RSA uses key sizes of 1024, 2048, and 3072 bits.

Additionally, the public and private key mechanism can be used to ensure the authenticity of the data source. Therefore, when private keys are used to digitally sign a message, it assures the receiver that only the owner of the private key could sign it correctly. This way, the destination that receives the message can validate whether the message came from the expected source, which is done through the use of the public key, as shown in Figure 6.3.

FIGURE 6.3 Signature using an asymmetric algorithm

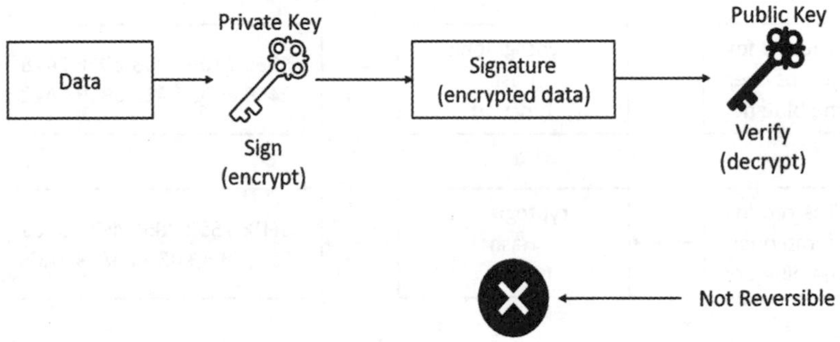

You can use a CMK with a key spec that represents an RSA key pair or an elliptic-curve cryptography (ECC) key pair, to sign messages and verify signatures, The key spec you choose is determined by the signing algorithm that you want to use. In some cases, the users who will verify signatures are outside AWS and can't call the verify signature operation. In that case, choose a key spec associated with a signing algorithm that these users can support in their local applications.

AWS Key Management Service (AWS KMS) supports postquantum hybrid key exchange for the Transport Layer Security (TLS) network encryption protocol that is used when connecting to KMS API endpoints. A large-scale quantum computer would break the current public key cryptography that is used for key exchange in every TLS connection, but AWS KMS also supports finite-field-based Diffie-Hellman ephemeral (FFDHE) and elliptic curve Diffie-Hellman ephemeral (ECDHE). For more information, see `aws.amazon.com/pt/blogs/security/post-quantum-tls-now-supported-in-aws-kms`.

Hash Algorithms

Another essential concept is the use of *hash algorithms*. Hashing is a feature that applies an algorithm to a piece of information, generating a message digest, which is a string of digits created by a one-way hashing to generate summary information, as shown in Figure 6.4.

As you can see in Figure 6.4, different input sizes generate different digest outputs, but with the same size. Even if you change a single letter in the input, you have a different digest output, but always with the same size. In reverse, different inputs, with the same hash function applied, result in different hashes (digests) but still with the same size. In this case, looking at the digest alone, you cannot infer the input data size or even the input data type.

FIGURE 6.4 Hash algorithm usage

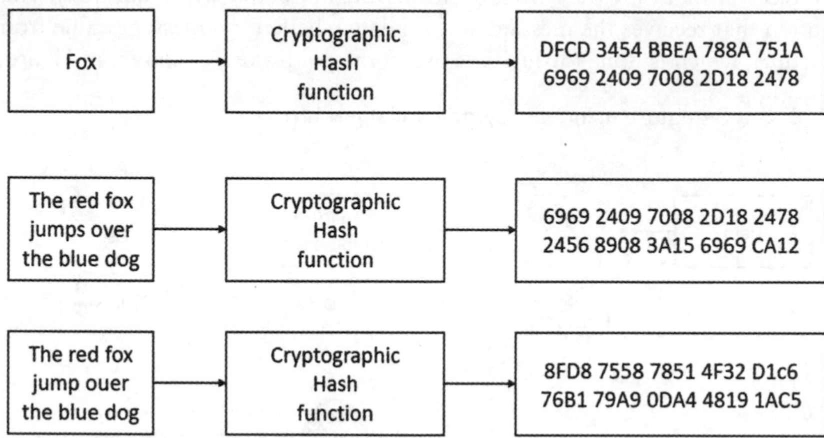

In a perfect scenario, based on the message digest, you cannot obtain the original information, so in theory, a good hash algorithm is irreversible. But since hashed values are generally smaller than the originals, a hash function can generate duplicate hashed values. These are known as *collisions*, and they occur when identical values are produced when using different data sources.

Collisions can be avoided by using larger hash values, or they can be resolved with multiple hash functions, overflow tables, or salts. Salts are often used to store passwords to prevent the use of precalculated password hash tables, known as *rainbow tables*, which can significantly accelerate brute forcing.

A salt is random data used as an additional input to safeguard a one-way function, like a hash algorithm. A new salt is randomly generated for each hash operation. You will find more examples of hash algorithms in Table 6.2.

TABLE 6.2 Hash algorithms examples

Name	Hash code size
Message-Digest 5 (MD5)	128
SHA-1	160
SHA-256	256
SHA-384	384
SHA-512	512

Table 6.2 shows the algorithm name, as well as the fixed output size in bits for each hash function.

The use of encryption is essential to increasing the level of data protection. However, encryption should be seen as a layer of defense and not the only defense. As one of the components of a data protection strategy, encryption should be used throughout the information lifecycle, including its creation, transport, and even when data is stored at rest, adopting an end-to-end encryption model.

However, in traditional environments, there are several challenges to the implementation of an end-to-end cryptographic model, such as

- Integration of distinct technology platforms
- Proper encryption key protection
- Implementation of encryption key use and audit trails
- Minimization of performance impact due to encryption deployed on various components of a solution and architecture
- Periodic rotation of cryptographic keys

The AWS Cloud enables the deployment of data protection mechanisms using large-scale cryptography, protecting data throughout its lifecycle, and natively addressing the challenges outlined earlier, enabling the implementation of an end-to-end encryption model that allows

- Protection of cryptographic keys based on the highest industry standards
- Identification of who is using cryptographic keys through native logs in the AWS Cloud, using the AWS CloudTrail service
- Large-scale encryption without impacting component performance, working natively and seamlessly with a range of AWS Cloud services
- Automatic and continuous rotation of cryptographic keys
- High availability

The next sections will demonstrate and explain how these capabilities are deployed in the AWS Cloud to provide data protection for your applications.

AWS Key Management Service

The AWS Cloud has a security service called *AWS Key Management Service (KMS)*, which allows you to natively encrypt data in a seamless and integrated manner with more than 50 available services in the AWS Cloud.

Here are some examples of services that can integrate with AWS KMS:

- Amazon Simple Storage Service (Amazon S3)
- Amazon Relational Database Services (Amazon RDS)

- Amazon Elastic Block Store (Amazon EBS)
- AWS CloudTrail
- Amazon DynamoDB
- Amazon Redshift
- Amazon EMR

The KMS service cannot be used to generate SSH access keys for your Amazon Elastic Compute Cloud (EC2) instances. Key pairs (public and private keys) are generated directly from the EC2 service.

A complete list of services that natively integrate with AWS KMS can be obtained directly from the service's public page in the AWS Service Integration section at `aws.amazon.com/kms/features/#AWS_Service_Integration` (see Figure 6.5).

FIGURE 6.5 AWS KMS service integration

aws

Contact Sales Support English My Account Create an AWS Account

Products Solutions Pricing Documentation Learn Partner Network AWS Marketplace Customer Enablement Explore More

AWS Key Management Service Overview Features Pricing Getting Started Resources FAQs

PAGE CONTENT

- Overview
- Centralized Key Management
- AWS Service Integration
- Audit Capabilities
- Scalability, Durability, and High Availability
- Secure
- Custom Key Store
- Compliance

AWS Service Integration

AWS KMS is seamlessly integrated with most AWS services. This integration means that you can easily use KMS master keys to control the encryption of the data you store within these services. When deciding to encrypt data in a service, you can chose to use an AWS managed master key that is created in KMS for you automatically by that service. You can track the usage of the key but it is managed by the service on your behalf.

If you need direct control over the lifecycle of a master key or wish to allow other accounts to use it, you can create and manage your own master keys that can be used on your behalf by AWS services. These customer managed master keys give you full control over the access permissions that determine who can use the key and under which conditions.

AWS Services Integrated with KMS

Alexa for Business*	Amazon EMR	Amazon S3
Amazon Athena	Amazon FSx for Windows File Server	Amazon SageMaker
Amazon Aurora	Amazon Glacier	Amazon Simple Email Service (SES)
Amazon CloudWatch Logs	Amazon Kinesis Data Streams	Amazon Relational Database Service (RDS)
Amazon Comprehend*	Amazon Kinesis Firehose	Amazon Simple Notification Service (SNS)
Amazon Connect	Amazon Kinesis Video Streams	Amazon Simple Queue Service (SQS)
Amazon DocumentDB	Amazon Lex	Amazon Translate
Amazon DynamoDB*	Amazon Lightsail*	Amazon WorkMail

Using the KMS service, you can implement an end-to-end encryption strategy, thus enabling you to encrypt data stored on Amazon Elastic Block Storage (EBS) attached to your servers, objects stored on Amazon S3 storage, and databases in your AWS Cloud environment.

Figure 6.6 shows how AWS KMS can provide encryption for various AWS Cloud services.

FIGURE 6.6 Implementing an end-to-end encryption strategy using AWS KMS

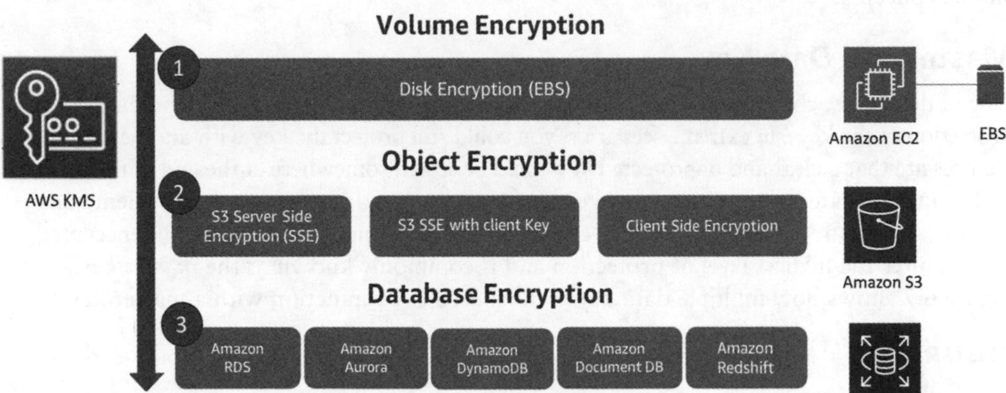

Figure 6.6 shows an example where AWS KMS service can be used to encrypt your data in three layers:

1. Data-at-rest in your EBS disks
2. Data-at-rest in your S3 buckets (object storage)
3. Data-at-rest in your database, like RDS, Aurora, DynamoDB, and Redshift

The AWS KMS service backs up cryptographic keys to maintain 11 nines of durability, 99.999999999%.

Although AWS KMS has its protection methods for cryptographic keys, AWS also allows the use of dedicated *hardware security modules (HSMs)* to provide more sophisticated protection of your keys. An HSM is dedicated hardware that has a variety of logical and physical controls designed to protect cryptographic keys, preventing their exposure and mitigating the risk of compromising the entire cryptographic model. AWS KMS natively uses HSMs to protect the master keys, but these HSMs are not dedicated to a single user, or in other words, they are multitenant. Nonetheless, with proper isolation and security controls implemented, the native HSMs behind the AWS KMS service can be securely shared among different users.

When you are using AWS KMS, you do not have access to manage the HSMs behind the service. Generally speaking, a dedicated HSM is usually required when regulatory and security policy compliance is needed, and this requirement can be addressed through an AWS/Amazon CloudHSM deployment.

AWS KMS Components

Before creating a cryptographic key and seeing how simple it is to administer and manage large-scale encryption in the AWS Cloud, you must understand how the AWS KMS service works in detail. In this section, we'll examine how encryption and decryption occur, and especially how these keys are securely generated and stored. Let's start with a couple of simple concepts.

Master and Data Key

One of the biggest challenges when you are implementing symmetric key encryption models is the protection of the keys. In extreme scenarios, you could still protect the key with another key, but chances are that a clear and unprotected key could be stored somewhere at the end of the process.

Because repeatedly encrypting one key with another would not solve the problem completely (since you will always have the challenge of protecting a key), the last unencrypted key requires the highest level of protection and is commonly known as the *master key*. Figure 6.7 shows how multiple data keys can be used in conjunction with a master key.

FIGURE 6.7 Master and data keys

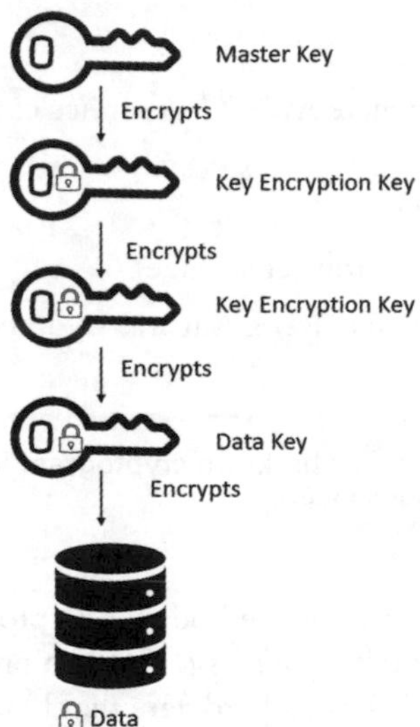

It is imperative to protect the master keys in your environments because these are the keys that ensure data key protection and guarantee data encryption. Consequently, AWS KMS creates the environment to manage and protect your master keys, as Figure 6.8 shows.

FIGURE 6.8 KMS master key protection

Using AWS KMS, your master key is protected and is never exposed in cleartext, so in this scenario, the key is never handled since cleartext is outside the protected boundary established by the KMS HSMs. The master key is used to encrypt and protect your data key, and the data key is used to encrypt and decrypt your data in many different services, as shown in Figure 6.8.

When you are using AWS KMS, you must interact with the service to use and manage your master keys using the console, CLI, or SDKs. All the interactions with the service are through API calls because the master keys never leave the AWS KMS unencrypted; thus, there is no exposure, and the master keys are protected by Federal Information Processing Standard (FIPS) 140-2 validated cryptographic modules (`csrc.nist.gov/projects/cryptographic-module-validation-program/Certificate/3139`).

When you're using the AWS SDKs to make programmatic API calls to AWS KMS, clients must support TLS 1.0, and we also highly recommend that you use TLS 1.2. Clients must also support cipher suites with perfect forward secrecy (PFS) such as Diffie-Hellman ephemeral (DHE) or ECDHE. Most modern systems such as Java 7 and later support these modules.

As you can see in Figure 6.9, you cannot access the master key directly. To access AWS KMS, you must use API calls using the console, SDK or CLI; be authenticated; and have the right level of access to interact with the service.

FIGURE 6.9 User access methods to the master key

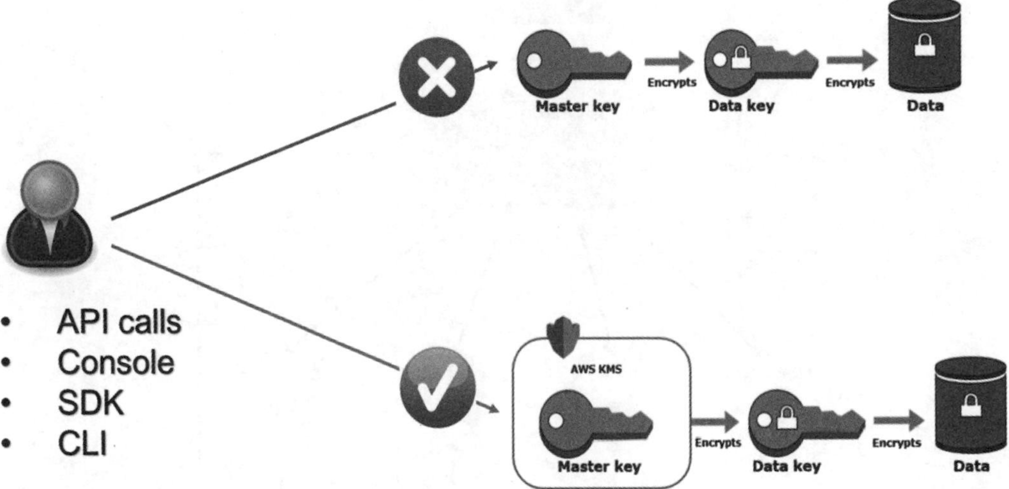

Customer Master Key and Key Hierarchy

A *customer master key (CMK)* is a 256-bit AES for symmetric keys that has a unique key ID, alias, and ARN (Amazon Resource Name) and is created based on a user-initiated request through AWS KMS. It resides at the top of your key hierarchy and is not exportable, spending its entire lifecycle within AWS KMS.

Figure 6.10 shows two customer master keys that were created in AWS KMS.

FIGURE 6.10 Customer master key examples

Key Management Service (KMS)

AWS managed keys
Customer managed keys
Custom key stores

KMS > Customer managed keys

Customer managed keys

Key actions ▼ Create key

sec

Alias	Key ID	Status	Creation date
securitybookawskey	1e0e2d55-5228-4262-8f60-7936b1180034	Enabled	Aug 24, 2019 18:15 GMT-3
securityawsbookkey	f2530a16-b249-4503-ba14-1f1645258aed	Enabled	Aug 24, 2019 17:45 GMT-3

Once you use the AWS KMS service, it is possible for a CMK to use multiple data keys to protect data in an integrated manner with other services in an AWS environment, as shown in Figure 6.11.

FIGURE 6.11 AWS KMS service integration

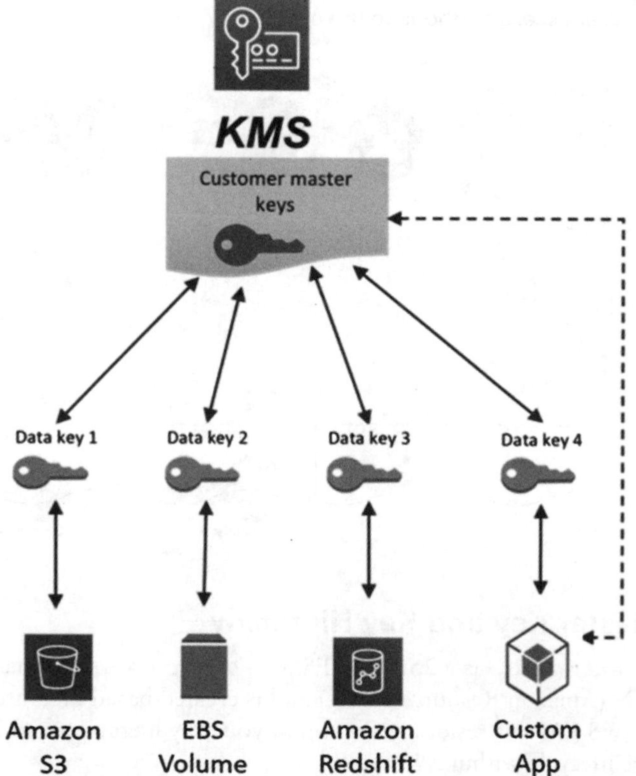

KeyID, Alias, and ARN

Customer master keys have three additional attributes that can be used for identification:

KeyID A unique key identifier for a CMK.

Alias A user-friendly name that can be associated with a CMK. The alias can be used interchangeably with the KeyID in many of the AWS KMS API operations. The alias is important when you are rotating keys with imported material.

ARN A file-naming convention used to identify a particular resource in the AWS public cloud, helping administrators and users to track and use AWS KMS keys across AWS products and API calls.

Figure 6.12 shows these attributes in the AWS console.

FIGURE 6.12 Customer master key details, ARN, alias, KeyID

Permissions

The permissions represent the level of access granted in a JSON policy that is attached to a CMK. Permission defines the principals (as defined in Chapter 3, "Identity and Access Management") that are allowed to use the keys for encryption and decryption, and also the account (or accounts) that can administer and add IAM policies to the key.

When you are creating CMKs, all the keys must have at least two policies roles (Figure 6.13):

- **Key Administrators:** IAM users or IAM roles that can manage the keys
- **Key Users:** IAM users or IAM roles that can use the keys to encrypt or decrypt data

Figure 6.13 shows two different IAM roles with distinct privileges. In this example, the Key Administrator role can create a key but cannot encrypt, decrypt, or generate a data key. On the right, the Key Users role can access and use the CMK to generate, decrypt, and encrypt a data key.

FIGURE 6.13 Two roles used to control access to the CMK

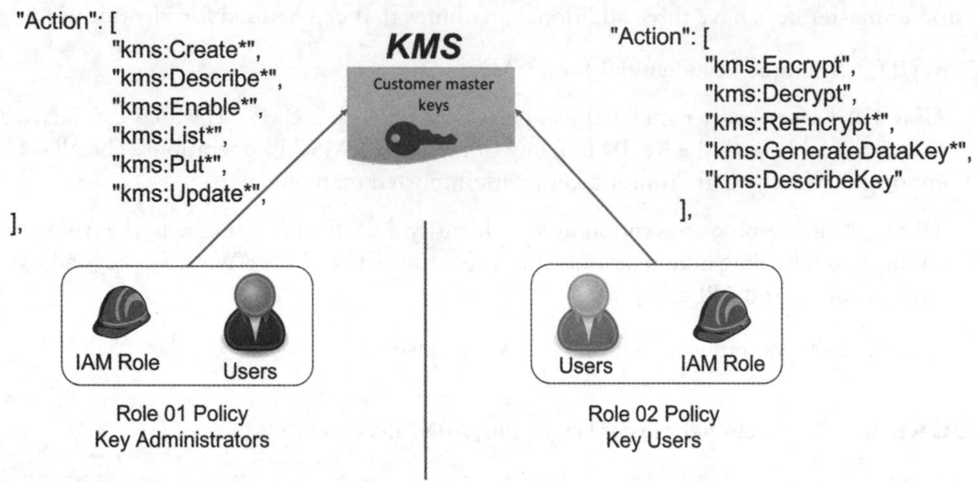

It is only possible to use IAM roles and IAM users—IAM groups cannot be used as principals in KMS policies.

Figure 6.14 shows two different users, with administrator and user access, respectively.

FIGURE 6.14 Role configuration in KMS to control access to the CMK

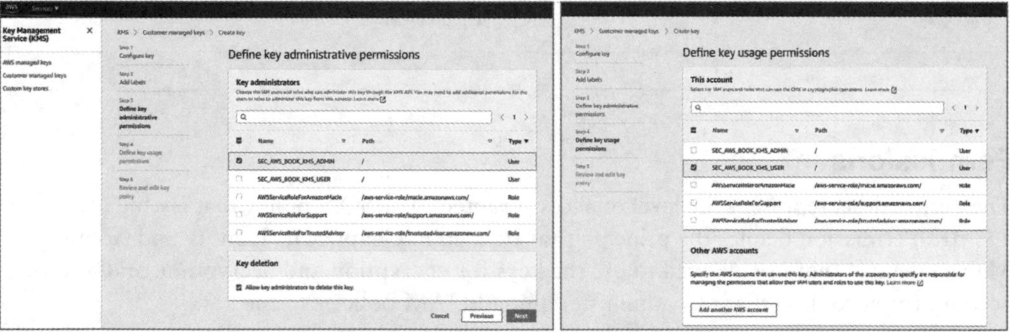

Figure 6.14 shows the AWS KMS Key policy option in the AWS console. Two IAM users are created for the specific key. `SEC_AWS_BOOK_KMS_ADMIN` is a key administrator and `SEC_AWS_BOOK_KMS_USER` is a key user.

Example 6.1 shows a KMS JSON policy created based on the access permissions defined in Figure 6.14.

Example 6.1: KMS JSON policy

```
{
    "Id": "key-consolepolicy-3",
    "Version": "2012-10-17",
    "Statement": [
        {
            "Sid": "Enable IAM User Permissions",
            "Effect": "Allow",
            "Principal": {
                "AWS": "arn:aws:iam::112233445566:root"
            },
            "Action": "kms:*",
            "Resource": "*"
        },
        {
            "Sid": "Allow access for Key Administrators",
            "Effect": "Allow",
            "Principal": {
                "AWS": "arn:aws:iam::112233445566:user/SEC_AWS_BOOK_KMS_ADMIN"
            },
            "Action": [
                "kms:Create*",
                "kms:Describe*",
                "kms:Enable*",
                "kms:List*",
                "kms:Put*",
                "kms:Update*",
                "kms:Revoke*",
                "kms:Disable*",
                "kms:Get*",
                "kms:Delete*",
                "kms:ImportKeyMaterial",
                "kms:TagResource",
```

```
                "kms:UntagResource",
                "kms:ScheduleKeyDeletion",
                "kms:CancelKeyDeletion"
            ],
            "Resource": "*"
        },
        {
            "Sid": "Allow use of the key",
            "Effect": "Allow",
            "Principal": {
                "AWS": "arn:aws:iam::112233445566:user/SEC_AWS_BOOK_KMS_USER"
            },
            "Action": [
                "kms:Encrypt",
                "kms:Decrypt",
                "kms:ReEncrypt*",
                "kms:GenerateDataKey*",
                "kms:DescribeKey"
            ],
            "Resource": "*"
        },
        {
            "Sid": "Allow attachment of persistent resources",
            "Effect": "Allow",
            "Principal": {
                "AWS": "arn:aws:iam::112233445566:user/SEC_AWS_BOOK_KMS_USER"
            },
            "Action": [
                "kms:CreateGrant",
                "kms:ListGrants",
                "kms:RevokeGrant"
            ],
            "Resource": "*",
            "Condition": {
                "Bool": {
                    "kms:GrantIsForAWSResource": "true"
                }
            }
        }
    ]
}
```

From now on, whenever you see a JSON policy example, take the time to read it more carefully. You should be able to interpret a KMS JSON policy to pass the AWS Certified Security Specialty exam. The remainder of this section will help you better understand how to identify a JSON policy's main blocks (see Figure 6.15):

AWS Root Account All AWS accounts have one root user credential, the credential of the account owner. This credential allows full access to all resources in the account, including the AWS KMS. You must adequately protect this credential, as defined in Chapter 3. The root user access to KMS CMKs is added by default in the policy to protect from key lockout. The default key policy gives the AWS account (root user) that owns the CMK full access to the CMK, which reduces the risk of the CMK becoming unmanageable and enables IAM policies to allow access to the CMK.

Key Administrator The `SEC_AWS_BOOK_KMS_ADMIN` user.

Key User The `SEC_AWS_BOOK_KMS_USER` user.

FIGURE 6.15 JSON permission policy example diagram

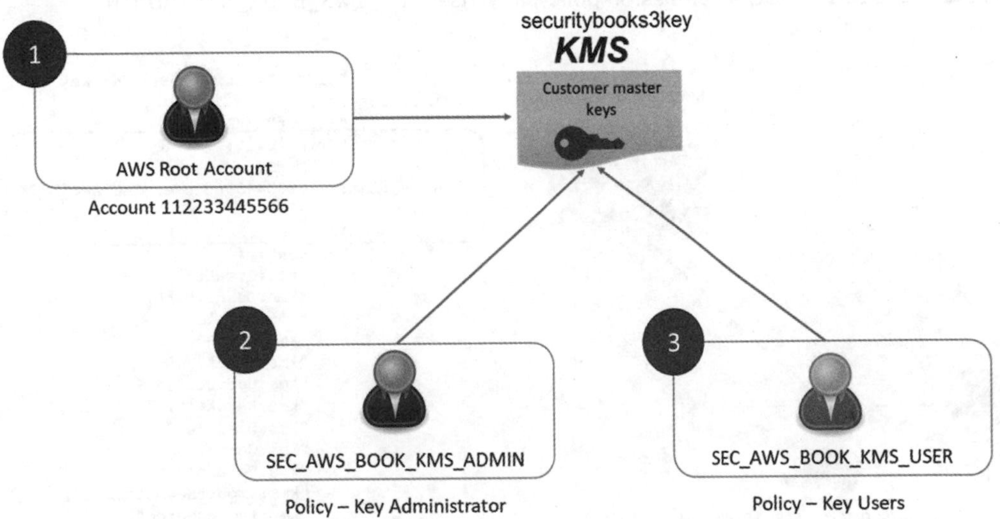

Each user has a set of permissions defined in JSON, allowing them to perform different activities with the keys. See Figure 6.16. Note that this is a default configuration that can be changed by the key administrator.

As Figure 6.16 shows, the `SEC_AWS_BOOK_KMS_ADMIN` IAM user can call all the admin APIs but cannot use encrypt or decrypt operations.

Going one step further in the analysis, Figure 6.17 shows the permissions for IAM users or IAM roles that can create, revoke, delete, and update the keys, among other API calls, and so can execute many different administrative actions within the respective key(s).

FIGURE 6.16 JSON permission policy, AWS root account

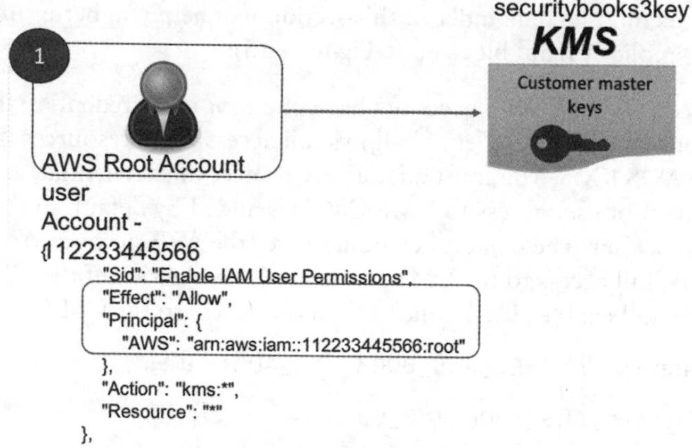

FIGURE 6.17 JSON permission policy, IAM user SEC_AWS_BOOK_KMS_ADMIN

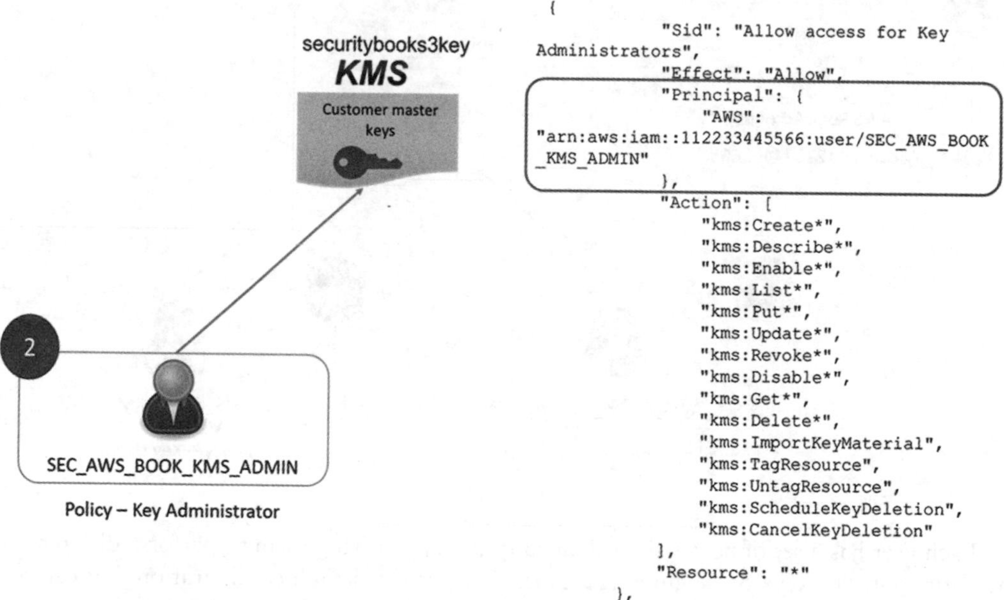

And finally, Figure 6.18 shows the permitted API calls that a typical IAM user or IAM role can execute based on the JSON policy. The SEC_AWS_BOOK_KMS_USER IAM user can call all the APIs to encrypt, decrypt, generate, reencypt, and describe a key and also to create, list, and revoke a grant, but cannot use administration API calls.

FIGURE 6.18 JSON permission policy, IAM user SEC_AWS_BOOK_KMS_USER

```
{
    "Sid": "Allow use of the key",
    "Effect": "Allow",
    "Principal": {
        "AWS": "arn:aws:iam::112233445566:user/SEC_AWS_BOOK_KMS_USER"
    },
    "Action": [
        "kms:Encrypt",
        "kms:Decrypt",
        "kms:ReEncrypt*",
        "kms:GenerateDataKey*",
        "kms:DescribeKey"
    ],
    "Resource": "*"
},
{
    "Sid": "Allow attachment of persistent resources",
    "Effect": "Allow",
    "Principal": {
        "AWS": "arn:aws:iam::112233445566:user/SEC_AWS_BOOK_KMS_USER"
    },
    "Action": [
        "kms:CreateGrant",
        "kms:ListGrants",
        "kms:RevokeGrant"
    ],
    "Resource": "*",
    "Condition": {
        "Bool": {
            "kms:GrantIsForAWSResource": "true"
        }
```

securitybooks3key
KMS
Customer master keys
3
SEC_AWS_BOOK_KMS_USER
Policy – Key Users

AWS KMS provides an additional set of predefined condition keys that you can use in key policies and IAM policies. You can use conditions with KMS, for instance, to control what accounts can use the key, using the `kms:CallerAccount` condition, or to control what specific AWS services can call the key using the `kms:ViaService` condition. You do not need to know in detail all the conditions for the exam, but you must know how to read and interpret a JSON KMS policy. If you need more details about KMS conditions, you can find them in the following KMS documentation: `docs.aws.amazon.com/kms/latest/developerguide/policy-conditions.html#conditions-kms`.

Creating a Customer Master Key in AWS KMS

In the AWS KMS service console shown in Figure 6.19, you can see that there are three categories of keys:

- **AWS managed keys** are the default master keys that protect S3 objects, Lambda functions, and Workspaces when no other keys (customer-managed keys) are defined for these services.

- **Customer-managed keys** are customer master keys (CMKs) that the users can create and administer using JSON policies.
- **Custom key stores** are used when you want to manage your CMKs using a dedicated AWS CloudHSM cluster, giving you direct control to the HSMs that generate and manage the key material for your CMKs and perform cryptographic operations with them. The section "Understanding the Cloud Hardware Security Module," later in this chapter, will address the AWS CloudHSMs and how you can use them to protect your environment.

FIGURE 6.19 Key categories in AWS KMS

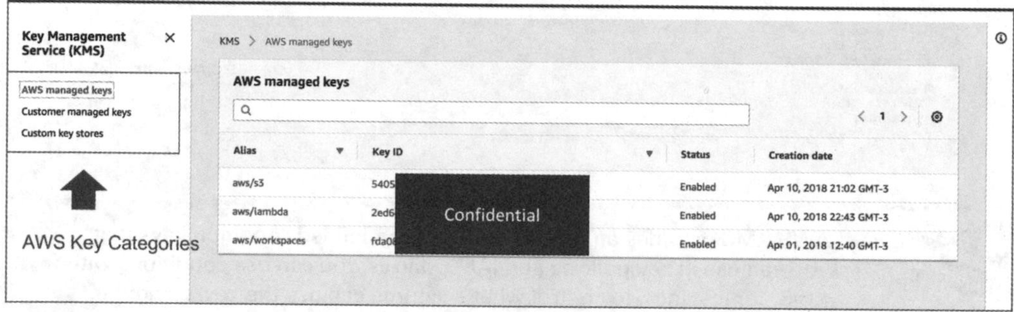

Creating a Key Using the Console

You can create a key directly from the AWS Console. Exercise 6.1 shows you how to do so.

EXERCISE 6.1

Create a KMS Key

Follow these steps to create a KMS key:

1. Log in with an account with administrative access that allows you to access the KMS service and create keys.
2. Access the AWS Key Management Services using the AWS Console.
3. Click the Create Key button.
4. Select Symmetric.

5. Click Advanced Options, and define the KMS key material origin.

KMS > Customer managed keys > Create key

Step 1
Configure key

Step 2
Add labels

Step 3
Define key administrative permissions

Step 4
Define key usage permissions

Step 5
Review and edit key policy

Configure key

Key type Help me choose

Symmetric
A single encryption key that is used for both encrypt and decrypt operations

Asymmetric
A public and private key pair that can be used for encrypt/decrypt or sign/verify operations

▾ Advanced options

Key material origin
Help me choose

KMS

External

Custom key store (CloudHSM)

Cancel Next

6. Click Next and create a CMK with an alias such as **`awssecuritycertificationkeytest`**.

7. Define the key description, such as **This is the key I'm using to study and pass the exam.**

8. Click Add Tag, and specify the tag key and tag value.

9. Click Next.

10. Select the key administrators (if you do not have any, you can create a user or a role by using the IAM Console)

11. Click Next.

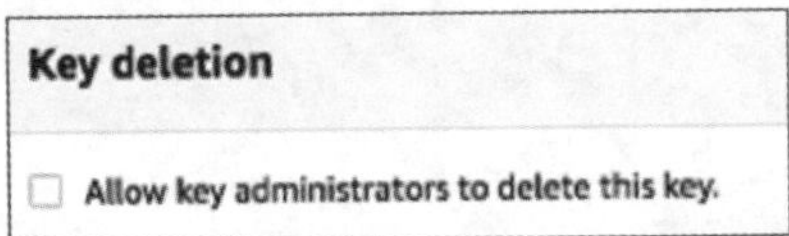

12. Select the IAM role and users that will be able to use the CMK to encrypt and decrypt data with the AWS KMS API, and click Next.

13. Review the KMS policy and click Finish.

14. Use the KMS Console to verify that your `awssecuritycertificationkeytest` was created.

awssecuritycertificationkeytest cfaee208-5524-45c9-8f5b-224a73b7b34a

It is crucial to use the Tag resource with AWS KMS. The tag can be used to help you evaluate costs per assets and resources, aggregating the costs by tags. So, when you use the Tag resource with AWS KMS, you can map costs for a project, application, or cost center. You can also use tags to define and categorize the keys per information type and projects.

Deleting Keys in AWS KMS

When you delete a CMK, you are also deleting all the metadata associated with it, and after that, you cannot decrypt data that was encrypted under that CMK anymore, which means that data encrypted with the deleted CMK becomes unrecoverable.

You should only delete a CMK when you are sure that you don't need to use it anymore. If you are in doubt, it is possible to disable the CMK and enable it again later if necessary, but you cannot recover a deleted CMK.

To help avoid a disastrous scenario where you might inadvertently delete a CMK, AWS KMS enforces a minimum of 7 days and a maximum of 30 days (default configuration) as a waiting period for deleting a CMK. Moreover, it is also important to remember that a pending CMK deletion cannot be used, and KMS does not rotate other derived keys from pending CMKs.

When you create the key, you still have the option to prevent the administrator from deleting it, thus adding another layer of protection for accidental deletion, as shown in Figure 6.20.

FIGURE 6.20 Allow Key Administrators To Delete This Key option

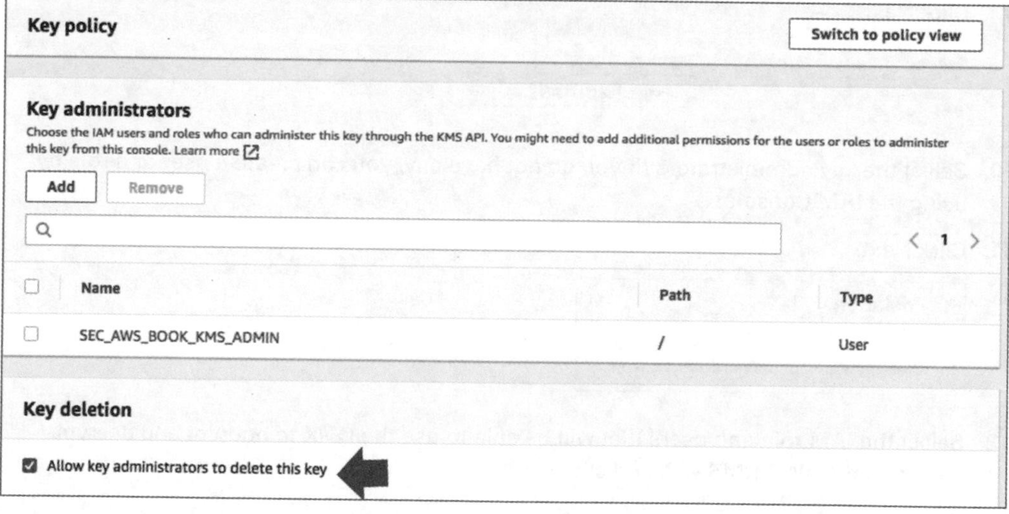

To delete a key in the AWS KMS console, perform the following steps:

1. Select AWS Key Management Services in the AWS Console.
2. Select the Customer Managed Keys option in the left panel.
3. Search for and select the key that you want to delete or disable.

4. Click the Key Actions button.
5. From the drop-down menu, select either Disable or Schedule Key Deletion. See Figure 6.21. If you choose the second option, define the waiting period.
6. Confirm your disable or deletion action from the previous step. Figure 6.22 shows the confirmation screen when you want to disable a key.

FIGURE 6.21 Key Disable and Schedule Key Deletion options

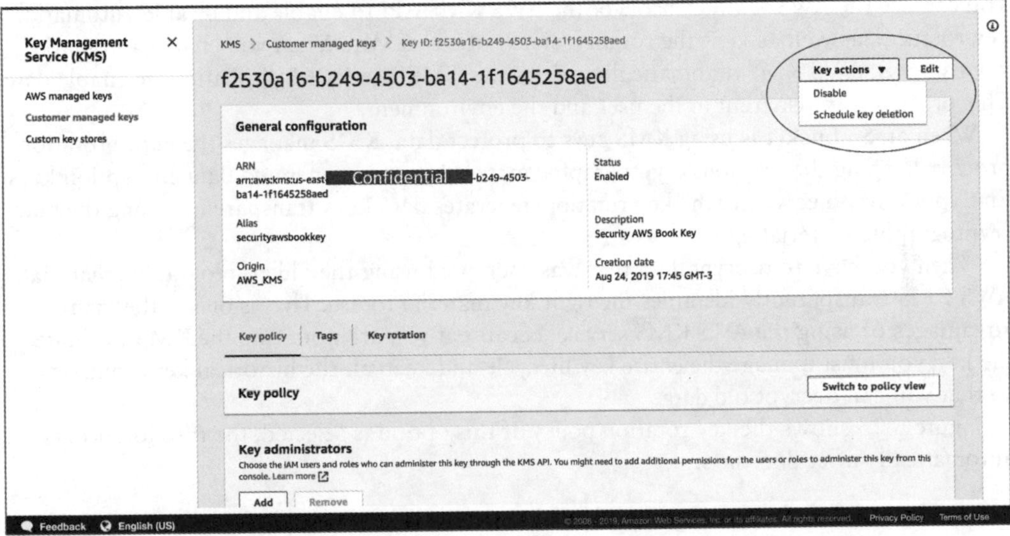

FIGURE 6.22 Confirm that you want to disable the key.

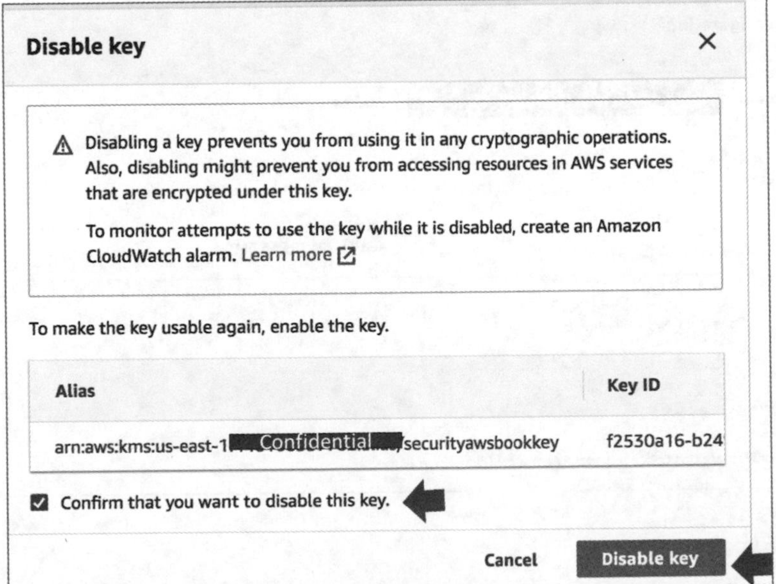

When considering deleting a key, even if there is a waiting period imposed by the AWS KMS service, you should disable the key for a period before performing the final deletion.

Rotating Keys in KMS

You can use the AWS KMS Console or the AWS KMS API to enable and disable automatic key rotation, as well as view the rotation status of any CMK. When you enable automatic key rotation, AWS KMS automatically rotates the CMK every 365 days after the enable date. This process is transparent to the user and the environment.

When an S3 bucket is using KMS keys to protect data, KMS manages the entire rotation process, keeping the previous cryptographic material used to generated data encryption keys. Encryption of objects after the key rotation generates data keys transparently using the new cryptographic material.

When you have to decrypt data that was encrypted using the old cryptographic material, AWS KMS transparently identifies the right key material to use. That is one of the many advantages of using the AWS KMS service, because if you are not using the KMS to rotate the key, you must manage the entire key lifecycle and keep all the historical keys somewhere so that you can decrypt old data.

Figure 6.23 shows the key rotation policy. If this option is selected, the rotation occurs automatically after 365 days.

FIGURE 6.23 Configuring and checking key rotation

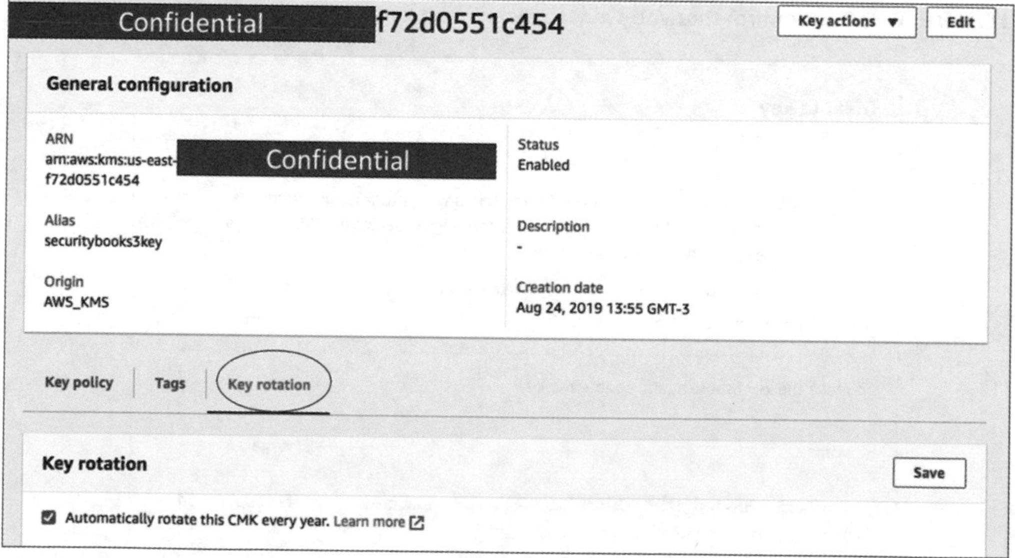

Manual key rotation may be needed because of rotation schedule or BYOK. More information on manual key rotation can be found at `docs.aws.amazon.com/kms/latest/developerguide/rotate-keys.html#rotate-keys-manually`.

In Exercise 6.2, you create an S3 bucket using a KMS key to protect your data.

EXERCISE 6.2

Create an S3 Bucket and Use a KMS Key to Protect the Bucket

In this exercise, you will create an S3 bucket and use the key created in Exercise 6.1 to protect the bucket content. Then you will upload a picture to the bucket, turn the object public, and try to access it as a standard/external unauthenticated Internet user.

1. Open the S3 service in the AWS Console.
2. Click the Create Bucket button.
3. Assign a unique name.
4. Click Create.
5. Create an S3 bucket with a unique name.
6. Select the bucket and select the Properties tab.
7. Click the Edit button for Default Encryption.

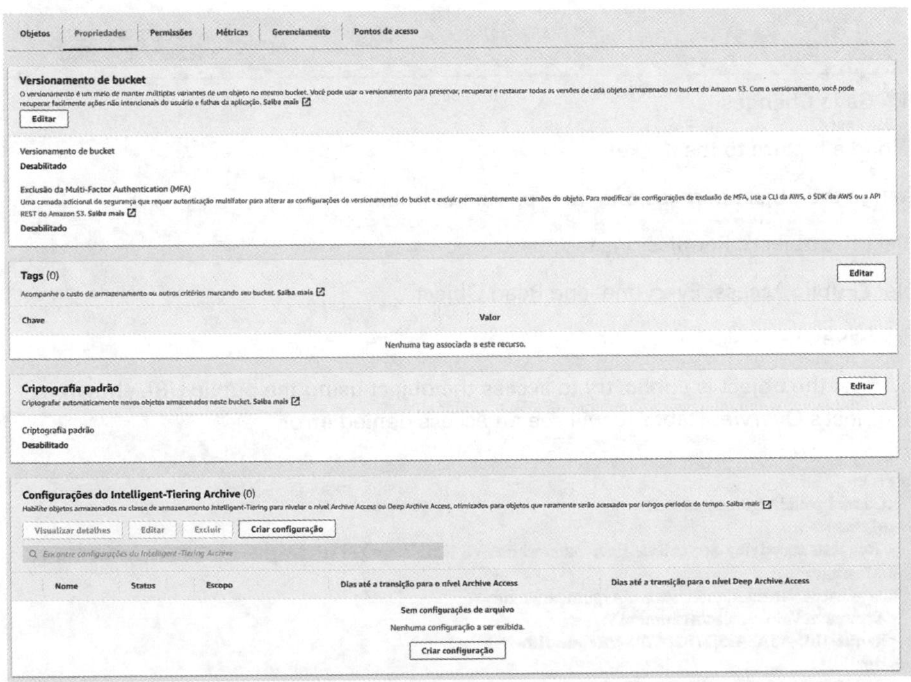

8. Select server-side encryption as Enable, encryption key type as AWS Key Management Service Key, AWS KMS Key as choose from your KMS master key, and search for the key that you created in Exercise 6.1.

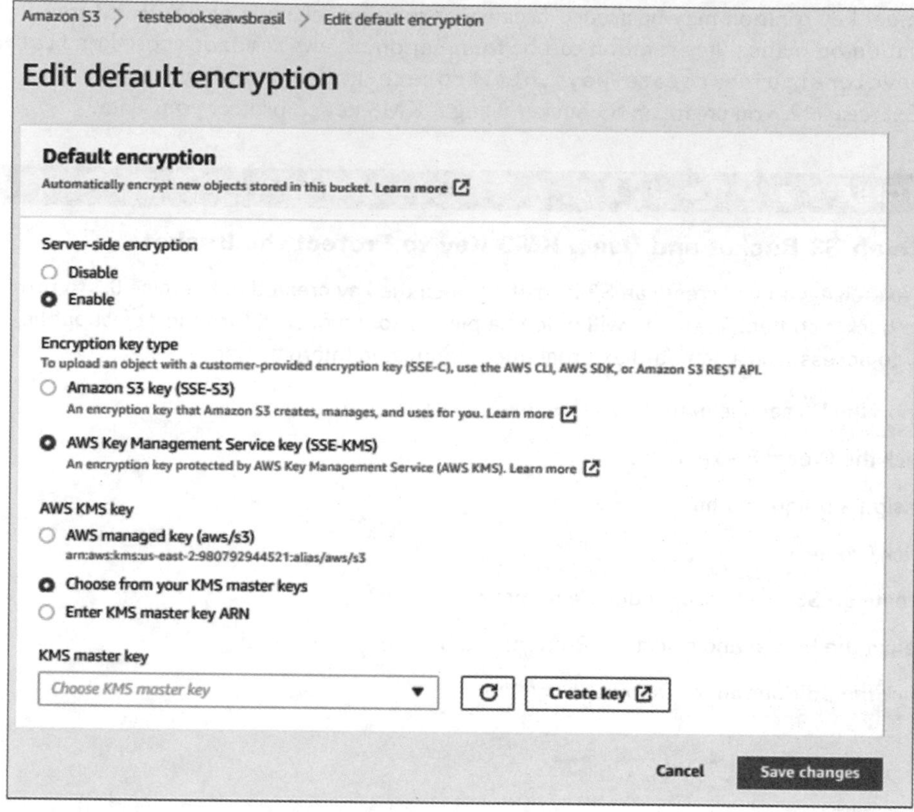

9. Click Save Changes.
10. Upload a picture to the bucket.
11. Change the object permissions from private to public.
12. Select the object's Permissions tab.
13. Select Public Access, Everyone, and Read Object.
14. Click Save.
15. Now that the object is public, try to access the object using the public URL shown in the object's Overview tab. You will see an access denied error.

```
-<Error>
   <Code>InvalidArgument</Code>
  -<Message>
     Requests specifying Server Side Encryption with AWS KMS managed keys require AWS Signature Version 4.
   </Message>
   <ArgumentName>Authorization</ArgumentName>
   <ArgumentValue>null</ArgumentValue>
   <RequestId>A5A3425D7B286298</RequestId>
  -<HostId>
     IIsKDOuf4nyYeFF40F3HQQI/fEGFPKKgApB14paF6zm/I1r0Mq7fnb8xQzDZz/MMCeJ4yg/JxXo=
   </HostId>
</Error>
```

16. Now try to access the object from the S3 Console by clicking Open.

Were you able to open the object now? Do you know why? Why could you not open in your browser even when you defined the object as a public object?

When you are opening the bucket using the link in the S3 Console and as a user who has access to the bucket and the KMS CMK, you can see the object. However, when you are trying to open it as an unauthenticated user from the Internet, even with a public S3 bucket, you cannot access the KMS service and decrypt the object. In that case, you have no access to decrypt and visualize the data, and the encryption works like another access control layer.

In Exercise 6.3, you create an RDS database using a KMS key to protect your data.

EXERCISE 6.3

Protecting RDS with KMS

In this exercise, you create an RDS database, create a KMS key (in the same ways that you did in Exercise 6.1) to use with the RDS service, and use that key to protect your RDS.

1. Log in with an account with administrative access that allows you to access the KMs service and create keys.
2. Access the KMS services using the AWS Console.
3. Click the Create Key button.
4. Click Advanced Options, and define the KMS key material origin.

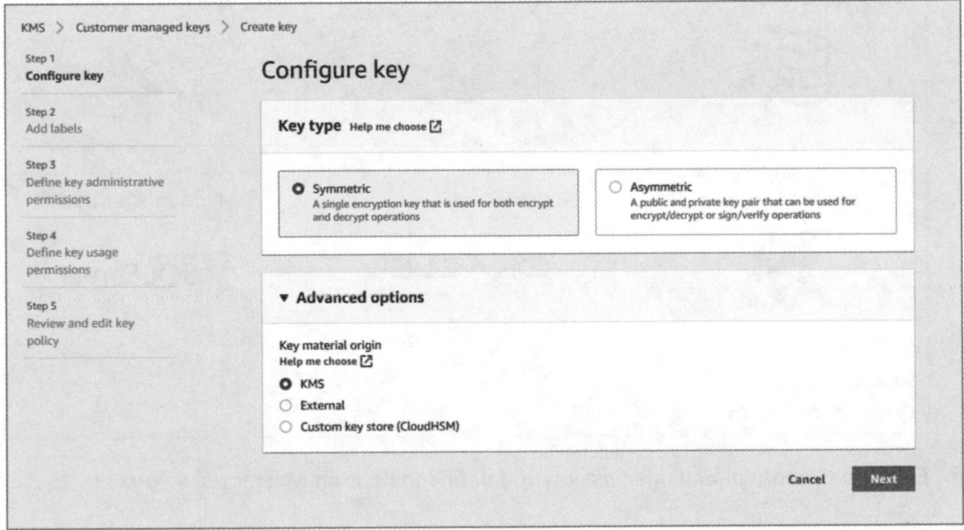

5. Click Add Tag and define the tag key and tag value.
6. Create a CMK with a unique name and define the alias for the key, such as **`RDSencryptionkey`**.

EXERCISE 6.3 *(continued)*

7. Define the key description, such as **This is the key I'm using to study, encrypt RDS, and pass the exam**.
8. Click Next.
9. Select the key administrators (if you do not have any, you can create a user or a role by using the IAM Console)
10. Click Next.
11. Select the IAM role and users that will be able to use the CMK to encrypt and decrypt data with the AWS KMS API, and click Next.
12. Review the KMS policy and click Finish.
13. Verify that `RDSencryptionkey` was created by using the KMS Console.

14. Create an RDS MySQL database using the AWS Console.

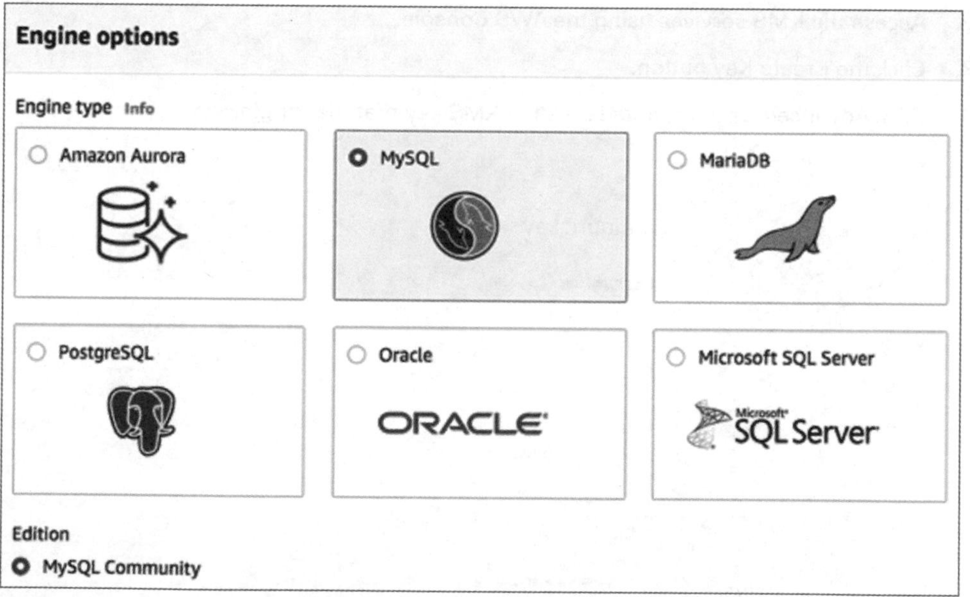

15. Find the Credential Settings session and define the admin Master password.

▼ **Credentials Settings**

Master username Info
Type a login ID for the master user of your DB instance.

admin

1 to 16 alphanumeric characters. First character must be a letter

☐ **Auto generate a password**
Amazon RDS can generate a password for you, or you can specify your own password

Master password Info

Constraints: At least 8 printable ASCII characters. Can't contain any of the following: / (slash), '(single quote), "(double quote) and @ (at sign).

Confirm password Info

16. Under Additional Configuration, select RDSencryptionkey. If you do not select the predefined key, the RDS service will encrypt the RDS using a default service key.

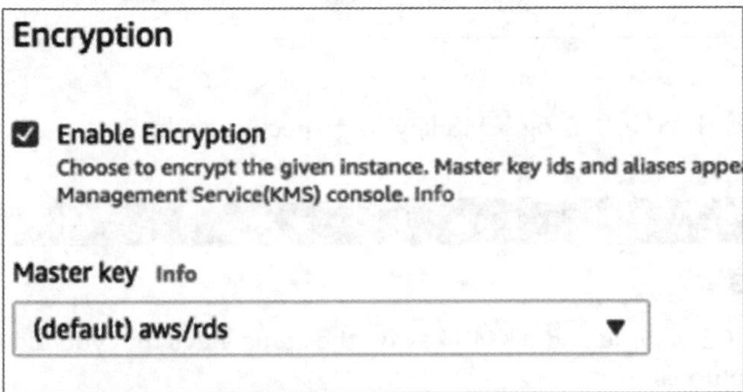

17. Click Create Database.
18. Check that your database was created using the right key.

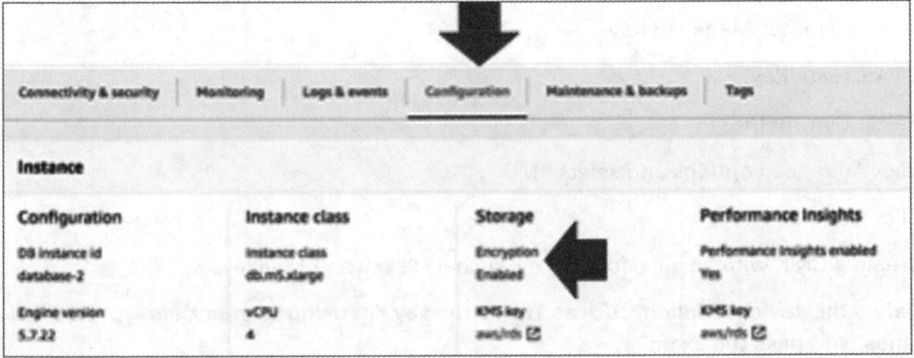

Now that you have created your database using a KMS key, you have an encrypted RDS. As you can see, the process is very simple; however, pay attention to the tips in the "Tips for Protecting RDS with KMS" sidebar, because they may be on your exam.

Tips for Protecting RDS with KMS

- You can only enable encryption for an Amazon RDS database instance when you create it, not after it is created.
- You cannot have an encrypted read replica of an unencrypted database instance or an unencrypted read replica of an encrypted database instance.
- You cannot restore a backup or unencrypted snapshot to an encrypted database instance.
- Encrypted read replicas must be encrypted with the same key as the source database instance.
- If you copy an encrypted snapshot within the same AWS region, you can encrypt the copy with the same KMS encryption key as the original snapshot, or you can specify a different KMS encryption key.
- If you copy an encrypted snapshot between regions, you cannot use the same KMS encryption key for the copy used for the source snapshot because the KMS keys are region specific. Instead, you must specify a valid KMS key in the target AWS region.

In Exercise 6.4, you create an EBS disk using KMS key to protect your data.

EXERCISE 6.4

Protecting EBS with KMS

In this exercise, you create an EBS volume and a KMS key (in the same ways that you did in Exercise 6.1) to use with EBS volumes.

1. Log in with an account with administrative access that allows you to access the KMs service and create keys.
2. Access the KMS services using the AWS Console.
3. Click Customer Managed Keys.
4. Click Create Key.
5. Select Symmetric.
6. Click Advanced options and select KMS.
7. Click Next.
8. Create a CMK with an alias for the key, such as `EBSencryptionkey`.
9. Define the key description, such as **This is the key I'm using to study, encrypt EBS volumes, and pass the exam**.
10. Click Add Tag.
11. Define the tag key and tag value.
12. Click Next.

13. Select the key administrators (if you do not have any, you can create a user or a role by using the IAM Console)
14. Click Next.
15. Select the IAM role and users that will be able to use the CMK to encrypt and decrypt data with the AWS KMS API, and click Next.
16. Review the KMS policy and click Finish.
17. Verify that `EBSencryptionkey` was created using the KMS Console.
18. Create an EBS using the AWS Console inside EC2. (If you need help, consult the documentation at `docs.aws.amazon.com/AWSEC2/latest/UserGuide/ebs-creating-volume.html`.)

19. Select the Encryption option.
20. Specify the master key.
21. Define the KMS key for encryption.

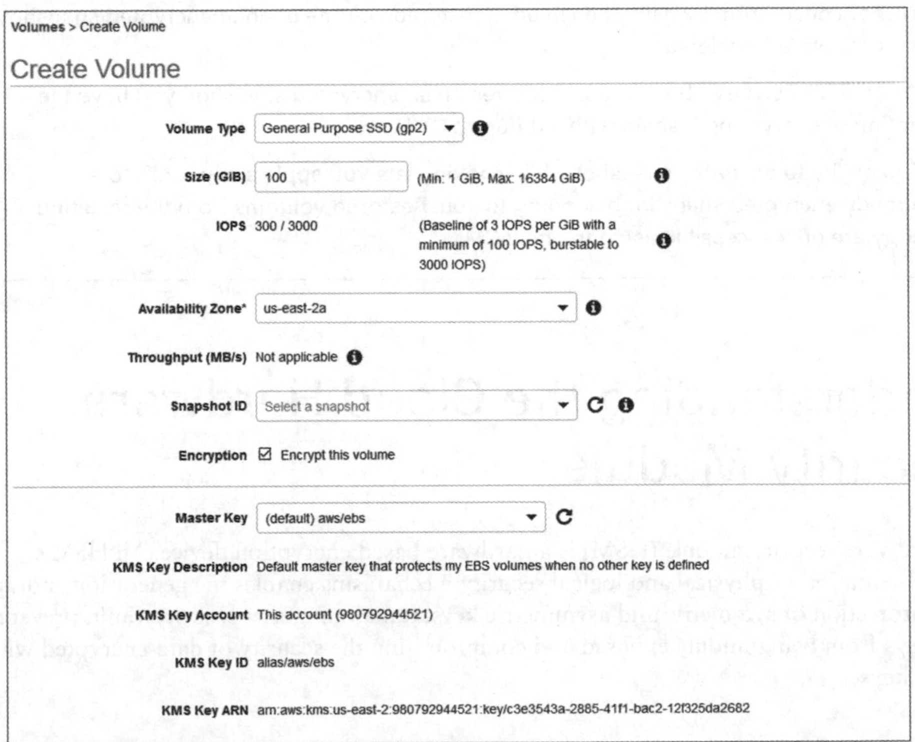

22. Click Create Volume.

Now that you have enabled the EBS encryption using a KMS key, you have EBS volumes that you can attach to an EC2 instance that support encryption volumes. As you can see, the process is very simple; however, pay attention to the "Tips for Protecting EBS with KMS" sidebar, because they may be on your exam.

Tips for Protecting EBS with KMS

- Encryption by default is a region-specific setting. If you enable it for a region, you cannot disable it for individual snapshots or volumes in that region. To enable the EBS encryption by default, you can use this command in the AWS CLI:

```
aws ec2 enable-ebs-encryption-by-default
```

- EBS volumes are encrypted by your account's default client master key unless you specify a customer-managed CMK in EC2 settings or on execution.
- Encryption by default does not affect existing EBS snapshots or volumes, but when copying encrypted snapshots or restoring unencrypted volumes, the resulting volumes or snapshots are encrypted.
- By enabling encryption by default, you can run an Amazon EC2 instance only if the instance type supports EBS encryption.
- Without encryption by default enabled, a restored volume of an unencrypted snapshot is unencrypted by default.
- When the `CreateVolume` action operates on an encrypted snapshot, you have the option of encrypting it again with a different CMK.
- The ability to encrypt a snapshot while copying lets you apply a new CMK to an already encrypted snapshot belonging to you. Restored volumes from the resulting copy are only accessible using the new CMK.

Understanding the Cloud Hardware Security Module

A hardware security module (HSM) is a hardware-based encryption device. An HSM's implementation of physical and logical security mechanisms enables the generation, storage, and protection of symmetric and asymmetric keys, functioning as a security vault, preventing the keys from being unduly exposed and compromising the security of data encrypted with those keys.

AWS CloudHSM is a managed service that automates administration tasks such as hardware provisioning, software patching, high availability configurations, and key backups. AWS CloudHSM lets you scale quickly by adding or removing on-demand HSM capabilities, in a pay-as-you-go model.

With AWS CloudHSM, you can still implement multiregional clustering and replication, further enhancing your level of protection, resiliency, and business continuity. You can also integrate the solution with your applications using APIs, Cryptography API: Next Generation (CNG) libraries, Public Key Cryptography Standards (PKCS) #11, and Java Cryptography Extensions (JCE).

Generally, the use of an HSM Cloud is directly related to meeting regulatory needs, such as FIPS 140-2 Level 3 standards. To create an HSM cluster in the AWS Console, you must configure the VPC, subnets, and their availability zones where cluster members will be provisioned.

Figures 6.24 and 6.25 show how Amazon CloudHSM is provisioned through the AWS Console.

FIGURE 6.24 CloudHSM configuration

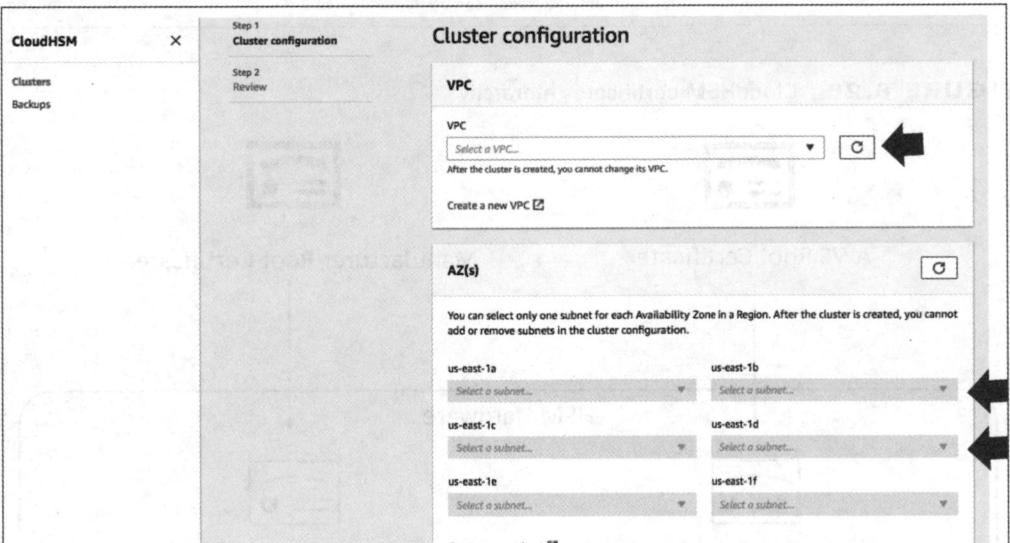

Once you have created a cluster, you need to kickstart it by validating the HSM certificate chains, verifying the identity of your cluster, and then importing the signed cluster certificate and your issuing certificate. Figure 6.26 shows the relationship between certificates.

FIGURE 6.25 CloudHSM configuration validation

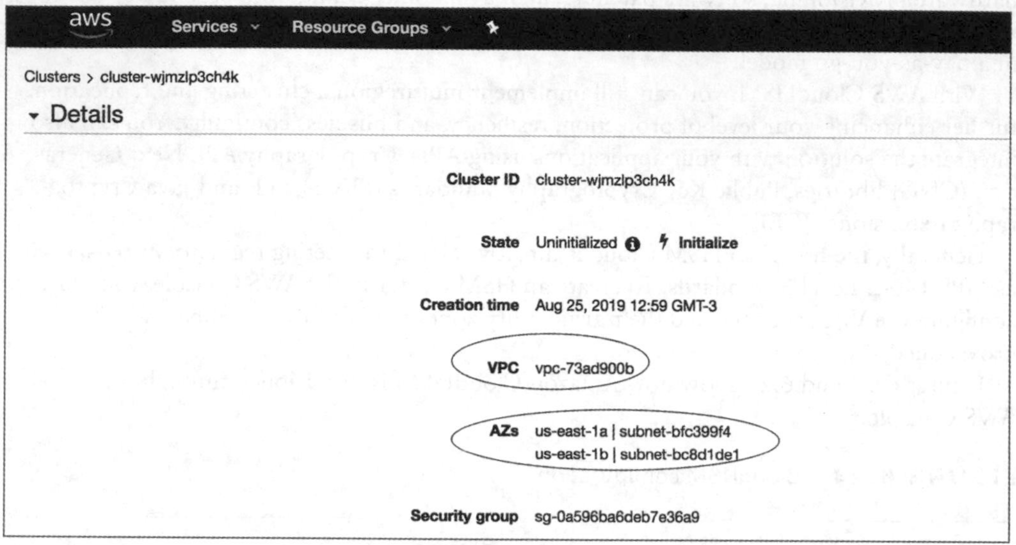

FIGURE 6.26 CloudHSM certificates hierarchy

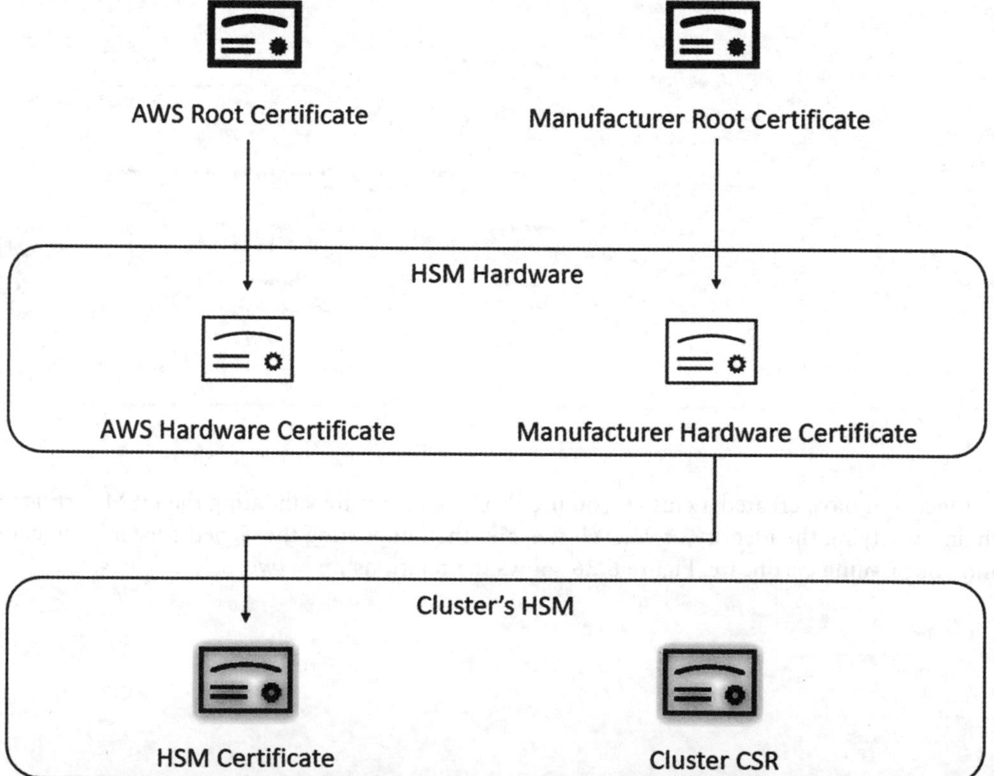

In order to understand the relationship between certificates, you first need to understand each of the certificates on its own:

- **AWS Root Certificate:** This is AWS CloudHSM's root certificate.
- **Manufacturer Root Certificate:** This is the hardware manufacturer's root certificate.
- **AWS Hardware Certificate:** AWS CloudHSM created this certificate when the HSM hardware was added to the fleet. This certificate asserts that AWS CloudHSM owns the hardware.
- **Manufacturer Hardware Certificate:** The HSM hardware manufacturer created this certificate when it manufactured the HSM hardware. This certificate asserts that the manufacturer created the hardware.
- **HSM Certificate:** The HSM certificate is generated by the FIPS-validated hardware when you create the first HSM in the cluster. This certificate asserts that the HSM hardware created the HSM.
- **Cluster CSR (certified signing request):** The first HSM creates the cluster CSR.When you sign the cluster CSR, you claim the cluster. Then, you can use the signed CSR to initialize the cluster.

Once the Cluster HSM (a collection of individual HSMs) is configured, the client can access the service through network interfaces and security group configurations directly from their VPC, as shown in Figure 6.27.

FIGURE 6.27 VPC architecture to access ClusterHSM

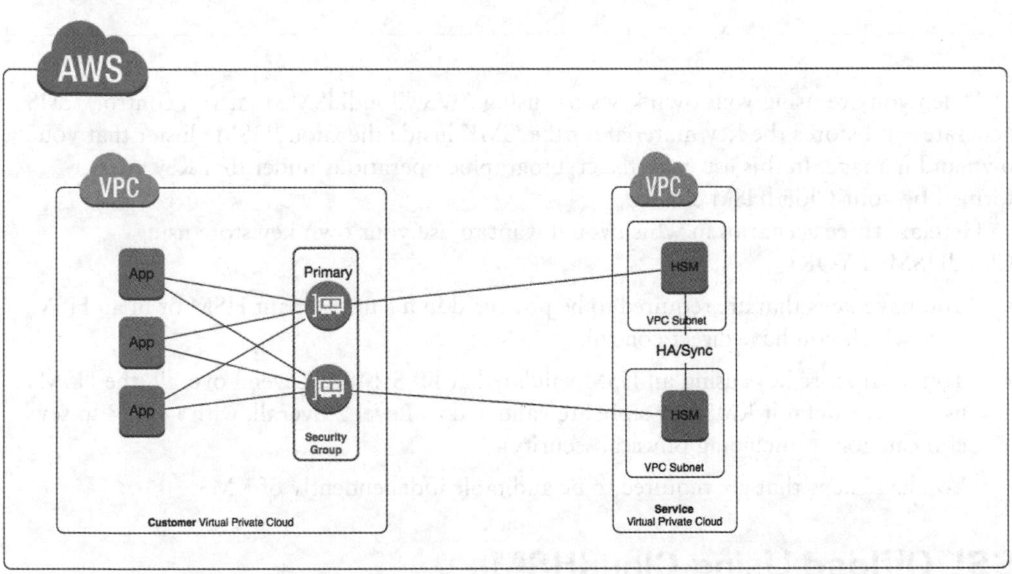

In Figure 6.27, applications in the Customer VPC must use an ENI to access CloudHMS and keys provisioned in the service VPC.

You don't need to know how to provision, export, validate, and start a CloudHSM for the certification exam, but if you want to do a complete lab, you can find step-by-step instructions in the CloudHSM documentation at `docs.aws.amazon.com/cloudhsm/latest/userguide/getting-started.html`.

Using CloudHSM with AWS KMS

It is also possible to integrate AWS CloudHSM with the AWS KMS service. This allows you to use an AWS CloudHSM cluster to protect the customer master keys (CMKs) and thus the data keys and data in the most diverse AWS cloud services.

Figure 6.28 shows how to configure AWS KMS custom key stores to use with a Cloud HSM.

FIGURE 6.28 AWS KMS Custom key stores configuration with HSM

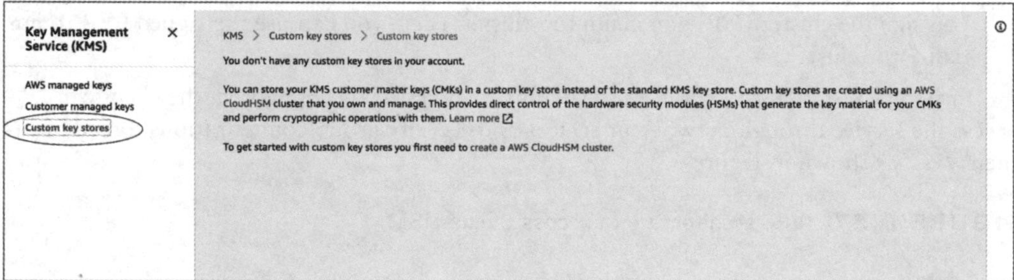

When you are using your own key store using AWS CloudHSMs that you control, KMS generates and stores the Key material for the CMK inside the CloudHSM cluster that you own and manage. In this use case, the cryptographic operations under that Key are performed by your CloudHSM cluster.

Here are three scenarios in which you'd want to use your own key store using CloudHSMs BYOK:

- You have keys that are required to be protected in a single-tenant HSM or in an HSM over which you have direct control.
- You must store keys using an HSM validated at FIPS 140-2 Level 3 overall (the HSMs used in the default KMS key store are validated to Level 2 overall, with Level 3 in several categories, including physical security).
- You have keys that are required to be auditable independently of KMS.

SSL Offload Using CloudHSM

You can use AWS CloudHSM to offload SSL encryption and decryption of traffic to your servers or instances, improving private key protection, reducing performance impact into your application, and raising your application security when using AWS Cloud.

The following steps describe the communication process followed by the client, the server, and CloudHSM once the configuration is built:

1. The client connects to the server.
2. The server responds and sends the server's certificate.
3. The client verifies that a trusted root certificate authority signs the SSL/TLS server certificate and extracts the public key from the server certificate.
4. The client generates a secret premaster key.
5. The client encrypts the premaster key with the server's public key and sends it to the server.
6. The server sends the client's premaster secret to the HSM.
7. The HSM uses the private key in the HSM to decrypt the premaster secret.
8. The HSM sends the premaster secret to the server.
9. The handshake process ends, and all subsequent messages sent between the client and the server are encrypted with derivatives of the master secret.

Figure 6.29 graphically represents these steps.

FIGURE 6.29 Custom Key Store KMS integration to CloudHSM

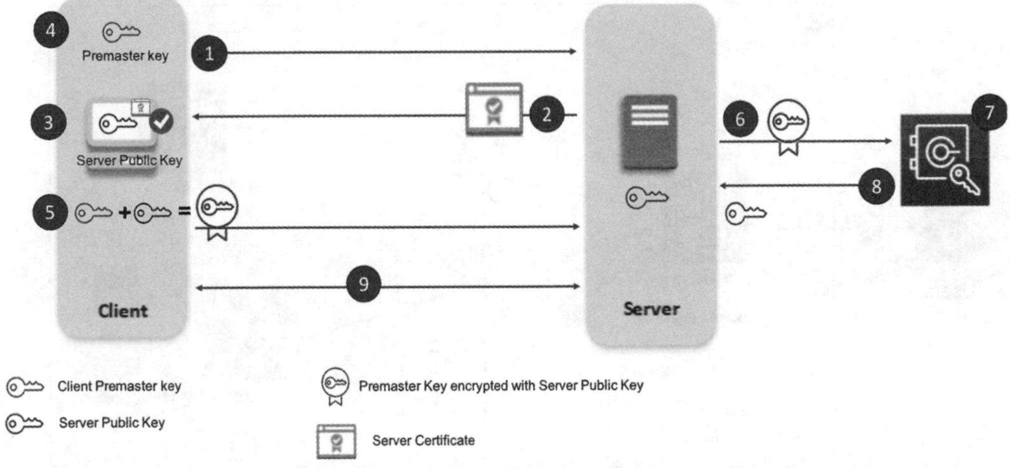

AWS Certificate Manager

With the increasing use of APIs, services exposed to the Internet, and integration with third parties, it is a requirement to implement secure protocols, especially when we talk about communications through Internet environments. The use of such protocols is fundamental to increase the security level of your applications and environments, as well as the confidentiality of your environment.

Consequently, with more elements exchanging information securely, the challenge to generate, manage, install, and control digital certificates for highly scalable environments also increases.

AWS Certificate Manager (ACM) is a managed service that allows you to quickly provision, manage, and deploy Secure Sockets Layer (SSL)/Transport Layer Security (TLS) certificates for use with both AWS Cloud–native services and your internal resources.

Through the AWS Certificate Manager service, you can quickly request an SSL certificate; deploy it to ACM-integrated AWS services such as Elastic Load Balancers, Amazon CloudFront distributions, and APIs on the Amazon API Gateway; and let AWS Certificate Manager administer the renewals of these certificates. The service can also be used for internal digital certificate generation, functioning as an internal *CA (certificate authority)*.

A CA issues SSL digital certificates accepted by most browsers, and is responsible for validating the ownership of a domain by a company or organization, ensuring that information is being exchanged with the correct entity.

ACM has no costs when used within the AWS-native environment and resources; however, when using it as an internal certificate authority for on-premises environments, it has a monthly cost.

Figure 6.30 shows a scenario where ACM is integrated to native AWS services.

FIGURE 6.30 ACM integration with AWS-native services scenario

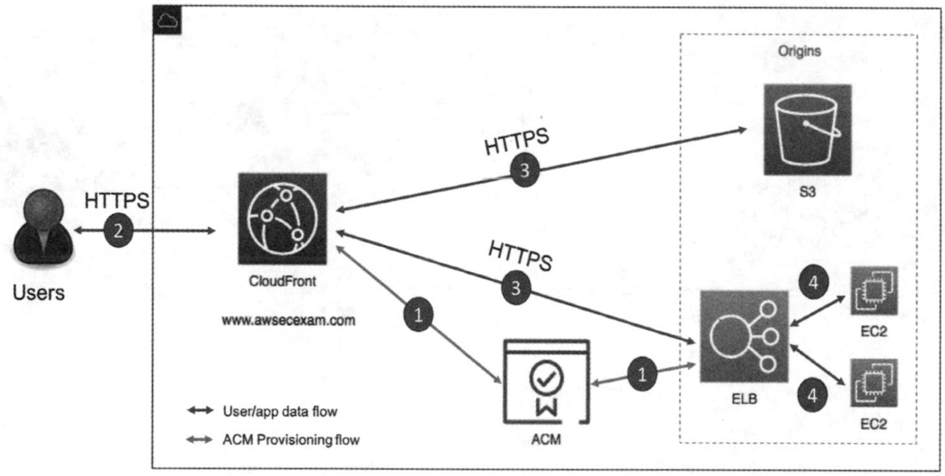

In Figure 6.30, ACM automates the creation and renewal of SSL/TLS certificates and deploys them to AWS CloudFront distributions and Elastic Load Balancer in step 1, considering your predefined configurations. The users communicate with CloudFront over HTTPS in step 2, and CloudFront terminates the SSL/TLS connection at the edge location. You can configure CloudFront to communicate to the origin over HTTPS in step 3, using an S3 bucket or even an ELB that can distribute the connections to different EC2 instances in the same AZ, or in multiple AZs, as defined in step 4.

Figure 6.31 shows how you can integrate your ACM in the AWS Cloud, generating certificates to your traditional, on-premises environments.

FIGURE 6.31 ACM private CA scenario

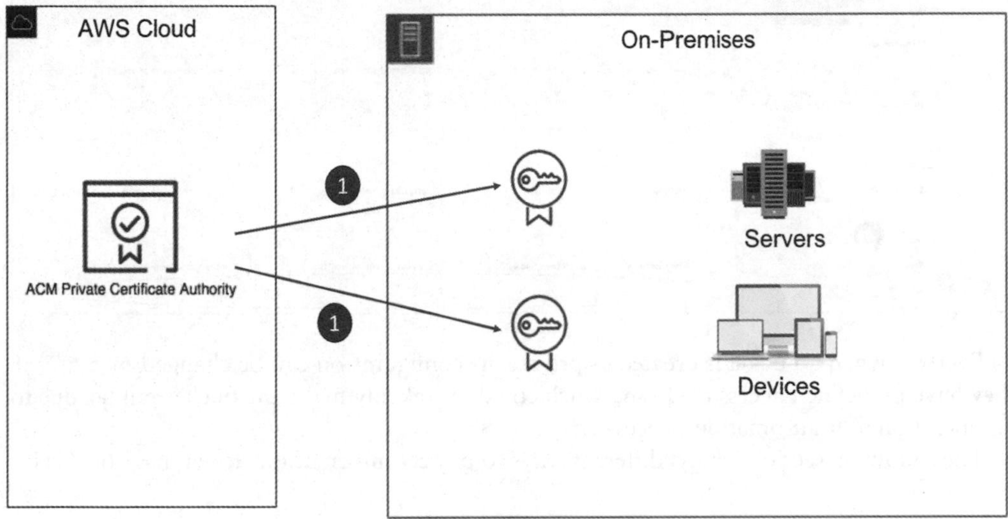

When used as a private CA, ACM can generate the certificates to your legacy, on-premises environment and protect IoT device communications.

Protecting Your S3 Buckets

Amazon Simple Storage Service (*Amazon S3*) is an object storage service that offers the ability to store large amounts of data for a variety of use cases, such as public site code that can be accessed by users, backing up and restoring files, images, business applications, and IoT devices. It is also a centerpiece for using big data and analytics in the AWS environment.

Since virtually any type of data can be stored in S3, it is crucial to apply the necessary security measures to protect sensitive information that may have been stored in this type of object storage. The following sections discuss fundamental mechanisms in the AWS environment that you should use to protect data when using S3 buckets.

Default Access Control Protection

Every bucket in S3 is created by default as a private bucket—that is, the bucket is initially protected from public external access, as shown in Figure 6.32.

FIGURE 6.32 Default S3 bucket created as a private bucket

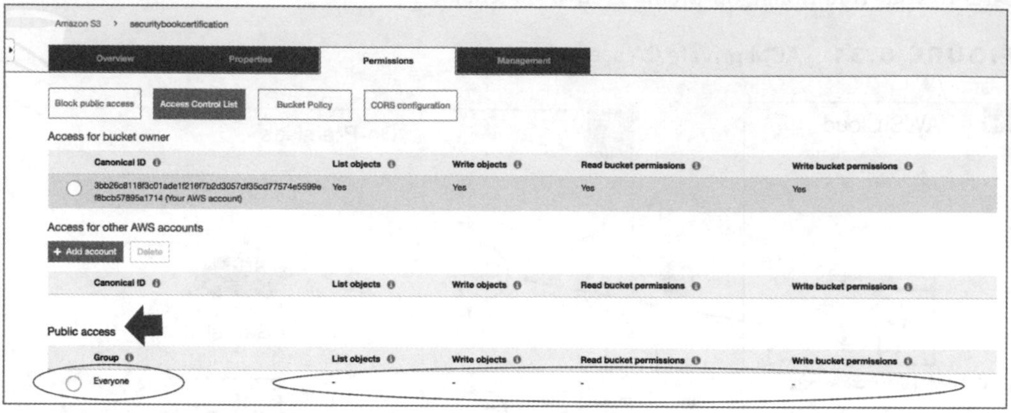

Even so, when a bucket is created as private, its configuration can be changed by a user if they have predefined access to do so, which could mistakenly make the bucket public, due to an operational or automation process error.

The following section details different ways to protect information stored in S3 buckets.

Bucket and Object Encryption

When created with the default settings, buckets are automatically defined as private. However, there are no encryption mechanisms defined by default, so the administrator or the bucket owner must determine which of the available encryption mechanisms to use.

Figure 6.33 shows the default encryption configuration when you create an S3 bucket.

The Amazon S3 service allows three different mechanisms to be used to encrypt stored data so that information is automatically encrypted when sent to buckets:

- **SSE-S3:** Server-side encryption with Amazon S3–managed keys
- **SSE-KMS:** Server-side encryption with KMS customer-managed master keys
- **SSE-C:** Server-side encryption with customer-provided encryption keys

Amazon S3 evaluates and applies bucket policies before applying bucket encryption settings. Even if you enable bucket encryption settings, your PUT requests without encryption information will be rejected if you have bucket policies to reject such PUT requests. So, it is very important to not only implement the encryption mechanism but also review your bucket policies.

FIGURE 6.33 Default S3 creation with no encryption

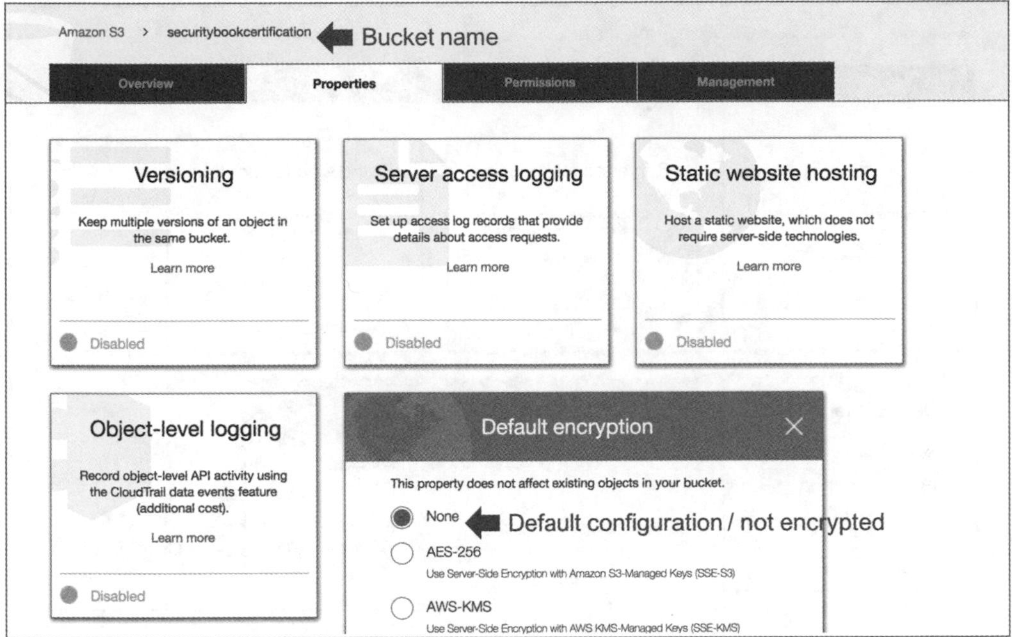

SSE-S3 Encryption

SSE-S3 is the native encryption functionality of the AWS S3 service. This functionality allows you to natively encrypt objects inserted into a bucket using an AES-256 symmetric key, which is automatically generated and managed directly by the S3 service, at no additional cost

In such a scenario, Amazon S3 encrypts each object with a unique key and additionally protects the data encryption key with a master key that is updated regularly. This feature can be enabled directly in the bucket's setting properties by following these steps through the AWS Console:

1. Select the Amazon S3 service inside the AWS Console.
2. Select the bucket that you want to encrypt by clicking its name in the list or by searching for it with the search tool at the top of the screen.
3. Click the Properties configuration tab of the bucket.
4. Select the option Default Encryption.
5. Select the AES-256 option.
6. Save the configuration.

Figure 6.34 shows which default encryption option corresponds to the SSE-S3 configuration.

FIGURE 6.34 SSE-S3 configuration

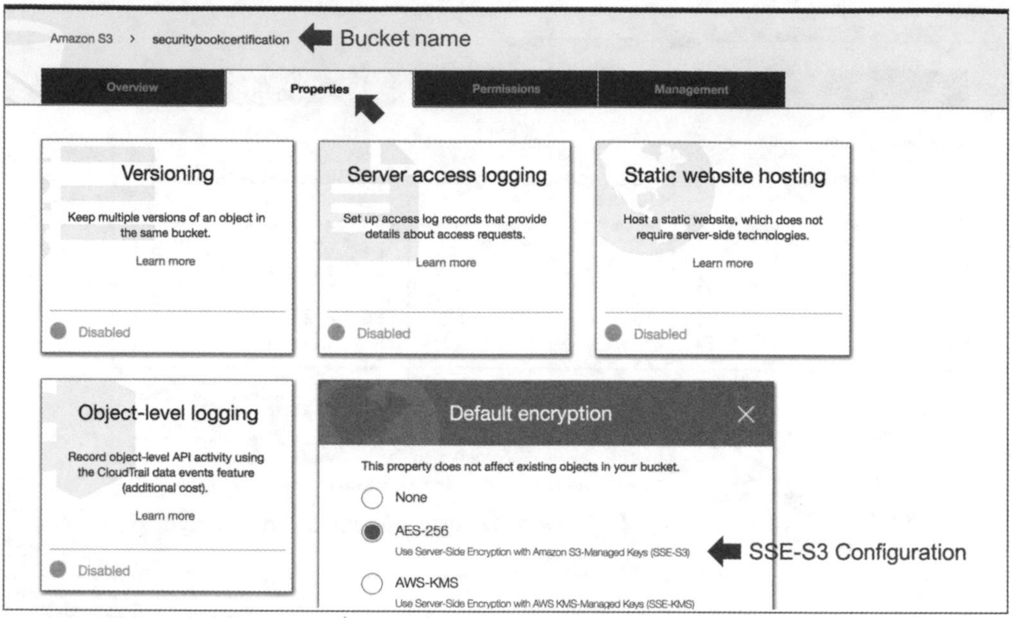

SSE-KMS Encryption

SSE-KMS is the encryption functionality of the S3 service that uses encryption keys managed with KMS. This functionality sets the behavior of S3 to encrypt by default every object inserted into the specified bucket using keys managed through KMS, regardless of whether they are AWS managed keys or customer-managed keys. Objects inserted in the bucket after this configuration is performed will be encrypted even if no encryption option is specified in the request.

The first time you add an SSE-KMS encrypted object to a bucket in a region, a default CMK is created and used for SSE-KMS encryption when you are using AWS Managed Keys (aws/s3).

It is also important to know that an extra cost might incur in this configuration. Figure 6.35 highlights how to configure the bucket encryption using the Properties tab, and Figure 6.36 shows how to select and use the AWS managed keys for S3 within KMS.

You can also select customer-managed keys (CMKs) previously created with KMS, which allows flexibility, including the ability to set access controls, a managed key rotation, and audit key usage to protect your data. In this scenario, the S3 service benefits from the full AWS KMS features such as auto-rotation, key management model, and usage auditability.

Figure 6.37 shows how to select a preexisting KMS CMK to use with an S3 bucket.

To enable the encryption service using AWS KMS, follow these steps:

1. Select the Amazon S3 service in the AWS Console.
2. Select the bucket that you want to encrypt by clicking its name in the list or by searching for it with the search tool at the top of the screen.

FIGURE 6.35 S3 SSE-KMS configuration

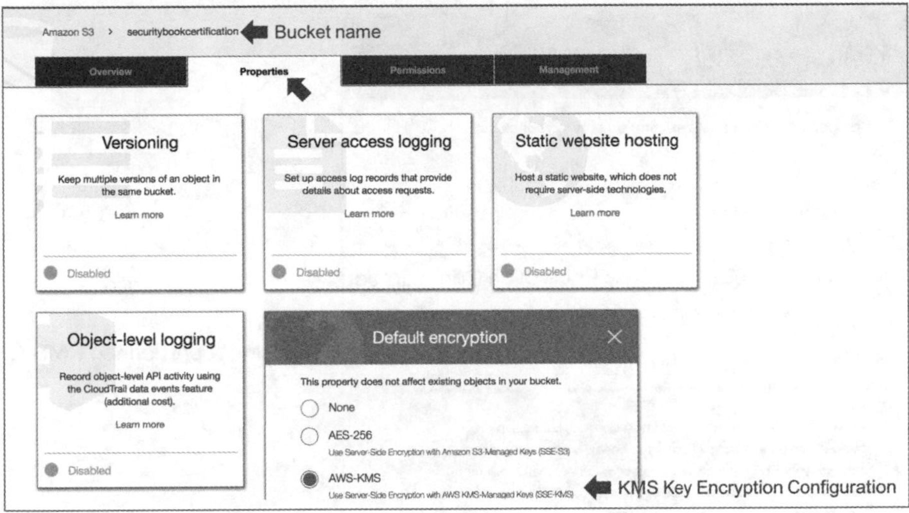

FIGURE 6.36 S3 SSE-KMS with default CMK

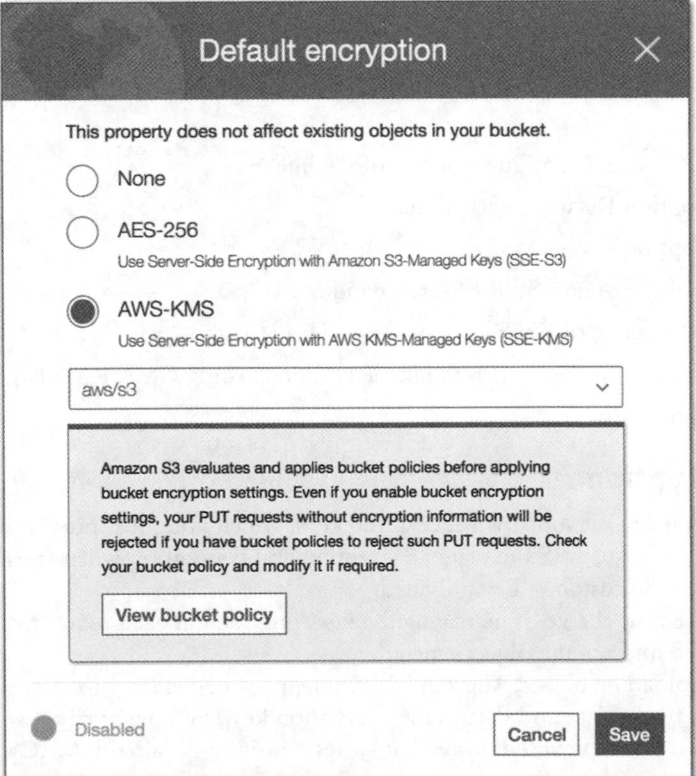

FIGURE 6.37 S3 SSE-KMS with preexisting CMK

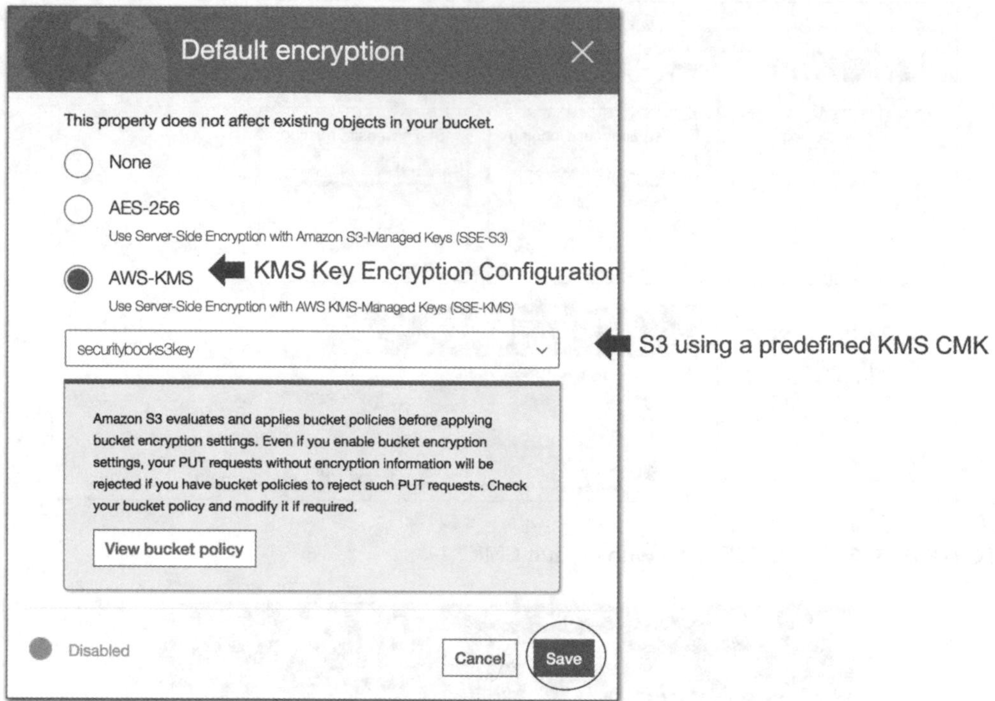

3. Select the Properties configuration tab of the bucket.
4. Select the option Default Encryption.
5. Select the option AWS-KMS.
6. Select one of the options in the Search window:
   - An AWS managed KMS key (aws/s3)—This is a standard CMK KMS key.
   - "KMS key name"—This is the name of a preexisting CMK KMS key.
7. Save the configuration.

SSE-C Encryption

Using SSE-C, you can set your own encryption keys, which you must provide as part of a request. So, in this case, the S3 manages encryption and decryption when storing and accessing objects using the customer key provided.

The customer is in charge of managing the keys provided in each request, and only the data is encrypted and not the object's metadata.

When you upload an object, Amazon S3 uses the provided encryption key to apply AES-256 encryption to the data and deletes the encryption key from memory, thus not storing the encryption key you provided. Instead, it stores a randomly salted HMAC value from the encryption key to validate future requests, preventing decryption of keys from that salted

HMAC value, key derivation, and decryption of protected data. So, if the customer loses the encryption key, the stored object data is also lost.

An HMAC (hash-based message authentication code) is a specific type of message authentication code (MAC) involving a cryptographic hash function and a secret cryptographic key. The cryptographic strength of the HMAC depends on the cryptographic strength of the underlying hash function, the size of its hash output, and the size and quality of the key.

When using the SSE-C feature, you must use HTTPS because requests made over general HTTP are rejected for security reasons and using HTTP may compromise the confidentiality of the keys sent. Also, since S3 does not store the keys used, the client is responsible for managing and controlling which key was used to encrypt each object. In this scenario, the client needs to manage which encryption key was used with each object. If the customer loses the encryption key, any GET request for an object without its encryption key fails, and the S3 object is lost.

SSE-KMS Encrypted Objects Replication

By default, Amazon S3 doesn't replicate objects that are stored using SSE-KMS. You must modify the bucket replication configuration to tell Amazon S3 to replicate these objects using the right KMS keys.

To configure the replication, you must change the replication definitions in the Management tab, adding a replication rule for the specific bucket, as shown in Figure 6.38.

FIGURE 6.38 S3 Replication configuration

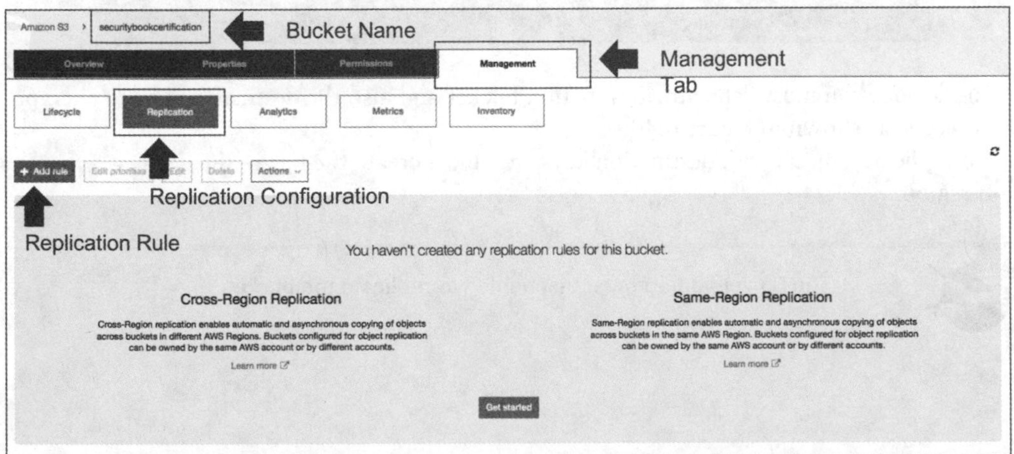

You must select the right CMK used to decrypt the objects in the source bucket, as you can see in Figure 6.39.

FIGURE 6.39 Key that must be used to decrypt the objects in the S3 origin bucket

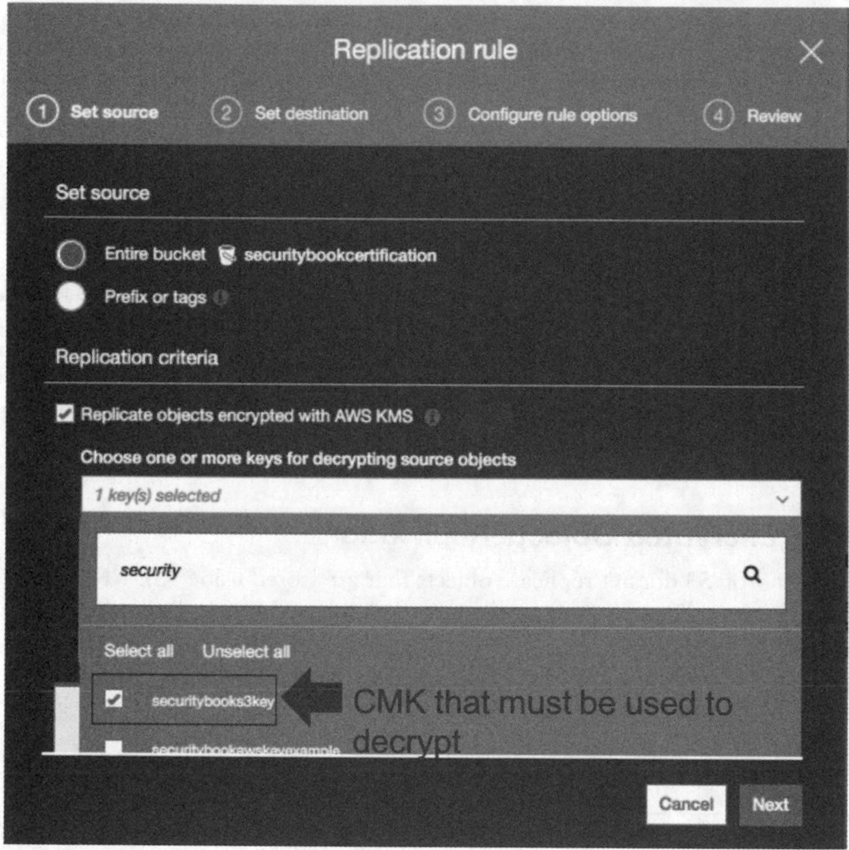

In the end, you must define the destination bucket and also the destination key to encrypt the objects, as shown in Figure 6.40.

To replicate objects with destination keys, you must create the key in the destination region.

The S3 versioning must be enabled to replicate the bucket.

FIGURE 6.40 Destination bucket and the destination encryption key

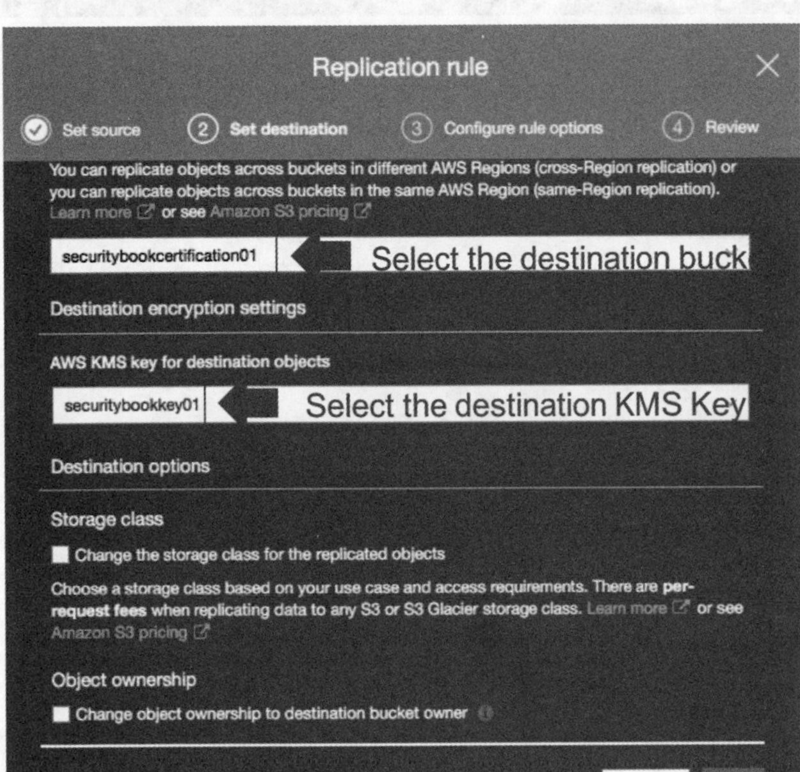

In Exercise 6.5, you create an S3 bucket using an SCP to protect access to your data.

EXERCISE 6.5

Protect Your S3 Buckets with Block Public Access Settings and SCP

In this exercise, you create an S3 bucket and use the Block Public Access functionality to protect and prevent an S3 bucket from becoming public. You will also configure an SCP to enforce a protection policy in your account. To complete the exercise, the account must be part of an AWS Organization and the user must have access to the organization master account to change the SCPs.

1. Open the S3 Console.
2. Select the account settings for Block Public Access.

EXERCISE 6.5 *(continued)*

Amazon S3

Buckets

Batch operations

Block public access (account settings)

3. Click Edit.
4. Select Block All Public Access, and click Save Changes.

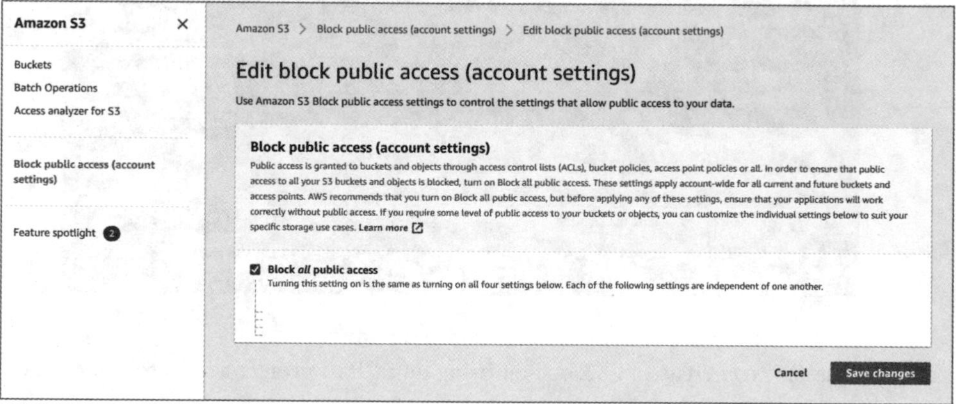

5. Click Confirm.

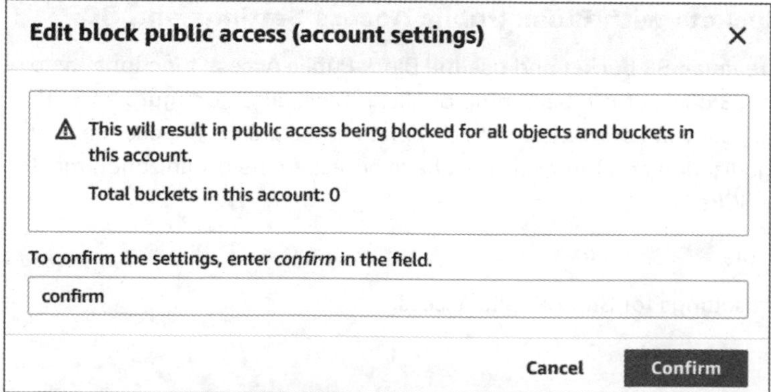

6. Make sure that you applied the configuration correctly.

7. Now you can create an S3 bucket, and try to change the configuration to make the bucket public. You will see an access error message.

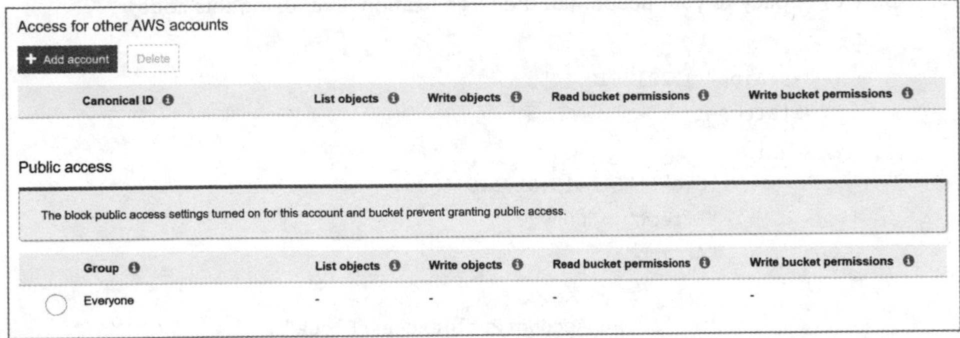

You received this message because the Block Public Access settings were configured, and you cannot change the bucket configuration to make that public.

8. Now try to change an existing bucket to public access. You will see a message that says you are blocked from changing the bucket to public access.

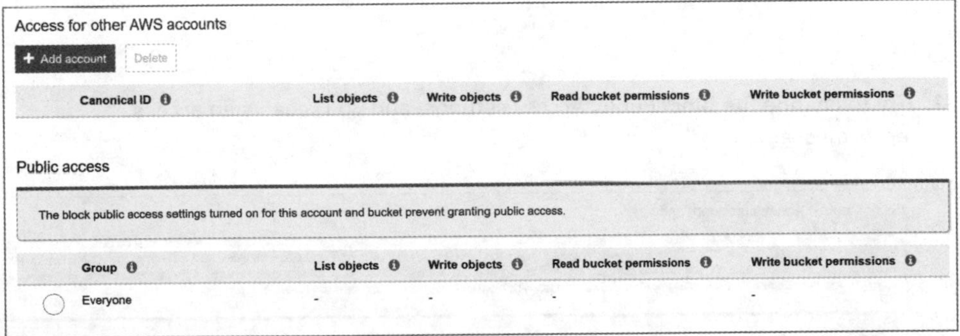

You can also create an SCP at the master account level in AWS Organizations that will apply to all child accounts to prevent someone from changing the Block Access policy configuration.

9. Open the AWS Organization console, and create an SCP.

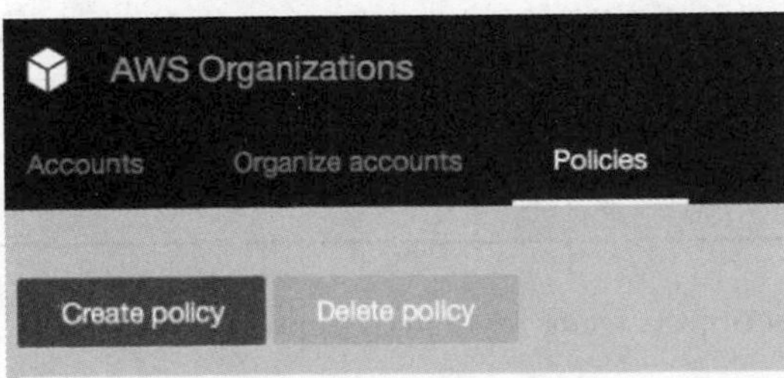

EXERCISE 6.5 ***(continued)***

10. Apply the policy to your account at the Organization level using this code:

```
{
    "Version": "2012-10-17",
    "Statement": [
        {
            "Sid": "Stmt1548173791000",
            "Effect": "Deny",
            "Action": [

                "s3:PutAccountPublicAccessBlock",
                "s3:PutBucketPublicAccessBlock"
            ],
            "Resource": [
                "*"
            ]
        }
    ]
}
```

11. Try to change the Block Public Access settings, and you receive an access error message.

Block public access (account settings)

Public access is granted to buckets and objects through access control lists (ACLs), bucket policies, or both. In order to ensure that public access to all your S3 buckets and objects is blocked, turn on Block *all* public access. These settings apply account-wide for all current and future buckets. AWS recommends that you turn on Block *all* public access, but before applying any of these settings, ensure that your applications will work correctly without public access. If you require some level of public access to your buckets or objects, you can customize the individual settings below to suit your specific storage use cases. Learn more

 You don't have access to view this configuration. Contact your account administrator to request access.

12. Use an SCP to block access to the following APIs:

- `s3:PutAccountPublicAccessBlock`
- `s3:PutBucketPublicAccessBlock`

You can block access to change the Block Public Access settings at the account level or the whole organization, so even if you log in as the root user, you will not be able to change the configuration.

It is also essential to notice that the SCP does not restrict the master account.

In Exercise 6.6, you replicate S3 bucket objects using KMS keys to protect your data across regions.

EXERCISE 6.6

Replicate Encrypted S3 Objects across Regions

In this exercise, you create an S3 bucket, and then configure the S3 bucket to replicate in different regions, using different encryption keys.

1. Create two different S3 buckets in two different regions.

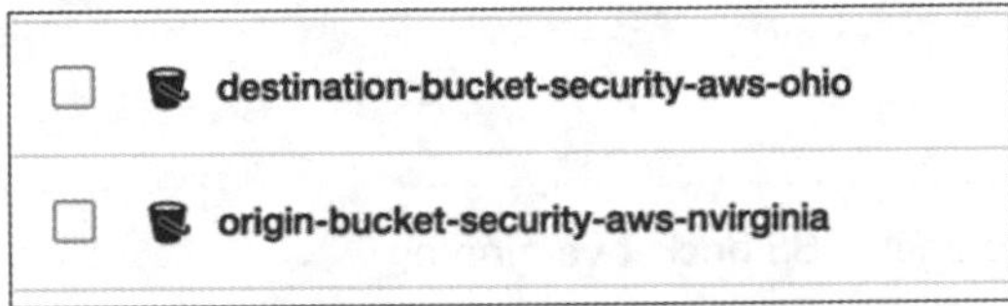

2. Create two different CMKs, one in each region in which you created the buckets (N.Virginia and Ohio, for example).
3. Select the origin bucket.
4. Click Properties.
5. Select Default Encryption.
6. Select the origin KMS key and click save

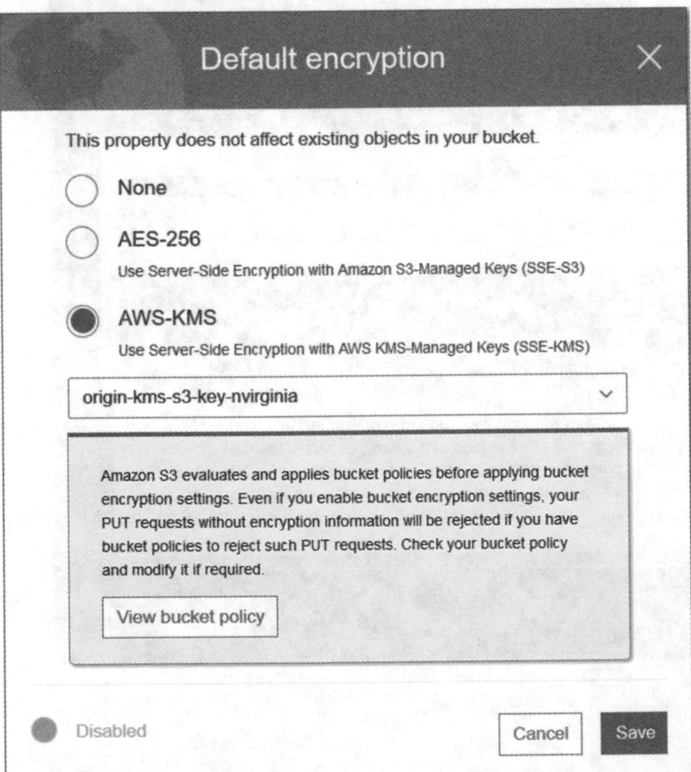

EXERCISE 6.6 *(continued)*

7. In the selected S3 bucket, click Management and then select Replication.

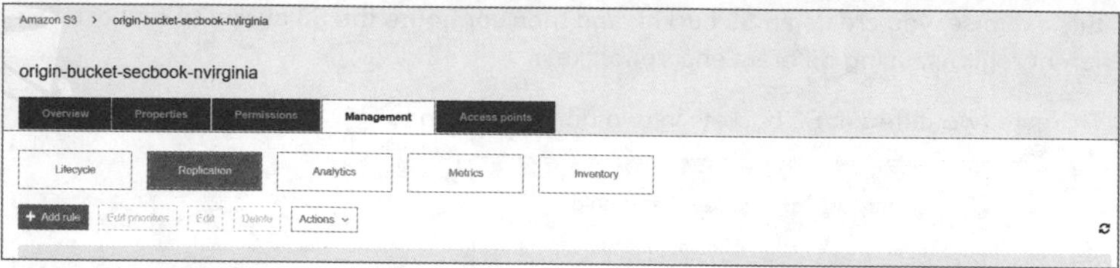

8. Add a rule (remember that you need to enable S3 bucket versioning).
9. Select the Replicate Objects Encrypted With AWS KMS option.

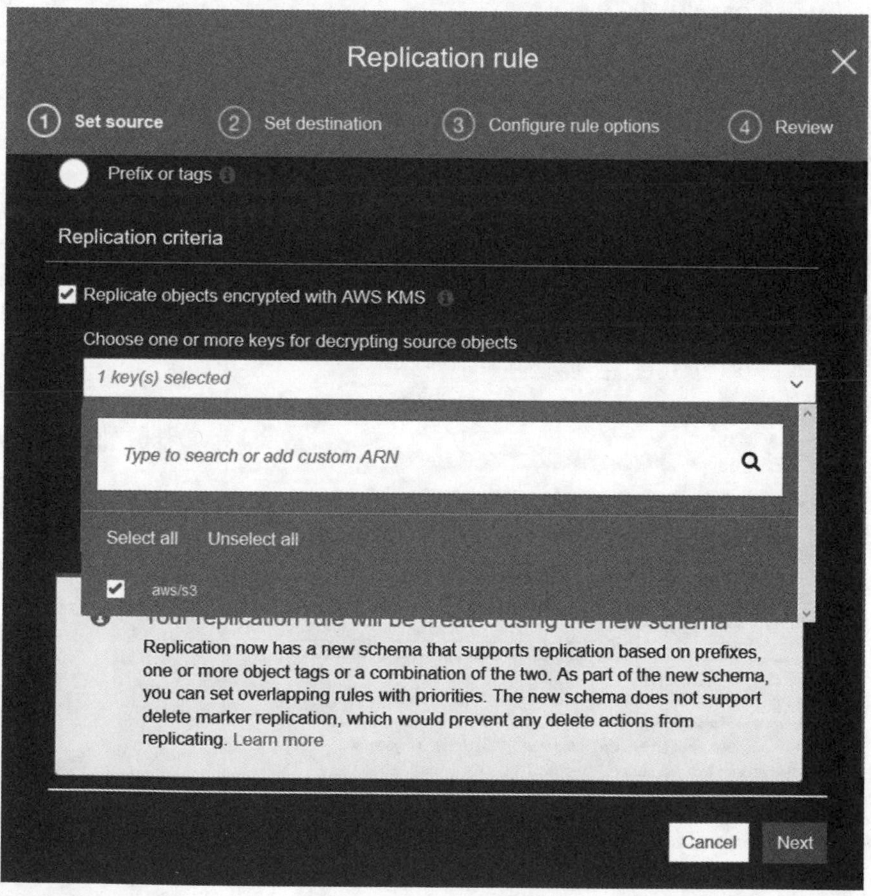

10. Select the key to decrypt the S3 buckets objects, and click Next.

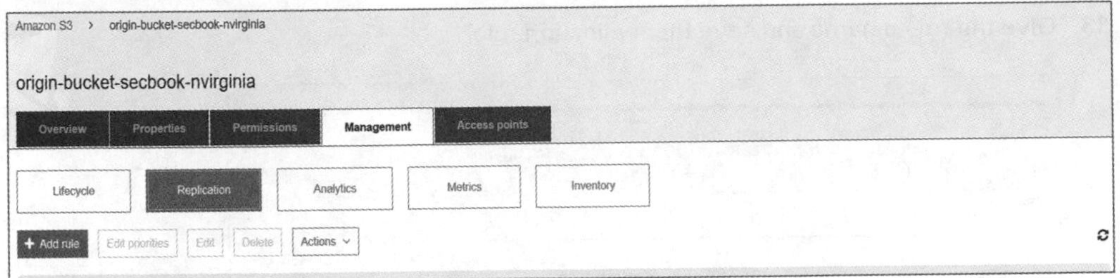

11. Select the bucket to replicate into the destination region and the respective key, and click Next.

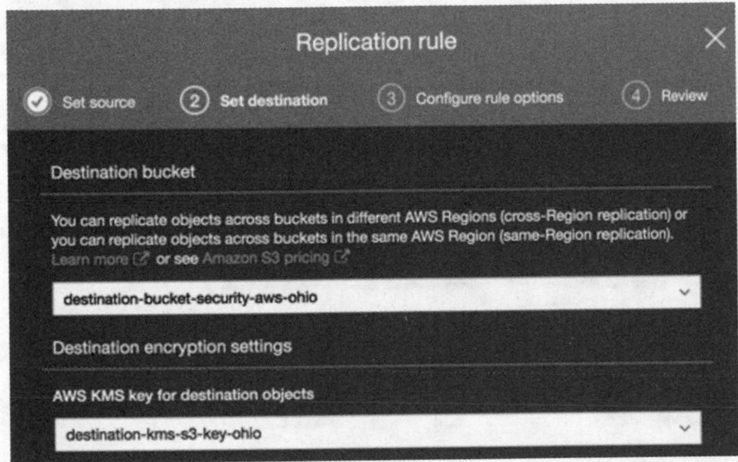

12. Define a new IAM role for replication.

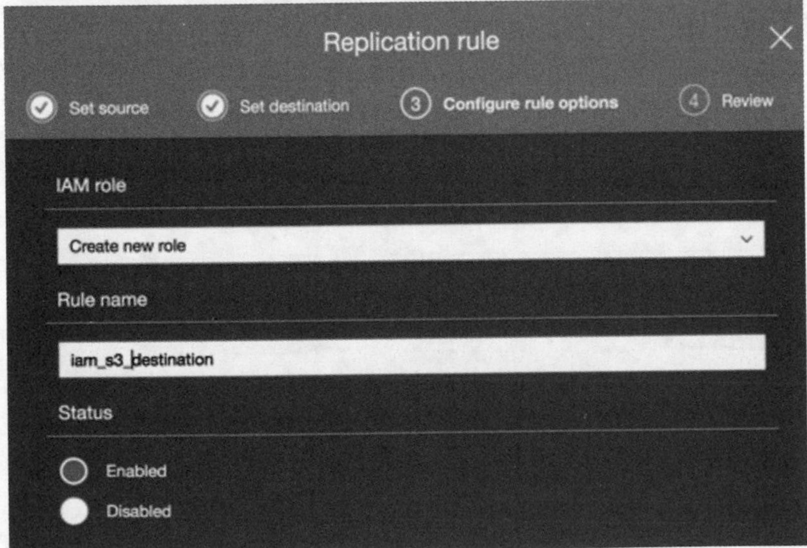

EXERCISE 6.6 *(continued)*

13. Give the rule a name and save the replication rule.

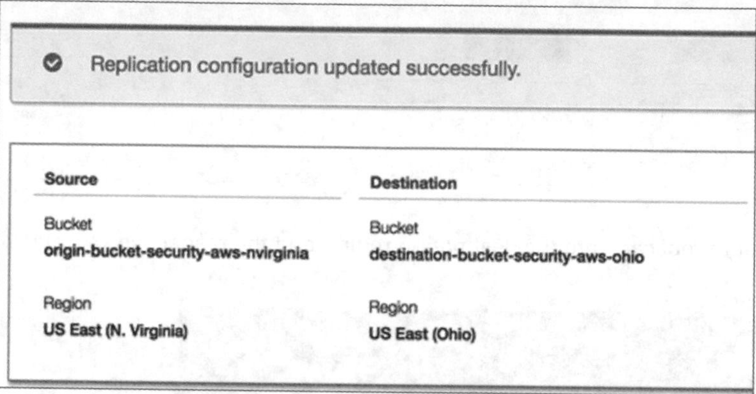

14. Insert a test object into the bucket and validate the replication.

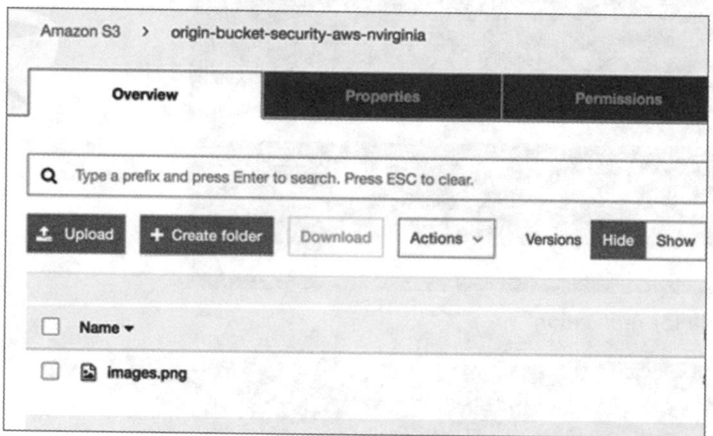

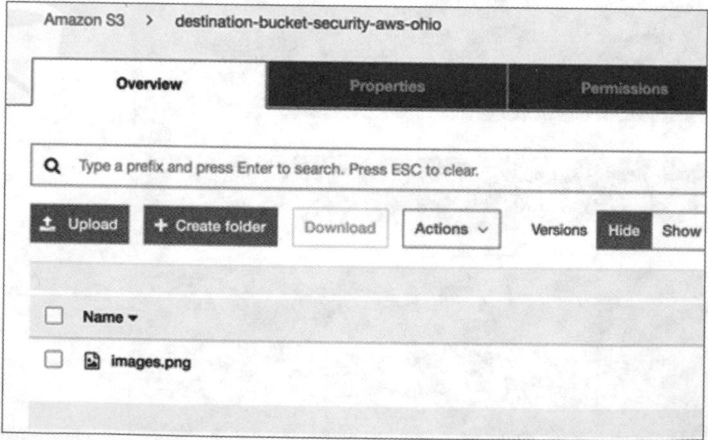

In Exercise 6.7, you protect data inside an S3 bucket object using a resource policy and VPC endpoints.

EXERCISE 6.7

Protect Your S3 Buckets with a Resource Policy and VPC Endpoints

In this exercise, you create an S3 bucket, and then you use an S3 bucket resource policy to limit access to a specific predefined VPC.

1. Create a new bucket.

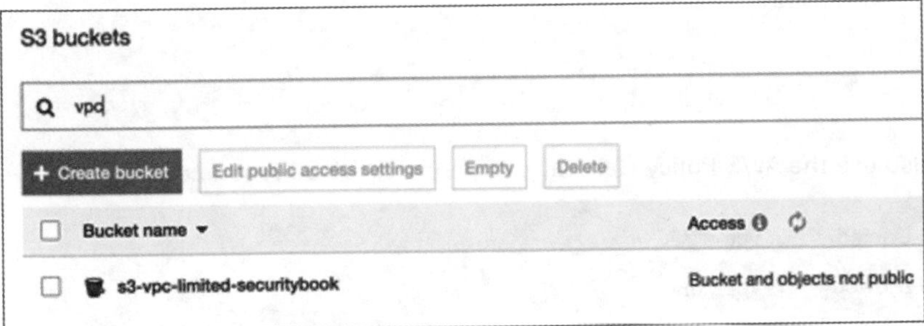

2. Create two different VPCs. (If you need more information on how to create a VPC, you can refer to `docs.aws.amazon.com/vpc/latest/userguide/vpc-getting-started.html`.)

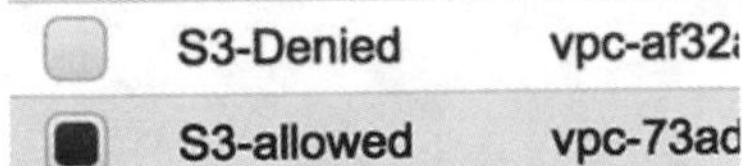

3. Start an EC2 instance in the S3-allowed and the S3-denied VPC so that you can use the AWS CLI to test access to the S3 bucket.

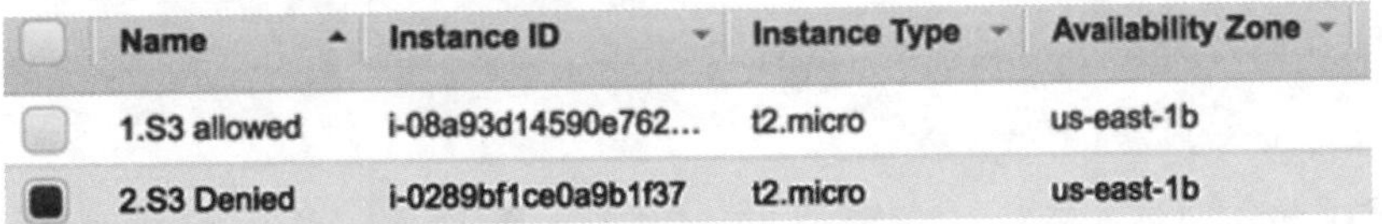

4. Create the following policy in your bucket. Change ***vpc-id*** to your corrected ID, and also change the S3 ARN to your ARN.

```
{
    "Id": "Policy1569592276562",
    "Version": "2012-10-17",
    "Statement": [
      {
        "Sid": "Stmt1569592272181",
        "Action": "s3:*",
```

EXERCISE 6.7 *(continued)*

```
        "Effect": "Deny",
        "Resource": ["arn:aws:s3:::s3-vpc-limited-securitybook",
                     "arn:aws:s3:::s3-vpc-limited-securitybook/*"],
        "Condition": {
          "StringNotEquals": {
            "aws:SourceVpc": "vpc-73ad900b"
          }
        },
        "Principal": "*"
      }
    ]
  }
```

You can also use the AWS Policy Generator to generate the S3 resource policy.

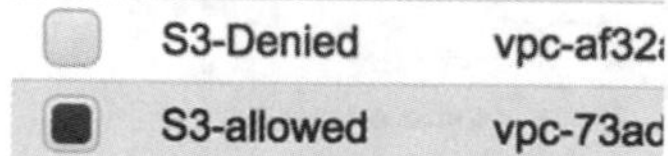

5. Insert an object inside the bucket, and apply the policy.
6. Create a VPC endpoint to the S3 service that is connected to your allowed VPC.

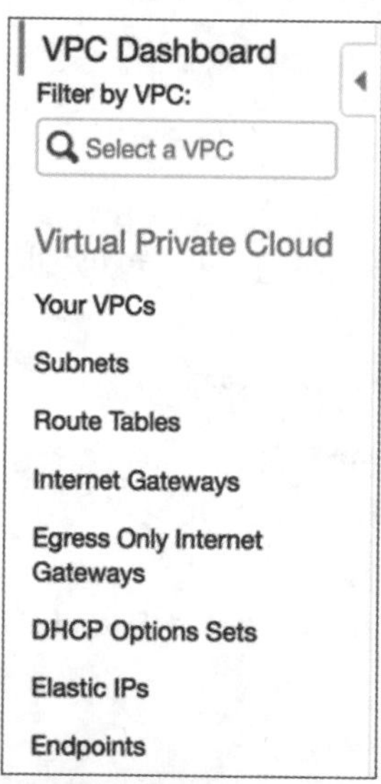

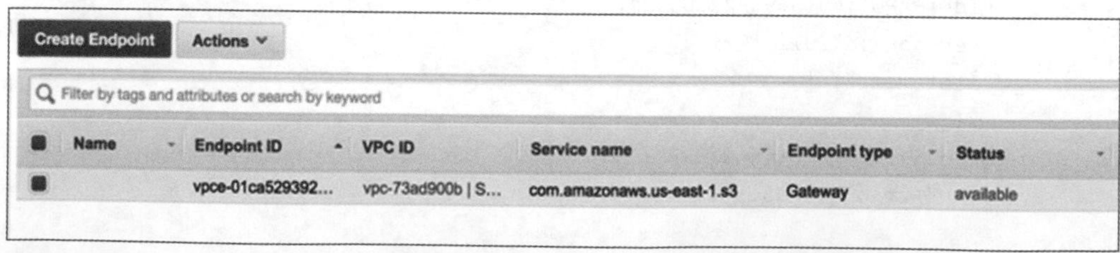

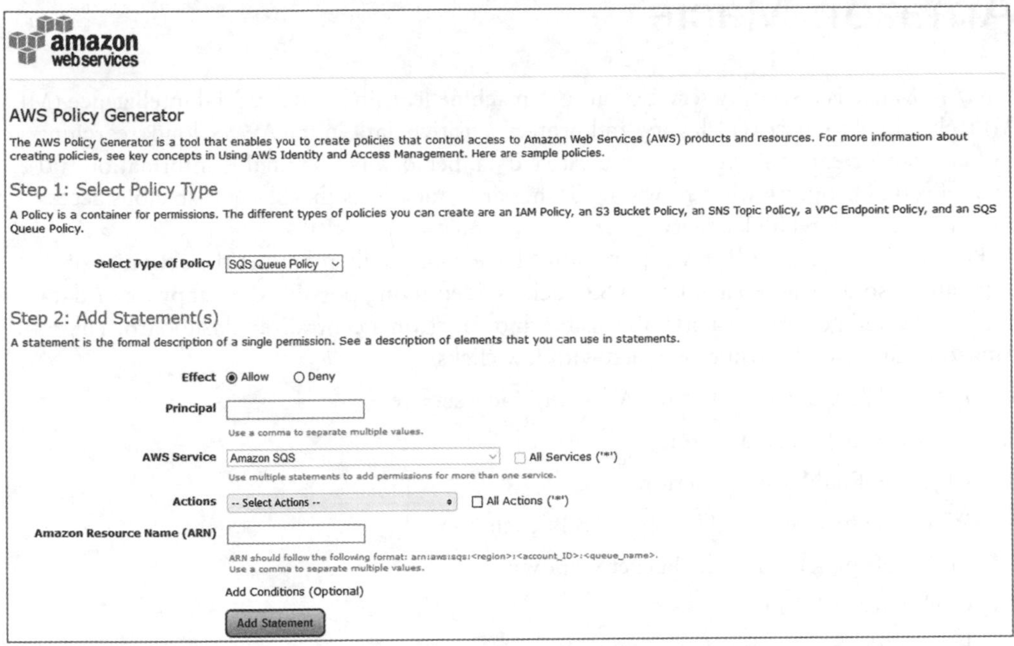

7. You will need to configure an EC2 AWS LINUX instance to run the CLI and execute the proposed tests. You will also need to configure an admin credential using the command AWS configure. If you need help with this, see `docs.aws.amazon.com/cli/latest/userguide/cli-chap-configure.html#cli-quick-configuration`.)

8. Try to access the bucket from the allowed VPCs using the EC2 instance

```
[ec2-user@ip-172-31-42-121 ~]$ aws s3 ls s3://s3-vpc-limited-securitybook
2019-09-27 13:46:45       4081 images.png
[ec2-user@ip-172-31-42-121 ~]$
```

   As you can see, it was possible to access the bucket, using the VPC endpoint and predefined resource policy.

9. Now try to access the bucket using another VPC that is not allowed to access the S3 bucket using another EC2 in this VPC. The access will be blocked because you can only access the bucket from the allowed VPC. Even if you define the bucket as public, you cannot access the bucket from the Internet, because only the predefined VPC, using the S3 endpoint, can access your bucket. Even if you try from the console now, you cannot access the bucket.

Amazon Macie

Amazon Macie is a security service that uses machine learning and artificial intelligence (ML/AI) technology to discover, classify, and protect sensitive data in the AWS Cloud, searching S3 buckets to create an inventory of sensitive data, personally identifiable information (PII), or intellectual property while providing dashboards and alerts that show suspicious access and unusual data-related activity.

Because it is a managed service, Amazon Macie continually monitors the activities of users and resources accessing data in S3 buckets, identifying possible data copying or data movement, and generating alerts of possible anomalies on a centralized dashboard. The Amazon Macie service can be enabled with few clicks:

1. In the AWS Console, select the Amazon Macie service.
2. Click the Get Started button.
3. Click the Enable Macie button.
4. When the service is enabled, click S3 Buckets.
5. In the left panel, select the bucket you own.
6. Click Create A Job.
7. Review the S3 buckets, and click Next.
8. For the scope, schedule a one-time job for this test, and click Next.
9. There are no custom identifiers, so click Next.
10. Define a name and description, and click Next. (You don't need to finish these steps from here, because doing so may generate costs, and our objective here is only to validate the console options.)
11. You can click Submit (remember that doing so may incur costs).

After these steps, Macie starts to monitor the data movements in the S3 bucket and use CloudTrail Events to identify bad behaviors and to generate alerts.

Once enabled, Amazon Macie uses the following methods to protect data:

- AWS CloudTrail Events
- AWS CloudTrail errors

Figure 6.41 shows an Amazon Macie dashboard after a monitoring process is enabled and configured.

FIGURE 6.41 Amazon Macie dashboard

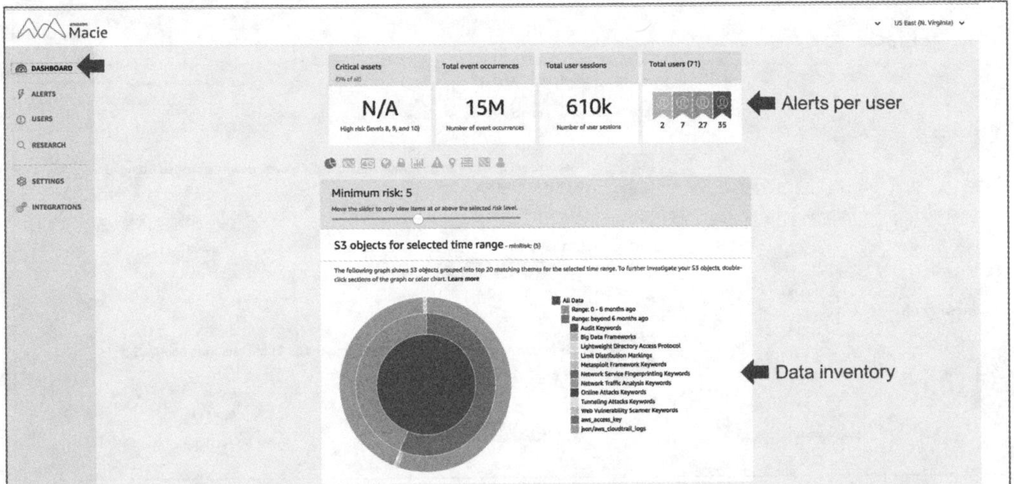

Figure 6.41 shows the S3 data inventory classification, and in the top-right corner, the alerts classification per user category. Macie categorizes the alerts based on four different categories: platinum, gold, silver, and bronze. Platinum and gold accounts should be monitored closely for signs of account compromise; silver and bronze accounts are not as important but should be monitored as well:

- **Platinum:** IAM users or roles that have a history of making high-risk API calls indicative of an administrator or root user. These accounts should be monitored closely for signs of account compromise.
- **Gold:** IAM users or roles that have a history of making infrastructure-related API calls indicative of a power user, such as running instances or writing data to Amazon S3.
- **Silver:** IAM users or roles that have a history of issuing high numbers of medium-risk API calls, such as `Describe*` and `List*` operations, or read-only access requests to Amazon S3.
- **Bronze:** IAM users or roles that typically execute lower numbers of `Describe*` and `List*` API calls in the AWS environment.

Figure 6.42 shows two alerts on the Amazon Macie console.

FIGURE 6.42 Amazon Macie Alerts details console

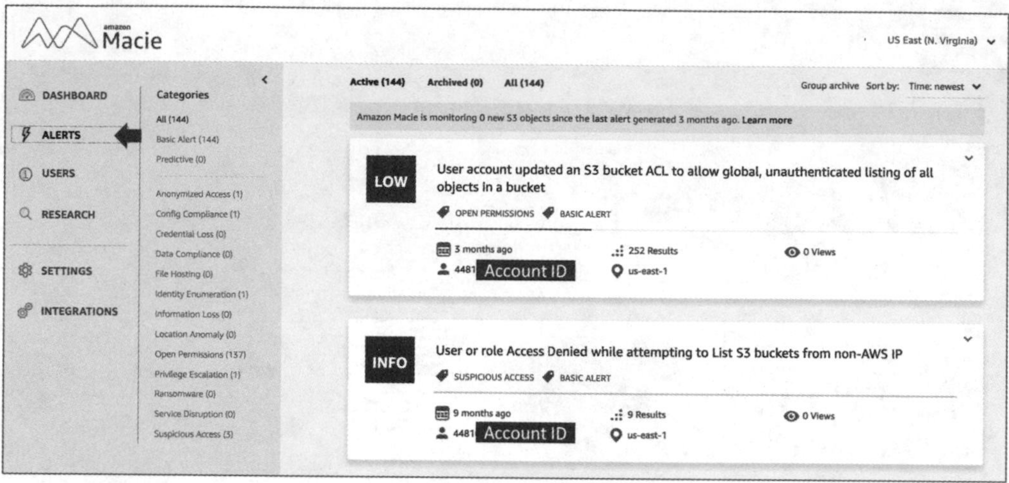

The first alert shows where a user changes an S3 ACL to allow a global, unauthenticated listing of all objects in a bucket's objects. The second alert shows a suspicious access where a non-AWS IP is trying to list S3 buckets but is receiving a denied access error. This might be an instance of trying to enumerate buckets to which the user or principal has no access, which could be an operation error only, but it should be investigated.

Once the service for inventory and data movement monitoring in S3 buckets is enabled, Amazon Macie executes a scan to identify and classify the data types within the selected buckets. It is essential to evaluate the data volume present inside the buckets and the cost of using the service before triggering an extensive data analysis, especially when the evaluation is related to the use of a large volume in data lakes and S3 buckets.

AWS CloudTrail Events

Amazon Macie uses *CloudTrail* Events as a data source for monitoring and learning of possible anomalous behaviors in an AWS customer environment, assigning a risk level between 1 and 10 for each of CloudTrail's supported events.

To have access to more details about the monitored events, as well as to enable or disable the service, follow these steps:

1. In the AWS console, select the Amazon Macie service.
2. Click Settings in the left panel.
3. Select AWS CloudTrail Events.

4. Select specific, monitored events.
5. Enable or disable the specific events in the console.

Figure 6.43 shows how you can access Amazon Macie CloudTrail events.

FIGURE 6.43 Amazon Macie CloudTrail monitored events

Figure 6.44 shows how to enable and disable the CloudTrail events monitoring the process in Amazon Macie.

FIGURE 6.44 Editing Amazon Macie CloudTrail event details

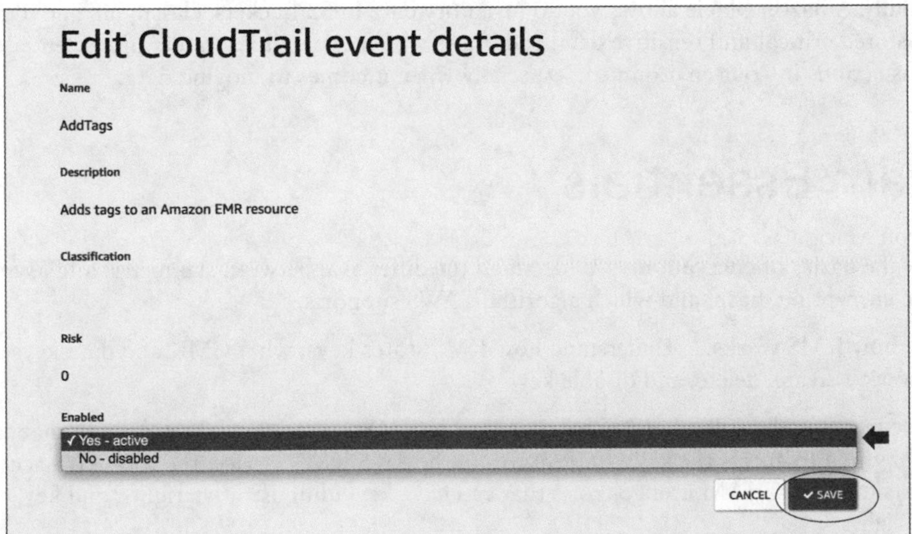

Summary

The implementation of encryption is a critical factor in the success of any data protection strategy. Although it does not solve every challenge related to secure data access, data ciphering is an important layer for increasing the level of data protection, resilience, and privacy.

Using native AWS Cloud data protection solutions enables you to solve many end-to-end security implementation difficulties that are usually observed in traditional environments, such as the ability to deploy cryptographic mechanisms without impacting environment performance, securely protecting and rotating keys automatically, transparently auditing key usage as well as scaling the environment without compromising security.

Using the AWS KMS service also allows you to implement encryption natively within various AWS services, such as RDS databases, EBS disks, and S3 storage of objects. In such integrations, the customer can use their own keys or keys automatically generated by AWS KMS service.

Key access can be granularly controlled, allowing you to define who can create and delete keys or who can access and use the keys to encrypt or decrypt data.

It is also possible to leverage AWS CloudHSM, thus implementing dedicated cryptographic hardware to protect your keys, meeting the highest security standards, such as FIPS140-2 Level 3.

A multiple AZ or even multi-regional architecture can be used to create a highly scalable, on-demand, and pay-as-you-go model.

You can use ACM for SSL/TLS digital certificate generation to secure communication of your applications by protecting data in transit in your AWS environment. You can also use it to generate and manage internal digital certificates in your traditional on-premises environments.

Finally, Amazon Macie allows you to inventory data in S3 buckets, classifying and identifying stored critical and sensitive data, and using ML/AI capabilities to identify potential suspicious actions in your environment, especially when it comes to moving data.

Exam Essentials

Know the basics of encryption. Understand the difference between symmetric and asymmetric encryption, hash, and which algorithms AWS supports.

Know how KMS works. Understand how KMS stores keys, what CMK and data keys are, and how to create, delete, and disable keys.

Be able to name the roles that you must control in KMS. You have three profiles that can be configured to access the keys and features of the AWS KMS service: the root AWS account that has full access, IAM users or roles that can have key administrative rights, and key usage rights.

Know how to create and use a KMS security policy. Make sure that you understand the different sessions in a JSON access control policy for CMKs, including the API calls that can be granularly controlled for administrative and nonadministrative access.

Know how to use KMS with other AWS-native services. Know how to use the KMS service with other services such as S3, EBS, RDS.

Understand the three S3 encryption models. You must understand the difference between SS3-S3, SSE-KMS, and SSE-C, as well as how to use and configure them.

Understand CloudHSM. Make sure that you know when to use a CloudHSM and the benefits of doing so. Remember that the HSM can generate and manage keys in compliance with the FIPS 140-2 Level 3 standard. Recall that you can use a multi-AZ, multiregion approach as a more resilient environment.

Know how to use ACM. Understand the scenarios in which you can use ACM, how to architect a solution that can generate SSL certificates to AWS-native services, and also how internal on-premises environments work.

Understand how Macie can protect your data. Make sure that you understand how Macie works, how it uses CloudTrail and ML/AI to protect your data, generate alerts, and allow visibility and cataloging of your PII and confidential data.

Review Questions

1. Which of the following methods can be used to encrypt data in S3 buckets? (Choose three.)
   A. ACM using symmetric keys
   B. SSE-S3
   C. SSE-KMS
   D. SSE-C
2. Which of the following methods is the cheaper encryption method that you can use in S3 buckets?
   A. SSE-S3
   B. SSE-KMS
   C. SSE-C
   D. The default S3 encryption method
3. You are configuring a CMK using the KMS service console. Which permissions you should define and configure in the JSON security policy? (Choose three.)
   A. The IAM groups that can read the key
   B. IAM users that can be the CMK administrators
   C. IAM roles that can be the CMK administrators
   D. The application pool that will access the CMK
   E. IAM roles that can use the CMK
   F. The asymmetric algorithms that can be used
   G. The Cognito pool that will be used to authenticate the user to read the keys
4. What happens when you delete a CMK using KMS?
   A. The key is deleted immediately.
   B. AWS KMS enforces a 60-day waiting period before you can delete a CMK.
   C. AWS KMS enforces a minimum of 7 days up to a maximum of 30 days waiting period before you can delete a CMK.
   D. It is impossible to delete a CMK.
5. Which AWS service should you use to implement a ubiquitous encryption strategy in your AWS environment?
   A. Amazon Macie
   B. Amazon Inspector
   C. ACM
   D. AWS KMS
   E. CloudHSM

6. When should you consider using CloudHSM? (Choose two.)
   - **A.** To meet regulatory needs, such as FIPS 140-2 Level 3 standards
   - **B.** To protect EC2 instances
   - **C.** For SSL offloading
   - **D.** All the times that you need to use KMS
7. How does key rotation work when you are using a CMK?
   - **A.** AWS KMS rotates automatically every 30 days.
   - **B.** AWS KMS cannot rotate the key, so the user must rotate it manually.
   - **C.** AWS KMS rotates the CMK every 365 days after the user enables automatic key rotation.
   - **D.** There is no key rotation functionality, and only ACM can rotate keys automatically.
   - **E.** EC2
   - **F.** EKS
   - **G.** S3
   - **H.** Workspaces
   - **I.** IAM
8. What symmetric algorithm is used when a CMK is created?
   - **A.** AES 128
   - **B.** 3DES
   - **C.** DES
   - **D.** AES 256

Incident Response

THE AWS CERTIFIED SECURITY SPECIALTY EXAM OBJECTIVES THAT LEVERAGE CONCEPTS EXPLAINED IN THIS CHAPTER INCLUDE THE FOLLOWING:

✓ **Domain 1: Incident Response**

- 1.1. Given an AWS abuse notice, evaluate the suspected compromised instance or exposed access keys
- 1.2. Verify that the Incident Response plan includes relevant AWS services
- 1.3. Evaluate the configuration of automated alerting, and execute possible remediation of security-related incidents and emerging issues

Introduction

In this chapter, you will learn about incident response best practices and how to identify the resources you will need in your incident response plan.

As you learned in Chapter 1, "Security Fundamentals," *incidents* are defined as a violation (or a threat of violation) of security policies, acceptable usage policies, or standard security practices. They can be as harmful as a full-on DDoS attack or as mundane as an incorrect configuration in a firewall rule. In either case, they demand action from responsible personnel—in the first example, to return to operating business as usual, and in the latter, because the misconfiguration can increase risk due to allowing unauthorized access to a specific resource, with the objective of keeping risk under the minimum acceptable level.

Incident responses can be *manual* or *automated.* Again, referring to the firewall misconfiguration example, you may receive a notification when a firewall rule is changed and manually decide if the rule change needs to be reverted. Or in the context of the AWS Cloud, you can establish an AWS Config rule that receives the change notification, automatically compares with the desired state, and takes immediate action to correct the misstep. The set of actions created to address incidents composes an incident handling program, which is also known as an *incident response plan.*

In Chapter 2, "Cloud Security Principles and Frameworks," you learned about the shared responsibility model. In a nutshell, AWS is responsible for the security *of* the cloud and the customer is responsible for security *in* the cloud. AWS deploys a security incident response plan as part of its accountability in the shared responsibility model (with evidence available to you through the security and compliance reports AWS Artifact creates). For the workloads you implement, you, the user, are responsible for developing the incident response plan, covering your part of the shared responsibility model.

In this chapter, you will learn best practices that will help you define and implement your own security incident response plan for workloads in the AWS Cloud. However, before we dive into specifics, we'll introduce a mental model that allows you to assess how mature an incident response plan is.

Incident Response Maturity Model

Incident response is a comprehensive and wide-scoped topic. It directly deals with the main goal of any security organization: risk reduction. It is also a process that involves external parties in addition to the internal organization.

A successful incident response plan deals with actions along the full lifecycle of a security event, from having the right tools for detecting and protection, going through the automation of security protections, and applying lessons learned from every incident. In other words, you cannot do a good job responding to incidents if you do not deploy security controls, consciously acknowledging that the incidents will happen. Therefore, you need to be prepared when a security incident arises.

To simplify the approach, think about three clearly visible components of an incident response plan: its *management* (or how it can improve over time), its *constituent factors* (people, technology, and processes), and the incident's *lifecycle* (detect, isolate, contain, remediate, recover, and forensics). Moreover, you can think of these factors as three axes of the maturity model depicted in Figure 7.1.

FIGURE 7.1 Incident response maturity model

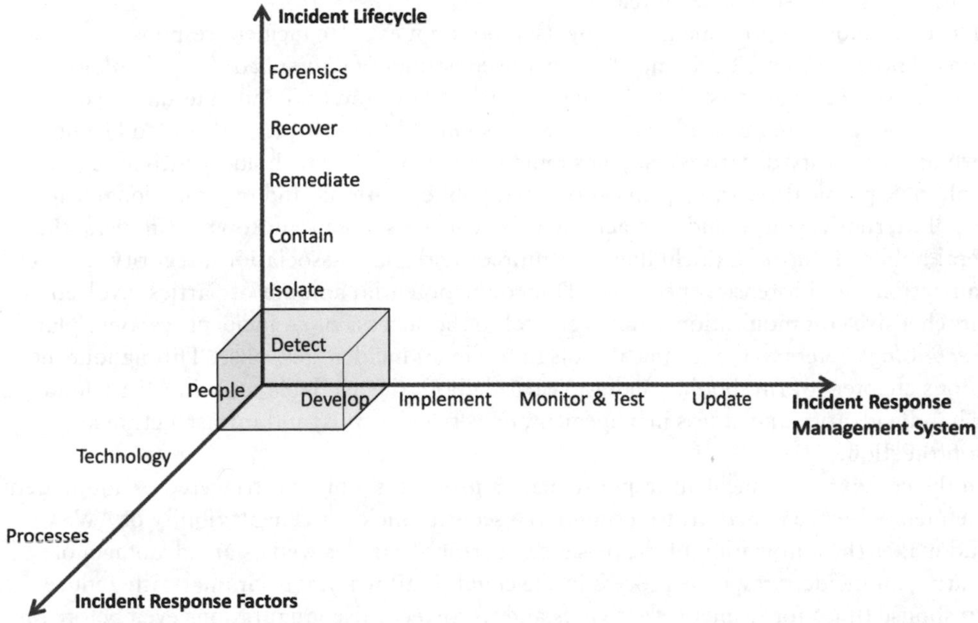

Because an incident response plan is inherently a process, it is subject to a continuous improvement cycle. Hence, it leverages the security wheel practical model, which we also discussed in Chapter 1. As a quick reminder, this model is based on a cyclical ever-enhancing execution of the following actions: develop a security policy; implement security measures; monitor & test (it is the actual response to an incident); and manage and update.

In the maturity model presented in Figure 7.1, *the develop* phase suggests that you gather as much information about your protected resources as you can and define your goals and important outcomes. You also define the adequate training level you require for involved *people* as well as any required improvements to the *processes* already in place. You also assess any gap between the current and the desired levels, including *technical* controls required to achieve your security goals.

In the *implement* phase, you carry out the actions and use tools to close the aforementioned gap. An important portion of this phase focuses on increasing incident visibility (along with incident notifications) in a comprehensive way for the responsible personnel.

In the *monitor & test* phase, you effectively put your security incident response plan into action. You can do that proactively by simulating security incident conditions, or alternatively, you can evaluate the performance of the process when facing a real security event situation. In either case, during the event you document and measure your capabilities to respond.

After executing the incident response plan, you most probably identify opportunities of improvement. Applying those improvements makes up the *update* phase, which brings you back to the first phase of a new cycle.

The continuous improvement cycle by itself does not execute incident response actions. Those actions are accomplished by the constituent factors: *people*, *technology*, and *processes*. *People* refers to the human resources, both internal and external to your organization, that are involved in an incident response. Internally, in addition to IT and information security departments, you should consider other stakeholders such as legal, compliance, physical security, business owners, public relations, and organizational leadership. Externally, you should also acknowledge entities such as your own customers, the general public, authorities (including law enforcement), class associations, security research organizations, and forensics specialists. Due to the potential amount of parties involved, a comprehensive communications plan is critical to the success of an incident response plan.

Technology refers to the technical tools to use in an incident response. Throughout the previous chapters of this book, you have learned about the available tools in AWS Cloud that handle identity and access management, detective controls, and infrastructure and data protection.

In the context of an incident response plan, a *process* is a human-triggered or automated predefined sequence of actions to respond to a security incident. The flexibility of AWS Cloud makes the automation of the processes a critical part (as well as an advantage) of executing an incident response process in the cloud. It allows you to dramatically reduce the response times for suspicious activities and to correct misconfigurations even before any malicious actor can exploit them.

To complete the incident response maturity model, consider the evolution of an incident itself: the *incident lifecycle*. Any incident should start with the *detection* of the suspicious activity. After confirming the negative impact of the incident, you can *isolate* the affected resources and *contain* the spreading to other resources. Then, you will apply corrective controls to *remediate* the affected resources. Afterward, you will *recover* your environment, confirming that it is performing business as usual. Finally, you will execute an analytical process (*forensics*) to identify the root causes of the security incident and understand how it behaved along its whole lifecycle. The outcome of the forensics phase is critical for the continuous improvement cycle. You will take the lessons learned from the incident into the planning phase, iterating over the management system cycle. As AWS CEO Andy Jassy once said, "There is no compression algorithm for experience."

As an example of how you could simplify the detection phase, in Exercise 7.1 you will use AWS CloudTrail console to automatically define a table that will allow you to query AWS CloudTrail logs using Amazon Athena. We assume you have already created an AWS CloudTrail trail (refer to Exercise 4.4 from Chapter 4: "Detective Controls").

EXERCISE 7.1

Automatically Create a Table for Querying AWS CloudTrail Logs with Amazon Athena

1. Access the AWS CloudTrail console.
2. Select the Event History menu.
3. Choose Create Athena Table or Run Advanced Queries In Amazon Athena (depending on the version of the AWS CloudTrail console you are using). A pop-up window appears.
4. Under Storage Location, select the Amazon S3 bucket where AWS CloudTrail logs are stored.
5. Click Create Table. After a few seconds, a message will confirm that the table was successfully created.

Exercise 7.2 is similar to Exercise 7.1, but here you will learn how to manually create the corresponding table in Amazon Athena that will allow you to query AWS CloudTrail logs. As in the previous exercise, we also assume you have already created an AWS CloudTrail trail.

EXERCISE 7.2

Manually Create a Table for Querying AWS CloudTrail Logs with Amazon Athena

1. Access the Amazon Athena console.
2. If this is your first query in Amazon Athena, you need to set up a query result location. You do this by choosing Settings and in the emerging dialog box defining a bucket or a folder (inside a bucket) in the Query Result Location field.

3. On the main panel, click the plus (+) sign to add an empty tab.
4. (Optional) Create a new database by running the following statement:

```
CREATE DATABASE IF NOT EXISTS security_chapter7_db
COMMENT 'Security-chapter 7 AWS CloudTrail logs'
WITH DBPROPERTIES ('creator'='<your name>', 'Chapter'='7');
```

5. In the left panel, select the database you want to create your table under.
6. In the main panel, run the following DDL statement:

```
CREATE EXTERNAL TABLE security_chapter7_cloudtrail_logs (
    eventVersion STRING,
    userIdentity STRUCT<
        type: STRING,
        principalId: STRING,
        arn: STRING,
        accountId: STRING,
        invokedBy: STRING,
        accessKeyId: STRING,
        userName: STRING,
        sessionContext: STRUCT<
            attributes: STRUCT<
                mfaAuthenticated: STRING,
                creationDate: STRING>,
            sessionIssuer: STRUCT<
                type: STRING,
                principalId: STRING,
                arn: STRING,
                accountId: STRING,
                userName: STRING>>>,
    eventTime STRING,
    eventSource STRING,
    eventName STRING,
    awsRegion STRING,
    sourceIpAddress STRING,
    userAgent STRING,
    errorCode STRING,
    errorMessage STRING,
    requestParameters STRING,
    responseElements STRING,
    additionalEventData STRING,
    requestId STRING,
```

```
    eventId STRING,
    resources ARRAY<STRUCT<
        arn: STRING,
        accountId: STRING,
        type: STRING>>,
    eventType STRING,
    apiVersion STRING,
    readOnly STRING,
    recipientAccountId STRING,
    serviceEventDetails STRING,
    sharedEventID STRING,
    vpcEndpointId STRING
)
COMMENT 'CloudTrail table for security-chapter7 exercise'
PARTITIONED BY (region STRING, year STRING, month STRING, day STRING)
ROW FORMAT SERDE 'com.amazon.emr.hive.serde.CloudTrailSerde'
STORED AS INPUTFORMAT 'com.amazon.emr.cloudtrail.CloudTrailInputFormat'
OUTPUTFORMAT 'org.apache.hadoop.hive.ql.io.HiveIgnoreKeyTextOutputFormat'
LOCATION 's3:// <cloudTrail_bucket_name>/AWSLogs/<account_id>/CloudTrail/'
TBLPROPERTIES ('classification'='cloudtrail');
```

For step 6, the PARTITIONED BY clause is optional. If you decide to partition the table, you will need to execute the optional steps 7 and 8.

7. (Optional) Use the ALTER TABLE ADD PARTITION command to load partitions, and be sure you use a date that contains data in the AWS CloudTrail trail:

```
ALTER TABLE security_chapter7_cloudtrail_logs ADD
  PARTITION (region='<region>',
             year='2020',
             month='11',
             day='30')
   LOCATION
   's3://<cloudTrail_bucket_name>/AWSLogs/<account_id>/CloudTrail/<reg ion>
   /2020/11/30/'
```

8. (Mandatory if you performed the step 7) Load partitions by executing the following query:

```
MSCK REPAIR TABLE security_chapter7_cloudtrail_logs;
```

Now that you have created the environment, Exercise 7.3 will guide you through the steps to query AWS CloudTrail logs in Amazon Athena.

EXERCISE 7.3

Query AWS CloudTrail Logs with Amazon Athena

1. Access the Amazon Athena console.
2. In the left panel, select the created database (`security_chapter7_db`).
3. In a new query window, execute a table preview by issuing the following command:

```
SELECT * FROM "security_chapter7_db"."security_chapter7_cloudtrail_logs" limit
10;
```

4. Try different queries, such as the following (adjusting the database and table names to match the names you defined in Exercises 7.1 and 7.2):

```
SELECT *
FROM "security_chapter7_db"."security_chapter7_cloudtrail_logs"
WHERE useridentity.type='AWSService' AND eventname='AssumeRole'
LIMIT 10;

SELECT useragent as "Calling Service"
FROM "security_chapter7_db"."security_chapter7_cloudtrail_logs"
WHERE useridentity.type='AWSService' AND eventname='AssumeRole'
LIMIT 10;

SELECT *
FROM "security_chapter7_db"."security_chapter7_cloudtrail_logs"
WHERE useridentity.type='AWSService' AND eventname='Decrypt'
LIMIT 10;

SELECT *
FROM "security_chapter7_db"."security_chapter7_cloudtrail_logs"
WHERE eventname='PutObject'
LIMIT 10;
```

With the three-dimensional model depicted in Figure 7.1, you will be able to visually gauge how mature your overall incident response plan is. As you position your plan in each one of the intersections, your readiness for incidents will be proportional to the amount and completeness of the resulting cubes (or *parallelepipeds*, to be more precise). By the same token, the parallelepipeds where your plan is less advanced represent the areas you should consider to improve.

In the next sections, you will learn about best practices to apply in accordance with the maturity model. These best practices will help you improve your incident response plan. If you are interested in going beyond the scope of the AWS Certified Security – Specialty certification, you can find additional information here:

AWS Well-Architected Framework Incident response is one of the five best practices areas defined for the security pillar. For more information, see `d1.awsstatic.com/whitepapers/architecture/AWS_Well-Architected_Framework.pdf`.

AWS Cloud Adoption Framework Incident response is one of the five core epics of the security perspective. For more information, see `d1.awsstatic.com/whitepapers/AWS_CAF_Security_Perspective.pdf`.

AWS Security Incident Response Guide This documentation discusses general incident response concepts and how they match with AWS Cloud capabilities. For more information, see `docs.aws.amazon.com/whitepapers/latest/aws-security-incident-response-guide/introduction.html`.

Incident Response Best Practices

Although incident response is a broad topic (and dependent on specific situations), in this section you will find general best practices to consider under any implementation in the AWS Cloud. If only for the sake of tidiness, you will learn about several best practices under the lens of the management system axis introduced in the earlier section "Incident Response Maturity Model."

Develop

In the develop phase, you should consider deploying the following best practices in your incident response plan:

- Identify the personnel required to deal with security incidents along the whole lifecycle.
- Establish the gap between the current and desired state in incident response training.
- Conduct risk assessment that clearly identifies information classification and the factors that define the severity of an incident.
- Establish an inventory of your monitored resources using AWS Config and AWS Systems Manager capabilities.
- Implement a tagging strategy for your monitored resources to help with the incident response. For example, tagging resources according to their classification level, owners, and workload name allows for faster identification of risk level at the time of the incident.
- Have a clear understanding of the different controls and countermeasures available in AWS Cloud.
- Establish a mechanism to stay up-to-date with the latest AWS services and features.

Implement

As you may remember, most of the preparation tasks for the incident response are actually executed in the implement phase. Therefore, you should contemplate the following best practices:

- Implement detailed logging and monitoring across the whole infrastructure, according with the detective controls explained in Chapter 4.
- Make sure to include logging at the different levels of the workload, including services, resources, and applications. Centralize logs and prepare the data structure for the analysis. For example, when delivering AWS CloudTrail logs to an Amazon S3 bucket, configure the data catalog in AWS Glue so that you will be able to query data using analytics tools like Amazon Athena or Amazon EMR.
- Create and update the data catalog for every centralized log delivered to the Amazon S3 repository, including logs from components like Elastic Load Balancing, AWS WAF, and Amazon API Gateway.
- Establish relevant metrics from the reported logs and plot them using Amazon CloudWatch metrics. For every metric, define thresholds and alarms.
- Configure notifications to be delivered through the right channels, providing relevant information and reaching the appropriate subscribers.
- Create AWS CloudFormation templates (infrastructure as code) for your AWS Cloud environment that define and implement the guardrails and technical specifications for detection of security events. Include technical specifications for the various detective controls defined in Chapter 4.
- Consider pre-provision tooling for incident response, including tools available from AWS, AWS Partner Network (APN) members, and other external parties (such as open-source tools or adequately licensed external solutions).
- Consider automation to take snapshots of the involved systems (including storage systems and volatile information like memory content). Establish and test backup and restore procedures.
- For forensics analysis, consider preparing a *clean room*, an isolated environment where you can deploy the infrastructure with the tools required for investigation. As a requirement for the clean room, keep an up-to-date Amazon EC2 AMI Image vetted by the security teams with the required set of tools.
- Use an AWS CloudFormation template to automate the creation of the clean room environment when needed.
- Put your incident response plan *in writing*. Document the processes to analyze findings, query logs, and metrics and respond to incidents following the lifecycle of the security incidents (from detection to forensics). Classify these documents and make sure they are accessible in case of an incident. Consider options to store these documents offline.
- Automate, as much as possible, the responses to security events.

You will learn more about automation in Chapter 8, "Security Automation."

- Implement a training and awareness program for personnel to know and successfully execute the documented incident response processes. Include topics such as how to query and analyze logs and findings, how to react when an alarm is notified, how to classify the severity of an incident, and how to respond, following the actions depending on the lifecycle of the incident. Make sure you provision access to the personnel dealing with incident response in accordance with the least privilege principle.
- Develop a clear communications guideline, establishing official communication mechanisms and points of contact. Make sure your contact information is up-to-date (both for internal and external contacts). In the case of external stakeholders, understand their operating model and, when applicable, whether you have a valid contract and SLA to use their services.
- Define how a *war room* (virtual or physical meeting of the team in charge of dealing with the incident) will be summoned and communicated. Also, take the appropriate measures to guarantee that all stakeholders have a clear understanding about the chain of communication, communication tools, war rooms, and PR guidelines during the incident response.

Monitor and Test

This phase corresponds to a thorough execution of the incident response plan. During the whole execution, you should document your responses with the goal of monitoring how your response plan performs and to gather metrics from your process. Therefore, you should do the following:

- Arrange to carry out the plan in a controlled environment (after all, it is better to find gaps in a simulation and not when dealing with a real incident in a production environment).
- Prepare and execute *security incident response simulations (SIRS)*, also known as incident response game days. Consider your simulations to be as realistic as possible, balanced with the requirement of not affecting production environments. Consider blind exercises where the response team does not know in advance about the simulation.
- Executing your incident response plan in a real situation is also part of the check phase.
- Regardless of whether it is a simulated or a real scenario, make sure you are *documenting every action* along the lifecycle of the incident. This includes having an activity log for both the manual and automated processes. Also, gather metrics during the process that will allow you to compare and establish improvement goals for future executions.

Update

After an incident response plan has been effectively executed, given a thoughtful monitoring of the process, you will probably uncover some gaps. You'll then have an opportunity to improve the plan's real value for your organization. Consequently, as part of the update phase, you should do the following:

- Document a *root cause analysis* (RCA) after every execution of the incident response plan. The RCA is a document in which you identify the reason behind the incident and describe the actions to avoid in the future, as well as any improvements to the plan.
- In addition to technical improvements, consider the people and processes dimensions. Human-related actions deviated from the documented processes can be improved by executing training and awareness activities.
- Review and update procedures that failed to solve the incidents at every stage of the lifecycle in a timely manner.

At this point, you will take the lessons learned from the execution of the incident response and enter them in the *develop* and *implement* phases, considering all three incident response factors: people, technology, and processes. This is an iterative cycle you will keep improving over time.

Reacting to Specific Security Incidents

In this section, you will learn how to react to well-known security incidents that may happen in your AWS Cloud. You should always remember that incidents happen, so it is better to be prepared to address them than to find out later what to do.

Abuse Notifications

The AWS Customer agreement, in section 6, "Temporary Suspension," specifies the following:

> 6.1 Generally. We may suspend your or any End User's right to access or use any portion or all of the Service Offerings immediately upon notice to you if we determine:
>
> (a) your or an End User's use of the Service Offerings (i) poses a security risk to the Service Offerings or any third party, (ii) could adversely impact our systems, the Service Offerings or the systems or Content of any other AWS customer, (iii) could subject us, our affiliates, or any third party to liability, or (iv) could be fraudulent;

As you can see, if your account gets compromised and a bad actor uses it to attack other accounts or third parties, AWS may suspend your account to prevent attacks from spreading through the Internet if you do not take proper countermeasures to contain the threat.

For this reason, it is particularly important that you protect your workloads in the AWS Cloud. Additionally, you should detect and contain compromised instances while also keeping your security contacts updated in the account information. With such information, AWS Security teams can contact your security engineers to warn them about suspicious activities in the account. Figure 7.2 shows where you should add the contacts related to your organization's security personnel.

FIGURE 7.2 AWS Account Security Contact

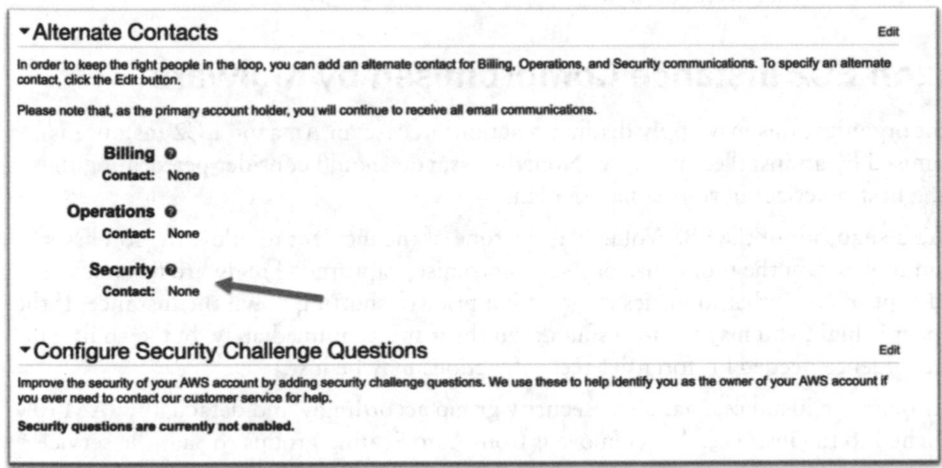

To reach that page, you access your AWS Management Console. In the upper bar, click the AWS account ID (or the AWS account alias if you defined one), select the option My Account, and look for the Alternate Contacts section.

It is also a best practice to define a dedicated alias (such as `aws-notifications@example.com`) that will deliver notifications to a team of security analysts. Make sure your team will receive instant messaging alerts when an email reaches this alias so that any member can act in time.

AWS may use that contact information to inform you about suspicious activity that could affect the operation of your account, such as detected leaked access keys from your account or if one of your Amazon EC2 instances is attacking someone else.

In Chapter 8, you will also learn about security automations that can be configured to isolate compromised instances, reducing the risk of account suspension.

Insider Threat and Former Employee Access

When a user with privileged access leaves the company, you as a security engineer need to remove all of the user's access according to your security policies. To remove privileges for the AWS environment, you should delete the AWS IAM user completely or revoke AWS IAM access keys while disabling their AWS Console password.

Alternatively, if you are using external authentication repositories such as Okta, OneLogin, or Microsoft Active Directory Federation Services, you need to disable or delete the user on that external identity provider solution.

If any security group with IP validation allowed access from the user's home IP address, you should remove that access as well.

Amazon EC2 Instance Compromised by Malware

Different organizations may apply distinct reactions in case an Amazon EC2 instance is compromised by an installed malware. Nonetheless, you should consider performing the following best practices in your response plan:

- Take a snapshot of the EBS Volume at the time of the incident to allow the forensics team to work on the root cause of the compromise, capture the malware for analysis, and capture any other forensics information prior to shutting down the instance. If the impact is high, you may want to shut down the instance immediately, but keep in mind that evidence needed for forensics reconstructions may be lost.
- To isolate the instance, change its security group accordingly and detach any IAM role attached to the instance. Also remove it from Auto Scaling groups so that the service creates a new instance from the template and service interruption is reduced.
- Tag the instance as Compromised together with an AWS IAM policy that explicitly restricts all operations related to the instance to the incident response and forensics teams. Following such a procedure is a great way to reduce the risk of unintentionally destroying the evidence due to human mistakes. These tags can be applied programmatically using Amazon CloudWatch Events upon the detection of specific Amazon GuardDuty finding types.
- When the incident forensics team wants to analyze the instance, they should deploy it into a totally isolated environment—ideally a private subnet (without Internet access) on an isolated Amazon Virtual Private Cloud that is exclusively accessed only by a forensics workstation. This special instance can be a hardened Amazon Workspaces virtual desktop preinstalled with the appropriate forensics tools (such as Wireshark) to speed up analysis.
- Analyze the logs and findings, such as operating system logs, application logs, AWS CloudTrail, Amazon VPC flow logs, or Amazon GuardDuty findings on that instance. Consider using Amazon Detective to assist in the root cause analysis.
- There are several options to automate incident responses. AWS Lambda functions can be an option if you prefer coding, but you can also use AWS Step Functions to define

responsive workflows. You can also leverage the Security Orchestration, Automation, and Response (SOAR) solution of your choice, such as Palo Alto Demisto, Splunk Phantom, or IBM Security Resilient.

Credentials Leaked

Developers sometimes enjoy sharing their code with their community of preference. If they used access keys and did not follow the best practices related to using temporary credentials (such as AWS IAM roles attached to Amazon EC2 instances), they may be inadvertently making their AWS credentials public. In addition, there are various reports that malicious actors are constantly looking for credentials of all sorts on shared repositories like GitHub.

If the AWS Security team finds those credentials, they will notify you by sending an email to your configured security contact. However, if a malicious actor finds your credentials first, they can easily generate an incident.

In consequence, as a best practice, if any access key is leaked to a shared repository (like GitHub)—even if only for a couple of seconds—you should assume that the access key was compromised and revoke it immediately.

In Exercise 7.4 you will practice rotating credentials for an AWS IAM user. Note that you will not assign access policies to this user.

EXERCISE 7.4

Rotate AWS IAM Credentials

1. Create a new AWS IAM user named **security-chapter7** and assign the following credentials: Console Password, Access Key, HTTPS Git Credentials, and Amazon Keyspaces.
2. Access the AWS IAM Management Console. Click Users under the Access Management category.
3. Click the security-chapter7 user.
4. Select the Security Credentials tab.
5. Under Access Keys, make the current access keys inactive.
6. Under HTTP Git Credentials for AWS Code Commit, make the current key inactive.
7. Under Credentials for Amazon Keyspaces, make the current key inactive.
8. Delete the security-chapter7 user.

Remember that rotating existing credentials will require you to update any system or application currently using the previous credentials.

The principle of least privilege is a critical factor in reducing risk in cases like this. If credentials are leaked, the impact depends on how restrictive your security policies are.

Also, if you upgrade your support plan to Business or Enterprise, you can use the AWS Trusted Advisor Exposed Access Keys check to monitor popular code repositories and learn whether your access keys have been exposed to the public.

Application Attacks

Some of the more frequent attacks are the ones that leverage a vulnerability on your web applications. Regardless of how you analyze the AWS WAF logs, as developers usually prioritize the development of functional aspects of the applications, there may be a delay in correcting vulnerabilities that could create an exposure window on your application.

As you learned in Chapter 5, "Infrastructure Protection," AWS WAF can effectively address such vulnerabilities. Keep in mind that AWS WAF, besides using AWS Managed Rules, also allows the creation of custom rules that can act as a virtual patch to the vulnerability until the development team fix the issue in their code.

If the type of attack you are receiving is a DDoS attack, consider using AWS Shield Advanced. AWS Shield Advanced will protect you from Layer 7 attacks as well and will grant you access to an AWS DDoS Response Team (DRT). This team will help you analyze and block the malicious traffic. AWS Shield Advanced will also protect your AWS bill; you will be able to request a refund of the charges related to your infrastructure growth due to the DDoS attack.

Summary

Dealing with incident response plans means understanding a wide spectrum of security services. Taking the three-axis model as a reference will help you navigate through the spectrum, considering best practices for the different activities related with the process.

First, it is important to understand that incident response is a continuous process under constant improvement. Enhancement comes from practice. So, it is critical to periodically test your incident response plan and consolidate the lessons learned.

Each iteration of your incident response plan follows the whole lifecycle of an incident, from detection to forensics. To be able to perform the actions in a timely and efficient way, you need to know the tools available. Be prepared to contain the spread of a security issue by isolating resources, rotating credentials, responding to notifications of suspicious activity, and using tools to analyze and understand root causes of the incidents.

As a dynamic business practice, the incident response cycle is subject to agents of change: people, processes, and technology. Those are the pillars to consider when implementing new actions as part of the plan. Regarding technology, AWS Cloud provides the tools to improve the effectiveness of an incident response plan. Arguably, one of the main factors that implies a more secure environment in the cloud is related to automation. By automating security responses, you can reduce the time required to react to a security incident, reducing your window of exposure and so reducing the overall risk. In the next chapter, you will learn more about the tools available in the cloud for automating your security responses.

Exam Essentials

Know that abuse notifications require attention. Keep in mind that when AWS Security teams send abuse notifications, they require attention from your security team and usually require your action as well. Ignoring them could potentially lead to account suspension. Respond to the notifications that you received from AWS Support through the AWS Support Center.

Know how to react to compromised credentials. When credentials are compromised, you need to ensure that no resource created by malicious actors remains in the account, including resources on your account that you didn't create, such as EC2 instances and AMIs, EBS volumes and snapshots, and IAM users. You need to rotate all potentially compromised credentials. Changing the password for other users is a safety measure as well.

Know how to react to compromised instances. Investigate compromised instances for malware, isolate them in the network, and stop or terminate them (ideally taking an Amazon EBS snapshot for the forensics team to do their root cause analysis). In AWS Marketplace you'll find available partner products that can help detect and remove malware.

Know how to use AWS WAF and AWS Shield to mitigate attacks on applications. Remember considering AWS Shield as a potential answer whenever you see DDoS attacks and preparing your architecture to withstand the load until AWS Shield acts. Using AWS CloudFront, AWS Elastic Load Balancing, and Route 53 helps as well. Remember that you can use AWS WAF to mitigate many different application attacks by adding custom rules, such as adding a rate limit to prevent scraping and other malicious bot activity.

Review Questions

1. What is the first action to take when a probable compromise of AWS IAM credentials is detected?
   - A. Update the security contact of the AWS account.
   - B. Deactivate the AWS IAM credentials.
   - C. Delete the AWS IAM credentials.
   - D. Modify the apps that use the AWS IAM credentials.

2. Which of the following AWS services (alone or combined) would suit better the remediate phase of an incident lifecycle?

   I. AWS Config

   II. AWS CloudTrail

   III. AWS Systems Manager

   A. Only I

   B. Only III

   C. Combination of II and III

   D. Combination of I and III

3. Which of the following is NOT a contact information you should always keep updated in your AWS account?

   A. Billing contact.

   B. Administrative contact.

   C. Security contact.

   D. Operations contact.

4. What should you do when the AWS team sends you an abuse report from your resources?

   A. Review only when you receive more than one abuse notice for the same incident.

   B. Review and reply to abuse report team, as soon as possible.

   C. Review and reply to abuse report team, only after you are totally sure about what caused the issue.

   D. Review and solve the issue. No need to reply to abuse team, unless you have questions about the notification.

5. Which of the following options minimizes the risk to your environment when testing your incident response plan?

   A. Automate containment capability to reduce response times and organizational impact.

   B. Develop an incident management plan that contains incidents and procedures to return to a known good state.

   C. Execute security incident response simulations to validate controls and processes.

   D. Use your existing forensics tools on your AWS environment.

6. The security team detected a user's abnormal behavior and needs to know if there were any changes to the AWS IAM permissions. What steps should the team take?

   A. Use AWS CloudTrail to review the user's IAM permissions prior to the abnormal behavior and compare them to their current IAM permissions.

   B. Use Amazon Macie to review the user's IAM permissions prior to the abnormal behavior and compare them to their current IAM permissions.

C. Use AWS Config to review the user's IAM permissions prior to the abnormal behavior and compare them to their current IAM permissions.

D. Use AWS Trusted Advisor to review the user's IAM permissions prior to the abnormal behavior and compare them to their current IAM permissions.

7. Amazon GuardDuty reported finding an instance of `Backdoor:EC2/C&CActivity.B!DNS` in the production environment, outside business hours, and the security team is wondering how to react. What would be the most appropriate action to take?

A. Instruct the forensics team to review the instance early tomorrow, since it does not reflect any immediate threat.

B. Investigate the image for malware, and isolate, stop, or terminate the instance as soon as possible.

C. Explicitly deny access to security groups to isolate the instance.

D. Use Amazon Inspector to analyze the vulnerabilities on the instance and shut down vulnerable services.

8. You, the IAM access administrator, receive an abuse notification indicating that your account may be compromised. You do not find any unrecognized resource, but you see one of your IAM users with the following policy attached, that you did not attach: `AWSExposedCredentialPolicy_DO_NOT_REMOVE`. What would be the most appropriate action to immediately start remediation?

A. Remove the policy since you did not create it and it may be the source of the issue.

B. Change the access keys for the user and detach the policy as the issue was remediated.

C. No action is needed since the policy restricts the usage of the user. The user should not be deleted. Open a support ticket for instructions on how to proceed.

D. Delete the user, and be sure to check all regions for unrecognized resources or other users with the policy attached.

9. Amazon GuardDuty reported the finding `UnauthorizedAccess:EC2/TorClient` related to an Amazon EC2 instance. You, as part of the security team, are determining how to react. What would be the most appropriate action to take?

A. Unless you know that the Amazon EC2 instance uses an anonymization network for valid business needs, you should isolate or stop the instance since it can indicate that your instance is compromised.

B. You should immediately terminate the instance.

C. You can safely ignore this finding since it's only informational, and it's probably an end user using TOR Browser to access your site for privacy reasons.

D. Use traffic mirroring to analyze the traffic to verify whether it is legitimate.

10. You are a security analyst at a company. You recently discovered that developers embed access keys on the code in many business applications. You are concerned about potential credentials being exposed by mistake. Which are the most simple and effective actions to mitigate the risk? (Choose three.)

A. Instruct the developers to use AWS Secrets Manager or AWS Systems Manager Parameter Store to avoid storing credentials in code.

B. Enable Amazon Macie to detect access keys exposed to the public.

C. Upgrade the support plan to Business or Enterprise Support and use AWS Trusted Advisor to detect exposed credentials.

D. Build an AWS Lambda function to check repositories and notify using Amazon Simple Notification Service.

E. Use Amazon CodeGuru to detect exposed credentials.

Security Automation

THE AWS CERTIFIED SECURITY SPECIALTY EXAM OBJECTIVES THAT LEVERAGE CONCEPTS EXPLAINED IN THIS CHAPTER INCLUDE THE FOLLOWING:

✓ **Domain 1: Incident Response**

- 1.3. Evaluate the configuration of automated alerting, and execute possible remediation of security-related incidents and emerging issues.

✓ **Domain 3: Implementation/Deployment**

- 3.1. Design edge security on AWS.

Introduction

In this chapter, you will learn about security concepts that will help you deal with automation. You will be prepared for incident response, implementation, and deployment, particularly in the following areas:

- Using event-driven security
- Using AWS Lambda for automated security response
- Understanding AWS Config Auto Remediation
- Automating resolution of findings using AWS Security Hub
- Aggregating and resolving issues with AWS Systems Manager
- WAF Security Automations
- Automating isolation of bad actors' access to applications

Security Automation Overview

This chapter focuses on how *security automation* allows security teams to scale by reducing the manual work involved in daily security operations. You will learn how automation can significantly improve the consistency of security controls, revert undesirable configuration drifts, correct insecure configurations that are usually caused by human error, and increase the speed of containment in the security incident response process, which in turn reduces the risk exposure by minimizing the window in which malicious actors can perform their activities.

Arguably, the most strained resources in organizations today are skilled technicians, and in particular, security engineers. As threats are always evolving in terms of complexity and volume, many organizations find it challenging to rely on a large team of specialists looking at dashboards to manage the emerging threats, for several reasons:

- When analyzing large amounts of data, humans can easily miss a security incident.
- Processes that involve humans routinely take longer than automated responses (which is especially important when you're trying to contain and mitigate the impact of a breach).

- Processes involving humans tend to generate inconsistent results.
- For many companies, having a large security operations center (SOC) with skilled and experienced security analysts with all the tooling required, such as security information and event management (SIEM) systems, user and entity behavior analytics (UEBA), and enough incident responders to manage all the alerts, can be economically prohibitive.
- Unlike software, humans cannot scale. Just imagine how many security analysts would be needed to protect large companies such as Amazon without any form of automation.

It has become necessary to automate the detection of potential security incidents (as with the solutions discussed in Chapter 4, "Detective Controls"). However, when you automate the creation of security tickets, a new problem comes to light: you end up with more tickets than your incident response team (also known as the *blue team*) can handle. For this reason, your focus should be on automating the *resolution* of these security incidents. Fortunately, automation can work continuously 24/7 and is capable of responding to multiple incidents in parallel.

The term *blue team* comes from the U.S. computer security defense initiative, where the red teams were in charge of producing the attacks, exploiting vulnerabilities, and simulating activities of a malicious entity trying to cause harm, and the blue teams were in charge of designing defensive measures, monitoring security events, responding to incidents, and in general ensuring all security controls continue to be effective in spite of the red team's efforts.

When AWS Chief Information Security Officer Stephen Schmidt gave his keynote address at *re:Invent* 2019, he said that 96.4 percent of the security incidents in our own infrastructure are resolved without human intervention. Instead of having a large blue team resolving issues, you should have the team focus on building automations. Your incident response playbook needs to include a final step of analysis so that you can scale incident response. If the incident calls for the creation of a mechanism so that the next time the same or a similar issue is raised, incidents should be handled without our scarcest resource: humans.

Event-Driven Security

When analyzing incident response playbooks (the set of rules that guide your response to events) to find opportunities for improving automation, you will often get to a logical sequence such as the one shown in Figure 8.1.

FIGURE 8.1 Security automation logical sequence

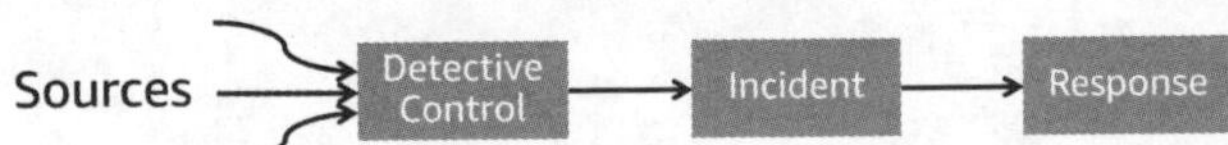

In Figure 8.1, the following steps are shown:

1. A detective control receives data from one or more data sources.
2. Using rules or machine intelligence, the detective control recognizes an undesired condition and then triggers an Amazon CloudWatch Event, creates a finding in AWS Security Hub, or creates a ticket in the Incident Response Platform or ticketing tool.
3. A response task is triggered that contains the threat, alerts the security team, and/or resolves the configuration drift.

The following elements are some examples of *common data sources:*

- **Logs:** AWS CloudTrail, DNS records, VPC flow logs, web application firewall logs, operating systems logs, application logs, or AWS CloudWatch logs
- **Infrastructure:** Configurations or inventory
- **Data:** Amazon S3 buckets data analytics

The following services are examples of *detective capabilities:*

- Amazon GuardDuty
- AWS Config
- Amazon Inspector
- Amazon Macie
- AWS IAM Access Analyzer

The following findings and events are frequently used to *trigger an automation*:

- Unsafe configurations (from AWS Config or Amazon Inspector), such as open buckets, RDP/SSH open to all IPs, and others.
- AWS Security Hub findings from AWS services and solutions from the AWS Partner Network, such as antivirus and endpoint detection and response (EDR) from CloudStrike, Symantec, and other partners.
- Potential security incidents, such as connections to anonymization networks (TOR), connections to botnets, or other malicious actors.
- Anomalies such as the abnormal usage of Amazon EC2 resources. For example, crypto-mining malware usually tries to consume as much CPU and GPU as is available, so abnormal usage might indicate attackers looking to exploit compute resources.
- Any event from Amazon CloudWatch Events can trigger a response task.

The Onion Router (TOR) Network routes traffic through a series of relays using cryptography for anonymization. The origin node can't know where the destination is located, and vice versa.

The following AWS service features are some examples of *common response tasks:*

- An AWS Lambda function can use AWS APIs to change security groups or network ACLs. In scenarios using attribute-based access control (ABAC), an AWS Lambda function can change tags to isolate access to the object or limit it to the blue team.
- Systems Manager Automation documents are frequently used to correct configuration drifts detected by AWS Config.
- If an action needs to be performed at the OS level, Systems Manager Run Command can be used to execute commands to multiple hosts at scale.
- Coordinated responses, especially when a human's confirmation is required, can be accomplished by using AWS Step Functions to follow a workflow of actions with conditionals, or by using AWS Systems Manager Automation documents, which support multiple steps, such as the following:
  1. Preserve evidence using a snapshot.
  2. Collect additional information on the incident from different sources to enrich the data available for the analysis.
  3. Contain the incident by isolating the compromised instances.

Depending on your objective for security automation, each of the boxes in Figure 8.1 will be mapped to a different component, with a different service or code. Throughout this chapter, you will explore a variety of automated processes that can be accomplished using AWS Services.

Know the Art of the Possible

Regarding security automations, it is important for you to know how a security objective can be achieved and which elements can be integrated toward the requested goal. Some questions may propose option A, to use a service that does not do what is requested, but perhaps something similar, or option B, an integration of two or more services that can achieve that goal.

Know Which Service Can Detect What Needs to Trigger the Automation

If you are trying to detect configuration drifts in the configuration of Amazon S3 Buckets, you could use Amazon Macie or AWS Config—both of which are capable of detecting weak configurations on Buckets—but AWS Config provides an auto-remediate feature to correct that configuration drift through an AWS Systems Manager Automation. If you are trying to

build an automation to react to a potential compromised instance or malicious actors' connections (based on their IP Reputation), then Amazon GuardDuty will be used to detect the instance and an AWS Lambda function will be used to isolate the instance.

One of the first services that offered capabilities for event-driven security was Amazon S3, which allows events such as an AWS Lambda execution to be triggered upon changes to files, deletions, creates, or other events within an S3 bucket. As an example, you can automate the parsing of certain log files as they arrive, to detect potential security issues or to add a malicious actor to a blacklist. This method, shown in Figure 8.2, is more efficient than periodic polling.

As you can see in Figure 8.2, Amazon S3 allows triggering an AWS Lambda function upon a change in the bucket. In this example, you can see how in a bucket where compressed logs are stored (using `gzip`), Amazon S3 is calling an AWS Lambda function that analyzes the log for enriching AWS WAF protection, as will be discussed in the "WAF Security Automations" section later in this chapter.

Another example is that at the creation of a new file (`PUT` operation), we can trigger an AWS Lambda function that analyzes the file looking for malware or sends the file to a malware sandboxing system for analysis. Malware sandboxing tools execute files in a controlled and monitored environment to evaluate whether they behave like malware. There are several solutions for malware sandboxing on the AWS Marketplace.

Using AWS Lambda for Automated Security Response

Many security automations use AWS Lambda functions, and there are a couple of reasons this makes sense. AWS Lambda is a service that allows executing custom code, including calls to AWS APIs. Being serverless, AWS Lambda is very appropriate for event-driven security for the following reasons:

- It does not generate costs while it is not invoked.
- It does not have the need for infrastructure management, which is also very valuable for security teams, where human operators are frequently the most constrained resource.

The following sections explore some common ways of using AWS Lambda for automating security responses.

FIGURE 8.2 Amazon S3 events triggering an AWS Lambda function

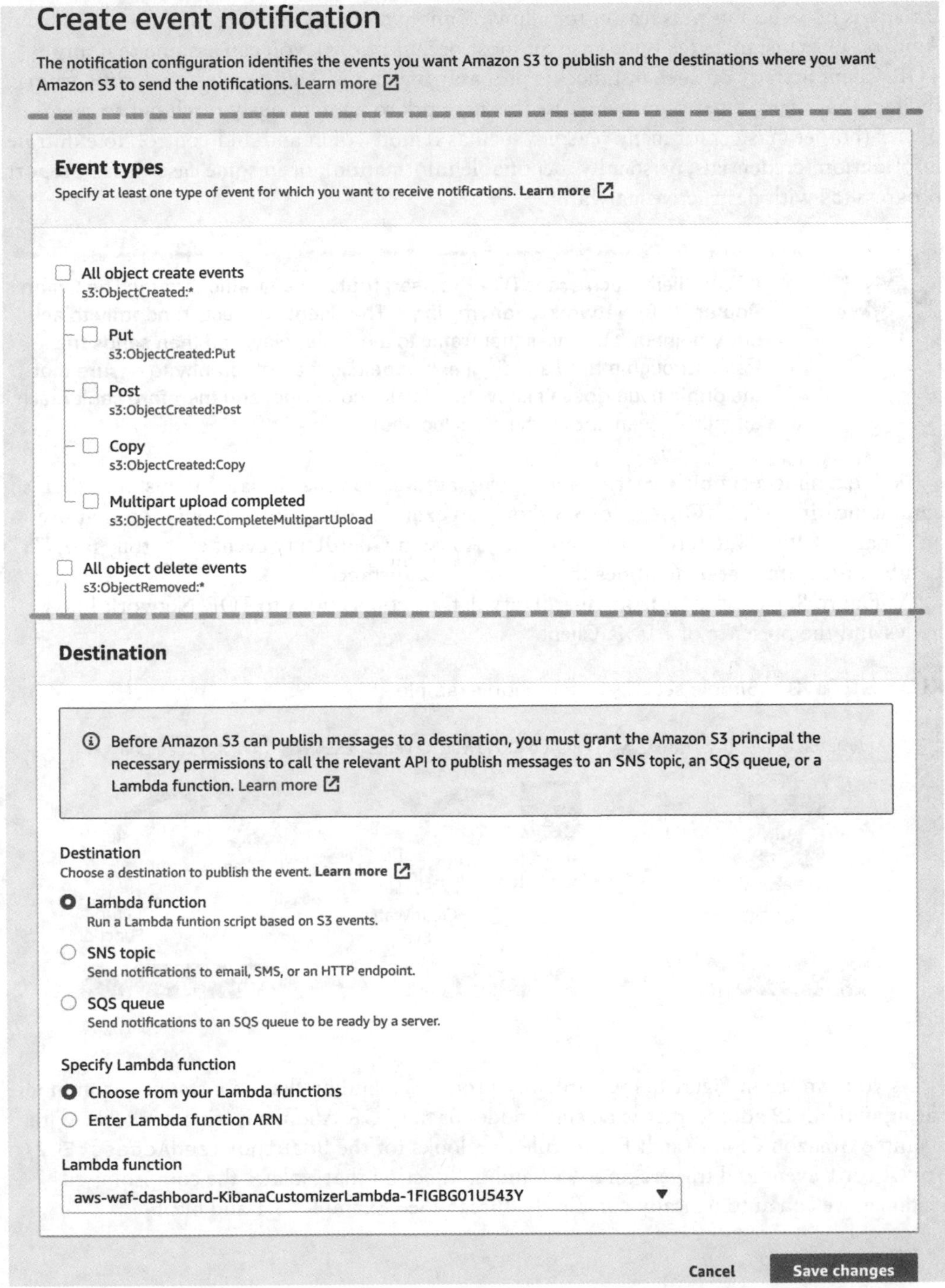

Create event notification

The notification configuration identifies the events you want Amazon S3 to publish and the destinations where you want Amazon S3 to send the notifications. Learn more

Event types

Specify at least one type of event for which you want to receive notifications. Learn more

All object create events
s3:ObjectCreated:*

Put
s3:ObjectCreated:Put

Post
s3:ObjectCreated:Post

Copy
s3:ObjectCreated:Copy

Multipart upload completed
s3:ObjectCreated:CompleteMultipartUpload

All object delete events
s3:ObjectRemoved:*

Destination

Before Amazon S3 can publish messages to a destination, you must grant the Amazon S3 principal the necessary permissions to call the relevant API to publish messages to an SNS topic, an SQS queue, or a Lambda function. Learn more

Destination
Choose a destination to publish the event. Learn more

Lambda function
Run a Lambda funtion script based on S3 events.

SNS topic
Send notifications to email, SMS, or an HTTP endpoint.

SQS queue
Send notifications to an SQS queue to be ready by a server.

Specify Lambda function

Choose from your Lambda functions

Enter Lambda function ARN

Lambda function

aws-waf-dashboard-KibanaCustomizerLambda-1FIGBG01U543Y

Cancel Save changes

Isolating Instances with Malware on Botnets

If there is no valid business reason for allowing anonymous access to remote resources from Amazon EC2 Instances (as is the case for most organizations), you can assume that any TOR Client activity on such instances is probably malicious. This conclusion derives from the fact that many types of malware use this network to anonymously reach out to their owner (botnet master) for many reasons, such as remote command-and-control, to exfiltrate information (credentials, personally identifiable information), or in some cases just to report progress (as with destructive malware).

A TOR Client (such as the TOR Browser) routes web traffic through The Onion Router (TOR) Network, anonymizing it. The Client connects randomly to any entry point that bounces that traffic to a middle relay, and then sends the traffic through a third and final exit node using cryptography to ensure that the origin node doesn't know the destination node (and therefore can't reach it directly or even know where it's located).

Let's examine a simple scenario of a security automation that isolates an instance that is communicating using TOR. Figure 8.3 shows an example of security automation that uses an Amazon CloudWatch rule to act upon the Amazon GuardDuty event executing an AWS Lambda function that quarantines the Amazon EC2 Instance.

As Figure 8.3 shows, Amazon GuardDuty detects connections to TOR Network Entry nodes and the presence of a TOR Client.

FIGURE 8.3 Simple security automation example

As you can see in Figure 8.4, GuardDuty produces a finding that an instance is communicating with an IP address that is an entry node for the TOR Anonymization network. With a simple Amazon CloudWatch Events rule that looks for the `UnauthorizedAccess:EC2/TorClient` event and triggers an AWS Lambda function that isolates the compromised instance, we can automatically contain the threat. (See Examples 8.1 and 8.2.)

FIGURE 8.4 GuardDuty's TOR Client detection message

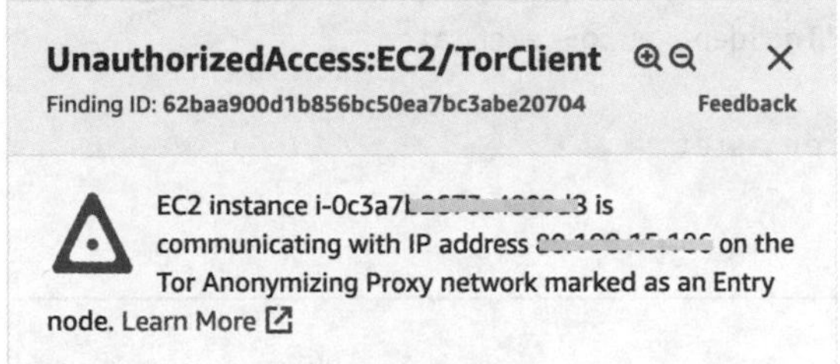

Example 8.1: Amazon CloudWatch Events rule

```
{
  "source": [ "aws.guardduty" ],
  "detail": { "type": [ "UnauthorizedAccess:EC2/TorClient" ] }
}
```

Example 8.2: AWS Lambda function (using Python 3.7 runtime)

```
import boto3
from botocore.exceptions import ClientError
import os

def lambda_handler(event, context):
    response = 'Error isolating the instance.'
    try:
        # Set Variables
        instanceID =
event['detail']['resource']['instanceDetails']['instanceId']
        security_group_id = os.environ['QUARANTINE_SG']

        # Get instance details
        ec2 = boto3.resource('ec2')
        instance = ec2.Instance(instanceID)
```

```
        # Change instance Security Group attribute
        instance.modify_attribute(Groups=[security_group_id])
        response = 'Incident auto-remediated'

    except ClientError as e:
        print(e)
    return response
```

As you can see in Example 8.2, the Python code sets the variable "security_group_id" to a value received as a parameter from the AWS Lambda Function, an environment variable called `QUARANTINE_SG`, which contains the identifier of the security group that closes all outgoing access to the instance and allows incoming traffic only from the Incident Forensics IP address. Therefore, the code is changing the security groups for that Amazon EC2 instance.

A best practice is to use a virtual desktop on Amazon Workspaces with all the forensics tools like Wireshark and nmap preinstalled to speed up investigation and to reduce the probability of infection of the security analyst's desktop.

As you can see in Figure 8.5, the security group is passed as a parameter to the AWS Lambda function. This security group allows the instance to be reached through the network only by the Forensics workstation's IP address and implicitly denies access for outgoing communications.

FIGURE 8.5 AWS Lambda environment variable pointing to the Forensics security group

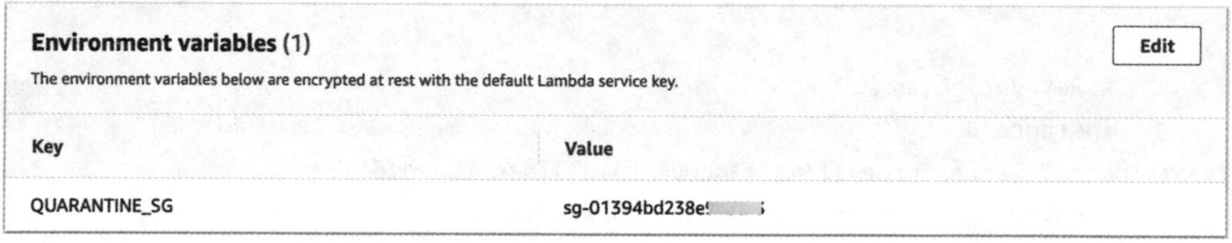

Environment variables (1) Edit

The environment variables below are encrypted at rest with the default Lambda service key.

Key	Value
QUARANTINE_SG	sg-01394bd238e[illegible]

For the AWS Lambda function to be able to change security groups and write its logs to Amazon CloudWatch logs, it needs an execution role granting the proper permissions. Therefore, you need to create a role including the AWS managed policy `AWSLambdaBasicExecutionRole` and add a policy for granting access to write Amazon CloudWatch logs such as the AWS managed policy `CloudWatchLogsFullAccess` (or one more specific for production) as well as a custom policy that allows changing the security group of Amazon EC2 instances.

An example of such a policy is shown in Example 8.3.

Example 8.3: IAM policy for modifying instance attributes (JSON)

```
{
    "Version": "2012-10-17",
    "Statement": [
        {
            "Action": [
                "ec2:ModifyInstanceAttribute",
                "ec2:DescribeInstances"
            ],
            "Resource": "*",
            "Effect": "Allow"
        }
    ]
}
```

You can see in the JSON policy in Example 8.3 that the ability to describe instances and modify instance attributes is given to the role that uses the AWS Lambda function while running.

With such security automation in place, the initial security group will be replaced with the Forensics security group once a TOR Client is detected, just minutes after it is discovered.

In Exercise 8.1, you will configure an automation to react to a TOR Client detection. This will allow you to gain hands-on experience with event-driven security and see a quick way to isolate potential connections to malicious actors using command-and-control tools leveraging the TOR network to protect their identity.

EXERCISE 8.1

Isolate Instances Using a TOR Anonymization Network

In this exercise, you will configure an automation to react to a TOR Client detection by Amazon GuardDuty. The automation will isolate the instance by changing the security group to an Incident-Forensics security group that allows access only from a specified IP address (used by that group).

1. Log in as an admin user in a sandbox or nonproduction account.
2. Create a security group called **Incident-Forensics** that allows inbound SSH only from the IP of the forensics team (optionally, it could be the IP address of a virtual desktop preinstalled with forensics tools in Amazon WorkSpaces), without allowing any outbound access.

EXERCISE 8.1 *(continued)*

3. Create an instance and configure a security group that allows RDP (or SSH if you chose to use a Linux instance).
4. Connect to the instance using RDP/SSH.
5. Download and install TOR Browser within the instance (`www.torproject.org/download`).
6. Configure an Amazon CloudWatch Events rule to trigger an AWS Lambda function upon finding `UnauthorizedAccess:EC2/TorClient`.
7. Write the code to change the security group to the Incident-Forensics security group.
8. Create a role that can be assumed by AWS Lambda with the permissions to change security groups and add it as an execution role.
9. Open the TOR Client on the instance.
10. Review the finding on Amazon GuardDuty (wait 10–20 minutes).
11. Verify that the security group was changed and that any connection was terminated.

Beware of More Complex Options When There Are More Straightforward Alternatives

In some exam questions, there is a native functionality that addresses what was requested, and another option that is technically feasible but would be more costly and harder to set up and maintain. These kinds of questions usually include a hint requesting the easiest or most effective way to accomplish the goal.

Automated Termination for Self-Healing Using Auto Scaling Groups

When working within AWS auto scaling groups of instances that do not have any state (when all data is stored externally in databases, or using services such as Amazon Elastic File Systems, or Amazon S3 buckets), you can terminate an instance as part of an automated action, since a new one will be created. This behavior certainly accomplishes self-healing, but always check with your Forensics team to know which information they will need for root cause analysis. They will probably require you to take a snapshot of the Amazon EBS volume before an instance can be terminated.

Automating Isolation of Bad Actors' Access to Web Applications

Amazon GuardDuty detects potential bad actors, which are adversaries, people, or groups that are interested in attacking your systems. A reasonable reaction, once a bad actor is detected, is to temporarily block access from their IP addresses to your web applications. You do this by adding them to an IP set and setting up a web ACL to block those IP addresses.

Bad actors can compromise an instance through a vulnerability, install malware, and launch reconnaissance actions from that instance. Such actions include scanning your network looking for open ports or expanding the scope of their attack by attempting to brute-force your SSH/RDP ports. Amazon GuardDuty detects these actions, and you can block the attacker's access to your applications by blacklisting their IP addresses on AWS WAF and adding network access control lists (NACLs) that deny access from the compromised instance.

Figure 8.6 shows how Amazon GuardDuty and AWS WAF can perform such duties.

FIGURE 8.6 Using Amazon GuardDuty and AWS WAF to automatically block suspicious hosts

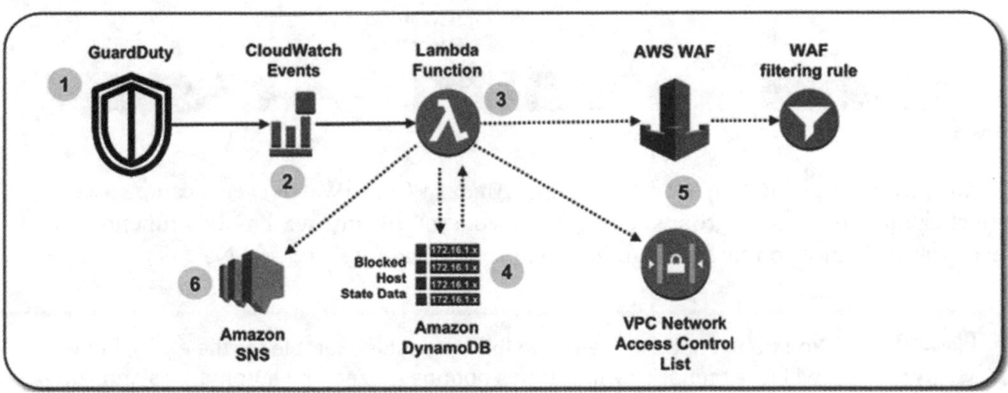

Figure 8.6 shows how Amazon GuardDuty triggers Amazon CloudWatch Events, which execute AWS Lambda functions that block access using AWS WAF and NACLs, creating a list on DynamoDB of the blocked hosts, and sending notifications using Amazon SNS.

More information about this security automation is available at the following blog post: `aws.amazon.com/blogs/security/how-to-use-amazon-guardduty-and-aws-web-application-firewall-to-automatically-block-suspicious-hosts`. Its video content is available in the AWS Online Tech Talk, "Automate Threat Mitigation Using AWS WAF and Amazon GuardDuty," published at `youtu.be/eLQIVLTALDk`.

Automating Actions upon Changes Detected by AWS CloudTrail

You can use AWS CloudTrail to detect a change by triggering Amazon CloudWatch events that execute an AWS Lambda function to automate security objectives. As Figure 8.7 shows, upon the creation or modification of an Amazon S3 bucket, an AWS Lambda function that forces encryption or versioning can be triggered.

As you can see in Figure 8.7, changes in the AWS infrastructure detected by AWS CloudTrail can be used to trigger Amazon CloudWatch events and execute AWS Lambda functions. These changes can include actions executed through API calls (via the AWS Web Console, AWS CLI, REST APIs, or software development kits).

FIGURE 8.7 Reacting to changes detected by AWS CloudTrail

Another example of such a strategy is how Amazon CloudWatch events can be used to detect changes to security groups to trigger remediation by an AWS Lambda function and then send a notification through Amazon Simple Notification Service (SNS).

You do not need to memorize this particular example for the exam, but you will face scenarios with various options for security automations and you should know which options are feasible, which accomplish the security objective in the question, and which are more effective and consistent.

WAF Security Automations

Web applications are a common point of entrance for attackers because they are frequently exposed to the public. Good implementation of security practices is needed to reduce the risk of a malicious actor exploiting a vulnerability. Generally, internal development teams need time to remediate security issues, and that time is even longer when the development is done by a third party.

For this reason, web application firewalls (WAFs) provide an additional layer of defense, blocking exploitation of vulnerabilities.

AWS WAF offers AWS managed rules and allows customers to leverage signatures from partners such as Fortinet, Cyber Security Cloud, GeoGuard, F5, and Imperva. Managed rules protect against common attacks on applications such as SQL injection and cross-site scripting. To cover other kinds of attacks such as bad bots, scrapers, HTTP floods, scanners, and probes, the implementation of other mechanisms such as the WAF Security Automation solution is needed. Figure 8.8 illustrates this solution.

FIGURE 8.8 WAF Security Automations architecture

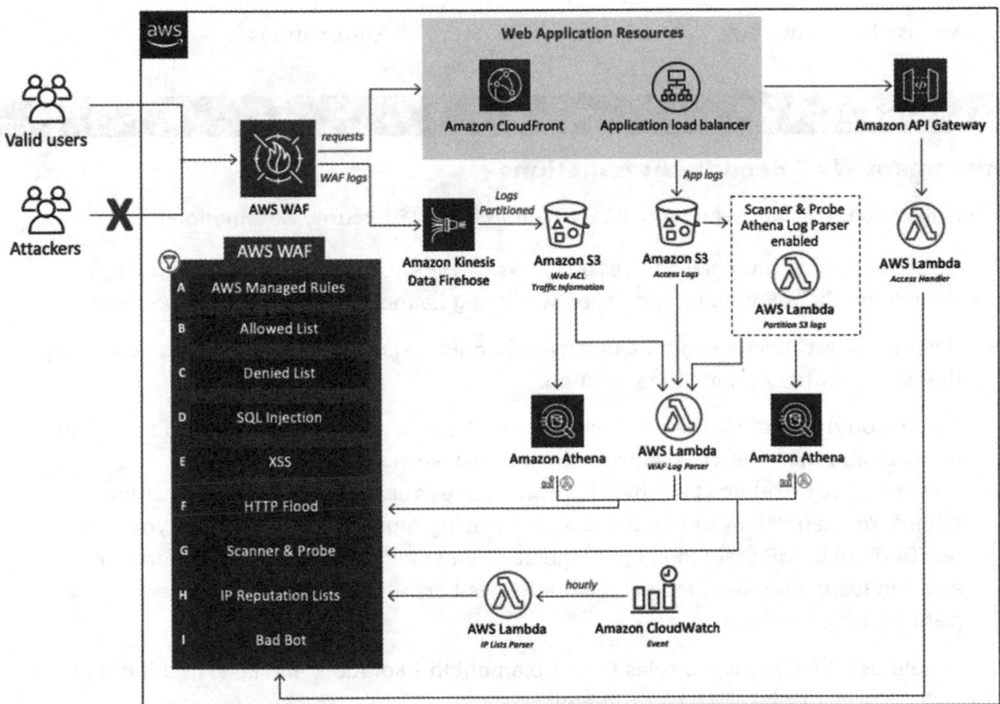

As Figure 8.8 shows, AWS WAF logs and application logs are stored on Amazon S3 and then analyzed to detect additional threats, such as malicious bots, including scrapers and spammers.

Malicious bots (also known as bad bots) are software applications that run automated tasks over the Internet that harm their victims in some way, or cause an undesired result such as a performance degradation. Scrapers are a particular type of malicious bot that collects data from the victim's website for malicious purposes, such as content reselling or price undercutting.

The WAF Security Automation solution includes an AWS CloudFormation template that you can use to launch and automatically build the entire architecture. You can find it on the AWS Solutions page with the deployment guide and documentation at `aws.amazon.com/solutions/aws-waf-security-automations`.

Not all vulnerabilities should be blocked by the WAF. Many need to be blocked in the applications, adding input validation and other controls. Blocking excessively on WAF can lead to false positives. Even if you have a WAF, your developers still need to understand application security concepts and scan their applications and code for vulnerabilities.

Exercise 8.2 shows how you can set up WAF Security Automations.

EXERCISE 8.2

Implement WAF Security Automations

In this exercise, you will set up the AWS Solution for WAF Security Automations.

1. Go to `aws.amazon.com/solutions/aws-waf-security-automations` and deploy the CloudFormation template by clicking Launch Solution in the AWS Console.
2. Review the architecture and the deployment guide, and protect your application using the WAF Security Automations solution.
3. If you would like to test the effectiveness of AWS WAF with the solution, you can find many deliberately insecure apps on the Internet, such as WebGoat (`owasp.org/www-project-webgoat`) or bWAPP (`www.itsecgames.com`) with many vulnerabilities. You can deploy one of these apps by using Amazon Linux AMIs, or you can use Bitnami LAMP Stack to simplify the deployment of bWAPP. Before performing any pen testing on AWS, review the guidelines here: `aws.amazon.com/security/penetration-testing`.

You should use AWS managed rules to complement this solution, and keep in mind that the Web ACL Capacity Unit (WCU) is a soft limit.

AWS Config Auto Remediation

One of the common challenges of securing workloads in the cloud is to maintain consistency of certain configurations that apply to all your accounts or resources. An example is certifying that logging (AWS CloudTrail) is turned on or that all your S3 buckets are configured to encrypt by default and are not publicly accessible.

AWS provides a service called AWS Config that allows you to overcome this challenge and perform many other security-related tasks, such as these:

- Maintaining an inventory of resources
- Comparing the infrastructure and configuration changes from one day to another
- Detecting compliance with a set of configuration rules, providing over 120 managed rules with common use cases, and allowing the creation of custom rules.
- Remediating configuration drifts by executing Systems Manager automations

AWS Config can check configurations on external resources such as GitHub repositories, Microsoft Active Directory resources, or any on-premises server using the API, as explained in the following announcement: `aws.amazon.com/about-aws/whats-new/2019/11/aws-config-launches-support-third-party-resources`.

Figure 8.9 shows the components that are part of an AWS Config flow.

FIGURE 8.9 AWS Config Flow

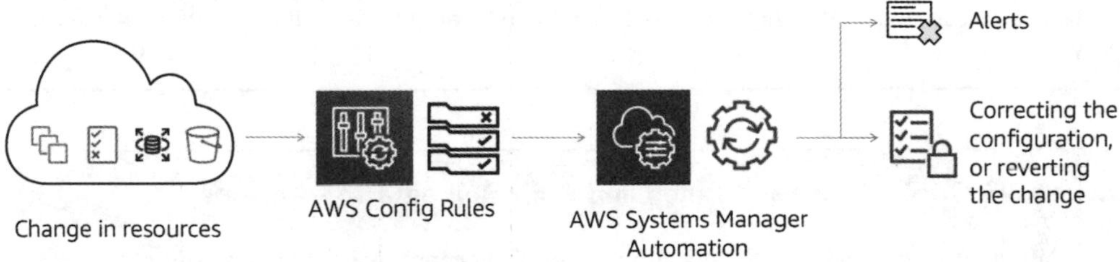

As you can see in Figure 8.9, changes to supported AWS resources are detected by AWS Config rules. If a noncompliance status is introduced, it can be automatically corrected using AWS Systems Manager Automation, with the generation of alerts via Amazon SNS.

Some of the security use cases covered by AWS managed rules are shown in Table 8.1.

TABLE 8.1 Common security use cases covered by AWS Config managed rules

Use case	Example remediation action
Detecting access keys that were not rotated in the past X days/months	Notify or disable or remove access keys
Detecting the use of unapproved AMIs	Stop or terminate noncompliant instances

TABLE 8.1 Common security use cases covered by AWS Config managed rules *(continued)*

Use case	Example remediation action
Detecting attached Amazon EBS volumes without encryption	Notify or stop Amazon EC2 instances, detach volume and encrypt volume (custom)
Ensuring Amazon GuardDuty and AWS CloudTrail are enabled	Enable Amazon GuardDuty and AWS CloudTrail
Running AWS IAM checks, such as detecting IAM policies attached directly to IAM users instead of using roles/groups, MFA, password policies, and unused credentials	Notify or disable noncompliant users
Running security groups checks, such as detecting the use of unrestricted access to common ports like RDP, SSH, or databases ports	Disable public access for security groups
Running Amazon S3 checks, such as whether public access is allowed or whether any buckets have default encryption set	Disable Amazon S3 public access; enable default encryption

Know AWS Config Managed Rules and Their Remediation Actions

Some exam questions ask you for the simplest way to accomplish a task and offer one option that can do what is requested but in a complex way, and another option that uses an AWS Config managed rule that accomplishes the same goal but takes only minutes to set up (and costs much less). Table 8.1 identifies remediation actions for various use cases.

Amazon S3 Default Encryption with AWS Config

As Werner Vogels (VP and CTO of `Amazon.com`) has repeatedly cautioned in several of his AWS keynotes: "Encrypt everything." And with AWS services supporting server-side encryption, this is a strongly recommended best practice—it's simple to implement, with low overhead and low cost.

But how can you automate the configuration of all Amazon S3 buckets to use secure encryption like AES256 by default? And furthermore, how can you ensure that even if an administrator sets encryption to None by mistake, the configuration reverts back to AES256?

A security automation based on AWS Config can be used to accomplish such goals. Exercise 8.3 shows what you need to configure.

EXERCISE 8.3

Automatically Configure All Buckets to Default to AES256 for Server-Side Encryption

In this exercise, you will set up an AWS Config rule with a remediation action that ensures all buckets have Amazon S3 Default Encryption configured to AES256. AWS Config will correct the configuration drift upon any future change remediating any noncompliance as it is discovered.

1. Log in as an admin user in a sandbox/nonproduction account.
2. Create an AWS IAM role called `Role-For-Enabling-S3-bucket-Encryption` with a trust relationship that allows the `ssm.amazonaws.com` service to assume the role.
3. Using JSON, add an AWS IAM policy for changing the encryption configuration on S3 buckets to a role that allows management of the Encryption setting on Amazon S3, as shown here:

```
{
    "Version": "2012-10-17",
    "Statement": [
        {
            "Sid": "VisualEditor0",
            "Effect": "Allow",
            "Action": "s3:PutEncryptionConfiguration",
            "Resource": "arn:aws:s3:::*"
        }
    ]
}
```

   This JSON policy grants permission to the AWS Systems Manager (SSM) service to correct the Amazon S3 configuration to enable encryption.

4. Create an Amazon S3 bucket with no encryption.
5. Enable the AWS Config rule `s3-bucket-server-side-encryption-enabled` and edit it to add a remediation action as shown here:

EXERCISE 8.3 *(continued)*

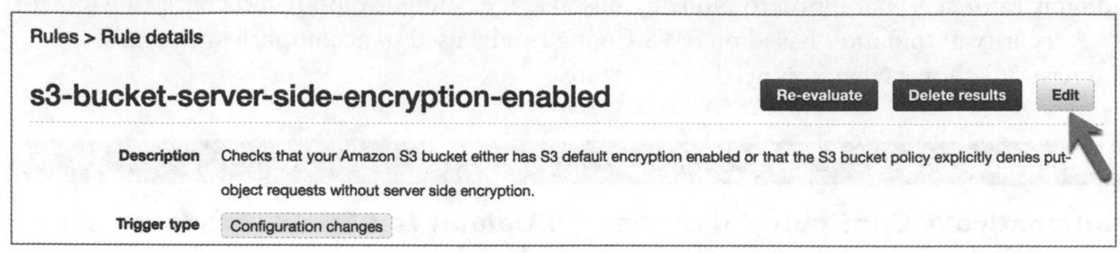

You can see an Edit button on each rule that allows configuration for remediation actions.

6. Configure a remediation action that executes `AWS-EnableS3BucketEncryption` with Auto Remediation set to Yes, Resource ID set to BucketName, SSEAlgorithm set to AES256, and AutomationAssumeRole set to the ARN of the role that you created earlier.

   AWS Config will monitor changes on S3 buckets to reevaluate the rule and execute the remediation action that sets encryption on the bucket automatically.

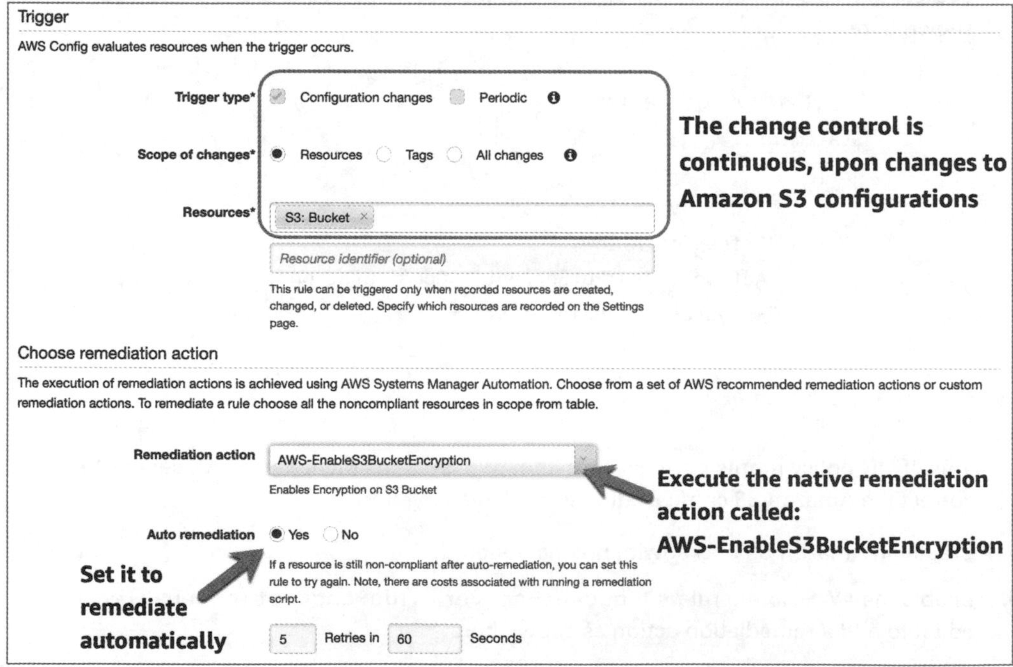

The remediation action used in this example has three parameters: the role to be used, the bucket name that we receive from Config as Resource ID parameter, and the algorithm to use.

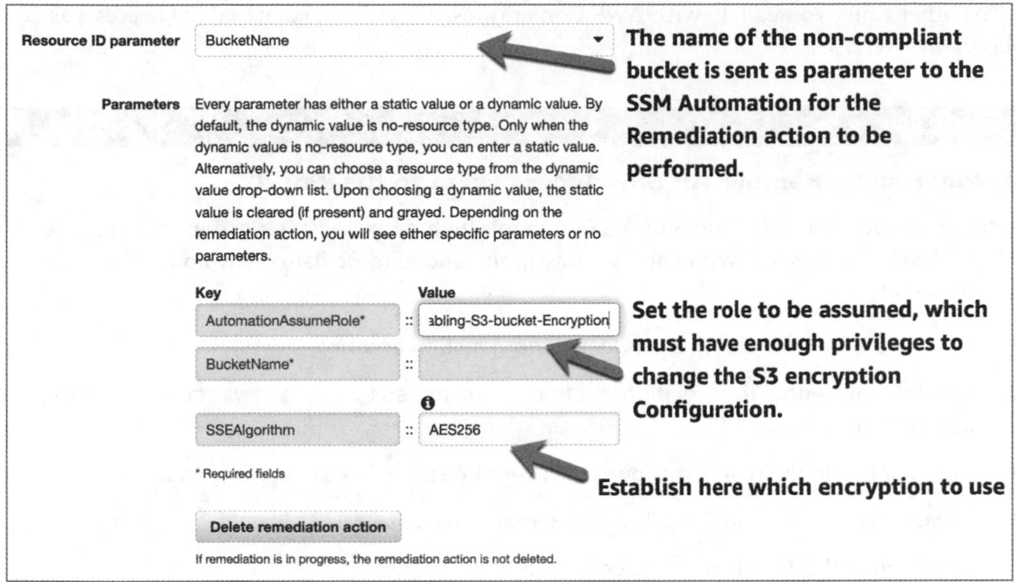

After a short period, all buckets on the account without default encryption will be changed to AES-256, and if someone changes the encryption to None again, AWS Config will change it back to AES-256.

7. Test this behavior as shown here:

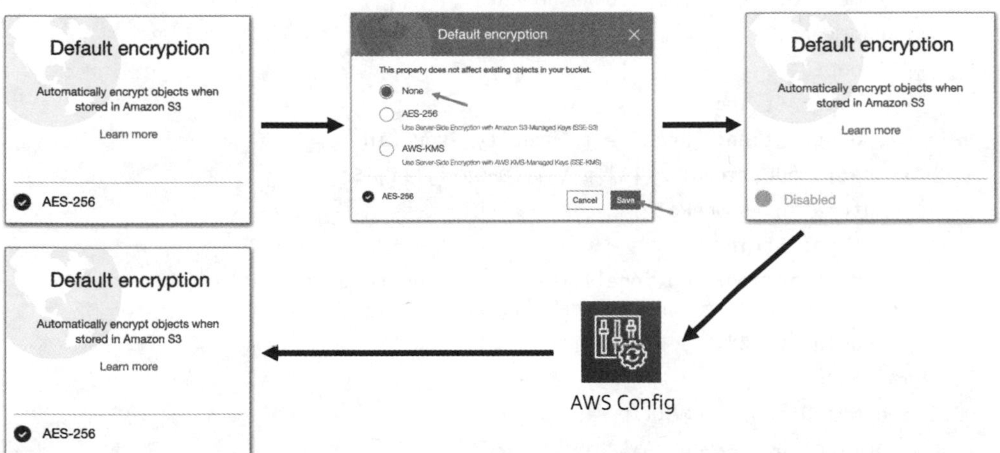

As you can see, AWS Config ensures that configurations are applied consistently and stay secure as intended.

Another thing you can do with AWS Config is restrict and remediate all SSH access, as shown in Exercise 8.4.

EXERCISE 8.4

Automatically Remove All SSH Access Open to the World

In this exercise, you will set up an AWS Config rule with its remediation action set to ensure that no SSH access is allowed in any security group and to remediate if any noncompliance is discovered.

1. Log in as an admin user in a sandbox/nonproduction account.
2. Create a role with a trust relationship that allows the `ssm.amazonaws.com` service to assume the role.
3. Add a policy to the role that allows `ec2:RevokeSecurityGroupIngress`.
4. Create a security group that allows SSH access to `0.0.0.0/0`.
5. Enable the AWS Config rule `restricted-ssh`.
6. Create an SSM document named `Disable-SSH-Ports-Opened-to-all-ip-addresses` with the following content:

```
---
description: Disable SSH ports opened all addresses.
schemaVersion: "0.3"
assumeRole: "{{ AutomationAssumeRole }}"
parameters:
  GroupId:
    type: String
    description: (Required) Security Group ID
    allowedPattern: ^([s][g]\-)([0-9a-f]){1,}$
  AutomationAssumeRole:
    type: String
    description: (Optional) The ARN of the role that allows Automation
to perform the actions on your behalf.
    default: ""
mainSteps:
- name: DisableFromAllIp
  action: aws:executeAwsApi
  inputs:
    Service: ec2
    Api:  RevokeSecurityGroupIngress
    GroupId: "{{GroupId}}"
```

```
        IpPermissions: [
            {"IpProtocol": "tcp", "FromPort": 22, "ToPort": 22,
            "IpRanges": [{"CidrIp": "0.0.0.0/0"}]},
            {"IpProtocol": "tcp", "FromPort": 22, "ToPort": 22,
            "Ipv6Ranges": [{"CidrIpv6": "::/0"}]}
        ]
    isEnd: true
```

7. Configure a remediation action that executes `Disable-SSH-Ports-Opened-to-all-ip-addresses` with Auto Remediation set to Yes, Resource ID set to GroupId, and AutomationAssumeRole set to the ARN of the role that you created earlier. You could also use the native `AWS-DisablePublicAccessForSecurityGroup` automation, but it will remove the RDP opened ports.
8. Check that all security groups that had SSH access no longer have it.

On the exam, you will be given several valid options to achieve the required end result, but one option would imply configuring several components or using custom code that is hard to build and maintain. If one of the options is a native feature that can achieve the same result in a simpler way, this option will be the right one. For example, one option might be to use a native AWS Config rule to detect and correct a configuration drift such as unapproved AMIs in use. Another option might be to use Amazon CloudWatch events to detect the launch of a new instance and then use an AWS Lambda function to query a list in DynamoDB with the approved AMIs to decide whether the instance should be terminated.

Automating Resolution of Findings Using AWS Security Hub

AWS Security Hub can help a lot with security automation. Because many different types of issues generate findings on AWS Security Hub, this service is the perfect place to centralize the remediation of such potential vulnerabilities in semi-automatic or automatic mode. Figure 8.10 shows the interaction of AWS Security Hub with other AWS services and third-party solutions.

As you can see in Figure 8.10, AWS Security Hub can receive findings from many AWS services (such as Amazon GuardDuty and Amazon Inspector) that provide detective controls, as well as solutions from AWS partners. Additionally, AWS Security Hub can trigger automated remediation actions through the events triggered in Amazon CloudWatch Events that can target AWS Lambda or Amazon SNS.

FIGURE 8.10 AWS Security Hub as the centerpiece of security automation

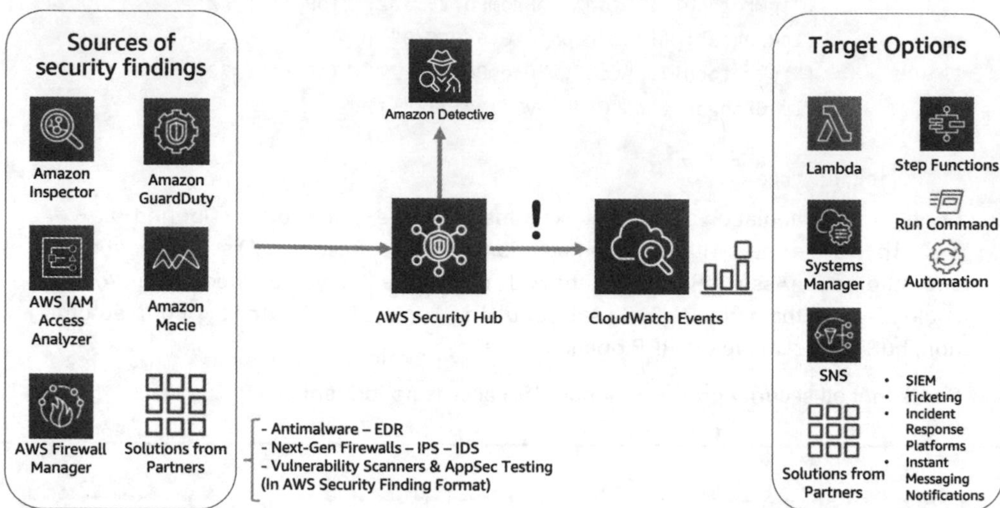

Within the AWS Security Hub, you can take one of the following three approaches to resolve a security finding:

- **Manual:** You can correct a finding manually (or archive it if you recognize it as a false positive).
- **Semi-Automatic:** With one or many predefined custom actions configured in AWS Security Hub, once you analyze a finding, you can decide that a remediation action should be launched by selecting the finding and selecting the desired action from the drop-down menu. For example, Close S3 Bucket enables Block Public Access at that bucket, or the action Resolve could trigger a response action that a different action will be triggered depending on the finding type.
- **Automatic:** All findings from AWS Security Hub generate Amazon CloudWatch Events, so a completely automated response can be triggered immediately. From the Amazon CloudWatch Events console, you can create a rule using Security Hub as the service name and setting Security Hub Findings - Imported as Even Type. You can also create a rule in JSON, as Example 8.4 shows.

Example 8.4: JSON rule

```
{
  "source": [
    "aws.securityhub"
  ],
  "detail-type": [
    "Security Hub Findings - Imported"
  ]
}
```

Using an AWS Lambda function as a target, an SSM Automation document, an SSM Run command, or an AWS Step Functions state machine can be used to automate a response. Such an approach is useful for containing threats such as worms that spread rapidly, or for known repeating issues that always require the same response. For more information on this capability go to `github.com/awsdocs/aws-security-hub-user-guide/blob/master/doc_source/securityhub-cloudwatch-events.md`.

Through this flow, you can automate responses using AWS services such as AWS Lambda to take snapshots, terminate instances, or isolate them by changing their security groups or disabling access keys for compromised users. Nevertheless, some AWS partners can also implement incident responses that are triggered via AWS Security Hub and Amazon CloudWatch Events. One example of an AWS partner that provides such useful tools and solutions is Atlassian. For example, when finding a high-risk vulnerability, you can configure an action that creates an "issue" to be resolved in Atlassian Opsgenie for developers to troubleshoot that code and remove the vulnerability. Alternatively, you can open a ticket using ServiceNow to ensure tracking of the vulnerability resolution process.

When the finding suggests a breach, you can launch an incident response plan on Demisto or Splunk Phantom, and send an instant message notification via Slack.

More information on AWS Security Hub Partners is available at `aws.amazon.com/security-hub/partners`. To learn more about automating response and remediation with AWS Security Hub, see `aws.amazon.com/blogs/security/automated-response-and-remediation-with-aws-security-hub`.

Automated Reasoning to Detect and Correct Human Mistakes

In late 2019, a new AWS service called AWS IAM Access Analyzer was launched. This service utilizes *automated reasoning* to analyze resource-based policies (such as bucket policies, key policies, and VPC endpoint policies) to detect when a resource is exposed outside of your AWS accounts and produce findings in AWS Security Hub.

AWS IAM Access Analyzer helps with the task of finding human errors that expose data to the public. It is also useful in unsecure situations such as when a developer sandbox account has access to a production resource.

Here is an example of security automation using AWS Security Hub taking IAM Access Analyzer as input. The use case's objective is to detect buckets that are open to the world (or accounts with less security controls, such a developer sandbox). To deploy this scenario, you will perform the following steps:

1. If you haven't done this already in your account for another automation, you should create the role for running the SSM automations. (You can review how to create the role at `docs.aws.amazon.com/systems-manager/latest/userguide/automation-setup.html`.) Then add the ARN to the SSM Automation document `AssumeRole` field. It should have this format: `arn:aws:iam::ACCOUNT:role/AutomationServiceRole`.

2. Create an AWS Systems Manager (SSM) Automation document and do the following:
   a. On the Builder tab, name it **DisableS3BucketPublicReadWrite.**
   b. Add an input parameter to the Document attributes called **BucketArn,** set Type to String, and set Required to Yes.
   c. At step 1 enter a name, like **Block_Public_Access,** and choose Run A Script (`aws:executeScript`) as Action Type.
   d. Using Python 3.6 Runtime, type **PutPublicAccessBlock** as the handler and enter the code shown in Example 8.5 in the Script area.
   e. In Additional Inputs, add an input with the name **InputPayload** and **`BucketArn: '{{ BucketArn }}'`** as Input Value.

Example 8.5: Script to enable Amazon S3 Block_Public_Access

```
def PutPublicAccessBlock(events, context):
    import boto3
    s3 = boto3.client('s3')
    Bucket = events['BucketArn'].split(':')[-1]
        response = s3.put_public_access_block(
            Bucket=Bucket,
            PublicAccessBlockConfiguration={
            'BlockPublicAcls': True,
            'IgnorePublicAcls': True,
            'BlockPublicPolicy': True,
            'RestrictPublicBuckets': True
        }
    )
    return response
```

3. Go to AWS Security Hub Settings and create a custom action, name it **Close S3 Bucket,** and type the following description: **Custom action to close Amazon S3 buckets opened for public access.** For Custom Action ID, enter **CloseS3Bucket.**

4. Open the Identity and Access Management (IAM) service, choose Access Analyzer ➢ Analyzers, and create a new analyzer, as shown in Figure 8.11. Your analyzer will analyze policies for all supported resources to identify access from outside the zone of trust. You can set your zone of trust to either Current Organization or Current Account. For this example, you will block only public access but you'll change the SSM Automation document. You could block access from other accounts in your organization as well.

FIGURE 8.11 AWS IAM Access Analyzer: creating an analyzer

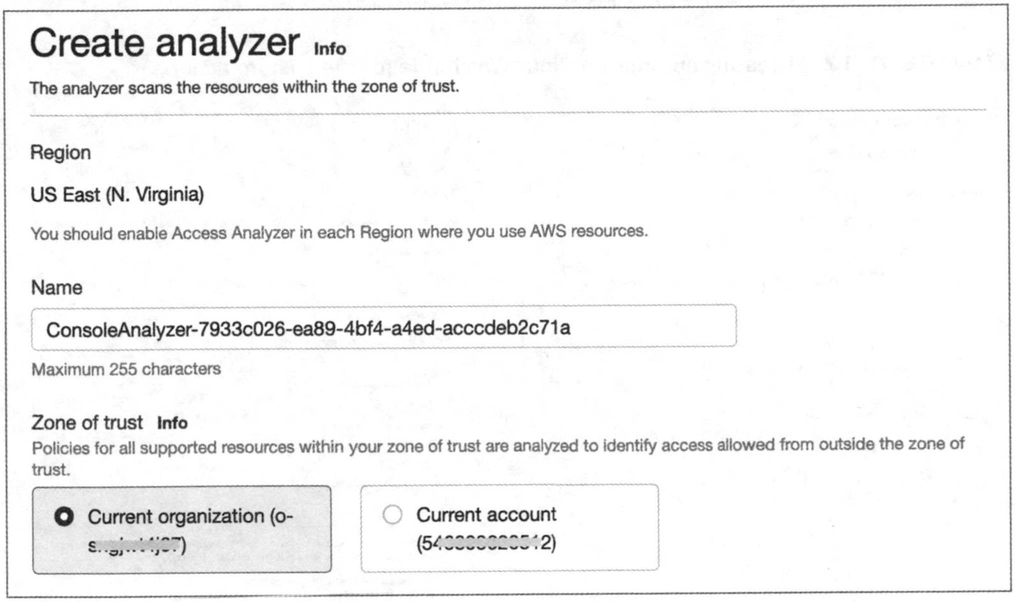

Figure 8.11 shows that the zone of trust can be your organization or your account.

5. Create an Amazon CloudWatch Events rule to detect the custom action with the event pattern described in Example 8.6.

Example 8.6: Amazon CloudWatch Event pattern

```
{
    "source": [
        "aws.securityhub"
    ],
    "detail-type": [
        "Security Hub Findings - Custom Action"
    ],
    "resources": [
        "arn:aws:securityhub:us-east-1:ACCOUNT:action/custom/CloseS3Bucket"
    ]
}
```

6. In Example 8.6, replace the word *ACCOUNT* with your account number and as Target, select an SSM automation, as shown in Figure 8.12.

FIGURE 8.12 Creating an Amazon CloudWatch rule for the custom action

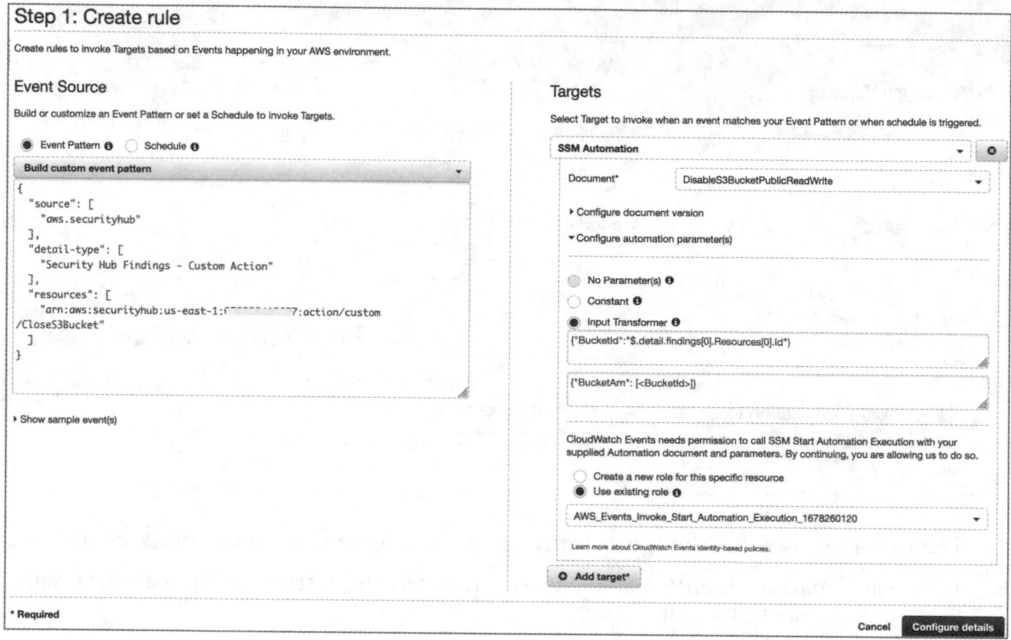

Figure 8.12 shows that since the full ARN is passed as a parameter and the SSM automation expects only the bucket name, Input Transformer is used with the following values:

```
{"BucketId":"$.detail.findings[0].Resources[0].Id"}
```

and

```
{"BucketArn": [<BucketId>]}
```

7. Create a bucket, removing the Block Public Access check marks, as shown in Figure 8.13.

   In Figure 8.13, Block All Public Access is set to Off.

8. Then, set up the bucket policy shown in Example 8.7, replacing the bucket's ARN with your own.

FIGURE 8.13 Creating the bucket without Block Public Access

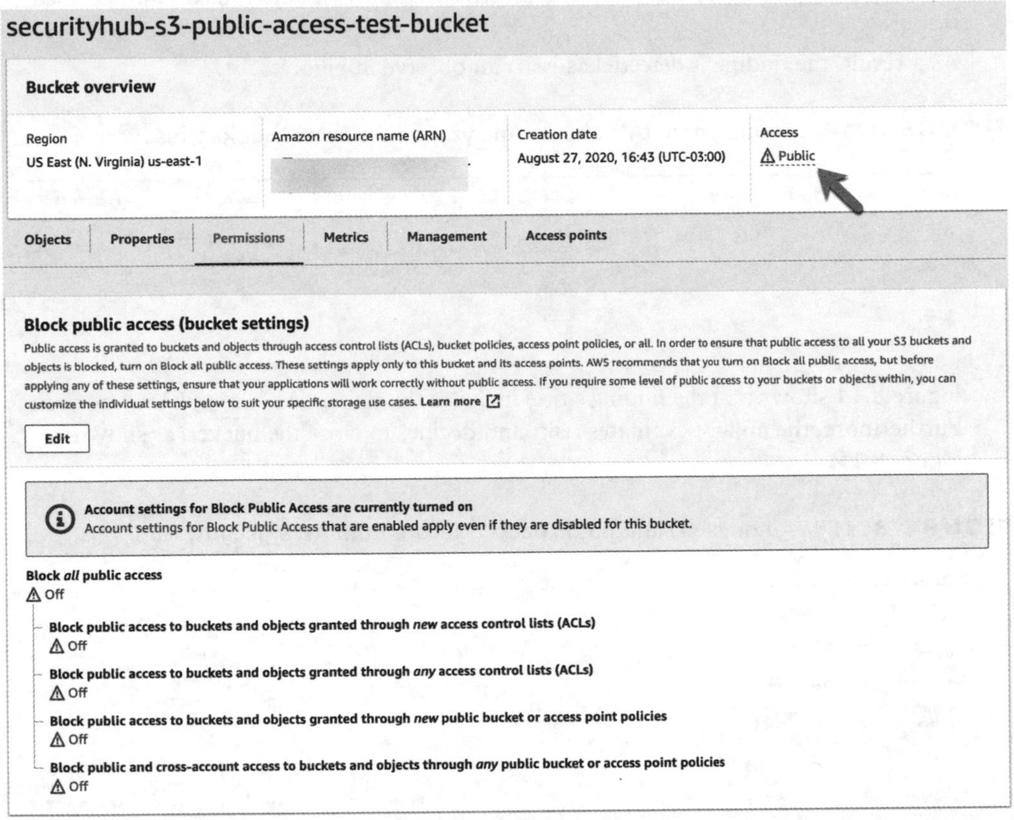

securityhub-s3-public-access-test-bucket

Bucket overview

Region
US East (N. Virginia) us-east-1

Amazon resource name (ARN)

Creation date
August 27, 2020, 16:43 (UTC-03:00)

Access
⚠ Public

Objects | Properties | Permissions | Metrics | Management | Access points

Block public access (bucket settings)

Public access is granted to buckets and objects through access control lists (ACLs), bucket policies, access point policies, or all. In order to ensure that public access to all your S3 buckets and objects is blocked, turn on Block all public access. These settings apply only to this bucket and its access points. AWS recommends that you turn on Block all public access, but before applying any of these settings, ensure that your applications will work correctly without public access. If you require some level of public access to your buckets or objects within, you can customize the individual settings below to suit your specific storage use cases. **Learn more**

Edit

Account settings for Block Public Access are currently turned on
Account settings for Block Public Access that are enabled apply even if they are disabled for this bucket.

Block *all* public access
⚠ Off

- **Block public access to buckets and objects granted through *new* access control lists (ACLs)**
  ⚠ Off
- **Block public access to buckets and objects granted through *any* access control lists (ACLs)**
  ⚠ Off
- **Block public access to buckets and objects granted through *new* public bucket or access point policies**
  ⚠ Off
- **Block public and cross-account access to buckets and objects through *any* public bucket or access point policies**
  ⚠ Off

Example 8.7: Amazon S3 Bucket Policy allowing public reads

```
{
    "Version": "2012-10-17",
    "Statement": [
        {
            "Sid": "PublicRead",
            "Effect": "Allow",
            "Principal": "*",
            "Action": "s3:GetObject",
            "Resource": "arn:aws:s3:::securityhub-s3-public-access-test-bucket/*"
        }
    ]
}
```

As you can see in Example 8.7, the principal is * and the action is `s3:GetObject`; therefore, the policy described in Example 8.7 will allow public reads on the specified resource.

As a result, the finding is detected as you can observe in Figure 8.14.

FIGURE 8.14 Finding from IAM Access Analyzer on the `AwsS3Bucket` resource

Severity	Company	Product	Title	Resource ID	Resource type
● MEDIUM	AWS	IAM Access Analyzer	AwsS3Bucket/arn:aws:s3:::securityhub-s3-public-access-test-bucket/ allows public access	arn:aws:s3:::securityhub-s3-public-access-test-bucket	AwsS3Bucket

Figure 8.14 shows that the finding's title includes the string `allows public access`. Furthermore, the analyst evaluates risks and decides to close the bucket, as shown in Figure 8.15.

FIGURE 8.15 Automated Amazon S3 bucket closure from AWS Security Hub

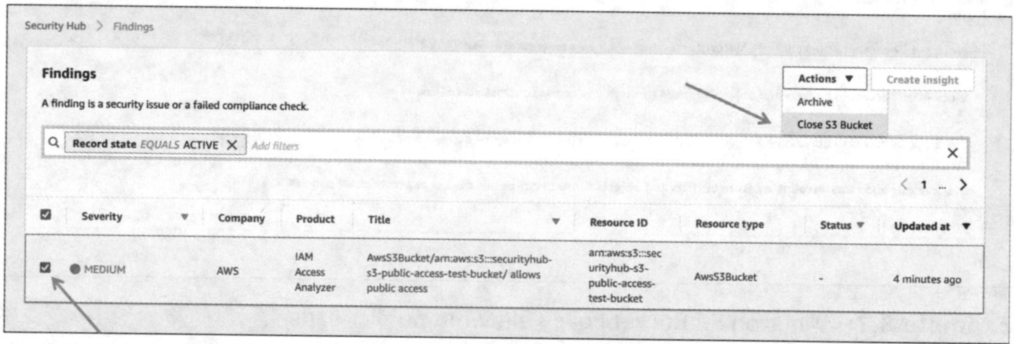

The bucket's public access will automatically be blocked, overriding the permissive bucket policy, as shown in Figure 8.16.

The example explained in these steps can be changed to alert AWS Security Hub on resources published to another account outside the zone of trust (your AWS accounts) to block access. Adding a `Deny` clause on the bucket policy would be effective (remember that explicit "deny" always overrides "allow").

FIGURE 8.16 Block All Public Access enabled

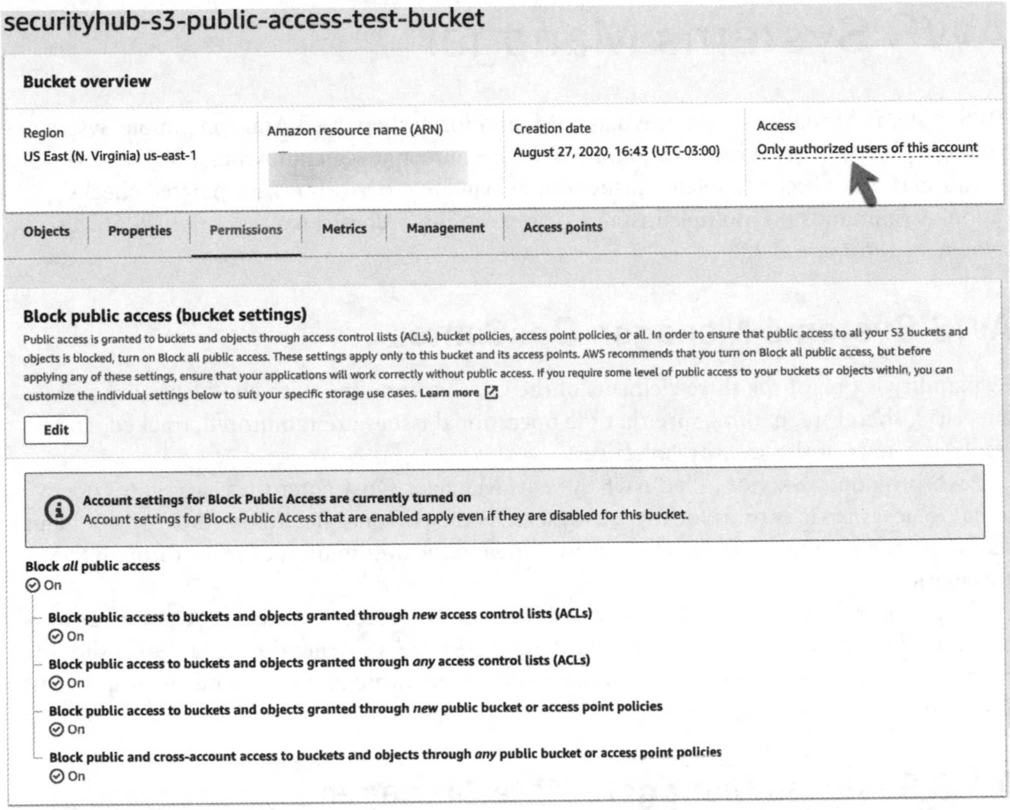

securityhub-s3-public-access-test-bucket

Bucket overview

Region	Amazon resource name (ARN)	Creation date	Access
US East (N. Virginia) us-east-1		August 27, 2020, 16:43 (UTC-03:00)	Only authorized users of this account

Objects | Properties | Permissions | Metrics | Management | Access points

Block public access (bucket settings)

Public access is granted to buckets and objects through access control lists (ACLs), bucket policies, access point policies, or all. In order to ensure that public access to all your S3 buckets and objects is blocked, turn on Block all public access. These settings apply only to this bucket and its access points. AWS recommends that you turn on Block all public access, but before applying any of these settings, ensure that your applications will work correctly without public access. If you require some level of public access to your buckets or objects within, you can customize the individual settings below to suit your specific storage use cases. **Learn more**

Edit

Account settings for Block Public Access are currently turned on
Account settings for Block Public Access that are enabled apply even if they are disabled for this bucket.

Block *all* public access
On

Block public access to buckets and objects granted through *new* access control lists (ACLs)
On

Block public access to buckets and objects granted through *any* access control lists (ACLs)
On

Block public access to buckets and objects granted through *new* public bucket or access point policies
On

Block public and cross-account access to buckets and objects through *any* public bucket or access point policies
On

Beware of Options That Do Not Work as Expected

Some exam questions mention the use of a service to do a task that sounds logical considering the name of the service, but it is just not the way that the service works. These types of questions are trying to prove that the candidate has real hands-on experience with the services, because if you've seen the console, you would know that the suggested option is not feasible. For example, in a question asking for the detection of a configuration drift, an option may say "Use AWS Config to execute a Step Functions state machine," and if you ever tried to configure AWS Config remediation you will know that it only executes Systems Manager Automation documents directly without any other intermediate service.

Aggregate and Resolve Issues with AWS Systems Manager

AWS Systems Manager (also known as SSM, and formerly named Amazon Simple Systems Manager) helps organizations to manage AWS resources at scale allowing a high degree of automation of security-related tasks such as patching, performing automated checks, running commands on multiple instances, or executing orchestrated tasks (which are also known as *automations*).

AWS Systems Manager: OpsCenter

Availability is one of the three elements of the CIA Triad (along with confidentiality and integrity); therefore, making sure that the operational issues are monitored, tracked, and resolved is part of the security objectives.

AWS provides a service called AWS Systems Manager OpsCenter that aggregates operational issues; provides tools for diagnosis, such as the personal health dashboard; and helps accelerate the resolution of those issues by allowing the automation of tasks through SSM automations.

Keep in mind that it's not recommended that you send security issues to OpsCenter to be centralized (you should use AWS Security Hub instead). As a general rule, IT teams should be monitoring OpsCenter (to centralize and resolve operational issues) while security teams should be monitoring AWS Security Hub.

AWS Systems Manager: State Manager

Availability is about keeping your services up and running without interruption as much as possible and depending on how critical an application is, indicated by its service level objective (99.5%, 99.9%, 99.99%, etc.).

If a service like an Apache Web Server goes down due to a failure, you will probably be interested in investigating what made the service go down. Before doing so, you may want to restart the service to reduce the impact on the end users and allow them to access the system again as soon as possible. AWS Systems Manager State Manager can help you by ensuring that if a service goes down, it will be restarted automatically.

This service can also help correct drifts of configurations within the instances through associations. An association is a configuration that is assigned to your managed instances, specifying a desired state, that will be reapplied periodically.

A common use case of this service is to ensure that the antimalware is running. If it's not installed, State Manager will install it automatically, and if it's not running, State Manager will start the service.

Automating Security Hygiene with AWS Systems Manager

As your infrastructure grows, manually maintaining the security hygiene becomes challenging. With *AWS Systems Manager* you can automate such management tasks at scale.

Something noteworthy of AWS Systems Manager is that it supports hybrid environments, so you can leverage this service to manage your on-premises infrastructure as well (or virtual machines on other cloud providers).

For an example of using AWS Systems Manager on multiple cloud providers, see `aws.amazon.com/blogs/mt/how-moodys-uses-aws-systems-manager-to-patch-servers-across-multiple-cloud-providers`.

AWS Systems Manager can help you manage the security of resources at scale in three ways:

- **Grouping** is creating groups of resources (such as grouping EC2 instances per application) to reflect an application stack or an environment using SSM resource groups.
- **Improving visibility** means centrally viewing patch compliance (using SSM Patch Manager) and operational issues (using SSM OpsCenter).
- **Taking actions** is automating remediation actions on groups of resources using SSM automations. Some of these actions are operating safely across resources by using SSM Session Manager, remediating issues by running scripts and commands on Amazon EC2 instances with the Run command, and remediating vulnerabilities while patching by using SSM Patch Manager.

Summary

Security automations allow you to contain or remediate security incidents, correct configuration drifts, and resolve issues consistently, without human intervention in a scalable manner.

Often security personnel only receive notifications so that they are aware of the situation that occurred. Or they receive notification about how a security incident was automatically handled, so they can evaluate if a new strategy is required to prevent this situation from reoccurring (such as training operators who made mistakes or removing bad actors from within the company).

AWS's detective capabilities provide a wealth of information that you can use in identifying anomalous behavior. You can use this knowledge to build effective automations.

If significant disruption to a service occurs (as when isolating an instance), you should test detective controls to ensure that they're triggered only when intended and that the architecture is designed to withstand the failure of that instance. For example, if the containment action is to terminate an instance infected with malware, you need to be sure that there is an Auto Scaling group that will take care of launching a new instance to make up for the one that was terminated, with minimal impact to the users.

Exam Essentials

Understand how to use CloudWatch Events. Amazon CloudWatch Events is frequently used to trigger response actions when a specific event is detected. This can include remediation using an AWS Lambda function.

Understand common remediation actions. Some of the most common remediation actions include executing AWS Lambda functions to isolate threats and running AWS Systems Manager Automation to fix configuration drifts.

Know what each service detects in order to trigger an automation. You can use Amazon Macie or AWS Config to detect weak configurations of Amazon S3 buckets. AWS Config also provides the Auto Remediation feature to correct configuration drift through AWS Systems Manager Automation. If you are trying to build an automation to react to a potential compromised instance or malicious actor's connections (based on their IP Reputation), then Amazon GuardDuty will be used to detect the instance, and an AWS Lambda function can be used to isolate the instance.

Be familiar with AWS Config managed rules and the available remediation actions. AWS Config managed rules allow you to quickly and cheaply perform a wide range of helpful remediation actions. Table 8.1 shows many use cases and their remediation.

Understand AWS Systems Manager's capabilities. The AWS Systems Manager OpsCenter helps aggregate operational issues. AWS Systems Manager State Manager helps ensure that services restart automatically when they go down; it also helps correct configuration drifts. AWS Systems Manager can help you manage the security of resources at scale by creating groups of resources, improving visibility of patch compliance and operational issues, and automating remediation actions on groups of resources.

Define the difference between AWS Security Hub and AWS OpsCenter. IT teams should be monitoring OpsCenter (to centralize and resolve operational issues) while security teams should be monitoring AWS Security Hub. You generally should not send security issues to OpsCenter to be centralized.

Review Questions

1. A company is worried about data loss and would like to detect the Amazon S3 buckets that allow access from outside their production account and let a security analyst decide whether to close the buckets or allow them to remain open. Which of the following services can be combined to accomplish such automation?

   A. Detect buckets with Trusted Advisor, and use an Amazon CloudWatch Events rule to trigger an AWS Lambda function to close the bucket.

   B. Use IAM Access Analyzer to detect buckets, and an AWS Security Hub custom action to trigger an Amazon CloudWatch Events rule that executes an AWS Lambda function to close the bucket.

   C. Use IAM Access Analyzer to detect buckets, and an Amazon CloudWatch Events rule that executes an AWS Lambda function to close the bucket.

   D. Use AWS Config rules to detect buckets, and auto-remediate with a Systems Manager automation.

2. A company wants to ensure that there are no buckets without default encryption enabled and that if by mistake any administrator removes the default encryption, it should be automatically corrected to comply with the company's policy. Which of the following automation options could accomplish the requested security objective? (Choose two.)

   A. Use AWS Security Hub's native finding "PCI.S3.4 S3 buckets should have server-side encryption enabled" and trigger an AWS Lambda function to remediate.

   B. Use AWS Config and trigger an AWS Lambda function to remediate.

   C. Use AWS Config to detect using `s3-bucket-server-side-encryption-enabled` and auto-remediate using the `AWS-EnableS3BucketEncryption` SSM automation.

   D. Use AWS CloudTrail to detect the change on the Amazon S3 bucket properties and trigger the Amazon CloudWatch Events rule that executes an AWS Lambda function to remediate.

3. A company wants to ensure that there are no buckets without default encryption enabled and that if by mistake any administrator removes the default encryption, it should be automatically corrected to comply with the company's policy. Which of the following automations could accomplish the requested security objective with the least effort?

   A. Use AWS Security Hub's native finding "PCI.S3.4 S3 buckets should have server-side encryption enabled" and trigger an AWS Lambda function to remediate.

   B. Use AWS Config and trigger an AWS Lambda function to remediate.

   C. Use AWS Config to detect `using s3-bucket-server-side-encryption-enabled` and auto-remediate using `AWS-EnableS3BucketEncryption` SSM automation.

   D. Use AWS CloudTrail to detect the change on the Amazon S3 bucket properties and trigger an Amazon CloudWatch Events rule that executes an AWS Lambda function to remediate.

4. A company requires you to detect failed login attempts in the operating system of a critical instance and to make that information available to security analysts to investigate and decide whether to ignore or isolate. Which of the following actions can be recommended? (Choose two.)

   A. Sending all the OS logs to a SIEM among the AWS Security Hub's partners and using a SIEM rule to create a finding in AWS Security Hub, then using AWS Security Hub's custom actions to ease isolation

   B. Sending all the OS logs to AWS Security Hub and AWS Security Hub's actions to automate resolution

   C. Sending OS logs to Amazon CloudWatch logs through the agent, creating a metric filter and an alarm, and triggering an AWS Lambda that creates the finding in AWS Security Hub, then using AWS Security Hub's custom actions to ease isolation

   D. Sending all the OS logs to a SIEM among the AWS Security Hub's partners and using a SIEM rule to create a finding in AWS Security Hub, then using Amazon CloudWatch Events to trigger an AWS Lambda function to isolate

5. A company's chief information security officer (CISO) wishes to stop all instances where crypto-mining is detected in an automated approach for nonproduction accounts and in a semi-automated way for the production accounts. Which of the following security automations could help the company achieve this result? (Choose two.)

   A. Using Amazon GuardDuty to detect crypto-mining, and create AWS Security Hub's custom actions to stop the instance

   B. Using AWS Config to detect crypto-mining and Amazon CloudWatch events rule to trigger an AWS Lambda function that changes the security groups isolating the instance

   C. Using Trusted Advisor to detect crypto-mining and Amazon CloudWatch events rule to trigger an AWS Lambda function that changes the security groups isolating the instance

   D. Using Amazon GuardDuty to detect crypto-mining, and an Amazon CloudWatch events rule to trigger an AWS Lambda function that changes the security groups isolating the instance

6. Which of the following services are more suited to detect and correct configuration drifts? (Choose two.)

   A. AWS Trusted Advisor

   B. AWS Config

   C. AWS Systems Manager State Manager

   D. AWS CloudTrail

   E. Amazon GuardDuty

7. Which of the following services are integrated in AWS Security Hub to generate findings? (Choose three.)

   A. Amazon EC2

   B. Amazon Inspector

   C. Amazon GuardDuty

   D. AWS CloudTrail

E. Amazon Macie

F. Amazon Cognito

8. The chief information security officer (CISO) of a company has just adopted Systems Manager Session Manager as the standard for managing remote access to their instances and bastions that accept inbound connections from specific IP addresses. Now, the CISO needs to detect any SSH opened to the world in the security groups and to revoke those accesses. What automation can be implemented to lock down these security groups?

   A. Use AWS Config to detect, and use Auto-Remediate.

   B. Use Trusted Advisor to detect, and use Auto-Remediate.

   C. Use AWS Config to execute an AWS Lambda function.

   D. Use AWS Systems Manager Session Manager to restrict access by other means.

9. A company's security analyst detected a malware (Remote Access Tool) on some instances that run web servers and are in an Auto Scaling group that maintains at least other 20 instances. No data is stored on those web servers, and while the Incident Forensics team analyzes how they got in, the security analyst wants to automate the rebuild of any compromised instance to ensure that the malware was removed. How would you suggest to proceed? (Choose three.)

   A. Run an antimalware software scan to remove the malware.

   B. Enable Amazon GuardDuty, and configure an Amazon CloudWatch Events rule to trigger a Run command execution to reinstall the web server.

   C. Enable Amazon GuardDuty, and configure an Amazon CloudWatch Events rule to trigger the termination of the instance when Remote Access Tools are detected.

   D. Use host intrusion prevention systems from the partners in the marketplace to harden the instances.

   E. Use AWS Systems Manager Patch Manager to patch the instances.

10. A company needs to ensure all buckets on an account (that has only static websites) are configured with versioning to recover quickly from defacement attacks and wants to make sure that if by mistake someone unconfigures versioning, it should automatically be turned on again. How can this be accomplished?

   A. Configure Amazon S3 Events to execute an AWS Lambda function that sets Versioning to Enabled when "Changes In Bucket Properties" occurs.

   B. Use a native AWS Config rule and Auto-Remediate.

   C. Use AWS Security Hub to detect Amazon S3 buckets without versioning and create a custom action to enable versioning.

   D. Use a custom AWS Config rule and Auto-Remediate.

Chapter

9

Security Troubleshooting on AWS

THE AWS CERTIFIED SECURITY SPECIALTY EXAM OBJECTIVES THAT LEVERAGE CONCEPTS EXPLAINED IN THIS CHAPTER INCLUDE THE FOLLOWING:

✓ **Domain 2: Logging and Monitoring**

- 2.2: Troubleshoot security monitoring and alerting
- 2.4: Troubleshoot logging solutions

✓ **Domain 3: Infrastructure Security**

- 3.3: Troubleshoot a secure network infrastructure

✓ **Domain 4: Identity and Access Management**

- 4.2: Troubleshoot an authorization and authentication system to access AWS resources

✓ **Domain 5: Data Protection**

- 5.2: Troubleshoot key management

Introduction

"Everything fails, all the time." With this famous quote from 2008, Werner Vogels (Amazon's vice president and chief technology officer) was arguably inciting a different attitude from IT professionals, one that abandoned blaming and finger-pointing and truly embraced preparation for problems that will happen.

Design best practices and frameworks such as the Well-Architected Framework (introduced in Chapter 2, "Cloud Security Principles and Frameworks") can greatly minimize the impact of failures that occur within AWS Cloud environments. Nonetheless, when you are dealing with the development and operation of complex and distributed systems, you should expect to run into scenarios where you need to understand abnormal behavior. This unusual behavior may be present not only in the application layer but also in all the infrastructure components that support it.

But how exactly can you deal with the unexpected? Well, it may help to take a look at what the past can teach you. Multiple reports point out human mistakes as the main cause for IT outages and data breaches (see, for example, `www.cnet-training.com/news/human-errors-the-biggest-challenge-to-data-center-availability-and-how-we-can-mitigate-them-part-1`, `https://journal.uptimeinstitute.com/examining-and-learning-from-complex-systems-failures/`, and `fortune.com/2020/05/20/data-breaches-privacy-cybersecurity-hacks`). And although automation can minimize configuration mistakes in repetitive implementations, planning for automation requires an adequate level of knowledge on how the services and features are being automated.

In this chapter, you will learn about several tools that will help you troubleshoot the operation of your AWS Cloud environments. You will examine a variety of abnormal behavior scenarios that are caused by common misconfigurations and integration mishandling. As you identify whether these mistakes apply to your situation, you will gain more perspective into what is causing the problem.

Using Troubleshooting Tools and Resources

As you saw in Chapter 4, "Detective Controls," AWS has several ways to identify events and correct problems. In this section, you will learn how to identify problems in the configuration and use of the following services: AWS CloudTrail, Amazon CloudWatch Logs, Amazon CloudWatch Events, and Amazon EventBridge. With such services correctly activated, you will have a much better chance of detecting and fixing abnormal behavior in your environments.

AWS CloudTrail

One of the essential security tools of AWS is CloudTrail. CloudTrail is a service that allows you to view the activities performed on your AWS account. The service provides the event history of the AWS account activity, including all API calls performed by the Management Console, the AWS SDKs, the command-line tools (CLI), and other AWS services.

CloudTrail is activated by default in your AWS account; however, to obtain a continuous record of events, you must create a trail. When you create a trail in CloudTrail, you need to provide the name of an S3 bucket for storing events.

Exercise 9.1 shows you how to create a trail.

EXERCISE 9.1

Creating a Trail in AWS CloudTrail

Please execute the following steps to create a new Trail:

1. While signed in as administrator, go to Services and select CloudTrail under Management & Governance.
2. Select Trails in the left menu.
3. Click the Create Trail button.
4. Enter **security-book-trail** as the trail name.
5. Select the Yes radio button in Apply Trail To All Regions.

EXERCISE 9.1 ***(continued)***

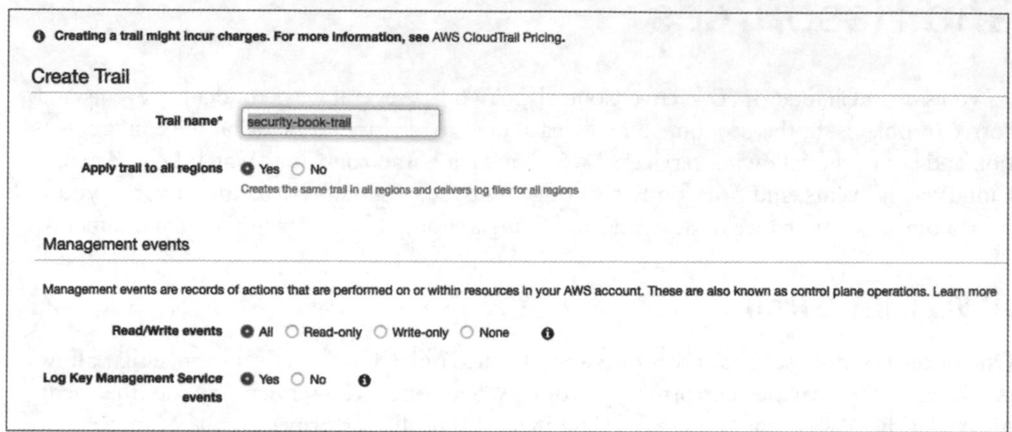

6. Select Data Events. This option can generate a high volume of information and is disabled by default.

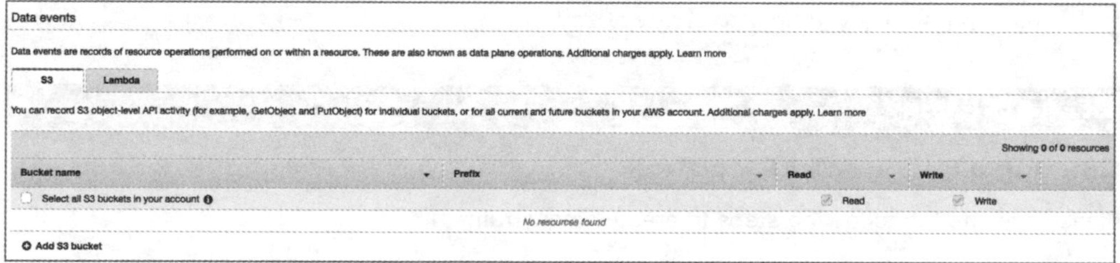

7. Select an existing bucket or create a new one by clicking Add S3 Bucket.

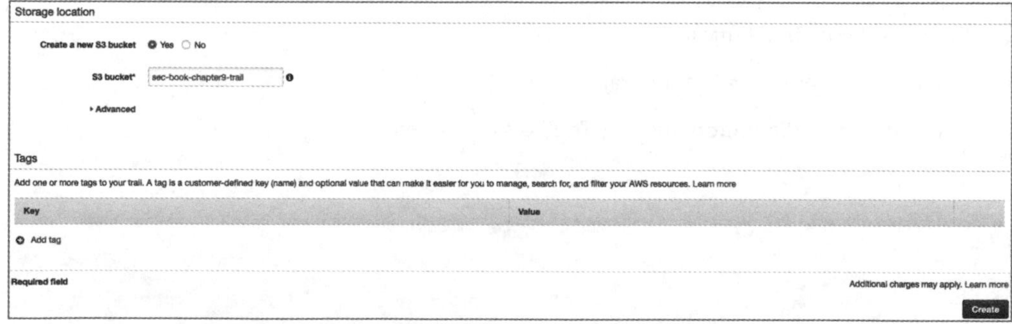

8. Click Create, and you will see your trail.

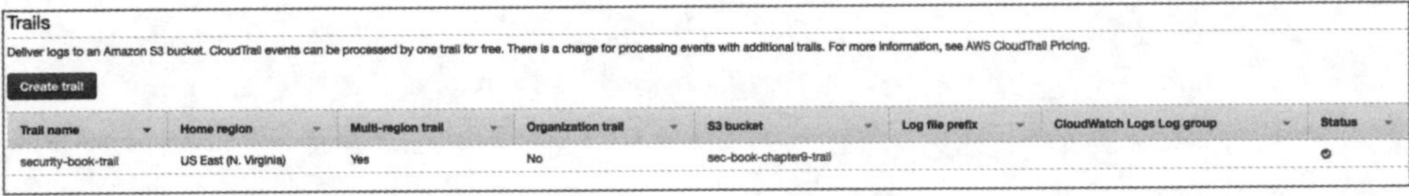

After you create the trail, it may take a few minutes for the first events to appear in the S3 bucket. If the records are not being saved, check that the trail has been created and is active on the console.

If the trail is active, check that the bucket name you provided is correct.

Check that the bucket policy allows CloudTrail to write events, as shown in Example 9.1.

Example 9.1: S3 bucket policy that allows CloudTrail to write events

```
{
    "Version": "2012-10-17",
    "Statement": [
        {
            "Sid": "AWSCloudTrailAclCheck20150319",
            "Effect": "Allow",
            "Principal": {
                "Service": "cloudtrail.amazonaws.com"
            },
            "Action": "s3:GetBucketAcl",
            "Resource": "arn:aws:s3:::<YOUR BUCKET NAME>"
        },
        {
            "Sid": "AWSCloudTrailWrite20150319",
            "Effect": "Allow",
            "Principal": {
                "Service": "cloudtrail.amazonaws.com"
            },
            "Action": "s3:PutObject",
            "Resource": "arn:aws:s3:::<YOUR BUCKET NAME>/AWSLogs/123456789012/*",
            "Condition": {
```

```
                "StringEquals": {
                    "s3:x-amz-acl": "bucket-owner-full-control"
                }
            }
        }
    ]
}
```

If you are having trouble accessing CloudTrail, make sure your user has read access to the service by using the `AWSCloudTrailReadOnlyAccess` policy.

Amazon CloudWatch Logs

You can use Amazon CloudWatch Logs to monitor, store, and access log files from EC2 instances, AWS CloudTrail, Route 53, and other sources. AWS CloudWatch Logs centralizes the logs of other services and applications in a robust, scalable, and managed solution.

To be able to view EC2 instance logs, you must have an agent installed on the instance. If you are unable to view the logs generated by the EC2 instance, verify that the agent is correctly installed, that the `awslogs` or `awslogsd` service has been started on the instance that the agent is installed on, and that the agent has the policy shown in Example 9.2 configured.

Example 9.2: CloudWatch agent policy example

```
{
    "Version": "2012-10-17",
    "Statement": [
      {
        "Effect": "Allow",
        "Action": [
          "logs:CreateLogGroup",
          "logs:CreateLogStream",
          "logs:PutLogEvents",
          "logs:DescribeLogStreams"
        ],
        "Resource": [
          "arn:aws:logs:*:*:*"
        ]
      }
    ]
}
```

For more details on agent settings, refer to `docs.aws.amazon.com/AmazonCloudWatch/latest/logs/AgentReference.html`.

Amazon CloudWatch Events

Amazon CloudWatch Events delivers a near real-time stream of system events that describe changes in AWS resources. Using simple rules, you can match events and route them to one or more target functions or streams.

CloudWatch Events becomes aware of operational changes as they occur, and you can build your own functions to take the necessary corrective actions, such as sending messages to respond to the environment, activating functions, making changes, and capturing state information.

You can also use CloudWatch Events to schedule automated actions that self-trigger at specific times using `cron` or `rate` expressions.

For example, you can create a Lambda function to perform automated tasks such as terminating unauthorized instances or those that may not have a specific tag filled. In this case, it is important to check if the Lambda that will be invoked by CloudWatch Events has the necessary permissions to perform the expected actions, in this case, terminating an EC2 instance. Additionally, you should check if the function policy allows the Lambda function to be invoked by CloudWatch Events.

Amazon EventBridge

Amazon EventBridge is a serverless event bus that facilitates application interconnection using data from the applications themselves, applications integrated into the software as a service model, and AWS services. EventBridge delivers a real-time data stream to destinations like AWS Lambda. You can configure routing rules that determine the destination of data to create event-driven application architectures.

Common Access Control Troubleshooting Scenarios

As you learned in Chapter 3, "Identity and Access Management," AWS Identity and Access Management (IAM) allows you to manage access to AWS services and resources securely. IAM helps you create and control AWS users and groups and use permissions to grant and deny access to AWS resources.

You can create users and groups in IAM, assign individual security credentials to them (access keys, passwords, and multifactor authentication devices), or request temporary security credentials to provide users with access to AWS services and resources. You can manage permissions to control what operations a user can perform.

You can create roles in IAM and manage permissions to control which operations can be performed by the entity or the AWS service that takes over the role. It is also possible to define which entity is allowed to assume the role. Also, you can use service-linked functions to delegate permissions to AWS services that create and manage AWS resources on your behalf.

You can enable identity federation to allow current identities (users, groups, and roles) in your company to access the AWS Management Console, call the AWS APIs, and access resources, without the need to create an IAM user for each identity. You can use any identity management solution that supports SAML 2.0 or any of our federation examples (AWS Console SSO or federation via APIs).

By default, access permissions on AWS are denied, meaning that you must be explicit about which permissions users and groups must have. When you are working with multiple policies, actions will only be allowed if no policies have explicit denial and at least one policy provides explicit access. That is, an explicit denial overrides permission.

Finally, if you are using resource-based access policies (such as Amazon S3 bucket policies), do not forget to verify how these policies are configured and make sure they are not conflicting with your IAM policies.

Permissions Boundary

A *permissions boundary* is a limit of permissions used to define the maximum permissions that a policy can grant to an IAM entity. An entity's permission limit allows the entity to perform only the actions permitted by both identity-based policies and their permission limits.

For example, the policy in Example 9.3 defines the maximum access limits for a given user.

Example 9.3: Permission boundary

```
{
    "Version": "2012-10-17",
    "Statement": [
        {
            "Effect": "Allow",
            "Action": [
                "s3:*",
                "ec2:*"
            ],
            "Resource": "*"
        }
    ]
}
```

When you use a policy to set the permissions boundary for the user, it limits the user's permissions but does not provide grants on its own, as you can see in Example 9.4.

Example 9.4: Policy attached directly to the user

```
{
  "Version": "2012-10-17",
  "Statement": {
    "Effect": "Allow",
    "Action": "iam:*",
    "Resource": "*"
  }
}
```

In this case, if the user tries to perform any operation in IAM, the call will fail because there is no explicit declaration in the permissions boundary allowing any operation in IAM. In other words, only the permitted operations defined in the user's policy and within the limits established in the permissions boundary will be allowed.

Figure 9.1 illustrates effective permissions when using a permissions boundary.

FIGURE 9.1 Effective permissions example

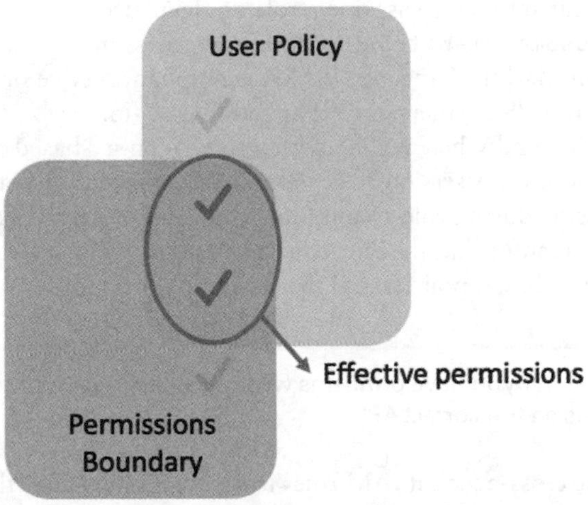

Service Control Policies

Service control policies (SCPs) are a type of organization policy that you can use to manage permissions in your organization. SCPs offer central control over the maximum available permissions for all accounts in your organization, and they are available only in an organization that has all features enabled.

Similar to the discussion about permissions boundaries in Chapter 3, SCPs alone are not sufficient for allowing or denying access in the accounts in your organization. However, SCPs define a guardrail for what actions the principals can perform.

For more information on how policies are evaluated on AWS, visit `docs.aws.amazon.com/IAM/latest/UserGuide/reference_policies_evaluation-logic.html`.

Identity Federation Problems

In AWS, there are three APIs that can be used with federated entities in the Security Token Service (STS): `AssumeRole`, `AssumeRoleWithWebIdentity`, and `AssumeRoleWithSAML`.

`STS:AssumeRole` is used when you need to assume a specific role after authenticating with your AWS account.

The `STS:AssumeRoleWithWebIdentity` API is used in cases of federation with OpenID Connect (OIDC) providers such as Amazon Cognito, Login with Amazon, Facebook, Google, or any OIDC-compatible identity provider. For example, after authenticating with an external provider, you must call the API `STS:AssumeRoleWithWebIdentity`, sending the web identity–generated token to assume a role on the platform.

Finally, the `STS:AssumeRoleWithSAML` API is used to assume a role when authenticated by a Security Assertion Markup Language (SAML)-compliant service or provider, such as Microsoft Azure AD or AWS partners like Okta and OneLogin.

One thing to keep in mind when dealing with a role's identity-based policies is how they interact with session policies. A session policy is an inline policy that you can create on the fly and pass in the session during role assumption to further scope the permissions of the role session. Therefore, be mindful that the effective permissions of the session are the intersection of the role's identity-based policies and the session policy.

Whenever you have problems with the authorization process, make sure you are using the correct API.

It is common to use cross-account IAM roles to access S3 buckets—that is, when an account needs to access a bucket that is in another AWS account. In this case, it is important to verify that the account that will make the request is registered as trusted and that the IAM role used to make the call has access to the STS `AssumeRole` API. Also, the IAM policy on the target account must authorize the source account to perform the assume role action, and there might also be a bucket policy in the destination account that could prevent access.

Encryption and Decryption Troubleshooting Scenarios

The AWS Key Management Service (AWS KMS) is a managed service that facilitates the creation and control of the encryption keys used to encrypt your data. The customer master keys that you create in AWS KMS are protected by hardware security modules (HSMs).

AWS KMS is integrated with most AWS services that enable the encryption of your data. AWS KMS is also integrated with AWS CloudTrail to provide logs of encryption key use to help meet your audit, regulatory, and compliance requirements.

You can use the encryption keys created in different AWS accounts. For that, you need to perform the cross-account access configuration for the KMS.

When configuring access to KMS through other accounts, you have to configure two types of policies: the key policy and the IAM policy. The key policy is a resource-based policy attached to the customer master key (CMK), and it defines controls for the management and use of the key. The IAM policy is responsible for defining which users, groups, and roles can perform operations such as `kms:Encrypt` or `kms:Decrypt`.

It is essential to know the most common problems when using CMK keys:

- The key policy must allow access to the key through an external account (trusted account) when using cross-account access.
- The external account must have an IAM policy allowing API calls to be made for the desired resource.

Network and Connectivity Troubleshooting Scenarios

One of the biggest challenges for professionals who operate distributed systems is the identification of network-related problems. In a cloud environment, it is no different. And as you saw in Chapter 5, "Infrastructure Protection," it is critical that you understand the operation of the main network components available on AWS to troubleshoot common connectivity scenarios in your environments.

The Amazon Virtual Private Cloud (VPC) allows the provisioning of a logically isolated network portion on AWS. In a VPC, you have total control over virtual networks, including choosing the IP address to use and creating subnets, routing tables, and network gateways.

Currently, VPC supports up to five IP address ranges, one primary and four secondaries for IPv4. Each of these ranges can have a size between /28 (in CIDR notation) and /16.

In IPv6, VPC has a fixed size of /56 (in CIDR notation). A VPC can have IPv4 and IPv6 CIDR blocks associated with it.

When planning the IP addressing of a VPC, you should always check whether the network assigned to a subnet is overlapping with IP networks from another VPC or on-premises data center. Doing so will help avoid connectivity problems when these environments are later interconnected.

VPC Security and Filtering

Keep in mind that two components can be used to filter traffic within the VPC, the security group, and network ACLs (NACLs).

Security groups can be used to help protect instances within the VPC. Security groups in a VPC are used to specify the allowed inbound and outbound network traffic to and from each Amazon EC2 instance. Traffic that is not explicitly permitted for an instance is automatically dropped. A security group is stateful—that is, it tracks traffic being allowed in one direction and automatically permits response traffic.

Security Group Example

A stateful filter that allows incoming traffic on TCP port 80 on a web server will allow return traffic to pass through the stateful filter between the client and the web server, usually on a high-numbered port (for example, port 63912). The filtering device maintains a status table that monitors the source and destination port numbers and IP addresses.

Security groups block all traffic by default, with the possibility of creating allow policies only; if you want to combine allows and denies, you must use a network ACL.

In addition to security groups, network traffic entering and leaving each subnet can be allowed or denied through network access control lists. NACLs operate at the subnet level and evaluate traffic coming in and out of a subnet. They can be used to define the Allow and Deny rules. NACLs do not filter traffic between instances on the same subnet.

If you need to filter traffic between instances on the same subnet, you can use security groups.

NACLs perform stateless filtering—that is, stateless filtering analyzes only the source and destination IP address and destination port, ignoring whether the traffic is a new request or a response to a request.

In the "Security Group Example" sidebar, it would be necessary to implement two rules on the filtering device: one rule to allow incoming traffic to the web server on TCP port 80 and another rule to allow outgoing traffic from the web server (TCP port range of 49152 to 65535).

Route Tables

A route table contains a set of rules, which are used to determine where network traffic is directed. Every subnet in the VPC must be associated with a route table. This table controls the routing for a subnet, and each subnet can be associated with only a single route table at a time. Still, it is possible to associate several subnets to the same route table.

When you are troubleshooting routing tables, you must remember the following:

- Your VPC already has implicit routing and comes with a standard route table that can be modified.
- It is possible to create more route tables for your VPC.
- It is not possible to delete the main route table. However, you can customize the routes in it; the VPC main route table will be automatically associated with newly created subnets.
- When traffic matches more than one entry on the route table, the most specific will be used.

Routing Priority

To determine how traffic should be routed, a route table prioritizes the most specific route in it. The routes for IPv4 and IPv6 addresses or CIDR blocks are independent of each other—that is, a route table uses the most specific route corresponding to IPv4 or IPv6 traffic.

Table 9.1 has a route for IPv4 Internet traffic (0.0.0.0/0) directed to an Internet gateway (IGW) and a route for IPv4 traffic 172.31.0.0/16 directed to a peering connection (pcx-1a2b3c4d). Any traffic on the subnet destined to the 172.31.0.0/16 IP address range uses the peering connection because this route is more specific than the route to the IGW. Any traffic to a VPC destination (10.0.0.0/16) is covered by the local route and is therefore routed within the VPC. All other traffic on the subnet uses the IGW.

TABLE 9.1 Routing table

CIDR	Destination
10.0.0.0/16	Local
172.31.0.0/16	pcx-1a2b3c4d
0.0.0.0/0	igw-11aa22bb

Network Gateways

AWS has several types of network gateways available for use: the NAT gateway, the Internet gateway, and the Transit gateway.

NAT gateways (see Figure 9.2) are used in network address translation (NAT) to allow instances on a private subnet to connect to the Internet or other AWS services and to prevent the Internet from initiating a connection to those instances. Each NAT gateway is created in a specific availability zone and implemented with redundancy, and it supports 5 Gbps of bandwidth and automatically scales up to 45 Gbps (at the time of this writing). If you require more bandwidth, you can distribute the workload into different subnets and create a NAT gateway.

FIGURE 9.2 Architecture of a NAT gateway

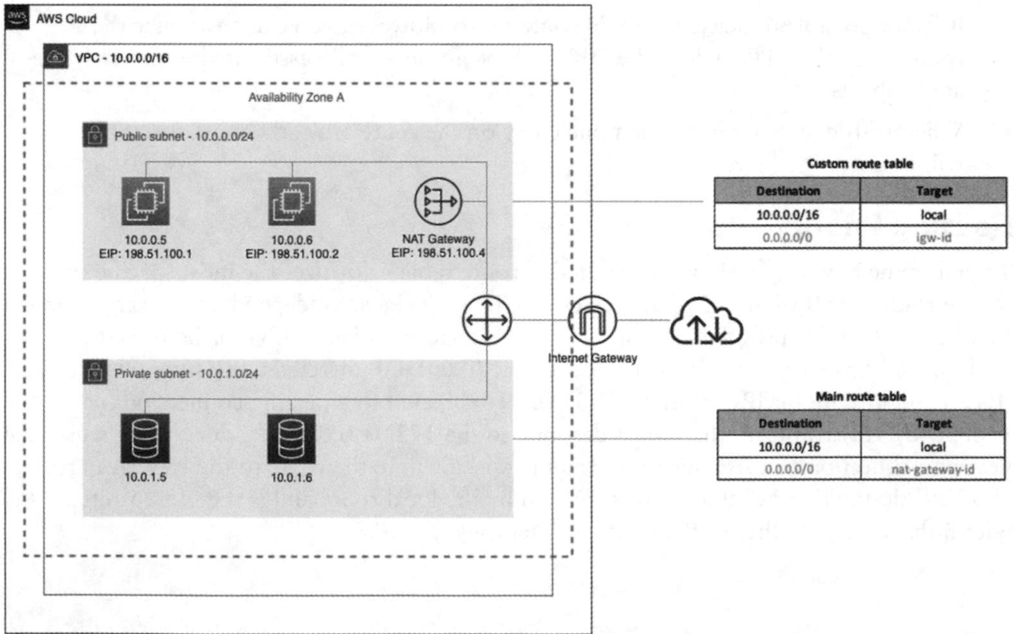

An Internet gateway (see Figure 9.3) is a redundant and highly available component of the VPC that allows communication between the instances in the VPC and the Internet. In this case, starting the connection from the Internet is allowed. To enable Internet communication for IPv4, your instance must have a public IPv4 address or an Elastic IP (EIP) associated with a private IPv4 address.

Since your instance only knows of the private address defined in the VPC, IGW provides a one-to-one NAT for your instance. When traffic leaves your subnet and goes to the Internet, the reply address field is defined as the public IPv4 address or Elastic IP (EIP) of your instance, not your private IP.

FIGURE 9.3 Architecture of an Internet gateway

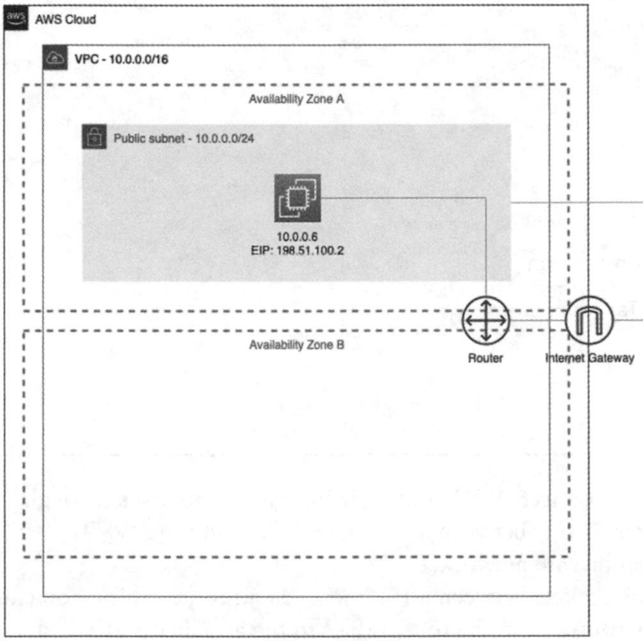
AWS Cloud
VPC - 10.0.0.0/16
Availability Zone A
Public subnet - 10.0.0.0/24
10.0.0.6
EIP: 198.51.100.2
Custom route table
Destination
Target
10.0.0.0/16
local
0.0.0.0/0
igw-id
Router
Internet Gateway
Availability Zone B

Exercise 9.2 shows you how to create an Internet gateway.

EXERCISE 9.2

Creating an Internet Gateway

Follow these steps to create an Internet gateway:

1. While signed in as administrator, go to Services and select VPC under Networking & Content Delivery.
2. Select Internet Gateways in the left menu.

EXERCISE 9.2 *(continued)*

3. Click the Create Internet Gateway button.
4. Type **security-book-ig** as the name.
5. Click Create Internet Gateway.
6. From the Actions menu, select Attach To VPC.
7. Select the VPC using the VPC field.
8. Click the Attach button.

   After creating the Internet gateway, you need to add the route.

9. Select Route Tables in the left menu.
10. Select the main route of your VPC.
11. Select the Routes tab.
12. Click the Edit Routes button.
13. Click the Add Route button.
14. Enter **0.0.0.0/0** in the Destination column.
15. Select Internet Gateway in the Target column.
16. Select security-book-ig.
17. Click the Save Routes button.

The AWS Transit gateway (TGW) connects VPCs and their local area networks through a central hub, such as a cloud router. Traffic between an Amazon VPC and the AWS Transit gateway remains on the AWS global private network.

Your TGW routes IPv4 and IPv6 packets between attachments using route tables. You can configure these tables to propagate routes from the route tables to the attached VPCs and VPN connections. Also, you can use static routes in your routing tables.

If by any chance you are using NAT instances, make sure you deselect Source/Destination Check and check whether the security group assigned to it correctly allows all desired traffic.

VPC Peering

It is a common scenario to need to connect two VPCs. In AWS, this functionality is delivered using a feature called VPC Peering. VPC Peering is a network connection between two VPCs that allows you to direct traffic between them using private IPv4 or IPv6 addresses. Instances in different VPCs can communicate with each other as if they were on the same network. You can create a peering connection between your VPCs or with a VPC from another AWS account. VPCs can also be in different regions.

Figure 9.4 shows the architecture of the peering between two VPCs.

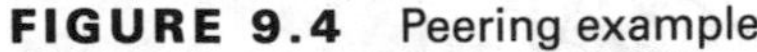

FIGURE 9.4 Peering example

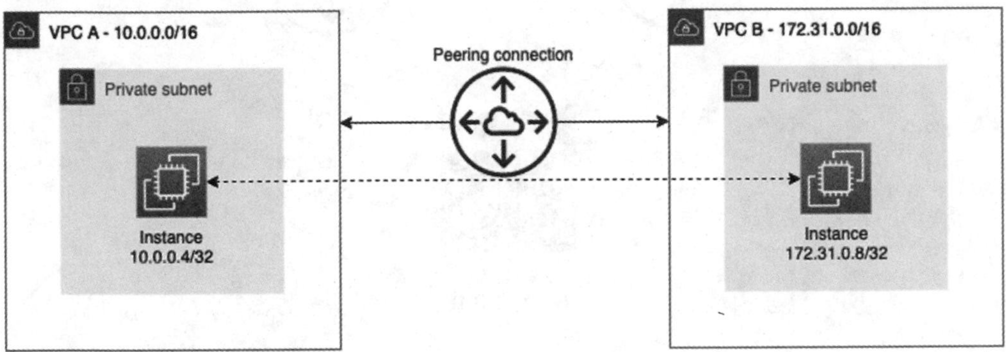

A VPC can have more than one peering configured; it is essential to note that there is no transitivity using an intermediate VPC. Figure 9.5 shows an example of peering between three VPCs. VPC B and VPC C can each communicate with VPC A. However, the communication between VPC B and VPC C via VPC A is not possible.

It is not possible to create a VPC peering connection between VPCs that have matching or overlapping IPv4 or IPv6 CIDR blocks.

Exercise 9.3 walks you through the steps for creating and routing a peering connection.

FIGURE 9.5 No transitivity example

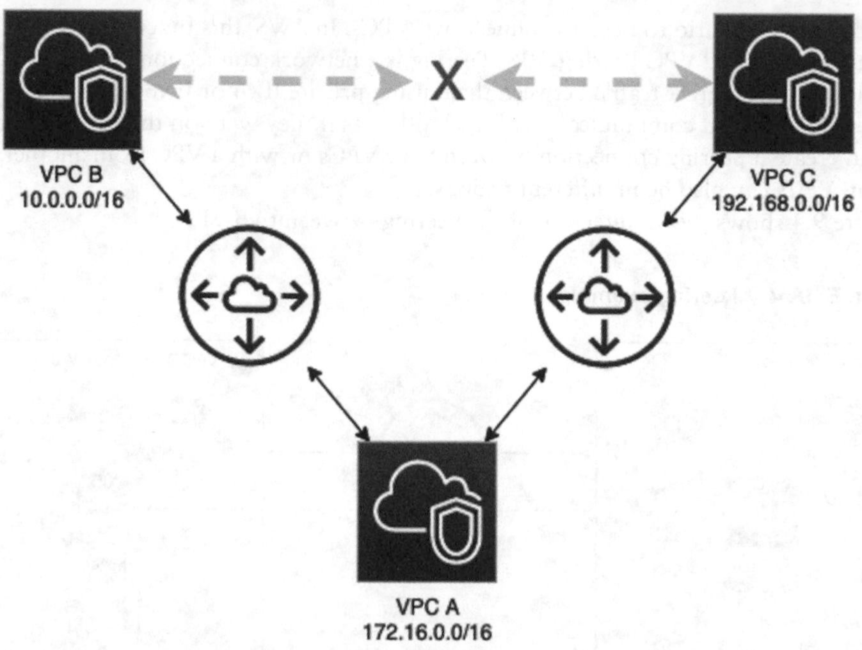

EXERCISE 9.3

Creating a Peering Connection

Follow these steps to create a new peering connection:

1. While signed in as administrator, go to Services and select VPC under Networking & Content Delivery.
2. Create two VPCs, one with a `172.31.0.0/16` CIDR and another with a `173.31.0.0/16` CIDR.
3. Select Peering Connections in the left menu.
4. Click the Create Peering Connection button.
5. Enter **security-book-peering** in the Peering connection name tag.
6. Select Requester VPC.
7. Select another VPC to peer with.
8. Click the Create Peering Connection button.

   After this, you need to accept the peering request.

9. Select the request with the Pending Acceptance status.
10. From the Actions menu, choose Accept Request.
11. Click Accept.

    After you accept the peering, you need to add routes:

12. Select Route Tables in the left menu.
13. Select the route `173.31.0.0/16` VPC.
14. Select the Routes tab.
15. Click Edit Routes.
16. Click Add Route.
17. Enter 172.31.0.0/16 in the Destination column.
18. Select Peering Connection in the Target column.
19. Select security-book-peering.
20. Click Save Routes.
21. Repeat steps 12–20 for the other route switching CIDRs block.

VPC Flow Logs

VPC Flow Logs is a feature that makes it possible to capture information about IP traffic on VPC network interfaces. Flow log data can be published to Amazon CloudWatch Logs and Amazon S3. When creating a flow log, you can use the standard flow log record format or specify a custom format; the custom format is only available for publication on Amazon S3.

The standard format for a flow log record is a space-separated string that has the following set of fields in this order:

```
<version> <account-id> <interface-id> <srcaddr> <dstaddr> <srcport> <dstport>
<protocol> <packets> <bytes> <start> <end> <action> <log-status>
```

To learn more about the fields available in VPC Flow Logs, see `docs.aws.amazon.com/vpc/latest/userguide/flow-logs.html`.

Troubleshooting Peering

Keep these factors in mind when troubleshooting peering connectivity:

- Check that the route is configured correctly on both VPCs.
- Check that the security group of the source and destination instances allow the necessary traffic.

- Check if there are any NACLs blocking requests. It is important to remember that network ACLs are stateless—that is, it is necessary to configure the rules for allowing IPs and ports in a bidirectional way (inbound and outbound), as explained at the beginning of this chapter.
- Use VPC Flow Logs to view accepted and rejected traffic in communication.

Exercise 9.4 walks you through the steps for creating a VPC flow log, and Exercise 9.5 shows how to remove a VPC.

EXERCISE 9.4

Creating a VPC Flow Log

Follow these steps to generate VPC flow logs:

1. While signed in as administrator, go to Services and select VPC under Networking & Content Delivery.
2. Select Your VPCs in the left menu.
3. Select one VPC.
4. Select the Flow Logs tab.
5. Click the Create Flow Log button.
6. Enter **security-book-peering** as the trail name.
7. Select the type of filter you need and the maximum aggregation interval.
8. Select the Send To An S3 Bucket destination.
9. Enter `arn:aws:s3:::`***<YOUR BUCKET NAME>*** in the S3 bucket ARN field.
10. Click Create.

EXERCISE 9.5

Removing a VPC Flow Log

If you need to remove a flow log, follow these steps:

1. Select the flow log.
2. From the Actions menu, choose Delete Flow Log.
3. Click the Yes, Delete button.

Summary

Be it for a malfunction of a single component or because of a not-so-perfect integration of multiple elements, IT professionals must always plan for situations when things do not work as they should.

In AWS Cloud environments, such plans can be based on best practices applied to their design, encompassing all pillars in the Well-Architected Framework: operational excellence, security, reliability, performance efficiency, and cost optimization. With such principles ingrained in your architecture, your environment will be able to continue to work during common failures and attacks. Nonetheless, the operational excellence pillar will reinforce that your environment also has tools that will help you handle problems that are caused by incorrect configurations and integrations. Therefore, you should take care of the appropriate activation of logging services (such as AWS CloudTrail, Amazon CloudWatch Logs, Amazon CloudWatch Events, and Amazon EventBridge) in your environments.

Given its key role in the authentication and authorization in AWS Cloud architectures, the AWS Identity and Access Management (IAM) service can incorrectly block the access of users or resources if it is not properly defined. If your logs show that such a situation may be happening, you should double-check your policy permissions, especially if you are using services that have resource-based policies, such as Amazon S3's bucket policies and AWS Key Management Service's (KMS) key policies.

If connectivity problems arise within your Amazon VPCs, a simple verification in your IP address distribution and route tables can help you detect their root cause. VPC peering, Internet gateways, and NAT gateways also require specific route table tweaks that may be missing. Although security groups and network ACLs provide a scalable and flexible way to filter traffic, careless configurations may actually block data communication that should be allowed. Therefore, be sure to check if these filtering techniques reflect your original intention for traffic within your VPCs. You can leverage VPC Flow Logs to accurately detect which component is interrupting the desired communication.

Now that you have learned how to design, deploy, and operate the most important security aspects of AWS Cloud environments, it is time to understand how these multiple services and configurations can be orderly put into action in real-world implementations. In the next (and final) chapter of this book, you will discover best practices and recommendations intended to help you through a complete secure cloud adoption journey.

Exam Essentials

Prepare for troubleshooting. Be aware of abnormal behavior and unusual situations via the activation and correct configuration of logging services such as AWS CloudTrail (to log all API calls in your environment), Amazon CloudWatch Logs (to get more detailed information in services such as Amazon EC2 and Route 53), Amazon CloudWatch Events (to obtain a near real-time stream of events), and Amazon EventBridge (to create a serverless event bus).

Understand common identity and access management issues. AWS IAM controls how users and resources can access your environment deployed on AWS Cloud. Therefore, be sure to check if your IAM user, IAM group, or IAM role has the proper identity-based policy permissions to access the desired resource. Moreover, if you are working with multiple policies, try to understand what exactly their combination implies. Additionally, if you are using Amazon S3 bucket policies, verify how these policies are configured and whether they are conflicting with your IAM policies. Finally, if you are deploying session policies, also check their intersection with the IAM user identity-based policy.

Understand common encryption and decryption issues. AWS Key Management Service (KMS) can greatly facilitate the creation and control of your encryption keys because it can be integrated with most AWS services that leverage data-at-rest encryption. AWS KMS key policies define access to a customer master key (CMK), restricting which users can manage and use them. However, an IAM policy controls which users, groups, and roles can actually perform operations with the key. Do not forget to check what their combination entails. For cross-account access problems, also verify if the same combination (key policy and IAM policy) works for the external account.

Understand common network and connectivity troubleshooting scenarios. The understanding of networking constructs and traffic filtering techniques applies to connectivity troubleshooting on both on-premises and AWS Cloud environments. In terms of IP addressing, you should always check if the network assigned to a subnet is not overlapping with another network in another connected VPC or on-premises data center. If you are using security groups or network ACLs, do not forget to check their influence across the connectivity path you are troubleshooting. Also, remember that security groups are stateful whereas network ACLs are not; you should therefore always check if traffic is allowed in both ways (inbound and outbound) in the latter. Route tables should always be checked (in both directions) whenever you are experiencing connectivity problems between two networked endpoints. Do not forget that each subnet can potentially have a different route table (which may be distinct from the main route table), and be mindful that routes are prioritized within each route table (more specific over less specific). You must also configure route tables to correctly direct traffic to your Internet gateway (do not forget to attach it first to your VPC) or VPC peering (if the request was accepted). If you are using a NAT gateway, be sure to position it on a public subnet (while also configuring your route table for the private subnets). VPC Flow Logs can increase the visibility of how traffic is being influenced by security groups, network ACLs, route tables, and gateways.

Review Questions

1. Which of the following services can you use to view activities performed on your AWS account?
   - A. AWS CloudTrail
   - B. IAM
   - C. Security Group
   - D. AWS CloudWatch Logs
2. Which of the following services can you use to monitor, store, and access log files?
   - A. AWS CloudTrail
   - B. AWS CloudWatch Logs
   - C. AWS CloudWatch Events
   - D. AWS VPC Flow Logs
3. Which AWS resource can be used to help protect instances within the VPC? (Choose two.)
   - A. Security groups
   - B. NACL
   - C. Routing tables
   - D. Instance firewall
4. NAT gateways are used in network address translation (NAT) to allow instances on which type of subnet to connect to the Internet?
   - A. Public
   - B. Private
   - C. DMZ
   - D. All types of subnet
5. Which type of gateway can you use if you need to start a connection from the Internet?
   - A. NAT gateway
   - B. Internet gateway
   - C. VPC gateway
   - D. External gateway
6. Which functionality can you use to connect two VPCs that allows you to have direct traffic between them?
   - A. AWS routing tables
   - B. AWS Internet gateway
   - C. AWS VPC peering
   - D. AWS Transit gateway

7. Which of the following features makes it possible to capture information about IP traffic on VPC?
   A. AWS CloudTrail
   B. AWS CloudWatch Logs
   C. AWS CloudWatch Events
   D. AWS VPC Flow Logs

8. What three APIs can you use in AWS when working with federated entities in the STS service? (Choose three.)
   A. `AssumeRole`
   B. `AssumeFederatedRole`
   C. `AssumeRoleWithWebIdentity`
   D. `AssumeRoleWithSAML`

9. Which feature is used to define the maximum permissions that a policy can grant to an IAM entity?
   A. IAM role
   B. Permissions boundary
   C. Groups
   D. IAM limits

10. Which AWS service facilitates the creation and control of the encryption keys used to encrypt your data?
    A. AWS KMS
    B. AWS security group
    C. AWS key policy
    D. AWS IAM

Creating Your Security Journey in AWS

THE AWS CERTIFIED SECURITY SPECIALTY EXAM OBJECTIVES THAT LEVERAGE CONCEPTS EXPLAINED IN THIS CHAPTER INCLUDE THE FOLLOWING:

✓ **Domain 1: Incident Response**

- 1.2. Verify that the Incident Response plan includes relevant AWS services.
- 1.3. Evaluate the configuration of automated alerting, and execute possible remediation of security-related incidents and emerging issues.

✓ **Domain 2: Logging and Monitoring**

- 2.1. Design and implement security monitoring and alerting.
- 2.3. Design and implement a logging solution.

✓ **Domain 3: Infrastructure Security**

- 3.1. Design edge security on AWS.
- 3.2. Design and implement a secure network infrastructure.
- 3.4. Design and implement host-based security.

✓ **Domain 4: Identity and Access Management**

- 4.1. Design and implement a scalable authorization and authentication system to access AWS resources.

✓ **Domain 5: Data Protection**

- 5.1. Design and implement key management and use.
- 5.3. Design and implement a data encryption solution for data at rest and data in transit.

Introduction

In traditional data centers, a security team is commonly responsible for the entire infrastructure stack, which includes the following:

- Physical Security: Access to facilities, camera systems, and monitoring centers
- Hardware: Servers, storage, and networking devices
- Software: Operating systems, databases, and applications in general

As a security professional acting on such environments, you must think about the security controls deployed on all of these technological layers. However, you should also plan how to enforce security processes and train the people who are necessary to achieve the level of security required by your organization's business and risk definitions.

Both old and new security concepts are necessary to build and manage AWS environments. Therefore, when planning your organization's journey into the AWS Cloud, you should be aware that a new context is in place: the *shared responsibility model*. In this model (which we explored in Chapter 2, "Cloud Security Principles and Frameworks"), AWS implements, operates, manages, and controls its infrastructure security components, from physical facilities to the virtualization layer. Consequently, this model greatly reduces the security operational efforts when compared to traditional environments.

With AWS being responsible for the security *of* the cloud, you remain accountable for security *in* the cloud. Therefore, you continue to develop the process of defining security controls and adopting best practices but with new and powerful tools in your hands. With a good understanding of the AWS security services, you will be able to evaluate how the landscape of your current security controls can be leveraged, adapted, or redefined as you make your first steps toward the cloud.

Drawing on the collective experience of the authors, the following sections recommend some first steps. As such guidelines and tips are presented, you will also have an opportunity to review the concepts explained in the previous chapters in a practical context.

Where to Start?

Before you begin, you need to understand the current security, compliance, and privacy practices that you have in place today in your organization. It is also essential to know the regulations and compliance requirements in your industry, making sure that you consider all the necessary security and privacy controls related to cloud computing adoption that are specific for your country, state, or even city. For instance, financial service companies and governmental entities have particular requirements that must be implemented and that vary greatly from location to location.

Once you understand such prerequisites, a great next step you can take is the assessment of which security practices and controls you can (or must) effectively migrate to the cloud, which ones can be optimized, or which ones should be fully transformed. Of course, this assessment will depend on your knowledge of the objectives and proposed architecture of the applications that will be deployed in the AWS Cloud.

Even if you cannot map these requirements because you are starting a new cloud environment from scratch, you should be careful to avoid a haphazard adoption of security frameworks and best practices. The authors have observed several real-world implementations that tried to use a lot of different frameworks and best practices at the same time and actually failed to follow their own organization's security objectives. You are better off if you initially define one framework and use it from beginning to end.

Once you have your security and compliance requirements analyzed and a single security framework chosen, you are in a good place to start designing your cloud security strategy and controls.

Chances are that you are probably wondering, "Do I really need to think about these controls and frameworks? Isn't there a shorter and more natural way?" In the authors' experience, there are surely quick wins that you can implement from day zero, which will be addressed in the upcoming sections. But also remember that security is a continuous process, so you must consider a daily effort across the board within different areas to implement any security best practice. For this reason, it is important to have your security framework and best practices identified as guidance.

Mapping Security Controls

With a tighter grip on the necessary security definitions for your cloud environment, you can start learning how to map these controls. Generally speaking, a good mental exercise for your future cloud security design can *start* with the analysis of how AWS native security services and features (as well as third-party security solutions) can replace your traditional security controls.

Table 10.1 compares controls that are commonly deployed on traditional on-premises data centers and potential AWS Cloud controls that can assume their function.

TABLE 10.1 Example matrix mapping current security controls to an AWS environment

Traditional security control	Potential AWS security control
Network segregation (such as firewall rules and router access control lists)	Security groups and network ACLs, Web Application Firewall (WAF)
Data encryption at rest	Amazon S3 server-side encryption, Amazon EBS encryption, Amazon RDS encryption, among other AWS KMS-enabled encryption features
Monitor intrusion and implementing security controls at the operating system level	Third-party solutions, including endpoint detection and response (EDR), antivirus (AV), and host intrusion prevention system (HIPS), anomaly detection, user and entity behavior analytics (UEBA), patching
Role-based access control (RBAC)	AWS IAM, Active Directory integration through IAM groups, temporary security credentials, AWS Organizations
Environment isolation	Multi-account strategy and AWS Organizations

You can definitely use such an approach to obtain quick wins in your deployments. However, you should also consider that this method is just an initial good practice—cloud computing usually allows much more in terms of security, as you will see in the following sections.

Security Journey Phased Example

As you learned in Chapter 1, "Security Fundamentals," one of the most interesting practical models for creating security design and operations is the security wheel. This model recognizes that the security practice has a continuous and cyclical nature and is structured in five basic stages:

1. Develop a security policy
2. Implement security measures
3. Monitor continuously
4. Test
5. Manage and update

You can leverage the model's continued improvement proposal by implementing it in multiple phases as you and your team learn new skills, gather more experience, and collect concrete results.

This section introduces a cloud journey example with three phases for a theoretical organization that has a great professional as their chief information security officer (CISO): you.

Here are the phases:

- Phase 1: Infrastructure Protection
- Phase 2: Security Insights and Workload Protection
- Phase 3: Security Automation

Of course, in real-world scenarios, you can implement more or fewer phases depending on multiple variables such as your team's cloud skills and legacy application dependency. However, remember that there is no silver bullet and no one-size-fits-all solution when dealing with cloud computing designs (or, in fact, any IT architecture). This example is intended to give you a small taste of factors that may influence a cloud adoption strategy.

In the next three sections, you will learn about actions that can be implemented at each phase. If you follow the security wheel model at each phase, you will be able to establish a solid foundation for the changes proposed in the subsequent phase as your organization becomes more proficient with cloud security concepts and tools.

Do not lose sight of the fact that "100 percent secure" does not exist. Therefore, the steps presented here cannot be considered all the necessary activities that are necessary for a security program, but they should be considered as important steps that deserve attention.

Phase 1: Infrastructure Protection

As you learned in Chapter 3, "Identity and Access Management," knowing *who does what* is crucial for cloud security. Therefore, phase 1 begins strongly focused in this discipline while also touching other subjects that are easier to activate and manage.

As this organization's CISO, you should recommend and implement the following key actions during this phase:

- Define and implement a multi-account model to isolate different departments (and their workloads) in order to reduce the *blast radius* (impact extension) in a compromised environment. You can use automation services such as AWS Control Tower to automatically set up and control new, multi-account AWS environments based on AWS best practices.
- Protect your root accounts. No one should be using root accounts for daily activities. They must be protected using multifactor authentication (MFA) and a rapid-response strategy for emergency situations. Only strictly necessary security personnel should

have access to the root account during an incident response or any another sensitive situation. Root access keys should not be used either, unless strictly required.

- Guarantee that your root accounts have the correct email addresses for all contacts (with corporate email addresses, not personal ones). It is also essential to use an email list as a best practice so that more than one person receives information about the root account.
- Integrate user authentication with a single point of truth (Active Directory, for instance) to create new cloud administration users via a profile with predefined roles. Doing so will give you better user control and user lifecycle management.
- Use service control policies at the right AWS Organizations level to protect specific resources and accounts.
- Implement MFA for all users who will access the AWS Console.
- Centralize and protect your AWS CloudTrail logs, leveraging a multi-account model with an audit account to concentrate and receive logs records from other accounts.
- Within your VPCs and subnets, create network ACLs and security groups to control not only inbound traffic but also outbound traffic. Adhere to the principle of least privilege as much as possible.
- Implement an end-to-end encryption strategy using AWS Key Management Service (KMS) to protect data in your buckets, storage, and databases.
- Turn on Amazon GuardDuty and leverage one of the most interesting aspects of the AWS Cloud: a unique perspective based on the experience of a thousand other users. Such a procedure is undoubtedly a quick win that will help you improve your awareness regarding common attacks in your environment.
- Assign one of your employees to regularly look into the Amazon GuardDuty events and act upon them, and consider generating alarms to your operations team as well. Discovering security events and then doing nothing about them is not much better than not observing them in the first place.
- Turn on helpful AWS Config basic rules. One example is detecting open buckets and using rule automation to fix the issue. Another example is identifying critical open ports such as SSH (22) and RDP (3389).
- If your organization has a security operations center (SOC), consider integrating the AWS CloudTrail logs and alerts into your traditional log solution.
- Run AWS Trusted Advisor periodically in your organization's accounts so that you can evaluate the basic security controls in your AWS Cloud environment. Remember that even the free version has important security evaluations such as Amazon EBS public snapshots and Amazon RDS public snapshots.
- Use AWS Systems Manager Session Manager or Amazon EC2 Instance Connect to access your Linux instances, and do not expose the SSH port to all Internet IP addresses on the planet. The same care is valid for Windows instances, especially because many ransomware attacks start by using exposed RDP ports. In both cases,

you can consider using bastion servers that are accessible via a VPN connection.

- It is also important to consider using S3 Block Access and IAM Access Analyzer to give you more visibility about possible incorrect access configurations.
- Although your team may be composed of professionals who may be able to fully operate your cloud environment, security is everyone's responsibility. A security-focused culture must be ingrained in all activities, so you will need to train other areas in your company too.

Using these approaches, you can improve your organization's resilience against common configuration errors, such as open buckets and open ports that can expose your AWS Cloud environment. You will also improve the way you protect cloud credentials, which is a crucial pillar in your strategy, especially when talking about a zero-trust strategy

Phase 2: Security Insights and Workload Protection

After you go through at least a couple of rounds of the security wheel model, phase 1 will be firmly established as the foundation of your cloud security journey. In phase 2, the security controls your team will deploy in AWS are more focused on the applications your organization is running in the cloud.

These actions include the following:

- If you are using Amazon EC2 instances, it is essential to define your patch and compliance strategy, using automation to improve your security posture continuously and quickly. You can use the EC2 Image Builder to help you create secure images.
- You should also consider using Amazon Inspector and AWS Patch Manager to increase your patch posture visibility and automate the mitigation processes.
- At this point, you are using Amazon GuardDuty, AWS Config, and Amazon Inspector. Therefore, your organization must have a lot of events to correlate. Now is the time to enable AWS Security Hub and leverage it as your single pane of glass to evaluate security findings and prioritize your actions.
- Consider using PCI/DSS, CIS Security, and AWS best practices standards available in AWS Security Hub to automatically evaluate your environment.
- You will also need to define your end-point security strategy. Select the most appropriate antimalware and endpoint detection and response (EDR) that you will use in your instances.
- If you have public-facing web applications, you must have a DDoS protection strategy considering services such as AWS Shield Standard, AWS Shield Advanced, AWS WAF, Amazon Route 53, AWS Auto Scaling, Amazon API Gateway, and Cloud Front.
- Your applications must use credentials to access resources like databases. In this case, it is essential to use AWS Secrets Manager to protect your database credentials and implement frequent rotation.

Phase 3: Security Automation

In this phase, your organization is looking for a higher level of automation, and you, as their CISO, will be implementing *security as code* and security automation strategies such as the following:

- Integrate security code evaluation into your pipelines, using Static Application Security Testing (SAST) and Dynamic Application Security Testing (DAST) technologies to protect your applications. You can also consider Amazon Code Guru and AWS partners to improve your code security evaluation process.
- If your organization is deploying infrastructure as code (IAC) strategies, you must also consider validating your AWS CloudFormation templates or any other IAC mechanism to detect insecure configurations such as unauthorized open ports, open buckets, and cleartext passwords.
- In this phase you can also start to deploy your incident response automation strategy, using the power of native cloud APIs to reduce the time between incident detection and mitigation. You can leverage AWS Lambda and other serverless services such as AWS Step Functions to automate incident response processes. But before doing so, be sure you have the right people involved and the right processes ingrained in these automations, including but not limited to the Cloud Operation, infrastructure, Security Operation, and DevSecOps teams.
- Speaking of automation, you can adopt different human resource strategies, starting with a dedicated team to automate the most common use cases detected, or decentralize the automation activity to each of the groups responsible for the environments. Still, you must be concerned with maintaining governance and standardization, reducing the risk of incorrectly automating actions that can disrupt your environment.
- Lastly, during a security incident, you do not have time to test a lot, so you need to prepare and train incident response processes in advance. Execute tabletop exercises (discussion-based sessions), create runbooks and playbooks, and consider executing game days and cyberattack simulations. Do not wait for a real incident to prepare your team.

As you can see, this phase also requires several rounds in the security wheel to provide an effective and efficient automatic response to security incidents in your cloud environments. As John F. Kennedy said in his State of the Union speech in 1962: "The time to repair the roof is when the sun is shining."

Summary

This chapter discussed the importance of creating a security strategy for a cloud journey. Based on the authors' collective experience, such a journey starts with the understanding of the industry regulations and necessary compliance requirements that govern your organization. Once you understand these requirements, you can assess which security controls you can migrate without modification to the AWS Cloud and which should be changed or transformed.

You also examined a phased cloud journey example, with its first phase focusing on environment preparation and adopting some quick wins delivered via easily activated services such as Amazon GuardDuty, AWS Config, and AWS Trusted Advisor. Phase 2 focused on new security controls at both application and infrastructure levels, with special attention to Amazon EC2 instances. And finally, phase 3 concentrated its attention on topics related to security automation, security by design, and incident response automation.

Although this example presents many interesting best practices and points of attention that were tested in real-world scenarios, you should always be mindful that there is no one-size-fits-all plan or strategy to deploy cloud computing environments security. As with any cross-domain discipline (and as many seasoned security experts can attest), the security practice is most fundamentally based on learning.

Perhaps a bit more than other professionals, the security expert commonly has a broad domain knowledge aligned with an insatiable curiosity. The authors sincerely hope that the content presented in this book has been enough to not only prepare you for the AWS Certified Security Specialty exam, but also to inspire a deeper understanding of cloud computing and its fascinating implications in the world of information security.

The authors sincerely wish you the best of luck in your exam as well as in all of your future endeavors!

Exam Essentials

Understand that a secure cloud deployment is a journey. Very few cloud computing implementations are immediate. In fact, because it depends on technology, people, and processes, cloud adoption is more similar to a *journey*, where different teams learn along with each migration, adaptation, or service activation. It is not different for security teams, as they learn new concepts such as the AWS shared responsibility model.

Know which first steps are important. If your organization decides to move (all or a part of) applications to the AWS Cloud, there are some real-world best practices that you can follow to develop a good plan: be mindful of which security practices and compliance regulations your organization must follow; analyze which security solutions will be migrated, optimized, or transformed; and focus on a single security framework. In addition, you can perform an assessment to verify which AWS security services and features (as well as third-party solutions) could potentially replace your traditional security controls. Refer to Table 10.1 for some recommendations.

Know that your implementation can take place in phases. If you define phases in your cloud computing deployment, you can establish objectives and milestones that better suit the reality of your organization in terms of skillset and processes. In each phase, you can leverage the security wheel model to fine-tune the implementation and provide a solid security foundation for all subsequent phases.

Review Questions

1. Before migrating to AWS Cloud, you want to leverage a native feature from the cloud provider to implement network segmentation. You currently deploy such segmentation in your data center via stateful firewall rules. Which of the following options better support your decision?

   A. Network ACLs and security groups

   B. Third-party firewall provider in AWS Marketplace

   C. Security groups

   D. Network ACLs

   E. AWS WAF

2. How can you deploy and manage host intrusion prevention system (HIPS) in your Amazon EC2 environment?

   A. AWS Config `run` command

   B. AWS CloudFormation

   C. Amazon GuardDuty

   D. AWS Firewall Manager

   E. Third-party solution

3. Your organization requires you to implement deep packet inspection solution such as an intrusion prevention system in their AWS environment. Which option is the easiest way to deploy such solution?

   A. Amazon GuardDuty

   B. Third-party solution from AWS Marketplace

   C. AWS Shield Advanced

   D. AWS Security Hub

   E. Amazon Inspector

4. Your organization currently deploys a role-based access control (RBAC) system based on an AAA server integrated with an Active Directory system. As their security officer, you will recommend which of the following options to deploy RBAC on your AWS Cloud environments?

   A. AWS Organizations

   B. AWS Account Management

   C. AWS RBAC

   D. AWS IAM, AD Integration, and AWS CloudTrail

   E. AWS IAM and AD Integration

5. As a CISO in a financial services conglomerate, you are requested to advise the strongest way to isolate applications from different lines of business (such as retail banking, corporate banking, payment, and investments) during an all-in migration to AWS Cloud. Which option better supports this request?
   A. Network ACLs
   B. Security groups
   C. Subnets
   D. VPCs
   E. Accounts

6. What is the easiest way to identify critical open ports such as SSH and RDP in your Amazon EC2 instances?
   A. Turn on AWS Config basic rules.
   B. Run AWS Trusted Advisor.
   C. Activate Amazon Guard Duty.
   D. Use AWS Systems Manager Session Manager.
   E. Look for logs in AWS CloudTrail.

7. Within your AWS environment, what is the easiest way to obtain log correlation from information from Amazon GuardDuty and Amazon Inspector?
   A. SIEM from AWS Marketplace
   B. AWS CloudTrail
   C. AWS Firewall Manager
   D. AWS Security Hub
   E. Amazon Trusted Advisor

8. Your organization intends to implement infrastructure as code to increase its application development agility. Which of the following elements should the company's security team focus on to detect insecure configurations on AWS Cloud?
   A. AWS Config file
   B. AWS Config `run` command
   C. AWS CloudFormation template
   D. AWS WAF Web ACL
   E. Amazon GuardDuty listings

9. You intend to deploy incident response automation via serverless technologies. Which two options will support your decision?
   A. AWS CloudFormation
   B. AWS Lambda
   C. Amazon Cloud Guru
   D. AWS Step Functions
   E. AWS Serverless

10. Which security practical model can provide a solid establishment of a better foundation in terms of deployment, skills and processes, at each phase of a cloud security deployment?
    A. Zero trust
    B. Attack continuum
    C. Security wheel
    D. Absolute security
    E. 3-phased migration

Appendix A

Answers to Review Questions

Chapter 1: Security Fundamentals

1. B. The concept of vulnerability is related to a fragility in a computer system, whereas a threat is defined by an entity exploiting a vulnerability. A security risk also considers the impact resulting from a threat being materialized. Therefore, options B and C are swapped.

2. A. Confidentiality is concerned with preventing unauthorized disclosure of sensitive information and ensuring that the suitable level of privacy is maintained at all stages of data processing. Integrity deals with the prevention of unauthorized modification of data and with ensuring information accuracy. Availability focuses on ensuring reliability and an acceptable level of performance for legitimate users of computing resources. All statements present valid methods of addressing such concepts.

3. B. The sentence refers to the undeniable confirmation that a user or system had in fact performed an action, which is also known as nonrepudiation.

4. D. The classic AAA architecture refers to authentication, authorization, and accounting.

5. A. The seven layers of the Open Systems Interconnection (OSI) model are Physical, Data Link, Network, Transport, Session, Presentation, and Application.

6. C. The Internet Control Message Protocol (ICMP) is not a dynamic routing protocol. All the other options are correct.

7. E. The intention of denial of service (DoS) is to exhaust processing resources (either on connectivity devices or computing hosts), thus keeping legitimate users from accessing the intended applications.

8. C. Some VPN technologies, such as Multiprotocol Label Switching (MPLS), do not natively provide data confidentiality features such as encryption. All the other options are correct.

9. C. The Payment Card Industry Data Security Standard (PCI DSS) requires that that credit card merchants meet minimum levels of security when they process, store, and transmit card holder data. The Health Insurance Portability and Accountability Act (HIPAA) is a set of security standards for protecting certain health information that is transferred or held in electronic form. The National Institute for Standards and Technology Cybersecurity Framework (NIST CSF) is a framework that assembles security standards, guidelines, and practices that have proved effective and may be used by entities belonging to any market segment. The General Data Protection Regulation (GDPR) is a set of rules created by the European Union (EU), requiring businesses to protect the personal data and privacy of EU citizens.

10. C. The zero-trust security model is based on the principle of least privilege, which states that organizations should grant the minimal amount of permissions that are strictly necessary for each user or application to work. Option A cites the phases of the security wheel model. Option B refers to the attack continuum model phases. Option D defines methods of data encryption. Option E is not directly related to the zero-trust model.

Chapter 2: Cloud Security Principles and Frameworks

1. A. AWS is always in charge of the facilities' security, including their data center, regardless of the type of service used. Options B and C are wrong because the customer is not accountable for AWS data center facilities security in the Shared Responsibility Model. Option D is wrong because the Shared Responsibility Model applies to all AWS regions.

2. C. When you are using an Amazon RDS database, AWS is in charge of most of the security layers, such as physical security, operating system security, database patching, backup, and high availability. However, you still need to define the maintenance windows to patch the operating system and applications. Options A and B are wrong because the customer does not manage the operating system in the Shared Responsibility Model for the container services category (which includes Amazon RDS). Option D is wrong because the Shared Responsibility Model applies to all AWS regions.

3. B. The AWS Artifact portal is your go-to resource for compliance-related information. It provides on-demand access to AWS's security and compliance reports and a selection of online agreements. Option A is wrong because there is no such portal. Option C is wrong because AWS GuardDuty is a service that provides monitoring on AWS Cloud environments. Option D is wrong because the AWS public website does not offer such certifications.

4. A. The AWS SOC 1 Type 2 report evaluates the effectiveness of AWS controls that might affect internal controls over financial reporting (ICFR), and the auditing process is aligned to the SSAE 18 and ISAE 3402 standards. Options B and C refer to definitions that do not apply to the mentioned report.

5. C. The AWS SOC 2 Security, Availability, & Confidentiality Report evaluates the AWS controls that meet the AICPA criteria for security, availability, and confidentiality. Options A and B refer to definitions that do not apply to the mentioned report.

6. C. The Well-Architected Framework was created to help cloud architects build secure, high-performing, resilient, and efficient infrastructure for their applications. The framework is freely available to all customers. Option A is wrong because the AWS Well-Architected Framework is not only related to security best practices. Option B is wrong because the framework is not a paid service. Option D is wrong because the framework is more than a tool.

7. D. The AWS Well-Architected security pillar dives deep into seven design principles for security in the cloud, and the seven principles are:

   Implement a strong identity foundation, enable traceability, apply security at all layers, automate security best practices, protect data in transit and at rest, keep people away from data, and prepare for security events.

   Options A, B, C, and E are wrong because they contain items that do not include all of the previous principles.

8. A. AWS is always in charge of the hypervisor security. When you start the operating system in your Amazon EC2 instance, you are in charge of updating the patches, implementing systems configuration best practices, and security policies aligned with your own security rules. Still, AWS is in charge of implementing the security patches, hardening and guidelines, and best practices in the hypervisor layer. Options B and D are wrong because the customer is not accountable for the hypervisor security in the AWS Shared Responsibility Model. Option C is wrong because the model applies for all Amazon EC2 instances that use AWS hypervisors.

9. A, B, D, F, H. In the Well-Architected security pillar, there are five best practices areas for security in the cloud:
   - Identity and access management
   - Detective controls
   - Infrastructure protection
   - Data protection
   - Incident response

Options C, E, and G do not refer to best practices areas in the Well-Architected security pillar.

10. D. The AWS Marketplace is where you can find many security solutions that you can use to improve your security posture. You can use strategic AWS security partners. You can also use your own licenses in a *Bring Your Own License* model. The pay-as-you-go model is also available to you. Option A is wrong because it is too general. Option B is wrong because the AWS website does not provide such a service. Option C refers to a web page that does not provide such services.

Chapter 3: Identity and Access Management

1. B, C, D. Options B, C, and D are correct because it is a best practice to activate MFA and define a strong password policy for the root account. You should avoid using the root account to manage your AWS account. Instead, you should create an IAM user with an `AdministratorAccess` role to perform day-to-day administrative tasks. Option A is incorrect because you should not create root account access keys, unless strictly necessary.

2. B. Option A is incorrect because an IAM group is cannot be identified as a principal in a resource-based or trust policy. Option B is correct because you can only use an IAM group to attach policies to multiple users at one time.

3. C. Option A is incorrect because the Resource element is implicitly defined when using resource-based policies. Options B and D are also incorrect because SID and Condition are not required elements when defining resource-based policies. Option C is correct because it specifies the Principal that has access to the bucket and the other minimum elements for a valid policy.

4. C. Option C is correct because a permissions boundary allows you to define the maximum permission an identity-based policy can grant to users or roles. Option A is incorrect because SCPs apply to the entire account, and option B is incorrect because session policies are used when you create a temporary session programmatically.

5. C. Option C is correct because when you enable cross-region replication for your Amazon S3 bucket, TLS/SSL communication is enforced by default.

6. C. Option C is correct because objects uploaded are owned by the account that uploaded them. For the bucket owner to manager these objects, the object owner must first grant permission to the bucket owner using an object ACL.

7. C. Option C is correct, because a user actually can renew the temporary credentials before their expiration as long as they have permission to do so.

8. D. The correct option is D because you need to change from Consolidated Billing to Enable All Features to start using SCPs.

9. B, C. Option B is correct because Amazon Cognito for identity federation provides guest users on your application with unique identities that, once they log in, can be replaced with temporary AWS credentials. Option C is correct because Amazon Cognito groups let users attach an IAM role with a policy that gives users access to Amazon S3.

10. B, D Option B is correct because the credential used to generate the Amazon S3 pre-signed URL must have permissions to access the object, or the access will fail. Option D is correct because the pre-signed URL has an expiration time that can be valid for up to 7 days.

Chapter 4: Detective Controls

1. B. By default, an AWS CloudTrail trail only delivers the events of type Management. You intentionally need to enable Data and Insights type events for them to appear in a trail.

2. B. In AWS Config terms, a configuration item is the representation of a single resource's attributes. A configuration snapshot is a JSON file containing the configuration of all the monitored resources. A configuration stream is the notification of a change in a monitored resource as soon as it happened, delivered in an Amazon SNS topic.

3. A. There are three types of AWS Config rules: custom rules (trigger a custom AWS Lambda function), managed rules (predefined by AWS Config), and service-linked rules (created by other AWS services).

4. C. AWS CloudTrail provides the CLI-based `validate-logs` command to validate the integrity of log files of the trail. In addition to this, you can use a custom method by validating the PKI-generated signature strings. No other AWS services (like Amazon S3 or AWS Config) provide a mechanism to validate integrity of the AWS CloudTrail files.

5. B. An AWS CloudTrail trail can be set up as an organizational trail if configured in a manager AWS Organization account. Another possible centralization mechanism is to store log files produced by different accounts into the same Amazon S3 bucket. There is no Consolidate Trails feature in AWS Organizations.

6. D. Amazon CloudWatch Logs offers the subscription mechanism to deliver a near real-time stream of events that can be directly delivered to Amazon Kinesis Data Streams, Amazon Kinesis Data Firehose, or an AWS Lambda function. The AWS Management Console provides a wizard that allows you to create a subscription linking an Amazon CloudWatch Logs log group to a predefined AWS Lambda function that will insert records into an Amazon Elasticsearch Service cluster.

7. C. High-resolution metrics (sub-minute reporting period) are only available for metrics reported by external sources (custom metrics). AWS Services publish metrics in Standard resolution. The metric's resolution is defined at the metric's creation time; there is no `modify-attribute` action in Amazon CloudWatch.

8. C. An Amazon EventBridge rule contains information about the event bus the rule is attached to, the event pattern (expression that matches the events of interest), and the target service. There is no remediation action in an Amazon EventBridge rule.

9. B. Amazon GuardDuty findings are automatically delivered to the default bus in Amazon EventBridge, and you can also specify to receive those findings in an Amazon S3 bucket you own. So, you can automate responses by creating an Amazon EventBridge rule and also linking an event to the Amazon S3 bucket you configured to receive the findings. Amazon GuardDuty does not provide an option to deliver findings to an Amazon SNS topic.

10. B. AWS Security Hub insights are filters and groupings that facilitate the analysis. A findings group is not a definition in AWS Security Hub. The security standard refers to a list of security controls that AWS Security Hub can check. Integrations refers to the capability of information received from third-party security products or your own applications.

Chapter 5: Infrastructure Protection

1. C. Statement I is wrong because a VPC is contained within an AWS Region. Statement II is right because a VPC can contain multiple AWS availability zones in a single region. Statement III is wrong because a subnet is contained within an AWS availability zone.

2. B. Option A is wrong because the VPC router address in this subnet is 172.16.100.129 (the first available address in the CIDR). Option B is correct because the DNS server in this subnet is 172.16.100.130 (the second available address in the CIDR). Option C is wrong

because the first available address in the subnet is 172.16.100.132 (the fifth available address in the CIDR). Option D is wrong because you can assign 172.16.100.128/25 as a CIDR block in a VPC.

3. A. Statement I is correct because both gateways allow Internet-outbound traffic in a VPC. Statement II is wrong because Internet gateways support only IPv4 and IPv6 whereas egress-only Internet gateways support only IPv6 traffic. Statement III is wrong because egress-only Internet gateways do not support NAT.

4. D. Options A, B, C, and E are correct. Option D is not correct because you cannot assign a security group to a NAT gateway.

5. B. Statements I and III are correct configurations in security groups. Statement II is not possible because security groups only have allow rules.

6. B. Option B is not correct because security groups are stateful; you therefore do not need to configure outbound rules for return traffic from permitted connections. Options A, C, and D are correct.

7. A. Statement I is correct because these load balancers indeed support such features. Statement II is incorrect because NLBs do not support AWS Lambda functions as targets. Statement III is incorrect because CLBs are not restricted to EC2-classic implementations.

8. C. Options A, B, and D represent traffic that, per definition, cannot be monitored via VPC flow logs. Option C is correct because traffic from a generic Windows instance can be monitored via VPC flow logs.

9. D. Options A, B, C, and E represent valid parameters on AWS WAF Web ACL rules. Option D is incorrect because AWS WAF can detect HTTP request headers, but not HTTP response headers.

10. B. Option A is incorrect because only AWS Shield Advanced offers support of the AWS DDoS response team (DRT). Option C is incorrect because AWS Shield Standard is enabled by default. Option D is incorrect because AWS Shield Advanced is enabled by default.

Chapter 6: Data Protection

1. B, C, D. There are three possible options for encrypting data using S3 buckets: SS3-S3, SSE-KMS, and SSE-C. ACM is not a valid option in this case and can work only with asymmetric certificates and not symmetric encryption.

2. A. There are no new charges for using SSE-S3 (server-side encryption with S3 managed keys). The S3 buckets do not have a default encryption method. When you create a bucket, by default it is private, but there is no default encryption defined.

3. B, C, E. When you are defining a CMK, you must define three levels of access: The AWS root account level of access to the CMK, the IAM roles or users that have admin rights, and the IAM roles or users that have access to use the keys to encrypt and decrypt data.

   It is also important to remember that you cannot use IAM groups inside the CMK JSON security policy.

4. C. AWS KMS enforces a minimum of 7 days up to a maximum of 30 days (default configuration) waiting period before you can delete a CMK.

5. D. AWS Key Management Service (KMS) allows you to encrypt data natively, in addition to the ability to integrate with more than 50 available services in the AWS Cloud.

6. A, C. Usually, the use of CloudHSM is directly related to meeting regulatory needs, such as FIPS 140-2 Level 3 standards. Another widespread use case is to protect web applications' private keys and offloading SSL encryption.

7. C. When you enable automatic key rotation, AWS KMS rotates the CMK every 365 days from the enabled date, so once a year automatically. This process is transparent to the user and the environment. The AWS managed keys are the default master keys that protect the S3 objects, Lambda functions, and WorkSpaces when no other keys (customer managed keys [CMKs]) are defined for these services.

8. C, D. The AWS managed keys are the default master keys that protect the S3 objects, Lambda functions, and WorkSpaces when no other keys are defined for these services.

9. D. CMK is a 256-bit Advanced Encryption Standard (AES) for symmetric keys that has a unique key ID, alias, and ARN and is created based on a user-initiated request through AWS KMS.

10. C. AWS KMS natively uses HSMs to protect the master keys, but these HSMs are not dedicated to a single client, so it is a multitenant HSM.

Chapter 7: Incident Response

1. B. If an AWS IAM credential is leaked, the best practice is to revoke it as soon as you detect the compromise. Only then you should modify the apps, and once the functionality is restored, you can proceed with the deletion of the credentials. It is important to keep the security contact on your AWS account updated, but it is not the more critical action to execute immediately after detecting a possible compromise.

2. D. Using AWS Config rules and the remediation feature with an AWS Systems Manager automation document is an effective way to remediate a deviation from a compliant configuration affecting a monitored resource. AWS CloudTrail helps with the detection phase of the suspicious activity.

3. B. You should keep all of the contacts for your AWS account updated because as they receive important notifications, some of them will require action to keep your account and services in good standing. Administrative is not a contact definition inside the AWS account; billing, operations and security are the alternate contact options within an AWS account.

4. B. You should constantly check and immediately review every abuse report you receive from AWS. To avoid any disruption, reply to the report as soon as possible explaining the actions you plan to take so that the AWS team is aware you are executing your incident response. Keep them informed until the incident is resolved.

5. C. Although all answers are valid mechanisms for developing a sound incident response plan, the security incident response simulations are specifically oriented to minimize the risk when testing your plan.

6. C. AWS Config is the most appropriate service to check if there were changes to an AWS resource. AWS CloudTrail gives you information of executed actions, Amazon Macie helps in the classification of information in Amazon S3 buckets (and detecting failures in protecting that information), and AWS Trusted Advisor informs you about your implementation of best practices.

7. B. First, the security team should be able to assess the criticality of the incident. A backdoor report in the production environment requires immediate attention. Isolation is part of the reaction, but it should be complemented with the root cause analysis of the incident to detect the blast radius.

8. D. The user had an IAM policy attached without the administrator's knowledge, which is suspicious. So, the first action is to delete the suspicious user and check other possible actions taken by that user. Removing the policy or changing access keys does not remediate the issue.

9. A. If you detect a suspicious activity (in this case an Amazon EC2 instance using a Tor client without a valid business need to do so), your next step is to try to isolate the incident; then you will contain, remediate, recover, and do a forensic analysis. Terminating the instance will not allow a comprehensive forensic analysis. Traffic mirroring is not effective since Tor clients use encryption to connect to the anonymization network. It is not a best practice to ignore a finding without further investigation (in addition, the finding reports an outbound traffic using a Tor client, not the other way around).

10. A, B, C. The constituent factors of an incident response plan are people, technology, and processes. Instructing the developers deals with *people*. Enabling Amazon Macie to detect access keys on Amazon S3 buckets deals with *technology* (use relevant AWS services). Using the right support plan helps with the *processes* that deal with incident. Although you can create an AWS Lambda function to check repositories, it is not the simplest way to do that. Amazon CodeGuru helps in checking code quality (such as discovering inappropriate handling of credentials) but not in mitigating the risk.

Chapter 8: Security Automation

1. B. Trusted Advisor and Config can be used to detect buckets with public access, but they are not designed to detect access from a sandbox account to an Amazon S3 bucket in the production account. For that, IAM Access Analyzer can be used. The question requested an analyst to have the final say on whether to close the bucket, so AWS Security Hub's action should be used instead of fully automated remediation. AWS Config rules can also be used with manual remediation action, but option D is not valid as it specifies "auto-remediate" and this option would execute the remediation automatically.

2. A, C. This question requires two things, not only to revert a change that removes default encryption, but also to go through all the Amazon S3 buckets and enable default encryption for them—that's why only acting upon AWS CloudTrail is not enough.
   Option B is not valid, since AWS Config executes SSM Automation documents to auto-remediate, not AWS Lambda functions. It can be done indirectly using Amazon CloudWatch Events, but it's not specified in the option.
   AWS Security Hub's PCI conformity pack includes a similar check to the Config rule (`securityhub-s3-bucket-server-side-encryption-enabled-898de88c`), and it's possible to write AWS Lambda code to enable the Amazon S3 bucket encryption. AWS Config natively includes a rule (`s3-bucket-server-side-encryption-enabled`) that can detect what was requested, and with the native SSM Automation for auto-remediation (`AWS-EnableS3BucketEncryption`) it can be corrected automatically.

3. C. The difference between question 2 and question 3 is that question 3 asks for you to solve it "with the least effort." While AWS Security Hub's PCI conformity pack includes the check, writing the AWS Lambda function to enable the Amazon S3 bucket encryption requires more effort than using the native AWS Config rule (`s3-bucket-server-side-encryption-enabled`) with the native SSM Automation for auto-remediation (`AWS-EnableS3BucketEncryption`).

4. A, C. Option B is not correct because AWS Security Hub should receive only findings, not all logs. It's not a SIEM solution.
   Option D is not correct because this option would automatically isolate and it's not the intended end result.
   Both options A and C are ways to collect the events, allow custom rules (for example, if a certain number of events arrive), then create the finding, and to simplify and accelerate the security analyst's task of isolation.

5. A, D. To accomplish what was requested, Amazon GuardDuty should be used as described in option A for production accounts so that a security analyst analyzes the impact of stopping an instance before doing it and, as described in option D, for nonproduction accounts. AWS Config detects changes on configurations, and Trusted Advisor does not include any checks that could detect crypto-mining.

6. B, C. AWS Config can detect configuration drifts and auto-remediate, and Systems Manager State Manager can also accomplish similar results for configurations within the instances through a State Manager association.

7. B, C, E. Amazon Inspector sends vulnerability findings to AWS Security Hub, Amazon GuardDuty sends its findings (potential threats) to AWS Security Hub, and Amazon Macie sends weak configurations on Amazon S3 buckets to AWS Security Hub. The other services currently do not offer any native integration to send findings to AWS Security Hub.

8. A. AWS Config has a native rule called `restricted-ssh` that checks whether security groups that are in use disallow unrestricted incoming SSH traffic. Editing that rule, adding a remediation action called `AWS-DisablePublicAccessForSecurityGroup`, setting Auto-Remediation to Yes, and specifying GroupId as the Resource ID parameter with a role that can be assumed by `ssm.amazonaws.com` can detect and auto-remediate.
   Option B is not correct because Trusted Advisor can't auto-remediate.
   Option C is not correct because AWS Config executes SSM automations to remediate, not AWS Lambda.
   Option D is not correct. Session Manager can't manage security groups, because it doesn't require inbound open ports on security groups to access the OS.

9. C, D, E. Option C is correct because the Auto Scaling group will regenerate the instance, rebuilding from the launch template and ensuring that the malware is gone.
   Options D and E are correct since they would help mitigate the risk of getting infected.
   Option A is not correct. Running a malware scan doesn't rebuild the instance as was requested.
   Option B is not correct because the steps described do not ensure that the malware is gone.

10. B. Option A is not correct because there is no "Changes In Bucket Properties" within Amazon S3 Events.
   Option B is correct because there is a native rule on AWS Config called `s3-bucket-versioning-enabled` to ensure that versioning is enabled on Amazon S3 buckets, and there is a remediation action called `AWS-ConfigureS3BucketVersioning` that can enable versioning.
   Option C is not correct because remediation would not be fully automated.
   Option D is not correct because it doesn't make sense to create a custom AWS Config rule when there is a native rule that does what's needed.

Chapter 9: Security Troubleshooting on AWS

1. A. AWS CloudTrail is a service that records all API calls performed on your AWS account. The service provides the event history of AWS account activity, including actions performed by the Management Console, the AWS SDKs, the command-line tools (CLI), and other AWS services.

2. B. Amazon CloudWatch Logs can be used to monitor, store, and access log files from EC2 instances, AWS CloudTrail, Route 53, and other sources. This service is used to centralize the logs of other services and applications in a robust, scalable, and managed solution.

3. A, B. Two components can be used to protect resources within the VPC: the security group and network ACLs (NACL).

4. B. NAT gateways are used in NAT to allow instances on a private subnet to connect to the Internet or other AWS services and to prevent the Internet from initiating a connection to those instances.

5. B. An Internet gateway is a redundant and highly available component of the VPC that allows communication between the instances in the VPC and the Internet. In this case, starting the connection from the Internet is allowed.

6. C. VPC peering is a network connection between two VPCs that allows you to direct traffic between them using private IPv4 or IPv6 addresses. Instances in any VPC can communicate with each other as if they were on the same network. You can create a peering connection between your VPCs or with a VPC from another AWS account. VPCs can also be in different regions.

7. D. VPC Flow Logs is a feature that makes it possible to capture information about IP traffic on VPC network interfaces. Flow log data can be published to Amazon CloudWatch Logs and Amazon S3. When creating a flow log, you can use the standard flow log record format or specify a custom format; the custom format is only available for publication on Amazon S3.

8. A, C, D. `STS:AssumeRole` is used when you need to assume a specific role after authenticating with your AWS account. The `STS:AssumeRoleWithWebIdentity` API is used in cases of federation with OpenID Connect (OIDC) providers such as Amazon Cognito, Login with Amazon, Facebook, Google, or any OIDC-compatible identity provider. The `STS:AssumeRoleWithSAML` API is used to assume a role when authenticated by a SAML-compliant service or provider, such as Active Directory.

9. B. A permissions boundary is a limit of permissions used to define the maximum permissions that a policy can grant to an IAM entity. An entity's permission limit allows the entity to perform only the actions permitted by both identity-based policies and their permission limits.

10. A. AWS Key Management Service (AWS KMS) is a managed service that facilitates the creation and control of the encryption keys used to encrypt your data. The customer master keys that you create in AWS KMS are protected by hardware security modules (HSMs). AWS KMS is integrated with most AWS services that enable the encryption of your data. AWS KMS is also integrated with AWS CloudTrail to provide logs of usage of encryption keys to help meet your audit, regulatory, and compliance requirements.

Chapter 10: Creating Your Security Journey in AWS

1. C. Security groups are native features that provide stateful network segmentation rules. Network ACLs are stateless, AWS Marketplace solutions are not considered native services, and AWS WAF is specific to web application attacks.

2. E. You will have to rely on third-party solution to deploy HIPS in your environment. Neither of the AWS services provides this functionality as of this writing.

3. B. None of the AWS services provide features that allow deep packet inspection. Therefore, you should rely on third-party solutions from AWS Marketplace.

4. D. AWS IAM and AWS CloudTrail address authentication, authorization, and accounting in AWS environments, whereas AD integration further approximates the solution to the described on-premises scenario. AWS Organizations is focused on providing hierarchy of AWS accounts, and the other services do not exist.

5. E. AWS accounts provide the strongest way to separate lines of business (LoBs) administratively. All the other options are possible within the same AWS account, making it possible that a root account, for example, can influence on multiple LoBs.

6. A. AWS Config basic rules can identify the ports open on Amazon EC2 instances.

7. D. AWS Security Hub aggregates, organizes, and prioritizes your security alerts, or findings, from multiple AWS services, such as Amazon GuardDuty, Amazon Inspector, Amazon Macie, AWS Identity and Access Management (IAM) Access Analyzer, and AWS Firewall Manager.

8. C. From all the options, AWS CloudFormation is the most appropriate service to deploy infrastructure as code. An AWS CloudFormation template describes the resources that you want to provision in your AWS CloudFormation stacks. Therefore, the company's security team should definitely look for insecure configurations on these elements.

9. B, D. AWS Lambda and AWS Step Functions are serverless technologies that can provide incident response automation.

10. C. The security wheel model recognizes that the security practice has a continuous and cyclical nature and is structured in five basic stages: develop a security policy; implement security measures; monitor and respond; test; and manage and update. The zero-trust model relies on the principle of least privilege whereas the Attack Continuum model establishes mechanisms for three different periods: before, during, and after the attack. Absolute security and 3-phased migration are not security practical models.

AWS Security Services Portfolio

AWS currently offers 175 cloud services across 23 regions and 69 availability zones. The company classifies 18 of these services as exclusively dedicated to security, identity, and compliance.

Because the authors of this book realized that remembering what each service does is a challenge for the novice cloud security practitioner, this appendix intends to give you a brief description of these dedicated services in alphabetical order, a summary of their relationship with other AWS services, and the icon that represents each of the services.

Much like a family photo, the AWS Security Service Portfolio will continue to change in the future with the addition of new members to the clan each year (and most probably announced during the company's conference: AWS re:Invent). Therefore, we highly recommend that you always check the following website to meet new "family members": `aws.amazon.com/security`.

Many of these AWS services are offered with a free trial for a certain period of time, like a month, or for a certain amount of storage, events, users, or other parameters. Charges, parameters, and offerings can change. Always refer to the AWS official documentation for the most current charges, updates, and other information.

Amazon Cognito

Amazon Cognito (see Figure B.1) allows you to add user sign-up, user sign-in, and user access control to web and mobile applications, sparing you the effort of designing or developing such components. Amazon Cognito has federation resources that support the use of identity providers such as Facebook, Google, and Amazon itself. Additionally, the service follows open identity standards such as Open Authorization (OAuth) 2.0, OpenID Connect (OIDC), and Security Assertion Markup Language (SAML) 2.0. Such integrations facilitate the management of user access control from these applications to AWS resources.

FIGURE B.1 Amazon Cognito icon

The feature set of Amazon Cognito includes multifactor authentication (MFA), data-at-rest and in-transit encryption, and a built-in customizable user interface. The service also offers protections such as adaptive authentication (detecting unusual sign-in requests from new locations or devices, risk score, additional verification, user blocking, SMS, and a time-based one-time password generator such as Google Authenticator) and Cognito Sync (allowing users to pick up application sessions where they left off between devices).

Amazon Cognito brings value to organizations by providing support for compliance regulations such as the Health Insurance Portability and Accountability Act (HIPAA), Payment Card Industry Data Security Standard (PCI DSS), System and Organization Control (SOC), International Standards Organization – International Electrotechnical Commission (ISO/IEC) 27001, ISO/IEC 27017, ISO/IEC 27018, and ISO 9001.

AWS currently offers Amazon Cognito for free for the first 50,000 monthly active users. Always refer to the AWS official documentation for updated information.

You can find the Amazon Cognito documentation at the following URL: `docs.aws.amazon.com/cognito`.

Amazon Detective

Amazon Detective (see Figure B.2) enables you to investigate, analyze, and identify root causes of security issues or suspicious activities in your AWS environments. Amazon Detective does this through the automatic collection of log data from AWS resources such as VPC flow logs, AWS CloudTrail, and Amazon GuardDuty. Within its engine, Amazon Detective leverages machine learning models, statistical analysis, and graph theory to build a data set that facilitates faster security investigations.

From an administrative perspective, Amazon Detective creates a consolidated and interactive view of resources, users, and the relationships among them over time in order to allow historical analysis and triage of real or false positives.

You can find the Amazon Detective documentation at the following URL: `docs.aws.amazon.com/detective`.

FIGURE B.2 Amazon Detective icon

Amazon GuardDuty

Amazon GuardDuty (see Figure B.3) is AWS's threat detection service that continuously searches for malicious activities and unauthorized operations in AWS resources deployed on your environment. Leveraging machine learning, anomaly detections, and threat intelligence from the AWS Security team and third parties such as CrowdStrike and Proofpoint, Amazon GuardDuty identifies potential threats across AWS CloudTrail, VPC flow logs, and DNS logs. It can also rely on AWS EventBridge and AWS Lambda to provide threat response automation.

FIGURE B.3 Amazon GuardDuty icon

Being able to act on multiple accounts simultaneously, Amazon GuardDuty detects crypto-currency mining, credential compromise behavior, communication with known command-and-control servers, API calls from well-known malicious IP addresses, unusual API activity, intra-VPC port scanning, unusual patterns of failed login requests, outbound denial-of-service activity, unusual high volume of network traffic, uncommon network protocols, data exfiltration using DNS, API calls from an unfamiliar geolocation, attempts to disable AWS CloudTrail logging, changes that weaken the account password policy, and unexpected infrastructure launches. It also can detect anomalies and threats in Amazon S3 buckets.

Amazon GuardDuty is currently eligible for a 30-day free trial period. Always refer to the Amazon GuardDuty official documentation for updated information: `docs.aws.amazon.com/guardduty`.

Amazon Inspector

Amazon Inspector (see Figure B.4) offers an automated assessment of the security posture and regulation compliance of applications deployed on AWS. The service searches for exposures, vulnerabilities, and deviations from best practices and produces a detailed list of security findings. These observations are then divided on different levels of severity, which can be reviewed directly or as a part of a detailed assessment report—available via the console or an API.

FIGURE B.4 Amazon Inspector icon

Amazon Inspector also helps you to discover network accesses that are not planned in your Amazon EC2 instances as well as potential vulnerabilities on those machines. These verifications are included in predefined rules packages, which a team of AWS security researchers regularly update with common security best practices and vulnerabilities definitions. Such care is especially valuable in development environments since security issues can be identified before instances are actually running productively.

Amazon Inspector currently is available as a free trial for accounts that have never activated it before. You can run Amazon Inspector for 250 agent assessments with host rules and 250 instance assessments with network reachability rules at no cost for 90 days.

Always refer to the Amazon Inspector official documentation for updated information: `docs.aws.amazon.com/inspector`.

Amazon Macie

Amazon Macie (see Figure B.5) automatically discovers, classifies, and protects sensitive data such as personally identifiable information (PII) or intellectual property via machine learning techniques. When Amazon Macie detects information such as credit card numbers, Social Security numbers, or a customizable pattern, it provides detailed alerts in a dashboard that shows which services, accounts, and S3 buckets are at risk.

FIGURE B.5 Amazon Macie icon

Currently, you will not be charged on Amazon Macie for the first gigabyte processed by its content classification engine and for the first 100,000 CloudTrail events. Additionally, Amazon Macie stores the generated metadata of classified S3 objects for 30 days at no additional cost. Always refer to the Amazon Macie official documentation for the latest information: `docs.aws.amazon.com/macie`.

AWS Artifact

AWS Artifact (see Figure B.6) is a service portal that empowers you to obtain compliance reports and online agreements related to your environments deployed on the AWS Cloud. Consequently, you can use AWS Artifact if you require formal information associated with regulations such as service organization control (SOC), Payment Card Industry (PCI), and agreements such as the business associate agreement (BAA) and nondisclosure agreement (NDA).

FIGURE B.6 AWS Artifact icon

This service intends to provide a comprehensive resource to auditors looking for reports, certifications, accreditations, and third-party attestations from regulation bodies across geographies and compliance industry organizations. It also provides governance for your agreements with AWS and insights from the AWS security control environment.

AWS Artifact is currently offered with no cost. Always refer to the AWS Artifact official documentation for updated information: `docs.aws.amazon.com/artifact`.

AWS Certificate Manager

Certificates are files that provide secure data communication and assure the identity of entities exchanging such data. The AWS Certificate Manager (see Figure B.7) makes it possible for you to provision, manage, and deploy public and private Secure Socket Layer (SSL) and Transport Layer Security (TLS) certificates—whether they are consumed by AWS services or on-premises resources. The AWS Certificate Manager centralizes the management of certificates and streamlines the traditional manual process of acquiring, uploading, and renewing these special files.

FIGURE B.7 AWS Certificate Manager icon

Within the AWS Cloud, the AWS Certificate Manager can directly assign certificates to Elastic Load Balancers, Amazon CloudFront distributions, APIs deployed on Amazon API Gateway, AWS Elastic Beanstalk, and AWS CloudFormation (for public email-validated certificates). In addition, you can audit the use of each certificate on the AWS Certificate Manager via Amazon CloudTrail logs and import certificates issued by third-party certificate authorities.

Any certificate for use with AWS Certificate Manager integrated services is currently free (you only pay for the AWS resources that consume these certificates). In addition, you can leverage the AWS Certificate Manager Private Certificate Authority service to generate a private certificate authority (which is offered as a free trial for 30 days). Always refer to the AWS Certificate Manager official documentation for updated information: `docs.aws.amazon.com/acm`.

AWS CloudHSM

A hardware security module (HSM) is a computing device that safeguards and manages encryption keys for authentication and also provides cryptoprocessing. AWS CloudHSM (see Figure B.8) is a cloud-based hardware security module that allows you to generate, manage, and use your own encryption keys. Because it is a cloud service, AWS CloudHSM performs its HSM duties without time-consuming administrative tasks such as hardware provisioning, software patching, high-availability deployment, and backup coordination. It also provides low latency to applications that leverage cloud services in AWS.

FIGURE B.8 AWS CloudHSM icon

This service is a Federal Information Processing Standard (FIPS) 140-2 Level 3–validated HSM that follows industry-standard APIs such as Public Key Cryptography Standards (PKCS) #11, Java Cryptography Extensions (JCE), and Microsoft Cryptography API: Next Generation (CNG) libraries. It is also compliant with regulations such as HIPAA, Federal Risk and Authorization Management Program (FedRAMP), and PCI.

As a dedicated hardware security module, AWS CloudHSM instances are deployed with single-tenant access inside your own Amazon Virtual Private Cloud (VPC). AWS CloudHSM has no visibility or access to your encryption keys while also providing a clear separation of management duties such as AWS administrator (role that manages the appliance) and crypto users (who perform key management and cryptographic operations).

You can access the AWS CloudHSM documentation at the following URL: `docs.aws.amazon.com/cloudhsm`.

AWS Directory Service

AWS Directory Service (see Figure B.9) is a managed Microsoft Active Directory deployed on the AWS cloud and built on actual Microsoft software. This service is also known as *AWS Managed Microsoft AD* and can be used both by your directory-aware workloads and AWS resources such as Amazon EC2 instances, Amazon RDS for SQL Server, and Amazon WorkSpaces.

FIGURE B.9 AWS Directory Service icon

With AWS Directory Service, you can use the same management tools that Microsoft AD administrators use to centrally manage application access and devices as well as to fully take advantage of Microsoft AD features such as Group Policies and Single Sign-On. Although this service does not require you to synchronize or replicate data from your existing AD to the AWS Cloud, you can easily deploy Microsoft AD trust relationships from existing domains to AWS Directory Service.

Similar to other AWS managed services, AWS Directory service simplifies administration by providing native high-availability through multi-AZ deployment, automatic monitoring to detect failures, data replication, automated daily snapshots, and no need of software installation, patching, or updates.

AWS Directory Service is available in two editions: Standard (for small and midsize businesses with up to 5,000 employees and 30,000 directory objects including users, groups, and devices) and Enterprise (for organizations with up to 500,000 directory objects).

AWS Directory Service is currently available as a 30-day free trial, limited to 1,500 domain controller hours. Always refer to the AWS Directory Service documentation for updated information: `docs.aws.amazon.com/directory-service`.

AWS Firewall Manager

AWS Firewall Manager (see Figure B.10) enables you to define and control firewall rules across accounts and applications deployed in AWS Organizations. As accounts, VPCs, and security policies grow in number in your environments, this service allows the creation and enforcement of firewall rules and security policies in a centralized way.

Through the AWS Firewall Manager, you can roll out AWS WAF rules for your application load balancers, Elastic IP addresses, and Amazon CloudFront distributions. In addition, you can control AWS Shield Advanced configurations, security groups for your Amazon EC2 instances, and Elastic Network Interfaces (ENIs) in Amazon VPCs. To achieve automatic protection on the aforementioned services deployed on your AWS environments, you can leverage group rules and policies that are centrally managed in AWS Firewall Manager. In summary, these constructs ensure compliance for new resources as they are created across accounts.

FIGURE B.10 AWS Firewall Manager icon

AWS Firewall Manager also brings zero-day vulnerability protection through AWS Web Application Firewall subscription to Managed Rules for WAF from the AWS Marketplace (for example, for Common Vulnerabilities and Exposures [CVE] patch updates). Furthermore, AWS Firewall manager provides a dashboard with compliance notifications to further help regulatory demands.

You can find the AWS Firewall Manager at the following URL: `docs.aws.amazon.com/firewall-manager`.

AWS Identity and Access Management

Also known as AWS IAM, AWS Identity and Access Management (see Figure B.11) is a security service that controls access to AWS services and resources. It creates and manages users, groups, and permissions, which allow and deny access to AWS resources in a granular way. AWS IAM enables such customizable access control through methods such as multifactor authentication (MFA), as well as encryption implementations such as SSL, source IP addresses, or time of day.

FIGURE B.11 AWS Identity and Access Management icon

AWS IAM adheres to the concept of zero-trust because, by default, users have no authorization to access any AWS resources until permissions are explicitly declared. Natively integrated in the majority of AWS services, AWS IAM differentiates the validation of public or cross-account access using policies from Amazon S3 buckets, AWS KMS keys, Amazon SQS queues, AWS IAM roles, and AWS Lambda functions. Moreover, the service can also be integrated with your corporate directory, such as Microsoft Active Directory, and is extensible via SAML 2.0.

There is currently no charge for using AWS IAM. Always refer to the AWS IAM official documentation for updated information: `docs.aws.amazon.com/iam`.

AWS Key Management Service

AWS Key Management Service (KMS) provides you with the means to create and control encryption keys across most AWS services and your applications. With AWS KMS (see Figure B.12), you can encrypt data in your applications as well as digitally sign and secure your data. AWS KMS also helps you to support your regulatory and compliance needs via AWS CloudTrail login of all key-related operations in your environment. Additionally, this service is validated under FIPS 140-2, SOC 1–3, PCI DSS Level 1, FedRAMP, and HIPAA.

FIGURE B.12 AWS Key Management Service icon

AWS KMS is currently free if you use fewer than 20,000 requests per month; however, AWS will charge you $1.00 per stored key across all regions in which the service is currently available. Always refer to the AWS KMS documentation for updated information: `docs.aws.amazon.com/kms`.

AWS Resource Access Manager

AWS Resource Access Manager (AWS RAM) gives you the power to securely share AWS resources with any other AWS account or with accounts within your AWS Organization. (See Figure B.13.) The service's main benefit is that, through the sharing of a resource among multiple accounts, it avoids duplication of cloud consumption as well as management efforts.

FIGURE B.13 AWS Resource Access Manager icon

Through three configuration steps (create a resource share, specify resources, and select accounts), AWS RAM allows you to securely use AWS Transit Gateways, AWS License Manager configurations, and Amazon Route 53 resolver rules, for example. In addition, to improve accountability, all API calls to this service are logged in AWS CloudTrail.

AWS RAM currently charges no additional fee. Always refer to the AWS RAM official documentation for updated information: `docs.aws.amazon.com/ram`.

AWS Secrets Manager

AWS Secrets Manager (see Figure B.14) enables you to rotate, manage, and retrieve secrets such as database credentials and API keys. Because this service releases you from storing sensitive information in clear text, AWS Secrets Manager protects secrets that are essential for your applications and resources.

FIGURE B.14 AWS Secrets Manager icon

This service provides secret rotation with built-in integration for Amazon Relational Database Service (RDS), Amazon Redshift, and Amazon DocumentDB. AWS Secrets Manager is also extensible to other types of secrets (such as OAuth tokens and API keys).

To better protect your secrets, AWS Secrets Manager transmits them securely over TLS, possesses fine-grained permissions, and does not save or cache them on any type of persistent storage. It also helps you adhere to compliance regulations such as HIPAA, PCI-DSS, ISO/IEC 27001, ISO/IEC 27017, ISO/IEC 27018, and ISO 9001.

AWS Secrets Manager is currently available without additional charge for a 30-day trial period. Always refer to the AWS Secrets Manager official documentation for updated information: `docs.aws.amazon.com/secretsmanager`.

AWS Security Hub

AWS Security Hub (see Figure B.15) provides a centralized view of security alerts and automated compliance verifications across your AWS accounts. Moreover, it collects information from multiple AWS services such as Amazon GuardDuty, Amazon Inspector, Amazon Macie, AWS IAM Access Analyzer, AWS Firewall Manager, and third-party solutions such as Check Point, CrowdStrike, Palo Alto Networks, Qualys, and Symantec.

FIGURE B.15 AWS Security Hub icon

All security findings in AWS Security Hub are collected via standardized AWS Security Findings Format. In addition, AWS Security Hub automates the verification of the Center for Internet Security (CIS) for AWS Foundations Benchmark, a program from Accenture that provides well-defined, unbiased, consensus-based industry best practices to help organizations assess and improve their security. AWS Security Hub also offers PCI-DSS and AWS Foundational Standards checks.

AWS Security Hub is currently available for free for a 30-day trial period. Always refer to the AWS Security Hub official documentation for updated information: `docs.aws.amazon.com/securityhub`.

AWS Shield

AWS Shield (see Figure B.16) offers managed distributed denial-of-service (DDoS) protection for applications running on AWS. It provides constant detections and automatic inline mitigations that minimize application downtime or performance degradation.

FIGURE B.16 AWS Shield icon

AWS Shield is available in two editions: Standard and Advanced. AWS Shield Standard is a no-cost version that defends your environments against the most common Network and Transport layers DDoS attacks that target your website or applications. This edition relies on detection techniques such as network flow monitoring, a combination of traffic signatures, and anomaly algorithms. Additionally, it mitigates attacks through in-line mechanisms, which include deterministic packet filtering, priority-based traffic shaping, and rules in AWS Web Application Firewall.

AWS Shield Advanced enables additional detection and mitigation against large and sophisticated DDoS attacks to Amazon EC2, ELB, Amazon CloudFront, AWS Global Accelerator, and Amazon Route 53 with near real-time visibility, integration with AWS WAF, 24×7 access to the AWS DDoS Response Team (DRT), and protection against DDoS-related spikes in charges related to those services. This version provides enhanced detection through network flow inspection, resource-specific monitoring, resource- and region-specific granular detection of DDoS attacks, and Application layer DDoS attacks like HTTP floods or DNS query floods through baselining traffic and identifying anomalies. It also offers advanced attack mitigation via routing techniques, DRT manual mitigations, AWS WAF free of charge for Shield-protected resources, visibility and attack notification (Amazon CloudWatch), DDoS cost protection, and global availability.

You can find the AWS Shield documentation at the following URL: `docs.aws.amazon.com/shield`.

AWS Single Sign-On

As its name implies, AWS Single Sign-On (SSO) centrally controls single sign-on access in your AWS accounts and business applications. (See Figure B.17.) This service manages SSO access and user permissions to all your accounts in AWS Organizations in a single place, while also including preconfigured integrations with Salesforce, Box, Office 365, Azure Active Directory, and Microsoft Active Directory. AWS Single Sign-On also has a configuration wizard that helps you extend SSO access to other applications via SAML 2.0.

FIGURE B.17 AWS Single Sign-On

AWS Single Sign-On is a managed service that has native high availability and logging in AWS CloudTrail. You can use AWS Single Sign-On to interact with portal, browser, command-line, or mobile interfaces.

You can find the AWS Single Sign-On documentation at the following URL: `docs.aws.amazon.com/singlesignon`.

AWS Web Application Firewall

Commonly known as AWS WAF, AWS Web Application Firewall (see Figure B.18) protects your web applications and APIs from known web attacks created to affect application availability, compromise data security, or provoke denial of service. With AWS WAF, you can create rules that block common attacks such as SQL injection and cross-site scripting, or specific traffic patterns you can define. You can filter any part of the web request, including IP addresses, HTTP headers, HTTP body, or URI strings.

FIGURE B.18 AWS Web Application icon

When applied to Amazon CloudFront, Application Load Balancer (ALB), or Amazon API Gateway, AWS WAF offers automated protection via managed rules for WAF, a preconfigured set of rules from AWS Marketplace that protects against vulnerabilities defined on OWASP's Top 10 Security Risks, threats specific to content management systems (CMSs), or emerging Common Vulnerabilities and Exposures (CVE). AWS WAF also includes a full-featured API that you can use to automate the creation, deployment, and maintenance of security rules.

In terms of monitoring and automated protection, AWS WAF offers near real-time visibility into your web traffic, allowing you to create new rules or alerts in Amazon CloudWatch. It also provides logging from each inspected web request for use in security automation, analytics, or auditing purposes.

You can find the AWS Web Application Firewall documentation at the following URL: `docs.aws.amazon.com/waf`.

DevSecOps in AWS

The DevSecOps practice is not yet covered by AWS security certification, but we believe it is essential to define the concept, introduce the AWS family of services that implement DevOps practices, and demonstrate in a practical way how security controls can be implemented in an automated pipeline.

Introduction

This appendix introduces you to the principles of DevSecOps and shows you how to implement a continuous integration and continuous deployment (CI/CD) process using security best practices. It will present a practical example of how to create an automated pipeline using AWS Developer Tools services (and some third-party tools) in order to illustrate such concepts.

A CI/CD pipeline helps you automate software delivery steps, such as building, testing, and deploying the application. The pipeline provides a standardized process of minimizing the chance of failures to improve the speed of feedback when errors occur during the process.

Before being properly introduced to DevSecOps, you will need to understand what a DevOps process is and the main benefits of implementing it in software development.

DevOps

The term "DevOps" first came up at the Velocity event in 2009, where John Allspaw and Paul Hammond presented the talk "10+ Deploys per Day: Dev and Ops Cooperation at Flickr," which explored the results and challenges of closer engagement between development and operations teams on Flickr. Patrick Debois, who attended the lecture online and would later co-create the term, came up with the idea of creating the "DevOps Days" event.

DevOps is a set of software development practices that combines software development and information technology operations to reduce the systems development lifecycle while delivering features, fixes, and frequent updates in close alignment with business objectives.

With the need for faster software deliveries, various techniques and tools have been created to automate development and release steps. Perhaps due to the strong mindshare some development tools possess, it is fairly common for people to confuse DevOps with the purchase or implementation of a toolkit. Nonetheless, the DevOps adoption process involves three complementary pillars: cultural philosophies, practices, and tools.

Cultural Philosophies

Many of the problems that occur during deployment processes are related to the lack of information from the operations team about what needs to be done at deployment time. In addition, developers are not always aware of the infrastructure that will support the application. To minimize these problems, information about what is being developed and how the application should behave after deploying it to environments must flow correctly among these teams.

To implement a DevOps process, both development and operations teams must work together, without silos, with shared responsibility from development to application support. Therefore, a philosophy of open communication has to drive their work on a daily basis.

Practices

DevOps practices mainly address the process of continuous integration, continuous delivery, continuous deployment, infrastructure as code, and monitoring.

Continuous integration is the practice of merging all developers' local copies of the software to a shared branch several times a day. With such a practice, it is possible to anticipate the problems that may occur when integrating the code of the various developers working within the same project and consequently fix it faster.

Continuous delivery is a software development practice where code changes are automatically prepared for production release. A cornerstone of modern application development, continuous delivery expands on continuous integration by deploying all code changes to a testing environment and, optionally, to a production environment after the build stage. When properly implemented, developers will always have access to a deployment-ready build artifact that has passed through a standardized test process.

Continuous delivery lets developers automate testing beyond just unit tests so that they can verify application updates across multiple steps before deploying to customers. These evaluations may include user interface testing, load testing, integration testing, and API reliability testing. Such processes help developers thoroughly validate updates and preemptively discover issues. One of the benefits of cloud computing in such scenarios is the ease of automating the creation and replication of multiple environments for testing, which is a difficult task in on-premises data centers.

Continuous deployment is a strategy for software releases where any code commit that passes the automated testing phase is automatically released to the production environment, implementing changes that are visible to users of the software being developed.

Other techniques should also be considered for a successful continuous deployment process. One of the main methods is the use of a development pattern called Feature Flag (also known as FeatureToggle). With this functionality, you can enable and disable parts of your code so that a specific feature can be enabled and disabled at runtime.

As an example, you can use Feature Flag when you need to enable a feature that has a specific date and time to go live to mobile users. In this situation, the code has already been delivered to the production environment, so now you will only be able to activate it when other areas are ready to consume the feature, or eventually when the application becomes available in its app store.

Figure C.1 depicts a comparison between both practices.

FIGURE C.1 Continuous delivery vs. continuous deployment

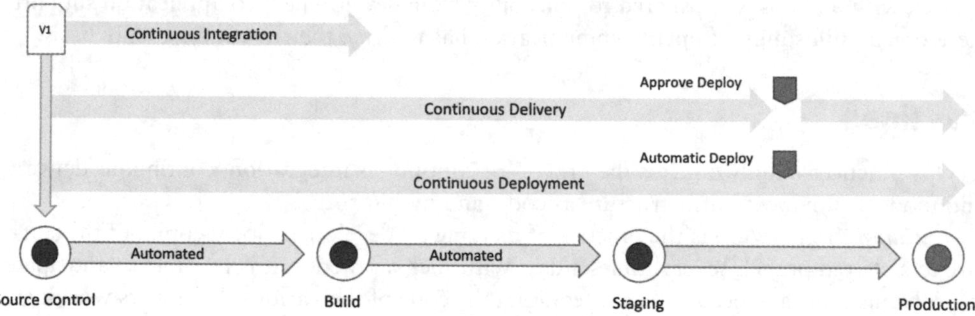

As shown in Figure C.1, with continuous delivery every code change is built, tested, and then pushed to a nonproduction testing or staging environment. There can be multiple parallel test stages before production deployment. Although continuous delivery requires human intervention through a manual approval for code deployment to production, continuous deployment does it automatically.

Infrastructure as code is the process of provisioning and managing cloud resources via a template file that is both human-readable and machine-consumable. Within the AWS Cloud, the built-in choice for infrastructure as code is the AWS CloudFormation service.

The code generated for the deployment of the infrastructure must be treated as the software of your application—it must be versioned and undergo tests, vulnerability checks, and compliance validation.

The *monitoring* practice is used to give teams visibility into application behavior, not only after production deployment but also during the build and deployment process.

Each organization may set different goals when implementing its DevOps process. Keep in mind that to achieve the highest levels of maturity, application changes may be required.

One of the most common changes observed in enterprise organizations today is the breaking down of monolithic applications into smaller parts, also known as *microservices*. With the adoption of microservices, you can speed up the software development process to achieve more frequent deliveries. Another significant benefit of adopting microservices is the ability to scale each component of your application independently, which could not be accomplished using monolithic applications.

Software engineering defines a monolithic application as a single-layered software application where the user interface and data access code are part of a single program.

A monolithic application describes a software application that is designed without modularity, is standalone, and is generally independent of other applications. It consists of an application that is not only responsible for a particular task but can also perform all the necessary steps to solve a problem.

As you break the application into smaller parts, multiple teams can be formed, each taking care of different components of the system. Each team becomes responsible for all stages of their components, from development to support.

It is important to note that when adopting the microservices strategy, you must clearly define how components will communicate with one another in the application. This is usually done by setting API contracts, which makes each part less dependent on the others. As a result, the evolution of the whole application is simpler.

Tools

To better understand the role of tools in DevOps, consider the steps of the software release process and what should be covered in each of the steps, as shown in Figure C.2.

FIGURE C.2 Steps of software release process

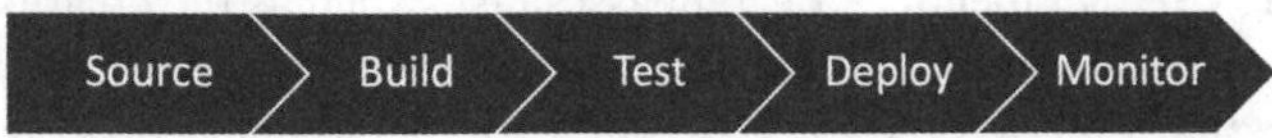

The *source* step is where source code versioning and revision of the committed codes are performed. The details behind the different strategies for branch management are beyond the scope of this appendix. Instead, we will focus on what should be controlled and the possible variations of implementation.

In the *build* step, you must compile the application, perform unit tests, perform code style checks, collect code metrics, package the software, and possibly generate container images.

In the *test* phase, you must run load tests, usability tests, and vulnerability tests, and perform integrated tests with other systems. In this phase, you address the application and its related infrastructure.

During the *deployment* stage, you deliver the artifacts generated to the production environment. Then, you should monitor the application metrics to identify any issues. One important observation: the term "monitor" here does not refer to metrics like CPU, memory, and disk usage. The process should be mostly concerned with business metrics, such as the percentage of successful responses in the API layer.

The closer the user is to a monitored metric, the more critical it should be considered. With metrics that reflect user experience, it is easier to understand whether they are being impacted by an incident or a change in the software that you just delivered to the production environment. For example, if an application typically has a failure rate of 0.3 percent and after the deployment of a new version, it increases to 0.8 percent, the change is directly impacting users as long as a correlation between both events is correctly identified.

Dev + Sec + Ops

"DevSecOps" (derived from "development," "security," and "operations") is the combination of cultural philosophies, practices, and tools that leverage the advances made in IT automation to achieve a state of production immutability, frequent delivery of business value, and automated enforcement of security policies.

To fully comprehend the need for DevSecOps, you should be aware of the competing demands that exist within organizations. The development team must deliver faster, the security team must ensure that deliveries are secure, and the operations team must keep systems stable.

DevSecOps is achieved through the integration and automation of the enforcement of preventive, detective, and responsive security controls into the pipeline. Its implementation has three main stages:

Security of the CI/CD Pipeline Encompasses tasks such as the creation of automated IAM roles, hardening of automation servers, and other configurations that protect the infrastructure that supports the software build and deployment process.

Security in the CI/CD Pipeline Includes security-related tasks such as automated security tests and code base analysis as part of the software development process.

Enforcement of the Pipeline Includes procedures that provide monitoring and proactive protection such as automated incident response remediation and forensics.

Tenets of DevSecOps

According to the Chalk Talk, "Building a DevSecOps Culture," presented during AWS re:Inforce 2019, DevSecOps has four tenets:

Test security as early as possible to accelerate feedback. It is essential to create mechanisms to test the application and to identify potential shortcomings as early as possible. It is common to see companies performing pipeline security checks only when they are going to make a production release. Sometimes they identify serious security issues that will take a longer time to fix and can sometimes cause production software to be delayed.

Prioritize preventive security controls to stop bad things from happening. When dealing with security issues, it is critical to avoid problems in the production application. For this reason, preventive safety controls must be implemented.

When deploying a detective security control, ensure that it has a complementary responsive security control. Even with the implementation of preventive safety controls, you must be ready to act in case of production failures. It is essential to keep the application runbooks always up to date and teams adequately trained to act in case of problems. It is usual for companies to adopt *Red Team* and *Blue Team* strategies to conduct application intrusion simulations to ensure that everyone knows what to do in a real security incident.

Application Runbook

An *application runbook* is a compilation of routine procedures and operations that the system administrator or operator carries out. People in IT departments use runbooks as a reference. Runbooks can be in either electronic or physical book form.

Automate, automate, and automate. To facilitate the identification and remediation of security issues, strive to automate everything in the system deployment process. Create automated scripts to contain security issues in production, such as isolating a compromised server so that a forensic team can evaluate it.

AWS Developer Tools

The AWS Cloud provides a series of services that support DevOps software development pipelines. This section will address which services can be used at each stage of the software release process and the main benefits of each service.

AWS CodeCommit

AWS CodeCommit is a fully managed source control service that hosts Git-based protected repositories. It enables teams to easily collaborate on code in a secure and highly scalable ecosystem. This service eliminates the need to operate your source control system or worry about infrastructure scalability. You can use CodeCommit to securely store anything from source code to binary files. In addition, it works perfectly with your existing Git tools.

AWS CodeBuild

AWS CodeBuild is a fully managed continuous integration service that compiles source code, performs testing, and produces ready-to-deploy software packages. With AWS CodeBuild, you don't have to provision, manage, and scale your build servers. AWS CodeBuild scales continuously and processes multiple builds at the same time, preventing them from waiting in a queue. You can quickly start using predefined build environments or create custom build environments with your build tools. When you are using AWS CodeBuild, the used computational resources are charged per minute.

AWS CodeBuild runs your builds in preconfigured build environments that contain the operating system, programming language runtime, and build tools like Apache Maven, Gradle, and npm, which are required to complete the task. Just specify your source code's location and select the settings for your build. AWS CodeBuild builds your code and stores the artifacts in an Amazon S3 bucket, or you can use a build command to upload them to an artifact repository.

To speed up the process of building your build scripts, you can use AWS CodeBuild's local testing support, which is available here: `aws.amazon.com/blogs/devops/announcing-local-build-support-for-aws-codebuild`.

Testing with AWS CodeBuild and Third-Party Tools

During the build process, you will need to perform different types of tests on your software. The most common are unit tests, load tests, integration or API tests, and vulnerability tests. In addition, to successfully implement a CI/CD process, you must automate an entire test suite.

With AWS CodeBuild you can add your test calls directly to your build script. In some cases, you will need to install third-party tools for testing. You can also install these features in your build script; however, because AWS CodeBuild charges for the computation time spent during the process, you will be spending money to install the tools and make the build time longer. For these cases, we recommend that you create a custom Docker image containing all the tools you will use in the build process so that your build process becomes faster and cheaper.

AWS CodeDeploy

AWS CodeDeploy is a fully managed deployment service that automates software deployments on a variety of computing services such as Amazon EC2, AWS Fargate, and AWS Lambda, as well as local servers. AWS CodeDeploy facilitates the rapid launch of new features, helps you avoid downtime while deploying applications, and deals with the complexity of updating them. You can use AWS CodeDeploy to automate software deployments and eliminate the need for error-prone manual operations. The service scales to meet your deployment needs.

AWS X-Ray

AWS X-Ray helps developers analyze and debug distributed production applications, such as those created by using a microservices architecture. With X-Ray, you can understand the performance of applications and their underlying services in order to identify and troubleshoot the root cause of performance issues and errors. X-Ray provides a complete view of requests as they move through the application, and it shows a map of the underlying components of the application. You can use X-Ray to analyze both development and production applications, varying from simple three-tier applications to complex microservices applications consisting of thousands of services.

Figure C.3 shows a service map that helps you identify the components of your application. You can quickly identify the percentage of affected customers in case of problems.

FIGURE C.3 AWS X-Ray service map

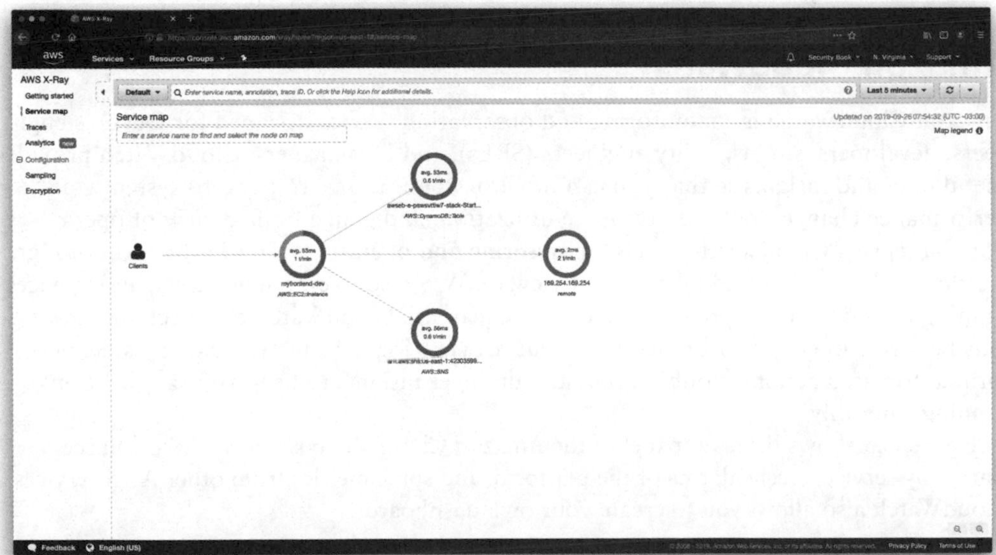

Figure C.4 shows a list of traces captured by X-Ray. You can see individual records where you can identify the origin request and some performance information to help you monitor your application.

FIGURE C.4 AWS X-Ray Traces

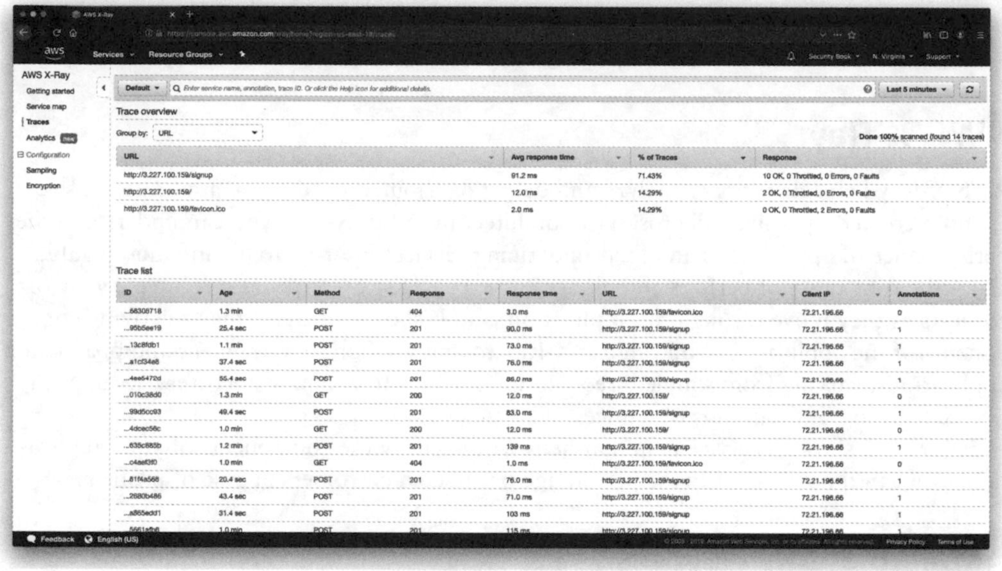

Amazon CloudWatch

Amazon CloudWatch is a monitoring and observation service designed for DevOps engineers, developers, site reliability engineers (SREs), and IT managers. CloudWatch provides useful data and insights so that you can monitor applications, respond to systemwide performance changes, optimize resource utilization, and gain a unified view of operational integrity. CloudWatch collects monitoring and operations data in the form of logs, metrics, and events, providing a unified view of AWS resources, applications, and services running on AWS and on-premises servers. You can use CloudWatch to detect anomalous behavior in your environments, set alarms, view logs and metrics side by side, perform automated actions, troubleshoot, and discover insights to keep your applications running smoothly.

Figure C.5 shows the main panel of the Amazon CloudWatch service, where you see alarms by service, recent alarms of the platform, and some metrics from other AWS services. CloudWatch also allows you to create your own dashboards.

FIGURE C.5 Amazon CloudWatch panel

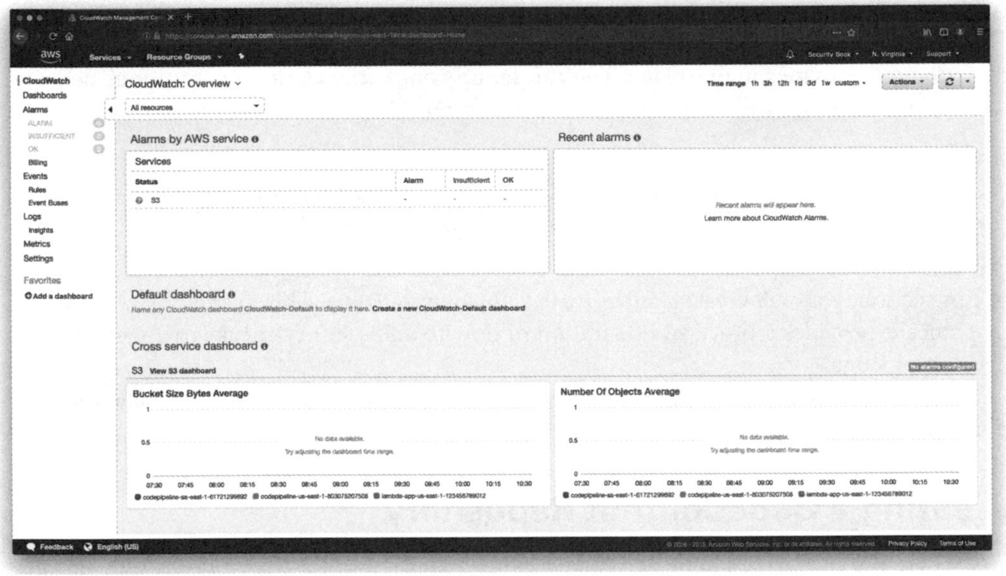

AWS CodePipeline

AWS CodePipeline is a managed continuous delivery service that helps automate release pipelines to provide fast and reliable application and infrastructure updates. CodePipeline automates the build, test, and deployment phases of the release process whenever a code change occurs, according to the release model you have defined. This enables you to make features and updates available quickly and reliably. You can easily integrate AWS CodePipeline with third-party services like GitHub or with your custom plug-in.

AWS Cloud9

AWS Cloud9 is a cloud-based IDE that allows you to write, execute, and debug code using your browser. The environment includes a code editor, a debugger, and a terminal. Cloud9 comes with essential tools for common programming languages. You don't have to install files or configure the development machine to start new projects. With Cloud9, you can quickly share the development environment with your team, which allows programming in pairs and mutual control of inputs in real time.

AWS CodeStar

AWS CodeStar allows you to develop, compile, and deploy applications on AWS. AWS CodeStar provides a unified user interface so that you can easily manage your software development activities in one place. You can set up your entire chain of continuous delivery tools easily, enabling you to start releasing code faster.

Creating a CI/CD Using AWS Tools

In this section, you will create a software development pipeline. This exercise is very important since it provides a practical illustration of how to add security checks to a software delivery pipeline.

As a first step, you will set up a code repository to save the source of a Lambda application. To create the repository, you will use the AWS CodeCommit service.

Creating a CodeCommit Repository

To execute the commands in this section, you need to install the AWS CLI tool. The installation steps can be found here: `docs.aws.amazon.com/cli/latest/userguide/cli-chap-install.html`.

After installing AWS CLI, you need to configure it. The configuration steps can be found here: `docs.aws.amazon.com/cli/latest/userguide/cli-chap-configure.html`.

Open your command-line interface tool such as Terminal in macOS and Linux or the command prompt in Windows.

```
aws codecommit create-repository --repository-name MyLambdaApp
--repository-description "My LambdaApp repository" --region us-east-1
```

This command will return a JSON file with details about the repository created:


```
{
    "repositoryMetadata": {
        "repositoryName": "MyLambdaApp",
        "cloneUrlSsh": "ssh://git-codecommit.us-east-
1.amazonaws.com/v1/repos/MyLambdaApp",
        "lastModifiedDate": 1567892089.859,
        "repositoryDescription": "My LambdaApp repository",
        "cloneUrlHttp": "https://git-codecommit.us-east-
1.amazonaws.com/v1/repos/MyLambdaApp",
        "creationDate": 1567892089.859,
        "repositoryId": "00000000-aaaa-bbbb-1111-aa000aaaaaa0",
        "Arn": "arn:aws:codecommit:us-east-1:123456789012:MyLambdaApp",
        "accountId": "123456789012"
    }
}
```

Figure C.6 shows your repository in the AWS Console.

FIGURE C.6 The repository you created in the AWS Console

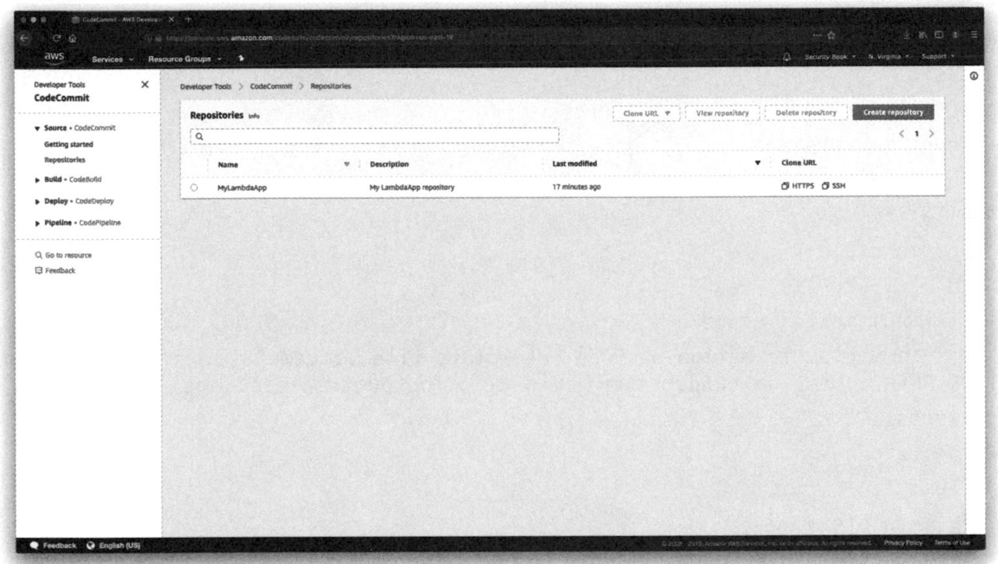

To clone the created repository, use the following command:

```
git clone https://git-codecommit.us-east-1.amazonaws.com/v1/repos/MyLambdaApp
```

After this process, open the `MyLambdaApp` folder and create a new folder called **`src`**:

```
cd MyLambdaApp
mkdir src
```

Open the `src` folder and create a new file named **`handler.js`** and insert the following code. This is the unique file inside the `src` folder.

```
var time = require('time');
exports.handler = (event, context, callback) => {
    var currentTime = new time.Date();
    currentTime.setTimezone("America/Los_Angeles");
    callback(null, {
        statusCode: '200',
        body: 'The time in Los Angeles is: ' + currentTime.toString(),
    });
};
```

Close the src folder using this command:

```
cd ..
```

Create a file named **buildspec.yml** and insert the following code in the file:

```
---
version: 0.2
phases:
  install:
    runtime-versions:
        nodejs: 10
  build:
    commands:
      - cd src
      - npm install time
      - aws cloudformation package --template-file ../template.yaml --s3-bucket
<YOUR BUCKET NAME> --output-template-file ../outputtemplate.yaml
artifacts:
  type: zip
  files:
    - template.yaml
    - outputtemplate.yaml
```

Replace *<YOUR BUCKET NAME>* with the name of an existing bucket in your AWS account.

Create a file named **template.yaml** and insert the following code in the file:

```
---
AWSTemplateFormatVersion : '2010-09-09'
Transform: AWS::Serverless-2016-10-31
Description: A sample SAM template for deploying Lambda functions.
Resources:
  # Details about the TimeFunction Lambda function
  TimeFunction:
    Type: AWS::Serverless::Function
    Properties:
      CodeUri: ./src
      Handler: index.handler
      Runtime: nodejs10.x
      # Grants this function permission to call lambda:InvokeFunction
      Policies:
        - Version: "2012-10-17"
          Statement:
```

```
        - Effect: "Allow"
          Action:
            - "lambda:InvokeFunction"
          Resource: '*'
```

Use the following `git` commands to send your source to AWS CodeCommit:

```
git add .
git commit -m "My First Commit"
git push origin master
```

Figure C.7 shows your repository with the committed source code.

FIGURE C.7 Committed source code

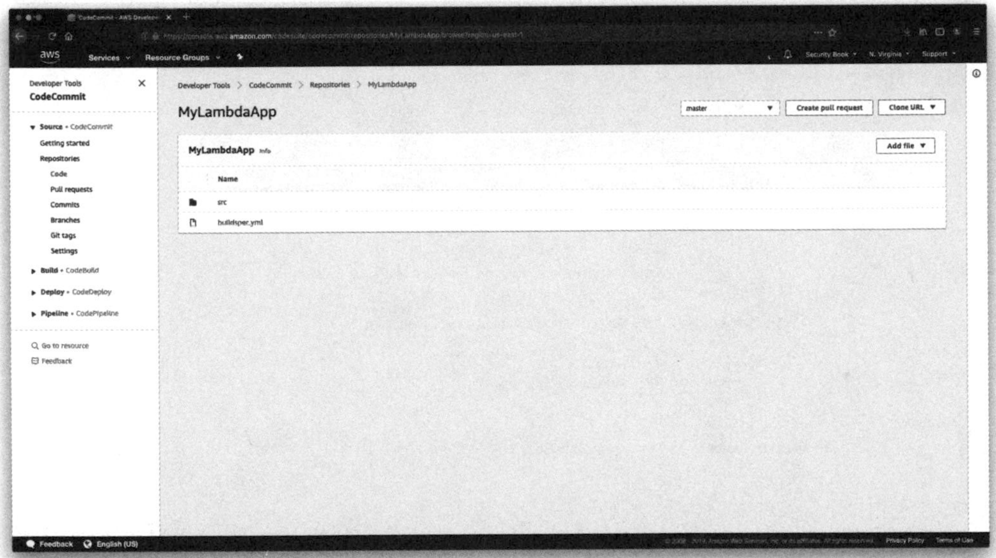

Creating an AWS CodePipeline Pipeline

Before creating a pipeline with AWS CodePipeline, you need to set up some other components such as an IAM role to execute AWS CloudFormation. You must also create an AWS CodeBuild project. The next sections will describe what you need to do.

Create a Role to AWS CloudFormation

Follow these steps to create a new IAM role:

1. While signed in as administrator or as a user with sufficient permissions, open IAM and create a CloudFormation-type role named **`cfn-lambda-pipeline`**.
2. Select the CloudFormation use case.
3. Type **`cfn-lambda-pipeline`** in the Role Name field.
4. Select the policy `AWSLambdaExecute`.
5. Review your role configurations (see Figure C.8) and click Create Role.

FIGURE C.8 Role configuration

Create role

1 2 3 4

Review

Provide the required information below and review this role before you create it.

Role name* cfn-lambda-pipeline

Use alphanumeric and '+=,.@-_' characters. Maximum 64 characters.

Role description Allows CloudFormation to create and manage AWS stacks and resources on your behalf.

Maximum 1000 characters. Use alphanumeric and '+=,.@-_' characters.

Trusted entities AWS service: cloudformation.amazonaws.com

Policies AWSLambdaExecute

Permissions boundary Permissions boundary is not set

No tags were added.

* Required

Cancel Previous Create role

6. Edit the created role and add an inline policy.
7. Select the JSON tab.
8. Enter the following code as a JSON policy:

```
{
    "Statement": [
        {
            "Action": [
                "codedeploy:*",
                "lambda:*",
                "cloudformation:CreateChangeSet",
                "iam:GetRole",
                "iam:CreateRole",
                "iam:DeleteRole",
                "iam:PutRolePolicy",
                "iam:AttachRolePolicy",
                "iam:DeleteRolePolicy",
                "iam:DetachRolePolicy",
                "iam:PassRole",
                "s3:GetObjectVersion",
                "s3:GetBucketVersioning"
            ],
            "Resource": "*",
            "Effect": "Allow"
        }
    ],
    "Version": "2012-10-17"
}
```

9. Click Review Policy.
10. Type **deploy-lambdaapp-policy** as the policy name.
11. Click Create Policy.

Create an AWS CodeBuild Project

Follow these steps to create a new AWS CodeBuild project:

1. While signed in as an administrator or as a user with ample permissions, open AWS CodeBuild.
2. Create a new project named **LambdaAppBuild**. See Figure C.9.

FIGURE C.9 Project configuration

Project configuration

Project name

LambdaAppBuild

A project name must be 2 to 255 characters. It can include the letters A-Z and a-z, the numbers 0-9, and the special characters - and _.

Description - *optional*

Build badge - *optional*

☐ Enable build badge

▶ **Additional configuration**
tags

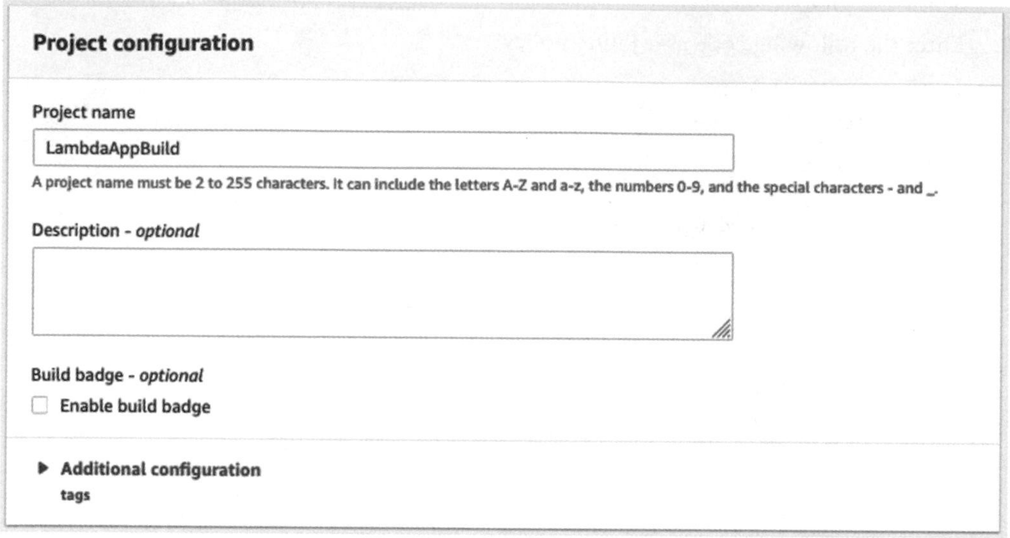

3. On the Source screen, select AWS CodeCommit from the Source Provider menu.
4. Select MyLambdaApp from the Repository menu.
5. Under Reference Type, select the Branch radio button, as shown in Figure C.10, and select Master from the Branch menu.
6. On the Environment screen, select Ubuntu from the Operating System menu.
7. Select the Standard runtime.
8. For Image, select the latest image using version as reference.
9. From the Image Version menu, choose "Always use the latest image for this runtime version," as shown in Figure C.11.
10. On the next screen, enter **`buildspec.yml`** as the file location and select "Use a buildspec file" option. See Figure C.12.

FIGURE C.10 Source screen

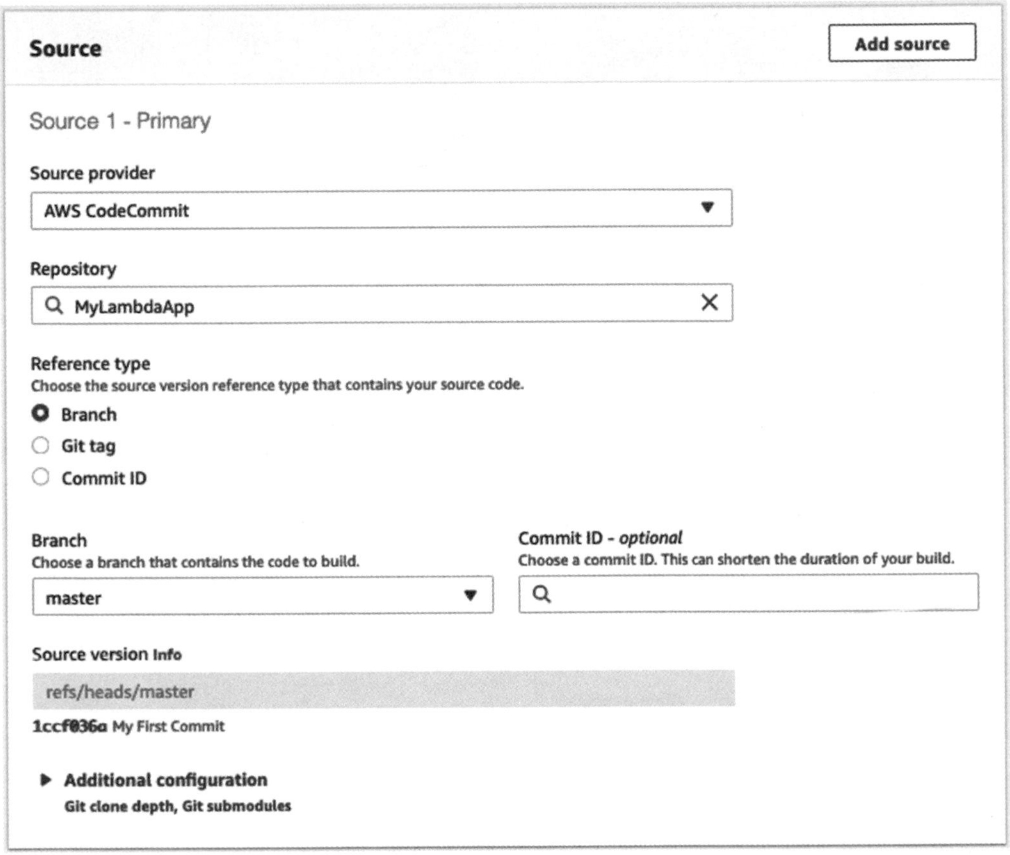

Source

Add source

Source 1 - Primary

Source provider

AWS CodeCommit

Repository

MyLambdaApp

Reference type

Choose the source version reference type that contains your source code.

Branch

Git tag

Commit ID

Branch

Choose a branch that contains the code to build.

master

Commit ID - *optional*

Choose a commit ID. This can shorten the duration of your build.

Source version Info

refs/heads/master

1ccf036a My First Commit

Additional configuration

Git clone depth, Git submodules

11. On the next screen, select the S3 bucket where you want to put the build artifacts.
12. Under Artifacts Packaging, select the Zip option, as shown in Figure C.13.
13. On the Logs screen, type **`LambdaAppBuild`** as the group name for CloudWatch logs. See Figure C.14.
14. Click Create Build Project.

FIGURE C.11 Environment screen

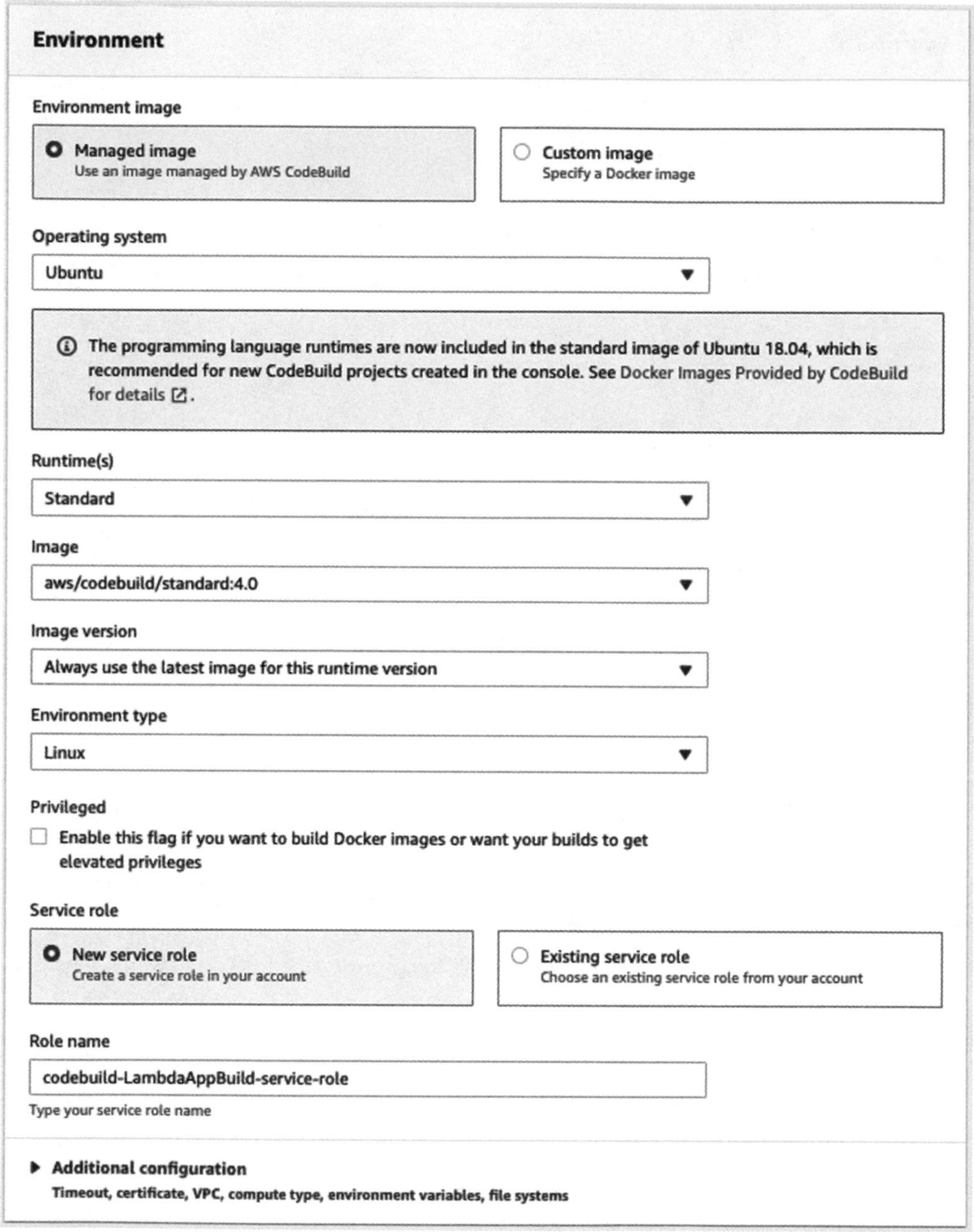

FIGURE C.12 Buildspec screen

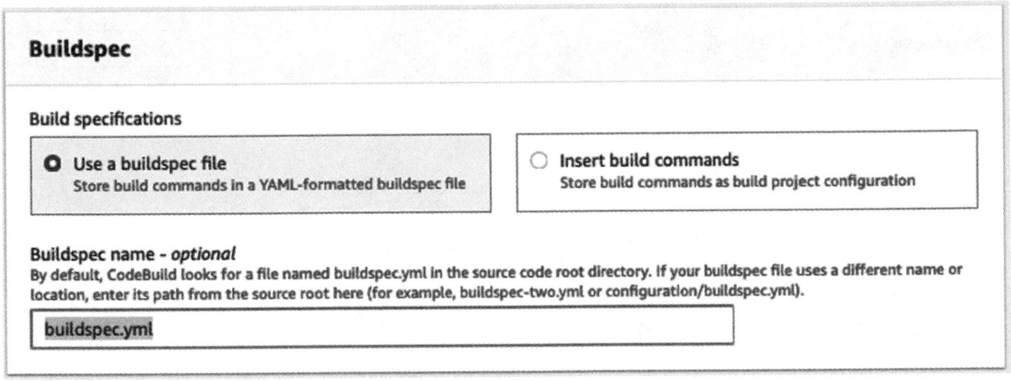

Create the Pipeline

Follow these steps to create a pipeline:

1. While signed in as administrator or as a user with ample permissions, open AWS CodePipeline.
2. Create a new pipeline named **`LambdaAppPipeline`**.
3. Click Next. See Figure C.15.
4. Select AWS CodeCommit as the source provider.
5. Select the repository MyLambdaApp.
6. Select the branch name Master.
7. Choose AWS CodePipeline as the detection mode.
8. Click Next. See Figure C.16.
9. Select AWS CodeBuild as the build provider.
10. Select the project LambdaAppBuild.
11. Click Next. See Figure C.17.

FIGURE C.13 Artifacts screen

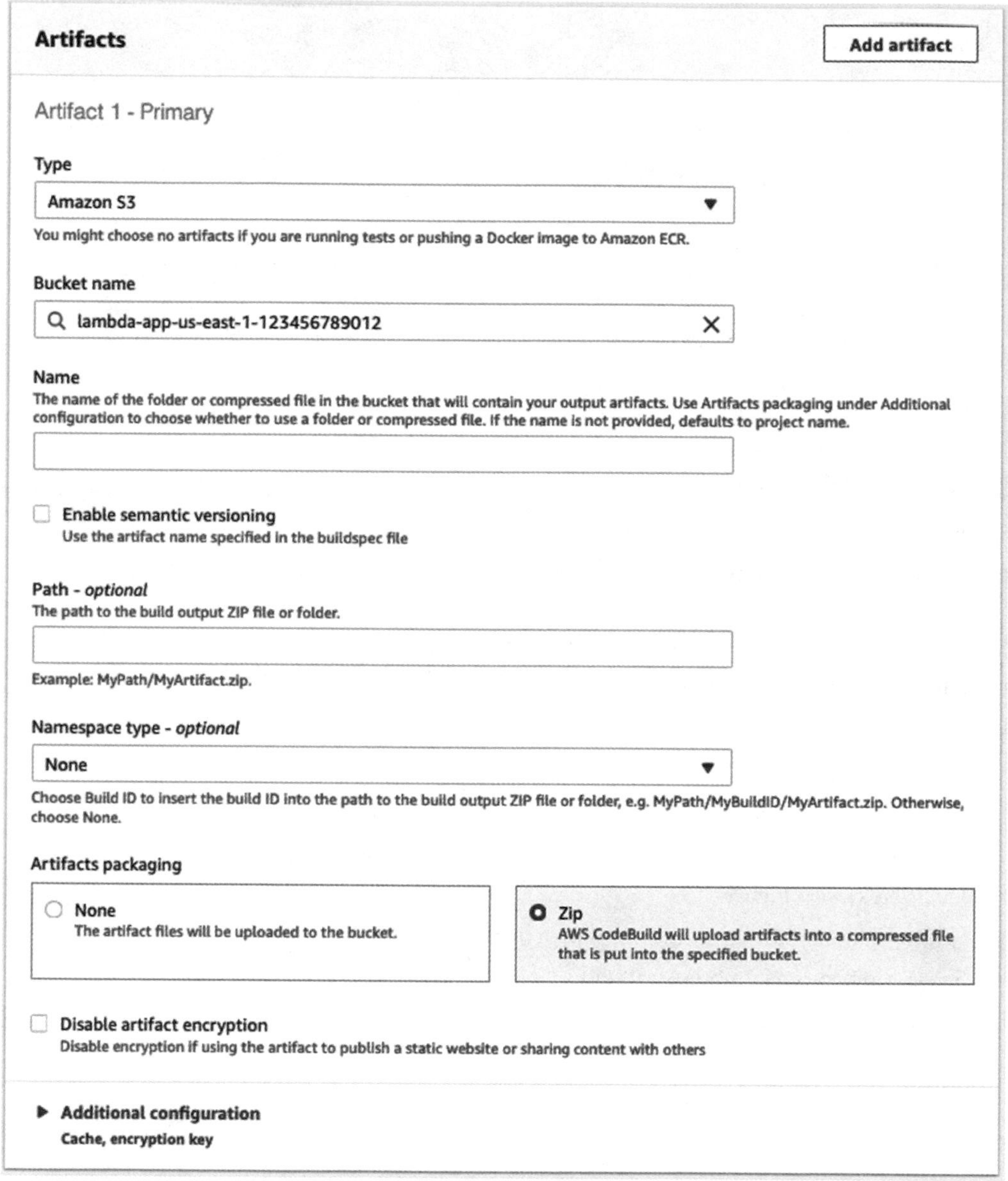

FIGURE C.14 Logs screen

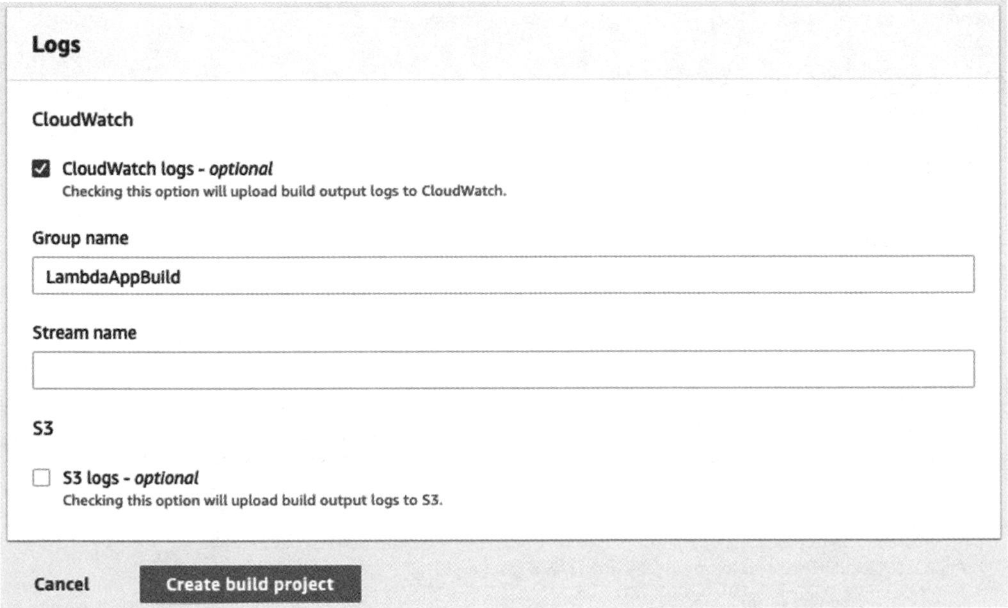

12. Select AWS CloudFormation as the deploy provider.
13. Select Create Or Update Stack as the action mode.
14. Select the stack name LambdaApp.
15. Select BuildArtifact from the Artifact Name menu.
16. Type **`outputtemplate.yaml`** in the File Name field.
17. Select `CAPABILITY_AUTO_EXPAND` and `CAPABILITY_IAM` under Capabilities.
18. Select the role name `arn:aws:iam::123456789012:role/cfn-lambda-pipeline`.
19. Click Next. See Figure C.18.
20. Review the configurations.
21. Click Create Pipeline.

After you finish the pipeline creation, click Release Change and wait for the complete pipeline execution. You can see the result in Figure C.19.

FIGURE C.15 Pipeline settings

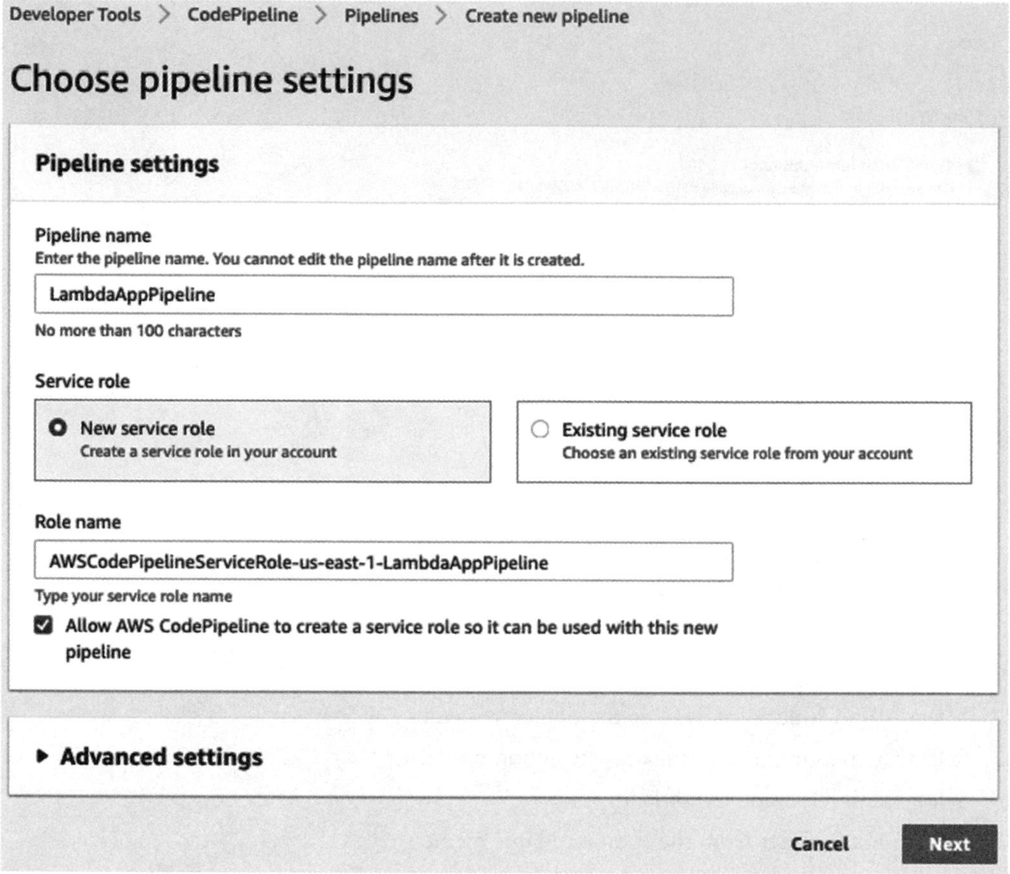

FIGURE C.16 Add Source Stage screen

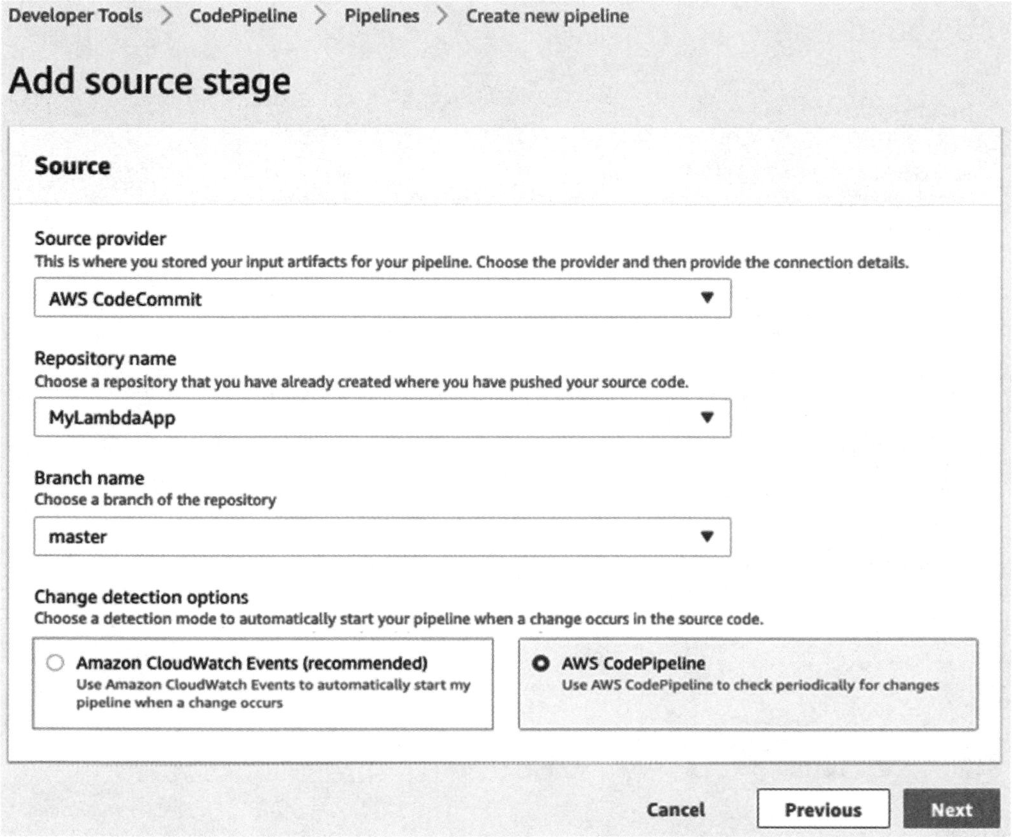

Developer Tools > CodePipeline > Pipelines > Create new pipeline

Add source stage

Source

Source provider
This is where you stored your input artifacts for your pipeline. Choose the provider and then provide the connection details.

AWS CodeCommit

Repository name
Choose a repository that you have already created where you have pushed your source code.

MyLambdaApp

Branch name
Choose a branch of the repository

master

Change detection options
Choose a detection mode to automatically start your pipeline when a change occurs in the source code.

Amazon CloudWatch Events (recommended)
Use Amazon CloudWatch Events to automatically start my pipeline when a change occurs

AWS CodePipeline
Use AWS CodePipeline to check periodically for changes

Cancel Previous Next

FIGURE C.17 Add Build Stage screen

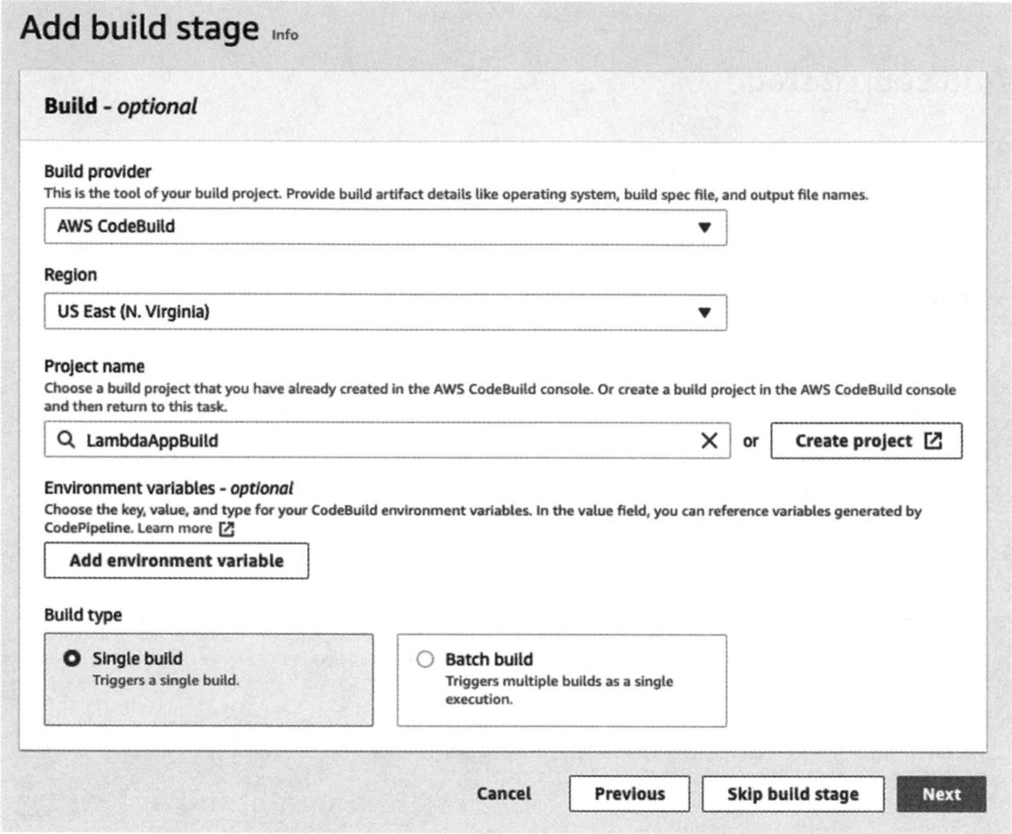

FIGURE C.18 Add Deploy Stage screen

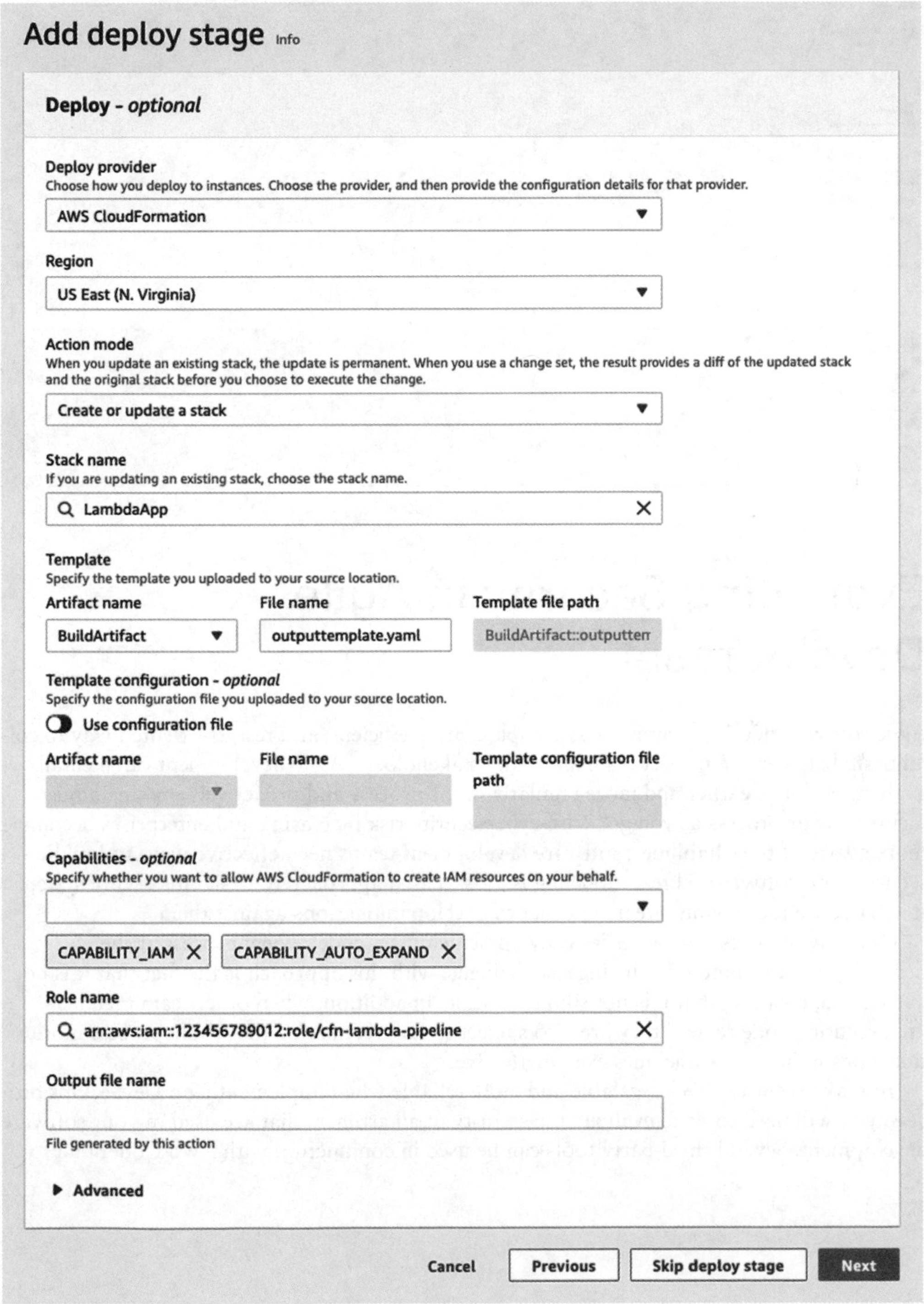

FIGURE C.19 Pipeline result

Evaluating Security in Agile Development

Agile software development is a less complex, more efficient, and results-oriented way to collaborate between the project team and other stakeholders. Agile development often entails evaluating things earlier and more regularly in the process and proactively making adjustments to your process as you go. With cybersecurity risk increasing and enterprises becoming more aware of their liabilities, software development teams need effective ways to build security into software. Threat modeling is a risk-based approach to designing secure systems. It is based on identifying threats in order to develop mitigations against them.

One way to check code security is by implementing a code review process at the beginning of your pipeline. The biggest challenge with this approach is the fact that it is not automated, meaning that it is not simple to scale. In addition, when other team members are executing code review, they are also subject to failure, making the whole process more time-consuming and sometimes even ineffective.

To make security checks scalable and more reliable when implementing a DevSecOps process, you will need tools to evaluate the security of all artifacts that are used in your software development. Several third-party tools can be used in conjunction with AWS CodeBuild to perform this task. Here is a list of solutions that you can integrate into the pipeline to help you identify security breaches:

Haskell Dockerfile Linter A smart Dockerfile *linter*, which is a static code analysis tool used to flag programming errors, bugs, stylistic errors, and suspicious constructs, can help you build best practice Docker images (`github.com/hadolint/hadolint`).

Detect-Secrets An aptly named module for (surprise, surprise) detecting secrets within a code base (`github.com/Yelp/detect-secrets`).

Anchore The Anchore Engine allows developers to perform detailed analysis on their container images, run queries, produce reports, and define policies that can be used in CI/CD pipelines. Developers can extend the tool to include new plug-ins that add new queries, new image analysis, and new policies (`anchore.com/opensource`).

Cfn_nag The cfn-nag tool looks for patterns in CloudFormation templates that may indicate insecure infrastructure. It will look for IAM rules or security groups that are too permissive, access logs that are not enabled, and encryption features that are not activated (`github.com/stelligent/cfn_nag`).

Now is the time to put in practice some of these concepts and tools. You should start by changing the pipeline you have already created in previous sections in order to include additional security checks. As a first step, change your `buildspec.yml` file to the following code. (Replace *<YOUR BUCKET NAME>* with the name of an existing bucket in your AWS account.)

```
---
version: 0.2
phases:
  install:
    runtime-versions:
        nodejs: 10
    commands:
      - pip install detect-secrets
  build:
    commands:
      - detect-secrets scan *--all-files > results.json
      - cat results.json
      - node -pe "if (Object.keys(JSON.parse(process.argv[1]).results).length
>=1) { process.exit(1) } else { process.exit() }" "$(cat results.json)"
      - cd src
      - npm install time
- aws cloudformation package --template-file ../template.yaml
```

```
--s3-bucket <YOUR BUCKET NAME> --output-template-file ../outputtemplate.yaml
artifacts:
  type: zip
  files:
    - template.yaml
    - outputtemplate.yaml
```

Now, change your `src/handler.js` file to the following code:

```
var time = require('time');
exports.handler = (event, context, callback) => {
    var key    = "AKIAWE7XI6O6QGGPDZEZ";
    var secret = "q5Kqj1qKYhlQLxjAiOwXOuwfao0bd1M/lUQq95Ax";

    var currentTime = new time.Date();
currentTime.setTimezone("America/Los_Angeles");
callback(null, {
        statusCode: '200',
        body: 'The time in Los Angeles is: ' + currentTime.toString(),
    });
};
```

Commit your changes, and after the pipeline finishes, you will see the failed status. See Figure C.20.

If you have problems using credentials, you can go to the following site to see how to solve that problem: `docs.aws.amazon.com/codecommit/latest/userguide/setting-up-https-unixes.html#setting-up-https-unixes-credential-helper`.

FIGURE C.20 Pipeline with failed status

This status results because we added a secret key to the Lambda function. By removing lines 3 and 4 from the `src/handler.js` file and committing your changes, the pipeline will finish with the Success status again. See Figure C.21.

FIGURE C.21 Pipeline with Success status

Creating the Correct Guardrails Using SAST and DAST

SAST and DAST are different styles of application security testing (AST) tools, which are tests performed automatically by specialized tools. *Static Application Security Testing* (SAST) is the source code scan for signs of vulnerable code. *Dynamic Application Security Testing* (DAST) corresponds to the analysis for conditions indicative of vulnerability performed with the application running, so the specialized tool will "navigate" the application, simulating known attack approaches.

SAST and DAST are often used in tandem because SAST will not find runtime errors and DAST is not going to flag coding errors (at least not down to the code line number). SAST performs well when it finds an error in a line of code, such as weak random number generation, but is usually not very efficient in finding data-flow flaws. Furthermore, SAST solutions are notorious for their large number of false positives or false negatives.

Security as Code: Creating Guardrails and Implementing Security by Design

The Open Web Application Security Project (OWASP) is a nonprofit community of software developers, engineers, and freelancers that provides resources and tools for web application security.

OWASP has several studies that you can use as the basis for your software development. These studies produce two main reports: The Top Ten Proactive Controls and The Ten Most Critical Web Application Security Risks. This section will summarize these reports and show how they can be leveraged in modern software development.

The Top 10 Proactive Controls

The OWASP Top Ten Proactive Controls 2018 is a list of security techniques that should be considered for every software development project. The report is written for developers to assist those new to secure development. One of the main goals of this project is to provide concrete, practical guidance that helps developers build secure software. These techniques should be applied proactively at the early stages of software development to ensure maximum effectiveness.

The full OWASP Top 10 Proactive Controls 2018 report can be accessed at `www.owasp.org/images/b/bc/OWASP_Top_10_Proactive_Controls_V3.pdf`.

Define Security Requirements

A security requirement is a statement of needed security functionality that ensures that one of many different security properties of software is being satisfied. Security requirements are derived from industry standards, applicable laws, and a history of past vulnerabilities. Security requirements define new features or additions for existing features to solve a specific security problem or eliminate a potential vulnerability. Examples of security requirements are authentication and authorization.

Security requirements provide a foundation of vetted security functionality for an application. Instead of developers creating a custom approach to security for every application, standard security requirements allow developers to reuse the definition of security controls and best practices. The same vetted security requirements provide solutions for security issues that have occurred in the past. Requirements exist to prevent the repeat of past security failures.

Leverage Security Frameworks and Libraries

Secure coding libraries and software frameworks with embedded security help software developers guard against security-related design and implementation flaws. A developer writing an application from scratch might not have sufficient knowledge, time, or budget to implement or maintain security features properly. Leveraging security frameworks helps accomplish security goals more efficiently and accurately.

Secure Database Access

This section describes secure access to all data stores, including both relational databases and NoSQL databases. Some areas to consider are as follows:

- **Secure Queries:** SQL injection occurs when untrusted user input is dynamically added to a SQL query in an insecure manner, often via basic string concatenation. SQL injection is one of the most dangerous application security risks. SQL injection is easy to exploit and could lead to the entire database being stolen, wiped, or modified. The application can even be used to run dangerous commands against the operating system hosting the database, thereby giving an attacker a foothold on the network.

  To mitigate SQL injection, you must prevent untrusted input from being interpreted as part of a SQL command. The best way to do this is with the programming technique known as *query parameterization*. This defense should be applied to SQL, Object Query Language (OQL), and stored procedure construction.

- **Secure Configuration:** Unfortunately, database management systems do not always ship in a "secure by default" configuration. Care must be taken to ensure that the security controls available from the database management system (DBMS) and hosting platform are enabled and properly configured. There are standards, guides, and benchmarks available for most common DBMSs.
- **Secure Authentication:** All access to the database should be properly authenticated. Authentication to the DBMS should be accomplished in a secure manner. Authentication should take place only over a secure channel. Credentials must be properly secured and available for use.
- **Secure Communication:** Most DBMSs support a variety of communications methods (such as services and APIs) that can be secure (authenticated or encrypted) or insecure (unauthenticated or unencrypted). It is a good practice to only use the secure communications options per the Protect Data Everywhere control.

Encode and Escape Data

Encoding and escaping are defensive techniques meant to stop injection attacks. Encoding (commonly called *output encoding*) involves translating special characters into some different but equivalent form that is no longer dangerous in the target interpreter—for example, translating the < character into the `<` string when writing an HTML page.

Escaping involves adding a special character before the character/string to avoid it being misinterpreted—for example, adding a `\` character before a `"` (double quote) character so that it is interpreted as text and not as closing a string.

Output encoding is best applied just before the content is passed to the target interpreter. If this defense is performed too early in the processing of a request, then the encoding or escaping may interfere with the use of the content in other parts of the program.

For example, if you escape the HTML content before storing that data in the database and the UI automatically escapes that data a second time, then the content will not display properly because it's double-escaped.

Validate All Inputs

Input validation is a programming technique that ensures that only properly formatted data can enter a software system component.

Input validation does not always make data "safe" since certain forms of complex input may be "valid" but still dangerous. For example, a valid email address may contain a SQL injection attack, or a valid URL may contain a cross-site scripting attack. Additional defenses besides input validation should always be applied to data, such as query parameterization or escaping. It's important to validate the input size, too, because of the vulnerability known as buffer overflow. A buffer overflow occurs when a program attempts to put more data in a buffer than it can hold or when a program attempts to put data in a memory area past a buffer. Writing outside the bounds of a block of allocated memory can corrupt data, crash the program, or cause the execution of malicious code.

Implement Digital Identity

Digital identity is the unique representation of a user (or other subject) as they engage in an online transaction. Authentication is the process of verifying that an individual or entity is who they claim to be. Session management is a process by which a server maintains the state of the user's authentication so that the user may continue to use the system without reauthenticating.

Enforce Access Controls

Access control (or authorization) is the process of granting or denying specific requests from a user, program, or process. Access control also involves the act of granting and revoking those least privileges. It should be noted that authorization (verifying access to specific features or resources) is not equivalent to authentication (verifying identity).

Access control functionality often spans many areas of software depending on the complexity of the access control system. For example, managing access control metadata and building caching for scalability purposes are often additional components in an access control system that need to be built or managed.

Protect Data Everywhere

Sensitive data such as passwords, credit card numbers, health records, personal information, and business secrets require extra protection, particularly if that data falls under privacy laws such as the European Union's General Data Protection Regulation (GDPR), financial data protection rules such as the PCI Data Security Standard (PCI DSS), or other regulations.

To see how to protect your data in AWS, please refer to Chapter 6, "Data Protection."

Implement Security Logging and Monitoring

Logging is a concept that most developers already use for debugging and diagnostic purposes. Security logging is an equally basic concept: logging security information during the runtime operation of an application. Monitoring is the live review of application and security logs using various forms of automation. The same tools and patterns can be used for operations, debugging, and security purposes.

Handle All Errors and Exceptions

Exception handling is a programming concept that allows an application to respond to different error states (such as network down, or database connection failed) in various ways. Handling exceptions and errors correctly is critical to making your code reliable and secure.

Error and exception handling occurs in all areas of an application, including critical business logic as well as security features and framework code.

Error handling is also important from an intrusion detection perspective. Certain attacks against your application may trigger errors, which can help you detect attacks in progress.

The 10 Most Critical Web Application Security Risks

A primary aim of the Top 10 Most Critical Web Application Security Risks report is to educate developers, designers, architects, managers, and organizations about the consequences of the most common and most critical web application security weaknesses. The report provides basic techniques to protect against these high-risk problem areas and guides on where to go from here.

Injection

Injection flaws, such as SQL, NoSQL, OS, and LDAP injection, occur when untrusted data is sent to an interpreter as part of a command or query. The attacker's hostile data can trick the interpreter into executing unintended commands or accessing data without proper authorization.

Broken Authentication

Application functions related to authentication and session management are often implemented incorrectly, allowing attackers to compromise passwords, keys, or session tokens, or to exploit other implementation flaws to assume other users' identities temporarily or permanently.

Sensitive Data Exposure

Many web applications and APIs do not properly protect sensitive data, such as financial, healthcare, and PII. Attackers may steal or modify this weakly protected data to conduct credit card fraud, identity theft, or other crimes. Sensitive data may be compromised without extra protection, such as encryption at rest or in transit, and requires special precautions when exchanged with the browser.

XML External Entities

Many older or poorly configured XML processors evaluate external entity references within XML documents. This feature can be used to disclose internal files, internal file shares, internal port scanning, remote code execution, and denial-of-service attacks.

Broken Access Control

Restrictions on what authenticated users are allowed to do are often not properly enforced. Attackers can exploit these flaws to access unauthorized functionality and/or data, such as accessing other users' accounts, viewing sensitive files, modifying other users' data, or changing access rights.

Security Misconfiguration

Security misconfiguration is the most commonly seen issue. This is usually a result of insecure default configurations, incomplete or ad hoc configurations, open cloud storage, misconfigured HTTP headers, and verbose error messages containing sensitive information. Not only must all operating systems, frameworks, libraries, and applications be securely configured, but they must be patched and upgraded in a timely fashion.

Cross-Site Scripting (XSS)

XSS flaws occur whenever an application includes untrusted data in a new web page without proper validation or escaping, or updates to an existing web page with user-supplied data using a browser API that can create HTML or JavaScript. XSS allows attackers to execute scripts in the victim's browser that can hijack user sessions, deface websites, or redirect the user to malicious sites.

Insecure Deserialization

Insecure deserialization often leads to remote code execution. Even if deserialization flaws do not result in remote code execution, they can be used to perform attacks, including replay attacks, injection attacks, and privilege escalation attacks.

Using Components with Known Vulnerabilities

Components, such as libraries, frameworks, and other software modules, run with the same privileges as the application. If a vulnerable component is exploited, such an attack can facilitate serious data loss or server takeover. Applications and APIs using components with known vulnerabilities may undermine application defenses and enable various attacks and impacts.

Insufficient Logging and Monitoring

Insufficient logging and monitoring, coupled with missing or ineffective integration with incident response, allows attackers to further attack systems, maintain persistence, pivot to more systems, and tamper, extract, or destroy data. Most breach studies show that the time to detect a breach is over 200 days, typically detected by external parties rather than internal processes or monitoring.

The full Top 10 Most Critical Web Application Security Risks report can be accessed at `owasp.org/www-project-top-ten/?`.

Index

A

B

E

J

K

L

M

N

O

P

R

S

T

U

V

W

X–Y–Z

Online Test Bank

Register to gain one year of FREE access to the online interactive test bank to help you study for your AWS Certified Security certification exam—included with your purchase of this book! All of the chapter review questions and the practice tests in this book are included in the online test bank so you can practice in a timed and graded setting.

Register and Access the Online Test Bank

To register your book and get access to the online test bank, follow these steps:

1. Go to `bit.ly/SybexTest` (this address is case sensitive)!
2. Select your book from the list.
3. Complete the required registration information, including answering the security verification to prove book ownership. You will be emailed a PIN code.
4. Follow the directions in the email or go to `www.wiley.com/go/sybextestprep`.
5. Find your book on that page and click the "Register or Login" link with it. Then enter the PIN code you received and click the "Activate PIN" button.
6. On the Create an Account or Login page, enter your username and password, and click Login or, if you don't have an account already, create a new account.
7. At this point, you should be in the test bank site with your new test bank listed at the top of the page. If you do not see it there, please refresh the page or log out and log back in.